Lecture Notes in Computer Science 13363

More information about this series at https://link.springer.com/bookseries/558

Mounîm El Yacoubi · Eric Granger ·
Pong Chi Yuen · Umapada Pal ·
Nicole Vincent (Eds.)

Pattern Recognition and Artificial Intelligence

Third International Conference, ICPRAI 2022
Paris, France, June 1–3, 2022
Proceedings, Part I

 Springer

Editors
Mounîm El Yacoubi [iD]
Télécom SudParis
Palaiseau, France

Pong Chi Yuen [iD]
Hong Kong Baptist University
Kowloon, Kowloon, Hong Kong

Nicole Vincent [iD]
Université Paris Cité
Paris, France

Eric Granger [iD]
École de Technologie Supérieure
Montreal, QC, Canada

Umapada Pal [iD]
Indian Statistical Institute
Kolkata, India

ISSN 0302-9743   ISSN 1611-3349 (electronic)
Lecture Notes in Computer Science
ISBN 978-3-031-09036-3   ISBN 978-3-031-09037-0 (eBook)
https://doi.org/10.1007/978-3-031-09037-0

This Springer imprint is published by the registered company Springer Nature Switzerland AG
The registered company address is: Gewerbestrasse 11, 6330 Cham, Switzerland

Preface

Welcome to the proceedings of the third International Conference on Pattern Recognition and Artificial Intelligence (ICPRAI 2022), held during June 1–3, 2022 in Paris, France. This conference follows the successful ICPRAI 2018, held in Montréal, Canada, in May 2018 and ICPRAI 2020, held in Zhongshan, China, in October 2020. It was organized by LIPADE (Laboratoire d'Informatique Paris Descartes) at Université Paris Cité with the co-operation of other French universities. The conference was endorsed by the International Association on Pattern Recognition (IAPR) and we hereby thank the organization for this support.

Pattern recognition and artificial intelligence (PRAI) techniques and systems have been applied successfully to solve practical problems in many domains. ICPRAI 2022 brought together numerous scientists from all over the world to present their innovative ideas, report their latest findings, and discuss the fruitful results of research laboratories in up to 43 countries in handwriting recognition, forensic studies, face recognition, medical imaging, deep learning, and classification techniques.

The Organizing Committee of ICPRAI 2022 consisted of well-known experts from all six (habited) continents of the world. The conference invited world-renowned keynote speakers to cover the new PRAI frontiers in depth and in breadth, and we are grateful for their insights. Due to the large number of high-quality papers submitted (a total of 152 submissions were received), the technical program included 81 presentations, as well as four special sessions, related to handwriting and text processing, computer vision and image processing, machine learning and deep networks, medical applications, forensic science and medical diagnosis, features and classification techniques, and various applications. The paper review process was carried out in a very professional way by the Program Committee members. In addition to the rich technical program, the conference also featured practical sessions, to encourage author-editor and inventor-investor interactions, and social events for all conference participants. A pre-conference doctorial consortium took place on May 31, 2022, as a satellite to the main event, offering PhD students the opportunity to present their work and meet senior researchers in their field of interest.

It was a great pleasure to organize this conference including all the above activities, promoting discussions on very innovative pieces of research work and we would like to thank all those involved for a superb technical program and conference proceedings: conference co-chairs, Edwin Hancock and Yuan Y. Tang; special session chairs, Jenny Benois-Pineau and Raphael Lins; and publication chairs, Camille Kurtz and Patrick Wang, along with all the Program Committee members.

We would like to express our gratitude to the numerous committee members who took care of the arrangement local organization, particularly to Florence Cloppet. Special thanks go to local arrangements team of the Université Paris Cité Faculty of Sciences and particularly to the Mathematics and Computer Science departments. All created a very warm and comfortable environment to work in.

Thanks are also due to the organizations listed in the proceedings and those of the organizers of ICPRAI 2022, along with the administration of Université Paris Cité, who gave us strong financial support and support in various forms and means.

Finally, we hope you found this conference to be a rewarding and memorable experience. We hope you enjoyed your stay in Paris.

April 2022

Ching Y. Suen
Nicole Vincent
Mounîm El Yacoubi
Umapada Pal
Eric Granger
Pong Chi Yuen

Organization

ICPRAI 2022 was hosted by Université Paris Cité and organized by LIPADE (Laboratoire d'Informatique Paris Descartes) of Université Paris Cité, France.

Honorary Chair

Ching Y. Suen   Concordia University, Canada

General Chair

Nicole Vincent   Université Paris Cité, France

Conference Chairs

Edwin Hancock   University of York, UK
Yuan Y. Tang   University of Macau, China

Program Chairs

Mounim El Yacoubi   Institut Polytechnique de Paris, France
Umapada Pal   Indian Statistical Institute, India
Eric Granger   École de technologie supérieure, Canada
Pong C. Yuen   Hong Kong Baptist University, China

Special Sessions Chairs

Jenny Benois-Pineau   Université de Bordeaux, France
Raphael Lins   Universidade Federal de Pernambuco, Brazil

Competition Chairs

Jean-Marc Ogier   La Rochelle Université, France
Cheng-Lin Liu   University of Chinese Academy of Sciences, China

Doctoral Consortium

Véronique Eglin   INSA de Lyon, France
Daniel Lopresti   Lehigh University, USA

Organization Chair

Florence Cloppet   Université de Paris, France

Publication Chairs

Camille Kurtz   Université Paris Cité, France
Patrick Wang   Northeastern University, USA

Exhibitions and Industrial Liaison

Alexandre Cornu   IMDS, Canada
Olivier Martinot   Telecom SudParis, France

Publicity Chairs

Jean-Christophe Burie   La Rochelle Université, France
Imran Siddiqi   Bahria University, Pakistan
Michael Blumenstein   University of Technology Sydney, Australia
Rejean Plamondon   Polytechnique Montréal, Canada

Sponsorship Chairs

Laurence Likforman   Telecom Paris, France
Josep Llados   Universitat Autònoma de Barcelona, Spain
Nicola Nobile   Concordia University, Canada

Web

Camille Kurtz   Université Paris Cité, France

Program Committee

Elisa H. Barney Smith   Boise State University, USA
Jenny Benois-Pineau   LaBRI, CNRS, University of Bordeaux, France
Saumik Bhattacharya   IIT Kanpur, India
Michael Blumenstein   University of Technology Sydney, Australia
Jean-Christophe Burie   L3i, La Rochelle Université, France
Sukalpa Chanda   Østfold University College, Norway
Jocelyn Chanussot   Grenoble INP, France
Christophe Charrier   Normandie Université, France
Rama Chellappa   University of Maryland, USA
Farida Cheriet   Polytechnique Montreal, Canada

Su Ruan	Université de Rouen, France
Friedhelm Schwenker	Ulm University, Germany
Imran Siddiqi	Bahria University, Pakistan
Nicolas Thome	Cnam, France
Massimo Tistarelli	University of Sassari, Italy
Seiichi Uchida	Kyushu University, Japan
Nicole Vincent	Universite de Paris, France
Richard Wilson	University of York, UK
Yirui Wu	Hohai University, China
Vera Yashina	Dorodnicyn Computing Center, Russian Academy of Sciences, Russia
Xiao Feng	Northwestern Polytechnical University, China

Keynote Speakers

ICPRAI 2022 was proud to host the following keynote speakers:

Bidyut B. Chaudhuri	Computer Vision & Pattern Recognition Unit, Indian Statistical Institute, India	"Bengali Handwriting Recognition with Transformative Generative Adversarial Net (TGAN)"
Robert B. Fisher	School of Informatics, University of Edinburgh, Scotland, UK	"The TrimBot2020 outdoor gardening robot"
Walter G. Kropatsch	Vienna University of Technology, Austria	"Controlling Topology-Preserving Graph-Pyramid"

Sponsors

Contents – Part I

Segmentation

Document

Video – 3D

Feature

Contents – Part II

Classification

Machine Learning

Computer Vision

Identifying, Evaluating, and Addressing Nondeterminism in Mask R-CNNs

Stephen Price$^{(\boxtimes)}$ ⓘ and Rodica Neamtu ⓘ

Computer Science Department, Worcester Polytechnic Institute, Worcester, MA, USA
{sprice,rneamtu}@wpi.edu

Abstract. Convolutional Neural Networks, and many other machine learning algorithms, use Graphical Processing Units (GPUs) instead of Central Processing Units (CPUs) to improve the training time of very large modeling computations. This work evaluates the impact of the model structure and GPU on nondeterminism and identifies its exact causes. The ability to replicate results is quintessential to research, thus nondeterminism must be either removed or significantly reduced. Simple methods are provided so that researchers can: (1) measure the impact of nondeterminism, (2) achieve determinable results by eliminating randomness embedded in the model structure and performing computations on a CPU, or (3) reduce the amount of variation between model performances while training on a GPU.

Keywords: Nondeterminism · Mask R-CNN · Determinable · GPU · NVIDIA · Computer vision · Embedded randomness · Replicability

1 Introduction

Recent advancements in computer vision using Convolutional Neural Networks (CNNs) have emphasized their ability to classify images and detect objects within images [16]. However, these tasks require significant computational resources and time to complete [25]. Fortunately, Graphics Processing Units (GPUs) are more capable of handling these advanced computations than Central Processing Units (CPUs) [9,27]. For example, models trained in this work require 20–30 min to complete on a GPU but take 10–14 h on a CPU. GPUs were originally configured to work with graphics. However, as researchers showed more interest in using GPUs for computations associated with machine learning, NVIDIA (the most commonly used GPU manufacturer for machine learning [20]) created the CUDA Library [12], thus enabling the use of GPUs for diverse machine learning tasks. Unfortunately, NVIDIA's GPU and CUDA library introduce nondeterminism reflected in two or more identically trained models sometimes producing different results. This GPU-related nondeterminism is distinct from the nondeterminism due to randomness embedded in the model structure by features such as Stochastic Data Augmentation and Stochastic Weight Initialization. The existence and impact of nondeterminism related to both the randomness embedded in the model structure and the GPU have gained increasing attention [20], and deserve continuous assessment and research to reduce it.

ⓒ Springer Nature Switzerland AG 2022
M. El Yacoubi et al. (Eds.): ICPRAI 2022, LNCS 13363, pp. 3–14, 2022.
https://doi.org/10.1007/978-3-031-09037-0_1

1.1   Motivation

This work is inspired and motivated by previous research [22] using a Mask R-CNN [28] to analyze metallic powder particles and detect deformations on the surface. Since these deformations known as satellites, impact the usability of metallic powders, accurate detection is very important. In the previous work, using a Mask R-CNN led to accurate detection, even on a diverse dataset composed of multiple powder types taken at varying magnification settings. However, upon deep analysis of results looking for determinism, it was discovered that, in some cases, two or more identically trained models could produce significantly different results. Figure 1, depicting two identically trained models, labeled Model A and B, highlights these differing results due to nondeterminism. These models were specifically selected to illustrate potential variation in outputs. In Fig. 1, the outlined green section highlights a small satellite detected in Fig. 1a more than tripling in size and losing its discernible shape in Fig. 1b. Similarly, in the section outlined red, two particles correctly identified to have no satellites in Fig. 1a are misidentified as satellites in Fig. 1b. Inspired by the nondeterminism causing these variations, this manuscript aims to quantify its impact and provide viable options to reduce or remove it to ensure replicability of experimental results.

1.2   Terminology

To avoid confusion due to various existing definitions, for the purpose of this work, determinism and nondeterminism are defined as follows: (1) An algorithm is said to be "determinable" if its current state uniquely determines its next state. Simply put, an algorithm at any state should produce exactly one output. (2) An algorithm is said to be "nondeterminable" if, at a given state, multiple potential outputs are possible given the same input [14]. In the context of this paper, *if all models trained within a given environment are identical, that training environment is determinable.*

1.3   Contributions

The ability to replicate results is quintessential to research [10]. Thus, being able to eliminate, or at least reduce nondeterminism in a Mask R-CNN is imperative. The contributions of this work are multi-fold:

1. Identifying and evaluating the causes and extent of nondeterminism in Mask R-CNN models with embedded randomness trained on an NVIDIA GPU.
2. Evaluating the extent of nondeterminism in Mask R-CNN models with no embedded randomness trained on an NVIDIA GPU.
3. Offering a simple method, requiring only eight additional lines of code, to achieve pure deterministic results through a combination of using a CPU and specific training configurations.

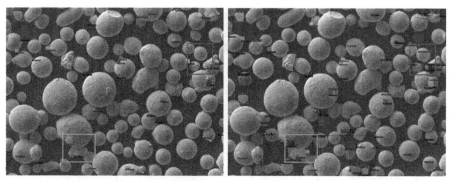

(a) Satellite Predictions from Model A   (b) Satellite Predictions from Model B

Fig. 1. Example of variation of performance in identically trained Mask R-CNN models as a result of nondeterminism (Color figure online)

2 Nondeterminism Introduced in Training

To measure nondeterminism in model training caused by GPUs, all other sources of nondeterminism must first be eliminated. Through rigorous examination of literature, documentation, and user manuals of the varying tools and packages [12,21,28], the following have been identified as potential sources of nondeterminism embedded in the model: *Random Number Generators* (used by Python Random Library, PyTorch, NumPy, and Detectron2), *Detectron2 Augmentation* Settings, and the *PyTorch implementation of CUDA Algorithms*. Figure 2 illustrates the general sources of nondeterminism that may be present in a Mask R-CNN, as well as the components of each source. The following subsections give some background information on each of these sources.

2.1 Random Number Generators

The training of a CNN employs randomness for large-scale computations to reduce training time and prevent bottlenecks [5,29]. Each instance of embedded randomness is enabled by a Pseudo-Random Number Generator (PRNG) that generates sequences of numbers designed to mimic randomness. Mersenne Twister (MT) [19] is one of the most frequently used PRNG algorithms by tools such as the Python Random Library [26]. MT simulates randomness by using the system time to select the starting index or seed in the sequence of numbers when a PRNG is created [26]. Without a set seed, each PRNGs starts at a unique index, leading to different outputs and introducing nondeterminism in training.

2.2 Model Structure

This model structure is configured by Detectron2 [28], which uses a fairly common training technique called Stochastic Data Augmentation to randomly mirror

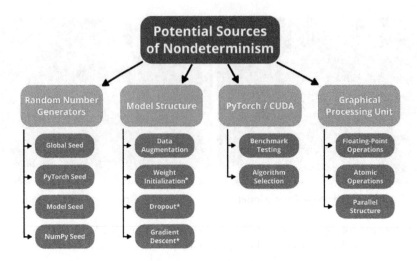

Fig. 2. General sources of nondeterminism that may be found in Mask R-CNNs (*not present in this work, but may be present in other implementations)

images prior to training [23]. The stochastic process of selection increases the nondeterminism in training. Augmentation is the only source of nondeterminism caused by the model structure here. However, this may not always be the case.

2.3 CUDA Algorithms and PyTorch

The PyTorch implementation of the CUDA Library [21], by default, contains two settings that increase nondeterminism in training. First, CUDA uses Benchmark Testing to select optimal algorithms for the given environment. However, as indicated in the documentation [21], this testing is "susceptible to noise and has the potential to select different algorithms, even on the same hardware." Second, by default, the library chooses nondeterminable algorithms for computing convolutions instead of their determinable counterparts. These nondeterminable algorithms are selected because they simplify computations by estimating randomly selected values instead of computing exact values for each layer [6]. Both configurations increase the nondeterminism present in model training.

3 Nondeterminism Introduced by Hardware

3.1 Floating-Point Operations

Many computer systems use floating-point numbers for arithmetic operations; however, these operations have a finite precision that cannot be maintained with exceptionally large or small numbers. In this work, values were stored using the IEEE 754 Single Precision standard [18]. Unfortunately, due to the finite precision of floating-point numbers, some calculations are approximated, causing a rounding error and rendering the associative property not applicable in floating-point operations [15]. Equations 1 and 2 provide an example in which the non-associativity of floating-points impacts the final result. In the intermediate sum in Equation 1, the 1 is rounded off when summed with 10^{100}, causing it to be lost in approximation. When computing the difference after rounding, $10^{100}–10^{100}$ returns **0**. By contrast, if $10^{100}–10^{100}$ is performed first, the result of computations will be 0 at the intermediate step, and when summed with 1, will return the correct value of **1**. In summary, due to the non-associativity of floating-points, the order in which operations are executed impacts the outputs. This becomes increasingly relevant when parallel computing is implemented, as further elaborated in Sects. 3.2 and 3.3.

$$(1 + 10^{100}) - 10^{100} = 0 \qquad (1) \qquad\qquad 1 + (10^{100} - 10^{100}) = 1 \qquad (2)$$

3.2   Atomic Operations

Shared memory is commonly implemented in parallel computing [3]. However, when multiple operations access the same location in memory at similar times, depending on when read and write methods are called, data can be "lost" due to overlapping operations [11]. Atomic Operations resolve this by performing a read and write call as an atomic action and preventing other operations from accessing or editing that location in memory until completed. Atomic operations are designed to ensure memory consistency but are unconcerned with the completion order consistency [11]. Effects of this are noted in the CUDA Library [12], stating "the following routines do not guarantee reproducibility across runs, even on the same architecture, because they use atomic operations" in reference to a list of algorithms used in convolutions.

3.3   Parallel Structure

With the introduction of the CUDA library, taking advantage of the benefits of parallel computing with GPUs became easier [8] and more frequently used [13]. Despite these benefits, there are inherent drawbacks to most multi-core or multi-threaded approaches. In parallel computing, large computations are broken into smaller ones and delegated to parallel cores/threads. Each sub-task has a variable completion time, which is amplified by the use of atomic operations. When considering the variable completion time of various tasks and the non-associativity of floating-point operations, it is not surprising that GPUs introduce nondeterminism. Figure 3 illustrates how a slight variation in the completion order of sub-tasks can lead to nondeterminable results due to floating-point operations. Figures 3a and 3b depict the process sum() adding sub-functions (labeled F1 to F5) together, in which each sub-function is dispatched to its own core/thread to be individually computed. The output (labeled O1 to O5) is collected in order of completion and summed. However, since completion order is not guaranteed, these outputs can be collected in different orders, resulting in differing output despite having identical inputs and hardware because of floating points non-associativity. [15].

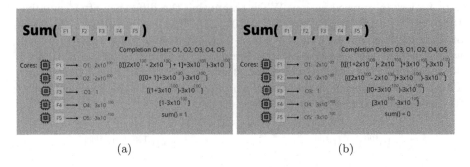

(a)	(b)

Fig. 3. Tracing the impact of variable completion times in parallel structures using floating-point operations

4   Experimental Setup

This work used the Detectron2 implementation of the Mask R-CNN with PyTorch (v1.8.1) [21] and CUDA (v10.2) [12]. Initial weights were pulled from the Detectron2 Model Zoo Library to remove any variation in weight initialization. The dataset used here is the same dataset used in [22], consisting of images of metallic powder particles collected from a Scanning Electron Microscope. It contains 1,384 satellite annotations across six powders and five magnifications and was separated using an 80:20 ratio between training and validation datasets.

4.1   System Architecture

To get a benchmark for variation in performance caused by embedded randomness in the model structure and the GPU, 120 models were trained using an NVIDIA V100 GPU. Of these models, 60 were left non-configured and 60 were configured, as shown in the source code [2], such that all embedded randomness within the model structure was disabled. This ensured that any nondeterminism present after configuring models was induced solely by the GPU. This experiment was then replicated using CPUs. However, due to the high time difference in training between GPUs and CPUs, a 5-Fold Cross Validation [4] was used instead of training 60 models. For example, based on results from the ten models trained on the CPU, training 120 models on a CPU would have taken between 50 and 70 days of computational time, instead of 48 h on a GPU. The 5-Fold Cross Validation was used only to evaluate if results were determinable over multiple iterations; due to the small number of data points it was not used to evaluate the extent of nondeterminism.

4.2   Measuring Performance

Identical to previous work [22], performance was measured by computing precision and recall, as defined in Equations 3 and 4. For every image in the validation set, each pixel was classified as True Positive (TP), False Positive (FP), True Negative (TN), and False Negative (FN) depending on its true value and the predicted output. Once these scores were computed for each image, they were averaged across all images in the validation set to get a final score for that model to be compared. Nondeterminism was evaluated by analyzing the average, standard deviation, and spread of each performance metric collected by models trained with identical configuration settings. If the training configurations and hardware are determinable, precision and recall will be identical for all models trained.

$$Precision \; = \; \frac{TP}{TP + FP} \quad (3) \qquad\qquad Recall \; = \; \frac{TP}{TP + FN} \quad (4)$$

4.3   Model Training Process

Previous work [22] discovered that in most cases, training beyond 10,000 iterations had little impact on performance. As a result, in an effort to prevent underfitting or overfitting, all models were trained to 10,000 iterations. Additionally, to prevent introducing any bias, hyperparameters were left at their default values. All calculations were completed in batch jobs dispatched to private nodes on Bridges2 [7], a High-Performance Computer (HPC) operated by Pittsburgh Supercomputing Center and funded by the National Science Foundation. Each node contained two NVIDIA Tesla V100 GPUs and two Intel Xeon Platinum 8168 CPUs.

4.4   Configuring Settings

To compare models with embedded randomness enabled and respectively disabled, specific configurations had to be set. Table 1, depicting configuration settings, shows the value of each configuration for models with and without embedded randomness. Configuring an RNG's seed only changes the starting index and has no further impact on the randomness [19]. As a result, so long as the seed remains constant, its specific value is arbitrary. Evidence for this is found in the Detectron2 Source Code stating the seed needs to be "any positive integer" and in the NVIDIA Determinism Repo stating "123, or whatever you choose" [1,28]. In light of this, all seeds were arbitrarily set to "42." After reviewing the CUDA Toolkit Documentation [12], the PyTorch Documentation [21], the Detectron2 Source Code [28], and NVIDIA Determinism Repository [1], the only possibility for achieving reproducible results that was not implemented was the PyTorch DataLoader. This was not configured because Detectron2 implements its own custom DataLoader class and the PyTorch version was not used.

Table 1. Configuration values for non-configured and fully configured models

Configuration name	Non-configured value	Fully configured value
Data augmentation	Horizontal	None
Benchmark testing	True	False
Determinable algorithms	False	True
RNG seeds	NA	42

5   Experimental Results

5.1   Data Collected from Models Trained on GPU

After training 120 models on a GPU (60 non-configured and 60 fully configured), regardless of configuration settings, there was clear evidence of nondeterminism. Table 2 shows all performance metrics gathered from models trained on a GPU for comparison, but attention will be drawn specifically to the standard deviation of precision and recall values (bolded and marked * and ** respectively). As can be seen in Table 2, configuring the embedded randomness in the model decreased the standard deviation of precision values by 1% (marked *) and recall by 0.1% (marked **). Despite the 1% reduction in variation of precision, only 25% of the nondeterminism is eliminated, leaving a remaining 3.1% standard deviation caused by the GPU. Figure 4 shows the distributions of precision values for non-configured and fully configured models. As can be seen, the distribution of Fig. 4a, corresponding to non-configured models, has a larger spread of data points than in Fig. 4b, corresponding to fully configured models.

Table 2. Performance metrics for non-configured and fully configured models

Model performance metrics on GPU	Non-configured	Fully configured
Average precision (%)	72.908%	70.750%
Precision std deviation (%)	**4.151%***	**3.135%***
Precision range (min:max)	63.5% : 82.7%	64.4% : 78.1%
Average recall (%)	61.581%	60.914%
Recall std deviation (%)	**2.733%****	**2.603%****
Recall range (min:max)	54.4% : 67.6%	55.8% : 66.5%
Average training time (min)	19.497	28.757
Training time std deviation (min)	0.359	0.304
Training time range (min:max)	19.0 : 21.32	28.25 : 29.5

5.2 Data Collected from Models Trained on CPU

Since only five models were trained on a CPU instead of 60 due to the expected very large training time as previously discussed, the presence or absence of nondeterminism can be observed but not quantified. Models trained on a CPU with all embedded randomness disabled produced perfectly determinable results. These results were identical up to the 16th decimal place (only measured to 16 decimal places) with a precision score and recall of approximately 76.2% and 56.2%, respectively. Among these models, there was a minimum training time of 606.15 min, a maximum of 842.05 min, and an average of 712.93 min. The variety in training times had no impact on the accuracy of the model. In contrast to every trained model with no embedded randomness on the CPU having identical precision and recall score, when embedded randomness was enabled, there wasn't a single duplicated value. As shown in Table 3 depicting a comparison of precision and recall scores of non-configured models trained on a CPU, each model produced quite different results, showing that nondeterminism is present. As a result of nondeterminism being present in CPU trainings when embedded randomness is enabled, nondetemrinism can, in part, be attributed to embedded randomness in the model.

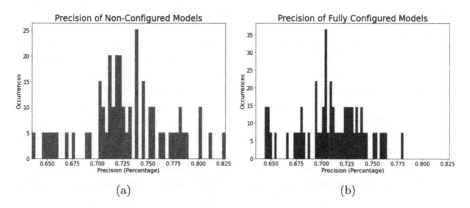

Fig. 4. Comparative results of the distribution of precision values collected from non-configured models (a) and fully configured models (b) trained on a GPU

Table 3. Performance metrics for non-configured models trained on CPUs

Training num	Precision (%)	Recall (%)	Time (min)
Model 1	0.7992862217337212	0.6222949769133339	646.07
Model 2	0.7321758705343052	0.6506021842415332	720.83
Model 3	0.7019480667622756	0.6118534248851561	606.23
Model 4	0.7585633387152428	0.6253458176827655	612.05
Model 5	0.7534353070389288	0.6330197085802262	616.65
Average	0.7490817609568948	0.628623222460603	640.37
Std deviation	0.0320522567741504	0.012918343823211	42.51

6   Discussion of Results

6.1   Impact of Embedded Randomness on Model Precision

As previously shown, randomness is deliberately embedded in machine learning models to improve their generalizability and robustness [17]. By eliminating the embedded randomness within the model, there is an associated reduction in the ability of the model to generalize for samples of data with more variation than those within the training set. In context, by decreasing the randomness embedded in the model structure during training, the model's ability to handle formations of satellites not included in the training set may decrease. This could explain why the average precision and recall values were lower in the fully configured model, and why there was a reduced number of models with precision scores above 75% out of the set of fully configured models (4 models) compared to the non-configured models (17 models). In summary, *by disabling embedded randomness, the model may be less capable of handling new data, and as a result, it may be less generalizable.*

6.2   Increase in Training Time After Configuring Randomness

Even though the reduction in performance variation was about 25% after disabling the randomness embedded in the model structure, the training time increased by nearly 50%. Non-Configured models took on average 19.5 min to train on a GPU, which rose to 28.8 min after configuring the embedded randomness. This increase was theorized to be the result of forcing CUDA algorithms to be determinable instead of their nondeterminable counterparts. To test this, 40 models were trained with all embedded randomness disabled except Determinable Algorithms. With these parameters, the models had nearly identical precision and recall scores to a fully configured model with an average score of 71.966% and 60.207% respectively, and standard deviations of 3.455% and 2.354%. However, the average training time decreased to 19.1 min with a standard deviation of 0.130 min, much closer to that of the non-configured models. As a result, *since forcing determinable algorithms has a minimal impact on the variation but increases the training time by approximately 50%, it is suggested to allow nondeterminable algorithms when response time is a priority.*

6.3   Impact of Seed Sensitivity

By disabling embedded randomness within the model structure, there was little adverse impact on performance. Between non-configured models and fully configured models on the GPU, precision and recall were reduced on average by 2% and 0.6%, respectively. Since each seed outputs different values than another seed and slightly impact performance, the model is seed-sensitive [24]. In this case, the seed was arbitrarily set to "42." However, other seed values may produce different results. Thus, *if hyperparameter tuning is being performed with a configured seed, users may consider testing multiple seed values to identify which works best for the given dataset and parameters.*

6.4 Conclusion

The methods and procedures highlighted in this manuscript aim to inform the selection process of parameters and hardware for training a Mask R-CNN model with respect to nondeterminism and training time. In cases where determinable results are of a priority, model training can be performed on a CPU with the embedded randomness in the model structure configured. This will guarantee fully determinable results and only requires an additional eight lines of code. These configurations can be found in the training files for the repository associated with this manuscript [2]. Unfortunately, by running computations on a CPU instead of a GPU, the training time increases from 20–30 min to 10–14 h. As a result, a CPU should only be used in cases where computational resources are not a concern and replicability is more important than speed and efficiency. If determinable results are not the first priority, in most cases performing training on a GPU is a better choice. However, in addition to the reductions in training time accomplished by using a GPU (at least 20 times faster), the nondeterminism present during model training will increase. Here, the standard deviation of this variation in non-configured models was approximately 4.2% and 2.7% for precision and recall respectively. Using the methods established above, this variation can be reduced to approximately 3.1% and 2.6% for precision and recall while still performing computations on a GPU. Each scenario will have different priorities, but this work can be used as a guide for configuring a training environment with respect to nondeterminism and training time.

Acknowledgements. This work used the Extreme Science and Engineering Discovery Environment (XSEDE), supported by NSF grant DMR200035. We thank Prof. Danielle Cote and Bryer Sousa for providing the dataset and insights.

References

1. Nvidia docs (2018). https://github.com/NVIDIA/framework-determinism
2. Identifying, evaluating, and addressing nondeterminism in mask R-CNNS source code (2021). https://github.com/Data-Driven-Materials-Science/Nondeterminism
3. Amza, C., et al.: Treadmarks: shared memory computing on networks of workstations. Computer **29**(2), 18–28 (1996)
4. Bengio, Y., Grandvalet, Y.: No unbiased estimator of the variance of k-fold cross-validation. J. Mach. Learn. Res. **5**, 1089–1105 (2004)
5. Bottou, L.: Large-scale machine learning with stochastic gradient descent. In: Proceedings of COMPSTAT'2010, pp. 177–186. Springer (2010). https://doi.org/10.1007/978-3-7908-2604-3_16
6. Bottou, L.: Stochastic gradient descent tricks. In: Montavon, G., Orr, G.B., Müller, K.-R. (eds.) Neural Networks: Tricks of the Trade. LNCS, vol. 7700, pp. 421–436. Springer, Heidelberg (2012). https://doi.org/10.1007/978-3-642-35289-8_25
7. Brown, S.T.E.A.: Bridges-2: a platform for rapidly-evolving and data intensive research. Pract. Exp. Adv. Res. Comput. (2021)
8. Buck, I.: GPU computing with Nvidia Cuda. In: ACM SIGGRAPH 2007 Courses, pp. 6-es (2007)

9. Chen, Z., Wang, J., He, H.: A fast deep learning system using GPU. In: 2014 IEEE International Symposium on Circuits and Systems (ISCAS). IEEE (2014)

10. Collaboration, O.S., et al.: Estimating the reproducibility of psychological science. Science **349**, 6251 (2015)

11. Defour, D., Collange, S.: Reproducible floating-point atomic addition in data-parallel environment. In: 2015 Federated Conference on Computer Science and Information Systems (FedCSIS), pp. 721–728. IEEE (2015)

12. Documentation, C.T.: v10. 2. Nvidia Corp., Santa Clara (2019)

13. Garland, M.E.A.: Parallel computing experiences with Cuda. IEEE Micro **28**(4), 13–27 (2008)

14. Gill, J.: Computational complexity of probabilistic turing machines. SIAM J. Comput. **6**(4), 675–695 (1977)

15. Goldberg, D.: What every computer scientist should know about floating-point arithmetic. ACM Comput. Surv. **23**(1), 5–48 (1991)

16. He, K., Gkioxari, G., Dollár, P., Girshick, R.: Mask R-CNN. In: Proceedings of the IEEE International Conference on Computer Vision, pp. 2961–2969 (2017)

17. He, Z., Rakin, A.S., Fan, D.: Parametric noise injection: trainable randomness to improve deep neural network robustness against adversarial attack. In: Proceedings of the IEEE/CVF Conference on Computer Vision and Pattern Recognition, pp. 588–597 (2019)

18. Kahan, W.: IEEE standard 754 for binary floating-point arithmetic. Lect. Notes Status IEEE **754**(94720–1776), 11 (1996)

19. Matsumoto, M., Nishimura, T.: Mersenne twister: a 623-dimensionally equidistributed uniform pseudo-random number generator. ACM Trans. Model. Comput. Simulat. **8**(1), 3–30 (1998)

20. Nagarajan, P., Warnell, G., Stone, P.: The impact of nondeterminism on reproducibility in deep reinforcement learning (2018)

21. Paszke, A.E.A.: Pytorch: an imperative style, high-performance deep learning library. Adv. Neural Inf. Process. Syst. **32**, 8026–8037 (2019)

22. Price, S.E., Gleason, M.A., Sousa, B.C., Cote, D.L., Neamtu, R.: Automated and refined application of convolutional neural network modeling to metallic powder particle satellite detection. In: Integrating Materials and Manufacturing Innovation, pp. 1–16 (2021)

23. Shorten, C., Khoshgoftaar, T.M.: A survey on image data augmentation for deep learning. J. Big Data **6**(1), 1–48 (2019)

24. Shuryak, I.: Advantages of synthetic noise and machine learning for analyzing radioecological data sets. PloS One **12**(1) (2017)

25. Steinkraus, D., Buck, I., Simard, P.: Using GPUS for machine learning algorithms. In: Eighth International Conference on Document Analysis and Recognition (ICDAR 2005), pp. 1115–1120. IEEE (2005)

26. VanRossum, G., Drake, F.L.: The Python Language Reference. Python Software Foundation, Amsterdam (2010)

27. Wang, Y.E., Wei, G.Y., Brooks, D.: Benchmarking TPU, GPU, and CPU platforms for deep learning. arXiv preprint arXiv:1907.10701 (2019)

28. Wu, Y., Kirillov, A., Massa, F., Lo, W.Y., Girshick, R.: Detectron2 (2019). https://github.com/facebookresearch/detectron2

29. Zhong, Z., Zheng, L., Kang, G., Li, S., Yang, Y.: Random erasing data augmentation. In: Proceedings of the AAAI Conference on Artificial Intelligence, vol. 34, pp. 13001–13008 (2020)

Structure-Aware Photorealistic Style Transfer Using Ghost Bottlenecks

Nhat-Tan Bui[1,3,4], Ngoc-Thao Nguyen[2,3(✉)], and Xuan-Nam Cao[2,3]

[1] International Training and Education Center, University of Science,
Ho Chi Minh City, Vietnam
`1859043@itec.hcmus.edu.vn`
[2] Faculty of Information Technology, University of Science, Ho Chi Minh City,
Vietnam
`{nnthao,cxnam}@fit.hcmus.edu.vn`
[3] Vietnam National University, Ho Chi Minh City, Vietnam
[4] Auckland University of Technology, Auckland, New Zealand

Abstract. Photorealistic style transfer synthesizes a new image from a
pair of content and style images. The transfer should express the visual
patterns in the former while preserving the content details following the
latter. However, most existing methods may generate an image that suffers disrupted content details and unexpected visual cues from the style
image; hence, they do not satisfy the photorealism. We tackle this issue
with a new style transfer architecture that effectively unifies a content
encoder, an Xception style encoder, a Ghost Bottlenecks subnet, and a
decoder. In our framework, the style features extracted from the Xception module balance well with the content features obtained from an
encoder; the Ghost Bottlenecks subnet then integrates these features
and feeds them into a decoder to produce the resulting style transferred
image. Experimental results demonstrate that our model surmounts the
structure distortion problem to satisfy photorealistic style transfer and
hence obtains impressive visual effects.

Keywords: Style transfer · Structure-preserving · Photorealism ·
Xception · Ghost Bottleneck

1 Introduction

Style transfer plays an essential part in the field of texture synthesis. From one
content image and one style image, the style transfer algorithms generate a result
image with the presence of the textures, colors, and brushstrokes from the style
while maintaining consistency with the content.

This field has recently drawn much attention since Gatys et al. [1] proposed a
pioneering work that uses a pretrained VGG19 [2] with a novel loss function. The
loss function considers both content and style aspects by taking the weighted
sum of the mean squared error (MSE) and the Gram matrix.

© Springer Nature Switzerland AG 2022
M. El Yacoubi et al. (Eds.): ICPRAI 2022, LNCS 13363, pp. 15–24, 2022.
https://doi.org/10.1007/978-3-031-09037-0_2

| Content | Style | AdaIN | Our |

Fig. 1. The original AdaIN layer of Huang et al. [11] tends to produce redundant style textures which make structure distortion while our model better captures the detailed structure of the content.

Most of the style transfer methods have one main issue is the spatial distortion which makes the results seem to be unrealistic by blurring meaningful information (e.g., edges, objects, contours, etc.) from the content images. Moreover, the chaos of colors and textures, which usually appears in almost all methods, is another reason for the inadequate quality of the stylized images.

Motivated by the observations above, we present a novel style transfer method that combines different pre-trained (CNN) models include GhostNet [3], Xception [4] and VGG [2] to obtain the content faithfulness, as shown in Fig. 1.

In summary, the contributions of this paper are threefold:

- We introduce a style transfer architecture which is able to generate an image based on any style/content image with plausible visual quality. The resulting image successfully blends the subtle details while preserving the primary edges and boundaries, hence better heading toward photorealism.
- Our research utilizes Xception as the feature extractor for style image and multilayer perceptron (MLP) to create parameters for Adaptive Instance Normalization in the Ghost Bottlenecks subnet to attain photorealistic style transfer.
- The effectiveness of our method is empirically verified to be superior to comparative methods on the publicly available dataset and objective metrics.

2   Related Work

Style Transfer. Traditional style transfer is related to texture transfer. Some early approaches had been explored in [5,6]. Gatys et al. [1] for the first time utilized convolution layers to match feature statistics of two images. Since then, several improvements had been introduced [7–10] to either achieve the quality and diversity of generated images or speed up the stylization.

Among them, Huang and Belongie [11] propose the Adaptive Instance Normalization (AdaIN) which matching feature statistics (channel-wise mean and variance) of the content images and style images by adaptively computing the mean and variance independently across spatial locations. Inspired by them, we also use AdaIN to perform the core style transfer for our model.

For the structure-preserving and artifact elimination, Li et al. [12] proposed the Laplacian loss to apprehend different scales of content images. Cheng et al. [13] introduced Structure-Representation Network which is the combination of a global structure extraction network and a local structure refinement network to detect the edge structures and the depth map of the content images. However, all of these methods require other loss functions which add unnecessary complexity for the model to achieve structure consistency.

Deep Generative Model. To address the Image-to-Image Translation in general and Style Transfer in particular, there are several frameworks, including auto-encoder [14], variational auto-encoders [15], generative adversarial networks (GANs) [16].

Convolutional Neural Network architectures. Recently, computer vision has witnessed a tremendous development of the CNN architecture in terms of both accuracy and number of parameters. This is demonstrated in the research of Khan et al. [17].

Xception [4], designed by Chollet, is entirely based on depthwise separable convolution with residual connections instead of normal convolution to achieve better efficiency without expensive computational cost. This inspires us to design a lightweight feature extractor for the style images.

In 2020, Han et al. [3] introduced GhostNet which applies a Ghost Module to create more features despite using fewer parameters. GhostNet is built on the Ghost Bottleneck which is constructed by stacking two Ghost Modules. Taking advantage of this research, we integrate the Ghost Bottleneck for our subnet to better capture the semantic features of the content images and the distribution characteristics of the style images.

3 Proposed Method

In this section, we first present the overall workflow of the proposed architecture (see Fig. 2) and then explain in detail each of the four core elements, including a content encoder, a style encoder, a Ghost Bootlenecks subnet, and a decoder.

3.1 Workflow

Our style transfer network takes one content image and one style image to synthesize a stylized image. The Xception style encoder takes a style image as input to extract the feature factors for the multilayer perceptron (MLP). The MLP produce a set of learnable parameters for the AdaIN algorithm from those features. On the other hand, an encoder aims to extract the content representations from a content image. After that, the content and style features are combined by the AdaIN layers in a subnet and fed into a decoder to generate the final result.

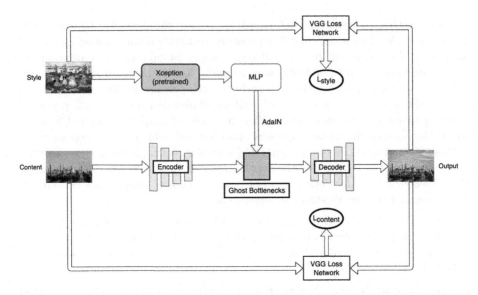

Fig. 2. The overall network architecture of our model. It mainly consists of an encoder-decoder architecture, the subnet which is multiple Ghost Bottlenecks, a pre-trained Xception, the MLP with AdaIN and a pre-trained VGG for the loss functions.

3.2   Architecture

Our content encoder comprises one standard convolution layer with 9×9 kernel and stride 1, the rest are convolution layers with 3×3 kernel and stride 2. The encoder use reflection padding, Instance Normalization (IN) [18] layers and LeakyReLU with slope 0.2 as the activation function.

We leverage Xception for style encoding, attaining two advantages compared to the previous methods [10,11,19] that use VGG19. First, the Xception can prevent the leaking of semantic information from the style images as well as the artifacts in the output images while successfully extracting *adequate* style features. Second, the Xception has fewer parameters than VGG19, thus it is a less laborious approach to generate the stylized images.

The subnet, which is the core of the encoder-decoder network, is two Ghost Bottlenecks. The Ghost Bottleneck helps creating more features for the content-style combination without introducing too many parameters and redundant feature maps. We use the multilayer perceptron (MLP) to provide parameters to the Ghost Bottlenecks, which is inspired by [20]. This MLP consist of a global average pooling layer, a flatten layer, and a fully-connected layer with ReLU followed by two fully-connected layers. We replace the batch normalization (BN) [21] layers in the original Ghost Bottlenecks by AdaIN layers which take parameters from the MLP.

$$AdaIN(x, \gamma, \beta) = \gamma \left(\frac{x - \mu(x)}{\sigma(x)} \right) + \beta \tag{1}$$

where γ and β are the dynamic parameters created by MLP, $\mu(x)$ and $\sigma(x)$ are the mean and standard deviation of previous layer, respectively. We empirically find that the combination of Ghost Bottlenecks subnet and the AdaIN can ensure the content details intact while still successful transfering the texture and color of the style image.

Our decoder which is symmetrical to the encoder comprises one convolution layer with 3×3 kernel and stride 2, two convolution layers with 3×3 kernel and stride 1, one convolution layer with 9×9 kernel and stride 1. Similar to the content encoder, all layers in the decoder utilize reflection padding and LeakyReLU with slope 0.2 except the last decoder layer which utilizes Tanh activation to guarantee the output in range [0,255]. Note that we do not use normalization layers for the decoder.

3.3   Loss Function

We use VGG19 [2] as our loss network to compute the loss function for our model.

$$\mathcal{L} = \mathcal{L}_{content} + \lambda \mathcal{L}_{style} \qquad (2)$$

where $\mathcal{L}_{content}$ is the content loss and $\mathcal{L}_{style}$ is the style loss with λ is a constant to regularize the contribution of the two losses into the joint loss. The content loss is the mean squared error between the content features and the stylized features of a specific layer in VGG19.

$$\mathcal{L}_{content} = ||\phi(D(E(x))) - \phi(x)||_2 \qquad (3)$$

where ϕ denotes a layer in VGG19 used to compute content loss, $D(E(x))$ is the features of output image and x is the features of the content image. We also leverage different layers in VGG19 to compute our style loss.

$$\mathcal{L}_{style} = ||\mu(\phi_i(D(E(x)))) - \mu(\phi_i(s))||_2 - ||\sigma(\phi_i(D(E(x)))) - \sigma(\phi_i(s))||_2 \qquad (4)$$

where μ and σ are the mean and standard deviation, respectively. ϕ_i denotes a layer in VGG19 used to compute style loss. $D(E(x))$ again is the features of stylization result while s is the features of style image.

4   Experiments

Datasets. Our model is trained on Microsoft COCO dataset [22] which has 82,783 content images and WikiArt [23] which has 79,433 style images. During training, we first apply smart resize (in Keras) to adjust the sizes of both the content and style images to 512×512 without aspect ratio distortion, then randomly crop regions of size 256×256. Note that during the testing, the content and style images can be any size.

Experiments Setting. We train our model in Google Colab with NVIDIA Tesla P100 for PCIe version 16GB CoWoS HBM2 GPU Memory. It takes roughly 1 h 15 min for training 1 epoch with 2 datasets.

Implementation Details. We adopt the *relu4_1* layer in VGG19 [2] for computing content loss and *relu1_1, relu2_1, relu3_1, relu4_1, relu5_1* layers for the style loss. The style loss weight is set to 10 and the learning rate is 0.0001 without any learning rate schedules. For the Xception [4] style encoder, we employ the layers *block7_sepconv1_act, block8_sepconv1_act, block9_sepconv1_act, block10_sepconv1_act* of a pre-trained Xception [4] in Keras for our style encoder. We train the model end-to-end with Adam optimizer [24] until the output is accepted.

Comparative Method. To evaluate the success of our model in the context of photorealistic style transfer, we compare our results with several previous methods in style transfer field. We use public source code in Github including Gatys et al. [1][1], AdaIN [11][2], AAMS [25][3], Wang et al. [26][4] and SAFIN [27][5] as the baselines for comparison. Note that all the baselines are implementation with default parameters.

4.1   Qualitative Results

For easy reading, we use the following notation, $[i, j]$, to refer to the image at row i and column j. We observe in Fig. 3 that the pioneer method of Gatys et al. introduces more excess textures than the others, severely distorting the primary details of the images (e.g., [3, 3], [4, 3], [5, 3] and [7, 3]). In this method, the balance of content and style is controlled by the α and β parameters ratio, and it is pretty challenging to search for an appropriate value across different contexts. On the other hand, the AdaIN method lets the style patterns intervene too much in the content layout, severely distorting the foreground objects. For example, the generated image in [2, 4] has a different countenance from the content image and the generated image in [6, 4] disrupts the face structure of the content image. The problem of distortion goes worse with the model of Wang et al. This model could not preserve the content details in most of the resulting images, especially those presenting faces (in images [3,6] and [4,6]). Meanwhile, the AAMS model blurs everything, bringing better measurements to metrics that average the pixel values yet negatively affecting the qualitative evaluation (see images in the fifth column). SAFIN has been proposed latest, and thus it is not surprising that SAFIN achieves stunning results. However, it occasionally makes the resulting image meaningless, which is especially obvious in the color of the eyes in [6, 7] image.

By contrast, our model can overcome the structure distortion issue, provide the balance and harmony between the stylized result and content preservation. Moreover, our method can prevent the artifacts from happening and enhance the semantic information of the content image with the art of the artworks.

---

[1] https://github.com/anishathalye/neural-style.
[2] https://github.com/naoto0804/pytorch-AdaIN.
[3] https://github.com/JianqiangRen/AAMS.
[4] https://github.com/mingsun-tse/collaborative-distillation.
[5] https://github.com/Aaditya-Singh/SAFIN.

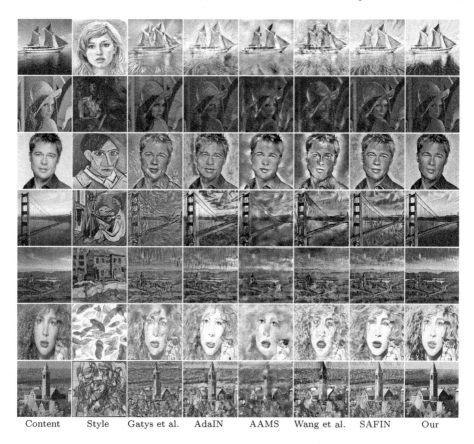

| Content | Style | Gatys et al. | AdaIN | AAMS | Wang et al. | SAFIN | Our |

Fig. 3. Qualitative comparison between our model and previous methods. The first column is the content images and the second column shows the style images. The rest columns illustrate the generated results of different methods.

Our approach is able to distinguish the foreground and background regions to retain the overall structure and embellish the images with colors, textures and paint strokes, thus generating plausible stylized results. The proposed method is comparative to the best one in each scenario and it is most stable across the six methods. We also illustrate more qualitative results of our model in Fig. 4.

4.2   Quantitative Results

To further validate the effectiveness of our model, we compute two quantitative evaluation metrics: Structural Similarity Index (SSIM) [28] and Root Mean Square Error (RMSE) by Scikit-image library. We randomly select 100 content images from the validation set of Microsoft COCO dataset [22], 10 style images from Wikiart website and combine 10 content images with 1 style image to generate 1000 stylized results and then use those results to compute different metrics. The average results are displayed in Table 1.

Fig. 4. More stylized examples generated by our model on different artworks. The first column is the content images, the first row shows the style images and the rest is the results.

Structural Similarity Index. The SSIM score, which is in range $[-1, 1]$, will represent the similarity measure between two images. The higher in SSIM, the better detail-preserving the model has. Based on the recorded scores, our model gets the highest score on the SSIM metric.

Root Mean Square Error. The RMSE is a common technique used to measure the distance of two images. The lower in RMSE, the higher change in two identical images is. We detect the edge detection results of the content and generated images by Canny algorithm [29] in OpenCV and compute the RMSE between those edge results. It is easy to recognize that our approach outperform other methods in term of RMSE score in the large margin.

Table 1. The SSIM and RMSE comparison to baseline models. The best score are emphasized in bold.

	Gatys et al.	AdaIN	AAMS	Wang et al.	SAFIN	Our
SSIM ↑	0.2142	0.2875	0.2379	0.2165	0.4077	**0.4086**
RMSE ↓	99.2631	85.1591	83.1870	88.7060	84.0963	**75.8293**

5   Conclusion

In this work, we have developed a novel style transfer model for enhancing the photorealism and persevering the content details for the stylized results. The combination of Xception network as the style extractor, AdaIN and Ghost Bottlenecks subnet has proven the effectiveness by comparisons against the previous state-of-the-art in terms of photorealistic style transfers. In the future, we will further explore the relation between structural consistency and artistic effect to ameliorate the quality of generated images.

References

1. Gatys, L.A., Ecker, A.S., Bethge, M.: Image style transfer using convolutional neural networks. In: IEEE Conference on Computer Vision and Pattern Recognition (CVPR) (2016)
2. Simonyan, K., Zisserman, A.: Very deep convolutional networks for large-scale image recognition. In: International Conference on Learning Representations (2015)
3. Han, K., Wang, Y., Tian, Q., Guo, J., Xu, C., Xu, C.: GhostNet: more features from cheap operations. In: IEEE Conference on Computer Vision and Pattern Recognition (CVPR) (2020)
4. Chollet, F.: Xception: deep learning with depthwise separable convolutions. In: IEEE Conference on Computer Vision and Pattern Recognition (CVPR) (2017)
5. Heeger, D.J., Bergen, J.R.: Pyramid-based texture analysis/synthesis. In: Proceedings of the 22nd Annual Conference on Computer Graphics and Interactive Techniques, pp. 229–238 (1995)
6. Efros, A.A., Freeman, W.T.: Image quilting for texture synthesis and transfer. In: Proceedings of the 28nd Annual Conference on Computer Graphics and Interactive Techniques, pp. 341–346 (2001)
7. Ulyanov, D., Vedaldi, A., Lempitsky, V.: Improved texture networks: maximizing quality and diversity in feed-forward stylization and texture synthesis. In: IEEE Conference on Computer Vision and Pattern Recognition (CVPR) (2017)
8. Chen, T.Q., Schmidt, M.: Fast Patch-Based Style Transfer of Arbitrary Style. arXiv preprint arXiv:1612.04337 (2016)
9. Johnson, J., Alahi, A., Fei-Fei, L.: Perceptual losses for real-time style transfer and super-resolution. In: European Conference on Computer Vision (ECCV) (2016)
10. Li, Y., Fang, C., Yang, J., Wang, Z., Lu, X., Yang, M.-H.: Universal style transfer via feature transforms. In: Proceedings of the 31st International Conference on Neural Information Processing Systems (NeurIPS) (2017)
11. Huang, X., Belongie, S.: Arbitrary style transfer in real-time with adaptive instance normalization. In: IEEE International Conference on Computer Vision (ICCV) (2017)
12. Li, S., Xu, X., Nie, L., Chua, T.-S.: Laplacian-steered neural style transfer. In: Proceedings of the 25th ACM international conference on Multimedia (2017)
13. Cheng, M.-M., Liu, X.-C., Wang, J., Lu, S.-P., Lai, Y.-K., Rosin, P.L.: Structure-preserving neural style transfer. IEEE Trans. Image Process. 29, 909–920 (2020)
14. Ranzato, M., Huang, F.-J., Boureau, Y.-L., LeCun, Y.: Unsupervised learning of invariant feature hierarchies with applications to object recognition. In: IEEE Conference on Computer Vision and Pattern Recognition (CVPR) (2007)

15. Kingma, D.P., Welling, M.: Auto-encoding variational Bayes. In: International Conference on Learning Representations (2014)
16. Goodfellow, I.J., et al.: Generative adversarial nets. In: Proceedings of the 27th International Conference on Neural Information Processing Systems (NIPS), vol. 2, pp. 2672–2680 (2014)
17. Khan, A., Sohail, A., Zahoora, U., Qureshi, A.S.: A survey of the recent architectures of deep convolutional neural networks. In: Artificial Intelligence Review (2020)
18. Ulyanov, D., Vedaldi, A., Lempitsky, V.: Instance Normalization: The Missing Ingredient for Fast Stylization. arXiv preprint arXiv:1607.08022 (2016)
19. Li, X., Liu, S., Kautz, J., Yang, M.-H.: Learning linear transformations for fast image and video style transfer. In: IEEE Conference on Computer Vision and Pattern Recognition (CVPR) (2019)
20. Huang, X., Liu, M.-Y., Belongie, S., Kautz, J.: Multimodal unsupervised image-to-image translation. In: European Conference on Computer Vision (ECCV) (2018)
21. Ioffe, S., Szegedy, C.: Batch normalization: accelerating deep network training by reducing internal covariate shift. In: Proceedings of the 32nd International Conference on International Conference on Machine Learning (ICML), vol. 37, pp. 448–456 (2015)
22. Lin, T.-Y., et al.: Microsoft COCO: common objects in context. In: European Conference on Computer Vision (ECCV) (2014)
23. Nichol, K.: Painter by numbers, wikiart. https://www.kaggle.com/c/painter-by-numbers
24. Kingma, D.P., Ba, J.: Adam: a method for stochastic optimization. In: International Conference on Learning Representations (ICLR) (2015)
25. Yao, Y., Ren, J., Xie, X., Liu, W., Liu, Y.-J., Wang, J.: Attention-aware multi-stroke style transfer. In: IEEE Conference on Computer Vision and Pattern Recognition (CVPR) (2019)
26. Wang, H., Li, Y., Wang, Y., Hu, H., Yang, M.: Collaborative distillation for ultra-resolution universal style transfer. In: IEEE Conference on Computer Vision and Pattern Recognition (CVPR) (2020)
27. Singh, A., Hingane, S., Gong, X., Wang, Z.: SAFIN: arbitrary style transfer with self-attentive factorized instance normalization. In: IEEE International Conference on Multimedia and Expo (ICME) (2021)
28. Wang, Z., Bovik, A.C., Sheikh, H.R., Simoncelli, E.P.: Image quality assessment: from error visibility to structural similarity. In: IEEE Transactions on Image Processing, vol. 13, pp. 600–612 (2004)
29. Canny, J.: A computational approach to edge detection. In: IEEE Transactions on Pattern Analysis and Machine Intelligence, pp. 679–698 (1986)

Analysing the Impact of Vibrations on Smart Wheelchair Systems and Users

Elhassan Mohamed$^{(\boxtimes)}$ ⒾD, Konstantinos Sirlantzis ⒾD, and Gareth Howells ⒾD

University of Kent, Canterbury CT2 7NT, UK
{enrm4,k.sirlantzis,w.g.j.howells}@kent.ac.uk

Abstract. Mechanical vibrations due to uneven terrains can significantly impact the accuracy of computer vision systems installed on any moving vehicle. In this study, we investigate the impact of mechanical vibrations induced using artificial bumps in a controlled environment on the performance of smart computer vision systems installed on an Electrical powered Wheelchair (EPW). Besides, the impact of the vibrations on the user's health and comfort is quantified using the vertical acceleration of an Inertial Measurement Unit (IMU) sensor according to the ISO standard 2631. The proposed smart computer vision system is a semantic segmentation based on deep learning for pixels classification that provides environmental cues for visually impaired users to facilitate safe and independent navigation. In addition, it provides the EPW user with the estimated distance to objects of interest. Results show that a high level of vibrations can negatively impact the performance of the computer vision system installed on powered wheelchairs. Also, high levels of whole-body vibrations negatively impact the user's health and comfort.

Keywords: Computer vision · Mechanical vibrations · Powered wheelchair · Semantic segmentation

1 Introduction

Smart computer vision systems based on Deep Learning (DL) are widely used in semi-autonomous and fully autonomous systems for several purposes such as object detection [2,5], scene understanding [11,16], and object interaction [9,15]. A hostile environment can negatively impact the performance of these systems, which may result in inaccurate human-system interaction. Mobile robots and smart vehicles are susceptible to mechanical vibrations due to traversing rough and uneven terrains. The ability to estimate the impact of vibration on the system performance is the first step to mitigating undesirable vibrations. This can enhance the system performance in challenging conditions; consequently, better human-system interaction can be attained.

Marichal et al. [10] investigated the impact of vibration produced by a helicopter on a vision system. It is concluded that the quality of the captured images

© Springer Nature Switzerland AG 2022
M. El Yacoubi et al. (Eds.): ICPRAI 2022, LNCS 13363, pp. 25–33, 2022.
https://doi.org/10.1007/978-3-031-09037-0_3

is negatively impacted due to the undesirable movement of the camera. The proposed semi-active frequency isolation technique has proved efficiency in improving the captured images with low vibrations. Consequently, the subsequent utilise of the captured images is enhanced. However, the proposed technique needs prior knowledge of the vibration frequency in order for the system to be able to isolate it.

Periu et al. [14] studied the impact of the vibrations on the performance of obstacle detection using a LIght Detection And Ranging (LIDAR) sensor. The LIDAR sensor is installed on a tractor for obstacle detection and guidance purposes. Generally, agriculture vehicles do not have a suspension system, similar to the EPW used in our experiments. The measurements of the LIDAR sensor can be significantly impacted by mechanical vibrations induced during the operation of the vehicle on rough and bumpy terrains. The study proposes supporting bars and stabilising systems to counteract the vibrations impact. It is concluded that with the increase in the tractor speed, the accuracy of the LIDAR decreases due to high levels of mechanical vibrations; consequently, the position estimation error increase. Thus, the mean error distance and the standard deviation between the actual and the detected position increase.

Vibrations due to ramps, damaged terrains, and uneven tarmacs are not only impacting the accuracy of the smart systems installed on the powered wheelchairs but also can impact the health and comfort of disabled users. This paper investigates the impact of vibrations on a semantic segmentation system used by visually impaired EPW users to understand their surroundings by providing environmental cues. Environmental cues can help visually impaired users to locate objects in their surroundings [12]. The paper also investigates the vibration impact on users' health and comfort and how it can be related to the impact on the computer vision systems of the powered wheelchair.

The paper is organised as follows: experimental setup is presented in Sect. 2. Section 3 discusses the results and the outcomes of the study. The study is concluded in Sect. 4, where future work is highlighted.

2 Methodology

A powered wheelchair is driven for 11 m on a carpet floor with and without artificial bumps in a controlled indoor environment. The chosen distance represents the maximum straight route of the corridor without turnings. The bumps, which are used to introduce the vibrations, are installed 1.5 m apart (Fig. 1) to keep the seven bumps equally distanced throughout the route length and to provide enough space for the powered wheelchair to stabilise before the next bump. Two kinds of data are collected: the accelerations using an IMU sensor installed on the powered wheelchair seat and videos using a camera installed beneath the joystick (Fig. 2). The acceleration data has been processed for the two scenarios (with and without bumps) to quantify the impact of whole-body vibrations on user's health and comfort with respect to the ISO-2631 standard [8]. The two 21-seconds videos are annotated on the pixel level for the assessment of the semantic segmentation system, with around 26.8 million pixels are annotated for each video.

The extracted 65 ground truth images from each video are compared with the corresponding predictions using a semantic segmentation system trained on data from the same distribution (the same indoor environment) [12]. The proposed system is based on Deep Lab Version 3 plus (DLV3+) [3] with some modifications [12]. The system [12] uses ResNet-18 [7] as its feature extraction network. ResNet-18 is a perfect choice as it uses residual blocks that help the system to process high-resolution images (960×540×3 pixels) using a deep network (many layers) without losing information because of the vanishing gradients problem [1,6]. Besides, using ResNet-18 as a base network for the DLV3+ has achieved better results and processing speed [12] compared to the usage of ResNet-50 or Xception [4] base networks that are used in the original implementation of DLV3+ [3].

Fig. 1. Artificial bumps to introduce vibrations fixed 1.5 m apart.

3 Results

Results show the impact of undesirable vibration on both the semantic segmentation systems and the user's health. Table 1 shows the impact of vibration on the user's health and comfort. The calculations are made according to the ISO-2631 standard [8]. Driving the powered wheelchair on the carpet floor presents neither a health risk nor discomfort to the user. The user of the powered wheelchair weighs 95 Kg and is 184 cm tall. As users' weight can impact the vibration levels [13], further studies with different weight users will be implemented in future work.

(a) Powered wheelchair weight: 59.5 Kg. (b) Intel® RealSense™ Depth Camera. (c) Mounting disk with IMU sensor.

Fig. 2. System installation for data collection.

On the other hand, the introduced bumps make the situation a potential health risk and uncomfortable to the user. Figure 3 shows the vertical acceleration of both scenarios (with and without the introduced vibrations). The vertical accelerations of the seven bumps can be clearly seen from the sudden changes in the signal's amplitude (blue signal). In contrast, the red signal, which represents the 'no vibration' scenario, does not have any sudden changes in the amplitude.

The analysis of the whole body vibration of the two scenarios is comparable with user 3 in [13], for which the user drives the powered wheelchair on the carpet floor for the no vibration case and the tiled concrete for the vibration case.

Table 1. Vibration impact on user's health and comfort.

State	No vibration					With vibration				
Assessment	Health				Comfort	Health				Comfort
Metric	$a_w(m/s^2)$	$MTVV(m/s^2)$	$MTVV/a_w$	$eVDV(7.5h)$	VTV	$a_w(m/s^2)$	$MTVV(m/s^2)$	$MTVV/a_w$	$eVDV(7.5h)$	VTV
Values	0.07	0.07	1.04	1.37	0.12	1.11	1.32	1.19	19.91	1.30
Result	No health risk				Not uncomfortable	Potential health risk				Uncomfortable

Figure 4 shows the detection performance of the system in the absence (first column) and the presence (second column) of the introduced vibrations. It can be seen that the vibrations have dramatically impacted the detection of objects such as the movable door handle, which the semantic segmentation system could not detect due to the sudden vibrations. Generally, the ability of the semantic

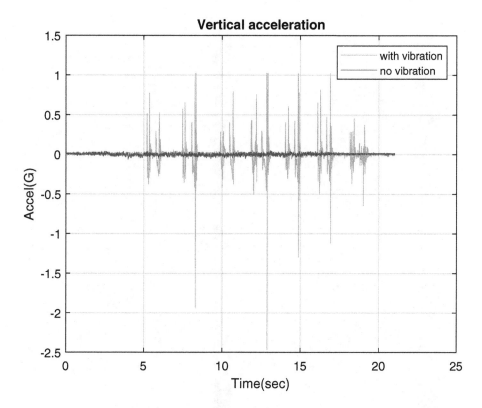

Fig. 3. Vertical accelerations with and without the introduced vibrations.

segmentation system to classify the image pixels has degraded due to the introduced vibrations. Qualitatively, the degradation can be seen in the fourth row of Fig. 4, where the intense green and magenta colours indicate these differences between the ground truth data and the system predictions. These pixels are unannotated or misclassified. The green colour shows the unannotated pixels which do not belong to objects of interest. At the same time, the magenta one shows the misclassified objects.

Quantitatively, the first two rows of Table 2 shows the evaluation metrics of the two scenarios (with and without the introduced vibrations). It can be observed that the performance of the semantic segmentation system degrades as a result of the introduced vibrations. Thus, it can be concluded from the results that the performance of the semantic segmenting system can be negatively impacted by the vibrations encountered while driving the powered wheelchair. Also, the change in performance is directly proportional to the amount of vibration.

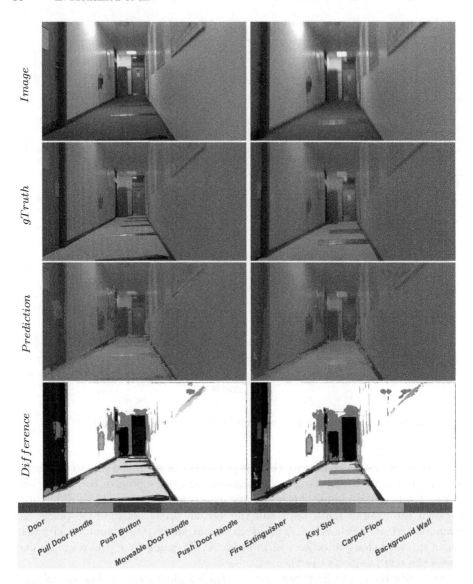

Fig. 4. The impact of vibrations on the performance of the semantic segmentation system. First column represents an image without vibrations and second one represents an image with vibration.

To further investigate the vibration impact on the semantic system accuracy, we segregate the images of the vibration dataset (when the artificial vibrations are introduced, the second row of Table 2) into two categories (last two rows of Table 2): images during the vibration incident and images before or after the vibration incident. The first group of images represents the times when the

Table 2. Evaluation metrics with and without the introduced vibration on the images level.

State	Metrics	Global accuracy	Mean accuracy	Mean IoU	Weighted IoU	Mean BF score
Without vibrations (65 images)	Mean	0.914	0.492	0.340	0.889	0.508
	Std	0.040	0.061	0.034	0.051	0.075
With vibrations (65 images)	Mean	0.877	0.475	0.309	0.842	0.472
	Std	0.062	0.054	0.041	0.081	0.075
Without vibration incident (50 images)	Mean	0.882	0.485	0.315	0.847	0.484
	Std	0.057	0.051	0.038	0.078	0.071
During vibration incident (15 images)	Mean	0.863	0.444	0.287	0.826	0.435
	Std	0.078	0.056	0.047	0.092	0.080

powered wheelchair encountered a bump, such as sub-figures b and d in Fig. 5. The second group of images represents the times when the powered wheelchair does not encounter a bump, such as sub-figures a and c in Fig. 5. Then, the mean and the standard deviation of accuracy, IoU, and Mean BF score on the level of the images are calculated. The number of captured images during a vibration incident due to a bump is 15. The remaining images (50) are considered as images without vibration incident, although the total 65 images are captured together. Table 2 shows the metrics of the two groups of images (last two rows).

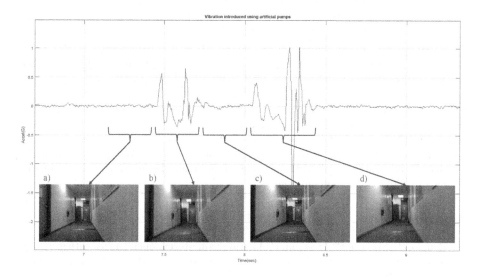

Fig. 5. Segregation method for the vibration dataset images.

It can be noticed that the portion of images from the vibration dataset that are collected without the incident of external vibration (before or after the bumps) has convergent metrics to the dataset which has been collected without any external vibrations. At the same time, the portion of images that are captured during the incident of vibration has been significantly impacted by the vibrations resulting in the lowest accuracy amongst all datasets. This emphasises the results and highlights the impact of vibrations on the semantic segmentation system.

The study has been conducted on a Roma powered wheelchair that does not have a suspension system, similar to the tractor used in [14]. A powered wheelchair suspension, mainly used to dampen vibrations, may negatively impact the system's performance by introducing more vibrations to counter the external ones. This will be investigated in the future work of this study.

4   Conclusion

In conclusion, we can anticipate a deterioration in the semantic segmentation system performance when driving a powered wheelchair on types of terrains that can cause health risks or discomfort for the user. Therefore, we recommend that the developers and researchers consider the impact of vibrations on the computer vision systems installed on powered wheelchairs. A shock absorption system or a camera stabiliser holder can reduce the negative effects of the vibrations on the system's accuracy, as shown in the literature. On the other hand, reducing the speed of the powered wheelchair can lower the potential risks to the users' health and comfort. Producing an accurate semantic segmentation system is beneficial for visually impaired disabled users to increase their independence. Besides, it can allow the approval of using electrical powered wheelchairs for those users who currently are not permitted to use powered wheelchairs due to their disabilities. The future step of this study is to investigate and compare the impact of vibrations on users' health and the performance of smart vision systems using powered wheelchairs with suspension systems.

Acknowledgment. This work is supported by the Assistive Devices for empowering dis-Abled People through robotic Technologies (ADAPT) project. ADAPT is selected for funding by the INTERREG VA France (Channel) England Programme which is co-financed by the European Regional Development Fund (ERDF). The European Regional Development Fund (ERDF) is one of the main financial instruments of the European Unions (EU) cohesion policy.

References

1. Bengio, Y., Simard, P., Frasconi, P.: Learning long-term dependencies with gradient descent is difficult. IEEE Trans. Neural Netw. **5**(2), 157–166 (1994). https://doi.org/10.1109/72.279181
2. Bruno, D.R., Osorio, F.S.: Image classification system based on deep learning applied to the recognition of traffic signs for intelligent robotic vehicle navigation purposes. In: 2017 Latin American Robotics Symposium (LARS) and 2017 Brazilian Symposium on Robotics (SBR), pp. 1–6 (2017). https://doi.org/10.1109/SBR-LARS-R.2017.8215287

3. Chen, L.C., Zhu, Y., Papandreou, G., Schroff, F., Adam, H.: Encoder-decoder with atrous separable convolution for semantic image segmentation. In: Proceedings of the European Conference on Computer Vision (ECCV), pp. 801–818 (2018)

4. Chollet, F.: Xception: deep learning with depthwise separable convolutions. In: Proceedings of the IEEE Conference on Computer Vision and Pattern Recognition, pp. 1251–1258 (2017)

5. Ess, A., Schindler, K., Leibe, B., Gool, L.V.: Object detection and tracking for autonomous navigation in dynamic environments. Int. J. Robot. Res. **29**(14), 1707–1725 (2010). https://doi.org/10.1177/0278364910365417

6. Glorot, X., Bengio, Y.: Understanding the difficulty of training deep feedforward neural networks. In: Teh, Y.W., Titterington, M. (eds.) Proceedings of the Thirteenth International Conference on Artificial Intelligence and Statistics, Proceedings of Machine Learning Research, PMLR, Chia Laguna Resort, Sardinia, 13–15 May 2010, vol. 9, pp. 249–256 (2010). http://proceedings.mlr.press/v9/glorot10a.html

7. He, K., Zhang, X., Ren, S., Sun, J.: Deep residual learning for image recognition. In: Proceedings of the IEEE Conference on Computer Vision and Pattern Recognition, pp. 770–778 (2016)

8. Mechanical vibration and shock - evaluation of human exposure to whole-body vibration - part 1: general requirements. In: Standard, International Organization for Standardization, Geneva, CH, May 1997 (1997)

9. Jiang, H., Zhang, T., Wachs, J.P., Duerstock, B.S.: Enhanced control of a wheelchair-mounted robotic manipulator using 3-d vision and multimodal interaction. Comput. Vis. Image Understand. **149**, 21–31 (2016). https://doi.org/10.1016/j.cviu.2016.03.015,https://www.sciencedirect.com/science/article/pii/S1077314216300066, special issue on Assistive Computer Vision and Robotics - "Assistive Solutions for Mobility, Communication and HMI"

10. Marichal, G.N., Tomás-Rodríguez, M., Hernández, Á., Castillo-Rivera, S., Campoy, P.: Vibration reduction for vision systems on board UAV using a neuro-fuzzy controller

11. Miyamoto, R., et al.: Vision-based road-following using results of semantic segmentation for autonomous navigation. In: 2019 IEEE 9th International Conference on Consumer Electronics (ICCE-Berlin), pp. 174–179 (2019). https://doi.org/10.1109/ICCE-Berlin47944.2019.8966198

12. Mohamed, E., Sirlantzis, K., Howells, G.: Indoor/outdoor semantic segmentation using deep learning for visually impaired wheelchair users. IEEE Access **9**, 147914–147932 (2021). https://doi.org/10.1109/ACCESS.2021.3123952

13. Mohamed, E., Sirlantzis, K., Howells, G., Dib, J.: Investigation of vibration and user comfort for powered wheelchairs. IEEE Sens. Lett. **6**(2), 1–4 (2022). https://doi.org/10.1109/LSENS.2022.3147740

14. Periu, C., Mohsenimanesh, A., Laguë, C., McLaughlin, N.: Isolation of vibrations transmitted to a lidar sensor mounted on an agricultural vehicle to improve obstacle detection. Canadian Biosyst. Eng. **55** (2013)

15. Quintero, C.P., Ramirez, O., Jägersand, M.: Vibi: assistive vision-based interface for robot manipulation. In: 2015 IEEE International Conference on Robotics and Automation (ICRA), pp. 4458–4463 (2015). https://doi.org/10.1109/ICRA.2015.7139816

16. Rashed, H., El Sallab, A., Yogamani, S., ElHelw, M.: Motion and depth augmented semantic segmentation for autonomous navigation. In: Proceedings of the IEEE/CVF Conference on Computer Vision and Pattern Recognition (CVPR) Workshops (2019)

Visual Microfossil Identification via Deep Metric Learning

Tayfun Karaderi[1,3(✉)], Tilo Burghardt[1], Allison Y. Hsiang[2], Jacob Ramaer[1], and Daniela N. Schmidt[3]

[1] Department of Computer Science, University of Bristol, Bristol, UK
vm19402@bristol.ac.uk, karaderitayfun@gmail.com
[2] Institutionen för geologiska vetenskaper, Stockholm University, Stockholm, Sweden
[3] School of Earth Sciences, University of Bristol, Bristol, UK

Abstract. We apply deep metric learning for the first time to the problem of classifying planktic foraminifer shells on microscopic images. This species recognition task is an important information source and scientific pillar for reconstructing past climates. All foraminifer CNN recognition pipelines in the literature produce black-box classifiers that lack visualisation options for human experts and cannot be applied to open set problems. Here, we benchmark metric learning against these pipelines, produce the first scientific visualisation of the phenotypic planktic foraminifer morphology space, and demonstrate that metric learning can be used to cluster species unseen during training. We show that metric learning outperforms all published CNN-based state-of-the-art benchmarks in this domain. We evaluate our approach on the 34,640 expert-annotated images of the Endless Forams public library of 35 modern planktic foramini-fera species. Our results on this data show leading 92% accuracy (at 0.84 F1-score) in reproducing expert labels on withheld test data, and 66.5% accuracy (at 0.70 F1-score) when clustering species never encountered in training. We conclude that metric learning is highly effective for this domain and serves as an important tool towards expert-in-the-loop automation of microfossil identification. Key code, network weights, and data splits are published with this paper for full reproducibility.

Keywords: Applied computer vision · Planktic foraminifers · Deep learning · Animal biometrics · Paleobiology · Climate science

1 Introduction

Motivation. Planktic foraminifers are an invaluable source of information for reconstructing past climate records [25]. Estimating ocean temperature, salinity, and pH using foraminifers involves quantifying the species composition of shell assemblages or picking individual specimens, often at low abundance, out of thousands of specimens. Identification of specimens to the species level is necessary as species-specific vital effects can result in different isotopic fractionation values [34]. Foraminifers grow their calcium carbonate shells by adding chambers in a spiral, where the main gross morphological traits used for taxonomic

© Springer Nature Switzerland AG 2022
M. El Yacoubi et al. (Eds.): ICPRAI 2022, LNCS 13363, pp. 34–46, 2022.
https://doi.org/10.1007/978-3-031-09037-0_4

identification are chamber form and arrangement, the size and position of an aperture, and other features [15] (see Figs. 1 and 2). The differences between species are often plastic along sliding morphological change [35] and human identifiers manipulate the specimen under the microscope to aid recognition. In contrast, single-view static image recognition confidence can be restricted by acquisition artefacts, imaging quality, and the viewpoint-dependent visibility limitations of traits. These factors pose a significant challenge with regard to the use of computer vision systems for automating single image identification.

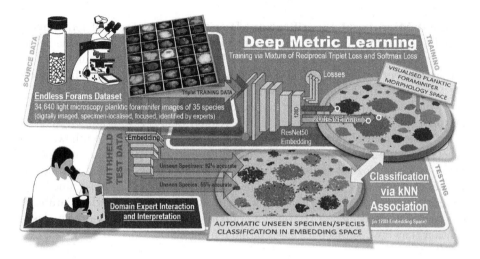

Fig. 1. Deep Metric Learning of Foraminifer Spaces. Schematic overview of the approach. Expert-annotated planktic foraminifer imagery (green) is used to metrically learn (blue) embeddings of specimen visuals in a 128D morphological appearance space via a Resnet50-based deep network using hybrid reciprocal triplet and Softmax loss minimisation. The built space naturally allows for a t-SNE visualisation of specimens and species including their geometric and topological relations. Unseen specimens and even unseen species not used for training can be projected into this space for automatic classification (red). Domain experts can now for the first time see the location of specimens in the morphological space and interpret results taxonomically. (Color figure online)

Paper Contributions. Inspired by classic machine learning (ML) applications for microfossils [4,5,48], recent pioneering works [19,30] started to evaluate convolutional neural networks (CNNs) for visual foraminifer recognition. However, none of the published pipelines so far allow for meaningful visualisations and expert interactions with the learned space of specimens, application to unseen species, or utilisation of contrastive gradients. In this paper, we address the above limitations for the first time via deep metric learning [2,40] in the domain. Figure 1 illustrates our approach visually. After a review of background and methodology, we will experimentally demonstrate that metric learning can outperform the current state-of-the-art (SOTA) in foraminifer classification benchmarks. In addition, we will show that our approach can generate grey-box foraminifer classification models with which domain experts can interact. Finally, we will explore how far the projection of unseen foraminifer species into this space (zero-shot scenario) can generalise learning beyond trained foraminifer classes.

2   Background

Manual Microfossil Identification. Despite the importance of foraminifers in paleoclimatology, few aggregated public resources exist to train people in the task of distinguishing morphologically similar taxa. Further, diverging views on species concepts and boundaries (e.g., 'clumpers' vs. 'splitters') result in conflicting taxonomies in the literature. As a result, the taxonomic agreement is sometimes only $\sim 75\%$ [1] for planktic foraminifera since they exhibit near-continuous morphological gradations between closely related taxa [11] (see Fig. 2). In some cases, morphological variation is unrelated to genetic differentiation; however in others genetic analysis has revealed the existence of some pseudo-cryptic species between morphological endmembers [20]. These difficulties resulted in different species concepts over time, which are particularly prominent in self-trained taxonomists [1]. Some of these challenges might be removed by growing databases of expert-classified images [7], opening opportunities for machine-driven classification that limit subjective biases of human classifiers.

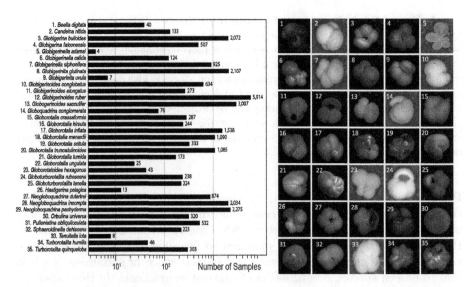

Fig. 2. Foraminifer Microscope Imagery. The Endless Forams public image library is used as our data source of modern planktonic foraminifera. *(left)* The distribution of the species classes varies strongly with a mean of 795 and a standard deviation of 1171. *(right)* Visualisation of a sample from each of the 35 species in the dataset.

Current Machine Vision for Microfossil Classification. Modern semantic image classification frameworks are almost without exception grounded in feed-forward CNNs, introduced in their earliest form by the ground-breaking work of Krizhevsky et al. [24] and leading to further milestone architectures including VGG16 [42], Inception [44], ResNet [14], ResNeXt [50], and deep transformer networks [47]. Taxonomic computer vision (CV) applications of these techniques for microfossils are still very rare in the literature, despite steep advances in general animal biometrics [26,46]. Nevertheless, ML-based species identification [8,33] has been applied to several microscopic taxa, including coccoliths [43], pollen [45], and phytoplankton [49]. While there have been early attempts for automatic classification on marine microfossils [4,48] the most successful focused on coccoliths which are predominantly flat [5,6]. There exist only very few papers which investigate the use of modern deep learning techniques on planktic foraminifers [19,30,32], all of which put forward traditional non-contrastive CNN architectures optimising for prediction correctness via SoftMax cross-entropy.

Metric Latent Spaces. Metric learning [2,40] moves away from focusing learning on optimising prediction correctness only; instead, a mapping into a class-distinctive latent space is constructed where maps to the same class naturally cluster together and distances directly relate to input similarity under the training task. A simple way of building a latent space of this form is to pass two inputs through an embedding function and then use a contrastive loss L_C [13]:

$$L_C = (1 - Y)0.5d(x_1, x_2) + 0.5Y \, max(0, \alpha - d(x_1, x_2)), \tag{1}$$

where x_1 and x_2 are the embedded input vectors, Y is a binary label denoting class equivalence/difference for the two inputs, and $d(\cdot, \cdot)$ is the Euclidean distance between two embeddings. However, this formulation cannot put similarities and dissimilarities between different pairs of embeddings in relation. A triplet loss formulation [41] instead utilises embeddings x_a, x_p and x_n denoting an anchor, a positive example of the same class, and a negative example of a different class, respectively. Minimising the distance between the same-class pair and maximising the distance between the different-class pair can be achieved by:

$$L_{TL} = max(0; d(x_a, x_p) - d(x_a, x_n) + \alpha), \tag{2}$$

where α is the margin hyper-parameter. Reciprocal triplet loss removes the need for this parameter [31] and accounts for large margins far away from the anchor:

$$L_{RTL} = d(x_a, x_p) + 1/d(x_a, x_n). \tag{3}$$

Including a SoftMax term in this loss can improve performance, as shown by recent work [17,27]. Thus, the SoftMax and reciprocal triplet losses can be combined into the standard formulation first published in [2] used in this paper:

$$L = \frac{-log(e^{x_{class}})}{\sum_i e^{x_i}} + \lambda L_{RTL}, \tag{4}$$

where λ is a mixing hyper-parameter. For the foraminifer classification problem in particular this allows both relative inter-species difference information captured by the reciprocal triplet loss component as well as overall species information captured by the SoftMax term to be used as backpropagation gradients.

Latent Space Partitioning for Classification. Once an embedding function has been learned for a metric space, any new sample – even one of the unseen classes – can be projected into this space. However, assigning a class label to this sample based on its position in the space eventually requires a partitioning of the latent space. Direct maps, as well as hierarchical [22] and partitional [12] clustering algorithms, have been used for this. We will experiment with a wide variety of partitioning options in Table 2 *(top right)* including Gaussian Mixture Models (GMMs) [36], Logistic Regression, Support Vector Machines (SVMs) [9], Multi-layer Perceptrons (MLPs) [8], and k-Nearest Neighbours [18]. Once partitioned, metric spaces expose model structure plus outlier information, can be visualised by mapping into lower-dimensional spaces, and often capture properties of the target domain beyond the specific samples used for training. Before using these techniques on the problem of foraminifer classification, we will first introduce the dataset and experimental settings.

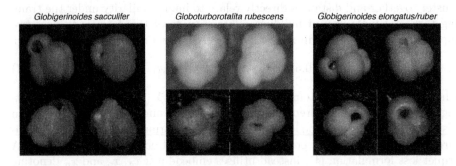

Fig. 3. Imaging Details and Classification Challenges. Microscopic imaging of 3D microfossils often obfuscates key taxonomic features due to variable viewpoint and acquisition conditions. *(left)* Within-class 3D viewpoint variability for *Globigerinoides sacculifer* yields 2D images with different visible chamber numbers rendering this key feature less informative. *(middle)* Out-of-focus acquisition can remove species-characteristic texture information, here of *Globoturborotalita rubescens*, blurred in the top images. Light microscopy images are also unable to capture fine grain wall texture details that would be useful for taxonomic identification. *(right)* Morphologically similar species such as *Globigerinoides elongatus* (top) and *G. ruber* (bottom) are difficult to distinguish from single-view static visuals alone. Ground truth labeling often requires additional information to establish secure taxonomic classification.

3   Dataset

Endless Forams. We use the Endless Forams image library [21] for all experiments. It is one of the largest datasets of its kind and publically available (at `endlessforams.org`). It contains 34,640 labelled images of 35 different foraminiferal species as detailed and exemplified in Fig. 2. This dataset was built based on a subset of foraminifer samples from the Yale Peabody Museum (YPM) Coretop Collection [10] and the Natural History Museum, London (NHM) Henry A. Buckley Collection [37]. The dataset is also associated with a taxonomic training portal hosted on the citizen science platform Zooniverse (`zooniverse.org/projects/ahsiang/endless-forams`). Species classification in this dataset is truly challenging compared to many other computer vision tasks since: (1) planktonic foraminifers exhibit significant intra-class variability (see Fig. 3 *(left)*); (2) critical morphological properties are not consistent across 3D viewpoint and acquisition conditions (see Fig. 3 *(left)*, *(middle)*); and 3) visual intra-species differences are barely apparent between some taxa (see Fig. 3 *(right)*).

4   Experimental Setup

Implementation Details. For all experiments, our PyTorch-implemented metric learning architecture extends a ResNet50 backbone pre-trained with ImageNet. The network is set to optimise the loss specified in Eq. 4 combining SoftMax and reciprocal triplet loss components with the mixing parameter $\lambda = 0.01$ as suggested in [17]. Training progresses via the SGD [38] optimiser for 100 epochs as quantitatively illustrated in Fig. 4. For full testing comparability with [21] we utilised their withheld test set for performance stipulation, whilst using the remaining 27,731 images augmented via rotations, scale, and Gaussian noise transforms for training (reported as **Ours**). In a second workflow and for full compatibility with [30], we also produced results via 5-fold cross-validation on random train-test data splits (reported as **Ours***). For sample selection during training of all workflows, we follow the 'batch hard' mining approach [16] where triplets are mined within mini-batches. This yields overall moderate triplets, i.e. training with the hardest examples within each mini-batch. The published source code [23] provides full details regarding all of the above for full result reproducibility. Training takes approx. 48 h on a P100 GPU system with 12 GB RAM. We obtain classifications for each test sample projected into the metric space via running kNN [18] with n=5 over the projected training samples.

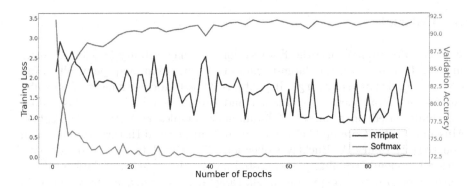

Fig. 4. Metric Learning Training Details. Curves quantifying the evolution of training losses and validation accuracy across all 100 epochs of training. Note that the two loss components are plotted separately showing the early conversion of the Softmax dimension, whilst RTriplet loss continues to alter the metric embedding space at higher magnitudes albeit at down-scaled weighting given $\lambda = 0.01$ in Eq. 4.

5   Results

Baseline Comparisons. The simplest baselines for the foraminifer species classification problem are given by using transfer learning via ImageNet-initialised off-the-shelf CNN architectures [30]. Table 1 *(rows 01–06)* compares key architectures and their performance against our setup using 5-fold cross-validation at standard resolution of 224×224. These results show that metric learning dominates such baselines without exception. Operating at 160×160 pixels, the original 2019 VGG-based benchmark by Hsiang et al. [21] achieved 87.4% accuracy on a withheld test set. Using the same test set, our metric learning approach improves on this performance significantly by 4.5% as shown in Table 1 *(rows 07–08)*.

Improving the State-of-the-Art. CycleNet used by Marchant et al. [30] claims current state-of-the-art performance on the data at an accuracy of 90.3% when using 5-fold cross-validation at 128×128. Table 1 *(rows 09–12)* compare their key results against our metric learning approach under this regime, showing improved metric learning accuracy of 91%. When using their best-performing CycleNet [30], scaling it up to a standard 224×224 resolution and using the testing regime of [21] their results improve slightly. However, our approach outperforms this new benchmark by another 1.2% as shown in Table 1 *(rows 13–14)*. Metric learning reaches top accuracy of 92% at resolution 416×416 as shown in Table 1 *(row 14)*. Figure 5 *(right)* depicts a detailed confusion matrix for this setting.

Table 1. Species Classification Results. Performance of our metric learning approach against SOTA techniques [21,30] quantified via accuracy, precision, recall and F1 score. Testing regime and input resolution were made to match the settings of previous works exactly where * indicates 5-fold cross-validation (see Sect. 4). *(A)* Metric learning supremacy against various off-the-shelf CNNs at 224 × 224 initialised via ImageNet as described in [30]. *(B)* Metric learning increases accuracy of [21] at 160×160 by 4.5%. *(C)* Critically, our approach outperforms SOTA CycleNet [30] at their published 128 × 128 resolution. *(D)* Finally, re-running CycleNet [30] under the regime of [21] and at 224 × 224 shows metric learning also dominating peaking at 92% at 416 × 416.

	Row	Method	Resolution (pixels)	Acc (weighted)	Prec (macro)	Rec (macro)	F1S (macro)
A	01	VGG19* [30]	224 × 224	77.1	70.5	64.9	66.9
	02	MobileNetV2* [30]	224 × 224	77.7	70.0	65.2	66.8
	03	InceptionV2* [30]	224 × 224	77.7	69.5	64.8	66.4
	04	DenseNet121* [30]	224 × 224	80.2	75.2	69.2	71.3
	05	ResNet50* [30]	224 × 224	81.8	76.7	71.4	73.4
	06	**Ours***	224 × 224	**91.6**	**88.2**	**78.3**	**81.3**
B	07	VGG16 [21]	160 × 160	87.4	72.4	69.8	70.0
	08	**Ours**	160 × 160	**91.9**	**91.3**	**81.9**	**84.6**
C	09	ResNet18Full* [30]	128 × 128	88.5	84.1	77.8	79.9
	10	ResNet50CycleFull* [30]	128 × 128	90.1	85.1	78.7	80.8
	11	BaseCycleFull* [30]	128 × 128	90.3	84.9	78.4	80.5
	12	**Ours***	128 × 128	**91.0**	**87.2**	**78.9**	**81.1**
D	13	BaseCycleFull [30]	224 × 224	90.5	84.5	79.6	81.5
	14	**Ours**	224 × 224	**91.7**	**88.1**	**77.0**	**80.7**
			416 × 416	**92.0**	**89.0**	**81.5**	**84.2**

Visualisation of Foraminifer Space. In contrast to basic CNN approaches, we can now visualise the learned 128D metric space, revealing an appearance-based distribution of planktic foraminifers. Figure 5 *(left)* shows this first scientific visualisation of phenotypic appearance space by projecting training and testing sets into the metric space before using t-SNE [28] to reduce dimensionality to 2.

Open Set Performance. By withholding some species[1] from training altogether, we can start to evaluate metric learning potential beyond seen training species, i.e. learning about the planktic foraminifer domain more generally. To do this, we project the unused training data of withheld classes during testing into the metric space together with the training data of used classes. We then utilise kNN with all these data points to measure how far test sets of seen or unseen classes are classified correctly. For the unseen species classes at 224×224, accuracy drops to 66.5% (at 0.70 F1-score) in our experiment. This result is remarkable since about 2/3 of never-seen species specimens can still be associated correctly amongst all 35 species. We thus conclude that metric learning does indeed capture important general features relevant for planktic foraminifer classification beyond any particular species appearance.

---

[1] Tail classes 1, 5, 9, 14, 22, 23, 26, 29, 33, and 34 were chosen as our open set to have maximum specimen counts available during training.

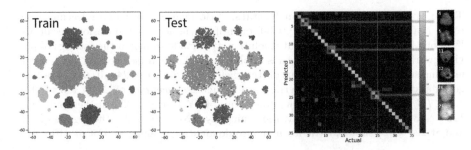

Fig. 5. Learned Metric Space Visualisation and Confusion Matrix. *(left)* 2D t-SNE visualisation of the training (RandIndex = 99.9) and testing (RandIndex=87.0) sets projected into the metric space; and *(right)* Confusion matrix detailing test performance where taxonomic similarities of prominent mix-ups are visually highlighted.

Ablations, Resolution, and Augmentation. Table 2 *(top)* details ablation experiments that demonstrate that the chosen metric learning loss functions and clustering algorithms are effective, contribute to performance, and indeed outperform other tested setups. An analysis of the dependency of our approach on resolution is presented in Table 2 *(bottom left)*. It outlines that above 160×160 pixels performance gains are widely diminished and flat-line, supporting the choices taken in [21]. Whilst SOTA competitor networks [30] also augment their data, augmentation can be essential for metric learning techniques generally [40]. Table 2 *(bottom right)* quantifies this fact and shows that performance in the foraminifer classification domain is indeed intricately linked to augmentation, with rotation variations producing the strongest component impact.

6   Taxonomic Reflection

Taxonomic Interpretation of Performance. We observe that species that are taxonomically related to each other are indeed the ones that are confused most often by the machine. For example, species from the same genus (e.g. 4 vs 5; 11 vs 12; 24 vs 25) are often misclassified symmetrically as highlighted in Fig. 5 *(right)*. This alignment is consistent with human classification difficulties and suggests that metric space distances are indeed related to visual properties humans use to differentiate species. Generally, we suggest three main reasons for lower classification performances, all of which would also present challenges for human classifiers. First, phylogenetic closeness, i.e. closely related sister taxa, can result in many shared taxonomic features that make differentiation difficult. Classes 4 and 5, for example, share many large-scale morphological features and are only distinguished by a lip at the aperture [29]. Secondly, some classes (e.g. 11 and 12) are not even typically distinguished in palaeontological studies, but are genetically distinct [3] and hence separated in the database. The distinguishing visual feature is a sliding scale of radial chamber compression which makes systematic labelling challenging. Thirdly, not all planktic foraminiferal species reach the same maximum size in the modern ocean [39], and size is an important

Table 2. Design Ablations, Resolution and Augmentation. Benchmarks use the testing regime of [21] and resolution 160×160 as standard; RI denotes the Rand Index. *(top left)* Performance of different loss functions confirm the superiority of L. *(top right)* Benchmark of various clustering approaches. *(bottom left)* Performance increases saturate around 160×160 providing only marginal gains if input resolution is increased beyond this point. *(bottom right)* Metric learning performance in this domain is intricately dependent on sufficient data augmentation. Rotation augmentation (R) in particular benefits accuracy, whilst scale augmentation (S), and Gaussian noise addition (G) have smaller effects. Applying all three (R+S+G) is most beneficial.

Loss	Acc	Prec	Rec	F1S	RI
Ours ($L_{RTL} + SM$)	**91.9**	**91.3**	**81.9**	**84.6**	**87.1**
SoftMax+L_{TL}	91.4	89.6	81.3	84.3	86.2
RTriplet (L_{RTL})	89.3	79.2	71.0	73.9	82.9
Triplet (L_{TL})	22.2	12	9.3	9.5	4.7
SoftMax	91.2	89.9	81.9	84.2	86.5

Alg	Acc	Prec	Rec	F1S	RI
Ours (kNN)	**91.9**	**91.3**	**81.9**	**84.6**	**87.1**
SVM	91.8	88.3	78.8	81.6	86.6
MLP	90.9	80.9	80.8	78.9	86.2
LR	91.5	84.6	74.7	78.0	86.4
GMM	-	-	-	-	63.8

Resolution	Acc	Prec	Rec	F1S	RI
416×416	**92.0**	89.0	81.5	84.2	**87.3**
224×224	91.7	88.1	77.0	80.7	86.8
160×160	91.9	**91.3**	**81.9**	**84.6**	87.1
120×120	91.0	88.4	79.2	82.1	86.3
80×80	90.0	84.8	78.1	80.2	84.1

Transform	Acc	Prec	Rec	F1S	RI
Ours (R+S+G)	**91.9**	**91.3**	**81.9**	**84.6**	**87.1**
R	91.2	86.8	79.3	81.5	85.8
S	88.4	87.6	76.3	80.0	81.1
G	85.0	75.0	66.2	69.1	76.3
–	82.7	75.2	66.2	69.0	72.4

feature used for taxonomic classification by human experts. As all the images have the same number of pixels, size information is lost in the database used and the amount of information per pixel will vary strongly between a species which is up to 5 times larger than another. For the smallest specimens, imaging often reaches the limits of typical optics, resulting in blur and other effects, as shown in Fig. 3 *(middle)* for class 24.

7   Conclusion

The accurate and efficient visual recognition of planktic foraminifers within shell assemblages in light microscopy imagery is an important pillar required for unlocking climatic archives. We have shown here for the first time that deep metric learning can be effectively applied to this task. We documented how deep metric learning outperforms all published state-of-the-art benchmarks in this domain when tested on one of the largest public, expert-annotated image libraries covering modern planktic foraminifera species. We further provided detailed result evaluation and ablation studies. Based on the metrically-learned feature spaces, we also produced the first scientific visualisation of a phenotypic planktic foraminifer appearance domain. Finally, we demonstrated that metric learning can be used to recognise specimens of species unseen during training by utilising the metric space embedding capabilities. We conclude that metric learning is highly effective for this domain and can form an important tool towards data-driven, expert-in-the-loop automation of microfossil identification.

Acknowledgements. TK was supported by the UKRI CDT in Interactive Artificial Intelligence under the grant EP/S022937/1. AYH was supported by VR grant 2020-03515. DNS was supported by NERC grant NE/P019439/1. We thank R Marchant and his team for making available source code and testing regime details to compare to [30]. Thanks to M Lagunes-Fortiz and W Andrew for permitting use and adaptation of source code related to metric learning.

References

1. Al-Sabouni, N., Fenton, I., Telford, R., Kučera, M.: Reproducibility of species recognition in modern planktonic foraminifera and its implications for analyses of community structure. J. Micropalaeontol. **37**, 519–534 (2018)
2. Andrew, W., Gao, J., Mullan, S., Campbell, N., Dowsey, A.W., Burghardt, T.: Visual identification of individual Holstein-Friesian cattle via deep metric learning. Comput. Electron. Agric. **185**, 106133 (2021)
3. Aurahs, R., Treis, Y., Darling, K., Kucera, M.: A revised taxonomic and phylogenetic concept for the planktonic foraminifer species Globigerinoides Ruber based on molecular and morphometric evidence. Mar. Micropaleontol. **79**, 1–14 (2011)
4. Balfoort, H., Snoek, J., Smiths, J., Breedveld, L., Hofstraat, J., Ringelberg, J.: Automatic identification of Algae: neural network analysis of flow cytometric data. J. Plankton Res. **14**, 575–589 (1992)
5. Beaufort, L., Dollfus, D.: Automatic recognition of coccoliths by dynamical neural networks. Mar. Micropaleontol. **51**, 57–73 (2004)
6. Beaufort, L., et al.: Sensitivity of coccolithophores to carbonate chemistry and ocean acidification. Nature **476**, 80–83 (2011)
7. Bown, P., Huber, B., Wade, B., Young, J.: pforams@mikrotax - introduction (2020). https://www.mikrotax.org/pforams/. Accessed 01 May 2021
8. Bozinovski, S., Fulgosi, A.: The use of artificial neural networks to classify primate vocalizations: a pilot study on black Lemurs. Am. J. Primatol. 1098–2345 (2009)
9. Cortes, C., Vapnik, V.: Support-vector networks. Mach. Learn. **20**(3), 273–297 (1995)
10. Elder, L.E., Hsiang, A.Y., Nelson, K., Strotz, L.C., Kahanamoku, S.S., Hull, P.M.: Sixty-one thousand recent planktonic foraminifera from the Atlantic Ocean. Sci. Data **5** (2018)
11. Franz, N.: On the lack of good scientific reasons for the growing phylogeny/classification gap. Cladistics **21**, 495–500 (2005)
12. Gandhi, G., Srivastava, R.: Review paper: A comparative study on partitioning techniques of clustering algorithms. International Journal of Computer Applications 87 (01 2014)
13. Hadsell, R., Chopra, S., LeCun, Y.: Dimensionality reduction by learning an invariant mapping. In: IEEE Computer Society Conference on Computer Vision and Pattern Recognition (CVPR 2006), vol. 2, pp. 1735–1742 (2006)
14. He, K., Zhang, X., Ren, S., Sun, J.: Deep residual learning for image recognition (2015)
15. Hemleben, C., Spindler, M., Anderson, O.: Modern Planktonic Foraminifera, p. 363. Springer, Cham (1989). https://doi.org/10.1007/978-1-4612-3544-6

16. Hermans, A., Beyer, L., Leibe, B.: In defense of the triplet loss for person re-identification (2017)
17. Hodan, T., Haluza, P., Obdrzalek, S., Matas, J., Lourakis, M., Zabulis, X.: T-LESS: An RGB-D dataset for 6D pose estimation of texture-less objects. In: Winter Conference on Applications of Computer Vision (WACV). IEEE, 880–888 (2017)
18. Hodges, L.: Nonparametric discrimination: Consistency properties. USAF School of Aviation Medicine (1951)
19. Hsiang, A.Y., et al.: Endless Forams: > 34,000 modern planktonic foraminiferal images for taxonomic training and automated species recognition using convolutional neural networks. Paleoceanography Paleoclimatol. **34**, 1157–1177 (2019)
20. Huber, B., Bijma, J., Darling, K.: Cryptic speciation in the living planktonic foraminifer Globigerinella siphoniphera (d'Orbigny). Paleobiology **23**, 33–62 (1997)
21. Hull., P.M., Hsiang, A.Y.: Endless Forams Most Beautiful (2020). http://endlessforams.org. Accessed 01 May 2021
22. Johnson, S.C.: Hierarchical clustering schemes. Psychometrika **32**, 241–254 (1967)
23. Karaderi, T.: Visual microfossil identification via deep metric learning (2022). https://github.com/TayfunKaraderi/ICPRAI-2022-Visual-Microfossil-Identification-via-Deep-Metric-Learning. Accessed 19 Mar 2022
24. Krizhevsky, A., Sutskever, I., Hinton, G.: ImageNet classification with deep convolutional neural networks. In: Advances in Neural Information Processing Systems, pp. 1097–1105 (2012)
25. Kucera, M.: Planktonic foraminifera as tracers of past oceanic environments. In: Hillaire-Marcel, C., De Vernal, A. (eds.) pp. 213–262 (2007)
26. Kühl, H.S., Burghardt, T.: Animal biometrics: quantifying and detecting phenotypic appearance. Trends Ecol. Evol. **28**(7), 432–441 (2013)
27. Lagunes-Fortiz, M., Damen, D., Mayol-Cuevas, W.: Learning discriminative embeddings for object recognition on-the-y. In: 2019 International Conference on Robotics and Automation (ICRA). IEEE, pp. 2932–2938 (2019)
28. van der Maaten, L., Hinton, G.: Visualizing data using t-SNE. J. Mach. Learn. Res. **9**, 2579–2605 (2008)
29. Malmgren, B., Kennett, J.: Biometric analysis of phenotypic variation in recent globigerina bulloides d'Orbigny in the southern Indian ocean. Mar. Micropaleontol. **1**, 2–25 (1976)
30. Marchant, R., Tetard, M., Pratiwi, A., Adebayo, M., de Garidel-Thoron, T.: Automated analysis of foraminifera fossil records by image classification using a convolutional neural network. J. Micropalaeontol. **39**(2), 183–202 (2020)
31. Masullo, A., Burghardt, T., Damen, D., Perrett, T., Mirmehdi, M.: Who goes there? Exploiting silhouettes and wearable signals for subject identification in multi-person environments. In: Proceedings of the IEEE International Conference on Computer Vision Workshops, pp. 1599–1607 (2019)
32. Mitra, R., Marchitto, T., Ge, Q., Zhong, B., Kanakiya, B., Cook, M., Fehrenbacher, J., Ortiz, J., Tripati, A., Lobaton, E.: Automated species-level identification of planktic foraminifera using convolutional neural networks, with comparison to human performance. Mar. Micropaleontol. **147**, 16–24 (2019)
33. Pacifico, L.D.S., Macario, V., Oliveira, J.F.L.: Plant classification using artificial neural networks. In: IJCNN, pp. 1–6 (2018)
34. Ravelo, A.C., Hillaire-Marcel, C.: The use of oxygen and carbon isotopes of foraminifera in paleoceanography. In: Developments in Marine Geology, vol. 1. Elsevier (2007)

35. Renaud, S., Schmidt, D.: Habitat tracking as a response of the planktic foraminifer Globorotalia truncatulinoides to environmental fluctuations during the last 140 kyr. Mar. Micropaleontol. **49**, 97–122 (2003)
36. Reynolds, D.A.: Gaussian mixture models. Encyclopedia Biometrics (2009)
37. Rillo, M.C., Whittaker, J., Ezard, T.H., Purvis, A., Henderson, A., Stukins, S., Miller, C.: The unknown planktonic foraminiferal pioneer Henry A. Buckley and his collection at The Natural History Museum. J. Micropalaeontol. **36**, 191–194 (2016)
38. Ruder, S.: An overview of gradient descent optimization algorithms. arXiv preprint arXiv:1609.04747 (2016)
39. Schmidt, D., Renaud, S., Bollmann, J., Schiebel, R., Thierstein, H.: Size distribution of Holocene planktic foraminifer assemblages: biogeography, ecology and adaptation. Mar. Micropaleontol. **50**, 319–338 (2004)
40. Schneider, S., Taylor, G.W., Linquist, S.S., Kremer, S.C.: Similarity learning networks for animal individual re-identification - beyond the capabilities of a human observer. WACV abs/1902.09324 (2019). http://arxiv.org/abs/1902.09324
41. Schroff, F., Kalenichenko, D., Philbin, J.: FaceNet: a united embedding for face recognition and clustering. Proc. IEEE Conf. Comput. Vis. Pattern Recognit. **2**, 815–823 (2015)
42. Simonyan, K., Zisserman, A.: Very deep convolutional networks for large-scale image recognition (2015)
43. Sluys, R.: The unappreciated, fundamentally analytical nature of taxonomy and the implications for the inventory of biodiversity. Biodivers. Conserv. **22**, 1095–1105 (2013)
44. Szegedy, C., et al.: Going deeper with convolutions. In: IEEE Conference on Computer Vision and Pattern Recognition (CVPR), pp. 1–9 (2015)
45. Tan, D., Ang, Y., Lim, G., Ismail, M., Meier, R.: From 'cryptic species' to integrative taxonomy: an iterative process involving DNA sequences, morphology, and behaviour leads to the resurrection of Sepsis pyrrhosoma (sepsidae: Diptera). Zoolog. Scr. **39**, 51–61 (2010)
46. Tuia, D., et al.: Seeing biodiversity: perspectives in machine learning for wildlife conservation. arXiv preprint arXiv:2110.12951 (2021)
47. Vaswani, A., et al.: Attention is all you need. CoRR 1706, 03762 (2017)
48. Weller, A., Harris, A., Ware, J.: Two supervised neural networks for classification of sedimentary organic matter images from palynological preparations. Math. Geol. **39**, 657–671 (2007)
49. Wägele, H., et al.: The taxonomist - an endangered race. A practical proposal for its survival. Front. Zool. **8**, 25 (2011)
50. Xie, S., Girshick, R., Dollár, P., Tu, Z., He, K.: Aggregated residual transformations for deep neural networks (2017)

QAP Optimisation with Reinforcement Learning for Faster Graph Matching in Sequential Semantic Image Analysis

Jérémy Chopin[1][(✉)], Jean-Baptiste Fasquel[1], Harold Mouchère[2],
Rozenn Dahyot[3], and Isabelle Bloch[4]

[1] LARIS, Université d'Angers, Angers, France
{jeremy.chopin,jean-baptiste.fasquel}@univ-angers.fr
[2] LS2N, Universite de Nantes, CNRS UMR, Nantes 6004, France
harold.mouchere@univ-nantes.fr
[3] Department of Computer Science, Maynooth University, Maynooth, Ireland
Rozenn.Dahyot@mu.ie
[4] Sorbonne Université, CNRS, LIP6, Paris, France
isabelle.bloch@sorbonne-universite.fr

Abstract. The paper addresses the fundamental task of semantic image analysis by exploiting structural information (spatial relationships between image regions). We propose to combine a deep neural network (CNN) with graph matching where graphs encode efficiently structural information related to regions segmented by the CNN. Our novel approach solves the quadratic assignment problem (QAP) sequentially for matching graphs. The optimal sequence for graph matching is conveniently defined using reinforcement-learning (RL) based on the region membership probabilities produced by the CNN and their structural relationships. Our RL based strategy for solving QAP sequentially allows us to significantly reduce the combinatorial complexity for graph matching. Preliminary experiments are performed on both a synthetic dataset and a public dataset dedicated to the semantic segmentation of face images. Results show that the proposed RL-based ordering significantly outperforms random ordering, and that our strategy is about 386 times faster than a global QAP-based approach, while preserving similar segmentation accuracy.

Keywords: Semantic image analysis · Structural information · Graph matching · Quadratic assignment problem · Reinforcement learning

1 Introduction

Semantic segmentation is a fundamental but challenging task in computer vision, often managed using deep neural networks such as U-Net [9]. Structural infor-

This research was conducted in the framework of the regional program Atlantic 2020, Research, Education and Innovation in Pays de la Loire, supported by the French Region Pays de la Loire and the European Regional Development Fund.

© Springer Nature Switzerland AG 2022
M. El Yacoubi et al. (Eds.): ICPRAI 2022, LNCS 13363, pp. 47–58, 2022.
https://doi.org/10.1007/978-3-031-09037-0_5

mation [2,5] such as spatial relationships is not explicitly used in such networks, although some recent works aim at exploiting it, e.g. CRF-based approaches [7] and CNN based semantic segmentation followed by inexact graph matching [3].

In this paper, we focus likewise on graph-based approaches exploiting relationships observed at high semantic level in annotated training images or provided by qualitative descriptions of the scene content [5]. In this context, graph vertices and edges encode regions and spatial relationships produced by a segmentation network and observed in annotated training images, leading to an inexact graph matching problem, expressed classically as a quadratic assignment problem (QAP) [16]. Note that some recent approaches solve graph matching with machine learning (e.g. graph neural networks [1]). Although promising for many application domains [17], large and representative training datasets of annotated graphs are required. Another difficulty is the definition of the appropriate architecture, and the management of both vertex and edge information, while edge features (related to relationships between regions) are often ignored [17].

One of the main drawbacks of QAP-based graph matching lies in its highly combinatorial nature [16]. In this context, our proposal is to solve it in a sequential manner, where vertices are progressively matched in order to reduce the complexity. This means that the semantic image analysis is done progressively: first identified regions are used to discover next ones [4,6] (this is closed to the notion of seeded graph matching [8]). The difficulty is to learn the optimal segmentation/graph matching order, to ensure that all regions are finally recovered. In this paper, we propose to solve this problem by reinforcement learning [12,14]. Note that, to our knowledge, such an approach has never been considered for graph-based semantic image segmentation, although it has been recently studied for graph matching (but in a different context [8]). Recent related works in computer vision focus on other tasks such as, for instance, object detection [10], object tracking [15], landmark detection [11] or control of regions of interest in video analysis [11].

This work is an extension of a recently proposed approach involving QAP-based graph matching that ignores this sequential alternative and therefore suffers from a high complexity [3]. The originality and contribution of this paper rely on challenging image understanding tasks by combining, on top of deep-learning-based segmentation, high-level structural information, inexact graph matching and a reinforcement-learning-based sequential strategy. Section 2 describes the proposed method while Sect. 3 presents experiments and results demonstrating the performance of our approach. We finally conclude in Sect. 4.

2   Reinforcement Learning for Sequential Graph Matching

Figure 1 provides an overview of the approach. A Convolutional Neural Network (CNN) is trained for image semantic segmentation using an annotated dataset (Fig. 1-Training). To correct segmentation errors (Fig. 1-Inference), we propose to use spatial relationships observed between identified regions of the annotated

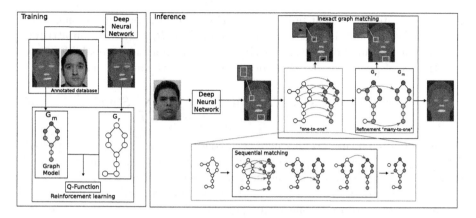

Fig. 1. Overview of the proposed approach. **Training**: Annotated data are used to train a CNN and learn the model graph. Segmentations over the training data are used with the graph model to learn the Q-function. **Inference**: Segmentation produced by the CNN is used to create image graph. A sequential one-to-one matching is done with a sequential refinement to improve the semantic segmentation.

training dataset, leading to an inexact-graph-matching procedure, between G_m (built from the training dataset) and G_r (built from the CNN output). When analysing an unknown image (Fig. 1-right), a hypothesis graph G_r is built from the initial CNN segmentation result. To identify regions, G_r is matched with G_m, which is an inexact graph matching problem, as there are more regions in G_r than in G_m due to artifacts. We propose to do this sequentially in two steps. First, an initial "one-to-one" matching is performed to recover one region candidate (vertex of G_r) per class (one vertex of G_m). This is done sequentially according to the ordering learned by reinforcement (based on a Q-Function resulting from a preliminary training - Fig. 1-Training). The second step (refinement) focuses on matching remaining artifacts, this being also done sequentially in any order. We hereafter detail each of these steps.

2.1 Neural Network and Graphs

When analysing an image, the neural network provides a tensor $S \in \mathbb{R}^{P \times N}$ with P the dimensions of the query image (e.g. $P = I \times J$ pixels for 2D images) and N is the total number of classes considered for segmentation. At each pixel location p, the value $S(p, n) \in [0, 1]$ is the probability of belonging to class n. The segmentation map $\mathcal{L}^*$ selects the label n of the class with the highest probability:

$$\forall p \in \{1, \ldots, P\}, \ \mathcal{L}^*(p) = \underset{n \in \{1, \ldots, N\}}{\arg\max} \ S(p, n). \tag{1}$$

From $\mathcal{L}^*$, we define a set R of all resulting connected components, and finally the graph $G_r = (V_r, E_r, A, D)$, where V_r is the set of vertices, E_r the set of edges, A a vertex attribute assignment function, and D an edge attribute assignment function. Each vertex $v \in V_r$ is associated with a region $R_v \in R$, with an attribute provided by the function A which is the average membership probability vector over the set of pixels $p \in R_v$, therefore computed on the initial tensor S:

$$\forall v \in V_r, \forall n \in \{1,\ldots,N\}, \ A(v)[n] = \frac{1}{|R_v|} \sum_{p \in R_v} S(p,n). \tag{2}$$

We consider a complete graph where each edge $e = (i,j) \in E_r$ has an attribute defined by the function D (hyperparameter in our method, detailed in experiments), associated with a relation between the regions R_i and R_j.

The model graph $G_m = (V_m, E_m, A, D)$ is built from the training set and is composed of N vertices (one vertex per class). The attribute of a vertex is a vector of dimension N with only one non-zero component (with value equal to 1), associated with the index of the corresponding class. The edges are obtained by calculating the average relationships (in the training set) between the regions (according to the relation D considered).

2.2 Sequential One-to-one Matching by Reinforcement Learning

The proposed sequential one-to-one matching between $G_r = (V_r, E_r, A, D)$ and $G_m = (V_m, E_m, A, D)$ is formulated as a QAP to be solved sequentially by Q-learning, for finally finding the best assignment X^*:

$$X^* = \arg\min_X \left\{ \text{vec}(X)^T K \, \text{vec}(X) \right\}, \tag{3}$$

where $X \in \{0,1\}^{|V_r| \times |V_m|}$, X_{ij} means that the vertex $i \in V_r$ is matched to the vertex $j \in V_m$, $vec(X)$ is the column vector representation of X, and T denotes the transposition operation. The matrix K is defined by:

$$K = \alpha \, K_v + (1-\alpha) \, K_e, \tag{4}$$

and embeds the dissimilarities between the two graphs: K_v embeds the dissimilarities between V_r and V_m (diagonal elements) and K_e embeds the dissimilarities between E_r and E_m (non-diagonal elements). The parameter $\alpha \in [0,1]$ allows weighting the relative contributions of vertex and edge dissimilarities.

For a sequential graph matching, one learns, by reinforcement, from interactions between the agent and the environment [12]. From a given state s_t (set of already matched nodes, at step t of the sequential matching procedure), the agent (the algorithm) selects and triggers an action (i.e. trying to match a new vertex of $|V_r|$ with a new one of $|V_m|$, or a new subset of vertices). The environment (encompassing image, semantic segmentation, graphs and graph matching computations) performs this action, and gives back to the agent the resulting new state s_{t+1} (matching result) together with a reward.

In this work, the considered reinforcement learning (RL) method is based on Q-learning using a Q-function defined by a Q-Table, that appeared appropriate for preliminary experiments. As underlined in [12], it is widely accepted that such a value-based RL algorithm is appropriate for a discrete RL scenario, which is the case of our graph matching problem (discrete decision making problem).

The design of the agent for our graph matching problem is detailed hereafter in terms of state, action and reward.

State. As in [8], the state $s_t \in \mathcal{S}$ (at the step t of the episode or matching procedure) is the subset $V_{r,t} \subseteq V_r$ of vertices matched with a subset $V_{m,t} \subseteq V_m$, where $|V_{r,t}| = |V_{m,t}|$, and $\mathcal{S}$ represents all possible partial matchings. The related bijective assignment matrix is $X_t \in \{0,1\}^{|V_{r,t}| \times |V_{m,t}|}$, so that $\forall p \in V_{m,t}, (\sum_{i=1}^{|V_{m,t}|} X_{pi} = 1) \wedge (\sum_{i=1}^{|V_{m,t}|} X_{ip} = 1)$. The matching procedure (episode) goes from $t = 0$ ($V_{r,0} = V_{m,0} = \emptyset$) to $t = \infty$ ($|V_{r,\infty}| = |V_m|$ and $V_{m,\infty} = V_m$). We observed experimentally that only a limited number of steps is needed.

Action. The action $a_t \in \mathcal{A}_t$, achieved by the agent at step t, consists in selecting a set of vertices of V_m not in $V_{m,t}$ (i.e. $V_m \setminus V_{m,t}$) and finding the corresponding ones in $V_r \setminus V_{r,t}$. $\mathcal{A}_t$ is the set of possible sets of vertices, and depends on t (i.e. already matched vertices at step t are ignored). In our case, at $t = 0$, sets of size larger than one element are considered, while, for $t > 0$, single nodes are investigated. The motivation is to begin by finding a small subgraph matching (seeded graph matching [8]) and then to consider only single nodes to ensure a low complexity. At each step, a QAP optimization is achieved to find the new matching(s), according to Eq. 3, where the assignment matrix is initialized according to X_t.

Reward. When learning, the agent receives a reward r, based on the quality of the resulting matching. Compared to [8], the reward is not based on the cost related to Eq. 3 but on the quality of the resulting semantic segmentation, similarly to [11], involving a similarity measurement between the recovered region(s) and the expected one(s). The motivation is to favor the matching with the most similar regions, as several regions (over-segmentation) of the image being analyzed can be associated (and therefore matched) with the same region of the reference segmentation. The reward, depending on both the state s_t and the selected action a_t, is the one considered in [11]:

$$r(a_t, s_t) = \begin{cases} DC + 1 & \text{if } DC > 0.1, \\ -1 & \text{otherwise} \end{cases} \tag{5}$$

where DC is the Dice index between the region(s) associated with the newly matched vertex (or vertices) and the expected one(s).

Sequential Matching. After the learning procedure leading to the Q function, the matching ordering (i.e. optimal action a_t to be selected at step t) is defined, at each step $t \in [0, \infty]$, by:

$$a_t = \underset{a \in \mathcal{A}_t}{\arg\max}(Q(s_t, a)). \tag{6}$$

where Q ($Q : \mathcal{S} \times \mathcal{A} \rightarrow \Re$) is the learned Q-Table [12], representing the maximum expected future rewards for actions at each state ($\mathcal{A}_t \subseteq \mathcal{A}$ in Eq. 6). Q is learned [12] over several episodes achieved on the training dataset, using previously defined notions of state, action and reward. Applying this policy leads to the one-to-one matching X^I.

Complexity. The complexity is directly related to the number of evaluated assignments according to Eq. 3, depending on the number of vertices involved and the related set of possible matchings (i.e. set of $X \in \{0,1\}^{|V_r| \times |V_m|}$). Without considering the proposed sequential approach, the number of evaluations NE_{QAP} equals the following number of $|V_m|$-permutations of $|V_r|$ (without repetitions), or arrangements (i.e. vertex sets from V_r, of size $|V_m|$, to be matched with the V_m vertices):

$$\text{NE}_{\text{QAP}} = P_{|V_m|}^{|V_r|} = \frac{|V_r|!}{(|V_r| - |V_m|)!} \tag{7}$$

With the sequential approach, the number of evaluations $\text{NE}_{\text{QAP-RL}}$ is:

$$\text{NE}_{\text{QAP-RL}} = P_{|S|}^{|V_r|} + \sum_{i=0}^{|V_m|-|S|} |V_r| - |S| - i \tag{8}$$

where $S \subseteq V_m$ is the set of vertices involved in the first step of graph matching procedure. Each following step involves only one vertex (right term of Eq. 8). Because $|S| \leq |V_m|$, the number of evaluations can be significantly reduced by minimizing $|S|$ (i.e. $|S| \ll |V_m|$).

2.3   Sequential Refinement: Many-to-one-or-none Matching

The unmatched remaining nodes are then matched sequentially but in a random manner. For each node $k \in V_r \setminus V_{r,\infty}$, one searches for the best assignment (element of V_m), minimizing the matching cost according to Eq. 3. In terms of complexity, this only involves the evaluation of $|V_m|$ assignment matrices per remaining $k \in V_r \setminus V_{r,\infty}$: $\text{NE}_{\text{Refinement}} = |V_r \setminus V_{r,\infty}| \times |V_m|$ (to be added to the complexity related to Eq. 7 or 8).

3   Experiments

3.1   Datasets

The datasets considered for our experiments are a synthetic dataset and the FASSEG-Instances[1] public dataset that has been created for these experiments (based on the FASSEG).

---

[1] https://github.com/Jeremy-Chopin/FASSEG-instances.

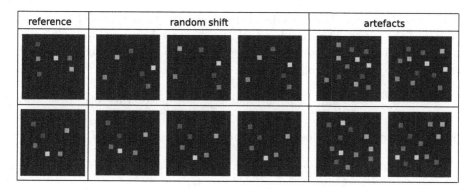

reference	random shift	artefacts

Fig. 2. Synthetic dataset. From reference images, altered ones are randomly created by first applying a random shift on region positions and by then integrating artifacts.

Synthetic dataset. Ten types of synthetic images are used (two are reported in Fig. 2). For each one, a reference image, composed of 6 regions/classes, is considered (from which G_m is built) together with 100 altered versions (from which 100 G_r are built). Altered images are generated from reference ones, by modifying region location (random shift around the initial position) and by incorporating randomly placed artifacts (one artifact per class). Note that the random shift for some regions is larger than for others, in order to simulate relationships variations that can differ between any two regions in realistic images. The considered relationships (D assignment function) are the distances between region barycenters: $\forall (i,j) \in V^2$, $D((i,j)) = \|\bar{R}_j - \bar{R}_i\|$, where $\bar{R}_i$ is the barycenter of the region associated with vertex i. The dissimilarity between two edges ($(i,j) \in E_m$ and $(k,l) \in E_r$) is computed as the difference between $D((i,j))$ and $D((k,l))$ (used to compute K in Eq. 3): $D1_{(i,j)}^{(k,l)} = \frac{D((k,l)) - D((i,j))}{C_s}$, where C_s is the length of the diagonal of the image, so as to keep the value in the interval $[0,1]$. To mimic the CNN output, each region is associated with an attributed vector representing a membership probability vector (A assignment function). For altered images, a probability is set randomly in $[0.7, 0.9]$ and assigned to the reference region/class, while the remaining quantity is randomly divided among the other classes.

FASSEG-Instances. This public dataset is based on the public FASSEG[2] dataset containing 60 human face images with the associated expert segmentation of face regions (eyes, nose, mouth...). We applied some modifications to the original FASSEG dataset in order to subdivide original labels (e.g. right-eye and left-eye instead of only eyes, i.e. two distinct instances of eyes), leading to 9 classes. Note that, although FASSEG includes faces in multiple poses, one considers frontal ones only because the considered graph matching technique may not be robust to face pose changes [3], except if spatial relations are defined in an intrinsic frame and not absolutely, this aspect being out of the scope of our study focusing

---

[2] FASSEG: https://github.com/massimomauro/FASSEG-repository.

on QAP optimization. For the sake of simplicity, the term FASSEG is used in the rest of the paper. The considered relationships are based on both minimum and maximum distances between regions, leading to the following assignment function $D((i,j)) = [d_{min}^{(i,j)}, d_{max}^{(i,j)}]$, where:

$$d_{min}^{(i,j)} = \min_{p \in R_i, q \in R_j} (|p - q|) \text{ and } d_{max}^{(i,j)} = \max_{p \in R_i, q \in R_j} (|p - q|) \qquad (9)$$

The resulting dissimilarity between two edges $(i,j) \in E_m$ and $(k,l) \in E_r$ is:

$$D2_{(i,j)}^{(k,l)} = \frac{\lambda}{C_s} \left(|d_{min}^{(i,j)} - d_{min}^{(k,l)}| \right) + \frac{(1 - \lambda)}{C_s} (|d_{max}^{(i,j)} - d_{max}^{(k,l)}|) \qquad (10)$$

where $\lambda \in [0, 1]$ is a parameter (set to 0.5 is our experiments) to balance the influence of the distances, and C_s the maximum diagonal length of the image.

3.2   Evaluation Protocol

On the synthetic dataset, for each reference image, the Q function is learned using 60 images, with 50 episodes per image, therefore leading to 3000 episodes. The remaining 40 images are used for testing purposes. Results are averaged over the 10 reference images. On this dataset, we considered two sub-experiments: one with attributes on edges only (Synthetic 1, with $\alpha = 0$ in Eq. 4 to favor structural information only) and one on both vertices and edges (Synthetic 2, with $\alpha = 0.5$ in Eq. 4). On the FASSEG dataset, 20 images are used for training both the U-Net [9] (used for the initial segmentation) and the Q function (with 50 episodes per image, i.e. 1000 episodes for this dataset). In both cases, a seed of 3 vertices is considered for the first step of the sequential graph matching (the seed composition being learned by reinforcement), while the next steps involve only single vertices.

Our sequential RL-based approach is compared to a random ordering (averaged over 100 random orderings for each of the synthetic test images and for FASSEG test ones). When possible, our approach is compared to the standard QAP. Due to the huge number of permutations, QAP may not be applied in some cases, in particular on FASSEG. We therefore consider a constrained QAP [3], by reducing the number of investigated assignment matrices (in Eq. 3): for a given vertex (region) $i \in G_m$, the considered candidates in G_r are not all possible vertices (regions) but only those with the highest membership probability, according to the U-Net, of being associated with class/vertex i.

Evaluation measures include the number of permutations (i.e. number of assignment matrices), and, when possible, the runtime (Intel i7-8850H CPU). One also measures, when possible, the segmentation accuracy (Dice index).

3.3   Results

Table 1 reports results on the segmentation accuracy for both synthetic and FASSEG datasets. The reinforcement learning significantly outperforms random

Table 1. Segmentation results (Dice index) obtained by the sequential approach (RL-based ordering and random ordering), the QAP, and the constrained QAP. FASSEG-R corresponds to segmentation results after the refinement step, while FASSEG concerns only the one-to-one matching. Some results are not available (too high a computation time).

Method	Synthetic 1	Synthetic 2	FASSEG	FASSEG-R
Reinforcement	0.6 ± 0.38	0.96 ± 0.08	0.82 ± 0.13	0.82 ± 0.13
Random ordering	0.21 ± 0.25	0.92 ± 0.14	0.71 ± 0.12	0.78 ± 0.1
QAP	0.72 ± 0.31	0.98 ± 0.05	NA	NA
Constrained QAP		0.99 ± 0.03	0.83 ± 0.06	0.84 ± 0.04

ordering, demonstrating the relevance of the proposed sequential approach. Compared to a global QAP-based matching, our approach is significantly less efficient on Synthetic 1, while only slightly less efficient on Synthetic 2. This illustrates that, even with an optimized ordering, considering few nodes (only 3 at the beginning compared to the global QAP that directly searches for the 6 ones) is not sufficient when only the relationships are considered (i.e. Synthetic 1 ignores vertex attributes), because one fails identifying the relevant matching among the large set of possible sub-graph matchings.

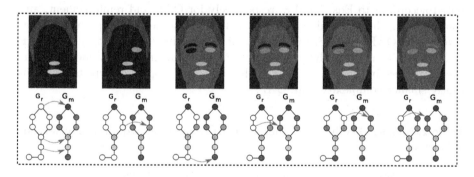

Fig. 3. Learned optimized ordering on FASSEG: starting with the nose, mouth and hair (initial seeded graph matching), before continuing with one eye, the skin, the second eye and finally eyebrows.

On FASSEG, the efficiency of our proposal is highly similar to the one of the constrained QAP (and significantly higher than the random ordering), although more classes (9) are involved, illustrating the relevance of our proposal. Figure 3 illustrates the learned optimized ordering on FASSEG, while Fig. 4 reports some examples of results on different faces (both our approach and constrained QAP fail for the second face), where $s_\infty = s_6$ and $V_{r,\infty} = V_{r,6}$. These examples qualitatively illustrate, in particular, the relevance of our approach compared to a random ordering.

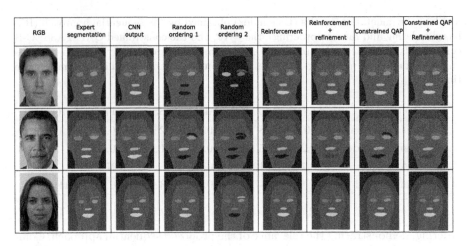

Fig. 4. Examples of segmentations obtained on FASSEG, using our approach (sequential matching before and after the refinement), the constrained QAP (before and after refinement) and random ordering (without considering the refinement). One also reports expert segmentation and CNN output (red boxes surround some initially misclassified regions).

Table 2 provides the required number of evaluated assignment matrices (computed according to Eqs. 7 and 8, respectively for QAP and reinforcement, and measured for the constrained QAP), as well as measured computation times (except for QAP on FASSEG because it is too time consuming). The QAP involves significantly much more evaluations than our proposal (values are averaged over test images on FASSEG): the sequential approach depicts a significantly smaller complexity than QAP.

Table 2. Number of evaluated assignment matrices and measured runtime (in seconds in brackets).

Method	Synthetic 1	Synthetic 2	FASSEG
Reinforcement	1344 (0.035s)		3570 (0.25s)
QAP	665280 (13.5s)		8.89 10^9 (NA)
Constrained QAP	665280 (13.5s)	64 (0.001s)	81 (0.57s)

This is confirmed by measured computation times: on the synthetic dataset, our proposal (0.035 s) is about 386 times faster that QAP (13.5 s). In our experiments, the constrained QAP is used to provide segmentations on FASSEG (too much time consuming for the QAP), by considering a global matching, to be compared with our sequential one. The counterpart is that we assume that the final identity/label of a region (final matching) initially corresponds to a label associated with the highest membership probability (CNN output), which may be the case in practice (e.g. when the CNN hesitates between two labels). Moreover, such a constrained QAP does not apply if vertex attributes do not embed membership probabilities (e.g. non CNN-based over-segmentation, such as for Synthetic 1 where the number of evaluated assignment is the same for both QAP and constrained QAP). In such a restrictive and less generic context, we measured that the number of permutations ranges from 1 (case of perfect CNN-based segmentation) to 1600 (many region candidates per class), with a mean value of 81 (see Table 2). Note that the measured computation time is, in average, equal to 0.57 s (mainly due to the application of the constraint, i.e. finding the list of region candidates) compared to 0.25 s with our sequential approach, although more assignment matrices are evaluated (3570).

4   Conclusion

We propose a reinforcement-learning-based framework for the sequential semantic analysis of image content by exploiting structural information formulated as a QAP-based inexact graph matching problem. Preliminary experiments on both a synthetic dataset and the FASSEG dataset are promising as they show that our approach dramatically reduces the complexity of this QAP-based inexact graph matching problem, while preserving the efficiency of the analysis.

Future works and additional studies will first evaluate our method on other applications with larger datasets. An important point to be studied, and ignored in this preliminary evaluation, is the influence of the size of the initial seed in the sequential approach based on reinforcement learning, as well as the ability to automatically learn its optimal size. Another aspect to be studied is the extension of this framework so that the ordering can be dynamically adapted, involving, for instance, the ability to integrate revocable actions [8]. Using a Dueling Deep Q-Networks approach [13] would allow adapting the strategy to the current image. Finally, the final refinement step, possibly involving outliers/artifacts, is managed by considering a random ordering. It would be interesting to investigate whether it could benefit from an optimized ordering, again based on reinforcement learning.

References

1. Bacciu, D., Errica, F., Micheli, A., Podda, M.: A gentle introduction to deep learning for graphs. Neural Netw. **129**, 203–221 (2020). https://doi.org/10.1016/j.neunet.2020.06.006
2. Bloch, I.: Fuzzy sets for image processing and understanding. Fuzzy Sets Syst. **281**, 280–291 (2015). https://doi.org/10.1016/j.fss.2015.06.017
3. Chopin, J., Fasquel, J.B., Mouchère, H., Dahyot, R., Bloch, I.: Semantic image segmentation based on spatial relationships and inexact graph matching. In: 2020 Tenth International Conference on Image Processing Theory, Tools and Applications (IPTA), pp. 1–6 (2020). https://doi.org/10.1109/IPTA50016.2020.9286611

4. Fasquel, J.B., Delanoue, N.: Approach for sequential image interpretation using a priori binary perceptual topological and photometric knowledge and k-means-based segmentation. J. Opt. Soc. Am. A **35**(6), 936–945 (2018). https://doi.org/10.1364/JOSAA.35.000936

5. Fasquel, J.B., Delanoue, N.: A graph based image interpretation method using a priori qualitative inclusion and photometric relationships. IEEE Trans. Pattern Anal. Mach. Intell. **41**(5), 1043–1055 (2019). https://doi.org/10.1109/TPAMI.2018.2827939

6. Fouquier, G., Atif, J., Bloch, I.: Sequential model-based segmentation and recognition of image structures driven by visual features and spatial relations. Comput. Vis. Image Underst. **116**(1), 146–165 (2012). https://doi.org/10.1016/j.cviu.2011.09.004

7. Kamnitsas, K., et al.: Efficient multi-scale 3D CNN with fully connected CRF for accurate brain lesion segmentation. Med. Image Anal. **36**, 61–78 (2017). https://doi.org/10.1016/j.media.2016.10.004

8. Liu, C., Wang, R., Jiang, Z., Yan, J., Huang, L., Lu, P.: Revocable deep reinforcement learning with affinity regularization for outlier-robust graph matching. CoRR (2020). https://arxiv.org/abs/2012.08950

9. Ronneberger, O., Fischer, P., Brox, T.: U-Net: convolutional networks for biomedical image segmentation. In: Navab, N., Hornegger, J., Wells, W.M., Frangi, A.F. (eds.) MICCAI 2015. LNCS, vol. 9351, pp. 234–241. Springer, Cham (2015). https://doi.org/10.1007/978-3-319-24574-4_28

10. Pirinen, A., Sminchisescu, C.: Deep reinforcement learning of region proposal networks for object detection. In: 2018 IEEE/CVF Conference on Computer Vision and Pattern Recognition, pp. 6945–6954 (2018). https://doi.org/10.1109/CVPR.2018.00726

11. Sun, M., Xiao, J., Lim, E.G., Xie, Y., Feng, J.: Adaptive ROI generation for video object segmentation using reinforcement learning. Pattern Recogn. **106**, 107465 (2020). https://doi.org/10.1016/j.patcog.2020.107465

12. Sutton, R.S., Barto, A.G.: Reinforcement Learning: An Introduction, 2nd edn. The MIT Press (2018). http://incompleteideas.net/book/the-book-2nd.html

13. Wang, Z., Schaul, T., Hessel, M., Van Hasselt, H., Lanctot, M., De Freitas, N.: Dueling network architectures for deep reinforcement learning. In: 33rd International Conference on International Conference on Machine Learning, vol. 48, pp. 1995–2003 (2016)

14. Yang, Y., Whinston, A.: A survey on reinforcement learning for combinatorial optimization (2020). https://arxiv.org/abs/2008.12248

15. Yun, S., Choi, J., Yoo, Y., Yun, K., Choi, J.Y.: Action-driven visual object tracking with deep reinforcement learning. IEEE Trans. Neural Netw. Learn. Syst. **29**(6), 2239–2252 (2018). https://doi.org/10.1109/TNNLS.2018.2801826

16. Zanfir, A., Sminchisescu, C.: Deep learning of graph matching. In: 2018 IEEE/CVF Conference on Computer Vision and Pattern Recognition, pp. 2684–2693 (2018). https://doi.org/10.1109/CVPR.2018.00284

17. Ziyao, L., Liang, Z., Guojie, S.: GCN-LASE: towards adequately incorporating link attributes in graph convolutional networks. In: 28th International Joint Conference on Artificial Intelligence (IJCAI), pp. 2959–2965 (2019). https://doi.org/10.24963/ijcai.2019/410

Towards a Unified Benchmark for Monocular Radial Distortion Correction and the Importance of Testing on Real-World Data

Christoph Theiß[1,2](✉) and Joachim Denzler[1,2](✉)

[1] Friedrich Schiller University Jena, 00743 Jena, Germany
{christoph.theiss,joachim.denzler}@uni-jena.de
[2] German Aerospace Center, Institute of Data Science, 07745 Jena, Germany

Abstract. Radial distortion correction for a single image is often over-looked in computer vision. It is possible to rectify images accurately when the camera and lens are known or physically available to take additional images with a calibration pattern. However, sometimes it is impossible to identify the camera or lens of an image, e.g., crowd-sourced datasets. Nonetheless, it is still important to correct that image for radial distortion in these cases. Especially in the last few years, solving the radial distortion correction problem from a single image with a deep neural network approach increased in popularity. This paper shows that these approaches tend to overfit completely on the synthetic data generation process used to train such networks. Additionally, we investigate which parts of this process are responsible for overfitting. We apply an explainability tool to analyze the trained models' behavior. Furthermore, we introduce a new dataset based on the popular ImageNet dataset as a new benchmark for comparison. Lastly, we propose an efficient solution to the overfitting problem by feeding edge images to the neural networks instead of the images. Source code, data, and models are publicly available at https://github.com/cvjena/deeprect.

Keywords: Radial distortion · Monocular images · Synthetic data

1 Introduction

The effects of lens distortion are often overlooked when knowledge about the geometry of 3D scenes or the pinhole camera model is integrated into deep learning-based approaches [10, 20, 31, 35]. Nevertheless, their effects are still visible on images taken with modern cameras, including mobile devices. In particular, wide-angle lenses, which are widely used due to their large field of view, suffer from geometric distortions. Additional difficulties arise when images are taken under uncontrolled conditions, e.g., crowd-sourcing or web-crawling scenarios. In these cases, conventional automatic algorithms for correcting radial distortions cannot be applied, and one would have to try correcting the image manually.

© Springer Nature Switzerland AG 2022
M. El Yacoubi et al. (Eds.): ICPRAI 2022, LNCS 13363, pp. 59–71, 2022.
https://doi.org/10.1007/978-3-031-09037-0_6

However, state of the art for radial distortion correction from a single image has improved dramatically recently with the ever-increasing success of machine learning and deep learning-based approaches [13,14,18,22,30,33]. While these methods achieve remarkable performance on benchmark datasets, they fail to estimate the radial distortion for real-world data correctly.

We show that the generalization to real-world data can be improved when edge detections of the images are fed to the network instead of the distorted images themselves. This way, information that is unnecessary for the radial distortion correction is removed, reducing the complexity of the search space and removing unintentional artifacts. Moreover, we demonstrate the influence of high-resolution images and that a combination of edge detections and high-resolution images improves the generalization even further. For that, we investigate the behavior of three previously published methods on a new high-resolution dataset, which is a subset of the ImageNet dataset [23]. Beyond that, we analyze the behavior of a classification-based approach with an explainability tool. This way, we can study which input areas the models focus on for their prediction.

2   Related Work

Many approaches exist for radial distortion correction with the help of a calibration pattern, video sequences, or when the camera is known and physically available. However, in many cases, none of these pieces of information are available. Hence, we focus on correcting radial distortion using a single image and describe more recent approaches that apply deep neural networks to solve this task.

Previous works on radial distortion correction from a single image focus almost exclusively on barrel distortion and omit pincushion or mustache distortion, which requires the estimation of at least two distortion coefficients. Rong et al. [22] cast radial distortion correction as a classification problem where each class corresponds to a radial distortion coefficient. This significantly limits the distortions they can estimate. Lutz et al. [18] proposed a data-driven approach in which a network is trained on a large set of synthetically distorted images. As common in regression tasks, they minimize the mean squared error between prediction and ground truth distortion coefficients. Shi et al. [24] extend a ResNet-18 model [12] by adding a weight layer with so-called inverted foveal models after the final convolutional layer to emphasize the importance of pixels closer to the border of the images. In addition to the distortion coefficients, Li et al. [13] estimate the displacement field between distorted and corrected images and use it to generate the corrected image.

An approach to estimate more than a single distortion parameter is presented by López-Antequera et al. [16], which simultaneously predicts tilt, roll, focal length, and radial distortion. They recover estimations for two radial distortion parameters from a large dataset with the help of Structure from Motion [27] reconstruction. They show that the parameters of the cameras used to acquire the dataset lie close to a one-dimensional manifold. While some cameras have this property, many do not, severely limiting the method's applicability.

Instead of predicting the radial distortion coefficients, Liao *et al.* [14] use generative adversarial networks (GANs) [11] to generate the undistorted image directly. The reconstructed images lack texture details, are partially distorted or differently illuminated, among other problems.

Other works focus on correcting fisheye images. Xue *et al.* [29] exploit that distorted lines generated by the fisheye projection should be straight after correction, or similarly that straight lines in 3D space should also be straight in the image plane [28]. However, both approaches require line segment annotations that are not easily acquirable, significantly limiting the available training data.

Finally, the current state of the art for correcting barrel distortion with a single image is achieved by Zhao *et al.* [33] integrating additional knowledge about the radial distortion model. They use a CNN to estimate the radial distortion coefficient and the inverse of the division model to calculate a sampling grid to rectify the distorted image by bilinear sampling. As a standard radial distortion model, we describe the division model in Sect. 3.1.

3   Data Generation

Ground truth data for radial distortion correction is difficult to obtain. Hence, previous work used synthetically distorted images for training. Following, we describe the division modell [9], which is often used to obtain distorted images. Afterward, we describe what datasets are used for that purpose and why they are unsuitable for radial distortion correction. Instead, we propose to use a subset of the ImageNet dataset that only contains high-resolution images. Lastly, we describe the proposed preprocessing strategy applied after the synthetic distortion of the input images.

3.1   Lens Distortion Models

A common way to model radial distortion is the division model

$$r^u = \frac{r^d}{1 + k_1(r^d)^2 + k_2(r^d)^4 + \dots} \tag{1}$$

w.r.t the radius $r^d = \sqrt{(\bar{x}^d)^2 + (\bar{y}^d)^2}$, proposed by [9], where $\bar{x}^d = x^d - x^0$, $\bar{y}^d = y^d - y^0$, and the coordinates of the distorted point (x^d, y^d). The distortion center is (x^0, y^0). In practice, the model is parameterized with up to three parameters k_1, k_2, k_3. It is also common that models for specific cameras only have one parameter. Barrel distortion occurs when all coefficients $k_1, k_2, \dots$ are negative and a pincushion distortion if all are positive. Mustache distortion can occur when the signs of the coefficients differ. It generally requires fewer coefficients to approximate large distortion compared to the radial model [4]. We assume that the center of distortion is the center of the image, and refer the interested reader to [26] for a more detailed comparison of various camera distortion models. A backward image warping is performed, which requires calculating the undistorted radius given the distorted radius when we distort an image.

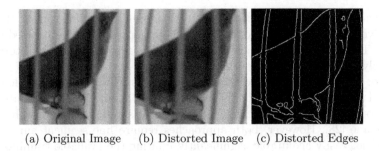

(a) Original Image   (b) Distorted Image   (c) Distorted Edges

Fig. 1. Example of the different types of input that are fed to the model. We compare the performance of models trained with images, and edge detection.

3.2 Preprocessing Strategy

We consider two input types to the neural network, as depicted in Fig. 1. As a baseline, we use natural images as is done in all previous deep neural network approaches for radial distortion correction. We show that models trained on synthetically distorted natural images overfit the data generation process and do not generalize to real-world data. Instead, we perform edge detection as the last preprocessing step with the Canny edge detector [6]. Previous non-parametric approaches [1,5,7,8,25,32] demonstrate that edge detection is well suited as a preprocessing step to estimate radial distortion. They provide enough context in the image to correctly estimate the coefficients while simultaneously reducing the amount of data. In the case of edge detections, the resulting inputs only have one channel. We adjust the first layer of the network accordingly.

3.3 Synthetically Distorted Datasets

In the literature [13,14,18,22,33], the model in Eq. (1) is often used to generate distorted images where the rectified images are assumed to be given as ground truth.

Previous work uses already available datasets to collect sufficient training data and synthetically distorts them. To that end, Rong et $al.$ [22] obtain a subset of the ImageNet dataset [23] with images that have a large amount of long straight lines relative to the image size. However, many images of the resulting dataset, counting roughly $68,000$, have undesirable properties, like tiny images or images not taken with a camera like, $e.g.$, screenshots. Additionally, all images of this dataset are resized to a resolution of 256×256 before conducting the synthetic radial distortion. In comparison, Li et $al.$ [13] use the Places365-Standard dataset [34]. They use images with a resolution of 512×512 as the original non-distorted images to generate a dataset of distorted images at a resolution of 256×256. Similarly, Lutz et $al.$ [18] use the MS COCO dataset [15] but resize all images to 1024 on their longer side before distortion.

In contrast, we focus on high-resolution images. Like Rong *et al.* [22], we construct an ImageNet subset containing 126, 623 the original 14.2 million images. However, we choose all images with a minimum width and height of at least 1200 pixels independent of straight lines. This results in a more diverse dataset with a vastly larger average resolution of 2011×1733 than other datasets like MS COCO with 577×484 or Places365-Standard with 677×551. We can leverage the high resolution to generate more realistically looking distortions because the resulting images appear significantly less blurry. We split the dataset into 106, 582 training, 5, 000 validation, and 10, 000 test samples.

To reduce the possibilities for the network to exploit the data generation process, we propose increasing the resolution at which the images are distorted and applying an edge detection preprocessing step. This way, we can decrease the possibility for artifacts that are not visible by a human observer but force the network to overfit the synthetic data generation process instead of the actual radial distortion. We leverage the high-resolution images available in the ImageNet dataset to distort the images. This makes it possible to distort the images at a resolution of 1024×1024 compared to 512×512 or 256×256 as is done in other work, which results in sharper, less blurry distorted images that more closely resemble the original undistorted image.

Besides evaluating the trained models qualitatively on real-world images, we also evaluate them quantitatively on a subset of a differently distorted dataset. For that, we use the dataset published by Bogdan *et al.* [3], who automatically generate distorted images based on panorama images and the unified spherical model [2]. Compared to Brown's and division models used in other work, the unified spherical model can describe a wider variety of cameras, including perspective, wide-angle, fisheye, and catadioptric cameras. Hence, we need to determine the subset of distorted images that the division model can correct. We first compute the corrected image for each sample in the dataset with the unified spherical model. Afterward, we sample coefficients for the division model between 0.0 and -0.2 to find the visually most similar-looking correction. We choose the subset of all images for which the peak signal-to-noise ratio (PSNR) between the two corrections is larger than 30, i.e., they are visually indistinguishable. Figure 2 shows the distribution of the model coefficients and PSNR of the resulting test dataset.

4   Experiments

4.1   Implementation Details

For the model, we follow previous works and choose a ResNet-18 [12] for all experiments. The models are initialized with ImageNet [23] weights. To avoid the unnecessary introduction of distortion, we resize all images while maintaining the aspect ratio. Then, the images are randomly cropped for training and center cropped for testing. We apply random horizontal and vertical flipping. Afterward, we randomly distort the images with the division model and distortion coefficients uniformly drawn between 0.0 and -0.2. We train each model

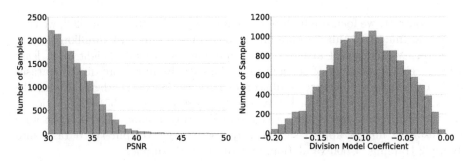

Fig. 2. PSNR and division model coefficient distributions for the subset of samples that are distorted by the unified spherical mode and can be corrected with the division model.

for 30 epochs and divide the learning rate by a factor of ten after 20 epochs. We used the AdamW optimizer [17] with $\beta_1 = 0.9$ and $\beta_2 = 0.999$. The experiments are implemented with PyTorch [19].

Following previous works in this area [29,30,33], we adapt the PSNR and the structural similarity index measure (SSIM) as evaluation metrics. A larger value corresponds to better correction quality. Additionally, we report the mean absolute error (MAE) between estimated and ground-truth coefficients.

4.2 Radial Distortion Estimation

We analyze different input types and their impact on the model's performance. We compare the models quantitatively on synthetically distorted validation data and qualitative on real-world images. The real-world samples are not synthetically distorted. Hence, they can give insight into whether the models learned to correct general radial distortion or overfitted to our data generation process. The quantitative results are shown in Fig. 3a. The results indicate that natural images without any further preprocessing outperform our preprocessing strategy on a synthetically distorted test dataset. However, the qualitative results on real-world images in Fig. 5 demonstrate that the models trained on natural images do not generalize to natural distortions. While models trained on edge images correctly predict a larger distortions coefficient when a severe distortion is visible in the image and do not overcorrect images with only a small visible distortion. This suggests that models trained on edge images can differentiate between severe and slight distortions.

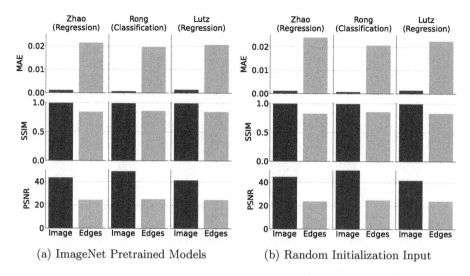

(a) ImageNet Pretrained Models   (b) Random Initialization Input

Fig. 3. Comparison between models trained on images and edge detections as inputs. It shows that natural images without any further preprocessing outperform the edges on a synthetically distorted test dataset. Moreover, the results are almost identical between pretrained and randomly initialized weights.

Besides the qualitative evaluation of the images shown in Fig. 5, we quantitatively test the trained models on a subset of the dataset proposed by Bogdan et al. [3] that are distorted with the unified spherical model and can be corrected with the division. Because the coefficients are not uniformly distributed, we put them evenly sized bins of 100 based on the ground truth distortion coefficient and report the MAE for each group separately, as depicted in Fig. 4. The models trained on natural images cannot detect any distortion at all. Hence, they consistently predict a coefficient close to 0.0 resulting in an MAE almost identical to the ground truth distortion coefficient. On the other hand, models trained on edge detections have a significantly lower MAE.

4.3 Influence of Pre-trained Weights

All trained networks in Sect. 4.2 all use pre-trained weights wherever possible. The weights are obtained by solving a classification task on the original ImageNet dataset. To train the neural networks to estimate the radial distortion coefficients, we use a subset of the ImageNet dataset containing only high-resolution images. Hence, it is reasonable to assume that the weights are a significant cause of the observed overfitting phenomenon.

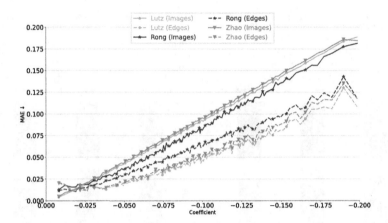

Fig. 4. MAE grouped by ground truth coefficients. While the MAE increases for both types of models with increasing distortion coefficients, models trained on edge detections are clearly more accurate.

One possible explanation for the improved generalization when we train a network with edge images is the random initialization of weights for the first convolutional layer. Instead, the layer is trained from scratch because no weights are readily available for single-channel inputs with the same model architecture.

We confirm that the behavior is independent of the initialized weights by repeating the same experiment outlined above with randomly initialized weights. The results in Fig. 3b support that choosing weights pre-trained for the classification task on ImageNet is not the cause of the significant overfitting that can be observed for the radial distortion correction task, as can be seen in the negligible difference between Figs. 3a and 3b.

4.4 Explainability of the Results

To better understand the behavior of our models, we apply local interpretable model-agnostic explanations (LIME) [21] to highlight areas of images that the models primarily use for their prediction. While applying this method to regression models is possible, the resulting explanations are not interpretable enough to be helpful, as stated by the authors. Hence, we apply LIME only to models trained with the method proposed by Rong *et al.* [22] because they are the only ones who cast radial distortion correction as a classification problem in a deep learning scenario. For radial distortion correction, areas with long lines are of particular interest. The results shown in Fig. 6 indicate that models trained on natural images specifically focus on homogenous areas without lines. In contrast, models that leverage edge detections prioritize areas with long edges.

Distorted Image   Lutz *et al.* [18]   Rong *et al.* [22]   Zhao *et al.* [33]

Fig. 5. Qualitative results on various real-world examples. The top right of each image shows the correction with models trained on edge detections with the edges overlayed for visualization purposes. The bottom left models trained on natural images. From left to right, it shows the distorted real-world images and the models trained with the following methods: Lutz *et al.* [18], Rong *et al.* [22], and Zhao *et al.* [33]

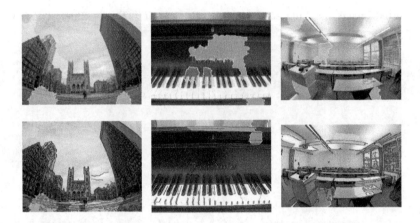

Fig. 6. LIME explanations for models trained with the method proposed by Rong *et al.* The top row shows explanations for a model trained on natural images and the bottom row for a model trained on edge detection. The edges depicted in the bottom row indicate the input of models trained on edge detections. The model trained on natural image focuses on homogenous areas of the image which do not contain information about the radial distortion. On the other hand, the model trained on edge detection focuses on long, distinct lines.

5   Conclusion

This work investigated the effect of edge detection as additional preprocessing on the generalizability of deep neural networks for radial distortion correction. We analyzed the performance and behavior of three different methods that leverage deep learning for radial distortion correction. We investigated the overfitting for neural networks when trained with synthetically distorted images. To that end, we explored the influence of pre-trained weights and the resolution at which the images are synthetically distorted. In addition, we proposed a new dataset of high-resolution images based on the popular ImageNet dataset.

Moreover, we applied LIME to explain the results of the classification-based approach, which showed that models trained on natural images focus on homogenous regions of the image, which should not be relevant for the task of radial distortion correction. We showed qualitatively on real-world examples and quantitatively on differently distorted images that edge detection as an additional preprocessing step is an effective measure to improve the generalization of these methods.

References

1. Alvarez, L., Gómez, L., Sendra, J.R.: An algebraic approach to lens distortion by line rectification. J. Math. Imag. Vis. **35**(1), 36–50 (2009). https://doi.org/10.1007/s10851-009-0153-2

2. Barreto, J.P.: A unifying geometric representation for central projection systems. Comput. Vis. Image Underst. **103**(3), 208–217 (2006)

3. Bogdan, O., Eckstein, V., Rameau, F., Bazin, J.C.: DeepCalib: a deep learning approach for automatic intrinsic calibration of wide field-of-view cameras. In: Proceedings of the 15th ACM SIGGRAPH European Conference on Visual Media Production, CVMP 2018, pp. 1–10. Association for Computing Machinery, New York (2018). https://doi.org/10.1145/3278471.3278479

4. Brown, D.C.: Decentering distortion of lenses. Photogrammetric Engineering and Remote Sensing (1966). https://ci.nii.ac.jp/naid/10022411406/

5. Bräuer-Burchardt, C., Voss, K.: Automatic lens distortion calibration using single views. In: Sommer, G., Krüger, N., Perwass, C. (eds.) Mustererkennung 2000. Informatik aktuell, pp. 187–194. Springer, Heidelberg (2000). https://doi.org/10.1007/978-3-642-59802-9_24

6. Canny, J.: A computational approach to edge detection. IEEE Trans. Pattern Anal. Mach. Intell. **6**, 679–698 (1986)

7. Claus, D., Fitzgibbon, A.W.: A plumbline constraint for the rational function lens distortion model. In: Proceedings of the British Machine Vision Conference 2005, pp. 10.1-10.10. British Machine Vision Association, Oxford (2005). https://doi.org/10.5244/C.19.10

8. Devernay, F., Faugeras, O.: Straight lines have to be straight. Mach. Vis. Appl. **13**(1), 14–24 (2001). https://doi.org/10.1007/PL00013269

9. Fitzgibbon, A.: Simultaneous linear estimation of multiple view geometry and lens distortion. In: Proceedings of the 2001 IEEE Computer Society Conference on Computer Vision and Pattern Recognition. CVPR 2001, vol. 1, pp. I (2001). https://doi.org/10.1109/CVPR.2001.990465, ISSN 1063-6919

10. Garg, R., B.G., V.K., Carneiro, G., Reid, I.: Unsupervised CNN for single view depth estimation: geometry to the rescue. In: Leibe, B., Matas, J., Sebe, N., Welling, M. (eds.) ECCV 2016. LNCS, vol. 9912, pp. 740–756. Springer, Cham (2016). https://doi.org/10.1007/978-3-319-46484-8_45

11. Goodfellow, I., et al.: Generative adversarial nets. In: Advances in Neural Information Processing Systems, vol. 27. Curran Associates, Inc. (2014)

12. He, K., Zhang, X., Ren, S., Sun, J.: Deep residual learning for image recognition, pp. 770–778 (2016)

13. Li, X., Zhang, B., Sander, P.V., Liao, J.: Blind geometric distortion correction on images through deep learning, pp. 4855–4864 (2019)

14. Liao, K., Lin, C., Zhao, Y., Gabbouj, M.: DR-GAN: automatic radial distortion rectification using conditional GAN in real-time. IEEE Trans. Circ. Syst. Video Technol. **30**(3), 725–733 (2020). https://doi.org/10.1109/TCSVT.2019.2897984

15. Lin, T.-Y., et al.: Microsoft COCO: common objects in context. In: Fleet, D., Pajdla, T., Schiele, B., Tuytelaars, T. (eds.) ECCV 2014. LNCS, vol. 8693, pp. 740–755. Springer, Cham (2014). https://doi.org/10.1007/978-3-319-10602-1_48

16. Lopez, M., Mari, R., Gargallo, P., Kuang, Y., Gonzalez-Jimenez, J., Haro, G.: Deep single image camera calibration with radial distortion, pp. 11817–11825 (2019)

17. Loshchilov, I., Hutter, F.: Decoupled weight decay regularization. arXiv:1711.05101 [cs, math] (2019). arXiv: 1711.05101

18. Lutz, S., Davey, M., Smolic, A.: Deep convolutional neural networks for estimating lens distortion parameters. Session 2: Deep Learning for Computer Vision (2019). https://doi.org/10.21427/yg8t-6g48
19. Paszke, A.,et al.: PyTorch: an imperative style, high-performance deep learning library. In: Advances in Neural Information Processing Systems, vol. 32. Curran Associates, Inc. (2019)
20. Ranjan, A., et al.: Competitive collaboration: joint unsupervised learning of depth, camera motion, optical flow and motion segmentation, pp. 12240–12249 (2019)
21. Ribeiro, M.T., Singh, S., Guestrin, C.: "Why should I trust you?": explaining the predictions of any classifier. In: Proceedings of the 22nd ACM SIGKDD International Conference on Knowledge Discovery and Data Mining, San Francisco, CA, USA, 13–17 August 2016, pp. 1135–1144 (2016)
22. Rong, J., Huang, S., Shang, Z., Ying, X.: Radial lens distortion correction using convolutional neural networks trained with synthesized images. In: Lai, S.-H., Lepetit, V., Nishino, K., Sato, Y. (eds.) ACCV 2016. LNCS, vol. 10113, pp. 35–49. Springer, Cham (2017). https://doi.org/10.1007/978-3-319-54187-7_3
23. Russakovsky, O., et al.: ImageNet large scale visual recognition challenge. Int. J. Comput. Vis. **115**(3), 211–252 (2015). https://doi.org/10.1007/s11263-015-0816-y
24. Shi, Y., Zhang, D., Wen, J., Tong, X., Ying, X., Zha, H.: Radial lens distortion correction by adding a weight layer with inverted foveal models to convolutional neural networks. In: 2018 24th International Conference on Pattern Recognition (ICPR), pp. 1–6 (2018). https://doi.org/10.1109/ICPR.2018.8545218, ISSN 1051-4651
25. Strand, R., Hayman, E.: Correcting radial distortion by circle fitting. In: Proceedings of the British Machine Vision Conference 2005, pp. 9.1-9.10. British Machine Vision Association, Oxford (2005). https://doi.org/10.5244/C.19.9
26. Tang, Z., Grompone von Gioi, R., Monasse, P., Morel, J.M.: A precision analysis of camera distortion models. IEEE Trans. Image Process. **26**(6), 2694–2704 (2017). https://doi.org/10.1109/TIP.2017.2686001
27. Ullman, S., Brenner, S.: The interpretation of structure from motion. Proc. R. Soc. Lond. Ser. B. Biol. Sci. **203**(1153), 405–426 (1979). https://doi.org/10.1098/rspb.1979.0006, https://royalsocietypublishing.org/doi/abs/10.1098/rspb.1979.0006
28. Xue, Z.C., Xue, N., Xia, G.S.: Fisheye distortion rectification from deep straight lines. arXiv:2003.11386 [cs] (2020). arXiv: 2003.11386
29. Xue, Z., Xue, N., Xia, G.S., Shen, W.: Learning to calibrate straight lines for Fisheye image rectification, pp. 1643–1651 (2019)
30. Yin, X., Wang, X., Yu, J., Zhang, M., Fua, P., Tao, D.: FishEyeRecNet: a multi-context collaborative deep network for Fisheye image rectification, pp. 469–484 (2018)
31. Yin, Z., Shi, J.: GeoNet: unsupervised learning of dense depth, optical flow and camera pose, pp. 1983–1992 (2018)
32. Ying, X., Hu, Z., Zha, H.: Fisheye lenses calibration using straight-line spherical perspective projection constraint. In: Narayanan, P.J., Nayar, S.K., Shum, H.-Y. (eds.) ACCV 2006. LNCS, vol. 3852, pp. 61–70. Springer, Heidelberg (2006). https://doi.org/10.1007/11612704_7
33. Zhao, H., Shi, Y., Tong, X., Ying, X., Zha, H.: A simple yet effective pipeline for radial distortion correction. In: 2020 IEEE International Conference on Image Processing (ICIP), pp. 878–882 (2020). https://doi.org/10.1109/ICIP40778.2020.9191107, ISSN 2381-8549

34. Zhou, B., Lapedriza, A., Khosla, A., Oliva, A., Torralba, A.: Places: a 10 million image database for scene recognition. IEEE Trans. Pattern Anal. Mach. Intell. **40**(6), 1452–1464 (2018). https://doi.org/10.1109/TPAMI.2017.2723009
35. Zhou, T., Brown, M., Snavely, N., Lowe, D.G.: Unsupervised Learning of depth and ego-motion from video, pp. 1851–1858 (2017)

Comparing Artificial Intelligence Algorithms in Computer Vision: The Weapon Detection Benchmark

Vincenzo Dentamaro⬩, Paolo Giglio⁽⊠⁾ ⬩, Donato Impedovo⬩, and Giuseppe Pirlo⬩

University of Bari "Aldo Moro", Bari, Italy
{vincenzo.dentamaro,paolo.giglio,donato.impedovo,
giuseppe.pirlo}@uniba.it

Abstract. The following work proposes a benchmark of performances of state of art AI algorithms for the weapons detection. Particularly, it is aimed to test three CNN based models on the task of detecting specific types of weapons. In order to accomplish this goal, four datasets are employed. Additionally, due to the lack of rich amounts of well-structured datasets in these field of research, new labeled data are produced as a new resource to test specific hypotheses about their impact on the performances of the models: different transfer-learning approaches are studied to understand how specific types of data could increase the generalization of the trained algorithms, with a peculiar attention to realistic scenarios. The whole work is designed with the intention to select the state-of-art algorithms that truly could be employed for realistic applications.

Keywords: Deep learning · Urban security · Weapons detection · Computer vision · Convolutional Neural Networks

1 Introduction

The field of object recognition has the intrinsic nature of being applicable to uncountable practical tasks. For same reason many challenges arise with the need to improve its transition from pure research to reliable applications for real world problems. This crucial transition is very sensitive to the complexity of the reality in terms of noise and disturbances of the input data as well as to the uncomplete representativity of reality provided by these data: for example, concerning the object detection, no training dataset will ever be able to include the totality of real case appearances of a specific object in terms of its peculiar attributes, perspectives, contingent backgrounds, its dynamics and so on. As a consequence, a fundamental problem emerges in terms of generalization of the trained algorithms for object detection when they are applied to reality. In this regard this field of research is always evolving towards new improvements that usually rely on new technologies and architectures, specifically AI algorithms during the last years, that redesign the way to perform detection and tracking of the objects appearing in a footage. As a consequence, there is the need to establish new benchmarks in order to

© Springer Nature Switzerland AG 2022
M. El Yacoubi et al. (Eds.): ICPRAI 2022, LNCS 13363, pp. 72–83, 2022.
https://doi.org/10.1007/978-3-031-09037-0_7

keep track of these improvements and to provide reliable comparative data of the state of art available technologies in order to understand what the research has achieved and what are the unresolved weaknesses that affect certain fields of applications. This work was born with the goal to address this specific issue specifically in the field of weapons detection.

2 State of Art

In accordance with the introduction, the majority of the studies here proposed are based on the employment of Convolutional Neural Networks (CNN) algorithms. As it will be shown, these have proved to outclass all the other technologies in the field of object recognition, classification and localization [1], which as a whole are referred to as the object detection task. All the following studies are focused on weapon detection as this is the specific field in which the authors of this work aim to provide a benchmark. It is important to highlight that each examined work usually starts from a Closed-Circuit Television (CCTV) system and redesign it in terms of a personalized detection system or in terms of a new dataset that could be useful for further studies in this field. The common challenges addressed by researchers are the following:

- Fast computation of videos while keeping good accuracy and a low number of false positives. The resulting system shall be able to alarm the security personnel promptly enough to respond with effectiveness to a potential threat.
- Lack of available and labeled datasets with the consequent need to design a new one from scratch with great expenditure of time and resources [4, 5].
- Concerning the weapons detection, the generalization is compromised by a substantial variability of shapes, colors, dimensions of the weapons even belonging to the same category, their potential similarity with other tools that are not dangerous [1] (such as pens, smartphones etc.).
- Additional variability is due to the diversity of viewpoints, perspectives of appearance of the weapons in real case scenarios, the noise of the input recorded data, the impact of external variables on the quality of the images [1, 5] (such as light condition, weather conditions, air pollution, reflections etc.)
- Another challenge comes from the partial or total concealment of the weapons during a real world episode: for example, the weapons are hold by hands and so partially visible when recorded [1].

Concerning the weapons detection state of art works, in [4] it is proposed an alarming system based on CNNs algorithms for the detection of typical guns used in crimes (revolvers, six-gun shooters, horse pistols or derringers, automatic or semi-automatic guns). Particularly, authors focus on reducing the number of false positives and evaluate a VGG-16 classifier by applying it with 2 different approaches: sliding window and region proposals. Additionally they adopt the weights of the VGG-16 pre-trained on ImageNet, a 1.28 million images dataset, then they perform a fine tuning on the weapons datasets. After training the classifier on 5 datasets and testing it on a 608 images test set, they compare the performances with the following results: a combination of the

Faster R-CNN (region proposal approach) with the VGG-16 classifier has the best performances with respect to the models based on the sliding window approach: a recall of 100%, and F1-score of 91.43%, a precision of 84.21% (which anyway is a fair value in this field). Furthermore, the speed of computation is enough to process 5.3 frames/s almost resulting in a real time detection of guns in a video. In [5] the authors propose one of the first works on the detection of knives with deep learning algorithms. Along with this goal the issue of low light conditions in indoor scenarios is also addressed. The latter is a problem that particularly affects the knives detection as their metallic surface reflects the light and can result in disturbing their appearance on the photograms. The detection models were built with the Tensorflow Object Detection API framework. Different combination of models were tested in order to perform both object detection and region selection: particularly SSD (InceptionV2), R-FCN (ResNet101), Faster R-CNN (Inception-ResNet-V2, ResNet50, ResNet101, InceptionV2). All the models were initialized with the pre-trained weights on the COCO dataset (over 200 thousands images) and then fine-tuned on a specific dataset, the Database-4 with 1250 images from the internet or retrieved from security videos downloaded from YouTube and Test-det. The most accurate model was the Faster R-CNN with Inception-ResNet-V2 with a F1 score of 95%. Its drawback is in the higher time expenditure for computation resulting in processing 1.3 fps, too low for real time applications. In this regard, the R-FCN (ResNet101) had a better tradeoff between the confusion matrix and a low latency (a precision of 100%, recall of 88.6%, F1 score of 93.97% and a speed of 10 fps). Concerning the light condition, the study concludes that the F1 score could undergo a drop of nearly 15% depending on the scarcity of light. In both [6] and [4] studies the problem of weapons detection is reformulated in terms of decreasing the number of false positives. In [6] particularly this issue is addressed with three models: CNN-based, Fast R-CNN and MobileNet CNN. The models are trained with two datasets: "Handgun Dataset for the sliding window approach" and "Handgun Dataset for the region proposals approach", both retrieved from [4]. The Mobile-SDD has the best performances with an accuracy of 90% for static images. In [7] a YOLOv2 algorithm is trained on two datasets rebuilt from those proposed in [4], particularly DB-2 which is the same present in [4] and DB-3 which is an edited version of the former with a compensated number of positives and negatives. A transfer learning procedure is performed starting with the pre-trained models on the COCO 2014 dataset. In order to provide comparable results, the YOLOv2 model is tested only on DB-2 with superior performances (100% of precision, recall of 89.15%). In [8] the authors aim to find the best model for detecting concealed or partially visible weapons on static images. A Faster R-CNN-Inception-V2-COCO model is used. The dataset for the training is retrieved from an open-source platform, with labeled images (2000 for the training and 100 for the test) with only 1 class for the "guns" over 4 (the others are "faces", "vehicles" and "hand"). The model performs with a floating precision from 99% to 64% depending on the contrast features of the image and a huge time expenditure for the detection (15 s) that makes its application unfeasible in real time. In [9] a weapon detection system is proposed based on the Faster R-CNN model. Two approaches are compared, one with the GoogleNet CNN architectures and another with SqueezeNet. The latter shows the best performance with an 85.44% average precision (IOU with a 50% threshold). In [10] a dataset is built with images of different weapons (guns, revolvers, rifles etc.) retrieved from the Internet Movie Firearm Database (IMFDB). The dataset is enriched with additional images from Google Images portraying tools that are similar to the weapons in terms of shapes and colors. The dataset is randomly split with a 90%-10% ratio. The YOLO algorithm is employed with the architecture based on the PASCAL VOC Challenge. The final results are a 96.26% accuracy and a 70% mAP. The technique is outstanding for its speed, allowing for real time applications. In [11] another dataset is proposed by merging ImageNet with a dataset of weapons portrayed from different perspectives. The Yolov3 algorithm is then applied on it with a transfer learning procedure. The detection system performances are then measured on four different videos with the main aim to reduce the number of false positives. Indeed a comparison is made with the Faster R-CNN model with comparable state of art results. In two cases Yolo performs even better with the following precisions: 98.64% vs 88.24% and 96.51% vs 82.46%. Additionally YOLOv3 is able to process at a speed of 45 fps against the 8 fps of the Faster R-CNN. In [12] a detection system is proposed by using CNN-based algorithms, such as SSD and Faster R-CNN. Two datasets are employed with the weapons being categorized into 5 classes. Faster R-CNN presents an accuracy of 84.6% and SSD an accuracy of 73.8%. On the contrary, the SSD is able to process 1.36 fps against the 0.62 fps of the Faster R-CNN. In [2] a comparison between state of art deep learning detection models is proposed for real-time applications. Both the sliding window/classification and region proposal/detection approaches are analyzed. For the sliding window/classification approach the VGG-16, InceptionV3, Inception ResNetV2 classifiers are chosen. Concerning the region proposal/detection approach, the SSD MobileNetV1, YOLOv3, Faster R-CNN-Inception ResNetV2, YOLOv4 models are selected. All the models are pre-trained on the ImageNet and COCO datasets. Three Datasets are created with frames from CCTV systems, YouTube, IMFDB and from the University of Granada as well as from other online repositories. All the datasets are split into two classes: Pistol/Not-Pistol. The Not-Pistol class includes objects and tools that can be confused with the weapons (phones, selfie sticks etc.). The models is compared with the standard metrics of F1-score, mAP, fps computational speed, in order to find the best tradeoff between accuracy and real time application feasibility. The YOLOv4 outclasses the others with a mAP of 91.73% (also the best results in terms of AP with a 91.73% value), and an F1-score of 91%. In [3] authors propose a new dataset made of images of robberies or portraying people with weapons, from YouTube, Instagram and Google. The images are categorized into two classes, those with the presence of weapons and the others. The images are preprocessed (resizing, data augmentation by rotations, capsizing etc.). A system is built with a Front End using a pre-trained YOLO system aimed to identify the images with subjects portrayed inside, and a Back End based on the employment of a VGG-Net to detect the presence of weapons in the images. The overall result is a concentration of the computational power to those parts of the videos where people are present with the consequent eventual presence of weapons. The recorded performances are 86% in terms of precision and recall. In [13] a comparison is provided between deep learning algorithms for the weapon detection on X-ray security images. The models are Faster CNN, R-FCN and YOLOv2, the latter performing better than the others. All these studies address the problem of weapon detection by pre-training the models and then fine tuning them with specific datasets. Unfortunately, weaknesses related to the weapons partial or total concealment as well as their appearance with different angles and perspectives remains an open issue. In [14] authors propose a different architecture that divides the analysis into two parts: the first one tries to understand the orientation of an object of interest and is combined with the procedure of cutting a sub region of interest (ROI) from the initial frame. The ROI is then classified by a Deep neural network based algorithm whose outcome is the probability that a weapon is depicted into the ROI. The architecture is called "Orientation Aware Object Detection (OAOD)". The organization of this work is designed to start from the previous studies found literature, specifically concerning the strategy of transfer learning and the typology of models involved, with the additional effort to test the best models on the ability to generalize from heterogeneous sets of data and accordingly to detect partially concealed weapons.

3   Datasets

As a consequence, the typology of data involved in this study is of paramount importance. In order to provide a new up to date benchmark on the detection of weapons from realistic images, this work relies on 4 different datasets. These contain static images categorized into 2 classes: "Handgun", with the presence of guns of different types and dimensions, shapes and colors, and "Knife" with images of a variety of different knives designed for different applications. These two categories are selected for practical reasons, as they represent the majority of the weapons used in crimes, especially in urban areas:

- in [18] authors suggest that stolen weapons are likely to be used in crimes and that the 60% of the stolen weapons are guns (60%, nearly 1.26 million over 2 million of stolen weapons, as highlighted by the FBI).
- in [2] authors claim that 95% of robberies shown in videos from YouTube, recorded with security cameras, are perpetrated with guns and revolvers.
- According to OMS, every year nearly 15 thousands people die due to violent crimes, 40% of these crimes are committed with knives [19].

The datasets employed are the followings:

- "training_dataset_1", which is a subset of images from Open Image Dataset (v4) [20], a dataset of 9 million labeled images with nearly 600 classes, including the "gun", "rifle" and "knives" ones. The subset consists of 1419 images and is balanced in terms of numbers of guns and knives. The images of this dataset typically are high resolution photos of the weapons on a monochromatic background, as it can be seen in Fig. 1A).
- "training_dataset_2", retrieved from the datasets of the University of Granada [5], whose design is described in [21]. This dataset was chosen as it gives the opportunity to make a comparison with the state of the art works, as it has already been employed in [4–7]. It is labeled, but it has been edited in order to remove images that were not related to the specific presence of a gun or a knife. The final dataset consists of 3250 images well balanced in terms of the number of guns and knives. The peculiarity of these images is that they are very close to realistic scenarios, with lower resolution and higher similarity with the features of the frames retrieved from CCTV systems, as shown in Fig. 1B).

- "training_dataset_3", which is built from the "training_dataset_2" by enriching it with more than 500 manually labeled images from the dataset in [3]. These additional images are extracted from movies and have been selected in order to show a partially concealed weapon or with the weapon occupying a small portion of the frame. Additionally, some data augmentation procedures have been applied to the images, such as producing grayscale ones, rotations, capsizing, noising and changing the luminosity along with other features of the original ones. The final dataset size is of 9192 images balanced in terms of number of guns and knives. An example image from this dataset is provided in Fig. 1C).
- "training_dataset_4", which is a new dataset built by merging the "training_dataset_1" and the "training_dataset_2". It finally accounts for 4669 balanced images. This dataset is designed in order to contain heterogeneous typologies of images (high resolution ones on monochromatic backgrounds, and those from realistic scenarios) and to verify if this quality could result in an improvement of the performances on the test set, or not.
- "Test", the dataset for testing the models. It is the same available in the repository where the "training_dataset_2" was retrieved and it is composed of 537 images balanced in terms of number of knives and guns. The main features of these images are very similar to those of the "training_dataset_2".

Fig. 1. A) two images from the "training_dataset_1", the weapons are portrayed with full details and on a monochromatic background. **B)** an image from the "training_dataset_2", a realistic scene of crime violence, with the weapon occupying a small part of the image. **C)** a frame retrieved from a movie, the weapon appears partially concealed.

4   Methods

There are three DNNs' architectures of particular interest for this analysis: Faster R-CNN-Inception-Resnet-V2, MobileNet-SSD-V1-FPN, and YOLOv4. These algorithms actually represent the state of art on performing the tasks of recognizing, classifying and localizing objects of interest appearing on video frames.

Faster-R-CNN-Inception-Resnet-V2: This model was chosen as it showed the best performances in terms of accuracy (mAP) in [5]. Furthermore, it also exhibits the best mAP (39.6%) when running on COCO. Another important aspect is the ease of training the model with fair time expenditure despite its relatively lower computational power. Its selection is based on the accuracy rather than its mean latency time of inference, which is relatively high (latency of 236 ms).

MobileNet-SSD-V1-FPN: This model is eligible for the study due to best results that SSD models achieve in terms of inference, time expenditure and sometimes also in terms of accuracy. These results are obtained even when they run on machines with lower computational power as a consequence of their algorithmic relatively low complexity [6, 12]. This specific model is very fast (latency of 48 ms) and it shows a mAP of 29.1% when applied to the COCO challenge, which is a fair value too.

These first two models belong to the Tensorflow 2 Model Zoo [16]: the ensemble of configurations and pretrained weights is available at the Tensorflow Object Detection API [15]. This library is used for the implementation, training and also the final evaluation of the Faster-R-CNN-Inception-Resnet-V2 and MobileNet-SSD-V1-FPN models. The configurations of these models are anyway edited in order to best suit their training on the specific dataset employed. Particularly, the "pipeline.config" file has been changed according to the official documentation of the library: a) the "num-classes" field was changed from 90 to only 2 classes, "Handgun" and "Knife", which are those targeted in this work; b) the "input_path" and "label_map_path" of the training configuration file "training_config" and "eval_inut_config" were edited by including the paths with ".record" or ".tfrecord" and "label_map.pbxt", where names and ids of the target classes are recorded; c) in order to perform fine-tuning from pretrained models, the "fine_tune_checkpoint" parameters were set with the checkpoint path to the weights and variables of the pretrained model, the "fine_tune_checkpoint_type" was set to "detection" value. Some "out of memory" critical errors led to secondary edits of configuration, such as resizing the images by means of a "fixed_shape_resizer" object with "height" and "width" parameters set to 416 pixels. As a consequence, the default image size of the MobileNet-SSD-V1FPN (640 × 640 pixels) and of the Faster-R-CNN-Inception-Resnet-V2 ("min_dimension" of 800 and "max_dimension" of 1333) were adapted to the available computational resources. In addition, for the latter of the models it was necessary to reduce the number of batches of the "batch_size" parameter from 16 to 8.

YOLO V4: This algorithm has the best performances in [2], thus it is inevitably selected as one of the three for the benchmark analysis. In this work YOLO V4 is implemented by using the Darknet library [17], which is quite efficient in terms of both mAP (67,5%) and latency (15 ms) when measured on COCO [24]. Even in this case the implementation is performed by using the pre-trained weights and configurations employed on COCO. Also for the YOLO V4 algorithm it has been necessary to edit the configuration by following the official guidelines of the Darknet library: a) it was created a "yolov4-obj.cfg" file with the architecture of the model designed in order to best fit the employed datasets: the "batch" parameter was set to 64, the "subdivisions" parameter to 16, the "width" and "height" to 512 (the highest affordable 32-multiple quantity without occurring in "out-of-memory" critical errors. The "max_batches" parameter was set to 6000 (this quantity is suggested by developers when the inference is between two classes), "steps" parameter set to 4800 (80% of the "max_batches") and 5400 (90% of the "max_batches), b) in the "yolov4-obj.cfg" the "filters" were edited on each one of the 3 layers preceding each "[yolo]" layer, and they were set to the value of 21, (number of classes + 5) * 3. After the three models were edited, it was possible to initialize them by using the configurations of the hyperparameters, of the layers and of the pre-trained weights on the COCO dataset, in order to perform later the fine-tuning on the new datasets. The models of the TensorFlow Object Detection API [15] were trained using the "model_main_tf2.py" script and specifying the model path by setting the "model_dir" parameter and its configuration with the "pipeline_config_path" parameter. The YOLOV4 model was trained by using a specific script available at the Darknet library [17] and specifying the "obg.data" file path, its configuration with the "yolov4-obj.cfg" and the pretrained weights with the "yolov4.conv.137" file. In order to restore the training phase after potential critical errors, during the operations the weights were recorded every one thousand steps on a training folder of the specific training model with files like "ckpt-x.index" and "ckpt-x.data" for the Tensorflow Object Detection API [15] and a "checkpoint" folder with files like "yolov4-obj_last.weights" for the YOLOV4 model. Additionally, the training phase was set with an early stopping procedure [25] in order to avoid overfitting. Particularly the "holdout-based early stopping" method discussed in [26] was employed in this work. Every dataset was split into a new training set and a validation set with a 9:1 proportionality. Every model was trained on the new training set by trying to optimize one or both the following aspects: minimizing the errors on the validation set (N.B. in this work the error represents both the loss on the classification task and localization task of the weapon appearing on the frame), maximizing the mean average precision with a threshold value IOU (Intersection Over Union) of the 50% on the validation set. Both the loss function and the mean average precision on the validation set were computed every one thousand steps during the previously mentioned training weights recording. The training was stopped once a decrease of the accuracy and/or an increase of the loss occurred with respect to the previous evaluation.

5 Results

Once the models were trained, they were tested on the test datasets (Fig. 24). For the models from the Tensorflow Object Detection API [15] the aforementioned "model_main_tf2.py" script was used with the only additional edit of the "pipeline.config": the "input_path" of the "eval_input_config" was set to the ".record" or ".tfrecord" files' paths of the test datasets. The Tensorflow Object Detection API [15] actually provides three protocols for the respective editable variants of the "pipeline.config" file in order to evaluate the detection tasks: these protocols are "PASCAL VOC 2010" detection, "COCO detection metrics" and "OID Challenge Object Detection Metric" [27]. Concerning the YOLOV4 model, a specific script was employed from the Darknet library: it is expected to receive the "obj.data" files' paths and the "yolov4-obj.cfg" personalized configuration file. The additional edit was the substitution of the pretrained weights with the new refined ones, "yolov4-obj_best.weights" after the early stopping of the fine tuning training. It is interesting to highlight how the process of detection is structured in order to understand the results. As it is derived from the

PASCAL VOC protocols, three different challenges are proposed: recognition, classification and segmentation, which indeed compose the more articulated detection process. The recognition process is measured with the average precision (AP) based on the overlapping region between the predicted bounding box (the area around the detected object) and the ground truth bounding box. A true positive detection happens when the Intersection Over Union of the two areas is greater than the 50%. This metric was activated in the "pipeline.config" file of the Tensorflow Object Detection API: the "metrics_set" parameter of the "eval_confi" file was set to the "pascal_voc_detection_metrics" value. Concerning the YOLOV4 model, the configuration process was edited with the "thresh 0.5" flag for the same metric. Darknet library [17] provides an ensemble of metrics (such as the mAP, average precision, recall, f1-score, IOU etc.) which are consistent with those that can be found in the PASCAL VOC Challenge protocol and COCO challenge [17], thus allowing for a reliable comparison of the results of the models when applied on the same final datasets. Indeed all the metrics in common within the Tensorflow Object Detection API [15] and Darknet library [17] were considered as a measuring framework to build a generalizable benchmark. Specifically the adopted metrics are the average precision (AP) with a IOU threshold of the 50% (it is used in the PASCAL VOC Challenge [22], and in the COCO Challenge [23] with some secondary variations, and on the Open Images Challenge [20]) and the mean average precision (an arithmetic average of the APs for both the knife and gun detections). Here it follows a set of tables of the resulted performances of the three models in terms of average precision and mean average precision (Table 1):

Table 1. The results of the three models in terms of the metrics *average precision (AP)* for an IOU with 0.5 threshold, and *mean average precision (mAP)*, which is the arithmetic average of the APs of both the gun and knife detection.

	Training Dataset 1			Training Dataset 2		
	AP Gun	AP Knife	mAP	AP Gun	AP Knife	mAP
Faster R-CNN-Inception-Resnet-v2	71.8%	17.41%	44.60%	92.64%	94.34%	93.49%
SSD-MobileNet-FPN-v1	62.57%	10.80%	36.68%	91.11%	94.47%	92.94%
YOLOv4 Darknet	69.63%	14.84%	42.24%	97.34%	97.83%	97.59%
	Training Dataset 3			Training Dataset 4		
	AP Gun	AP Knife	mAP	AP Knife	AP Gun	mAP
SSD-MobileNet-FPN-v1	87.47%	90.04%	88.75%	89.14%	91.11%	90.13%
YOLOv4 Darknet	88.50%	92.70%	90.60%	91.73%	89.91%	90.82%
Faster R-CNN-Inception-Resnet-v2	93.78%	94.58%	94.18%	95.76%	95.91%	95.83%

6   Discussion

From the previous tables it is possible to derive a series of observations:

- The worst results were recorded when the models were applied to the "training_dataset_1". An explanation could be due to the presence of pistols and knives portrayed as in the foreground of high resolution images. These weapons also appear on monochromatic backgrounds which in turn become a bias for the recognition of weapons when the models are applied on real case scenario video frames.
- The best results were obtained when the models were trained on the "training_dataset_2". The images in this dataset are realistic scenes where the weapons appear from different perspectives and with a small relative size with respect to the realistic, fully detailed scenario. Additionally these images exhibit a lower resolution, indeed they are similar to those retrievable from video-surveillance cameras.

Suboptimal and comparable results were achieved when the models were trained on the "training_dataset_3" and "training_dataset_4". Both of them are a slight variation of the "training_dataset_2". Furthermore the "training_dataset_3" also includes images with partial or total concealment of the weapons as well as low resolution or noisy photos. The employment of the "training_dataset_4", which is a combination of the "training_dataset_1" and the "training_dataset_2" did not produce an increment of performances with respect to those obtained by the only usage of the "training_dataset_2". Therefore, the presence of weapons' high resolution photos shall not be considered a prerequisite for enhancing the detection performances, on the contrary they seem to reduce the generalization of the models. Many studies combine the problem of weapons detection with that of reducing the number of false positives, such as [2, 4, 6, 11]. This metric is provided by default by the Darknet library, which in turn has recorded a very low number of false positives when the YOLOv4 worked on the "training_dataset_2": the results were of only 12 false positives over 537 cases on the test dataset.

7   Conclusion

This work proposes a benchmark of performances of three detection models which are considered the most representative and best performing of their categories. The YOLOV4 was the best performing model in terms of both class average precision with an overlapping bounding box IOU threshold of the 50% and mean average precision. As it can be retrieved from the scientific literature, this algorithm is also one with the lowest time expenditure for computation [2].

In the security field of application, the need to reduce the occurrence of true positives is demanding as well as that of reducing the false negatives. The former is due to the applicability of technology as an extension of the alarm systems. Indeed a huge amount of false positives would lead to an unsustainable activation of alarms and security procedures, which is not realistically feasible. The latter is due to obvious reasons of security and performances. In this regard, YOLOv4 was the best performing algorithm on lowering the number of false positives. From these considerations it appears that

YOLOv4 from the Darknet library is the optimal candidate as an automated module for real time applications of detection of guns and knives in real case scenarios.

References

1. Debnath, R., Bhowmik, M.K.: A comprehensive survey on computer vision based concepts, methodologies, analysis and applications for automatic gun/knife detection. J. Vis. Commun. Image Represent. **78**, 103165 (2021)
2. Bhatti, M.T., Khan, M.G., Aslam, M., Fiaz, M.J.: Weapon detection in real-time CCTV videos using deep learning. IEEE Access **9**, 34366–34382 (2021)
3. Romero, D., Salamea, C.: Convolutional models for the detection of firearms in surveillance videos. Appl. Sci. **9**(15), 2965 (2019)
4. Olmos, R., Tabik, S., Herrera, F.: Automatic handgun detection alarm in videos using deep learning. Neurocomputing **275**, 66–72 (2018)
5. Castillo, A., Tabik, S., Pérez, F., Olmos, R., Herrera, F.: Brightness guided preprocessing for automatic cold steel weapon detection in surveillance videos with deep learning. Neurocomputing **330**, 151–161 (2019)
6. Elmir, Y., Laouar, S.A., Hamdaoui, L.: Deep learning for automatic detection of handguns in video sequences. In: JERI (2019)
7. Cardoso, G., Simões, V., Ciarelli, P.M., Vassallo, R.F.: Use of deep learning for firearms detection in images. In: Anais do XV Workshop de Visão Computacional, pp. 109–114. SBC (2019)
8. Dubey, S.:Building a gun detection model using deep learning. Program Chair & Proceedings Editor: M. Afzal Upal, Ph.d. Chair of Computing & Information Science Department Mercyhurst University 501 (2019)
9. Fernandez-Carrobles, M.M., Deniz, O., Maroto, F.: Gun and knife detection based on faster R-CNN for video surveillance. In: Morales, A., Fierrez, J., Sánchez, J.S., Ribeiro, B. (eds.) IbPRIA 2019. LNCS, vol. 11868, pp. 441–452. Springer, Cham (2019). https://doi.org/10.1007/978-3-030-31321-0_38
10. de Azevedo Kanehisa, R.F., de Almeida Neto, A.: Firearm detection using convolutional neural networks. In: ICAART 2019, pp. 707–714 (2019)
11. Warsi, A., Abdullah, M., Husen, M.N., Yahya, M., Khan, S., Jawaid, N.: Gun detection system using YOLOv3. In: 2019 IEEE International Conference on Smart Instrumentation, Measurement and Application (ICSIMA), pp. 1–4. IEEE (2019)
12. Jain, H., Vikram, A., Kashyap, A., Jain, A.:Weapon detection using artificial intelligence and deep learning for security applications. In: 2020 International Conference on Electronics and Sustainable Communication Systems (ICESC), pp. 193–198. IEEE (2020)
13. Akcay, S., Kundegorski, M.E., Willcocks, C.G., Breckon, T.P.: Using deep convolutional neural network architectures for object classification and detection within x-ray baggage security imagery. IEEE Trans. Inf. Forensics Secur. **13**(9), 2203–2215 (2018)
14. Iqbal, J., Munir, M.A., Mahmood, A., Ali, A.R., Ali, M.:Leveraging orientation for weakly supervised object detection with application to firearm localization. arXiv preprint arXiv:1904.10032 (2019)
15. Huang, J., et al.: Speed/accuracy trade-offs for modern convolutional object detectors. In: CVPR 2017 (2017)
16. Goldsborough, P.: A tour of tensorflow. arXiv preprint arXiv:1610.01178 (2016)
17. Bochkovskiy, A., Wang, C.Y., Liao, H.Y.M.: Yolov4: optimal speed and accuracy of object detection. arXiv preprint arXiv:2004.10934 (2020)

18. Guns used in crime, Washington, DC: US Department of Justice: Bureau of Justice Statistics Selected Findings, publication NCJ-148201 (1995)
19. World Health Organization: European report on preventing violence and knife crime among young people. World Health Organization. Regional Office for Europe (2010)
20. Kuznetsova, A., et al.: The open images dataset v4: unified image classification, object detection, and visual relationship detection at scale. arXiv preprint arXiv:1811.00982 (2018)
21. Pérez-Hernández, F., Tabik, S., Lamas, A., Olmos, R., Fujita, H., Herrera, F.: Object detection binary classifiers methodology based on deep learning to identify small objects handled similarly: application in video surveillance. Knowl. Based Syst. **194**, 105590 (2020)
22. Everingham, M., Winn, J.: The pascal visual object classes challenge 2012 (voc2012) development kit. Pattern Analysis, Statistical Modelling and Computational Learning, Technical report, 8, 5 (2011)
23. Lin, T.-Y., et al.: Microsoft coco: common objects in context. In: Fleet, D., Pajdla, T., Schiele, B., Tuytelaars, T. (eds.) Computer Vision – ECCV 2014: 13th European Conference, Zurich, Switzerland, September 6–12, 2014, Proceedings, Part V, pp. 740–755. Springer, Cham (2014). https://doi.org/10.1007/978-3-319-10602-1_48
24. Bochkovskiy, A., Wang, C.-Y., Liao, H.-Y.M.:Yolov4: optimal speed and accuracy of object detection. arXiv preprint arXiv:2004.10934 (2020)
25. Mahsereci, M., Balles, L., Lassner, C., Hennig, P.: Early stopping without a validation set. arXiv preprint arXiv:1703.09580 (2017)
26. Prechelt, L.: Early stopping - but when? In: Orr, G.B., Müller, K.-R. (eds.) Neural Networks: Tricks of the trade, pp. 55–69. Springer, Heidelberg (1998). https://doi.org/10.1007/3-540-49430-8_3
27. Shetty, S.: Application of convolutional neural network for image classification on Pascal VOC challenge 2012 dataset. arXiv preprint arXiv:1607.03785 (2016)

Metrics for Saliency Map Evaluation
of Deep Learning Explanation Methods

Tristan Gomez[1]([✉]), Thomas Fréour[2], and Harold Mouchère[1]

[1] Nantes Université, Centrale Nantes, CNRS, LS2N, 44000 Nantes, France
{tristan.gomez,harold.mouchere}@univ-nantes.fr
[2] CRTI, Inserm UMR 1064, Nantes University Hospital Inserm, 44000 Nantes, France
thomas.freour@chu-nantes.fr

Abstract. Due to the black-box nature of deep learning models, there is a recent development of solutions for visual explanations of CNNs. Given the high cost of user studies, metrics are necessary to compare and evaluate these different methods. In this paper, we critically analyze the Deletion Area Under Curve (DAUC) and Insertion Area Under Curve (IAUC) metrics proposed by Petsiuk et al. (2018). These metrics were designed to evaluate the faithfulness of saliency maps generated by generic methods such as Grad-CAM or RISE. First, we show that the actual saliency score values given by the saliency map are ignored as only the ranking of the scores is taken into account. This shows that these metrics are insufficient by themselves, as the visual appearance of a saliency map can change significantly without the ranking of the scores being modified. Secondly, we argue that during the computation of DAUC and IAUC, the model is presented with images that are out of the training distribution which might lead to unexpected behavior of the model being explained. To complement DAUC/IAUC, we propose new metrics that quantify the sparsity and the calibration of explanation methods, two previously unstudied properties. Finally, we give general remarks about the metrics studied in this paper and discuss how to evaluate them in a user study.

Keywords: Interpretable machine learning · Objective evaluation · Saliency maps

1 Introduction

Recent years have seen a surge of interest in interpretable machine learning, as many state-of-the-art learning models currently are deep models and suffer from their lack of interpretability due to their black-box nature. In image classification, many generic approaches have been proposed to explain a model's decision by generating saliency maps that highlight the important areas of the image concerning the task at hand [1,3,14,16,20,21,23,27]. The community of

Supported by Nantes Excellence Trajectory (NExT).

M. El Yacoubi et al. (Eds.): ICPRAI 2022, LNCS 13363, pp. 84–95, 2022.
https://doi.org/10.1007/978-3-031-09037-0_8

interpretable deep learning has yet to find a consensus about how to evaluate these methods, the main difficulty residing in the ambiguity of the concept of interpretability. Indeed, depending on the application context, the users' requirements in terms of interpretability may vary a lot, making it difficult to find a universal evaluation protocol.

This has started a trend in literature where authors confront users with models' decisions along with explanations to determine the users' preference on a particular application [2, 24, 25]. The main issues of this approach are its financial cost and the difficulty to establish a correct protocol, which mainly comes from the requirement to design an experiment whose results will help understand the users' needs and also from the fact that most machine learning researchers are not used to run experiments involving humans.

Because of these issues, another trend proposes to design objective metrics to evaluate generic explanation methods [3, 14, 20]. In this paper, we chose to follow this trend, by proposing three new metrics.

We focus our work on the DAUC and IAUC metrics proposed by [20]. First, we study several aspects of these metrics and we show that the actual saliency score values given by the saliency map are ignored as they only take into account the ranking of the scores. This shows that these metrics are insufficient by themselves, as the visual appearance of a saliency map can change significantly without the ranking of the scores being modified. We also argue that during the computation of DAUC and IAUC, the model is presented with images that are out of the training distribution which might lead to unexpected behavior of the model and of the method used to generate the saliency maps. We then introduce a new metric called Sparsity, which quantifies the sparsity of a saliency map, a property that is ignored by previous work. Another property that was not studied until now is the calibration of the saliency maps. Given it could be a useful property for interpretability, we also propose two new metrics to quantify it, namely Deletion Correlation (DC) and Insertion Correlation (IC). Finally, we give general remarks about all the metrics studied in this paper and discuss how to evaluate these metrics in a user study.

2 Existing Metrics

Various metrics have been proposed to automatically evaluate saliency maps generated by explanation methods [3, 14, 20]. These metrics consist to add or remove the important areas according to the saliency map and measure the impact on the initially predicted class score. For example, Chattopadhay et al. proposed "increase in confidence" (IIC) and "average drop" (AD) [3]. These metrics consist to multiply the input image with an explanation map to mask the non-relevant areas and to measure the class score variation. Jung et al. proposed a variant of AD where the salient areas are masked instead of the non-salient, called Average Drop in Deletion (ADD) [14]. In parallel, Petsiuk et al. proposed DAUC and IAUC which study the score variation while progressively masking/revealing the image instead of applying the saliency map once [20].

Given the similarity of these metrics, we will focus our study on DAUC and IAUC, which we will now describe.

2.1 DAUC and IAUC

To evaluate the reliability of the proposed attention mechanism, Petsiuk et al. proposed the Deletion Area Under Curve (DAUC) and Integration Area Under Curve (IAUC) metrics [20]. These metrics evaluate the reliability of the saliency maps by progressively masking/revealing the image starting with the most important areas according to the saliency map and finishing with the least important.

The input image is a 3D tensor $I \in \mathbb{R}^{H \times W \times 3}$ and the saliency map is a 2D matrix $S \in \mathbb{R}^{H' \times W'}$ with a lower resolution, $H' < H$ and $W' < W$. First, S is sorted and parsed from the highest element to its lowest element. At each element $S_{i'j'}$, we mask the corresponding area of I by multiplying it by a mask $M^k \in \mathbb{R}^{H \times W}$, where

$$M_{ij}^k = \begin{cases} 0, & \text{if } i' + r < i < i' + 2r \text{ and } j' + r < j < j' + 2r \\ 1, & \text{otherwise,} \end{cases} \tag{1}$$

where $r = H/H' = W/W'$. After each masking operation, the model m runs an inference with the updated version of I, and the score of the initially predicted class is updated, producing a new score c_k :

$$c_k = m(I \cdot \prod_{\tilde{k}=1}^{\tilde{k}=k} M^{\tilde{k}}), \tag{2}$$

where $k \in \{1, ..., H' \times W'\}$. Examples of input images obtained during this operation can be seen in Fig. 1. Secondly, once the whole image has been masked, the scores c_k are normalized by dividing them by the maximum $\max_k c_k$ and then plotted as a function of the proportion p_k of the image that is masked. The DAUC is finally obtained by computing the area under the curve (AUC) of this function. The intuition behind this is that if a saliency map highlights the areas that are relevant to the decision, masking them will result in a large decrease of the initially predicted class score, which in turn will minimize the AUC. Therefore, minimizing this metric corresponds to an improvement.

Instead of progressively masking the image, the IAUC metric starts from a blurred image and then progressively unblurs it by starting from the most important areas according to the saliency map. Similarly, if the areas highlighted by the map are relevant for predicting the correct category, the score of the corresponding class (obtained using the partially unblurred image) is supposed to increase rapidly. Conversely, maximizing this metric corresponds to an improvement.

2.2 Limitations

DAUC and IAUC Generate Out of Distribution (OOD) Images. When progressively masking/unblurring the input image, the model is presented with samples that can be considered out of the training distribution, as shown in Fig. 1.

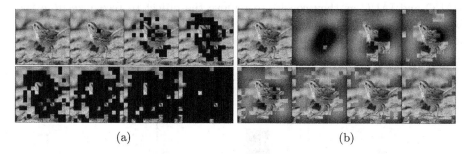

(a)   (b)

Fig. 1. Examples of images passed to the model during the computation of (a) DAUC and (b) IAUC. Masking and blurring the input images probably lead to OOD samples.

Indeed, the kind of distortions produced by the masking/blurring operations do not exist naturally in the dataset and are different from the kind produced by the standard data augmentations like random crop, horizontal flip, and color jitter, meaning that the model has not learned to process images with such distortions. Therefore, the distribution of the images presented to the model is different from the one met during training. However, it has been documented that CNNs and more generally deep learning models have poor generalization outside of the training distribution [8]. This shows that DAUC and IAUC may not reflect the faithfulness of explanation methods as they are based on a behavior of the model that is different from that encountered when facing training distribution (e.g. during the test phase).

To verify this hypothesis we visualize the UMAP [17] projections of the representations of 100 masked/blurred samples obtained during the computation of DAUC and IAUC on the CUB-200-2011 dataset [26]. We also added the representation of 500 unmodified test images (in blue) to visualize the training distribution. The model used is a ResNet50 [11] on which we applied Grad-CAM++ [3]. Figure 2 shows that, during computation of DAUC, the representations gradually converge towards a unique point, which is not surprising as, at the end of the computation, all images are fully masked, i.e. plain black. However even when only a proportion of 0.4 of the image is masked, the corresponding representation is distant from the blue point cloud indicating the training distribution. A similar phenomenon happens with IAUC, where blurring the image causes the representation to move away from the training distribution. This experiment demonstrates that the DAUC and IAUC metrics indeed present OOD samples, which might lead to unexpected behavior of the model and of the method used to generate the explanation maps. However, as suspected by [20], the blurring operation seems to create samples that are less far from the training distribution compared to the masking operation, probably because a blurred image still contains the low-frequency parts of the original image. Another explanation is that most current classification models are designed with the assumption that an input image contains an object to recognize, which is in contradiction with DAUC and IAUC as they consist to remove the object to recognize from the image. This suggests that modifying these metrics in such a way as to always leave an object to recognize in the input image would solve this issue.

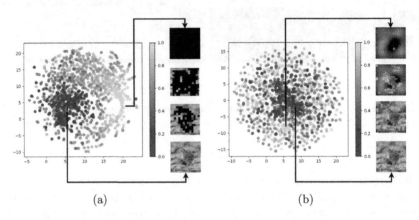

(a)   (b)

Fig. 2. UMAP projection of representations obtained while computing (a) DAUC and (b) IAUC on 100 images. The color indicates the proportion of the image that is masked/unblurred. The model used is a ResNet50 on which we applied Grad-CAM++ on the CUB-200-2011 dataset. We also plotted representations from 500 points of the test set to visualize the training distribution (in blue). By gradually masking the image, the representations converge towards a point (in yellow) that is distant from the points corresponding to unmasked images (in blue). Similarly, blurring the image causes the representation to move away the training distribution. This shows that masking/blurring indeed creates OOD samples. (Color figure online)

DAUC and IAUC Only Take the Pixel Score Rank into Account. When computing DAUC and IAUC, the saliency map is used only to determine in which order to mask/reveal the input image. Hence, only the ranking of the saliency scores S_{ij} is used to determine in which order to mask the image, leaving the actual values of the scores ignored.

However, pixel ranking is not the only characteristic that should be taken into account, as the visual appearance can vastly vary between two attention maps without changing the ranking. Figure 3 shows examples of a saliency map with various score distributions artificially modified. We used a saliency map produced by the Score-CAM [27] explanation method and altered its score distribution by multiplying all values by a coefficient followed by the application of a softmax function. By increasing the coefficient we alter the visual appearance of the maps, without changing the pixel ranking, which maintains the same DAUC and IAUC scores. This illustrates the fact that DAUC and IAUC ignore the score dynamic of the saliency map, which can vastly affect the visual appearance. To complement DAUC and IAUC, we propose new metrics that take the score values into account in the following section.

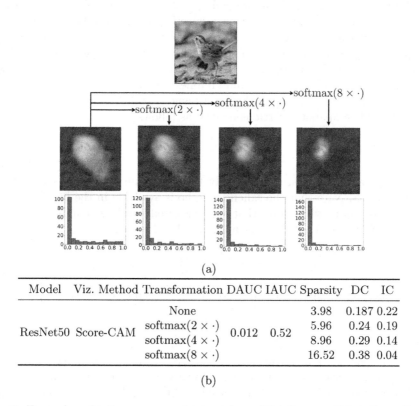

(a)

Model	Viz. Method	Transformation	DAUC	IAUC	Sparsity	DC	IC
ResNet50	Score-CAM	None			3.98	0.187	0.22
		softmax(2 × ·)	0.012	0.52	5.96	0.24	0.19
		softmax(4 × ·)			8.96	0.29	0.14
		softmax(8 × ·)			16.52	0.38	0.04

(b)

Fig. 3. Examples of saliency maps obtained by artificially sparsifying the saliency scores. The original saliency map is generated using Score-CAM applied on a ResNet50 model tested on the CUB-200-2011 dataset. Despite having different visual appearances, the four maps have the same DAUC and IAUC metric values because these metrics ignore the score values and only take into account the ranking of the scores. On the other hand, the Sparsity metric depends on the score distribution and reflects the amount of focus of the map. In this figure, only the saliency map is modified, the decision process is left unchanged.

3 Score Aware Metrics

As mentioned in the previous paragraph, DAUC and IAUC ignore the actual score values and only take into account the saliency score S_{ij} ranking. To complement these metrics, we propose three new metrics, namely Sparsity, Deletion Correlation (DC), and Insertion Correlation (IC).

3.1   The Sparsity Metric

An important visual aspect of saliency maps that has not been studied until now by the community is what we call sparsity. As shown by Fig. 3, Saliency maps can be more or less focused on a specific point depending on the score distribution, without changing the score ranking. This aspect could impact the interpretability of the method, as it significantly changes the visual aspect of the map and therefore could also affect the perception of the user. For example, one could argue that a high sparsity value implies a map with a precise focus that highlights only a few elements of the input image, making it easier to understand for humans. The Sparsity metric is defined as follows:

$$\text{Sparsity} = \frac{S_{max}}{S_{mean}} \tag{3}$$

where S_{max} and S_{mean} are respectively the maximum and mean score of the saliency map S. Note that the saliency methods available in the literature generate saliency maps with scores that are comprised in a large number of ranges. Therefore, the map should be first normalized as follows:

$$S' = \frac{S - S_{min}}{S_{max} - S_{min}} \tag{4}$$

This means that, after normalization, $S'_{max} = 1$ and Eq. (3) can be simplified to

$$\text{Sparsity} = \frac{1}{S'_{mean}} \tag{5}$$

A high sparsity value means a high S_{max}/S_{mean} ratio, i.e., a low mean score S_{mean} which indicates that the map's activated areas are narrow and focused. As shown by Fig. 3b, this metric is indeed sensitive to the actual saliency scores values and reflects the various amount of focus observed in the saliency maps.

3.2   The DC and IC Metrics

As previously mentioned, the DAUC and IAUC metrics ignore the score values of the saliency maps and only take into account the ranking of the scores. This means that these metrics ignore the sparsity of the map, which is why we proposed to quantify this aspect. Another potentially interesting property of saliency maps is the calibration. The concept of calibration has seen a recent surge of interest in the deep learning community [10,19,28], but previous work focused exclusively on calibrating prediction scores. A pixel S_{ij} from a well-calibrated saliency map S would reflect through its luminosity the importance it has on the class score. More precisely, we say that an explanatory map S is perfectly calibrated if for any two elements S_{ij} and $S_{i'j'}$, we have $S_{ij}/S_{i'j'} = v/v'$, where

v and v' are respectively the impact of S_{ij} and $S_{i'j'}$ on the class score. To evaluate this, we propose to quantify how correlated the saliency scores and their corresponding impact on the class score are. To the best of our knowledge, this is the first time that an objective metric is proposed to measure the calibration of explanation methods. In practice, such a metric could be used in a user study to evaluate to what extent the calibration property is useful.

We take inspiration from the DAUC and IAUC metrics and propose to gradually mask/reveal the input image by following the order suggested by the saliency map, but instead of computing the area under the class score vs. pixel rank curve, we compute the linear correlation of the class score variations and the saliency scores. The correlation measured when masking the image is called Deletion Correlation (DC) and the one measured when revealing the image is called Insertion Correlation (IC). The following paragraph details the computation of these two metrics.

DC is computed using the same progressive masking and inference method as DAUC. Once the scores c_k have been computed, we compute the variation of the scores $v_k = c_k - c_{k+1}$. Finally, we compute the linear correlation between the v_k and the s_k where s_k is the saliency score of the area masked at step k. For the IC metric, we take inspiration from IAUC, and instead of masking the image, we start from a blurred image, and gradually reveal the image according to the saliency map. Once the image is totally revealed, the score variations are computed $v_k = c_{k+1} - c_k$ and we compute the linear correlation of the v_k with the s_k. Note that the order of the subtraction is reversed compared to DC because when revealing the image, the class score is expected to increase.

When computing DC/IC on a well-calibrated saliency method, we expect that when the class score variation is high, the saliency score should also be high, and conversely, when the class score variation is low, the saliency score should be also low.

The DC and IC metrics measure the calibration, which is an aspect that is ignored by the DAUC and IAUC metrics but also by the Sparsity metric. To illustrate, the DC and IC metrics are computed for the examples visible in Fig. 3.

3.3 Limitations

The Sparsity Metric Does Not Take into Account the Prediction Scores. Indeed, this metric only considers the saliency score dynamic and ignores the class score produced by the model. However, this is not necessarily a problem as this metric was designed to be used as a complement to other metrics like DAUC, IAUC, DC, or IC, which takes the class score into account.

The DC and IC Metrics also Generate OOD Images. As we took inspiration from DAUC and IAUC and also passed masked/blurred examples to the model, one can make the same argument as for DAUC/IAUC to show that the reliability of DC and IC could probably be improved by preventing OOD samples.

4   Benchmark

We compute the five metrics studied in the work (DAUC, IAUC, DC, IC, and Sparsity) on post-hoc generic explanation methods and attention architectures that integrate the computation of the saliency map in their forward pass. The post-hoc methods are Grad-CAM [21], Grad-CAM++ [3], RISE [20], Score-CAM [27], Ablation CAM [6]. The architectures with native attention are B-CNN [12], BR-NPA [9], the model from [13] which we call IBP (short for Interpretability By Parts), ProtoPNet [4], and ProtoTree [18]. These attention models generate several saliency maps (or *attention* maps) per input image but the metrics are designed for a single saliency map per image. To compute the metrics on these models, we selected the first attention map among all the ones produced, as, in these architectures, the first is the most important one.

Table 1 shows the performances obtained. The most important thing to notice is the overall low values of correlation, especially for IC, where most values are very close to 0, meaning the saliency scores reflect the impact on the class score as much as random values. This highlights the fact that attention models and explanation methods are currently not designed for this objective, although it could be an interesting property.

Table 1. Evaluation of the interpretability on the CUB-200-2011 dataset.

Model	Viz. method	Accuracy	DAUC	IAUC	DC	IC	Sparsity
ResNet50	Ablation CAM	0.842	0.0215	0.26	0.36	−0.04	8.54
	Grad-CAM		0.0286	0.16	0.35	−0.12	5.28
	Grad-CAM++		0.0161	0.21	0.35	−0.07	6.73
	RISE		0.0279	0.18	**0.57**	−0.11	6.63
	Score-CAM		0.0207	0.27	0.32	−0.05	5.96
	AM		0.0362	0.22	0.31	−0.09	4.04
B-CNN	–	0.848	0.0208	0.3	0.27	−0.02	12.74
BR-NPA		**0.855**	0.0155	**0.49**	0.41	−0.02	**16.02**
IBP		0.819	0.0811	0.48	0.23	−0.04	6.56
ProtoPNet		0.848	0.2964	0.37	0.1	−0.06	2.18
ProtoTree		0.821	0.2122	0.43	0.17	**0.04**	13.75

5   Discussion

One common limit of all the metrics discussed here is that they are designed for methods and architectures producing single saliency maps, making their use for multi-part attention architectures like B-CNN, BR-NPA, IBP, ProtoPNet, and ProtoTree less straightforward. In Table 1, we chose to only select the most important attention map but the other ones should also be taken into account to fully reflect the model's behavior. We also could have computed the mean attention maps from all the ones produced by the model but this would also not be faithful towards the model. Indeed, that would amount to considering that all attention maps have the same weight in the decision, which is not true, as the first attention map has more importance in the decision than the second, which is more important than the third, etc. One possibility would be to estimate the weight of each map and to compute a pondered mean but there remains the issue of computing the weight, which may be difficult in the general case, due to the variety of architectures.

Note that the low values of DC and IC in Table 1 do not imply that the models and methods provide unsatisfying performance, but simply show that the calibration property has not been studied until now.

We propose to quantify the sparsity and the calibration of the saliency maps as these properties have not been studied until now and may be relevant for interpretability. However, to what extent this is true remains to be tested in a subjective experiment. More generally, all the metrics discussed in this paper should be tested against a user experiment. As shown by [5,7], there is a great variety of possible experimental setups depending on what should be explained, in which context, and for who the explanation is targeted.

Notably, how the explanation is presented to the user is still an open question. For example, [22] applies a mask on the input image whereas [2] proposed to superimpose the explanation over the image. Also, various tasks can be given to the user to evaluate the explanation. Slack et al. proposed to mask the input image at the most salient areas and ask users to try to recognize the object with the mask [22]. Instead of guessing the label, Alqaraawi et al. asked users to predict the network's prediction to evaluate if the access to a saliency map helps to improve their prediction [2]. We could use a similar setup with various saliency map methods and evaluate the users' accuracy. Then we could rank the methods according to the impact they have on the users' accuracy and see how this ranking relates to the ranking provided by the objective metrics. Like this, we could deduce which metrics best reflect the impact of an explanation method on the user's understanding of the model.

The main issue is that current user studies seem to show that providing saliency maps to the user affects little their understanding of the model and also does not affect the trust in the model [15]. One study found that the presence of a saliency map helps users to better predict the model's output [2]. However, the effect size measured was small and it could be argued that the effect of changing the explanation method would be smaller or even difficult to observe.

6   Conclusion

In this work, we first studied two aspects of the DAUC and IAUC metrics. We showed that they may generate OOD samples which might negatively impact their reliability. Also, we show that they only take into account the ranking of the saliency scores and show that the visual appearance of a saliency map can significantly change without the DAUC and IAUC metrics being affected. Then, we propose to quantify two aspects that were previously unstudied on saliency maps, the sparsity and the calibration (DC and IC). Finally, we conclude with general remarks on the studied metrics and discuss the issues of a user study that could be used to evaluate the usefulness of these metrics.

References

1. Adebayo, J., Gilmer, J., Goodfellow, I., Kim, B.: Local explanation methods for deep neural networks lack sensitivity to parameter values (2018)
2. Alqaraawi, A., Schuessler, M., Weiß, P., Costanza, E., Berthouze, N.: Evaluating saliency map explanations for convolutional neural networks: a user study. In: IUI 2020, pp. 275–285. Association for Computing Machinery, New York (2020). https://doi.org/10.1145/3377325.3377519
3. Chattopadhay, A., Sarkar, A., Howlader, P., Balasubramanian, V.N.: Grad-CAM++: generalized gradient-based visual explanations for deep convolutional networks. In: 2018 IEEE Winter Conference on Applications of Computer Vision (WACV), pp. 839–847 (2018). https://doi.org/10.1109/WACV.2018.00097
4. Chen, C., Li, O., Barnett, A., Su, J., Rudin, C.: This looks like that: deep learning for interpretable image recognition. In: NeurIPS (2019)
5. Chromik, M., Butz, A.: Human-XAI interaction: a review and design principles for explanation user interfaces. In: Ardito, C., et al. (eds.) INTERACT 2021. LNCS, vol. 12933, pp. 619–640. Springer, Cham (2021). https://doi.org/10.1007/978-3-030-85616-8_36
6. Desai, S., Ramaswamy, H.G.: Ablation-CAM: visual explanations for deep convolutional network via gradient-free localization. In: 2020 IEEE Winter Conference on Applications of Computer Vision (WACV), pp. 972–980 (2020). https://doi.org/10.1109/WACV45572.2020.9093360
7. Ferreira, J.J., Monteiro, M.S.: What are people doing about XAI user experience? A survey on AI explainability research and practice. In: Marcus, A., Rosenzweig, E. (eds.) HCII 2020. LNCS, vol. 12201, pp. 56–73. Springer, Cham (2020). https://doi.org/10.1007/978-3-030-49760-6_4
8. Ghosh, S., Shet, R., Amon, P., Hutter, A., Kaup, A.: Robustness of deep convolutional neural networks for image degradations. In: 2018 IEEE International Conference on Acoustics, Speech and Signal Processing (ICASSP), pp. 2916–2920. IEEE (2018)
9. Gomez, T., Ling, S., Fréour, T., Mouchère, H.: Improve the interpretability of attention: a fast, accurate, and interpretable high-resolution attention model (2021)
10. Guo, C., Pleiss, G., Sun, Y., Weinberger, K.Q.: On calibration of modern neural networks. In: Precup, D., Teh, Y.W. (eds.) Proceedings of the 34th International Conference on Machine Learning. Proceedings of Machine Learning Research, 06–11 August 2017, vol. 70, pp. 1321–1330. PMLR (2017)
11. He, K., Zhang, X., Ren, S., Sun, J.: Deep residual learning for image recognition. In: 2016 IEEE Conference on Computer Vision and Pattern Recognition (CVPR), pp. 770–778 (2016)
12. Hu, T., Qi, H.: See better before looking closer: weakly supervised data augmentation network for fine-grained visual classification. CoRR abs/1901.09891 (2019)

13. Huang, Z., Li, Y.: Interpretable and accurate fine-grained recognition via region grouping (2020)
14. Jung, H., Oh, Y.: LIFT-CAM: towards better explanations for class activation mapping. arXiv arXiv:2102.05228 (2021)
15. Kenny, E.M., Ford, C., Quinn, M., Keane, M.T.: Explaining black-box classifiers using post-hoc explanations-by-example: the effect of explanations and error-rates in XAI user studies. Artif. Intell. **294**, 103459 (2021). https://doi.org/10.1016/j.artint.2021.103459
16. Lundberg, S.M., Lee, S.I.: A unified approach to interpreting model predictions. In: Proceedings of the 31st International Conference on Neural Information Processing Systems, pp. 4768–4777 (2017)
17. McInnes, L., Healy, J., Melville, J.: UMAP: uniform manifold approximation and projection for dimension reduction (2020)
18. Nauta, M., van Bree, R., Seifert, C.: Neural prototype trees for interpretable fine-grained image recognition (2021)
19. Nixon, J., Dusenberry, M.W., Zhang, L., Jerfel, G., Tran, D.: Measuring calibration in deep learning. In: CVPR Workshops, vol. 2 (2019)
20. Petsiuk, V., Das, A., Saenko, K.: RISE: randomized input sampling for explanation of black-box models (2018)
21. Selvaraju, R.R., Cogswell, M., Das, A., Vedantam, R., Parikh, D., Batra, D.: Grad-CAM: visual explanations from deep networks via gradient-based localization. In: 2017 IEEE International Conference on Computer Vision (ICCV), pp. 618–626 (2017)
22. Slack, D., Hilgard, A., Singh, S., Lakkaraju, H.: Reliable post hoc explanations: modeling uncertainty in explainability. In: Advances in Neural Information Processing Systems, vol. 34 (2021)
23. Smilkov, D., Thorat, N., Kim, B., Viégas, F., Wattenberg, M.: SmoothGrad: removing noise by adding noise (2017)
24. Tsai, C.H., Brusilovsky, P.: Evaluating visual explanations for similarity-based recommendations: user perception and performance, pp. 22–30. Association for Computing Machinery, New York (2019)
25. van der Waa, J., Nieuwburg, E., Cremers, A., Neerincx, M.: Evaluating XAI: a comparison of rule-based and example-based explanations. Artif. Intell. **291**, 103404 (2021). https://doi.org/10.1016/j.artint.2020.103404
26. Wah, C., Branson, S., Welinder, P., Perona, P., Belongie, S.: The Caltech-UCSD Birds-200-2011 Dataset. Technical report, CNS-TR-2011-001, California Institute of Technology (2011)
27. Wang, H., et al.: Score-CAM: score-weighted visual explanations for convolutional neural networks. In: Proceedings of the IEEE/CVF Conference on Computer Vision and Pattern Recognition Workshops, pp. 24–25 (2020)
28. Zhang, J., Kailkhura, B., Han, T.Y.J.: Mix-n-Match: ensemble and compositional methods for uncertainty calibration in deep learning. In: Singh, A., et al. (eds.) Proceedings of the 37th International Conference on Machine Learning. Proceedings of Machine Learning Research, 13–18 July 2020, vol. 119, pp. 11117–11128. PMLR (2020)

Image Classification via Multi-branch Position Attention Network

Ke Zhang[1,2], Jun Yang[1], Kun Yuan[1], Qing-Song Wei[3], and Si-Bao Chen[3(✉)]

[1] State Grid Power Research Institute, Hefei 230086, China
[2] School of Information Science and Technology, University of Science
and Technology of China, Hefei 230026, China
[3] School of Computer Science and Technology, Anhui University, Hefei 230601, China
sbchen@ahu.edu.cn

Abstract. Image classification is a hot spot in the field of pattern recognition and artificial intelligence. When there are apparent inter-class similarity and intra-class diversity, such as in the area of remote sensing, image classification becomes very challenge. With the continuous development of convolutional neural networks, a major breakthrough has been made in image classification. Although good performance have been achieved, there is still some room for improvement. First, in addition to global information, local features are crucial to image classification. Second, minimizing/maximizing the distance from the same/different classes allows the key points in image classification to be given full attention. In this paper, we propose an image classification method which is named multi-branch position attention network (MBPANet). We design a channel attention module containing position information, called Position Channel Attention Module (PCAM), and synthesize a new attention module Position Spatial Attention Module (PSAM) with a spatial attention module Local Spatial Attention Module (LSAM). The features obtained by the attention weighting method not only obtain local neighborhood semantic information but also contain global semantic information. Extensive experiments on three benchmark datasets show that our approach outperforms state-of-the-art methods.

Keywords: Image classification · Remote sensing scene classification · Attention module · Convolutional neural networks

1 Introduction

Image classification is an important area in pattern recognition and artificial intelligence. Lots of deep convolutional neural networks are proposed for image classification, which improve the classification performance and promote wide applications of image classification. Remote sensing image scene classification is one of important application of image classification.

Supported by Science and Technology Project of SGCC (No. 5500-202140127A).

M. El Yacoubi et al. (Eds.): ICPRAI 2022, LNCS 13363, pp. 96–108, 2022.
https://doi.org/10.1007/978-3-031-09037-0_9

During the development of remote sensing technology, the resolution (spatial resolution, spectral resolution, radiometric resolution and temporal resolution) and quality of remote sensing images have been continuously improved. High-resolution remote sensing images are characterized by rich texture information and many imaging spectral bands, which make them contain a large amount of complex background information and variable scene structures, of which the two most prominent characteristics are inter-class similarity and intra-class diversity, which make the scene categories more difficult to distinguish and bring great challenges to the interpretation of remote sensing images.

Due to the increase in the number of available datasets and recent advances in data-driven algorithms, a large number of experimental studies have been conducted on practical applications. Existing scene classification methods are usually classified into three main categories based on the kind of features used: manual feature learning-based methods, unsupervised feature learning-based methods, and deep feature learning-based methods. Most of the early remote sensing image scene classification methods use traditional manual algorithms to extract the underlying visual features of images. These methods can not only be time-consuming and labor-intensive, but also rely excessively on a priori knowledge and expertise, which greatly affects the classification performance. In recent years, due to the great success of Convolutional Neural Networks (CNNs) in the field of computer vision, a large number of CNN-based models have been applied to remote sensing images. Although CNNs eliminate the complex human feature extraction process in classification algorithms and have substantially improved in recognition accuracy compared with traditional algorithms, there is still much room for CNNs to improve on the problem of large intra-class variability and high inter-class similarity in remote sensing images.

The problems of remote sensing images are mainly due to the fact that the top view covers a large area, which contains many different types of features and contains much richer high-level semantic information. But not all of this spatial information is useful, and they make humans understand the world more clearly on the one hand, and bring troubles to the interpretation of images on the other. In recent years, the Attention Model (AM) [1], inspired by the human visual system, has been proposed and used to select the information that is more critical to the current task goal from the many information. SENet [2] proposed in 2017 is a representative work of channel domain attention, which learns to use global information, selectively emphasizes informative features and suppressing less useful features. ECANet [3] focuses on some improvements to the SENet module, proposing a local cross-channel interaction strategy without dimensionality reduction and an adaptive selection of the one-dimensional convolutional kernel size, resulting in performance improvements. In the literature [4], a hybrid domain attention module combining spatial attention mechanism and channel attention mechanism, called the convolutional block attention module (CBAM), is proposed. It combines channel branches and spatial branches in a sequential manner, which not only significantly improves the accuracy of image classification and target detection, but also saves parameters and computational power.

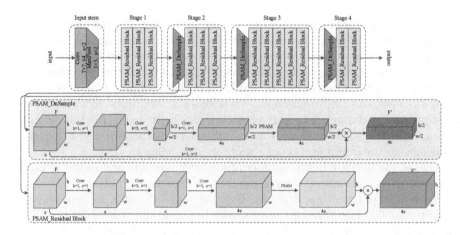

Fig. 1. Structure overview of the proposed MBPANet. Downsampling blocks and residual blocks are embedded with Position Spatial Attention Module (PSAM_DnSample and PSAM_ResBlock) in each stage of ResNet50 backbone. The PSAM consists of two parts: Position Channel Attention Module (PCAM) and Local Spatial Attention Module (LSAM).

Based on the above works, we propose an image classification method which is named Multi-Branch Position Attention Network (MBPANet).

MBPANet proposes a Position Space Attention Module (PSAM) that combines channel position information and spatial semantic information. The PSAM can be fused with any known classical backbone network so that the feature map contains channel location information as well as local spatial neighborhood similarity information. Given a convolutional feature map, we use the Position Channel Attention Module (PCAM) and the Local Space Attention Module (LSAM) in parallel, then add the results element by element, and finally multiply the input convolutional feature map element by element, so that the attention-weighted feature map is obtained. The feature map contains the channel position information as well as the local spatial neighborhood similarity information. In addition, to reveal the effectiveness of our method, we conduct extensive experiments on three benchmarks (UC Merced LandUse [5], AID [6] and NWPU-RESISC45 [7] datasets) and compare them with many state-of-the-art methods.

2   The Proposed Method

The general structure of the proposed MBPANet is shown in Fig. 1. In each stage of ResNet50 backbone, downsampling and residual blocks are embedded in Position Spatial Attention Module (PSAM_DnSample and PSAM_ResBlock). The PSAM consists of two parts: Position Channel Attention Module (PCAM) and Local Spatial Attention Module (LSAM).

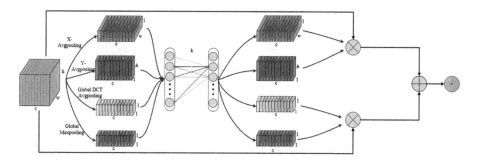

Fig. 2. Detailed structure diagram of Position Channel Attention Module (PCAM)

2.1 Position Channel Attention Module (PCAM)

The detailed structure of Position Channel Attention Module (PCAM) is shown in Fig. 2. For an input feature map size of $H \times W \times C$, two global pooling operations of kernel size $(H, 1)$ and $(1, W)$ are first performed to encode each channel along H-direction and W-direction of input image to obtain location channel feature descriptors, h-average pooling features F_c^h and w-average pooling features F_c^w, respectively, expressed by the following equations.

$$F_c^h = \frac{1}{W} \sum_{0 \leq i \leq W} x_c(h, i) \tag{1}$$

$$F_c^w = \frac{1}{H} \sum_{0 \leq j \leq H} x_c(j, w) \tag{2}$$

Then F_c^h and F_c^w are integrated in feature map by local cross-channel interaction strategy to obtain F_c^{eh} and F_c^{ew}, which avoids the loss caused by the dimensionality reduction operation and the introduction of additional parameters. The formulae of local cross-channel interaction strategy and adaptive kernel size k are shown below.

$$F_c^e = C1D_k(F) \tag{3}$$

$$k = \psi(C) = \left| \frac{log_2 C}{\gamma} + \frac{b}{\gamma} \right|_{odd} \tag{4}$$

where $C1D$ denotes one-dimensional convolution, k denotes the size of the 1-dimensional convolution kernel for the coverage of local cross-channel interaction, C is the number of channels, $|t|_{odd}$ denotes the odd number closest to t, γ and b are generally set to 2 and 1.

Meanwhile, for the input feature F of size $H \times W \times C$, two $1 \times 1 \times C$ channel feature descriptors, average pooling feature F_c^a and maximum pooling feature F_c^m, are obtained using global average pooling and global maximum pooling based on discrete cosine transform, and feature maps F_c^{ea} and F_c^{em} are

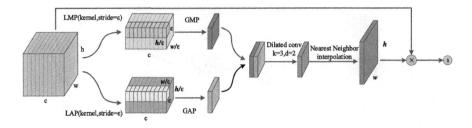

Fig. 3. Detailed structure diagram of Local Spatial Attention Module (LSAM)

also obtained using local cross-channel interaction strategy. The global average pooling formula based on discrete cosine transform is shown below.

$$FGAP = cat\left(\left[Freq^0, Freq^0, \cdots, Freq^{n-1}\right]\right) \tag{5}$$

$$Freq^i = \sum_{h=0}^{H-1} \sum_{w=0}^{W-1} X^i_{:,h,w} B^{u_j,v_i}_{h,w} \\ s.t.\ i \in \{0, 1, \cdots, n-1\} \tag{6}$$

where $[u_j, v_i]$ is the 2D index of the frequency component corresponding to X^i and $Freq^i \in \mathbb{R}^{C'}$ is the compressed dimensional vector.

Finally F_c^{eh}, F_c^{ew}, F_c^{ea} and F_c^{em} are multiplied with the original input feature map, and then the feature maps of the two branches are subjected to element-by-element addition operation to obtain the final channel attention weighted feature map $M_c^p(F)$. The formula is as follows.

$$M_c^p = \sigma((C1D_k\left(FGAP\left(F\right)\right) \times C1D_k\left(FGAP\left(F\right)\right)) \times F \\ + \left(C1D_k\left(HAP\left(F\right)\right) \times C1D_k\left(WAP\left(F\right)\right)\right) \times F) \tag{7} \\ = \sigma\left(W\left(F_c^a\right) \times W\left(F_c^m\right) \times F + W\left(F_c^h\right) \times W\left(F_c^m\right) \times F\right)$$

where, $W \in \mathbb{R}^{C \times C}$, σ is the sigmoid-type activation function, $\times$ denotes element-by-element multiplication and $+$ is element-by-element summation.

2.2   Local Spatial Attention Module (LSAM)

To focus on semantically similar features in the spatial neighborhood, LSAM enhances the spatial semantic representation of features by generating a spatial attention weight map containing the spatial semantic information of the neighborhood through the local neighborhood parameter ε.

Figure 3 shows the structure of LSAM. First, two compressed spatial attention descriptors F_ε^{lm} and F_ε^{la} are generated by applying local spatial max pooling and local average pooling (with pooling kernel and step size equal to ε) to all channels of the input feature map F in parallel. F_ε^{lm} and F_ε^{la} are compressed to $1/\varepsilon$ of their original size at the spatial scale compared to the original feature map F, while remaining unchanged at the channel level. Subsequently, two traditional global maximum pooling and global average pooling are used to further

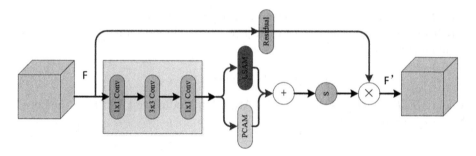

Fig. 4. Schema of PSAM-integrated CNNs units with Positional Channel Attention Module (PCAM) and Local Spatial Attention Module (LSAM) combined in parallel to obtain both channel and spatial attentions.

aggregate the channel information of the feature maps to generate two new feature maps that are spatially unchanged in scale compared to the feature maps obtained after the local pooling operation, but contain semantic information of all channels. $F_{\varepsilon,avg}^{la}$ and $F_{\varepsilon,max}^{lm}$ represent average pooled features and maximum pooled features respectively. Then, the two features are fused by a cascade operation to reduce the computational cost. Then the 3×3 expanded convolution is applied to the fused feature map to further learn the features and mitigate the feature loss caused by the multi-step pooling operation. The dilation convolution improves the nonlinear representation of spatial attention descriptors. Finally, the output feature map is upsampled by nearest-neighbor interpolation so that the size of the output feature map is scaled to be the same as the original input feature map to obtain the spatial attention feature map $M_s^\varepsilon(F)$.

$$F_\varepsilon^{lm} = LMP_{k,s=\varepsilon}\left(F\right) \tag{8}$$

$$F_\varepsilon^{la} = LAP_{k,s=\varepsilon}\left(F\right) \tag{9}$$

$$M_s^\varepsilon\left(F\right) = \sigma\left(f_n\left(f^{3\times3}\left[F_{\varepsilon,max}^{lm}; F_{\varepsilon,avg}^{la}\right]\right) \times F\right) \tag{10}$$

where $LMP(\cdot)$ and $LAP(\cdot)$ denote the local max/average pooling operations with kernel and stride ε over the spatial domain, $F_{\varepsilon,max}^{lm}$ and $F_{\varepsilon,avg}^{la}$ are the feature maps obtained from the global max/average pooling operations along the channel direction, f_n represents the null convolution, $f^{3\times3}$ is the nearest neighbor interpolation upsampling operation, $\times$ denotes element-by-element multiplication, and σ is the sigmoid activation function.

2.3 Integrating Attention Modules into Backbone Networks

The final Position Spatial Attention Module (PSAM), which contains the encoding of the position information, consists of PCAM for the channel attention branch and LSAM for the spatial attention branch. The two branches can be combined in parallel and in sequential execution. Through experiments we find that the parallel combination works better. The final combination of PSAM and ResNet network is the element-by-element parallel operation. The detailed structure diagram is shown in Fig. 4. The whole computational process can be summarized as follows.

$$F' = \sigma \left(M_c^p (F) + M_s^\varepsilon (F) \right) \times F \tag{11}$$

where $M_c^p (F)$ is the Position Channel Attention Module and $M_s^\varepsilon (F)$ is the Local Space Attention Module.

3   Experiments

To evaluate the image classification performance of the proposed MBPANet, we mainly focus on remote sensing image scene classification (RSSC) due to its wide applications. The proposed MBPANet is conducted extensive experiments comparing with state-of-the-art.

3.1   Implementation Details

Datasets. The UC Merced LandUse (UCM) [5] of the University of California, Merced is one of the oldest datasets in the RSSC domain with 21 categories and 2100 images, which were extracted from the USGS National Map, Urban Areas image collection. Each scene category contains 100 images with a size of 256×256 pixels and an image resolution of 0.3 m.

Aerial Image Data Set (AID) [6] is a large-scale dataset for aerial scene classification with a large number of 10,000 images with a size of 600×600 pixels. All images were acquired using Google Earth imagery and tagged by experts in the field of remote sensing image interpretation. The images are multi-resolution and their spatial resolution can vary from half a meter to 8 m.

NWPU-RESISC45 [7] was created by a team of researchers at Northwestern Polytechnic University in 2017 using Google Earth images. It contains 45 classes. Each class contains 700 RGB images, each with a size of 256×256 pixels. In the scene class, the spatial resolution varies from 30.0 m per pixel to 0.2 m. Some special terrain classes may have images with lower resolution, such as islands, lakes, regular mountains, and snow-capped peaks. The rich image variation, some differences in scene classes, and some similarities between scene classes make the dataset quite challenging.

Experimental Settings. We segmented the dataset using the following strategy: 20% and 50% of the images of AID [6] were randomly selected for training. Similarly, we randomly selected 10% and 20% of the NWPU-RESISC45 [7] images for training and the rest for validation. And 80% of the UCM [5] dataset was used as the training set. All experimental results are implemented based on the Pytorch framework, the learning rate of SGD is initialized to 0.01, the cosine learning rate decay strategy is selected to iterate 100 epochs, and the weight decay is changed to 5e−4.

Table 1. Overall accuracy (%) comparison with state-of-the-art on UCM dataset with 80% training ratio

Method	Publication & year	Overall accuracy
CTFCNN [8]	RS2019	98.44 ± 0.58
CNN-CapsNet [9]	RS2019	99.05 ± 0.24
SCCov [10]	TNNLS2019	99.05 ± 0.25
ARCNet-VGG [11]	TGRS2019	99.12 ± 0.40
GBNet [12]	TGRS2020	98.57 ± 0.48
ResNet-50 + EAM [13]	GRSL2021	98.98 ± 0.37
MG-CAP [14]	TIP2020	99.00 ± 0.10
BiMobileNet (MobileNetv2) [15]	Sensors2020	99.03 ± 0.28
Pretrained ResNet-50 [16]	CVPR2016	98.81 ± 0.23
ViT-B-16 [17]	ICLR2021	99.28 ± 0.23
Pretrained ResNet-50+CBAM [4]	ECCV2018	90.04 ± 0.23
MBLANet [18]	TIP2022	99.53 ± 0.21
MBPANet (ours)		**99.64 ± 0.12**

3.2 Compared to State-of-the-Art Methods

To evaluate the performance of the proposed MBPANet method, we compared it with some algorithms of recent years. From Table 1 to Table 3, the comparison results are reported for UCM, AID, and NWPU-RESISC45, respectively.

Table 1 shows the overall accuracy comparison of classification performance between the proposed MBPANet and state-of-the-art methods on the UCMerced dataset. The classification accuracy on the UCM dataset tends to saturate and is difficult to improve. Although the improvement of MBPANet is less significant compared to other methods, the improvement in classification accuracy still indicates that our model still outperforms the previous methods and further validates that adding the attention module can indeed enhance the classification performance of CNNs.

Table 2 shows the experimental results of the existing methods on the AID dataset. It can be found that our proposed MBPANet achieves the best performance with 95.71% and 97.23%, respectively. The method obtains significant classification results when the training rates are 20% and 50%, respectively, compared to the state-of-the-art methods used in recent years. Even compared with MBLANet, our model shows different degrees of improvement. Although the improvement in classification accuracy is only 0.1%, which is not very significant, it likewise shows that the encoding of location information added by the channel branches is effective and can truly capture the long-range dependence of spatial information in the images.

NWPU-RESISC45 dataset has the largest amount of image data and categories compared to the other datasets. Therefore, the complexity and diversity

Table 2. Overall accuracy (%) comparison with state-of-the-art on AID dataset with training ratios 20% and 50%

Method	Publication & year	Overall accuracy	
		20% training	50% training
CNN-CapsNet [9]	RS2019	93.79 ± 0.13	96.32 ± 0.12
SCCov [10]	TNNLS2019	93.12 ± 0.25	96.10 ± 0.16
ARCNet-VGG [11]	TGRS2019	88.75 ± 0.40	93.10 ± 0.55
GBNet [12]	TGRS2020	92.20 ± 0.23	95.48 ± 0.12
MF^{2}Net [19]	GRSL2020	93.82 ± 0.26	95.93 ± 0.23
ResNet-50 + EAM [13]	GRSL2021	94.26 ± 0.11	97.06 ± 0.19
MG-CAP [14]	TIP2020	93.34 ± 0.18	96.12 ± 0.12
BiMobileNet (MobileNetv2) [15]	Sensors2020	94.83 ± 0.24	96.87 ± 0.23
Pretrained ResNet-50 [16]	CVPR2016	94.67 ± 0.15	95.74 ± 0.10
ViT-B-16 [17]	ICLR2021	93.81 ± 0.21	96.08 ± 0.14
Pretrained ResNet-50+CBAM [4]	ECCV2018	94.66 ± 0.39	96.90 ± 0.04
MBLANet [18]	TIP2022	95.60 ± 0.17	97.14 ± 0.03
MBPANet (ours)		**95.71 ± 0.10**	**97.23 ± 0.13**

of the samples increases as well. Table 3 shows the comparison between the proposed models and existing models on NWPU-RESISC45 dataset. At a training rate of 10%, our method is ahead of state-of-the-art methods with a very large improvement. When the training rate is 20%, our method is only just equal to MBLANet, which may be due to the redundancy of features. Similar features are extracted by location information encoding and some of the features are extracted by spatial branch.

3.3   Reports of Confusion Matrix

To better understand the performance of the proposed MBPANet classification method, we illustrate the classification results by confusion matrices. Only the confusion matrix results of MBPANet on the NWPU-RESISC45 dataset are given, which is shown in Fig. 5. When the training rates are 10% and 20%, a total of 38 and 40 class images of 45 class images have classification accuracies greater than 90%, respectively. The palace has the lowest accuracy at two different training rates of 0.70 and 0.79. Compared with the other work, the classification performance of the proposed MBPANet on the class of palace images is still a significant improvement. This indicates that for images with high inter-class similarity, the inclusion of location information can effectively enhance the acquisition of global semantic features.

Table 3. Overall accuracy (%) comparison with state-of-the-art on NWPU-RESISC45 dataset

Method	Publication & year	Overall accuracy	
		10% training	20% training
Two-Fusion [20]	CIN2018	80.22 ± 0.22	83.16 ± 0.18
CNN-CapsNet [9]	RS2019	89.03 ± 0.21	89.03 ± 0.21
SCCov [10]	TNNLS2019	89.30 ± 0.35	92.10 ± 0.25
MF^{2}Net [19]	GRSL2020	90.17 ± 0.25	92.73 ± 0.21
MG-CAP [14]	TIP2020	90.83 ± 0.12	92.95 ± 0.11
ResNet-50 + EAM [13]	GRSL2021	91.91 ± 0.22	94.29 ± 0.09
BiMobileNet (MobileNetv2) [15]	Sensors2020	92.06 ± 0.14	94.08 ± 0.11
MVFLN + VGG-VD16 [21]	MTA2021	92.03 ± 0.24	94.46 ± 0.17
Pretrained ResNet-50 [16]	CVPR2016	90.09 ± 0.13	94.10 ± 0.15
ViT-B-16 [17]	ICLR2021	90.96 ± 0.08	93.36 ± 0.17
Pretrained ResNet-50+CBAM [4]	ECCV2018	92.10 ± 0.04	94.26 ± 0.12
MBLANet [18]	TIP2022	92.32 ± 0.15	94.66 ± 0.11
MBPANet (ours)		$\mathbf{92.40 \pm 0.16}$	$\mathbf{94.70 \pm 0.13}$

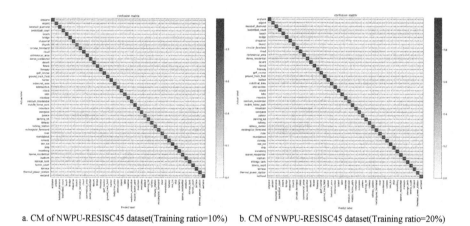

a. CM of NWPU-RESISC45 dataset(Training ratio=10%)   b. CM of NWPU-RESISC45 dataset(Training ratio=20%)

Fig. 5. Confusion matrices (CM) of the proposed MBPANet on NWPU-RESISC45 dataset, where training ratios are 10% and 20% respectively.

3.4   Ablation Study

Convolutional Kernel Size k. We first focus on the effect of convolutional kernel size k on the local cross-channel interaction strategy. This part of the experiments evaluates its impact on PCAM and verifies the effectiveness of our approach in adaptively selecting the kernel size. For this purpose, we used

ResNet50 as the backbone model and set k to 3–9 for the experiments, respectively. The results are shown in Table 4, from which it can be observed that MBPANet achieves the best results at $k = 5$ when k is fixed in all convolutional blocks. Since small convolution kernels have a small field of perception, it is difficult to obtain good global features, which is not good for dealing with intra-class diversity in remote sensing images. However, too large convolution kernels have a large field of perception and can obtain good global features, but they introduce a large number of calculations and tend to ignore the features of small targets, which is precisely an important information in remote sensing images.

In addition, the proposed method which adaptively determined convolutional kernel size is better than the method with fixed convolutional kernel size, which not only can avoid the manual adjustment of parameters, but also the adaptive value has the adaptive size of the perceptual field. It will not make the global feature information missing due to the small perceptual field and will not ignore the important micro-target features due to the large perceptual field. The above results demonstrate that our adaptive selection of the convolutional kernel size can achieve good and stable results.

Table 4. Effect of the value of convolutional kernel size k on NWPU-RESISC45 dataset

Value of k	Overall accuracy
3	94.50 ± 0.07
5	94.63 ± 0.11
7	94.53 ± 0.14
9	94.58 ± 0.18
Adaptive	**94.70 ± 0.13**

The Way of Combination Between Attention Module and Backbone Network. Then we focus on the combination way of attention module and backbone network. Table 5 shows the experimental results of different combinations, and it can be found that the combination using the parallel approach works better.

The experiments on the combination of channel branches and spatial branches are also carried out in this section, as shown in Table 6. From the data in the table, it can be seen that the summation operation is more accurate than branch multiplication. The element-by-element addition operation can further enhance the feature representation, while the element-by-element multiplication emphasizes a feature weighting.

Table 5. Effect of combination way between channel branch (c) and spatial branch (s)

Way of combination	UCM (80%)	AID (%)		NWPU-RESISC45 (%)	
		20%	50%	10%	20%
c + s	**99.64 ± 0.12**	**95.71 ± 0.10**	**97.23 ± 0.13**	**92.40 ± 0.16**	**94.70 ± 0.13**
c × s	99.05 ± 0.24	95.35 ± 0.14	97.01 ± 0.08	92.32 ± 0.09	94.54 ± 0.18

Table 6. Effect of the way of attentional module combined with backbone network

Way of combination	UCM (80%)	AID (%)		NWPU-RESISC45 (%)	
		20%	50%	10%	20%
Serial	99.12 ± 0.12	95.01 ± 0.31	96.98 ± 0.21	92.26 ± 0.14	94.56 ± 0.17
Parallel	**99.64 ± 0.12**	**95.71 ± 0.10**	**97.23 ± 0.13**	**92.40 ± 0.16**	**94.70 ± 0.13**

4   Conclusion

In this paper, we propose an image classification method based on multi-branch position attention network (MBPANet) by introducing position information coding into channel attention branch. MBPANet is also a location space attention module (PSAM) embedded in the backbone network ResNet by fusing channel attention branch and spatial attention branch. The channel attention branch PCAM of PSAM consists of two small branches. One is the location information encoding features and the other is the pooling encoding features. The location information encoding feature branch is a feature map containing location information using one-dimensional global pooling in parallel along the spatial horizontal and vertical directions; the pooling encoding feature branch is a complementary channel attention feature map obtained in parallel using global average pooling based on the discrete cosine transform and global maximum pooling. The feature maps obtained by all operations use a local cross-channel information interaction strategy to integrate the information and both are weighted with the original image to obtain the final channel attention feature maps. PCAM and LSAM are fused and embedded into the ResNet50 network in a parallel and element-by-element summation manner. Finally experiments are conducted on three remote sensing image scene classification datasets, whose results validate the advantages of the proposed MBPANet.

References

1. Bahdanau, D., Cho, K., Bengio, Y.: Neural machine translation by jointly learning to align and translate. arXiv preprint arXiv:1409.0473 (2014)
2. Hu, J., Shen, L., Sun, G.: Squeeze-and-excitation networks. In: Proceedings of the IEEE Conference on Computer Vision and Pattern Recognition, pp. 7132–7141 (2018)

3. Wang, Q., Wu, B., Zhu, P., Li, P., Zuo, W., Hu, Q.: ECA-Net: efficient channel attention for deep convolutional neural networks. In: IEEE/CVF Conference on Computer Vision and Pattern Recognition (CVPR), pp. 11531–11539 (2020)

4. Woo, S., Park, J., Lee, J.-Y., Kweon, I.S.: CBAM: convolutional block attention module. In: Ferrari, V., Hebert, M., Sminchisescu, C., Weiss, Y. (eds.) ECCV 2018. LNCS, vol. 11211, pp. 3–19. Springer, Cham (2018). https://doi.org/10.1007/978-3-030-01234-2_1

5. Yang, Y., Newsam, S.: Bag-of-visual-words and spatial extensions for land-use classification. In: Proceedings of the 18th SIGSPATIAL International Conference on Advances in Geographic Information Systems, pp. 270–279 (2010)

6. Xia, G.S., et al.: AID: a benchmark data set for performance evaluation of aerial scene classification. IEEE Trans. Geosci. Remote Sens. **55**(7), 3965–3981 (2017)

7. Cheng, G., Han, J., Lu, X.: Remote sensing image scene classification: benchmark and state of the art. Proc. IEEE **105**(10), 1865–1883 (2017)

8. Huang, H., Xu, K.: Combing triple-part features of convolutional neural networks for scene classification in remote sensing. Remote Sens. **11**(14), 1687 (2019)

9. Zhang, W., Tang, P., Zhao, L.: Remote sensing image scene classification using CNN-CapsNet. Remote Sens. **11**(5), 494 (2019)

10. He, N., Fang, L., Li, S., Plaza, J., Plaza, A.: Skip-connected covariance network for remote sensing scene classification. IEEE Trans. Neural Netw. Learn. Syst. **31**(5), 1461–1474 (2019)

11. Wang, Q., Liu, S., Chanussot, J., Li, X.: Scene classification with recurrent attention of VHR remote sensing images. IEEE Trans. Geosci. Remote Sens. **57**(2), 1155–1167 (2018)

12. Sun, H., Li, S., Zheng, X., Lu, X.: Remote sensing scene classification by gated bidirectional network. IEEE Trans. Geosci. Remote Sens. **58**(1), 82–96 (2019)

13. Zhao, Z., Li, J., Luo, Z., Li, J., Chen, C.: Remote sensing image scene classification based on an enhanced attention module. IEEE Geosci. Remote Sens. Lett. **18**(11), 1926–1930 (2021)

14. Wang, S., Guan, Y., Shao, L.: Multi-granularity canonical appearance pooling for remote sensing scene classification. IEEE Trans. Image Process. **29**, 5396–5407 (2020)

15. Yu, D., Xu, Q., Guo, H., Zhao, C., Lin, Y., Li, D.: An efficient and lightweight convolutional neural network for remote sensing image scene classification. Sensors **20**(7), 1999 (2020)

16. He, K., Zhang, X., Ren, S., Sun, J.: Deep residual learning for image recognition. In: Proceedings of the IEEE Conference on Computer Vision and Pattern Recognition, pp. 770–778 (2016)

17. Dosovitskiy, A., et al.: An image is worth 16 × 16 words: transformers for image recognition at scale. arXiv preprint arXiv:2010.11929 (2020)

18. Chen, S.B., Wei, Q.S., Wang, W.Z., Tang, J., Luo, B., Wang, Z.Y.: Remote sensing scene classification via multi-branch local attention network. IEEE Trans. Image Process. **31**, 99–109 (2022)

19. Xu, K., Huang, H., Li, Y., Shi, G.: Multilayer feature fusion network for scene classification in remote sensing. IEEE Geosci. Remote Sens. Lett. **17**(11), 1894–1898 (2020)

20. Yu, Y., Liu, F.: A two-stream deep fusion framework for high-resolution aerial scene classification. Comput. Intell. Neurosci. **2018**(8639367), 1–13 (2018)

21. Guo, Y., Ji, J., Shi, D., Ye, Q., Xie, H.: Multi-view feature learning for VHR remote sensing image classification. Multimedia Tools Appl. **80**(15), 23009–23021 (2020). https://doi.org/10.1007/s11042-020-08713-z

UGQE: Uncertainty Guided Query Expansion

Firat Oncel[1(✉)] , Mehmet Aygün[1,2] , Gulcin Baykal[1] , and Gozde Unal[1]

[1] Istanbul Technical University, Istanbul, Turkey
oncelf@itu.edu.tr
[2] The University of Edinburgh, Edinburgh, Scotland

Abstract. Query expansion is a standard technique in image retrieval, which enriches the original query by capturing various features from relevant images and further aggregating these features to create an expanded query. In this work, we present a new framework, which is based on incorporating uncertainty estimation on top of a self attention mechanism during the expansion procedure. An uncertainty network provides added information on the images that are relevant to the query, in order to increase the expressiveness of the expanded query. Experimental results demonstrate that integrating uncertainty information into a transformer network can improve the performance in terms of mean Average Precision (mAP) on standard image retrieval datasets in comparison to existing methods. Moreover, our approach is the first one that incorporates uncertainty in aggregation of information in a query expansion procedure.

Keywords: Uncertainty · Image retrieval · Self attention

1 Introduction

Image retrieval methods rely mainly on a projection from a high dimensional input data to a relatively low-dimensional vector space.

Due to several sources of error such as occlusions or loss of information during projection to the vector space, image search is enriched with a query expansion idea that depends on constructing a latent model, which is based on aggregating a collection of responses from an initial query [7,29]. On the other hand, in the recent years, image retrieval methods are dominated by Convolutional Neural Networks (CNNs), which replace hand-crafted features in feature extraction phase of image retrieval systems [4,13,22,24].

As important as a role feature extraction plays in performance of image retrieval systems, a set of related tools such as database augmentation [31], query expansion [7], hashing [8] and so on play crucial roles in image retrieval systems. Particularly, Query expansion (QE) is regarded as one of the most powerful tools, as it increases the performance of an image retrieval system no matter how the features are extracted [7,14]. The basic idea of a QE method is to enhance the

M. El Yacoubi et al. (Eds.): ICPRAI 2022, LNCS 13363, pp. 109–120, 2022.
https://doi.org/10.1007/978-3-031-09037-0_10

quality of the search vector through an augmentation of the query vector space using some priors. The latter is provided by an initial search that results in a collection of vectors that lead to a richer latent feature representation of the query. One of the main limitations of QE algorithms [3,7,13,24] is that the assigned weights to neighbors of the query are monotonic. In the recent work of Gordo et al. [14], a self-attention mechanism was used via transformers [32] in order to predict weights which do not have to be monotonic so that irrelevant neighbors, which are not true neighbors, can be eliminated.

While neural networks have the flexibility to create and assign different weights in QE algorithms, they are famous for their overconfidently wrong predictions [15], which might hurt the quality of the expanded query feature vector. In recent years, there has been a lot of interest on how to incorporate uncertainty estimation into deep neural network models [12,18,21,28] to alleviate their problem in making overconfident predictions. These works enable integrating the ability of saying "I am not sure about this prediction". In this paper, we integrate a dedicated pairwise uncertainty estimation between a query and each of its neighbors in creation of an enriched image representation. The latter is in terms of image features relative to the original extracted features which in combination provide a tool in generating more powerful expanded queries. To that end, we design an uncertainty-guided transformer encoder, which relies on and expands on the self-attention-based Learnable Attention-based Query Expansion (LAttQE) model by [14] via incorporating an uncertainty that is estimated with the Evidential Deep Learning (EDL) framework [28].

Our proposed new module, which is called the Uncertainty Guided Query Expansion (UGQE), first takes a query and features of retrieved top-k neighbors and estimates the uncertainty in whether the neighbors are from the same landmark with the query or not, using the EDL setting within a transformer encoder architecture. Next, our model utilizes the obtained uncertainty information in order to generate a new feature representation via concatenating transformed features and original features. Finally, the LAttQE model is used to form the expanded query by aggregating these new generated features of the nearest neighbors.

Our main contributions in this paper can be summarized as follows: (i) a method to create uncertainty guided features to enrich the original image representations; (ii) a demonstration of how to use EDL for quantifying the pair-wise uncertainty. Our experiments demonstrate that the proposed UGQE method increases the performance of the traditional QE methods and outperforms the LAttQE model when the uncertainty is integrated, in most settings.

2   Related Work

Image Retrieval and Query Expansion: Image retrieval systems generally consist of two parts. The first part extracts a representation from an image, and the second part performs the search by utilizing a distance measure in the representation space. Before the revival of (deep) neural networks, the representation extraction part was based on hand-crafted feature engineering methods such as SIFT [20], Fisher Vectors [23] and VLAD [16]. Further extensions of those methods are also introduced for improving whole retrieval pipelines [3]. Recently, the feature extraction phase is dominated by deep neural networks. Bottleneck features, or activations at the output of certain later layers are used as the representations for the input data. In an early work by Babenko et al. [4], pre-trained networks are used as feature extractors. However, in recent works, CNNs are fine-tuned in unsupervised [24] and supervised [2,13,22] settings for learning more efficient representations. Generally, the supervised methods use noisy data for fine-tuning. To improve the feature representation of query images, Chum et al. [7] introduced the idea of QE for image retrieval, which first appeared in text retrieval systems [6,26]. The QE idea is very simple: after the first search, highly ranked images are filtered with a spatial verification step to retain high quality results. Next, using the original query description along with the descriptions of retrieved presumably high quality results, a new expanded query description is generated. A number of methods are suggested for generating the newly expanded vector, however the most commonly used one just averages the initial query and the high quality ranked ones for generating the expanded vector.

While the QE methods were first introduced for hand-crafted features in image retrieval systems, deep learning based image retrieval systems also used QE in their pipelines for improving their performance since QE methods do not rely on how features are extracted. Moreover, lately, state of the art results are obtained with QE methods that are combined with deep representations in the feature extraction phase [13,24,30], or more recently, with learning the QE weights [14] using the attention mechanism [32].

Transformers - Visual Transformers: The transformer [32] architecture has become the default choice for most of the natural language processing tasks [5,9, 19]. Transformer architectures are capable of grasping the relationship between sequential inputs using a self-attention mechanism. Transformers are also lately used in computer vision tasks [10], via representing images as sequence of patches. El-Nouby et al. [11] extends visual transformers to a metric learning setting to perform image retrieval. While this work focuses on the initial representation of images, in our work we focus on how to expand the initial representations using transformers in the QE framework.

Graph Attention Networks [33] are used in the metric learning setting to weigh the feature vectors in a batch [27]. Most recent and relevant work in query expansion that includes the attention setting is by Gordo et al. [14]. They utilized a self attention mechanism to weigh the nearest neighbors of the query image for integrating their information. Our work expands on the transformer idea, strengthening it with the uncertainty information. The uncertainty that we introduce is captured from the neighborhood relationships between feature vectors, and integrated into generation of an expanded query feature vector.

Uncertainty in Deep Learning: Predicting model uncertainty is an emerging field in deep learning. MC Dropout [12] is one of the earliest and widely utilized works in the related literature. In this method, a dropout mechanism is applied not only in training time but also in test time, and a multitude of predictions are averaged to get the prediction, and the variance among predictions is used to calculate the uncertainty. This approach presents high computation time requirements since multiple forward passes are needed. Deep Ensembles [18] and their variants are also related to MC Dropout, bearing a similar approach in incorporating an indirect uncertainty estimation into deep neural networks. In contrast to deep ensemble methods, a line of recent research work, known as Evidential Deep Learning directly estimates both data and model uncertainty. The latter, which is also known as epistemic uncertainty, deals with how certain a neural network can be when making predictions. Sensoy et al. [28] estimate the classification uncertainty collecting evidence for each class by placing a Dirichlet distribution on the class probabilities instead of a softmax to allow the neural network models to directly quantify the uncertainty in their outputs. Amini et al. [1] extends this idea into continuous outputs by placing an Inverse Gamma distribution at the end of the regression task. In our work, we integrate the uncertainty estimation between a query image and its top-k neighbors to generate new features. With these features, the image representations are enhanced while the estimated uncertainty is integrated into the query expansion procedure. To our knowledge, our work is the first to introduce an uncertainty guidance through gauging the reliability of neighboring feature vectors into the QE framework.

3   Method

As we deploy an uncertainty quantification through the Evidential Deep Learning approach into the Attention-Based QE setting, we give a brief overview of both frameworks.

Attention-Based Query Expansion Learning: LAttQE [14] utilizes the self-attention mechanism to form the expanded query based on the original query and its k-nearest neighbors by predicting the weights for each of the respective feature vectors. They formulate the problem as a metric learning problem. Let ϕ be a CNN feature extractor, which takes an input image, and transforms it into a D-dimensional feature vector. The query image is denoted by q, and its feature vector is denoted by $\mathbf{q} = \phi(q)$. The positive pair, the i-th negative pair and the k-th nearest neighbor of the query image are denoted as $\mathbf{p}$, $\mathbf{n_i}$ and $\mathbf{d_k}$, respectively. $\hat{\mathbf{q}}$ can be formulated as: $\hat{\mathbf{q}} = \mathbf{w_q}\mathbf{q} + \sum_{n=1}^{k} \mathbf{w_{d_k}}\mathbf{d_k}$, where w_q and w_{d_k} are assigned weights to the query and its neighbors. Additionally, the transformer outputs whether the retrieved neighbors are from the same landmark as the query or not. To account for that, an additional variable y is defined such that y is set to 1 if we have a positive pair, and set to 0 otherwise. The corresponding contrastive loss can be formulated as follows:

$$L_{qe}(\hat{\mathbf{q}}, \mathbf{f}, y) = y \, \|\hat{\mathbf{q}} - \mathbf{f}\| + (1 - y) \max(0, m - \|\hat{\mathbf{q}} - \mathbf{f}\|), \tag{1}$$

where $\mathbf{f}$ is either $\mathbf{p}$ or $\mathbf{n_i}$, and m is a selected margin.

Evidential Deep Learning (EDL): For estimating the uncertainty or inversely the reliability of a neighbor in contributing to the feature description of a query, we utilize the objective proposed in [28]. Let us denote the evidence collected from the k-th class of a multi-class (e.g. K-class) classification problem as e_k, and Dirichlet distribution parameters as $\alpha_k = e_k + 1$. Then the Dirichlet strength is given by $S = \sum_{k=1}^{K} \alpha_k$. Belief masses are defined as $b_k = \dfrac{e_k}{S}$, and the expected probability for the k-th class is $\hat{p}_k = \dfrac{\alpha_k}{S}$. Finally, the uncertainty in the prediction can be calculated as the residual belief remaining when we subtract the sum of our beliefs from unity: $u = 1 - \sum_{k=1}^{k} b_k$. Given N input samples and labels, the classification uncertainty can be quantified by minimizing the following objective function:

$$\mathcal{L}(\Theta) = \sum_{i=1}^{N} \mathcal{L}_i(\Theta) = \sum_{i=1}^{N} \sum_{j=1}^{K} (y_{ij} - \hat{p}_{ij})^2 + \frac{\hat{p}_{ij}(1 - \hat{p}_{ij})}{(S_i + 1)} \tag{2}$$

where Θ denotes neural network parameters, y_i is a one-hot vector encoding of ground-truth of sample x_i with $y_{ik} = 0$ and $y_{ij} = 1$ for all $k \neq j$, and i denotes the index of a data sample for $i = 1, ..., N$. Here, the objective entails minimization of the sum of the squared prediction errors and an estimate of the variance in the second term to obtain the evidential distribution parameters. Although this is a non-Bayesian neural network approach, by placing evidential priors over the classification output, this framework outputs the uncertainty u in the form of what is left beyond our beliefs and collected evidence that are based on the assumed evidential distribution.

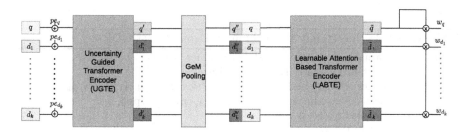

Fig. 1. Uncertainty Guided Query Expansion: UGTE takes input features, calculates the uncertainty between the query and each neighbor, and outputs the uncertainty guided features. Then, LABTE takes a combination of new features and original features, and outputs the weights for the query and its nearest neighbors to generate the expanded query.

Uncertainty Guided Query Expansion Learning: Leveraging on the evidential distribution idea, we propose the Uncertainty Guided Query Expansion (UGQE) model, which adapts and fuses ideas from both the EDL and LAttQE to create an improved attention-based architecture that enables and exploits uncertainty learning in query expansion. Our complete UGQE model is depicted in Fig. 1. UGQE involves two transformer encoders, the first one generates the uncertainty guided features. The first transformer encoder integrates a pairwise uncertainty quantification, by employing a $K = 2$-class evidential classification, which outputs a target label y that is 1 if the i-th neighbor $\mathbf{d_i}$ of the query $\mathbf{q}$ is relevant, and 0 otherwise. The first transformer is trained end-to-end with the second transformer encoder, i.e. the LAttQE architecture, to produce the final weights that are used in the query expansion.

The details of the UGQE algorithm is described in Algorithm 1. Input feature vectors, which are the query ($\hat{\mathbf{q}}$) and its top-k nearest neighbors ($\mathbf{n_1}, \mathbf{n_2}, ..., \mathbf{n_k}$), are 2048-Dimensional. The output vectors of this model is also 2048-D, same as the input size. Our model takes these features (line 1 in Algorithm 1), as inputs and then sends the output vectors to the GeM Pooling layer [24], which reduces the dimensions of vectors from 2048-Dimensions (2048D) to 512D (line 2 in Algorithm 1). As the point of this model is to learn informative features, we observe that the reduced features were able to retain the useful information in the original features. These 512D features, which are later concatenated to the original features, are fed to a multilayer perceptron (MLP). Then the EDL Loss (Eq. 2) is minimized, and an uncertainty estimate is produced for each neighbor, which is a quantity that signifies a kind of confidence in the neighbor status of each neighbor. Then, the obtained uncertainty feature vectors are concatenated to the original features to be input to the second transformer, i.e. the LAttQE model (line 3 in Algorithm 1). LAttQE is trained end-to-end with the first transformer encoder, and the output of the overall model are the weights of the query and its nearest neighbors that provide construction of the final expanded query ($\hat{\mathbf{q}}$) (lines 4–10 in Algorithm 1).

Algorithm 1: Uncertainty Guided Query Expansion (UGQE)

---

    input   : Learnable Attention Based Transformer Encoder ($LABTE$)
                   Uncertainty Guided Transformer Encoder ($UGTE$)
                   features of query and k-nearest neighbors: $F = \{\mathbf{q}, \mathbf{d_1}, \mathbf{d_2}, ..., \mathbf{d_k}\}$
                   positional encodings: $PE = \{\mathbf{pe_q}, \mathbf{pe_{d_1}}, \mathbf{pe_{d_2}}, ..., \mathbf{pe_{d_k}}\}$
    output : expanded query: $\hat{\mathbf{q}}$
1 $F' \leftarrow UGTE([F; PE])$
2 $F' \leftarrow GeMPooling(F')$ ▷ Uncertainty guided features
3 $\{\tilde{q}, \tilde{d}_1, \tilde{d}_2, ..., \tilde{d}_k\} \leftarrow LABTE([F'; F])$
4 **for** $i \leftarrow 1$ **to** K **do**
5 | $w_i \leftarrow normalizeddotproduct(\tilde{q}, \tilde{d}_i)$
6 **end**
7 $\hat{\mathbf{q}} \leftarrow \mathbf{q}$
8 **for** $i \leftarrow 1$ **to** K **do**
9 | $\hat{\mathbf{q}} = \hat{\mathbf{q}} + w_i \mathbf{d_i}$
10 **end**
11 **return** $\hat{\mathbf{q}}$

Implementation Details: UGQE model has 2 attention layers (each one with 64 heads) and created features are 512D. Only EDL Loss is used to train this model. We use Adam optimizer [17] with initial learning rate of $1e^{-4}$, a weight decay of $1e^{-6}$, and an exponential learning rate scheduler with a decay of 0.99. Then we concatenate the original features with the created ones to train the second self-attention model, which is the LAttQE, which has 3 attention layers (each one with 64 heads). We use the contrastive loss in Eq. (1), with a margin parameter of 2.1, and the binary-cross entropy loss to train this model. In the implementation of the EDL, we use the exponential activation layer at the end of our uncertainty MLP block. We use 2048 queries per epoch and 15 negative samples, which is chosen empirically, for each positive sample, selected from a pool of 40000 samples. Choice of the number of negative samples for a positive sample and the margin is essential as the loss is usually 0 with a low number, i.e. 5 or 10, of negative samples, and a low margin, i.e. 0.1. Queries and the pool of samples are updated at every epoch. We also use Adam optimizer with initial learning rate of $1e^{-4}$, a weight decay of $1e^{-6}$, and an exponential learning rate scheduler with decay of 0.99 for the second transformer. We train our setting for 300 epochs with a batch size of 64, and 127 neighbors. We do not use neighborhood dropping, which is proposed in [14], as it does not improve the scores in our experiments. Both models have learnable positional encodings to integrate the positional information. As there is no publicly available official implementation of [14][1], we implemented the LAttQE architecture, which constitutes our baseline. Using the original hyperparameters reported in the paper[2], slightly lower performance values are obtained than the reported results. We report both results in our paper, however, we take our implementation as the baseline to compare it with the proposed UGQE.

4   Experiments

Training Dataset: We use rSfM120k dataset [24] for training the models in our experiments. The training part of the dataset has 91642 images and 551 landmarks, while validation part has 6403 images and 162 landmarks, distinct from the training ones. To extract features, we use ResNet101, which is trained on the Google Landmarks dataset [22], with GeM pooling and a whitening layer. Resulting feature vectors are 2048-D vectors. Single scale vectors are extracted at the original scale, with the input image size of 1024, while multi scale vectors are extracted at 3 scales; $1024 * (1, \sqrt{2} \text{ and } 1/\sqrt{2})$, and then mean-aggregated. Both single scale and multi scale vectors are l_2 normalized. We use Python Image Retrieval Toolbox[3] to extract all features. We conduct our experiments

---

[1] https://github.com/filipradenovic/cnnimageretrieval-pytorch/issues/68.

[2] Unfortunately it was not possible to reproduce the performance results reported in the paper. This is also reported by researchers via issues opened in the github repo of the paper.

[3] https://github.com/filipradenovic/cnnimageretrieval-pytorch.

with both single scale and multi scale vectors, whereas training with single scale vectors gives slightly better results so that we report this setting.

Test Datasets: We conduct our tests over three publicly available datasets using the suggested test protocols as described in [25]. The training dataset and the test dataset do not contain overlapping images. We provide test results on the Medium (M) and Hard (H) protocols.

- Revisited Oxford ($\mathcal{R}$Oxford ($\mathcal{R}$Oxf)): 4993 images with 70 query images.
- Revisited Paris ($\mathcal{R}$Paris ($\mathcal{R}$Par)): 6322 images with 70 query images.
- Distractor set (1 million distractors ($\mathcal{R}$1M)): 1 million distractors, which are irrelevant from ($\mathcal{R}$Oxf) and ($\mathcal{R}$Par) datasets, are added to the two datasets to evaluate the performance in the harder setup.

All test feature vectors are extracted at the multiscale setting, as described in the training dataset part to make a fair comparison with the existing methods. We use the commonly used mAP (mean Average Precision) to evaluate the performance.

Comparison to State-of-the-Art: All experimental results are presented in Table 1. Results of AQE [7], AQEwD [13], DQE [3], αQE [24] and LAttQE (depicted in gray) are given as reported in [14]. Our implementation of the LAttQE is given by LAttQE*. In both settings, the UGQE improves the baseline method [14] in terms of the reported performance measure. On the ($\mathcal{R}$Oxf) dataset, the UGQE performs better than other existing methods, and gives similar performance on the ($\mathcal{R}$Par). Furthermore, compared to the traditional methods and the LAttQE, the UGQE gives more balanced results as the mean mAP outperform the traditional methods. There are some mixed performance outputs where the αQE outperformed the transformer based techniques in some scenarios. A possible explanation is that after some point as the number of neighbors taken into account in the expansion increases, the performance in ($\mathcal{R}$Oxford) decreases while the performance in ($\mathcal{R}$Paris) increases. This indicates that there is a trade-off in the performance of the two test datasets using traditional methods. However, even then it can be observed that the addition of the uncertainty guidance in the self-attention transformer framework helped UGQE surpass the performance results of the baseline in all settings. Although the results of LAttQE reported in [14] are not reproducable[4], the proposed UGQE outperforms the reproducable baseline method. Some sample visual results are given in Fig. 2, where the UGQE tends to retrieve irrelevant images (red framed) in later ranks than the others.

Database Side Augmentation: We employ a Database-side Augmentation (DBA) approach that is similar to that of [14], which entails dividing the weights by the temperature parameter T that regularizes the softmax inputs. Hence,

---

[4] We will release our codes and pretrained models for the reproducable baseline (LAttQE) as well as the UGQE at the time of publication.

the softmax function is applied to the regularized logits. After calculating the expanded query with the tempered weights, the resulting vector is l_2 normalized. For a given query, the weights and the expanded query are calculated as follows: $\mathbf{w} = \text{Softmax}\left(\text{normalizeddotproduct}\left(\tilde{\mathbf{q}}, \left[\tilde{\mathbf{d}}_0, \tilde{\mathbf{d}}_1, \ldots, \tilde{\mathbf{d}}_k\right]\right)/T\right)$, and $\hat{\mathbf{q}} = \mathbf{w_q}\mathbf{q} + \sum_{n=1}^{k} \mathbf{w_{d_k}}\mathbf{d_k}$, and finally $\hat{\mathbf{q}} = \dfrac{\hat{\mathbf{q}}}{||\hat{\mathbf{q}}||_2}$.

All database vectors are augmented beforehand *offline* as described above. This strategy gives the best results for database side augmentation. In Table 1, DBA+QE section shows the performance results when the described DBA procedure was applied before all QE models. The DBA-added UGQE method again outperforms its baseline in all scenarios. Again, there are mixed results where for $\mathcal{R}$Paris ($\mathcal{R}$Paris), the DBA-added αQE outperforms the others.

Table 1. Mean average precision (mAP) of $\mathcal{R}$Oxford ($\mathcal{R}$Oxf) and $\mathcal{R}$Paris ($\mathcal{R}$Par) with and without 1 million distractors ($\mathcal{R}$1M). Our uncertainty guided query expansion method outperforms both traditional and learning based expansion methods on most of the settings. (* with our implementation, gray lines with † as reported in [14], and all other scores also taken from [14]).

		$\mathcal{R}$Oxf		$\mathcal{R}$Oxf + $\mathcal{R}$1M		$\mathcal{R}$Par		$\mathcal{R}$Par + $\mathcal{R}$1M		
		M	H	M	H	M	H	M	H	Mean
No QE										
—		67.3	44.3	49.5	25.7	80.6	61.5	57.3	29.8	52.0
QE										
[7]	AQE	72.3	49.0	57.3	30.5	82.7	65.1	62.3	36.5	56.9
[13]	AQEwD	72.0	48.7	56.9	30.0	83.3	65.9	63.0	37.1	57.1
[3]	DQE	72.7	48.8	54.5	26.3	83.7	66.5	64.2	38.0	56.8
[24]	αQE	69.3	44.5	52.5	26.1	**86.9**	**71.7**	**66.5**	**41.6**	57.4
[14]	LAttQE†	73.4	49.6	58.3	31.0	86.3	70.6	67.3	42.4	59.8
[14]	LAttQE*	73.2	49.7	57.1	30.0	84.3	67.2	63.9	37.8	57.9
	UGQE	**73.3**	**50.1**	**58.3**	**31.0**	86.2	70.8	65.0	39.3	**59.2**
DBA + QE										
[7]	ADBA + AQE	71.9	53.6	55.3	32.8	83.9	68.0	65.0	39.6	58.8
[13]	ADBAwD + AQEwD	73.2	53.2	57.9	34.0	84.3	68.7	65.6	40.8	59.7
[3]	DDBA + DQE	72.0	50.7	56.9	32.9	83.2	66.7	65.4	39.1	58.4
[24]	αDBA + αQE	71.7	50.7	56.0	31.5	**87.5**	**73.5**	**70.6**	**48.5**	61.3
[14]	LAttQE + LAttDBA†	74.0	54.1	60.0	36.3	87.8	74.1	70.5	48.3	63.1
	LAttQE + LAttDBA*	73.8	54.4	57.8	33.0	85.8	70.6	67.2	42.7	60.7
	UGQE + UGQEDBA	**75.5**	**56.3**	**58.0**	**31.6**	87.3	73.3	67.7	43.7	**61.7**

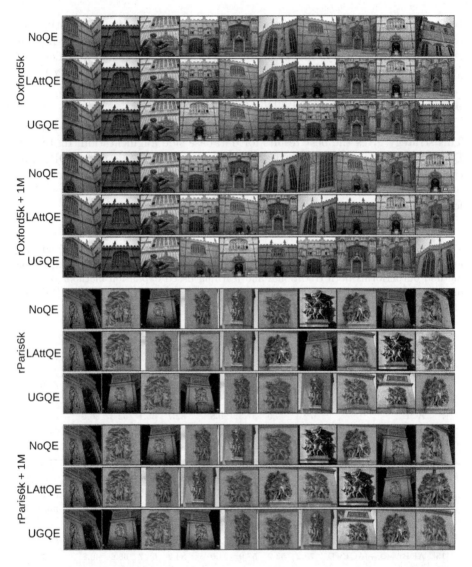

Fig. 2. Sample Visual Results: Color codes are as follows: Yellow Frame: Query Image, Blue or Green Frame: Relevant Image, Red Frame: Irrelevant Image, Cyan Frame: Distractor Image. As can be seen from examples, uncertainty information helps to remove some of the irrelevant retrievals. (Color figure online)

5   Conclusion

In this work, we proposed an uncertainty guided self-attention mechanism to learn query expansion in an end-to-end fashion. We built a novel feature generation method that is compatible with the traditional methods such as the QE, AQEwD and the learning based LAttQE method. Our work provides evidence to our hypothesis that the integration of uncertainty information on the neighborhood relationships in image retrieval methods can lead to the creation of more robust retrieval systems.

References

1. Amini, A., Schwarting, W., Soleimany, A., Rus, D.: Deep evidential regression. In: Advances in Neural Information Processing Systems, vol. 33 (2020)
2. Arandjelovic, R., Gronat, P., Torii, A., Pajdla, T., Sivic, J.: NetVLAD: CNN architecture for weakly supervised place recognition. In: Proceedings of the IEEE Conference on Computer Vision and Pattern Recognition (CVPR), June 2016 (2016)
3. Arandjelovic, R., Zisserman, A.: Three things everyone should know to improve object retrieval. In: CVPR (2012)
4. Babenko, A., Slesarev, A., Chigorin, A., Lempitsky, V.: Neural codes for image retrieval. In: Fleet, D., Pajdla, T., Schiele, B., Tuytelaars, T. (eds.) ECCV 2014. LNCS, vol. 8689, pp. 584–599. Springer, Cham (2014). https://doi.org/10.1007/978-3-319-10590-1_38
5. Brown, T., et al.: Language models are few-shot learners. In: Advances in Neural Information Processing Systems, vol. 33, pp. 1877–1901 (2020)
6. Buckley, C.: Automatic query expansion using smart: TREC 3. In: Proceedings of the 3rd Text REtrieval Conference (TREC-3), pp. 69–80 (1994)
7. Chum, O., Philbin, J., Sivic, J., Isard, M., Zisserman, A.: Total recall: automatic query expansion with a generative feature model for object retrieval. In: 2007 IEEE 11th ICCV (2007)
8. Datar, M., Indyk, P.: Locality-sensitive hashing scheme based on p-stable distributions. In: Proceedings of the 20th Annual Symposium on Computational Geometry, SCG 2004, pp. 253–262. ACM Press (2004)
9. Devlin, J., Chang, M.W., Lee, K., Toutanova, K.: BERT: pre-training of deep bidirectional transformers for language understanding. In: NAACL (2019)
10. Dosovitskiy, A., et al.: An image is worth 16 × 16 words: transformers for image recognition at scale. In: 9th International Conference on Learning Representations, ICLR (2021)
11. El-Nouby, A., Neverova, N., Laptev, I., Jégou, H.: Training vision transformers for image retrieval. CoRR abs/2102.05644 (2021)
12. Gal, Y., Ghahramani, Z.: Dropout as a Bayesian approximation: representing model uncertainty in deep learning. In: ICML, pp. 1050–1059. PMLR (2016)
13. Gordo, A., Almazán, J., Revaud, J., Larlus, D.: End-to-end learning of deep visual representations for image retrieval. Int. J. Comput. Vis. **124**(2), 237–254 (2017)
14. Gordo, A., Radenovic, F., Berg, T.: Attention-based query expansion learning. In: Vedaldi, A., Bischof, H., Brox, T., Frahm, J.-M. (eds.) ECCV 2020. LNCS, vol. 12373, pp. 172–188. Springer, Cham (2020). https://doi.org/10.1007/978-3-030-58604-1_11
15. Guo, C., Pleiss, G., Sun, Y., Weinberger, K.Q.: On calibration of modern neural networks. In: International Conference on Machine Learning, pp. 1321–1330 (2017)
16. Jégou, H., Douze, M., Schmid, C., Pérez, P.: Aggregating local descriptors into a compact image representation. In: 2010 IEEE Computer Society Conference on Computer Vision and Pattern Recognition, pp. 3304–3311 (2010)
17. Kingma, D.P., Ba, J.: Adam: a method for stochastic optimization. arXiv:1412.6980 (2014)

18. Lakshminarayanan, B., Pritzel, A., Blundell, C.: Simple and scalable predictive uncertainty estimation using deep ensembles. In: Advances in Neural Information Processing Systems, vol. 30 (2017)
19. Liu, X., Duh, K., Liu, L., Gao, J.: Very deep transformers for neural machine translation. arXiv preprint arXiv:2008.07772 (2020)
20. Lowe, D.: Object recognition from local scale-invariant features. In: Proceedings of the 7th IEEE ICCV (1999)
21. Malinin, A., Gales, M.: Predictive uncertainty estimation via prior networks. arXiv preprint arXiv:1802.10501 (2018)
22. Noh, H., Araujo, A., Sim, J., Weyand, T., Han, B.: Large-scale image retrieval with attentive deep local features. In: Proceedings of the IEEE International Conference on Computer Vision (ICCV), October 2017 (2017)
23. Perronnin, F., Sánchez, J., Mensink, T.: Improving the fisher kernel for large-scale image classification. In: Daniilidis, K., Maragos, P., Paragios, N. (eds.) ECCV 2010. LNCS, vol. 6314, pp. 143–156. Springer, Heidelberg (2010). https://doi.org/10.1007/978-3-642-15561-1_11
24. Radenovic, F., Tolias, G., Chum, O.: Fine-tuning CNN image retrieval with no human annotation. IEEE Trans. Pattern Anal. Mach. Intell. **41**(7), 1655–1668 (2019)
25. Radenović, F., Iscen, A., Tolias, G., Avrithis, Y., Chum, O.: Revisiting Oxford and Paris: large-scale image retrieval benchmarking. In: CVPR (2018)
26. Salton, G., Buckley, C.: Improving retrieval performance by relevance feedback. J. Am. Soc. Inf. Sci. **41**(4), 288–297 (1990)
27. Seidenschwarz, J., Elezi, I., Leal-Taixé, L.: Learning intra-batch connections for deep metric learning. In: 38th International Conference on Machine Learning (ICML) (2021)
28. Sensoy, M., Kaplan, L., Kandemir, M.: Evidential deep learning to quantify classification uncertainty. In: Advances in Neural Information Processing Systems (2018)
29. Tolias, G., Jégou, H.: Visual query expansion with or without geometry: refining local descriptors by feature aggregation. Pattern Recogn. **47**(10), 3466–3476 (2014)
30. Tolias, G., Sicre, R., Jégou, H.: Particular object retrieval with integral max-pooling of CNN activations. In: Bengio, Y., LeCun, Y. (eds.) 4th International Conference on Learning Representations, ICLR (2016)
31. Turcot, T., Lowe, D.G.: Better matching with fewer features: the selection of useful features in large database recognition problems. In: ICCV Workshop (2009)
32. Vaswani, A., et al.: Attention is all you need. In: NeurIPS (2017)
33. Veličković, P., Cucurull, G., Casanova, A., Romero, A., Liò, P., Bengio, Y.: Graph attention networks. In: International Conference on Learning Representations (2018)

Controlling the Quality of GAN-Based Generated Images for Predictions Tasks

Hajar Hammouch[1,2(✉)], Mounim El-Yacoubi[1(✉)] ⓘ, Huafeng Qin[3(✉)] ⓘ,
Hassan Berbia[2(✉)], and Mohamed Chikhaoui[4(✉)]

[1] Institut Polytechnique de Paris, Palaiseau, France
{hajar.hammouch,mounim.el_yacoubi}@telecom-sudparis.eu
[2] Mohammed V University, Rabat, Morocco
h_berbia@yahoo.com
[3] Chongqing Technology and Business University, Chongqing, China
qin_huafeng@163.com
[4] Institute of Agronomy and Veterinary Medicine, Rabat, Morocco
mchikhaoui@gmail.com

Abstract. Recently, Generative Adversarial Networks (GANs) have been widely applied for data augmentation given limited datasets. The state of the art is dominated by measures evaluating the quality of the generated images, that are typically all added to the training dataset. There is however no control of the generated data, in terms of the compromise between diversity and closeness to the original data, and this is our work's focus. Our study concerns the prediction of soil moisture dissipation rates from synthetic aerial images using a CNN regressor. CNNs, however, require large datasets to successfully train them. To this end, we apply and compare two Generative Adversarial Networks (GANs) models: (1) Deep Convolutional Neural Network (DCGAN) and (2) Bidirectional Generative Adversarial Network (BiGAN), to generate fake images. We propose a novel approach that consists of studying which generated images to include into the augmented dataset. We consider a various number of images, selected for training according to their realistic character, based on the discriminator loss. The results show that, using our approach, the CNN trained on the augmented dataset generated by BiGAN and DCGAN allows a significant relative decrease of the Mean Absolute Error w.r.t the CNN trained on the original dataset. We believe that our approach can be generalized to any Generative Adversarial Network model.

Keywords: Deep neural networks · Generative Adversarial Networks · Control of GAN output quality · Regression task

The authors thank Campus France and Morocco CNRST for the financial support of this research, and Telecom SudParis, and Univ. Mohammed V during the different phases of this study. This work was also supported in part by the National Natural Science Foundation of China under Grant 61976030 and the funds for creative research groups of Chongqing Municipal Education Commission under Grant CXQT21034.

M. El Yacoubi et al. (Eds.): ICPRAI 2022, LNCS 13363, pp. 121–133, 2022.
https://doi.org/10.1007/978-3-031-09037-0_11

1   Introduction and Related Work

Over recent decades, the decrease in water available for irrigation around the world has become a major issue especially in arid and semi-arid regions [1]. A useful solution involves estimating the amount of water required based on soil moisture [2]. Deep Learning has shown great potential in many agriculture tasks such as fruit counting, plant diseases recognition and soil moisture prediction [3]. Convolutional Neural Networks (CNNs) are ones of the most common deep learning models, but they require large amounts of training data. To overcome this problem, Generative adversarial networks (GANs) are a well-known effective technique for augmenting the training data sets [4,5]. Although GANs provide excellent results, not all their generated samples are realistic [6]. Evaluating GANs, or more specifically, the samples generated by GANs, is a challenging process [7]. From the state of the art, structural similarity (SSIM) and Peak Signal to Noise Ratio (PNSR) are the most two used image quality assessment metrics. They are based on the realism and diversity of the generated images [7]. SSIM compares the corresponding pixels and their neighborhoods in two images based on the luminance, the contrast and the structure, while PNSR computes the peak signal-to-noise ratio between two samples [7]. Although SSIM and PNSR are currently the most popular metrics, they are increasingly criticized [8,9]. They may fail capturing fine features in the images and provide high scores to images with bad quality [7]. Furthermore, the scores are not always well correlated with human perception [10]. In other words, the generated sample with high metrics values does not always appear better to humans than the sample with lower metrics values [10]. In addition to the image quality metrics mentioned above, some other measures such as Inception Score (IS) and Fréchet Inception Distance (FID) [11], have been widely adopted for evaluating GANs [12]. These two measures use a pre-trained Inception neural network trained on the ImageNet dataset to extract the features and capture the required properties of generated images [7]. However, the two Inception-based measures do not consider real images at all, and so cannot measure how well the generator approximates the real distribution [7]. In other words, these scores are limited to measuring only the diversity of the generated images [11]. Furthermore, IS and FID focus on the evaluation of the generative models, which cannot be utilized to evaluate the quality of each single fake image [13]. In addition, better FID (i.e., lower) does not always imply better image quality [14]. The authors in [15], aimed to increase their original limited agriculture data set using GAN for a segmentation task, by proposing a GAN that automatically generates realistic agriculture scenes. They only generate instances of the objects of interest in the scene, not all the image. Furthermore, they proposed an empirical evaluation where they extract features from the original and generated samples to calculate performance using various metrics such as: IS and FID. These measures showed that the fake samples' quality was similar to original samples' quality. Then, without selecting the best generated images, all the augmented synthesized images were added to the original data set to train a CNN model for a crop segmentation purpose. The results showed that the GAN enhanced dataset improved the performance of four different state-of-the art segmentation architectures. The authors in [4], have proposed a model to develop a deep learning based framework to recognize the tomato plant diseases by investigating tomato leaf images. They generated synthetic images from the PlantVillage dataset using conditional GAN model for a classification purpose. The generated samples were first evaluated visually and then using two metrics: PNSR and IS. The comparable values of PNSR and IS showed that the quality of images generated by C-GAN were very close to the quality of real images. Then, in the second experiment, the models were trained first on the original data set and then on the augmented data set. The results show that the augmented data set gives better accuracy as compared to the original dataset. In [13], the authors used a GAN-based data augmentation technique to improve the training performance. In this work, the proposed GAN model has been assessed by various metrics such as: Inception Score, Fréchet Inception Distance, Precision and Recall. The results showed that, by adding the generated samples to the original set, the proposed model results in significant performance accuracy. Overall, GANs technology is quickly evolving and is being used in more and more agriculture applications for classification or segmentation. State of the art methods, however, add all the generated images into the augmented data for a classification or a segmentation purpose [4,13,15]. Sometimes, they just evaluate the generated data, but do not assess which ones to select for the addition. However not all generated images are realistic and relevant [6]. Our study is devoted to handle this issue by proposing a framework that studies which generated images to include in the augmented dataset. This approach allows to train a deep learning model using only the most realistic generated images. In this paper, and as presented in our previous work [16], we are interested in the prediction of soil moisture dissipation rates from synthetic aerial images using a CNN model. This entails a regression task where the CNN, given an input image, has to predict a vector of regression values associated with the dissipation rates at different locations of the agricultural field. CNNs, however, require large data sets to successfully train the deep network. To this end, we propose and compare between two Generative adversarial networks models: (1) Deep Convolutional Generative Adversarial Network (DCGAN) and (2) Bidirectionnal Generative Adversarial Network (BIGAN) using the same architectures for generating fake agriculture images. Then, we conduct several experiments to study which generated images to include in the augmented dataset. We consider different numbers of generated images, namely from 250 to 1200 images, with four scenarios regarding the discriminator loss ranges: (1) 0.20–0.80, (2) 0.30–0.70, (3) 0.40–0.60 and (4) 0.45–0.55. Additional augmented data did not improve the results. Following that, we use the baseline CNN model trained on the original data set to predict the regression vector serving as its ground truth in the augmented dataset. The results show that the CNN trained on the augmented data set generated by BiGAN and DCGAN models allowed respectively a relative decrease of the Mean Absolute Error by 19.34% and 14.23% instead of 16.05% and 12.40% (using all the generated images) w.r.t to the CNN trained on the original data set. This shows that the proposed GANs-based generated images quality assessment approach can add high-quality agriculture images to the training set efficiently, leading to performance improvement of the regression model. To the best of our knowledge, this is the first paper using this approach, that can be applied to any Generative Adversarial Network model.

In summary, the main contributions of this article are outlined as follows:

- By adding conv layers and an encoder on the standard GAN respectively, we compare two known models using the same architectures: (1) Deep Convolutional Generative Adversarial Network (DCGAN) and (2) Bidirectional Generative Adversarial Network (BiGAN) for generating fake agriculture images.
- We propose a framework where we study which images to include into the augmented dataset by considering different sizes of images that are generated from 250 to 1200 images with four scenarios regarding the discriminator loss ranges: (1) 0.20–0.80, (2) 0.30–0.70, (3) 0.40–0.60 and (4) 0.45–0.55.
- We use the basic CNN model to generate the regression ground truth corresponding to the generated images.
- To evaluate the performance of our proposed approach, a publicly available agriculture RAPID data set has been used in the experiments. The presented approach is applicable using any other Generative adversarial networks model.

The remainder of this paper is as follows. The background is briefly presented in Sect. 2. The used methods and materials are described in Sect. 3. Then, in Sect. 4, we evaluate the experimental results, followed by a discussion. The last section, Sect. 5, concludes the paper.

2   Background

Generative Adversarial Network: GAN is a deep learning model consisting of two modules: a discriminator D and a generator G [17]. D determines whether the data is real or fake, and G transforms a random vector into a realistic data, by fooling the discriminator into accepting its generated data as original data [17]. During training, G improves on generating fake samples, while D learns to distinguish between the original and generated examples [15]. The equilibrium is reached when G generates realistic images similar to real samples [17]. The discriminator will be totally confused in the ideal case, when guessing with 50% probability that all samples, whether original or generated, are fake [17]. GAN aims to reduce the probability distribution distance between real and generated samples. GAN training involves optimizing the following loss function:

$$\min_{G} \max_{D} \mathbb{V}(D, G) = \mathbb{E}_{x \sim p_{\text{data}}(x)}[\log D(x)] + \mathbb{E}_{z \sim p_{\text{generated}}(z)}[\log(1 - D(G(z)))] \quad (1)$$

where $E_{x \sim p_{\text{data}}(x)}$ is the expectation over the original samples, $E_{z \sim p_{\text{generated}}(z)}$ is the expectation over the generated samples, $p_{\text{generated}}(z)$ is the noise vector, $D(x)$ is the discriminator loss given the probability that x comes from the training data distribution, $G(z)$ is the generator loss and x represents the original dataset.

During training, the generator and discriminator networks are trained in competition with each other, and both play a two players minimax game, i.e., the generator aims to minimize (1), while the discriminator aims to maximize it. The characteristics of (1) are that $\log D(x)$ is maximized by the discriminator, so that the original and generated samples are properly classified. Besides, $\log (1 - D(G(z))$ is minimized by training the generator. Theoretically, achieving $p_{generated} = p_{data}$ is the solution to this minimax game when D starts randomly guessing whether the inputs are real or generated.

Bidirectionnal Generative Adversarial Network: The encoder is the difference between BiGAN and GAN models. The original GAN can generate an image for any random noise vector but cannot generate the corresponding random noise for any given generated image. Donahue et al. [18] proposed the bidirectional GAN which contains an additional encoder component E [18]. In addition to the encoder E which maps the data space to the latent space, BiGAN allows for the extraction of additional data characteristics and to perform the learning process [19]. With three components, encoder E, generator G and discriminator D, true images are fed into the encoder E to learn the feature representation E(x) while z, considered as a noise vector in the latent space, is input into the generator G to generate synthetic representation data G(z), and finally the obtained pairs (z, G(z)) and (E(x), x) are used to train the discriminator D. As a result, $\hat{z}$ = E(x) can be used as low-dimensional characteristics extracted by the encoder from data images. The structure of discriminator D is altered. Instead of using x or $\hat{x}$ = G(z) as the input of D, the discriminator discriminates joint pair (x,$\hat{z}$) or ($\hat{x}$, z) from data space and latent space, respectively. As GAN model, the purpose of BiGAN can be defined as a minimax objective:

$$\min_{G,E} \max_{D} \mathbb{E}_{x \sim p_{data}(x)}[\log D(x, E(x))] + \mathbb{E}_{z \sim p_{generated}(z)}[\log(1 - D(G(z), z)] \quad (2)$$

3   Materials and Methods

Dataset: We use RAPID [20], the only public available dataset. The examples are pairs of synthetic aerial images and corresponding soil moisture dissipation rate values. It contains 1400 aerial images of a vineyard with known soil moisture levels. The dataset is originally split into a train and test sets, of 1200 and 200 images respectively [20]. Each image contains 200 equidistant plants distributed in 10 columns and 20 rows, associated with a vector of 200 values of soil moisture values. Figure 1 shows an example of three images resized to 128×128. Yellow refers to higher dissipation rates, whereas green refers to lower rates.

Convolution Neural Network: We use a CNN regression model with Euclidean loss. To evaluate the accuracy, we use the Mean Absolute Error (MAE) metric (3), where y_{ij} is the actual output value (ground truth), i.e., the dissipation rate at plant j in image i, $\hat{y}_{ij}$ represents the predicted value, n the number of image plants, p the number of dataset elements, $1 \leq i \leq p$, $0 \leq j \leq n$, and the values of MAE are positive. The closer MAE to zero, the better the prediction.

Fig. 1. Original images resized to 128 × 128. (Color figure online)

$$MAE = \frac{1}{p}(\frac{1}{n}\sum_{i=1}^{p}\sum_{j=0}^{n}|\hat{y}_{ij} - y_{ij}| \tag{3}$$

Our CNN contains six convolution layers, followed by a fully connected layer, with ReLU as the activation function. Inputs to the CNN are images of size 128 × 128 × 3. The first layer contains 32 filters of size (3 × 3), followed by a dropout layer. The second layer has 32 filters of size (3 × 3), followed by a max pooling layer with size 2 × 2 and stride 0. The third layer is composed of 64 filters with size 3 × 3 and stride 0, followed by a dropout layer. The fourth layer has 64 filters with size 3 × 3. The following max pooling is of size 2 × 2 and stride 0. The fifth layer contains 128 filters of size (3 × 3), followed by a dropout layer. The last convolution layer has 128 filters of size (3 × 3), and is followed by dropout and max pooling layers of pooling size 2 × 2 with stride 0. This is followed by a fully connected layer of dimension 200 that predicts the vector of 200 soil moisture dissipation rates. The CNN architecture, is obtained by a Greedy optimization method on the validation set, of various hyperparameters such as: filter size, batch size, optimizer, learning rate, number of epochs, dropout.

Proposal and Experimental Design: In this work, we aim to develop an effective framework assessing the quality of the generated images, that allows selecting the generated images to be included into the augmented data. To this end, we use two GANs: DCGAN and BiGAN. In our scheme, not all generated images are added into the augmented data set, but only those who satisfy a quality criterion given by the discriminator loss, as the latter gives us a quantitative hint to how similar a generated image is to an original one. Concretely, we conduct several experiments where we consider different sizes of images that are generated from 250 to 1200 images with four scenarios regarding the discriminator loss. In one of the scenarios, for instance, we do not want to include very easy images for which the discriminator loss is close to 0, as these samples are too different from the real images, so inclusion may actually hinder the quality of the training data. We want rather realistic images that show variability and diversity with respect to the training data. We consider the first experiment where we include only images really close to the real ones by considering a loss between 0.45 and 0.55, so we are 5% on each size of the middle (of 50%), where the discriminator has total confusion on whether the image is real or fake. The second range is between 0.40 and 0.60, where we can afford more variability in the training data. We can go further with a loss between 0.40 and 0.60 or even further with a discriminator loss between 0.20 and 0.80 that allows for more variability. Subsequently, the resulting samples along with their predicted soil moisture dissipation rates, used as their ground truths, will be used to augment the training set for a more robust CNN parameter estimation.

Experimental Details: For all the experiments, an Adam optimizer (LR = 0.0002) is used in our architectures to update the classifier parameters. The number of epochs and batch size were set respectively to 200 and 128, and the binary cross entropy is used as loss function.

Generator Network: The generator, shown in Fig. 2(b), takes, as input, a 100×1 random noise, and generates an image of size $128 \times 128 \times 3$. It is composed of four conv layers and three dense layers. The activation function LeakyReLU is applied for all layers except for the output layer that uses Tanh. An Upsampling layer is used after all conv layers, except after the input layer. Finally, batch normalization is used for the first two dense layers to stabilize the learning process by normalizing the input to have zero mean and unit variance.

Discriminator Network: The discriminator (see Fig. 2(c)) classifies whether the images are real or generated [17]. It takes as input images of size $128 \times 128 \times 3$. In this architecture, the input sample undergoes transformation embeddings through two conv layers and three Dense layers, followed by the Sigmoid activation function to predict whether the sample is real or generated. The LeakyReLU activation function follows each conv and dense layers except for the output layers. Finally, dropout layer is used for the first two dense layers.

Encoder Network: Our BiGAN generator and discriminator architectures are similar to our Deep Convolutional GAN (DCGAN). The architecture of the encoder E (see Fig. 2(a)), contains four convolutional layers and three Dense layers followed by batch normalization layers, with LeakyReLU as activation function. The BIGAN discriminator concatenates both the data point x and its latent z as input, which is then passed through two convolutional layers and three dense layers serving as fully connected layers before obtaining a scalar as output.

Ground truth Prediction: To get a full augmented dataset, we use the same CNN to generate the ground truth of the fake samples generated by GAN and BiGAN models (Fig. 3). The latter, therefore, consist of GAN-based and BiGAN-based generated images, along with their generated ground truth vector.

4 Results

Convolutional Neural Network: As a baseline, we consider the CNN of Sect. 3, applied to the original data only, without data augmentation. Table 1 shows the accuracy and loss for the training, validation, and test sets.

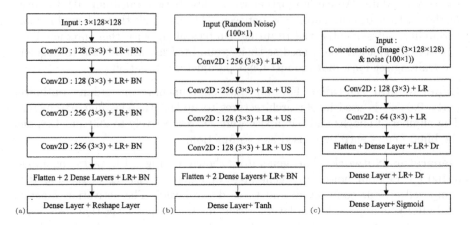

Fig. 2. (a) Encoder Architecture, (b) Generator Architecture, (c) Discriminator Architecture; LR: LeakyReLU, US: UpSampling2D, Dr: Dropout, BN: BatchNormalization.

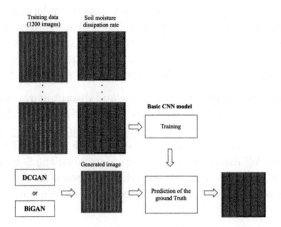

Fig. 3. Prediction of the ground truth using DCGAN or BiGAN model.

Table 1. CNN results using the original data.

	Loss: MSE	Metric: Mae
Train	0.0014	0.0288
Validation	0.0013	0.0267
Test	0.0013	0.0274

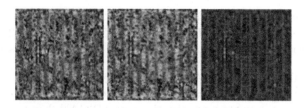

Fig. 4. Images with a discriminator loss close to 0.

Deep Convolutional GANs: DCGAN was able to produce samples that look like the real data at about 80 epochs. The quality of these fake samples continued to improve until roughly 200 epochs. However, and as mentioned above, not all generated samples are realistic. It makes sense, therefore, not to include very easy images, where the discriminator loss is close to 0, as shown in Fig. 4. Therefore, we considered different numbers of generated images, from 250 to 1200 images, with four scenarios regarding the discriminator loss ranges: (1) 0.20–0.80, (2) 0.30–0.70, (3) 0.40–0.60 and (4) 0.45–0.55. Figure 5(a), (b), (c) shows a grid of real and generated samples corresponding to (1) and (4). Visually, the number of columns is the same for all cases. Furthermore, the distribution of the colors is the same, except for (1) and (2), where the distribution of yellow color is quite different w.r.t the original samples. As shown in Fig. 5(c), the best generated images correspond to the last case, where the discriminator loss is between 0.45 and 0.55. Therefore, we conclude that the more the discriminator loss is closer to 0.5, the better the quality of the images is.

$$Absolute\ change = Mae_{final} - Mae_{initial} \qquad (4)$$

$$Relative\ change = (\frac{Mae_{final} - Mae_{initial}}{Mae_{initial}}) \times 100 \qquad (5)$$

For each case study, the selected best synthesized images were added to the original training dataset to show how much the regression performance can be improved by our quality assessment framework. The evaluation is performed based on the MAE metric. First, we set 1000 original images and 200 original images in the training validation sets respectively. 250, 500, 750, 1000, 1200 fake images were added gradually to the original training data to get respectively: 1250, 1500, 1750, 2000 and 2200 augmented training data sets. Additional augmented data did not improve the results. The results show that for all cases, the more generated images are added, the better the result is. For all cases, the best result was the last case when adding 1200 generated images reaching a validation MAE of 3.18%, 2%, 3.10% and 2.72% where the discriminator loss is respectively between: (1) 0.20–0.80, (2) 0.30–0.70, (3) 0.40–0.60 and (4) 0.45–0.55. We considered, therefore, this optimal configuration, and tested for each case the associated trained model on the held-out 200 test images. We obtained a MAE of 2.93%, 2.92%, 2.91% and 2.35%. The best result was the last case, when discriminator loss was set between 0.45 and 0.55, and when adding 1200 generated images reaching a validation MAE of 2.35% instead of 2.74%, which amounts to a relative decrease of the MAE of 14.23% instead of 12.40% without using our approach (i.e., adding all the generated images) (see Eqs. (4) and (5)).

Bidirectionnal Generative Adversarial Networks: BiGAN was trained using the same hyperparameters as DCGAN model. The architectures of the generator and discriminator were also the same. BiGAN, however, was able to produce samples that look like the real data at about just 20 epochs. The quality of these generated samples continued to improve until roughly 200 epochs. Figure 5(a), (b'), (c') shows a grid of real and generated samples corresponding to (1) and (4). Visually, the number of columns is the same in all cases. Furthermore, the distribution of the colors is the same except for the first two cases (1) and (2) where the distribution of yellow color is quite different w.r.t the original data. The best generated images correspond to the last two cases (3) and (4), where the discriminator loss is between 0.40–0.60 and 0.45–0.55. Visually, the quality of images generated by BiGAN model outperforms those generated by DCGAN. However, in both cases, the generated images continue to improve when the discriminator loss gets closer to 0.5. Using the same DCGAN experiments, we note again that, for all cases, the more generated images are added, the better the result is. Here again, for each case, the best result was the last when adding 1200 generated images, reaching respectively a validation MAE of 2.66%, 2.44%, 2.34% and 2.25% where the discriminator loss is between

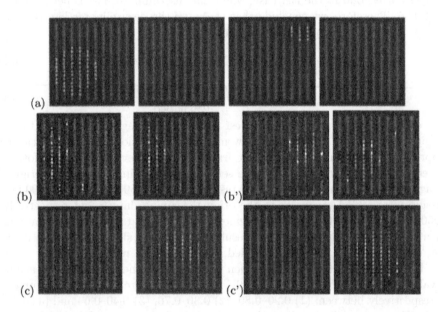

Fig. 5. (a) Original images; Generated images using DCGAN and BiGAN respectively and corresponding to a discriminator loss between: (b)–(b') 0.20 and 0.80, and (c)–(c') 0.45 and 0.55.

(1) 0.20–0.80, (2) 0.30–0.70, (3) 0.40–0.60 and (4) 0.45–0.55. We considered, therefore, this optimal configuration, and tested the associated trained model on the held-out 200 test images. We obtained a MAE of 2.39%, 2.30%, 2.27% and 2.21%. The best result was the last case where the discriminator loss is between 0.45 and 0.55 and when adding 1200 generated images reaching a validation MAE of 2.21% instead of 2.74%, which amounts to a relative decrease of the MAE of 19.34% instead of 16.05% without using our approach (i.e., adding all the generated images). Additional augmented data did not improve the results. Table 2, summarizes the best results (i.e., generating 1200 images) obtained by both DCGAN and BiGAN, using and without using our approach. Thus, the performance of the CNN model has been further improved by a relative decrease of the MAE of 12.40% and 16.05% (including all the generated images), 14.23% and 19.34% (using our approach) through the DCGAN and BiGAN models respectively. Another interesting finding is that, for all cases, the time consumption for generating images using DCGAN model was much larger than that of generating images using BiGAN model. In addition, using our approach on four cases, we showed that our BiGAN model provides better performances in terms of the MAE metric and also in terms of images generation quality compared to the DCGAN model. This result is explained by the good feature extraction capability of the encoder. In other words, by adding the encoder, BiGAN is able to better extract the features from the data. Overall, our proposed selection framework improves significantly the CNN prediction performance using either DCGAN or BiGAN.

Table 2. Final results; W.A: Without using our approach, R.C: Relative Change, Case1: 0.20–0.80, Case2: 0.30–0.70, Case3: 0.40–0.60, Case4: 0.45–0.55

Baseline	Mse-Train		Mae-Train			Mse-Val		Mae-Val		Mae-Test	
	0.0014		0.0288			0.0013		0.0267		0.0274	
	BiGAN Model					DCGAN Model					
	Train set		Validation set		Test set	R.C	Train set		Validation set		Test set	R.C
	MAE	MSE	MAE	MSE	MAE		MAE	MSE	MAE	MSE	MAE	
W.A	7.07.10−4	0.0197	0.0011	0.0246	0.0230	**16.05%**	4.67.10−4	0.0150	0.0013	0.0261	0.0240	**12.40%**
Case 1	9.95.10−4	0.0222	0.0012	0.0266	0.0239	–	6.08.10−4	0.0172	0.0018	0.0318	0.0293	–
Case 2	0.0013	0.0254	0.0010	0.0244	0.0230	–	6.67.10−4	0.0181	6.90.10−4	0.02	0.0292	–
Case 3	3.01.10−4	0.0116	9.84.10−4	0.0234	0.0227	–	7.10−4	0.0187	0.0018	0.0310	0.0291	–
Case 4	4.93.10−4	0.0155	8.66.10−4	0.0225	0.0221	**19.34%**	7.11.10−4	0.0181	7.20.10−4	0.0272	0.0235	**14.23%**

5 Conclusion

In this work, we have proposed a quality GAN-based generated images framework, where we control the discriminator loss to augment the training data set with the most realistic generated agricultural images for a regression task. We used and compared two generative adversarial networks models (DCGAN and BiGAN) to generate fake images from 250 to 1200 with four scenarios, with a baseline CNN used to generate the regression ground truth vector for each fake image. We have shown that BiGAN model outperforms DCGAN model in terms of the MAE metric and of the quality of the generated images. Augmenting the training data set, using our approach, is effective and allows significantly improving the regression performance with a relative decrease of the Mean Absolute Error (MAE) of 19.34% and 14.23% using BiGAN and DCGAN respectively instead of 16.05% and 12.40% where all the generated images were added into the training data. In our future work, we intend to build our own dataset from an agriculture field in Morocco. We will also apply our approach using the new collected dataset with various other GAN-based network architectures.

References

1. Papadavid, G., Hadjimitsis, D., Fedra, K., Michaelides, S.: Smart management and irrigation demand monitoring in Cyprus, using remote sensing and water resources simulation and optimization. Adv. Geosci. **30**, 31–37 (2011)
2. Hassan-Esfahani, L., Torres-Rua, A., Jensen, A., Mckee, M.: Spatial root zone soil water content estimation in agricultural lands using Bayesian-based artificial neural networks and high resolution visual, NIR, and thermal imagery. Irrig. Drain. **66**, 273–288 (2017)
3. Jha, K., Doshi, A., Patel, P.: Intelligent irrigation system using artificial intelligence and machine learning: a comprehensive review. Int. J. Adv. Res. **6**(10), 1493–1502 (2018)
4. Abbas, A., Jain, S., Gour, M., Vankudothu, S.: Tomato plant disease detection using transfer learning with C-GAN synthetic images. Comput. Electron. Agric. **187**, 106279 (2021)
5. Qin, H., El Yacoubi, M., Li, Y., Liu, C.: Multi-scale and multidirection GAN For CNN-based single palm-vein identification. IEEE Trans. Inf. Forensics Secur. **16**, 2652–2666 (2021)
6. Gu, S., Bao, J., Chen, D., Wen, F.: GIQA: generated image quality assessment. arXiv preprint arXiv:2003.08932 (2020)
7. Borji, A.: Pros and cons of GAN evaluation measures. Comput. Vis. Image Underst. J. **179**, 41–65 (2019)
8. Zhu, X., et al.: GAN-Based Image Super-Resolution with a Novel Quality Loss. Mathematical Problems in Engineering (2020)
9. Jean-François, P., Rhita, N.: Limitations of the SSIM quality metric in the context of diagnostic imaging. In: International Conference on Image Processing, ICIP 2015, pp. 2960–2963. IEEE, Canada (2015). https://doi.org/10.1109/ICIP.2015.7351345
10. Kovalenko, B.: Super resolution with Generative Adversarial Networks (n.d.)
11. Borji, A.: Pros and cons of GAN evaluation measures: new developments (2021). http://arxiv.org/abs/2103.09396
12. Shmelkov, K., Schmid, C., Alahari, K.: How good is my GAN? In: Ferrari, V., Hebert, M., Sminchisescu, C., Weiss, Y. (eds.) ECCV 2018. LNCS, vol. 11206, pp. 218–234. Springer, Cham (2018). https://doi.org/10.1007/978-3-030-01216-8_14
13. Qin, Z., Liu, Z., Zhu, P., Xue, Y.: A GAN-based image synthesis method for skin lesion classification. Comput. Meth. Program. Biomed. **195**, 0169–2607 (2020)
14. Zhao, Z., Zhang, Z., Chen, T., Singh, S., Zhang, H.: Image augmentations for GAN training (2020). http://arxiv.org/abs/2006.02595

15. Fawakherji, M., Ptena, C., Prevedello, I., Pretto, A., Bloisi, D.D., Nardi, D.: Data augmentation using GANs for crop/weed segmentation in precision farming. In: CCTA 2020 Conference, Montréal, pp. 279–284. IEEE Xplore (2020). https://doi.org/10.1109/CCTA41146.2020.9206297

16. Hammouch, H., El Yacoubi, M., Qin, H., Berrahou, A., Berbia, H., Chikhaoui, M.: A two-stage deep convolutional generative adversarial network-based data augmentation scheme for agriculture image regression tasks. In: International Conference on Cyber-physical Social Intelligence, CSI 2021, Beijing. IEEE Xplore (2021)

17. Goodfellow, I., Pouget-Abadie, J., Mirza, M.: Generative adversarial networks. Commun. ACM **63**(11), 139–144 (2020)

18. Donahue, J., Krähenbühl, P., Darrell, T.: Adversarial feature learning (2016). http://arxiv.org/abs/1605.09782

19. Cui, L., Tian, X., Shi, X., Wang, X., Cui, Y.: A semi-supervised fault diagnosis method based on improved bidirectional generative adversarial network. Appl. Sci. **11**(20), 9401 (2021). https://doi.org/10.3390/app11209401

20. Tseng, D., et al.: Towards automating precision irrigation: deep learning to infer local soil moisture conditions from synthetic aerial agricultural images. In: CASE 2018 Conference, Munich, pp. 284–291. IEEE (2018). https://doi.org/10.1109/COASE.2018.8560431

A Framework for Registration
of Multi-modal Spatial Transcriptomics
Data

Yu Qiang[1,2(✉)], Shixu He[1], Renpeng Ding[1], Kailong Ma[1], Yong Hou[1],
Yan Zhou[1], and Karl Rohr[2]

[1] MGI, BGI-Shenzhen, Shenzhen 518083, China
yuqiang@mgi-tech.com
[2] Heidelberg University, BioQuant, IPMB, and DKFZ Heidelberg, Biomedical
Computer Vision Group, INF 267, 69120 Heidelberg, Germany

Abstract. Observing the spatial characteristics of gene expression by
image-based spatial transcriptomics technology allows studying gene
activity across different cells and intracellular structures. We present
a framework for the registration and analysis of transcriptome images
and immunostaining images. The method is based on particle filters and
jointly exploits intensity information and image features. We applied
our approach to synthetic data as well as real transcriptome images and
immunostaining microscopy images of the mouse brain. It turns out that
our approach accurately registers the multi-modal images and yields better results than a state-of-the-art method.

Keywords: Spatial transcriptomics · Multi-modal images ·
Registration

1   Introduction

Spatial transcriptomics (ST) technologies based on next generation sequencing (NGS) systematically generate spatial measurements of gene expression in
an entire tissue sample, which bridge the gap between spatial information and
the whole transcriptome [1]. Advanced spatial transcriptomics platforms, like
Stereo-seq [2] or Seq-scope [3], achieve nanoscale resolution, enabling determining subcellular compartmentalization and visualization of RNA sequencing data.

However, for the current ST technologies with nanoscale resolution it is difficult to accurately assign spots of the transcriptome images (gene expression
images) to specific organelles or cells [1]. The information about gene expression
can be exploited in different ways, for example, to characterize gene expression
patterns or to classifiy cell types in the tissue [4–6]. However, lack of distinct cell
boundaries in the transcriptome images presents a big challenge for automated
analysis. Fast and accurate registration of transcriptome images and immunostaining images can facilitate the assignment of expressed genes to specific cells
to enable studying sub-cellular gene expression patterns.

© Springer Nature Switzerland AG 2022
M. El Yacoubi et al. (Eds.): ICPRAI 2022, LNCS 13363, pp. 134–145, 2022.
https://doi.org/10.1007/978-3-031-09037-0_12

Cell nuclei in gene expression matrix images can be located by spots with intron sequence aggregation, while the morphological features of the cell membranes and nuclei can be visualized in situ using immunostaining before permeabilization the tissue slice for RNA sequencing. Although in situ sequencing (to generate transcriptome images) and immunostaining are carried out on the same tissue, there are multiple factors that can cause spatial shifting, for example, the sample preparation process and dispersion of RNAs after tissue permeabilization. Manual alignment of two images is time consuming, and only enables partial alignment in most cases [3,6]. Therefore, methods are needed for efficient and accurate registration of large-scale transcriptome images and immunostaining images with tens of thousands of cells.

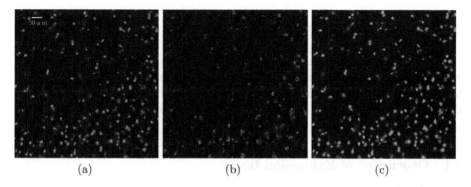

(a)   (b)   (c)

Fig. 1. Registration result of our approach for an image section: (a) Immunostaining image, (b) transcriptome image (gene expression image), and (c) overlay of registered images.

Data fusion of transcriptome images and immunostaining images is very important. The redundancy of information captured by the different modalities increases the reliability and robustness of the ST technology. However, despite the advantages mentioned above, using different modalities raises new problems such as multi-modal image registration. Image registration algorithms can be classified into intensity-based and feature-based methods (e.g., [7,8]). Intensity-based methods exploit intensity patterns in images via different similarity metrics, while feature-based methods determine correspondences between image features such as points, lines, or contours. Besides classical methods, recently deep learning methods for multi-modal registration of medical images were proposed (e.g., [9]).

In previous work on automatic registration of spatial transcriptomics image data only few methods were introduced. [10] described a multi-information-based method for registration of multiplexed in situ sequencing (ISS) datasets from the Human Cell Atlas project. Multi-information is defined as KL divergence between a joint distribution and a product of marginal distributions, and used in conjunction with FRI (finite rate of innovation) sampling and swarm optimization. However, the method is computationally expensive since multi-information is costly to compute.

In this work, we introduce a novel framework for registration and analysis of transcriptome images and immunostaining images. The approach is based on a probabilistic Bayesian framework and uses particle filters to determine the transformation between the multi-modal images. Intensity information and image features are jointly taken into account. We applied our approach to synthetic data as well as real transcriptome images and immunostaining microscopy images of the mouse brain (cf. Fig. 1) section. It turns out that our approach successfully registers the multi-modal images and yields better results than a state-of-the-art method.

2   Methodology

Our registration framework consists of three main steps: (i) Generation of gene expression image, (ii) global to local registration framework, and (iii) Voronoi-based cell region determination. For registration, we use mutual information and the point set distance jointly as metric and employ particle filters for the optimization process.

2.1   Generation of Expression Image

The gene expression matrix can be transformed to a gene expression hypercube format by using x and y coordinates in the matrix as pixel position in an image and employing the unique molecular identifier (UMI) count value of each position as the intensity value. The gene class of each pixel is treated as the layer of hypercube as shown in Fig. 2. The gene expression image (transcriptome images) is generated by including all pixels from different layers into one single layer image.

The intron of the genes can be used to locate cell nuclei. Eukaryotic genes are composed of exons, which correspond to protein-coding sequences, and intervening sequences called introns, which may be involved in gene regulation. In RNA transcription and maturation, intron sequences are removed through RNA-splicing before mRNAs are transported to the cytoplasm for translation. As shown in Fig. 3, the spikes of intronic gene expression are present within nuclei locations, which can be used to improve the accuracy of spot detection within our registration framework.

2.2   Framework for Registration

Our aim is to study the relationship between the spatial cell structure in the immunostaining image and the corresponding gene expression distribution in the gene expression image (transcriptome image). The goal of registration is to assign N_g gene expression spots to N_c cells (each gene expression spot is

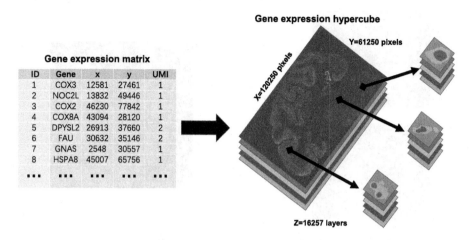

Fig. 2. (Left) Gene expression matrix. Each row shows one captured gene with (x, y) coordinate, gene ID, and unique molecular identifier (UMI) count value. (Right) Gene expression hypercube visualization based on the gene expression matrix.

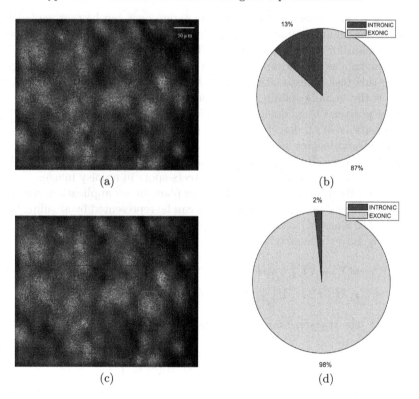

Fig. 3. Statistical results of intronic and exonic gene expression for real data (image section): (a) Gene expression image with a manually selected red circle ROI, (b) statistical results of intronic and exonic gene expression for red circle ROI, (c) gene expression image with a manually selected blue circle ROI, (d) statistical results of intronic and exonic gene expression for blue circle ROI. (Color figure online)

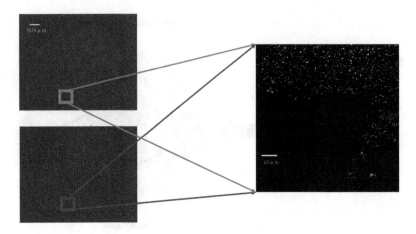

Fig. 4. (Left) Immunostaining image (top), and globally aligned gene expression image (bottom). (Right) Enlarged ROI of overlayed images after global registration.

assumed as a cell nucleus region). Such an assignment can be represented by a non-negative assignment matrix ω with elements $\omega_{n_g}^{n_c}$ that denote the strength of gene expression for a spot n_g within a cell n_c (using a binary assignment $\omega_{n_g}^{n_c} \in \{0, 1\}$). Some nodes may be assigned to no cells. In a Bayesian framework, we can formulate this task by estimating the posterior probability density $p(\omega \mid I^i, I^g)$, where I^i is the immunostaining image and I^g is the gene expression image. We denote the positions of all detected spots in the immunostaining image by $\boldsymbol{Y}^i_{1:N_c}$ and the positions of all detected spots in gene expression image by $\boldsymbol{Y}^g_{1:N_g}$.

To detect and localize multiple bright spots in an image, the spot-enhancing filter [11,12] is used. It applies an LoG (Laplacian of Gaussian or Mexican Hat) filter to a 2D image, and enhances and detects spots in a noisy image.

Since all cells are located within the same plane in our application, the transformation between the multi-modal images can be represented by an affine transformation $\boldsymbol{H}$. Since $\boldsymbol{Y}^i_{1:N_c}$ and $\boldsymbol{Y}^g_{1:N_g}$ are conditionally independent of I^i and I^g, by using Bayes' theorem, we can write

$$p(\boldsymbol{Y}^i_{1:N_c}, \boldsymbol{Y}^g_{1:N_g}, \boldsymbol{H} \mid I^i, I^g) =$$
$$p(\boldsymbol{H} \mid I^i, I^g, \boldsymbol{Y}^i_{1:N_c}, \boldsymbol{Y}^g_{1:N_g}) p(\boldsymbol{Y}^i_{1:N_c} \mid I^i) p(\boldsymbol{Y}^g_{1:N_g} \mid I^g). \tag{1}$$

In our work, the transformation matrix is represented by

$$\boldsymbol{H}(\boldsymbol{x}) = \begin{pmatrix} s_x \cos(\theta) & -\sin(\theta) & t_x \\ \sin(\theta) & s_y \cos(\theta) & t_y \\ 0 & 0 & 1 \end{pmatrix}. \tag{2}$$

To determine $\boldsymbol{H}$, we need to compute the $5D$ parameter vector $\boldsymbol{x} = (s_x, s_y, \theta, t_x, t_y)$ with rotation angle θ, scaling s_x, s_y, and translation t_x, t_y. As similarity metric between corresponding images we suggest using a combination

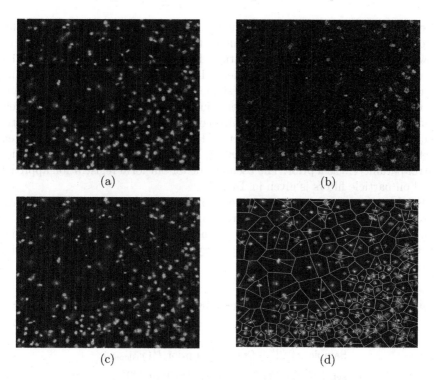

(a)   (b)

(c)   (d)

Fig. 5. Results of our method for real data (image section): (a) Immunostaining image, (b) gene expression image, (c) overlay of registered images, (d) computed cell regions (red crosses: detected center points of nuclei in immunostaining image using the spot-enhancing filter [11], blue points: detected spots in gene expression image, yellow lines: computed cell regions). (Color figure online)

of mutual information (MI) for the image intensities and the point set distance. The metric is maximized to align the multi-modal images.

Let $\mathrm{MI}\left(I^i, \boldsymbol{H}(\boldsymbol{x})I^g\right)$ be the mutual information of I^i and $\boldsymbol{H}(\boldsymbol{x})I^g$, and $\mathrm{D}(\boldsymbol{Y}^i, \boldsymbol{H}(\boldsymbol{x})\boldsymbol{Y}^g)$ be the sum of distances to closest points (nearest neighbors) between points from $\boldsymbol{Y}^i$ and $\boldsymbol{H}(\boldsymbol{x})\boldsymbol{Y}^g$. We search the optimal parameter vector $\boldsymbol{x}^*$ by maximizing the following likelihood function

$$\arg\max_{\boldsymbol{x}} p(\mathrm{MI}(I^i, \boldsymbol{H}(\boldsymbol{x})I^g))p(\mathrm{D}(\boldsymbol{Y}^i, \boldsymbol{H}(\boldsymbol{x})\boldsymbol{Y}^g)) =$$

$$\arg\max_{\boldsymbol{x}} \exp\{\frac{\mathrm{MI}(I^i, \boldsymbol{H}(\boldsymbol{x})\boldsymbol{Y}^g))}{2\sigma_{MI}^2}\}\exp\{\frac{\mathrm{D}(\boldsymbol{Y}^i, \boldsymbol{H}(\boldsymbol{x})\boldsymbol{Y}^g))}{(-1) * 2\sigma_D^2}\}, \quad (3)$$

where σ_{MI} is the standard deviation of MI and σ_D is the standard deviation of the point set distance. Since $\mathrm{MI}(r) \geq 0$ and $\mathrm{D}(r) \geq 0$, the first term and the second term in Eq. (3) have opposite monotonicity.

We could naively search the whole parameter space to find the maximum likelihood to achieve the best alignment between the two images. However, this is time consuming. In our framework, we use a two-step global-to-local strategy for efficient registration. For global registration, we apply the CPD algorithm introduced in [13], and coarsely estimate the transformation matrix. Figure 4 shows the result after global registration. In order to reduce the computation time, a grid average downsampling method is applied in our framework. Points within the same box are merged to a single point in the output. Then, we split the whole image into 1000×1000 pixels squares and apply our novel joint likelihood metric for local registration, which combines mutual information and the point set distance in the similarity metric. Here, we suggest using particle filters to efficiently determine the optimal x^* in Eq. (3), given global transformation matrix parameters as a prior. The pseudocode for our local registration approach based on particle filters is given in Table 1.

Furthermore, we can estimate the elements of the assignment matrix $\omega_{n_g}^{n_c}$ representing the strength of gene expression for each gene expression spot n_g at each cell n_c for given observations $Y_{n_c}^i$ and $Y_{n_g}^g$. We use Voronoi tessellation [14] to identify cell regions (rough boundary of a cell) to assign gene expression spots to cells.

Table 1. Pseudocode for our local registration approach based on particle filters.

At $t = 0$
Sample $x_i^{t=0}\big|_{i=1}^n$ from initial prior $P(x_{\text{Global}})$
set $(\pi_i^{t=0}, x_i^{t=0})\big|_{i=1}^n$ with $\pi_i^{t=0} = P(x_i^{t=0})$
For $t = 1$ to N
    For $i = 1$ to n
        Sample $x_i^t \sim P(x_i^t \mid x_i^{t-1})$
        Compute error e_i^t
        Evaluate $\pi_i^t = P(e_i^t \mid x_i^t)$
    end
    Normalize weights $\pi_i^t = \frac{\pi_i^t}{\sum_i \pi_i^t}$
    Set new $(\pi_i^t)\big|_{i=1}^n$
end

3   Experimental Results

We compared our registration framework with the state-of-the-art registration approach [10] using synthetic as well as real immunostaining images and gene expression images. For synthetic data, we generated immunostaining images (500×500 pixels) using SimuCell [15] and randomly determined transformations as ground truth (GT) transformations. For the real data of the mouse brain (Stereo-seq [2], 120.250×61.250 pixels, pixel size $0.65 \times 0.65 \,\mu m^2$), the GT transformation was obtained by manual alignment.

The target registration error (TRE) is used to quantify the registration result. The TRE is the average distance between the positions determined by the computed transformation parameters and the positions using the GT parameters. We employed M control point pairs, which were selected randomly and uniformly, to compute the TRE and determined the average position error in the x and y directions of the corresponding points. Let $H(x^*)$ be the computed transformation matrix and $p_q, q \in \{1, \cdots, M\}$, the manually selected points, then the TRE is computed by

$$TRE_x = \frac{1}{M} \sum_{q=1}^{M} d_x \left(p_q^i, H(x^*)p_q^g\right)$$

$$TRE_y = \frac{1}{M} \sum_{q=1}^{M} d_y \left(p_q^i, H(x^*)p_q^g\right)$$

(4)

where d_x, d_y denote the distance between two corresponding points in x and y direction. p_q^i, p_q^g are two corresponding points in the immunostaining image and the gene expression image. For our experiment, we chose 20 corresponding points manually as control point pairs.

In our registration approach, we used 50 random samples and 20 time steps for the particle filters to determine the transformation matrix in Eq. (2).

Table 2. Target registration error for synthetic images.

Image	#Cells	Method [10]		Ours	
		TRE_x	TRE_y	TRE_x	TRE_y
1	5	8.32	15.65	2.27	9.78
2	20	15.14	17.37	2.88	13.37
3	80	6.84	20.74	3.29	15.38
4	320	12.89	23.84	5.17	17.16
Average	106	10.80	19.40	3.40	13.92

Table 3. Target registration error for real images.

Images	#Cells	Method [10]		Ours	
		TRE_x	TRE_y	TRE_x	TRE_y
1	256	22.68	23.17	12.21	16.56
2	153	18.14	15.37	8.44	15.42
3	175	22.84	27.74	10.29	13.38
4	208	23.89	22.84	10.17	14.16
Average	198	21.89	22.28	10.28	14.88

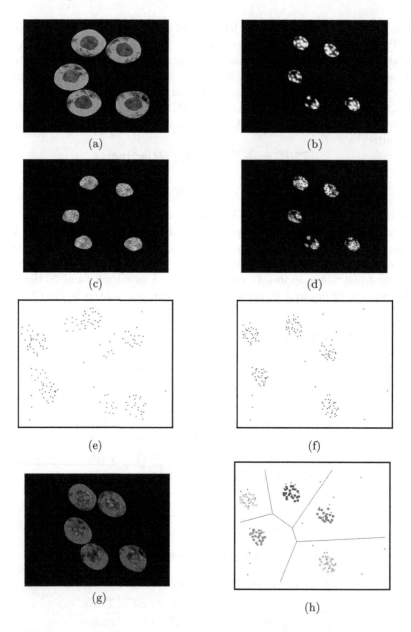

Fig. 6. Results of our method for synthetic data: (a) Immunostaining image (green region: cytoplasm), (b) gene expression image, (c) detected spots in immunostaining image (red), (d) detected spots in gene expression image (blue), (e) overlay of detected spots in both images before registration (red: detected spots in immunostaining image, blue: detected spots in gene expression image), (f) overlay of detected spots in both images after registration, (g) overlay of registered immunostaining image and gene expression image, (h) computed cell regions by Voronoi tesselation (each cell is represented by a different color). (Color figure online)

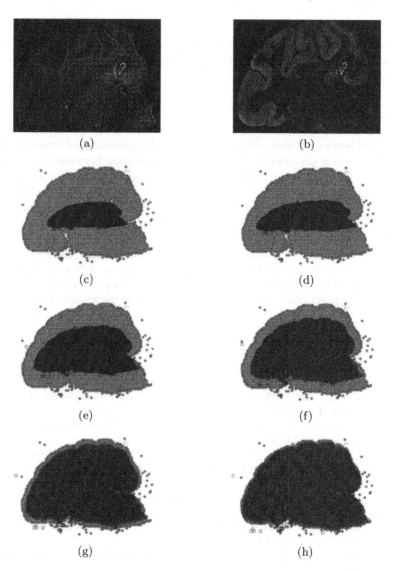

Fig. 7. Global registration process of our method for real data of the mouse brain: (a) Immunostaining image, (b) gene expression image, (c) overlay of registered downsampled point set (red denotes detected spots in immunostaining image, blue denotes detected spots in gene expression image), (d) first step optimization result, (e) second step optimization result, (f) third step optimization result, (g) fourth step optimization result, (h) fifth step optimization result. (Color figure online)

Table 2 and Table 3 provide the TRE of our registration approach and the method in [10] for 4 pairs of synthetic images and 4 pairs of real images. For all image pairs, the TRE of our approach is much lower than that of method

[10]. Thus, our approach is much more accurate than the previous method for the considered challenging data. Further, the computational performance of our approach is about 3 times faster than the previous method [10]. Example results are provided in Fig. 5, Fig. 6, and Fig. 7.

4   Conclusions

We have presented a framework for multi-modal registration of transcriptomics image data. Our approach determines the transformation between immunostaining images and gene expression images. The method jointly exploits intensity information and image features. Our approach has been successfully applied to synthetic data and real spatial transcriptomics data of the mouse brain, and we found that our approach yields better results than a state-of-the-art method.

Acknowledgements. This work was supported by BGI Research and the Institute of Neuroscience (ION) of the Chinese Academy of Sciences. The authors gratefully acknowledge Prof. Mu-Ming Poo, Qing Xie, and Ao Chen for providing the mouse brain spatial transcriptomics data and many helpful discussions during the development.

References

1. Rao, A., Barkley, D., França, G.S., Yanai, I.: Exploring tissue architecture using spatial transcriptomics. Nature **596**(7871), 211–220 (2021)
2. Chen, A., et al.: Large field of view-spatially resolved transcriptomics at nanoscale resolution. bioRxiv (2021)
3. Cho, C.-S., et al.: Microscopic examination of spatial transcriptome using SEQ-scope. Cell **184**(13), 3559–3572 (2021)
4. Yoosuf, N., Navarro, J.F., Salmén, F., Ståhl, P.L., Daub, C.O.: Identification and transfer of spatial transcriptomics signatures for cancer diagnosis. Breast Cancer Res. **22**(1), 1–10 (2020)
5. Saiselet, M.: Transcriptional output, cell-type densities, and normalization in spatial transcriptomics. J. Mol. Cell Biol. **12**(11), 906–908 (2020)
6. Chen, W.-T., et al.: Spatial transcriptomics and in situ sequencing to study alzheimer's disease. Cell **182**(4), 976–991 (2020)
7. Rohr, K.: Landmark-Based Image Analysis. Springer, Dordrecht (2001). https://doi.org/10.1007/978-94-015-9787-6
8. Goshtasby, A.A.: 2-D and 3-D Image Registration: For Medical Remote Sensing, and Industrial Applications. Wiley (2005)
9. Islam, K.T., Wijewickrema, S., O'Leary, S.: A deep learning based framework for the registration of three dimensional multi-modal medical images of the head. Sci. Rep. **11**(1), 1860 (2021)
10. Chen, R., Das, A.B., Varshney, L.R.: Registration for image-based transcriptomics: parametric signal features and multivariate information measures. In: Proceedings of the 2019 53rd Annual Conference on Information Sciences and Systems (CISS), pp. 1–6. IEEE (2019)
11. Sage, D., Neumann, F.R., Hediger, F., Gasser, S.M., Unser, M.: Automatic tracking of individual fluorescence particles: application to the study of chromosome dynamics. IEEE Trans. Image Process. **14**(9), 1372–1383 (2005)

12. Qiang, Y., Lee, J.Y., Bartenschlager, R., Rohr, K.: Colocalization analysis and particle tracking in multi-channel fluorescence microscopy images. In: Proceedings of the ISBI 2017, pp. 646–649. IEEE (2017)
13. Myronenko, A., Song, X.: Point set registration: coherent point drift. IEEE Trans. Pattern Anal. Mach. Intell. **32**(12), 2262–2275 (2010)
14. Bock, M., Tyagi, A.K., Kreft, J.-U., Alt, W.: Generalized Voronoi tessellation as a model of two-dimensional cell tissue dynamics. Bull. Math. Biol. **72**(7), 1696–1731 (2010)
15. Rajaram, S., Pavie, B., Hac, N.E., Altschuler, S.J., Wu, L.F.: SimuCell: a flexible framework for creating synthetic microscopy images. Nat. Meth. **9**(7), 634–635 (2012)

Extracting and Classifying Salient Fields of View from Microscopy Slides of Tuberculosis Bacteria

Marios Zachariou[1]([✉]), Ognjen Arandjelović[1], Evelin Dombay[2], Wilber Sabiiti[2], Bariki Mtafya[3], and Derek Sloan[2]

[1] School of Computer Science, St Andrews KY16 9SX, Scotland
marios.zachariou@hotmail.com
[2] School of Medicine, St Andrews KY16 9TF, Scotland
[3] Mbeya Medical Research Center, Mbeya, Tanzania

Abstract. Tuberculosis is one of the most serious infectious diseases, and its treatment is highly dependent on early detection. Microscopy-based analysis of sputum images for bacilli identification is a common technique used for both diagnosis and treatment monitoring. However, it a challenging process since sputum analysis requires time and highly trained experts to avoid potentially fatal mistakes. Capturing fields of view (FOVs) from high resolution whole slide images is a laborious procedure, since they are manually localized and then examined to determine the presence of bacteria. In the present paper we propose a method that automates the process, thus greatly reducing the amount of human labour. In particular, we (i) describe an image processing based method for the extraction of a FOV representation which emphasises salient, bacterial content, while suppressing confounding visual information, and (ii) introduce a novel deep learning based architecture which learns from coarsely labelled FOV images and the corresponding binary masks, and then classifies novel FOV images as salient (bacteria containing) or not. Using a real-world data corpus, the proposed method is shown to outperform 12 state of the art methods in the literature, achieving (i) an approximately 10% lower overall error rate than the next best model and (ii) perfect sensitivity (7% higher than the next best model).

Keywords: Whole slide images · Fluorescence microscopy · Image processing · Artificial intelligence · Medicine · Infection · Respiratory system

1   Introduction

Tuberculosis (TB) is the biggest infectious disease-related cause of mortality globally [10]. *Mycobacterium tuberculosis* (Mtb) is the causative bacterium of TB, spread by droplet and aerosol, with up to 85% of cases affecting the lungs [38]. Other organs or tissues, such as the brain, kidneys, bone, and skin, can be infected by these pathogens. The present work focuses on microscopy

© Springer Nature Switzerland AG 2022
M. El Yacoubi et al. (Eds.): ICPRAI 2022, LNCS 13363, pp. 146–157, 2022.
https://doi.org/10.1007/978-3-031-09037-0_13

images for identifying Mtb bacilli, with an emphasis on pulmonary tuberculosis. According to the WHO, up to 2 billion people worldwide have Mtb bacteria in their bodies, with up to 10 million instances of active illness and 2 million deaths every year [38]. Since the 1940s, TB was treatable, but things began to deteriorate with the advent of Drug Resistant TB variations such as Multi Drug Resistant, eXtensive Drug Resistant, and Total Drug Resistant forms of the bacterium [12]. The largest burden of morbidity and death from tuberculosis occurs in poor and middle-income nations, where healthcare resources are limited [30]. Early TB testing improves patient chances for treatment and recovery while also assisting in the prevention of disease spread, and lowering the probability of drug resistant pathogen emergence [7,20,38].

Sputum smear microscopy has traditionally been the primary method for diagnosing tuberculosis. Sputum samples from symptomatic individuals are heat-fixed onto slides and stained using laboratory techniques that identify acid-fast bacteria (AFB) like Mtb cells. For light microscopy (typically at ×1000 magnification), the older Ziehl-Neelsen treatment stains AFB red on a blue background, but newer Auramine-based protocols stain it yellow-green against a black background for fluorescence microscopy (usually at ×400 magnification). Semi-quantitative grading methods have been created to measure the bacterial burden in a patient's lungs. The findings of sputum smear microscopy are often described as 'negative', 'scanty', '1+', '2+', or '3+' [34], in ascending order of disease severity.

1.1 Importance of Microscopy

Many centres throughout the globe have switched their attention away from smear microscopy and towards new tools (such as the Xpert MTB/RIF test) for TB diagnosis in recent years [17]. Sputum smear gradings, on the other hand, remain effective for triaging disease severity and prognosis, with implications for therapeutic individualisation [34] and treatment response where new assays are not currently suggested [38].

Smear microscopy provides data considerably faster than waiting for Mtb to develop in culture in clinical microbiology practice [31]. When properly done, it has a high specificity (99%) for detecting Mtb cells [34]. Smear microscopy has become more sensitive since switching from classic Ziehl-Neelsen to fluorescent Auramine-based microscopy (from 0.34–0.94 to 0.52–0.97 according to one systematic review) [3,32]. Although microscopy laboratory materials are typically affordable, the method is time-consuming, which has an impact on laboratory staffing costs. The large ranges of diagnostic sensitivity reported for TB smear microscopy also reflect the complexity and subjectivity of the process.

Disadvantages of Microscopy and Motivation for Computer Based Automatic Detection. There are obstacles to using microscopy effectively for clinical patient treatment and scholarly research on Mtb. As a microscopist, maintaining a high level of skill necessitates a consistent commitment of time. To stay proficient, practitioners should study at least 25 slides every day according to general guidelines [22]. Each slide is divided into small regions that are examined sequentially, with human error (e.g. due to weariness) reducing the specificity and sensitivity of analysis [25]. Some slides are also difficult to interpret because AFB can exhibit unusual appearance or because non-bacterial components (artefacts) inside the sputum matrix resemble Mtb cells. A promising direction of addressing these challenges lies in the removal of the human from the loop, that is by employing modern artificial intelligence approaches [36].

2   Related Work

To the best of our knowledge, there is no published work that is specific to the collecting of enlarged FOV images containing probable microorganisms. Most datasets used in tuberculosis research comprise images that have been manually magnified and cropped by a microbiologist specialist.

The work of Forero *et al.* [6] was one of the earliest attempts at the use of automatic methods for the analysis of fluorescence microscopy slides with Mtb bacteria. The authors' primary objective was to develop a diagnostic tool, and they used autofocus functions to crop FOVs from microscopic slides. Autofocus was accomplished by a two-pass algorithm that determines whether or not a specific area is void of bacterial content before bringing the image into focus [18]. The initial run of the algorithm analyses slides at three z-axis points to assess if there is sufficient variance between them to signal the presence of salient content in the field. As the authors note, Mtb bacteria occupy extremely small areas of the image, i.e. most of the image is taken up by the background, and their experiments demonstrate that a narrow scanning window (256×256 pixels) must be used for accurate FOV localization. Using auramine stained slides, out of the four focusing methods examined by the authors, two, namely the wave and auto-correlation based ones, produced promising results.

A more recent attempt to make use of autofocus functions is that of Zhai *et al.* [41]. The primary distinction between theirs and previous work lies in the use of conventional rather than fluorescent microscopy. Amongst others, a notable difference as compared with the approach introduced in the present paper lies in the scanning process. In particular, Zhai *et al.* employ a row-wise scanning strategy whereas herein we proceed in a spiral manner. The authors employed three different autofocus measurement, namely the sum of gray-level differences, the Laplacian, and the Tenengrad function with the Sobel operator, and found that the latter outperforms the former two. Nevertheless, the reported empirical accuracy of the method is much lower than that of other methods in the literature that perform diagnosis without collecting FOVs [19,24,37].

Kant and Srivastava's work processes entire slides in a bottom-up manner, that is by aggregating information extracted from small patches [12]. They used a five-layer patch-wise classifier to load each tile from a microscopic slide and a 20×20 pixel window which moves through the FOV to assess the presence of germs. Although the authors claim 99.8% accuracy, this number is rather misleading. The reason stems from the observation that the vast majority of the area of a microscopic slide is occupied by the background, resulting in high accuracy owing to accurate background classification (i.e. in effect, false negative errors are deprioritized). Indeed, when sensitivity and specificity are considered, the reported rates of 83.8% and 67.6% respectively are comparable to or *worse* than those of other methods discussed in the present paper.

3   Proposed Method

We begin our process of cropping the slide by putting each tile into memory (as the entire slide is too big ≈ 19 GB) and cropping 200×400 pixel patches from each tile. Our slides include a total of 2700 tiles which are anisotropically scaled by a factor of 4.83 in the x direction and 3.24 in the y direction, so as to match FOVs created manually by a specialist.

3.1   Discrimination Enhanced Representation Extraction

A human specialist detects Mtb microorganisms by inspecting the green channel of a FOV. The more acid fast a bacterium is, the more prominent is its appearance [5]. Additionally, Mtb bacteria that store non-polar lipids intracellularly are classified as lipid-rich (LR) cells, as opposed to lipid-poor (LP) cells. It is hypothesised that resistant LR bacteria play a critical role in patient relapse [21,27]. As a result, their acid resistance begins to deteriorate, and they become less visible in the green channel. Fortunately, in this case they become more apparent in the red channel [8,23] using Nile red staining as opposed to Auramine-O. While the evidence that the presence of LR Mtb bacteria indeed does predict poor treatment outcome is still insufficiently strong, there are numerous studies on non-polar lipids in Mtb bacteria and Nile red staining which point in this direction [2,4,13,14]. Thus, both the red (Nile red staining) and the green (Auramine-O) channel remain of relative importance in both research and clinical terms.

Additionally, the ability to generate high-quality microscopic images is contingent upon the quality of clinical samples collected and the details of smear preparation and staining processes. Thick smears from highly mucous samples can have an excessive amount of background staining, which makes bacteria harder to localize. To increase the robustness of our method, as well as to reduce the complexity of the learning task, we propose a pre-processing stage that enhances image content of interest while at the same time suppressing confounding information e.g. in the form of staining artefacts [39].

Considering that the bacteria of interest form largely straight, thin, and elongated structures, we employ a ridge detector [1]. In particular, we make use of the Hessian matrix approximation (at the scale of 2×2 pixels in the present work). Its eigendecomposition allows for a differentiation between different kinds of local image behaviour leading to a straightforward process of distinguishing between blob-like structures, uniform regions, and elongated structures of interest herein [15]. Considering that bacilli form elongated structures, we are interested in the loci which exhibit significant change in one principal direction (perpendicular to a bacterium) and little change in the other (along a bacterium), and these can be readily identified using the corresponding Hessian matrix eigenvalues. In particular, to create an enhanced image (in the context of our end goal), each pixel in the original image is replaced with the absolute value of the lower magnitude value of the Hessian eigenvalue computed at the locus. The at first sight appealing alternatives which take into account both eigenvalues, such as the use of the ratio of the two eigenvalues, were found unsuitable due to an increase in noise and the dynamic range.

3.2   The Learning

Our end goal is to classify cropped FOVs as positive or negative for Mtb microorganisms. By doing so, that is by filtering out uninteresting FOVs, the burden of the manual workload required from a lab worker is dramatically reduced. In addition, the aforementioned classification can also be used to simplify and improve further automatic processing, e.g. diagnostic inference or bacterial culture analysis.

Proposed Model. Evidence from previous work on non-automatic smear analysis, that is analysis performed by humans, suggests that for the detection of Mtb bacteria the use of both texture and shape information is superior to the use of either of the two in isolation [6,29,37]. Herein we introduce a network that reflects this finding by employing two encoders to generate two separate feature maps. One of these is trained on the discrimination enhanced representation of FOVs introduced in Sect. 3.1, while the other is trained on the binary masks corresponding to the FOVs, which distinguish between the objects of interest (bacteria) and the uninteresting content (background and artefacts). The encoder outputs are concatenated to generate the input matrix for another smaller network ($16 \times 32 \times 512$); see Fig. 1. The weights of the two encoders are frozen, and no gradient computation is done during the training of the smaller network. As a result, the smaller network makes an effort to infer the probability distribution from the two encoders which independently infer texture and shape. To train the two encoders, a further layer with adaptive max pooling and a linear layer leading to a single output unit with a sigmoid activation function were added. The same environmental and hyper-parameters as previously employed were utilized to train the two encoders and the smaller network.

4   Evaluation

4.1   Data

The data used in the present work consists of microscopic slides captured from a clinical cohort study in Mbeya, Tanzania. Between February 2017 and March 2018, 46 persons with sputum smear positive pulmonary tuberculosis (40 newly

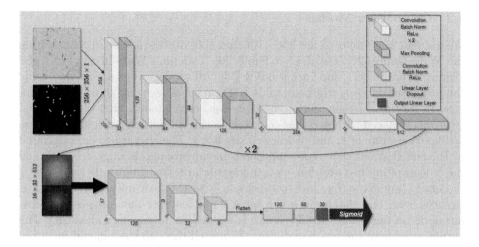

Fig. 1. Diagram of information flow through the architecture proposed in the present paper: following an encoding process, information passes through a convolutional network, leading to the eventual inference of the bacterial presence in a FOV.

diagnosed and 6 previously diagnosed) were recruited and tracked until the conclusion of a 6-month course of conventional tuberculosis therapy. Sputum samples were taken pre-treatment and at the end of months 2, 4, and 6 of therapy. Smears on microscope slides were made from the sputum samples. The slides were dyed using normal Auramine-O procedures, and the smears were systematically scanned through a fluorescein isothiocyanate filter using a Leica DMLB epifluorescence microscope at ×1000 magnification by an experienced microscopist. A digital camera was used to capture and save all fields having auramine-stained, yellow-green AFB. A total of 230 slides were inspected, and for each AFB positive slide 30 images were created.

The training dataset for this experiment included 46 patients with around 150 FOV images per patient from diagnosis through therapy completion. Around 800 FOVs were randomly chosen from the Tanzanian corpus. To verify that the automated image analysis method being developed is not affected by changes in the morphology of Mtb cells during or after TB therapy, images were picked across all time periods of sample collection. These images were re-examined by a microscopist who was not involved in the original experiment. Each FOV was then assessed as positive or negative by a microscopy specialist.

Two additional slides from a separate facility and technician were used to evaluate our method. The test set consists of 130 FOVs extracted from the slides using the approach proposed in the present paper, chosen using balanced random sampling that ensures that the set is balanced in terms of positive and negative examples.

4.2   Competitor Models

We compare the proposed method with a number of state of the art models from the VGG family [26], the ResNet family [9] (including Wide-Resnet [40]), the Densenet family [11], and InceptionV3 [33]. All models were pre-trained using the ImageNet dataset, which contains 1000 target classes and three input channels. Regardless of their initial configuration, each model's first convolutional layer was replaced with one that comprises a single input channel, kernel of size 3×3, stride value of 1, and padding of size 3×3. The alterations are motivated by the fact that our slide representation is monochrome (i.e. single channel) and the objects of interest are thin, elongated structures that frequently appear near the image boundary. The last modification is to the final linear layer, which is replaced with one that retains the same input features but has just one output node (in InceptionV3, this change is applied to its auxiliary classifier). The output weights of the last linear layer are passed through the sigmoid function.

4.3   Hyper-parameter Learning

To ensure a fair comparison, all models, including the proposed one, were trained using the same set of hyper-parameters. To begin, the batch size was chosen to be 16 in order to achieve a balance between generalization, accuracy, and computing speed. Adam optimizer with the values of the β parameters (that is, the initial decay rates used when estimating the first and second moments of the gradient) equal to 0.50 and 0.99 was used. For the training process, following evidence from prior research [28], the base and maximum learning rates were set to 0.00001 and 0.0004, respectively, and the learning scheduler used was the novel circular scheduler with a step size equal to five times the size of the dataset (which varies according to batch size). Finally, binary cross entropy was used as the loss function; see Fig. 2.

4.4   Results and Discussion

A microbiological specialist classified 73 of the 130 FOV images in our test set as positive and 57 as negative. The same expert manually created binary masks corresponding to all of the 130 FOVs, which were treated as the ground truth. In order to facilitate a comprehensive and nuanced comparison between models [35], we assess performance using a number of metrics, namely overall accuracy, recall (sensitivity) and precision (specificity), receiver operating characteristics (ROC), and the area under the ROC curve (AUC).

A summary of our experimental results is shown in Table 1. To start with, consider the overall performance metric in the form of the classification error (in the rightmost column of the table) and observe that the proposed method achieved the best performance of all 13 methods compared. The error rate of the next best model, namely ResNet50, is more than 11% greater. InceptionV3 and the best DenseNet family model, DenseNet201, performed next best (23% higher error rate than the proposed model). While there is significant variation

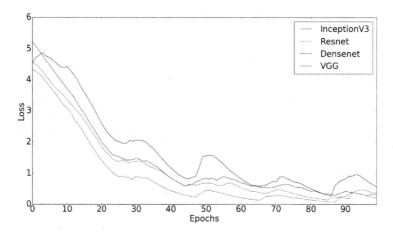

Fig. 2. With the exception of VGG family, all models converge around the 65th epoch and exhibit the same overall learning behaviour. The poor performance of the VGG family suggests that the present task requires greater architectural sophistication than that achieved by merely stacking convolutional layers.

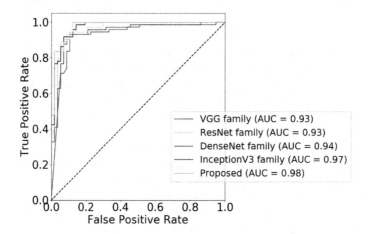

Fig. 3. Comparison of ROC curves and the areas under the curves, both show that the proposed solution outperforms the current state of the art. For the sake of clarity, each model family is illustrated using the average performance of its evaluated models.

between different specific models within all families, generally speaking ResNet performed better than DenseNet, and VGG networks fared the worst (45–101% higher error rate than the proposed model).

A more nuanced insight into the behaviour of different models can be gained by examining the specific error types (in columns 3 and 5 of Table 1; also see Fig. 3). Importantly, note that the proposed method performed best in terms of the false positive error rate – indeed, it made no incorrect positive calls at all. This is extremely important in this context for reasons already noted in Sect. 2,

Table 1. Summary of results. All VGG models were trained using batch normalization (BN). The best performing model with respect to each statistic is shown in bold.

Model name	True +ve	False +ve	True −ve	False −ve	Error rate
VGG11 (w/ BN)	68	5	49	8	0.100
VGG13 (w/ BN)	67	6	47	10	0.123
VGG16 (w/ BN)	67	6	46	11	0.131
VGG19 (w/ BN)	63	10	50	7	0.131
ResNet18	65	8	51	6	0.108
ResNet34	66	7	51	6	0.100
ResNet50	68	5	**52**	**5**	0.077
ResNet50-Wide	68	5	49	8	0.100
DenseNet121	66	7	51	6	0.100
DenseNet169	67	6	45	12	0.139
DenseNet201	68	5	51	6	0.085
InceptionV3	67	6	**52**	**5**	0.085
Proposed	**73**	**0**	48	9	**0.069**

to wit the vast majority of FOVs do not contain bacteria and it is of paramount importance that these are filtered out as a means of reducing expert human labour thereafter. No other method comes close to ours, with DenseNet201, ResNet50, ResNet50-Wide, and VGG11 erring in approximately 7% of the cases. On the other hand, the proposed method was not superior in terms of the false positive rate. In the context of this metric InceptionV3 and ResNet50 performed best, achieving the error rate of approximately 9%. However, here it is important to observe the asymmetry of the importance of type I and type II errors on the task at hand [16]. As we noted earlier, the former are of primary importance as low type I error rate means that the vast amount of irrelevant information is not passed on further for human analysis which is where the practical bottleneck lies. On the other hand, type II errors, while of course undesirable (as any error is), are far less important, as clinically salient information about a bacterial culture can be readily derived from only a sample of bacteria, without there being a need for the entirety of the culture to be examined. Of course, this is predicated on the sample being representative which is why the type II error rate must not be excessively high. As witnessed by our results in Table 1 this is not a major challenge here as none of the methods compared produced a high number of false negatives.

5   Conclusion

Although sputum smear microscopy is being phased out in many settings in favour of Xpert MTB/RIF and other molecular tests, it still serves a function in some aspects of disease severity assessment and therapy monitoring. Since microscopic examination of Mtb cells is critical as a research tool, work on the development of improved automated tools for standardising and expediting image analysis remains important. To this end, in this paper we described a novel solution based on a newly crafted deep learning based architecture tailored specifically for the task, which learns from coarsely labelled FOV images and the corresponding binary masks, and then classifies novel FOV images as bacteria containing or not. The fully automated nature of the model and its empirically evidenced vanishing false positive rate, demonstrate the potential of the proposed method to significantly reduce human expert labour.

Acknowledgements. We will like to express our appreciation to the McKenzie Institute for providing the necessary funding to complete this work.

References

1. Arandjelović, O., Cipolla, R.: A new look at filtering techniques for illumination invariance in automatic face recognition, pp. 449–454 (2006)
2. Baron, V.O., et al.: Label-free optical vibrational spectroscopy to detect the metabolic state of M. tuberculosis cells at the site of disease. Sci. Rep. **7**(1), 1–9 (2017)
3. Costa Filho, C.F.F., Costa, M.G.F., Júnior, A.K.: Autofocus functions for tuberculosis diagnosis with conventional sputum smear microscopy. In: Current Microscopy Contributions to Advances in Science and Technology, pp. 13–20 (2012)
4. Daniel, J., Kapoor, N., Sirakova, T., Sinha, R., Kolattukudy, P.: The perilipin-like PPE15 protein in Mycobacterium tuberculosis is required for triacylglycerol accumulation under dormancy-inducing conditions. Mol. Microbiol. **101**(5), 784–794 (2016)
5. Deb, C., et al.: A novel in vitro multiple-stress dormancy model for mycobacterium tuberculosis generates a lipid-loaded, drug-tolerant, dormant pathogen. PLoS ONE **4**(6), e6077 (2009)
6. Forero, M.G., Sroubek, F., Cristóbal, G.: Identification of tuberculosis bacteria based on shape and color. Real-Time Imaging **10**(4), 251–262 (2004)
7. Gele, A.A., Bjune, G., Abebe, F.: Pastoralism and delay in diagnosis of TB in Ethiopia. BMC Public Health **9**(1), 1–7 (2009)
8. Greenspan, P., Fowler, S.D.: Spectrofluorometric studies of the lipid probe, nile red. J. Lipid Res. **26**(7), 781–789 (1985)
9. He, D., Xia, Y., Qin, T., Wang, L., Yu, N., Liu, T.Y., Ma, W.Y.: Dual learning for machine translation. Adv. Neural Inf. Process. Syst. **29**, 820–828 (2016)
10. Holmes, C.B., Hausler, H., Nunn, P.: A review of sex differences in the epidemiology of tuberculosis. Int. J. Tuberc. Lung Dis. **2**(2), 96–104 (1998)
11. Huang, G., Liu, Z., Van Der Maaten, L., Weinberger, K.Q.: Densely connected convolutional networks. In: IEEE Conference on Computer Vision and Pattern Recognition, pp. 4700–4708 (2017)
12. Kant, S., Srivastava, M.M.: Towards automated tuberculosis detection using deep learning. In: IEEE Symposium Series on Computational Intelligence, pp. 1250–1253 (2019)

13. Kayigire, X.A., Friedrich, S.O., van der Merwe, L., Donald, P.R., Diacon, A.H.: Simultaneous staining of sputum smears for acid-fast and lipid-containing Myobacterium tuberculosis can enhance the clinical evaluation of antituberculosis treatments. Tuberculosis **95**(6), 770–779 (2015)

14. Kennedy, J.A., Baron, V., Hammond, R.J.H., Sloan, D.J., Gillespie, S.H.: Centrifugation and decontamination procedures selectively impair recovery of important populations in Mycobacterium smegmatis. Tuberculosis **112**, 79–82 (2018)

15. Kumar, N.C.S., Radhika, Y.: Optimized maximum principal curvatures based segmentation of blood vessels from retinal images. Biomed. Res. **30**(2) (2019)

16. Lomacenkova, A., Arandjelović, O.: Whole slide pathology image patch based deep classification: an investigation of the effects of the latent autoencoder representation and the loss function form. In: Proceedings of IEEE International Conference on Biomedical and Health Informatics (2021). https://doi.org/10.1109/BHI50953.2021.9508577

17. Mehta, P.K., Raj, A., Singh, N., Khuller, G.K.: Diagnosis of extrapulmonary tuberculosis by PCR. FEMS Immunol. Med. Microbiol. **66**(1), 20–36 (2012)

18. Merchant, F.A., Castleman, K.R.: Computer-assisted microscopy. In: The Essential Guide to Image Processing, pp. 777–831 (2009)

19. Panicker, R.O., Kalmady, K.S., Rajan, J., Sabu, M.K.: Automatic detection of tuberculosis bacilli from microscopic sputum smear images using deep learning methods. Biocybernetics Biomed. Eng. **38**(3), 691–699 (2018)

20. Peter, J.G., van Zyl-Smit, R.N., Denkinger, C.M., Pai, M.: Diagnosis of TB: state of the art. Eur. Respir. Monograph **58**, 123–143 (2012)

21. Phillips, P.P.J., et al.: Limited role of culture conversion for decision-making in individual patient care and for advancing novel regimens to confirmatory clinical trials. BMC Med. **14**(1), 1–11 (2016)

22. Rieder, H.L., et al.: Priorities for Tuberculosis Bacteriology Services in Low-Income Countries. International Union Against Tuberculosis and Lung Disease (2007)

23. Rumin, J., Bonnefond, H., Saint-Jean, B., Rouxel, C., Sciandra, A., Bernard, O., Cadoret, J.P., Bougaran, G.: The use of fluorescent Nile red and BODIPY for lipid measurement in microalgae. Biotechnol. Biofuels **8**(1), 1–16 (2015)

24. Sadaphal, P., Rao, J., Comstock, G.W., Beg, M.F.: Image processing techniques for identifying Mycobacterium tuberculosis in Ziehl-Neelsen stains. Int. J. Tuberc. Lung Dis. **12**(5), 579–582 (2008)

25. Shea, Y.R., et al.: High sensitivity and specificity of acid-fast microscopy for diagnosis of pulmonary tuberculosis in an African population with a high prevalence of human immunodeficiency virus. J. Clin. Microbiol. **47**(5), 1553–1555 (2009)

26. Simonyan, K., Zisserman, A.: Very deep convolutional networks for large-scale image recognition. arXiv preprint arXiv:1409.1556 (2014)

27. Sloan, D.J., et al.: Pharmacodynamic modeling of bacillary elimination rates and detection of bacterial lipid bodies in sputum to predict and understand outcomes in treatment of pulmonary tuberculosis. Clin. Infect. Dis. **61**(1), 1–8 (2015)

28. Smith, L.N.: Cyclical learning rates for training neural networks. In: IEEE Winter Conference on Applications of Computer Vision, pp. 464–472 (2017)

29. Sotaquira, M., Rueda, L., Narvaez, R.: Detection and quantification of bacilli and clusters present in sputum smear samples: a novel algorithm for pulmonary tuberculosis diagnosis. In: International Conference on Digital Image Processing, pp. 117–121 (2009)

30. Spence, D.P., Hotchkiss, J., Williams, C.S., Davies, P.D.: Tuberculosis and poverty. Br. Med. J. **307**(6907), 759–761 (1993)

31. Steingart, K.R., et al.: A systematic review of commercial serological antibody detection tests for the diagnosis of extrapulmonary tuberculosis. Postgrad. Med. J. **83**(985), 705–712 (2007)
32. Steingart, K.R., et al.: Fluorescence versus conventional sputum smear microscopy for tuberculosis: a systematic review. Lancet Infect. Dis. **9**(6), 570–581 (2006)
33. Szegedy, C., et al.: Going deeper with convolutions. In: IEEE Computer Society Conference on Computer Vision and Pattern Recognition, pp. 1–9 (2015)
34. Toman, K.: Toman's Tuberculosis: Case Detection, Treatment and Monitoring: Questions and Answers. World Health Organization (2004)
35. Valsson, S., Arandjelović, O.: Nuances of interpreting X-ray analysis by deep learning and lessons for reporting experimental findings. Sci **4**(1), 1–13 (2022)
36. Vente, D., Arandjelović, O., Baron, V., Dombay, E., Gillespie, S.: Using machine learning for automatic counting of lipid-rich tuberculosis cells in fluorescence microscopy images. In: Proceedings of AAAI Conference on Artificial Intelligence Workshop on Health Intelligence, pp. 57–68 (2019)
37. Veropoulos, K., Learmonth, G., Campbell, C., Knight, B., Simpson, J.: Automated identification of tubercle bacilli in sputum: a preliminary investigation. Anal. Quant. Cytol. Histol. **21**(4), 277–282 (1999)
38. World Health Organisation: Global Tuberculosis Report. Technical report (2018). https://apps.who.int/iris/bitstream/handle/10665/274453/9789241565646-eng.pdf
39. Zachariou, M., Arandjelović, O., Sloan, S., Sabiiti, W., Mtafya, B.: Tuberculosis bacteria detection and counting in fluorescence microscopy images using a multistage deep learning pipeline. Information **13**(2), 96 (2022)
40. Zagoruyko, S., Komodakis, N.: Wide residual networks. arXiv preprint arXiv:1605.07146 (2016)
41. Zhai, Y., Liu, Y., Zhou, D., Liu, S.: Automatic identification of mycobacterium tuberculosis from ZN-stained sputum smear: algorithm and system design. In: IEEE International Conference on Robotics and Biomimetics, pp. 41–46 (2010)

Segmentation

Deep Learning for Fast Segmentation of E-waste Devices' Inner Parts in a Recycling Scenario

Cristof Rojas$^{(\boxtimes)}$, Antonio Rodríguez-Sánchez⬤, and Erwan Renaudo⬤

Faculty of Mathematics, Computer Science and Physics, University of Innsbruck, 6020 Innsbruck, Austria
cristof.rojas@student.uibk.ac.at,
{antonio.rodriguez-sanchez,erwan.renaudo}@uibk.ac.at

Abstract. Recycling obsolete electronic devices (E-waste) is a dangerous task for human workers. Automated E-waste recycling is an area of great interest but challenging for current robotic applications. We focus on the problem of segmenting inner parts of E-waste devices into manipulable elements. First, we extend a dataset of hard-drive disk (HDD) components with labelled occluded and non-occluded points of view of the parts, in order to increase the diversity and the quality of the learning data with different angles. We then perform an extensive evaluation with three different state-of-the-art models, namely CenterMask, BlendMask and SOLOv2 (including variants) and two types of metrics: the average precision as well as the frame rate. Our results show that instance segmentation using state-of-the-art deep learning methods can precisely detect complex shapes along with their boundaries, as well as being suited for fast tracking of parts in a robotic recycling system.

Keywords: Instance segmentation · Deep learning · Recycling E-waste · Hard-drive disks dataset

1 Introduction

Due to the increasing use of home electronics, the volume of obsolete electronics devices (E-waste) is growing fast, calling for efficient recycling methods. However, existing destructive approaches are problematic: the presence of toxic materials endangers human workers [21]; precious materials (e.g. gold) are lost whereas their extraction from waste is much more efficient than from ore [16]. For these reasons, the automation of E-waste recycling is an important step towards better recycling processes. However, the variety of devices as well as their shape and size makes it tedious to design specialized machines; thus adaptable robotic manipulation is required. The latter requires the recycling robot to have a relevant visual representation of the parts of a device to interact with. Instance segmentation allows to learn these parts and detect not only the object center but also its boundaries. The robot thus gets an estimate of the object shape useful for manipulation.

The state-of-the-art approach to Instance Segmentation is a deep learning *two-stage* pipeline that first, defines the area of interest in the image, then produces labelled object

© Springer Nature Switzerland AG 2022
M. El Yacoubi et al. (Eds.): ICPRAI 2022, LNCS 13363, pp. 161–172, 2022.
https://doi.org/10.1007/978-3-031-09037-0_14

masks [4]. It has been successfully applied to the E-waste use-case [22] in combination with specialized screw and gap detectors. But one important limitation is that two-stage pipelines are slow, as they process the image twice.

We are thus interested in whether *single-stage* pipelines can achieve comparable segmentation results while reaching a sufficient frame rate to be used as a naive part tracking method. In this work, we focus on two key points: investigating a set of deep learning methods that can predict the part of a learned device with state-of-the-art accuracy as well as a "high enough" frame per second rate (FPS); making the learning robust to the object motion resulting from the interaction of the robot on the device. We address the first point by evaluating real-time capable deep learning models and comparing them to the baseline set by Mask R-CNN, as done in [22]. This evaluation is conducted on the extended version of the dataset used in [22], where we added new view angles of the device.

The remaining of this paper is organized as follows: Sect. 2 surveys existing approaches for instance segmentation and object tracking; Sect. 3 presents the extended HDD dataset used in this study as well as the evaluated deep learning models. Section 4 reports the performance of the selected methods trained and tested on the dataset, as well as the recorded inference time.

2   Related Work

Instance Segmentation. In [22], the authors highlight different constraints for the analysis of a disassembly scene: the detection of parts has to be accurate enough to allow manipulation; due to tight assembly, there is a high level of occlusion on the different parts; and there is substantial intra-class variance for specific parts on the device brand, model or the potential damage to the part. Therefore, the authors formulate the problem as an *instance segmentation* problem and state that deep learning methods are the best suited to solve it.

Deep learning methods use Convolutional Neural Networks [6] (CNN) to achieve pixelwise segmentation of images. Mask R-CNN [4] uses a Region Based Convolutional Neural Networks (R-CNN) for predicting segmentation masks for each instance. It is based on a two-stage detector using the *detect-then-segment* approach, thus quite slow and inadequate for applications requiring minimal frame rates.

In the last years, there have been many studies of *single-stage* instance segmentation detection methods:

- **YOLACT++** [1]. Separates instance segmentation into two tasks that run in parallel: generating a set of prototype masks and predicting per-instance mask coefficients. Furthermore, they introduced a faster non-maximum suppression (Fast-NMS) algorithm, and added deformable convolutions in the encoder's backbone network.
- **PolarMask++** [20]. Predicts the contours of objects in polar coordinates. This representation combines instance segmentation (masks) and object detection (bounding boxes) into a single framework. In addition, a Refined Feature Pyramid was introduced.

- **SipMask** [2]. Introduced a spatial preservation module, a pooling mechanism to store the spatial information of an object, which generates a separate set of spatial coefficients for each sub-region within a bounding box.

Based on their AP on the COCO *test-dev* dataset and their inference time, we chose these single-stage models for our use case: CenterMask [9], BlendMask [3] and SOLOv2 [18].

Object Tracking. Most tracking methods focus on tracking of individual instances of cars and pedestrians (e.g. MOT benchmark [7]). The standard for tracking algorithms is the *tracking-by-detection* approach, where the instances are extracted of each frame and are used for the tracking process. MOT algorithms can be separated into two different methods: *batch* [14] and *online* methods [19]. In *batch tracking*, all frames (including frames in the future) are used to determine the object instance at a specific time (i.e. in a certain frame). On the other hand, *online tracking* algorithms can only use the current and past information.

Instance Segmentation for Disassembly and Recycling. Instance segmentation is used in several domains, but as already mentioned in [22], still to this date and to the best of our knowledge, almost no work currently addresses the domain of automated recycling of E-Waste. One of the few exceptions was the thesis [13] where deep learning networks were used to recycle flat panel displays.

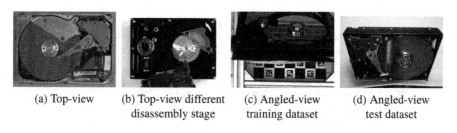

(a) Top-view   (b) Top-view different   (c) Angled-view   (d) Angled-view
                 disassembly stage   training dataset   test dataset

Fig. 1. Example of different HDD images.

3   Methods

3.1   Dataset

We use a dataset of annotated HDD parts, separated into 11 classes. Each of these parts' type has to be recognized by the system in order to be recycled differently. The original dataset had 500 images, containing only top-views of the hard-drives. This limits the system, as it can not recognize the parts with good accuracy when the hard-drive is rotated or moved by the robot.

Our extended dataset contains an additional 400 annotated images, including tilted views of the device. Figure 1 shows examples of the hard-drives in top- and angled-view, and the number of instances for each part are listed in Table 1. The angled-views were created with the HDDs rotated around the axis of their length, in a variety of angles and disassembly stages (Figs. 1c and 1d). Although more angles could be added, we consider this tilting angle sufficient within the scope of this study, as it covers most of the situations experienced by the robot. The ground-truth in the dataset was manually annotated using the online tool makesense.ai. The complete taxonomy of HDD parts can be found on the IMAGINE project website.

The dataset includes images of 7 different brands and several models, including damaged devices, and various stages of disassembly. The highest occurring part is the drive bay, which is seen in almost all the images, while the lowest occurring parts are the top dumper and the head contacts. Top dumpers are aimed to protect the platter, and only a few HDDs are equipped with it. Head contacts are the connection between PCB and R/W-Head, it is often hidden behind the PCB in the backside and can only be seen when the PCB was removed. All the other parts are present in about the same quantity.

Although the dataset has relatively low number of images for deep learning, we achieve reasonably good results (over 60% average precision, Sect. 4), which is due to the lower variance between certain HDD parts between different brands and models, such as the platter, spindle Hub, platters clamp, drive bay and drivers lid. We noticed that certain parts would benefit from more instances in the dataset, for example the top dumper, due to its higher variability and low occurrence, it has significantly lower average precision compared to the other parts at only around 30%. The evaluated neural networks have been pre-trained on the COCO dataset [11].

Table 1. Number of images and instances of our train and test-dataset. The name of taxonomy refers to the HDD part names defined in the IMAGINE project. The name of the classes and their corresponding colors are used for the detection results in Fig. 4.

ID	Name in taxonomy	Name of class	Colors	Train inst.	Test inst.
0	Magnets	magnet	Red	265	70
1	Flexible Printed Circuit	fpc	Green	199	93
2	Read/Write-Head	rw_head	Yellow	246	61
3	Spindle Hub	spindle_hub	Blue	301	101
4	Platters Clamp	platters_clamp	Orange	220	70
5	Platter(s)	platter	Turquoise	267	124
6	Drive Bay	bay	Rose	**612**	**228**
7	The Drivers Lid	lid	Pink	197	78
8	PCB	pcb	Teal	154	51
9	Head Contacts	head_contacts	Violet	42	45
10	Top Dumper	top_dumper	Light Brown	11	40
Total inst.				**2514** (72%)	**961** (28%)
Total img.				**695** (74%)	**242** (26%)

3.2   Precision

The precision of the models are evaluated using the COCO [11] evaluation metric. This method, known as Average Precision (AP) measures the accuracy for object detection and instance segmentation. The AP relies on of the *Intersection over Union* metric (IoU) defined in Eq. (1):

$$IoU = \frac{area(Mask_p \cap Mask_{gt})}{area(Mask_p \cup Mask_{gt})}. \tag{1}$$

$Mask_p$ and $Mask_{gt}$ correspond to the predicted mask and ground-truth mask, respectively. The IoU (Eq. 1) calculates the intersection between the ground-truth and the predicted mask. The predicted mask is correctly detected if the IoU is equal or greater to a given threshold (e.g. 50% for $AP_{IoU=.5}$). AP is the area under the precision and recall curve of 10 IoU values, from 50% to 95% in 5% increments.

3.3   Inference Time

We measure the *inference time* of a network, defined as the computational time between the presentation of an input image and the output of the prediction. We calculate this time for the whole test-dataset and deduce the average framerate the network can achieve. This metric is very dependent on the hardware used. On embedded robotic systems, Jetson computers are gaining popularity (e.g. Jetson Xavier), but since this setup is for a stationary recycling system, we went with a desktop with a GTX 1080. Therefore, all time measurements in this work were done using a single GTX 1080 GPU card, with a batch-size of 1.

Having a low inference time is crucial for tracking the movement of the hard-drive parts. However, we do not aim to achieve closed-loop control but analysis of robotic actions' effects at a decision-making level. The camera streams 4k images over a local network, thus providing raw images at 5 FPS. Given the speed at which the disassembly actions are executed, we set 2 FPS as a minimal acceptable FPS rate for this task. We additionally evaluated the number of parameters and number of floating point operations (GFlop) for the models with the best results.

3.4   Instance Segmentation

Since its introduction, Mask R-CNN [4] has been the state-of-the-art method for instance segmentation. It uses a *top-down approach* (also known as *detect-then-segment approach*) where the bounding boxes around the classes are first detected, using a two-stage object detector, and then the instance mask in each bounding box is created to differentiate the instances of the objects. Mask R-CNN is precise enough for the use-case of recycling HDDs [22] therefore its performance defines our baseline for precision. The *single-stage* models must at least achieve an equivalent average precision to be considered a good replacement. The drawback of Mask R-CNN has been the inference time, delivering only 2 FPS. Our experiments (Sect. 4) show that the best models for our use-case are BlendMask [3] and SOLOv2 [18]. These algorithms will be described briefly below.

3.5 Tracking

For tracking, we used only the information of the previous frame, instead of multiple past frames, and therefore we follow a simple frame-by-frame approach for tracking, which showed to be sufficient for this use case. To track the movement, we calculate the contours of each predicted instance mask, and afterwards the midpoint of each contour. This delivers a more accurate result than the midpoint of the bounding boxes. The segmentation predictions are bitmasks where 1 corresponds to the bits of the instance of one of the objects parts, and 0 is the rest of the image. We find the outermost contours of the given bitmasks individually, and the midpoint is calculated by the weighted average of the pixels for each contour. In case there are multiple instances of the same part detected, we choose the part with the smallest euclidean distance between the midpoints.

To evaluate the tracking of the chosen models on our dataset, we used a sequence of hard-drive images during movement. For each image of the sequence, the AP was calculated to determine the accuracy during movement of an HDD.

BlendMask. This model [3] uses the *detect-then-segment* approach, where at first an object detection network generates instance proposals and afterwards for each instance, a sub-network predicts the instances. It simplifies the head of Mask R-CNN from a four layer CNN to a tensor-product operations (called *Blend*) by reusing a predicted global segmentation mask. BlendMask is build upon FCOS [15], a fully convolutional single-stage object detection framework. For instance segmentation, a lightweight top and bottom modules are added to FCOS, which are adopted from the top-down and bottom-up approaches. Top-down approaches rely on features to predict the entire instance, while bottom-up approaches create local predictions by grouping pixels into instances [12].

These approaches are merged for BlendMask. The bottom module of BlendMask predicts a set of object bases from the backbone. The top module is a single-layer neural network that predicts attention maps, which is the coarse shape and pose of the object. For the final segmentation, the blender module combines the position-sensitive bases according to the attentions.

SOLOv2. This model [17] stands for Segment Objects by Locations and is a simple framework for instance segmentation, where the task is split into two simultaneously performed classification tasks. An input image is divided in uniform grids, if the center of an object is inside the current grid cell, the semantic class is predicted and the object's instance is segmented. Furthermore, they introduced "instance categories" which assigns categories to each pixel within an instance depending on the instance's location and size, hence the name SOLO. This model is a single-stage instance segmenter, that uses a more direct approach, instead of using the *detect-then-segment* approach. The network is not restricted by anchors, benefits from the advantages of Fully Connected Networks, and outputs instance masks and their class probabilities directly.

SOLOv2 [18] improves on some shortcomings of SOLO by using a dynamic scheme. The mask generation process was divided into a mask kernel prediction and mask feature learning. The mask kernels are predicted dynamically depending on the input, while the appropriate location categories are assigned to different pixels. The feature representation is afterwards constructed in a unified and high-resolution instance-aware segmentation. Furthermore, SOLOv2 reduced the inference time by introducing a matrix non-maximum suppression (NMS) technique, with parallel matrix operations in one shot.

3.6   Training

The models were trained for 20000 iterations with a batch size of 5, using the Google Colaboratory interactive environment. All the models were pre-trained on the COCO dataset.

The precision and inference time of some models depend highly on the resolution of the input image: a higher resolution image leads to results of higher precision at the cost of a higher inference time, and vice-versa. We train some models in higher and lower resolution input images, to evaluate the resulting trade-off between precision and inference time. In the models with higher resolution, the smaller side of the image was randomly scaled from 640 to 800 pixels for training, while the model with lower resolution were trained with scaling from 256 to 608 pixels, except for CenterMask V19-FPN which was trained between 580 and 600. Furthermore, all the models have the same augmentations of random lightning, random brightness and random horizontal flips.

4   Results

4.1   Precision and Speed

Precision of the models is evaluated using the AP metric (Sect. 3.2). Previous evaluation [22] showed that Mask R-CNN is precise enough to allow the disassembly of HDDs. We then included Mask R-CNN as the baseline model to evaluate on our dataset and to compare the results of the more real-time capable models. For Mask R-CNN we chose the Residual Neural Network (R50 and R101) [5] with a Feature Pyramid Network (FPN) [10] backbone, and got an AP of 67.7% with an inference speed of about 2 FPS. Therefore, we set the minimum required precision at 67%, and the minimum inference speed to 2 FPS. The state-of-the-art single-stage real-time capable models evaluated on our dataset are CenterMask-Lite [9], BlendMask [3] and SOLOv2 [18].

Experimental results are shown in Fig. 2, where we can see the trade-off between precision and speed: deeper backbones consistently result in higher precision, compared to the shallower one with lower precision, but higher inference speed. The models were evaluated on different image sizes, and the AP with the smaller image sizes is always lower, but the inference speed is higher.

The highest AP is achieved by SOLOv2 with the R101-FPN backbone. The fastest model was the SOLOv2 R50-FPN, with 5 times the speed of Mask R-CNN, while only showing a decrease of 0.2% in terms of AP. The second-best model was Blend-Mask using the Deep Layer Aggregation (DLA34) [23] backbone with about 8 FPS and

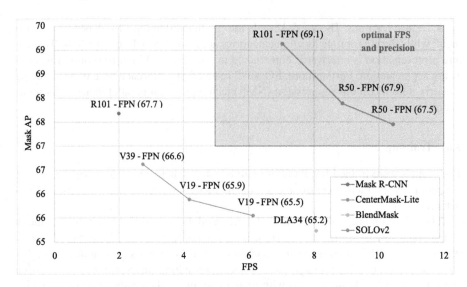

Fig. 2. Speed and Accuracy AP for the various methods and backbones evaluated. The graph shows the relative positions of the methods based on their inference time and accuracy (AP) using different backbones and input image sizes. The labels of each marker indicates the used backbone and the AP in parentheses. The evaluated shorter side of the input image were resized to: 512 for BlendMask DLA34, 512 and 800 for SOLOv2, 600 and 800 for CenterMask V19-FPN, and 800 for the V39-FPN backbone. The models with smaller image sizes and shallower backbones result in higher inference speed, but lower AP.

2% less AP compared to SOLOv2 R50-FPN. CenterMask-Lite with VoVNet [8] (V19-FPN and V39-FPN) had slightly better precision than BlendMask, but was significantly slower than BlendMask. Generally, deeper networks provide better precision, however the inference time also increases. For a more complete evaluation, we added the deeper backbones R101 and V39, to see which options provide the best precision and speed trade-off. Our results indicate that for our use-case the shallower backbones are better suited, as the improvement in speed is more significant than the improvement in precision. SOLOv2 with the R50-FPN backbone has the best trade-off between precision and inference speed, with only 0.2% lower precision than Mask R-CNN, and 5 times the speed. The R101-FPN also can be used for higher precision if the inference speed of 7 FPS is deemed to be high enough, or if a more powerful GPU is used.

4.2   Tracking

We analyze next the precision of the faster models on images of HDDs during motion. Figure 3 shows a sequence of frames example with the ground-truth and the predicted masks of the different models. This HDD is part of our test-dataset, where where the conditions in which the images were taken were quite different from the ones used in training in order to analyze robustness. While the images in the training set were taken with the camera mounted to the disassembly robot (Fig. 1c), these images were taken

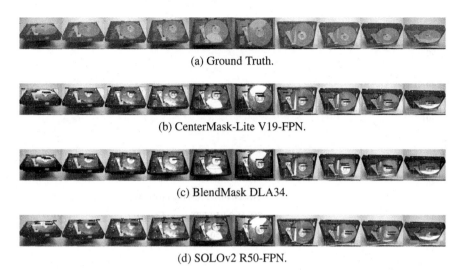

(a) Ground Truth.

(b) CenterMask-Lite V19-FPN.

(c) BlendMask DLA34.

(d) SOLOv2 R50-FPN.

Fig. 3. Predicted masks with the models using lower image sizes. Sample images part of our test-dataset, the top row corresponds to the ground-truth masks, and the models are the same as in Fig. 2. The colors and name of classes correspond to Table 1, where next to each class the confidence score of each mask is shown. We can already see the difference in AP between each model, where SOLOv2 R50-FPN has the most accurate masks.

on a simple mount that could change its angle (Fig. 1d). Because of the difference in mounts, these HDD images cast a shadow, which was partially wrongly detected as part of the drive bay by the CenterMask-Lite and SOLOv2 models. BlendMask showed to be more robust, detecting the drive bay, but generally smaller than it actually is.

Figure 4 shows the corresponding AP for each frame presented in Fig. 3. In this figure we see that the models have lower AP the more angled the HDD is, but the precision still stays over 50% for all frames and models, while SOLOv2 has about 60% as the lowest AP result. The observed decrease of performance with higher angles is probably due to the unbalance between top- and angled-views in our dataset. While several images in different views and angles were added, the dataset still has a majority of the parts in top-view. The reason for this is that in top-views, there are multiple disassembly stages shown, with different inner component configurations, whereas these various configurations are not visible on the most angled-views; thus, there is a natural imbalance in the dataset towards top-views (Fig. 1b). To show the improvement of our extended dataset, we compare the AP results of a SOLOv2 R50-FPN model trained on the older dataset [22], which only included top-views of HDDs. The results show us that on higher angled-views, the old model is significantly worse on the first and last frames, where the HDD had wider angles. We can see a small drop in precision in frame 3 compared to nearby frames. This is the due to that the FPC part was not detected in this frame by SOLOv2 and BlendMask In General the FPC is difficult to detect when the HDD is angled, because its appearance changes more from different perspectives compared to the other parts in this dataset. Further expanding the dataset with more variations of FPCs in different orientations would be beneficial.

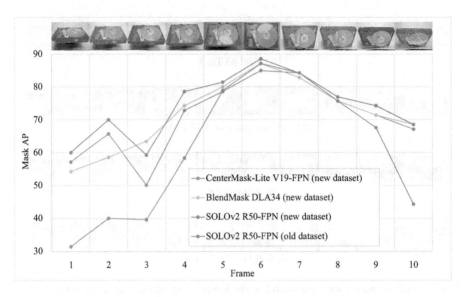

Fig. 4. AP on the frames of Fig. 3. The images over the diagram are the corresponding ground-truth masks. In the images where the HDD is angled more, the AP of all the models decrease. SOLOv2 has the highest AP for all the frames with over 60%. Furthermore, we compare our extended dataset to the old dataset [22] by additionally training the SOLOv2 R50-FPN model solely on the older dataset that only contained top-views. We can see that the SOLOv2 model trained on the old dataset has significantly worse AP for the images where the HDD is angled more, while the AP for the top-view images have about the same AP.

Table 2. Number of parameters and GFlops per model. The number of parameters in millions and the number of GFlops. The image size row explains how the shorter side of the input image was resized. The number of parameters is independent of the input image size, while GFlops decrease with lower image sizes. Mask R-CNN has the most number of parameters and GFlops, while BlendMask has the least.

	Mask R-CNN	BlendMask	SOLOv2		
Backbone	R101	DLA-34	R101	R50	
Image size	800 × ∗	512 × ∗	800 × ∗	800 × ∗	512 × ∗
FPS	2	8	7	8.9	10.4
GFlops	314.8	87.2	287.6	220.8	132.3
Total params [M]	62.9	25.5	65.5	46.5	
Backbone params [M]	45.7	17.3	45.7	26.8	

In Table 2 we further analyzed the models by inspecting their number of parameters and GFlops. The number of parameters is independent on the input image size. Mask R-CNN has the highest number of parameters, while SOLOv2 with the same R101-FPN backbone has lower total parameters. BlendMask has the lowest number of parameters, while Mask R-CNN has the most. The GFlops are the number of operations required to run a single instance of the given mode, and in our case we calculated them over the average of 100 input images.

5   Conclusion

In this work, we extended an HDD dataset for the detection of HDD parts in a motion recycling scenario, by adding HDD images with different angles and views. With this dataset, we compared several state-of-the-art single-stage instance segmentation models and compared them to Mask R-CNN. The best results were achieved using the single-stage SOLOv2 model with the R50-FPN backbone, achieving AP of 67.5% and inference speed of 10 FPS on our test-dataset. These results have on-par precision with the previously used Mask R-CNN with 5 times the speed.

The predicted masks were used to track the movement of an HDD during disassembly. We evaluated the tracking precision by evaluating the AP of an HDD during movement. The results showed that even on images with a high level of occlusion on different parts, we achieve an AP of at least 60%. Furthermore, we compared the old dataset [22] with our extended dataset, by also training SOLOv2 model on the old dataset, and comparing the AP of an HDD during movement. The AP with our extended dataset significantly improved the precision on images with wider angles and higher level of occlusion. Overall, these results show that single-stage deep learning-based instance segmentation can be used in an online setup without compromising precision. This strengthens the idea of autonomous and adaptive recycling system for E-waste processing.

Acknowledgements. We acknowledge the European Union's Horizon 2020 program for the grant agreement no. 731761 (IMAGINE).

References

1. Bolya, D., Zhou, C., Xiao, F., Lee, Y.J.: YOLACT++: better real-time instance segmentation. IEEE Trans. Pattern Anal. Mach. Intell. **44**(2), 1108–1121 (2020)
2. Cao, J., Anwer, R.M., Cholakkal, H., Khan, F.S., Pang, Y., Shao, L.: SipMask: spatial information preservation for fast image and video instance segmentation. CoRR abs/2007.14772 (2020). https://arxiv.org/abs/2007.14772
3. Chen, H., Sun, K., Tian, Z., Shen, C., Huang, Y., Yan, Y.: BlendMask: top-down meets bottom-up for instance segmentation. CoRR abs/2001.00309 (2020). http://arxiv.org/abs/2001.00309
4. He, K., Gkioxari, G., Dollár, P., Girshick, R.B.: Mask R-CNN. CoRR abs/1703.06870 (2017). http://arxiv.org/abs/1703.06870
5. He, K., Zhang, X., Ren, S., Sun, J.: Deep residual learning for image recognition. CoRR abs/1512.03385 (2015). http://arxiv.org/abs/1512.03385
6. Krizhevsky, A., Sutskever, I., Hinton, G.E.: ImageNet classification with deep convolutional neural networks. In: Pereira, F., Burges, C.J.C., Bottou, L., Weinberger, K.Q. (eds.) Advances in Neural Information Processing Systems, vol. 25. Curran Associates, Inc. (2012)
7. Leal-Taixé, L.: Multiple object tracking with context awareness. CoRR abs/1411.7935 (2014). http://arxiv.org/abs/1411.7935

8. Lee, Y., Hwang, J., Lee, S., Bae, Y., Park, J.: An energy and GPU-computation efficient backbone network for real-time object detection. CoRR abs/1904.09730 (2019). http://arxiv.org/abs/1904.09730

9. Lee, Y., Park, J.: CenterMask: real-time anchor-free instance segmentation. CoRR abs/1911.06667 (2019). http://arxiv.org/abs/1911.06667

10. Lin, T., Dollár, P., Girshick, R.B., He, K., Hariharan, B., Belongie, S.J.: Feature pyramid networks for object detection. CoRR abs/1612.03144 (2016). http://arxiv.org/abs/1612.03144

11. Lin, T.-Y., et al.: Microsoft COCO: common objects in context. In: Fleet, D., Pajdla, T., Schiele, B., Tuytelaars, T. (eds.) ECCV 2014. LNCS, vol. 8693, pp. 740–755. Springer, Cham (2014). https://doi.org/10.1007/978-3-319-10602-1_48

12. Neven, D., Brabandere, B.D., Proesmans, M., Gool, L.V.: Instance segmentation by jointly optimizing spatial embeddings and clustering bandwidth. CoRR abs/1906.11109 (2019). http://arxiv.org/abs/1906.11109

13. Sanderson, A.: Intelligent robotic recycling of flat panel displays. Master's thesis, University of Waterloo (2019). http://hdl.handle.net/10012/14730

14. Son, J., Baek, M., Cho, M., Han, B.: Multi-object tracking with quadruplet convolutional neural networks. In: 2017 IEEE Conference on Computer Vision and Pattern Recognition (CVPR), pp. 3786–3795 (2017)

15. Tian, Z., Shen, C., Chen, H., He, T.: FCOS: fully convolutional one-stage object detection. CoRR abs/1904.01355 (2019). http://arxiv.org/abs/1904.01355

16. United Nations Environment Programme, P., ITU, I., UNIDO, U.N.U.: A new circular vision for electronics time for a global reboot (2019)

17. Wang, X., Kong, T., Shen, C., Jiang, Y., Li, L.: SOLO: segmenting objects by locations. CoRR abs/1912.04488 (2019). http://arxiv.org/abs/1912.04488

18. Wang, X., Zhang, R., Kong, T., Li, L., Shen, C.: SOLOV2: dynamic, faster and stronger. CoRR abs/2003.10152 (2020). https://arxiv.org/abs/2003.10152

19. Xiang, J., Zhang, G., Hou, J.: Online multi-object tracking based on feature representation and Bayesian filtering within a deep learning architecture. IEEE Access 7, 27923–27935 (2019)

20. Xie, E., Wang, W., Ding, M., Zhang, R., Luo, P.: PolarMask++: enhanced polar representation for single-shot instance segmentation and beyond. CoRR abs/2105.02184 (2021). https://arxiv.org/abs/2105.02184

21. Yang, J., et al.: Arsenic burden in e-waste recycling workers-a cross-sectional study at the Agbogbloshie e-waste recycling site, Ghana. Chemosphere 261, 127712 (2020)

22. Yildiz., E., et al.: A visual intelligence scheme for hard drive disassembly in automated recycling routines. In: Proceedings of the International Conference on Robotics, Computer Vision and Intelligent Systems - ROBOVIS, pp. 17–27. INSTICC, SciTePress (2020)

23. Yu, F., Wang, D., Darrell, T.: Deep layer aggregation. CoRR abs/1707.06484 (2017). http://arxiv.org/abs/1707.06484

Improving Semantic Segmentation with Graph-Based Structural Knowledge

Jérémy Chopin[1]([✉])(iD), Jean-Baptiste Fasquel[1](iD), Harold Mouchère[2](iD),
Rozenn Dahyot[3](iD), and Isabelle Bloch[4](iD)

[1] LARIS, Université d'Angers, Angers, France
{jeremy.chopin,jean-baptiste.fasquel}@univ-angers.fr
[2] LS2N, Universite de Nantes, CNRS UMR 6004, Nantes, France
harold.mouchere@univ-nantes.fr
[3] Department of Computer Science, Maynooth University, Maynooth, Ireland
Rozenn.Dahyot@mu.ie
[4] Sorbonne Université, CNRS, LIP6, Paris, France
isabelle.bloch@sorbonne-universite.fr

Abstract. Deep learning based pipelines for semantic segmentation often ignore structural information available on annotated images used for training. We propose a novel post-processing module enforcing structural knowledge about the objects of interest to improve segmentation results provided by deep learning. This module corresponds to a "many-to-one-or-none" inexact graph matching approach, and is formulated as a quadratic assignment problem. Using two standard measures for evaluation, we show experimentally that our pipeline for segmentation of 3D MRI data of the brain outperforms the baseline CNN (U-Net) used alone. In addition, our approach is shown to be resilient to small training datasets that often limit the performance of deep learning.

Keywords: Graph matching · Deep learning · Image segmentation · Volume segmentation · Quadratic assignment problem

1 Introduction

Deep learning approaches are now widely used in computer vision [11], and in particular for semantic image segmentation [10]. Through a set of convolution layers, semantic segmentation with Convolutional Neural Networks (CNNs) is intrinsically based on information embedded at low-level, *i.e.* at pixel and its neighborhood levels. CNNs do not explicitly model the structural information available at a higher semantic level, for instance the relationships between annotated regions that are present in the training dataset. High-level structural

This research was conducted in the framework of the regional program Atlanstic 2020, Research, Education and Innovation in Pays de la Loire, supported by the French Region Pays de la Loire and the European Regional Development Fund.

information may include spatial relationships between different regions (e.g. distances, relative directional position) [2] or relationships between their properties (e.g. relative brightness, difference of colorimetry) [8,9].

This type of high-level structural information is very promising [2,6,8,9,19] and it has found applications in medical image understanding [4,7,18] but also in document analysis (e.g. [5,12] for handwriting recognition) or in scene understanding (e.g. [13] for robotic). In some domains, the relations between objects have to be identified to recognize the image content [12] but in other domains these relations help the recognition of a global scene as a complementary knowledge [5,8,9,13]. Our work falls in this second category. This high-level information is commonly represented using graphs, where vertices correspond to regions, and edges carry the structural information. The semantic segmentation problem turns then into a region or node labeling problem, often formulated as a graph matching problem [8,9,16]. In this paper, we propose a new approach involving a graph-matching-based semantic segmentation applied to the probability map produced by CNNs for semantic segmentation, in order to take into account explicitly this high-level structural information observed in the training dataset but intrinsically ignored by convolutional layers. Our proposal aims at improving the semantic segmentation of images, in particular when the size of the training dataset is low. As such, our work also addresses, to some extent, one key limitation of deep learning: the requirement of a large and representative dataset for training purposes, this being often addressed by generating more training data (data augmentation) [21] or by considering a transfer learning technique [23]. By focusing on the high level global structure of a scene, our approach is expected to be less sensitive to the lack of diversity and representativity of the training dataset.

This paper extends [3] by combining the high level structural information observed in the training dataset with the output of the semantic segmentation produced by a deep neural network. It uses a graph matching approach formulated as a quadratic assignment problem (QAP) [17,24,25]. We deploy two types of relationships for capturing structural information and our approach is shown experimentally to perform well for segmenting 3D volumetric data (cf. Fig. 1)[1].

2   Proposed Method

Structural information, such as spatial relationships, is encoded in a graph model G_m that captures the observed relationships between regions in an annotated training dataset. Vertices and edges correspond respectively to regions of the annotated dataset and spatial relationships between them. A hypothesis graph G_r is similarly created from the semantic segmentation map of a query image using the same label taxonomy as the training set. Graph matching (GM) of G_r onto G_m allows matching the vertices (and thus the underlying regions of the query image) with those of the model. Correspondences between G_r and G_m

---

[1] The open-source code and data are to be shared with the community https://github.com/Jeremy-Chopin/APACoSI/.

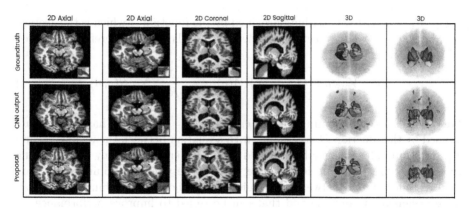

Fig. 1. Example of semantic segmentation of a brain (slices and 3D view) performed by the expert (reference segmentation - top), by the CNN (middle) and by our method (bottom). 100% of the training dataset is considered. Surrounded boxes and red arrows indicate segmentation errors that are corrected by our method. (Color figure online)

computed with GM provide a relabelling of some of the regions (vertices) in G_r hence providing a enhanced semantic segmentation map of the query image with additional high-level structural information.

Semantic Segmentation. A query image or volume is segmented providing a tensor $S \in \mathbb{R}^{P \times N}$ with P the dimensions of the query ($P = I \times J$ pixels for 2D images, or $P = I \times J \times K$ voxels in 3D volumes) and N is the total number of classes considered for segmentation. At each pixel or voxel location p, the value $S(p, n) \in [0, 1]$ is the probability of belonging to class n with the constraints:

$$(\forall n \in \{1, \dots, N\}, \ 0 \leq S(p, n) \leq 1) \wedge \left(\sum_{n=1}^{N} S(p, n) = 1 \right)$$

The segmentation map $\mathcal{L}^*$ selects the label n of the class with the highest probability. Note that in practice semantic segmentation of a query image can be performed using deep neural networks such as, for instance, U-Net [21] or segNet [1].

2.1   Graph Definitions

From the segmentation map $\mathcal{L}^*$, a set R of all resulting connected components is defined. Additionally, to constrain graph matching (described in Sect. 2.2), we define a set $R^* = \{R_1^*, \dots, R_N^*\}$, where, for each class $n \in \{1, \cdots, N\}$, R_n^* is a set of regions corresponding to the connected components belonging to class n. From the set R, the graph $G_r = (V_r, E_r, A, D)$ is defined, where V_r is the set of vertices, E_r the set of edges, A a vertex attribute assignment function and D an edge attribute assignment function. Each vertex $v \in V_r$ is associated with a region $R_v \in R$ with an attribute provided by the function A which is the average membership probability vector over the set of pixels $p \in R_v$, therefore computed on the initial tensor S:

$$\forall v \in V_r, \forall n \in \{1, \ldots, N\}, A(v)[n] = \frac{1}{|R_v|} \sum_{p \in R_v} S(p, n) \tag{1}$$

We consider a complete graph where each edge $e = (i, j) \in E_r$ has an attribute defined by the function D, associated with a relation between the regions R_i and R_j. Two functions D have been tested in our experiments. They are capturing the relative directional position or the trade-off between the minimal and maximal distances found between two regions. The choice of the function D is an hyperparameter in our method that can be tuned to improve performance for the considered application (cf. Sect. 2.3).

The model graph $G_m = (V_m, E_m, A, D)$ is composed of N vertices (one vertex per class) and is constructed from the annotated images of the training set. The attribute of a vertex is a vector of dimension N with only one non-zero component (with value equal to 1), associated with the index of the corresponding class. The edges are obtained by calculating the average spatial relationships (in the training set) between the regions (according to the relation D considered).

2.2 Graph Matching

We propose to identify the regions by associating each of the vertices of G_r to a vertex of the model graph G_m. The most likely situation encountered is when more regions are found in the image associated with G_r than in the model (i.e. $|V_r| \geq |V_m|$). To solve this, we propose here to extend the many-to-one inexact graph matching strategy [3, 16] to a many-to-one-or-none matching. The "none" term allows some vertices in G_r to be matched with none of the vertices of the model graph G_m, which corresponds to removing the underlying image region (e.g. merged with the background). Graph matching is here formulated as a quadratic assignment problem (QAP) [25]. The matrix $X \in \{0,1\}^{|V_r| \times |V_m|}$ is defined such that $X_{ij} = 1$ means that vertex $i \in V_r$ is matched with vertex $j \in V_m$. The objective is to estimate the best matching X^* as follows:

$$X^* = \arg \min_X \left\{ \text{vec}(X)^T K \, \text{vec}(X) \right\} \tag{2}$$

where $\text{vec}(X)$ is the column vector representation of X and T denotes the transposition operator. This optimal matching is associated with the optimal matching cost $C^* = \text{vec}(X^*)^T K \, \text{vec}(X^*)$.

The matrix K embeds the dissimilarity measures between the two graphs G_r and G_m, at vertices (diagonal elements) and edges (non-diagonal elements):

$$K = \alpha \, K_v + (1 - \alpha) \, \frac{K_e(D)}{\max K_e(D)} \tag{3}$$

where K_v embeds dissimilarities between vertices (e.g. L2 Euclidean distance between class membership probability vectors) - more details for computing K

can be found in [25]. The matrix $K_e(D)$ is related to dissimilarities between edges, and depends on the considered relation D. K_e terms are related to distances between regions (normalized in the final K matrix). The α parameter ($\alpha \in [0,1]$) allows weighting the relative contribution of vertex and edge dissimilarities: K_v terms range between 0 and 1, and K_e is also normalized in Eq. 3. Due to the combinatorial nature of this optimization problem [25] (i.e. set of possible X candidates in Eq. 2), we propose a two-steps procedure:

1. Search for an initial one-to-one matching.
2. Refinement by matching remaining vertices, finally leading to a many-to-one-or-none matching.

Initial Matching: One-to-One. One searches for the optimal solution to Eq. 2 by imposing the following three constraints on X, thus reducing the search space for eligible candidates:

1. $\sum_{j=1}^{|V_m|} X_{ij} \leq 1$: some vertices i of G_r may not be matched.
2. $\sum_{i=1}^{|V_r|} X_{ij} = 1$: each vertex j of G_m must be matched with only one vertex of G_r.
3. $X_{ij} = 1 \Rightarrow R_i \in R_j^*$: vertex $i \in V_r$ can be matched with vertex $j \in V_m$ if the associated R_i region was initially considered by the neural network to most likely belong to class j (i.e. $R_i \in R_j^*$).

The first two constraints ensure to search for a one-to-one matching thanks to the third constraint, one reduces the search space by relying on the neural network: one assumes that it has correctly, at least to some extent, identified the target regions, even if artifacts may still have been produced as well (to be managed by refining the matching). This step allows us to retrieve the general structure of the regions (thus verifying the prior structure modeled by G_m) with a cost $C^I = \text{vec}(X^I)^T K \text{vec}(X^I)$ related to the optimal initial matching X^I (I stands for "initial").

Refinement: Many-to-One-or-None. Unmatched nodes are integrated into the optimal matching X^I or removed (i.e. assigned to a "background" or "none" node) through a refinement step leading to X^* considered in Eq. 2. This many-to-one-or-none matching is performed through an iterative procedure over the set of unlabeled nodes $U = \{k \in V_r \mid \sum_{j=1}^{|V_m|} X_{kj}^I = 0\}$. For each node $k \in U$, one searches for the best assignment, among all possible ones, related to the set of already labeled nodes $L = \{k \in V_r \mid \sum_{j=1}^{|V_m|} X_{kj}^I = 1\}$. Mathematically, the best label candidate for a given node $k \in U$ is:

$$l_k^* = \arg\min_{l \in L}\{\text{vec}(X^I)^t K_{k \to l} \text{vec}(X^I)\} \qquad (4)$$

where $K_{k \to l}$ corresponds to the matrix K after having merged both underlying regions (i.e. $R_l = R_l \cup R_k$) and updated relations (leading to the graph G_r', where both k and l vertices are merged). The cost related to the merging of k to l_k^* is $C_{k \to l_k^*}$. Figure 2 illustrates this iterative procedure.

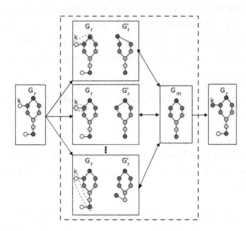

Fig. 2. Refinement: finding the best matching for a given unlabeled node $k \in U$ (white node). Only three possible matchings are reported for clarity (dashed surrounded nodes). The one in the middle is finally kept (smallest deformation of G_r' with respect to the model G_m).

The best candidate is retained if the related cost is smaller than a chosen threshold T, otherwise the related node k is discarded (i.e. $k \to \emptyset$, $\emptyset$ corresponding to the "none" vertex, meaning that the underlying image region is merged with the background). The optimal matching is updated according to the condition:

$$\begin{cases} X_{kl}^* = 1, & \text{if } C_{k \to l_k^*} < T \\ X_{kl}^* = 0, & \text{otherwise} \end{cases}$$

This enables to manage the removal of regions to be considered as artifacts and this was not managed in our earlier work [3].

Algorithm 1 provides an implementation of the proposed refinement. For each unlabeled vertex $k \in U$, the optimal cost is initially set to infinity (Line 2). Then, for each candidate $l \in L$, one creates an image region (temporary variable R_l') corresponding to the union of both unlabeled and merging candidate regions (Line 4). We update the dissimilarity matrix (leading to the temporary variable $K_{k \to l}$ - Line 5), and then compute the cost of this union (Line 6). If this union decreases the matching cost, the merging candidate is considered as the best one (Lines 8 and 9). After having evaluated the cost of the matching with the best candidate $l \in L$, we finally accept the resulting best matching, if the value of the associated cost is lower than the predefined threshold T (Lines 12 to 16). If the cost is higher, the vertex $k \in U$ is discarded (and the image region is removed).

Algorithm 1. Refinement algorithm

Require: U, L, T, X^I
1: **for** $k \in U$ **do**
2:      $C^*_{k \to l} \leftarrow \infty$
3:      **for** $l \in L$ **do**
4:          $R'_l \leftarrow R_l \cup R_k$
5:          $K_{k \to l} \leftarrow$ Update-K(R'_l)
6:          $C_{k \to l} \leftarrow vec(X^I)^t \, K_{k \to l} \, vec(X^I)$
7:          **if** $C_{k \to l} < C^*_{k \to l}$ **then**
8:              $l^*_k \leftarrow l$
9:              $C^*_{k \to l^*_k} \leftarrow C_{k \to l}$
10:         **end if**
11:     **end for**
12:     **if** $C_{k \to l^*_k} < T$ **then**
13:         $k \to l^*_k$ {k is assigned}
14:         $R_{l^*_k} \leftarrow R_{l^*_k} \cup R_k$
15:     **else**
16:         $k \to \emptyset$ {k is discarded}
17:     **end if**
18: **end for**

2.3   Modelling Spatial Relationships

Two types of spatial relationships are considered (cf. Fig. 3), each being associated to a specific dissimilarity function D (used to compute the term $K_e(D)$ in Eq. 3). The first spatial relationship involves two distances (leading to two components on an edge attribute), corresponding to the minimal and maximum distances between two regions R_i and R_j (cf. Fig. 3-left):

$$d^{(i,j)}_{\min} = \min_{p \in R_i, q \in R_j} (|p - q|) \tag{5}$$

$$d^{(i,j)}_{\max} = \max_{p \in R_i, q \in R_j} (|p - q|) \tag{6}$$

Based on these relationships, the considered dissimilarity function is defined as:

$$D1^{(k,l)}_{(i,j)} = \frac{\lambda}{C_s} \left(|d^{(i,j)}_{\min} - d^{(k,l)}_{\min}| \right) + \frac{(1 - \lambda)}{C_s} (|d^{(i,j)}_{\max} - d^{(k,l)}_{\max}|) \tag{7}$$

where λ is a parameter balancing the influence of the dissimilarities on both distances. C_s corresponds to the largest distance observed in an image, ensuring that values range within $[0, 1]$.

The second spatial relationship is the relative directional position of the centroids of two regions, as in [20]. For two regions R_i and R_j, the relative position is defined by the vector $\vec{v_{ij}} = \overline{R}_j - \overline{R}_i$ (edge attribute), where $\overline{R}$ denotes the coordinates of the center of mass of region R. Based on this relationship, the considered dissimilarity function is:

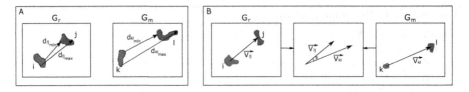

Fig. 3. Spatial relationships considered in experiments. A: Relationship based on distances (corresponding to the D_1 dissimilarity function). B: Relationship based on relative directional positions (corresponding to the D_2 dissimilarity function).

$$D_2{}_{(i,j)}^{(k,l)} = \lambda \frac{|\cos\theta - 1|}{2} + (1-\lambda)\frac{||\vec{v_{ij}}| - |\vec{v_{kl}}||}{C_s} \tag{8}$$

where θ is the angle between them $\vec{v_{ij}}$ and $\vec{v_{kl}}$ vectors, computed using a scalar product (Eq. 9):

$$\cos(\theta) = \frac{\vec{v_{ij}}.\vec{v_{kl}}}{|\vec{v_{ij}}|.|\vec{v_{kl}}|} \tag{9}$$

As for the first spatial relationship, the C_s term is the maximum distance value observed in an image, ensuring that values range within $[0, 1]$. The term $\lambda \in [0, 1]$ is a parameter balancing the influence of the difference in terms of distance and orientation.

Concerning the complexity, the computation time is mainly affected by the refinement step involving many relabelling (cf. Fig. 2). In Algorithm 1, the complexity of this second step of the matching linearly depends on the cardinalities of both U and L entities as well as on the complexity of the cost computation (i.e. union of regions, Update-K(R'_l) and $vec(X)^T K vec(X)$ reported in lines 4–6 of Algorithm 1).

3   Application to Segmentation of 3D MRI

IBSR Dataset: The IBSR[2] public dataset provides 18 3D MRI of the brain, together with the manual segmentation of 32 regions. In our experiments, similarly to the work by Kushibar et al. [14], only 14 classes (i.e. 14 regions) of the annotated dataset are considered: thalamus (left and right), caudate (left and right), putamen (left and right), pallidum (left and right), hippocampus (left and right), amygdala (left and right) and accumbens (left and right).

CNN Backbone: 3D U-Net neural network is used for creating three instances of a trained CNN for segmentation using training sets of different sizes:

- *100% (10/18):* 10 images are used for training (training set) out of the 18 available, an additional 4 are used validation (validation set) and the last 4 are used for testing (test set).

---

[2] The IBSR annotated public dataset can be downloaded at the following address: https://www.nitrc.org/projects/ibsr.

- *75% (8/18):* In this case, out of the 10 images available in the original training set, only 8 are used. Results reported correspond to an average over several CNNs trained with randomly selecting 8 images amongst the 10 in the training set. Validation and test sets remain the same.
- *50% (5/18):* out of the 10 images available in the original training set, only 5 are used. Results reported correspond to an average over several CNNs trained with randomly selecting 5 images amongst the 10 in the original training set. Validation and test sets remain the same.

50 epochs are used for training the network and an early stopping politic is applied to prevent over-fitting. The training process was terminated if there was no improvement on the loss (using cross entropy loss function) for 8 consecutive epochs. We used a 3D patch-based approach [15] since classes are highly unbalanced (i.e. small size of target regions with respect to other brain tissues and background). Patches are volumes of size 48^3 voxels, that have been extracted around the centroid of each label (random selection) using the *Torchio* library [22]. 150 patches are selected for each MRI volume, with a frequency that is proportional to the inverse prior probability of the corresponding class.

Measures for Assessment: The Hausdorff distance (HD) is widely used in this application domain [14] ($HD = 0$ corresponding to a perfect segmentation). The pixel-wise Dice index (DSC) is also reported and it is ranging within $[0, 1]$ where 1 corresponds to a perfect segmentation. The hyperparameters are chosen empirically without optimisation: $\alpha = 0.5$ and $\lambda = 0.5$.

Quantitative Results: Table 1 compares performances for both spatial relationships D_1 and D_2. Our pipeline improves the results of the CNN used alone either in terms of Dice index (best DSC with D_2) or in terms of Hausdorff distance (best HD with D_1). Structural information modelled with either D_1 or D_2 in our pipeline allows us to improve segmentation results.

Table 1. Comparing dissimilarity functions D_1 and D_2 for modelling spatial relationships. The evaluation measures are the pixel-wise Dice index (DSC) and the Hausdorff distance (HD).

Method	CNN		Ours (D_1)		Ours (D_2)	
Tr.dataset (%)	DSC↑	HD↓	DSC↑	HD↓	DSC↑	HD↓
100%	0.66	55.21	0.67	**7.52**	**0.7**	24.45
75%	0.6	63.2	0.63	**9.58**	**0.66**	24.51
50%	0.59	57.83	0.64	**9.38**	**0.65**	24.4

Table 2 details the results for each class using D_2 that significantly improves the Dice index while also significantly reducing the Hausdorff distance. For

DSC, the improvement fluctuates between 4% (Tr. dataset 100%) and 6% (Tr. dataset 50%). The improvement is significant for large regions (e.g. "Tha.L" and "Put.L"). In terms of Hausdorff distance, the improvement is significant (58% on average) for most considered classes and size of the training dataset used.

Table 2. Comparison of segmentations provided by the CNN and by our proposal, for the second spatial relationships (D_2 dissimilarity function), considering the Dice index related to pixelwise precision and Hausdorff distance compared to the manual segmentation. Results are provided as average and for each class: Tha.L(left thalamus), Tha.R(right thalamus), Cau.L(left caudate), Cau.R(right caudate), Put.L(left putamen), Put.R(right putamen), Pal.L(left pallidum), Pal.R(right pallidum), Hip.L(left hippocampus), Hip.R(right hippocamus), Amy.L(left amygdala), Amy.R(right amygdala), Acc.L(left accumbens), Acc.R(right accumbens). Results are also provided for different sizes of the training/validation sets.

| | 100% (10/18) | | | | 75% (8/18) | | | | 50% (5/18) | | | |
| | DSC (highest best) | | HD (lowest best) | | DSC (highest best) | | HD (lowest best) | | DSC (highest best) | | HD (lowest best) | |
class	CNN	Ours	CNN	Ours	CNN	Ours	CNN	Ours	CNN	Ours	CNN	Ours
Tha.L	0.82	**0.85**	69.64	23.97	0.7	**0.84**	68.3	27.87	0.75	**0.83**	66.33	28.05
Tha.R	0.79	**0.83**	66.86	22.65	0.73	**0.81**	68.83	23.98	0.76	**0.79**	58.52	28.17
Cau.L	0.63	**0.66**	75.86	23.65	**0.66**	**0.66**	68.43	22.41	0.64	**0.62**	73.16	26.81
Cau.R	0.52	**0.56**	68.88	27.2	0.52	**0.54**	72.14	23.69	0.5	**0.48**	68.04	24.02
Put.L	0.75	**0.86**	58.91	22.31	0.62	**0.82**	71.04	27.08	0.61	**0.82**	69.42	21.85
Put.R	0.75	**0.78**	67.7	22.37	0.63	**0.73**	75.8	18.09	0.65	**0.74**	71.41	21.39
Pal.L	0.71	**0.8**	48.68	19.9	0.64	**0.79**	61.79	25.11	0.57	**0.78**	57.93	27.44
Pal.R	**0.64**	0.62	47.43	31.1	**0.56**	0.52	60.15	22.52	**0.5**	0.48	62.95	25.3
Hip.L	0.59	**0.69**	69.51	27.28	0.58	**0.67**	73.75	29.25	0.52	**0.65**	69.95	28.19
Hip.R	0.65	**0.72**	67.61	29.69	0.6	**0.7**	72.19	30.17	0.46	**0.66**	73.06	26.73
Amy.L	0.71	**0.73**	53.99	25.46	0.66	**0.69**	67.99	27.7	0.69	**0.7**	61.57	27.01
Amy.R	**0.6**	0.56	21.35	15.65	**0.61**	**0.61**	65.69	22.47	**0.61**	0.59	51.06	22.83
Acc.L	**0.58**	**0.58**	33.45	23.42	**0.38**	0.37	28.35	21.61	**0.51**	**0.51**	17.62	18.22
Acc.R	**0.56**	0.55	23.14	27.66	**0.52**	**0.52**	30.38	21.25	**0.49**	0.48	8.63	15.53
Mean	0.66	**0.7**	55.21	24.45	0.6	**0.66**	63.2	24.51	0.59	**0.65**	57.83	24.4

Qualitative Results: Figure 1 provides an example of a 3D image processed by the CNN only and by our pipeline. The CNN (Fig. 1-CNN Output) provides a visually acceptable semantic segmentation: at the exception of many surrounding artefacts (particularly visible on 3D views), most target structures are globally recovered. Despite these surrounding artefacts, segmentation errors occur in parts of the target structures that need to be relabelled (see 2D slices, bounding boxes and arrows in 3D views). Our pipeline succeeds in correcting most segmentation errors: many parts of the structures of interest are correctly relabeled and most surrounding artefacts are removed. Note that artefacts removal corresponds to the matching with the class "none" in our "many-to-one-or-none" graph matching strategy, and it is managed using the threshold T (cf. Algorithm 1) that needs to be correctly tuned as it affects computation of HD.

4 Conclusion

We have proposed a post-processing technique for improving segmentation results using a graph matching procedure encoding structural relationships between regions. This correction of deep learning segmentation with the exploitation of structural patterns is performed thanks to inexact graph matching formulated as a two-steps Quadratic Assignment Problem (QAP). We validated our approach with experiments on 3D volumetric data, and we have shown significant improvements can be observed. When training the neural network on a limited dataset, our approach provides a very clear advantage by outperforming the baseline. Future work will investigate how to reduce the high computational time resulting from the complexity of operations (segmentation, graph matching and refinement) of our approach that may hinder real time applications.

References

1. Badrinarayanan, V., Kendall, A., Cipolla, R.: SegNet: a deep convolutional encoder-decoder architecture for image segmentation. IEEE Trans. Pattern Anal. Mach. Intell. **39**(12), 2481–2495 (2017). https://doi.org/10.1109/TPAMI.2016.2644615
2. Bloch, I.: Fuzzy sets for image processing and understanding. Fuzzy Sets Syst. **281**, 280–291 (2015). https://doi.org/10.1016/j.fss.2015.06.017
3. Chopin, J., Fasquel, J.B., Mouchère, H., Dahyot, R., Bloch, I.: Semantic image segmentation based on spatial relationships and inexact graph matching. In: 2020 Tenth International Conference on Image Processing Theory, Tools and Applications (IPTA), pp. 1–6 (2020). https://doi.org/10.1109/IPTA50016.2020.9286611
4. Colliot, O., Camara, O., Bloch, I.: Integration of fuzzy spatial relations in deformable models - application to brain MRI segmentation. Pattern Recogn. **39**, 1401–1414 (2006). https://doi.org/10.1016/j.patcog.2006.02.022
5. Delaye, A., Anquetil, E.: Fuzzy relative positioning templates for symbol recognition. In: International Conference on Document Analysis and Recognition, Beijing, China, September 2011. https://doi.org/10.1109/ICDAR.2011.246
6. Deruyver, A., Hodé, Y.: Qualitative spatial relationships for image interpretation by using a conceptual graph. Image Vis. Comput. **27**(7), 876–886 (2009). https://doi.org/10.1016/j.imavis.2008.10.002, 7th IAPR-TC15 Workshop on Graph-based Representations (GbR 2007)
7. Fasquel, J.B., Agnus, V., Moreau, J., Soler, L., Marescaux, J.: An interactive medical image segmentation system based on the optimal management of regions of interest using topological medical knowledge. Comput. Methods Programs Biomed. **82**, 216–230 (2006). https://doi.org/10.1016/j.cmpb.2006.04.004
8. Fasquel, J.B., Delanoue, N.: An approach for sequential image interpretation using a priori binary perceptual topological and photometric knowledge and k-means based segmentation. J. Opt. Soc. Am. A **35**(6), 936–945 (2018). https://doi.org/10.1364/JOSAA.35.000936
9. Fasquel, J.B., Delanoue, N.: A graph based image interpretation method using a priori qualitative inclusion and photometric relationships. IEEE Trans. Pattern Anal. Mach. Intell. **41**(5), 1043–1055 (2019). https://doi.org/10.1109/TPAMI.2018.2827939

10. Garcia-Garcia, A., Orts-Escolano, S., Oprea, S., Villena-Martinez, V., Martinez-Gonzalez, P., Garcia-Rodriguez, J.: A survey on deep learning techniques for image and video semantic segmentation. Appl. Soft Comput. **70**, 41–65 (2018). https://doi.org/10.1016/j.asoc.2018.05.018

11. Goodfellow, I.J., Bengio, Y., Courville, A.: Deep Learning. MIT Press, Cambridge (2016)

12. Julca-Aguilar, F., Mouchère, H., Viard-Gaudin, C., Hirata, N.S.T.: A general framework for the recognition of online handwritten graphics. Int. J. Doc. Anal. Recogn. (IJDAR) **23**(2), 143–160 (2020). https://doi.org/10.1007/s10032-019-00349-6

13. Kunze, L., et al.: Combining top-down spatial reasoning and bottom-up object class recognition for scene understanding. In: 2014 IEEE/RSJ International Conference on Intelligent Robots and Systems, pp. 2910–2915. IEEE (2014). https://doi.org/10.1109/IROS.2014.6942963

14. Kushibar, K., et al.: Automated sub-cortical brain structure segmentation combining spatial and deep convolutional features. Med. Image Anal. **48**, 177–186 (2018). https://doi.org/10.1016/j.media.2018.06.006

15. Lee, B., Yamanakkanavar, N., Choi, J.Y.: Automatic segmentation of brain MRI using a novel patch-wise U-Net deep architecture. PLOS ONE **15**(8), 1–20 (2020). https://doi.org/10.1371/journal.pone.0236493

16. Lezoray, O., Leo, L.: Image Processing and Analysis with Graphs: Theory and Practice. CRC Press, Cambridge (2012)

17. Maciel, J., Costeira, J.P.: A global solution to sparse correspondence problems. IEEE Trans. Pattern Anal. Mach. Intell. **25**(2), 187–199 (2003). https://doi.org/10.1109/TPAMI.2003.1177151

18. Moreno, A., Takemura, C., Colliot, O., Camara, O., Bloch, I.: Using anatomical knowledge expressed as fuzzy constraints to segment the heart in CT images. Pattern Recogn. **41**(8), 2525–2540 (2008). https://doi.org/10.1016/j.patcog.2008.01.020

19. Nempont, O., Atif, J., Bloch, I.: A constraint propagation approach to structural model based image segmentation and recognition. Inf. Sci. **246**, 1–27 (2013). https://doi.org/10.1016/j.ins.2013.05.030

20. Noma, A., Graciano, A.B., Cesar, R.M., Jr., Consularo, L.A., Bloch, I.: Interactive image segmentation by matching attributed relational graphs. Pattern Recogn. **45**(3), 1159–1179 (2012). https://doi.org/10.1016/j.patcog.2011.08.017

21. Ronneberger, O., Fischer, P., Brox, T.: U-Net: convolutional networks for biomedical image segmentation. In: Navab, N., Hornegger, J., Wells, W.M., Frangi, A.F. (eds.) MICCAI 2015. LNCS, vol. 9351, pp. 234–241. Springer, Cham (2015). https://doi.org/10.1007/978-3-319-24574-4_28

22. Pérez-García, F., Sparks, R., Ourselin, S.: TorchIO: a Python library for efficient loading, preprocessing, augmentation and patch-based sampling of medical images in deep learning. arXiv:2003.04696 [cs, eess, stat], March 2020

23. Weiss, K., Khoshgoftaar, T.M., Wang, D.D.: A survey of transfer learning. J. Big Data **3**(1), 1–40 (2016). https://doi.org/10.1186/s40537-016-0043-6

24. Zanfir, A., Sminchisescu, C.: Deep learning of graph matching. In: 2018 IEEE/CVF Conference on Computer Vision and Pattern Recognition, pp. 2684–2693 (2018). https://doi.org/10.1109/CVPR.2018.00284

25. Zhou, F., De la Torre, F.: Factorized graph matching. IEEE Trans. Pattern Anal. Mach. Intell. **38**(9), 1774–1789 (2016). https://doi.org/10.1109/TPAMI.2015.2501802

Application of Rail Segmentation in the Monitoring of Autonomous Train's Frontal Environment

Mohamed Amine Hadded[1](✉)(iD), Ankur Mahtani[1](✉)(iD), Sébastien Ambellouis[2](✉)(iD), Jacques Boonaert[3](✉)(iD), and Hazem Wannous[4](✉)(iD)

[1] FCS Railenium, 59300 Famars, France
{mohamed-amine.hadded,ankur.mahtani}@railenium.eu
[2] Gustave Eiffel University, Villeneuve d'Ascq, Lille, France
sebastien.ambellouis@univ-eiffel.fr
[3] IMT Lille-Douai, Douai, France
jacques.boonaert@imt-lille-douai.fr
[4] IMT Lille Douai, Villeneuve-d'Ascq, France
hazem.wannous@imt-lille-douai.fr

Abstract. One of the key factors in achieving an autonomous vehicle is understanding and modeling the driving environment. This step requires a considerable amount of data acquired from a wide range of sensors. To bridge the gap between the Roadway and Railway fields in terms of datasets and experimentation, we provide a new dataset called RailSet as the second large dataset after Railsem19, specialized in Rail segmentation. In this paper we present a multiple semantic segmentation using two deep networks UNET and FRNN trained on different data configuration involving RailSet and Railsem19 datasets. We show comparable results and promising performance to be applicable in monitoring autonomous train's ego perspective view.

Keywords: Semantic segmentation · Rail segmentation · Frontal train monitoring · Railway

1 Introduction

For decades, the industry has sought to replace or augment drivers in various modes of transportation with autonomous, programmed computers that would be more efficient, cost-effective, and safer than human operators.

The concept of developing self-driving trains is not new; indeed, the "Victoria" metro line (inaugurated in 1968 in London-UK) is considered to be the first large-scale automatic rail system [1,2]. This train is currently classified as GoA2 [3]: the driver is still present in the cab but only deals with closing doors and starting orders, and the train moves automatically to the next stop. As of July 2016, 789 km of automated metro in operation consisting of 53 lines and 822 stations in 36 cities around the world according

---

IRT Railenium, SNCF, Alstom Crespin, Thales, Bosch, and SpirOps.
For now only 10% of our dataset RailSet are provided in this link, will publish the rest shortly.

© Springer Nature Switzerland AG 2022
M. El Yacoubi et al. (Eds.): ICPRAI 2022, LNCS 13363, pp. 185–197, 2022.
https://doi.org/10.1007/978-3-031-09037-0_16

Fig. 1. Examples from RailSet: front views of train taken from different setups, climatic conditions and different acquisition periods.

to the International Union of Public Transport (UITP) [2]. Half of the automated metro infrastructure is concentrated in four countries: France, South Korea, Singapore and the United Arab Emirates [UITP, 2016] [2], but these sophisticated systems are limited and located in urban areas relatively isolated from certain potential hazards. The most sophisticated driverless trains, particularly in urban guided transport, are automatic but not autonomous.

The absence of a driver in the cabin is therefore not enough to classify a train as autonomous. It is its on-board decision-making capacity that makes a train autonomous. Moreover, autonomous trains are different from automatic trains regarding the fact that autonomous trains evolve in an open and dynamic environment. Some elements of the environment have an unpredictable behavior that can lead to unexpected and potentially hazardous situations. These autonomous rolling stocks will encounter a very heterogeneous environment and will operate on tracks equipped with various signaling systems. Therefore, one of the most important aspects for ensuring a vehicle's autonomy is to remain self-aware of its surroundings, first by perceiving (identifying and classifying) all external risks, possible anomalies or hazards; then by acting on the information through the control system to position themselves correctly in their environment in order to better adapt to external conditions [4], this implies the use of more advanced applications and technologies.

Inspection and detection of the structural condition of the railway infrastructure [5–8] is crucial to ensure safety and to enable more advanced applications such as driver automation. At the very heart of this challenge comes the rail and the rail track, which constitute one of the most important components of the railway environment, as they are in direct contact with the train's wheels determining its trajectory. Any alteration in the structure of these components [8] through wheels interaction [7], imperfections in either of them due to severe loading conditions heavier axles and vehicles, due to traffic growth, gives rise to severe dynamic effects such as vibrations and track deformations that can lead to catastrophic vehicle derailment, the consequences of which can result in fatalities, injuries and economic losses. Alternatively, external objects such as obstructions and passengers at the vicinity of the rails have the same bad impact on the normal flow of the train. This makes detecting Rails a central key in monitoring frontal environment of the train and in decision making in autonomous trains, similar to detecting road lanes for autonomous vehicles in order to localize its flow in reference to other users.

In this paper, we discuss various semantic segmentation experiments based on UNET [9] and FRNN [10] methods to assess their performance on rail segmentation from various train frontal scenes taken from two railway datasets including the largest datasets, Railsem19 scenes and our RailSet dataset with 8500 and 6600 scenes respectively, see Fig. 1. When creating our RailSet dataset, we strived to bring more complex scenes in terms of rail visibility, weather conditions, and long distance rail detection, not just noisy images due to vibration and flow movement. This brings more scenes to Railsem19 [11], more semantic use cases, and helps enrich public rail datasets and test scenarios like the semantic experiences detailed in this paper, which summarize our contribution in this work.

2   Related Works

2.1   Dataset

Railsem19 [11] is the first public contribution to the segmentation task of multiple objects in the railway environment. It contains 8500 annotated short sequences, including various scenes taken from the perspective of the train and streetcar driver. Yin et al. [12] proposed a railroad segmentation dataset called RSDS, which consists of 3000 images taken in the environment of low-speed trains in China. Yin et al. [12] employed manual annotation with the VIA tool [13] to label only the active railroad track on which the train is moving. The data is not made available to the public.

Then comes our RailSet dataset as a second public dataset consisting of 6600 manual annotations using the open source software CVAT [14]. We process all visible rails in the scenes, where only rail and track classes are labeled.

However, with road-oriented datasets such as Cityscapes [15], Mapillary vistas [16], COCO-stuff [17], and KITTI [18], some railway elements can be found in the images. The rail scenes in these datasets represent a combination of interior views, road views, and pedestrian views, but perspective scenes of the driver are almost non-existent.

2.2   Segmentation

Our proposed dataset, RailSet, is intended to solve the task of segmenting the rails from the train's ego view. This task is important for monitoring the railway environment from an onboard video surveillance system at the front of the train. The rail segmentation task has been the subject of some existing research. Among these works, Kaleli and Akgul [19] propose a driver assistance solution, in which they use dynamic programming to extract the active track ahead of the train. Ukai and Tomoyuki [20] also focus on front track extraction, an important step to detect fixed or moving obstacles in front of the train. To extract the railroad tracks, they divide the scene into a near and far area and apply a set of image processing techniques and an iterative algorithm for each to extract the rail parts.

With the emergence of deep learning and convolution neural network reasoning, a number of works have begun to exploit the semantically segmented neural network for rail detection in frontal train scenes. Zendel et al. [11] propose a full-resolution residual network (FRNN) [10] as a benchmark method for fully segmenting Railway scenes from an ego-perspective view. This model is first trained on the Cityscape dataset and then refined on the Railsem19 dataset. This approach achieves a good level of segmentation on the different classes in the rail and streetcar configurations, and in particular on the rail-specific labels, with 71.5% mIoU on elevated railroads, 45% mIoU on embedded railroads, 81.9% mIoU on railroads, and 40.1% mIoU on streetcar tracks. Yin et al. proposed RailNet, a custom convolutional model designed to segment the active track region of low-speed trains. Yin et al. [12] proposed RailNet, a custom end-to-end model that combines feature extraction and segmentation, where they integrate multi-convolution feature extraction based on pyramid structure to make the features have a top-bottom propagation. It achieves better performance that fully convolutional FCN and detection based methods Mask RCNN. Gibert and Patel [21] demonstrate a custom full convolution network to segment railroad track scenes for visual inspection of rail components. This approach is tested on the Northeast Corridor dataset by ENSCO Rail's Comprehensive Track Inspection Vehicle (CTIV) and shows good accuracy and low false positive segmentation rates.

3   Rail Segmentation

3.1   RailSet

We selected 23 videos from the train driver's perspective to create the RailSet dataset. Of these videos, 22 are accessible via the YouTube platform[1], one of which is owned by the SNCF[2]. These videos cover more than 34 h of train traffic from different countries and in various conditions: weather conditions, camera models, editing positions and lighting conditions. To avoid redundancy and overlapping scenes, we choose an average of 280 frames per video, with each frame relatively distinct from the previous one. We also adjust an SSIM metric [22] to measure the difference in structure between the selected frames and filter out repetitive scenes. We include empty scenes where the rails are invisible, such as in tunnels with no lighting, and snowy scenes where the rails are fully or partially covered, in order to evaluate the consistency of existing models over more variable situations (see Table 1).

Unlike Railsem19, we provide links to the collected videos and the index of each processed scene. This allows us to provide more similar scenes for testing purposes, and also serves as pseudo-labels where we can take a sequence of unlabeled images around the labeled scenes for semi-supervised learning and for temporal processing like tracking and matching.

We annotate the data based on the basic concept of rail structure, where the rails are the components in direct contact with the train wheels, while the areas between each pair of rails define the rail tracks. The rail class is annotated using the CVAT computer vision annotation tool [14]. Each rail is annotated with a polyline extended to the widest range of visibility of the rail, then smoothed with spline interpolation to remove wobbles and sharp edges. The rail track class is automatically inferred from the rail labels

---

[1] These videos are licensed permissive or free to use except for commercial purposes or with explicit consent to allow experimentation and dissemination.

[2] Société Nationale des Chemins de fer Français.

by applying rail pairing. Rail pairing consists of grouping two rails belonging to the same track which we performed manually using the CVAT tool [14]. We represent the rail track class in two forms, either by a midline or by an enclosing polygon. To form the polygonal representation, we simply connect each pair of lines and then fill in the surrounding space. For the midline shape, we fit a line between each pair of rails by taking the midpoint coordinates of the points that lie on the same horizontal level (Fig. 2). The purpose of using different shapes of the rails class is to detect which of them will allow the models to achieve better performance in detecting rails and neglecting other objects semantically similar to rails.

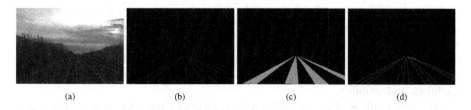

(a)   (b)   (c)   (d)

Fig. 2. RailSet different annotations masks. (**a**) raw-image, (**b**) rail class, (**c**) rail and rail-track (enclosing polygon representation) classes and (**d**) rail and rail-track (mid-line representation) classes.

Railsem19 [11] labeling policy contains more rail-specific labels than in our work. For the SBDS data, only the active rail track is annotated, which is different from our dataset and Railsem19, and since it is private data, we cannot consider it in our comparison. To ensure comparability between the RailSet and Railsem19 datasets in our experiment we take four of these labeled classes and we transform them following the policy described previously taking the rail-raised (Fig. 6 (a)) and the rail-embedded (Fig. 6 (b)) labels as rail class, while the rail-track (Fig. 6 (a)) and the tram-track (Fig. 6 (b)) labels as rail-track class.

Table 1. RailSet dataset properties

Number of Data	Number_of_videos	Acquisition time	Number of rails	Less visibility
6600	23	Day light = 4376, Sunny = 56, Rain = 395, Snow = 1033, Dusk time = 299, Night = 441	Pairs = 15223, Single-tracks = 139, Total = 30585, >4 rails per frame = 25%, <4 rails per frame = 75%	Before bridge or tunnel = 393 Inside tunnels = 604 Snow = 517 Night = 320
Annotation shapes	Presence in frames	Empty_images	Percentage_covered_areas	Mean_frames_per_video
rail = polyline rail-track = polygon rail-track = poly-line(mid-line)	Rails = 98.74% Rail-track(polygon, mid-line) = 98.28%	83	Rails = 0.89% Rail-tracks = 8.26%	280 ≃ 0.41%

3.2   Experiments

We have two semantic segmentation networks deployed to solve the rail track segmenta-tion task, UNET [9] and FRNN [10] which represent the baselines for our experiments. The training, validation, and testing distributions are based on different combinations of data, including the RailSet and Railsem19 [11] datasets. Both architectures, UNET [9] and FRNN [10] are configured for an input shape of $512 \times 512 \times 3$ and a batch size of 20 images, with the Adam optimizer (learning rate = 0.01, decay rate = 0.9) [23]. As a model evaluation metric, we use the Jaccard index, called the IoU metric. This metric provides the amount of overlap between the predicted labels and the ground truth labels. The models are implemented in the NVIDIA V100 GPU.

For each segmentation model, we validate its performance and test it on both RailSet and Railsem19. The test set is composed of 1419 images from both datasets in a pro-portion of 10% each. For the training set, depending on the experience, it varies at proportion of 80% of the involved data. All these sets are selected equitably by tak-ing into account various level of complexity presented on the number of rails, climatic conditions and visibility.

We apply to the RailSet and Railsem19 datasets an augmentation using two trans-formations which are mirroring with horizontal shift and zooming by warping the per-spective of the region that contains all the rails to the full size image, see Fig. 3. We also add 1290 crops of objects semantically similar to the rails, such as poles and wires, to the empty images where the rails are not visible due to lighting, such as in tunnels. The goal is to test whether this improves the discrimination ability of the models, thereby reducing false positives.

Our data present a strong intrinsic imbalance, and to avoid having biased segmenta-tion models, we generate for each batch of images and masks the corresponding weights to penalize misclassifications.

(a)   (b)

Fig. 3. Data augmentation. (**a**) Mirror via horizontal-shift augmentation, (**b**) Zooming to rails via image stretching transformation.

We compare eight different experimental scenarios in which we refer to the results of Zendel et al. [11] on the Railsem19 dataset. Since the relevant datasets are based on two classes, while in Railsem19 they have dealt with several rail-specific classes, we derive the average results of Zendel et al. [11] to obtain an overall segmentation performance on the rail and track classes. Thus, we introduce the following equation: 1, in which we use the presence rate in the images "in-frame" and the individual "mIoU" performance provided in [11].

$$mIoU(Rails) = \frac{In - Frames_{(Rail-raised)} \times mIoU_{(Rail-raised)} + In - Frames_{(Rail-embedded)} \times mIoU_{(Rail-embedded)}}{(In - frames_{(Rail-raised)} + In - Frames_{(Rail-embedded)})} \quad (1)$$

In all different scenarios, we opted for the dice-coefficient loss function that allows us to obtain the best performance. The process of how we select the suitable loss function is based on an experiment with UNET [9] and FRNN [10] on the RailSet dataset, we compare different loss functions among many such as AsymLoss, Tversky Loss, Sensitivity-Specifity Loss, SoftDice loss and TopKLoss, see Table 2. Their implementations are described in [24].

Scenarios on Rail Class. In the scenario (1) and (2) we used RailSet and Railsem19 respectively with only the rail class, to study the impact of data augmentation on UNET and FRNN segmentation performance. Therefore, we tested 3 data configurations; without data augmentation, with data augmentation using only zooming and mirroring, then we add the empty crops and images. We see an overall performance improvement on both datasets, see Fig. 4. Since we proved the importance of data augmentation applied on RailSet and Railsem19, that allows the models to learn more features and different situations, we opt for this technique in the remaining scenarios.

Under full data augmentation, UNET and FRNN models perform better overall more complex scenes in the test set when trained on RailSet than on Railsem19 (see Table 3), given that only 40% of the test set comes from our RailSet dataset. In the scenario (1), we also tested the models on only tramway scenes, that yielded to comparable results to Zendel et al. [11]. That shows the consistency of our dataset in more specific environment setups. Otherwise, in the scenario (2), we observe a drop in performance when testing the models on RailSet which is a dataset specific to only railways (see Fig. 5). This drop of performance can be explained by the fact that training models on a more general dataset that contains mix of railways and tramways data would produce a domain shift[3]. We therefore set an assumption that neglecting these tramway scenes and training only with an in-domain data would improve performance. This assumption is treated in the next scenario (3).

In scenario (3), we addressed the previously mentioned assumption. We trained UNET and FRNN models on the Railsem19 dataset with only railway scenes, and tested it against the RailSet dataset. We note that there is no significant improvement in performance (see Fig. 5). This is can be due to the high variability of RailSet scenes, which potentially contain a more complex environment configuration. This explains the importance of introducing this new dataset to handle more specific environment complexity in the railway domain.

Scenarios on Rail and Rail Track Classes. Previously, only the rail class is treated. In the scenario (4) and (5), we include the rail-track class when training the models on RailSet and Railsem19 respectively. This additional class lead to a better segmentation performance and provides a visual representation of the rail track region. In the

---

[3] A change in the data distribution between an algorithm's training dataset, and a dataset it encounters when deployed.

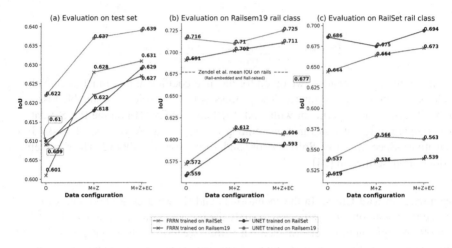

Fig. 4. Evaluation of FRNN and UNET on test set (a), rail class of Railsem19 dataset (b) and rail class of RailSet dataset (c) taken from the scenarios (1) and (2). The effect of the different data-augmentations O: without augmentation, M+Z: Mirror+Zoom, M+Z+EC:Mirror+Zoom+Empty-Crops(1290 scenes without rails+83 empty images).

scenario (4), we observe an improvement in rail segmentation, especially the results on Railsem19 with almost 1,5% gain compared to scenario (1) where we trained with only the rail class, see Fig. 5. In the scenario (5), we observe an enhancement when testing on RailSet with almost 1%. Moreover, rail-track class yields more direct local features on the rails and leads the models to focus on the low region of the images, which reduces the false positive rate, i.e., the detection of wires as rails. This improves rail detection in reduced visibility conditions in tunnels, at night and also in stormy conditions, as shown in the Table 3 of the test set.

In the scenario (6), we study the impact of changing the rail-track representation in the RailSet dataset. The rail-tracks in their standard representation as enclosing-polygons produce better performance results than the mid-line form, see Fig. 5. This may be due to the area similarity covered by the mid-lines with the surrounding areas, resulting in more confusion and false positive segmentation. Such discontinuities or shifts in the mid-lines position can cause the same on the rails segments.

Scenarios on Mix Dataset RailSet and Railsem19. In the scenarios (7) and (8) we highlight the importance of mixing both datasets RailSet and Railsem19 when training models, in which we obtained the best results on the test set as shown in Fig. 5. We also notice that training with the two classes rail and rail-track in scenario (8) achieves rails segmentation precision of 67% mIoU on test set, 70% mIoU on Railsem19 and 69% mIoU on RailSet almost similar performance results compared to training with only the rail class in scenario (7). In the Table 3, we can see in bold the best performances on various scene categories of the test set are obtained by training on both datasets, as well as adding the rail track class which improves the segmentation accuracy on less visible rails. This experiment confirms the need of obtaining more training data to get more scene situations and features. See Fig. 7 for more visual results.

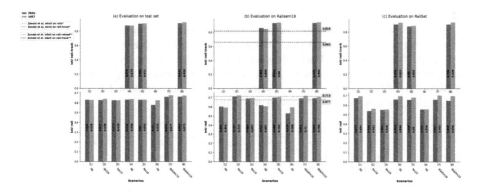

Fig. 5. Evaluation results of UNET and FRNN on test set (a), Railsem19 (b) and RailSet (c) across all the eight cases where all the data-augmentations were applied. The three lower plots deal with performance on rail class and the three upper plots with performance on rail-track class. **RS** = RailSet dataset, **Rm19** = Railsem19 dataset, **RS&Rm19** = RailSet dataset and Railsem19 dataset. In legends, * refers to results deduced from the Eq. (1), while ** refers to individual results taken from zendal et al. [11] paper.

In perspective, along with the semantic segmentation, these data will serve for anomaly detection by taking the location of the rails and processing it by auto-encoders. Alternatively as in [25], we can take this data and explore the semantic labels, whether they are ground truth labels or pseudo-labels composed of a sequence of ground truth labels and the underlying unlabeled scenes, as secondary guiding features for the 3D reconstruction of frontal train scenes to detect geometric deformation of the rails and holes in the rails and tracks.

Table 2. Evaluation of UNET and FRNN models trained on RailSet under various state-of-the-art segmentation losses on the overall datasets. **EC**: Empty Crops with objects semantically similar to rails, **M+Z**: Mirror+Zooming. The evaluation metric is the mIoU. The shortcut SS-loss refers to Sensitivity-Specifity loss.

Model	Training-parameters					Test-data	Valid-data	Railsem19			RailSet
	Data	Loss	Class	Augmentation				Train-scenes	Tram-scenes	Shared scene	
				M+Z	EC						
UNET	RailSet	Dice-coefficient	Rails	✓	✓	**0.642**	**0.637**	**0.627**	0.382	**0.621**	0.716
		Assymloss		✓	✓	0.585	0.574	0.587	0.335	0.587	0.597
		Tversky		✓	✓	0.639	0.636	0.607	0.382	0.596	**0.721**
		SS-loss		✓	✓	0.638	0.635	0.621	0.398	0.616	0.708
		DC_and_topk		✓	✓	0.629	0.625	0.615	0.373	0.61	0.695
FRNN	RailSet	Dice-coefficient	Rails	✓	✓	0.63	0.631	0.625	**0.418**	0.62	0.673
		Assymloss		✓	✓	0.603	0.605	0.564	0.399	0.558	0.692
		Tversky		✓	✓	0.548	0.555	0.512	0.35	0.505	0.631
		SS-loss		✓	✓	0.609	0.612	0.581	0.386	0.572	0.682
		DC_and_topk		✓	✓	0.622	0.623	0.587	0.395	0.583	0.699

Table 3. Detailed results of UNET and FRNN performance on various scenes in the test set, taking into account weather conditions and the number of rails per scene that alter rail visibility and make segmentation more complex. Training is performed on different data configurations and classes: "Rail" and "Rail Track" (polygon, centerline). <4 rails refers to scenes with less than four rails and <4 rails for scenes with more than four rails that represents 20% of test set. Values in bold indicate the best results on rail and track segmentation. For the rail midline configuration, we only shows the results on the rail class.

Model	Data	Classes	Test-data					
			Night	Snow	Tunnels	Rain	<4 rails	>4 rails
UNET	RailSet	Rail	0.58	0.647	0.544	0.66	0.627	0.633
		Rail | Rail track (midline)	0.546	0.6	0.514	0.621	0.593	0.594
		Rail | Rail track (polygon)	0.61 | 0.81	0.65 | 0.866	0.556 | 0.802	0.677 | 0.909	0.631 | 0.871	0.633 | 0.844
	Railsem19	Rail	0.562	0.559	0.525	0.616	0.617	0.657
		Rail | Rail track (polygon)	0.554 | 0.831	0.553 | 0.853	0.524 | 0.83	0.613 | 0.913	0.615 | 0.905	0.651 | 0.894
	RailSet + Railsem19	Rail	0.615	0.659	0.566	0.681	**0.677**	**0.675**
		Rail | Rail track (polygon)	**0.635 | 0.844**	**0.666 | 0.892**	**0.592 | 0.86**	**0.701 | 0.939**	0.675 | **0.923**	**0.675 | 0.903**
FRNN	RailSet	Rail	0.561	0.598	0.521	0.681	0.628	0.64
		Rail | Rail track (midline)	0.497	0.573	0.49	0.614	0.58	0.57
		Rail | Rail track (polygon)	0.552 | 0.763	0.592 | 0.823	0.535 | 0.801	0.682 | 0.897	0.634 | 0.88	0.639 | 0.869
	Railsem19	Rail	0.457	0.5	0.456	0.625	0.597	0.655
		Rail | Rail track (polygon)	0.505 | 0.763	0.522 | 0.814	0.494 | 0.787	0.615 | 0.909	0.613 | 0.895	0.645 | 0.894
	RailSet + Railsem19	Rail	0.561	0.619	0.541	0.662	0.655	0.674
		Rail | Rail track (polygon)	0.564 | 0.77	0.61 | 0.839	0.542 | 0.819	0.667 | 0.924	0.659 | 0.91	0.671 | 0.90

Fig. 6. FRNN test example on Railsem19's scenes. The first row displays the input images: (a) train scene, (b) tramway scene and (c) shared scene, the second row displays the ground truth of the input images and the last row displays the FRNN predictions.

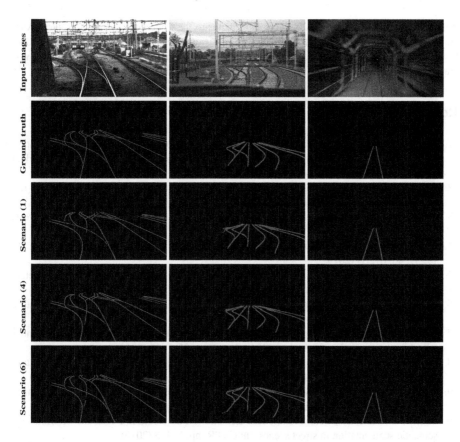

Fig. 7. Further examples of the results of UNET trained on different configurations of RailSet detailed in *scenario (1)*, *scenario (4)* and *scenario (6)*. Only the rail segmentation masks are displayed.

4 Conclusion

We present a new dataset for Rail and Rail-track segmentation in railway scenes: RailSet. Manual annotations are made to generate the Rail class masks, and from these initial annotations, the Rail-track labeling is generated automatically. We conducted multiple experiments using the UNET and FRNN architectures on different data configurations. These experiments yielded results comparable to those recorded on the Railsem19 dataset. That in turn proved the valuability of the RailSet dataset, along a number of pre-treatments such as the data augmentation, the inclusion of the Rail-track class in training and merging the two datasets. Adding temporal indexes of RailSet scenes would yield more data for testing, and would serve as input for other tasks such as semantic pattern matching and tracking. For now, only a part of the RailSet dataset is provided for public and will publish the remaining sooner.

Acknowledgements. This research work contributes to the french collaborative project TASV (autonomous passengers service train), with SNCF, Alstom Crespin, Thales, Bosch, and SpirOps. It was carried out in the framework of IRT Railenium, Valenciennes, France, and therefore was granted public funds within the scope of the French Program "Investissements d' Avenir".

References

1. Powell, J., Fraszczyk, A., Cheong, C., Yeung, H.: Potential benefits and obstacles of implementing driverless train operation on the Tyne and wear metro: a simulation exercise. Urban Rail Transit **12**, 1–12 (2016)
2. Wang, Y., Zhang, M., Ma, J., Zhou, X.S.: Survey on driverless train operation for urban rail transit systems. Urban Rail Transit **2**, 106–113 (2016)
3. Stene, T.: Automation of the Rail-Removing the Human Factor? pp. 1947–1955. CRC Press, Cambrige (2018)
4. Carre, M.: Autonomic framework for safety management in the autonomous vehicle, pp. 18, 19, 39, 40, 67, 69 (2019)
5. Sadeghi, J., Askarinejad, H.: Influences of track structure, geometry and traffic parameters on railway deterioration. Trans. B Appl. **3**, 292–300 (2007)
6. Kumaran, G., Menon, D., Nair, K.: Dynamic studies of railtrack sleepers in a track structure system. J. Sound Vibr. **268**, 488–490 (2003)
7. Bian, J., Gu, Y., Murray, M.: A dynamic wheel-rail impact analysis of railway track under wheel flat by finite element analysis. Veh. Syst. Dyn. **51**, 1–16 (2013)
8. Cannon, D., Edel, K.-O., Grassie, S., Sawley, K.: Rail defects: an overview. Fatigue Fracture Eng. Mater. Struct. **26**, 865–886 (2003)
9. Olaf Ronneberger, T.B., Fischer, P.: U-Net: convolutional networks for biomedical image segmentation. MICCAI, arxiv:1505.04597, pp. 2–4 (2015)
10. Pohlen, T., Hermans, A., Mathias, M., Leibe, B.: Full-resolution residual networks for semantic segmentation in street scenes. In: CVPR, pp. 1, 4, 5 (2016)
11. Zendel, O., Murschitz, M., Zeilinger, M., Steininger, D., Abbasi, S., Beleznai, C.: Railsem19: a dataset for semantic rail scene understanding. In: CVPRW, pp. 1, 5, 6 (2019)
12. Wang, Y., Wang, L., Hu, Y.H., Qiu, J.: RailNet: a segmentation network for railroad detection. IEEE Access **7**, 143772–143779 (2019)
13. Dutta, A., Zisserman, A.: The VGG image annotator (VIA). CoRR arXiv:1904.10699 (2019)
14. Sekachev and Boris: Computer vision annotation tool: a universal approach to data annotation (2019)
15. Cordts, M., et al.: The cityscapes dataset for semantic urban scene understanding. CoRR, pp. 1–3 (2016)
16. Neuhold, G., Ollmann, T., Rota Bulo, S., Kontschieder, P.: The mapillary vistas dataset for semantic understanding of street scenes. In: ICCV, pp. 1, 2, 4 (2017)
17. Lin, T., et al.: Microsoft COCO: common objects in context. CoRR, pp. 5–7 (2014)
18. K.I. of Technology and T.T.I. at Chicago. Kitti
19. Kaleli, F., Akgul, Y.: Vision-based railroad track extraction using dynamic programming. In: ITSC, pp. 4–6 (2009)
20. Ukai, M., Tomoyuki, B.: Obstacle detection on railway track by fusing radar and image sensor. In: WCRR, p. 12 (2011)
21. Gibert, V., Patel, M., Chellappa, R.: Semantic segmentation of railway track images with deep convolutional neural networks. In: ICIP, pp. 1–5 (2015)
22. Brunet, D., Vrscay, E.R., Wang, Z.: On the mathematical properties of the structural similarity index. IEEE Trans. Image Process. **21**(4), 1488–1499 (2012)

23. Chollet, F., et al.: Keras (2015). https://github.com/tensorflow/tensorflow/blob/master/tensorflow/python/training/adam.py
24. JunMa11. Segloss (2020). https://github.com/JunMa11/SegLoss/
25. Guizilini, V., Hou, R., Li, J., Ambrus, R., Gaidon, A.: Semantically-guided representation learning for self-supervised monocular depth. In: International Conference on Learning Representations (2020)

DR-VNet: Retinal Vessel Segmentation via Dense Residual UNet

Ali Karaali[1,2(✉)] [ID], Rozenn Dahyot[2,3] [ID], and Donal J. Sexton[1,2,4] [ID]

[1] The Irish Longitudinal Study on Ageing (TILDA), School of Medicine, Trinity College Dublin, Dublin, Ireland
{karaalia,dosexton}@tcd.ie
[2] ADAPT: Science Foundation Ireland (SFI) Research Centre for Digital Media Technology, Dublin, Ireland
rozenn.dahyot@mu.ie
[3] Department of Computer Science, Maynooth University, Maynooth, Ireland
[4] Department of Nephrology, St. James's Hospital, Dublin, Ireland

Abstract. Accurate retinal vessel segmentation is an important task for many computer-aided diagnosis systems. Yet, it is still a challenging problem due to the complex vessel structures of an eye. Numerous vessel segmentation methods have been proposed recently, however more research is needed to deal with poor segmentation of thin and tiny vessels. To address this, we propose a new deep learning pipeline combining the efficiency of residual dense net blocks and, residual squeeze and excitation blocks. We validate experimentally our approach on three datasets and show that our pipeline outperforms current state of the art techniques on the sensitivity metric relevant to assess capture of small vessels.

Keywords: Retinal image · Vessel segmentation · Eye

1 Introduction

Retinal fundus images have been widely used as a supportive tool to screen, diagnose and treat various systemic diseases, such as cardiovascular disorders [20], kidney diseases [3], and eye-related pathologies, as the retina is the only tissue in the human body where vascular structures can be visualized in a non-invasive manner for clinical examination. Most of the aforementioned diseases might manifest as changes in the morphological structure of retinal blood vessels, consequently various salient and dangerous diseases (e.g. cardiovascular diseases, high blood pressure) can be detected before they create more dangerous and irreversible conditions. Segmentation of the retinal blood vessels is one of the crucial steps for retinal fundus image analysis. However, segmenting the retinal blood vessels manually is a very time consuming and intensive task, and requires not only specific medical training but also technical expertise. In order to mitigate the workload of the health workers, computerized segmentation strategies have garnered great interest in recent years, and many segmentation methods have been proposed [2,6,14]. However, one of the main drawbacks of existing retinal

© Springer Nature Switzerland AG 2022
M. El Yacoubi et al. (Eds.): ICPRAI 2022, LNCS 13363, pp. 198–210, 2022.
https://doi.org/10.1007/978-3-031-09037-0_17

vessel segmentation methods is that they present a poor sensitivity rate where the thin and tiny vessel branches are located, and they tend to be miss-classified by most of the existing methods.

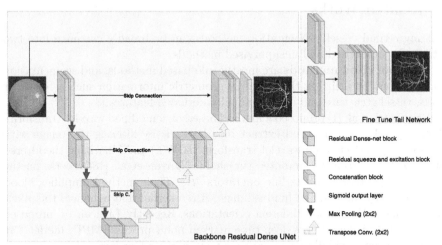

(a) Overview: Residual Dense-Net (pink blocks) is explained Fig. 1(b), Residual squeeze and excitation block architecture (blue blocks) is explained Fig. 1(c).

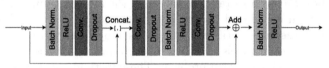

(b) Residual dense-net (RDN) block architecture.

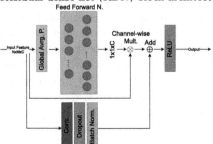

(c) Residual squeeze and excitation block architecture.

Fig. 1. Our proposed architecture uses a modified Backbone Residual Dense UNet that is extended with a Fine Tune Tail Network.

In this paper we propose a supervised method called DR-VNet for retinal vessel segmentation based on Convolutional Neural Network (CNN), aiming to overcome the aforementioned sensitivity rate problem while keeping the other accuracy metrics (e.g. specificity, accuracy, Area Under the ROC Curve (AUC)) at a high level. The technical details of each part of our pipeline are presented in Sect. 3 and validated on three datasets (cf. Sect. 4) against the current leading state of the art methods (reviewed Sect. 2).

2 Related Works

Existing retinal vessel segmentation methods can be broadly classified into two categories: supervised and unsupervised methods.

Unsupervised methods are mostly rule-based methods, and segmentation is carried out by utilizing the visual or geometric information such as contrast levels, vessel structure and other manually designed features [2].

Bankhead et al. [1] proposed a method based on a modified wavelet transform. More precisely, their method extract blood vessels by filtering the image with the isotropic undecimated wavelet transform (IUWT) and binarizing the filtered image with a percentile-computed threshold. Nguyen et al. [18]'s work, on the other hand, is based on the line operators [21]. Their method amplifies blood vessel pixels by filtering the fundus image with a kernel that enhances the pixels that belong to the lines at different orientations. Recently, Li et al.[14] proposed a method that is based on a deep tube marked point process (MPP) model [13], which has been originally proposed to detect short and/or long tubes in a given hyper-spectral image. As the blood vessel in retinal fundus images are visually similar to tubes, the authors take advantage of the already trained MPP model bypassing the need for labeled images.

Supervised methods utilize a group of samples to train a classifier that discriminates the vessel pixels from the background eye tissue, which can be referred as a binary classification problem. These methods are machine learning and/or deep neural network (DNN) based methods.

Soares et al. [23] proposed a supervised segmentation algorithm that utilizes the two dimensional - multi scale Gabor wavelet filter responses as features. Then, three types of classifiers is used to segment vessel pixels: Gaussian mixture model (GMM), K-nearest neighbor (KNN) and least mean square error (LMSE). More recently, Liskowski et al. [15] proposed a CNN based method that consists of consecutive convolutional & max pooling and fully connected layers. The proposed network inputs 27×27 image patches, and classifies them whether centered on vessel pixels or not. Moreover, Guo et al. proposed a UNet [22] based method called Structured Dropout UNet [7]. The method is inspired by a recently developed neural block called DropBlock [4], which does not exploit the traditional dropout at convolutional layers, but instead, utilizes a structured dropout block. Their work is extended in [5] by employing a modified residual block structure and a spatial attention block [25]. Later on, Guo et al. [6] introduced a new block called Modified Efficient Channel Attention (MECA). Their module enhances the discriminative capacity of the modified UNet shape architecture by weighting the feature map channels independently.

Following the vast majority of recent methods relying on deep learning, we present next a new deep learning pipeline aiming at improving sensitivity for detecting thin blood vessels (see Fig. 1).

3 Proposed Method

Our proposed CNN architecture DR-VNet consists of two cascaded sub-networks: a *Backbone Residual Dense* network and a *Fine-tune Tail* network.

The *Backbone Residual Dense* sub-network is inspired by the well known UNet [22], where three down-sampling and up-sampling blocks are used instead of four, and the original convolutional layers are replaced by two novel blocks: (i) Residual dense-net block (Fig. 1(b)); (ii) Residual squeeze and excitation block (Fig. 1(c)). *The Fine-tune Tail sub-network*, on the other hand, is a shallow network that consists of three consecutive RDN and RSE blocks, which combine the output of the *Backbone Residual Dense* sub-network and the input retinal image. The aim is to fine-tune the output of the *Backbone Residual Dense* sub-network to produce the final retinal vessel segmentation image.

Residual dense-net (RDN) block is a novel neural architecture that is based on DenseNet [11] and ResNet [8] types of neural structures (see Fig. 1(b)). The proposed neural block consists of two sequentially connected sub-blocks that utilize dense and residual connectivity patterns.

The first sub-block, which employs the dense connectivity pattern, is based on the idea of connecting a layer's output to the following layer's input in a feed-forward fashion, as in [11]. In contrast to summation as in a residual block, the connection is performed by concatenation. To do that, we define a composite function of $\mathcal{H}$ that consists of consecutive Batch Normalization, ReLu, Convolution and Dropout operations, and applied to the input features X. More formally, the process can be defined as $y_d = [\mathcal{H}(X; \{W_i\}), X]$, where [.] represents the concatenation operation, and y_d is the output of the first sub-block. Although this sub-block might have more than one composite function $\mathcal{H}$ (i.e. a deeper architecture), we opt to use a single unit to keep the network light-weight.

The second sub-block, on the other hand, employs the residual connectivity pattern, which consists of a mapping function $\mathcal{F}$ with 2-layers of Convolution, Dropout, Batch Normalization, and ReLu operations (see Fig. 1(b)). More precisely, the RDN block is defined as $y_{RDN} = \delta(\mathcal{BN}(\mathcal{F}(y_d; \{W_i\}) + y_d))$, where y_{RDN} represent the output of the RDN block, $\mathcal{BN}$ represents the Batch Normalization operation, and δ represents the second non-linearity function ReLu. This block is designed as a feature extractor inspired by DenseNet and ResNet neural architectures, as they present a good leverage for many CNN tasks [8,11].

Residual squeeze and excitation (RSE) block is inspired by ResNet [8] and a recently developed Squeeze and Excitation (SE) types of neural architectures [10]. In general, SE neural blocks aim at exploring channel interdependencies so as to selectively emphasize informative channels and suppress less useful ones. Residual blocks are designed to smooth the information flow across the layers so as to facilitate the optimization process. Given the success of ResNet blocks [8] and SE blocks [10], we propose to combine ResNet onto SE block to design a novel neural block (Fig. 1(c)) to enhance the extracted features and to facilitate the optimization process.

The proposed RSE block consists of two parallel branches:

1. a SE computational branch that transforms the given input $X \in \mathbb{R}^{N' \times M' \times C'}$ to a calibrated feature map $\hat{X} \in \mathbb{R}^{N \times M \times C}$,
2. and a standard convolutional block with dropout and batch normalization layers that represents the residual mapping function for the RSE block.

More formally, we define the RSE block as $y_{RSE} = \delta(\mathcal{F}(X; \{W_i\}) + \hat{X})$, where X and y_{RSE} represent the input and output feature maps of the RSE block, $\hat{X}$ represents the output of SE computational branch, $\mathcal{F}(X; \{W_i\})$ illustrates the residual mapping function with weights W_i, and δ is the final non-linearity function ReLu. In this work, we use a single $\mathcal{F}$ composite function of Convolution, Dropout and Batch Normalization respectively.

In the SE computational branch, firstly, the input features undergo a squeeze operation so as to shrink the feature maps across their spatial dimensions and produce a channel descriptor vector $v \in \mathbb{R}^{C'}$ that defines a statistic for each channel of the input features. This is accomplished by using the global average pooling operation:

$$v_c = \frac{1}{N \times M} \sum_k \sum_l X_c(k, l), \tag{1}$$

where k and l represent the spatial locations, c is the channel of interest, N and M are the spatial dimensions. The channel-wise statistic vector v is then re-calibrated through two fully-connected (FC) layers of one hidden layer of size $\frac{C}{r}$ with ReLU activations and one output layer of size C with Sigmoid activations. Formally, the recalibration is obtained via a simple gating mechanism $u_c = \sigma(W_2\, \delta(W_1 v))$, where σ and δ represent the Sigmoid and ReLu activation functions, and W_1 & W_2 are the weights of the fully connected layers respectively. Then, the output of the SE branch is obtained by rescaling the input features with the re-calibrated channel-wise statistic vector $\hat{X} = X \otimes u_c$, where $\otimes$ refers to channel-wise multiplication. This neural block is proposed as a transition block in order to modify the weights of each channel of feature maps so that the informative channels can be emphasized further during the information flow in the network.

The network architecture is designed as a light-weight encoder-decoder type neural network (Fig. 1(a)). The network contains two consecutive cascaded sub-networks. First sub-network, as noted previously, is based on the famous UNet architecture, which is referred as *Backbone Residual Dense* sub-network; and the second sub-network is based on a shallow CNN, which is referred as *Fine-tune Tail* sub-network.

The *Backbone Residual Dense* sub-network consists of three down-sampling layers, a latent layer, three up-sampling layers and an output block. Each layer contains a RDN block and a transition RSE block. RDN block is carried out as a feature extractor by using the DenseNet and ResNet connectivity patterns [8,11]. RSE block is utilized as a transition block that modifies the weights of each channel so as to emphasize the informative ones further. None of these blocks alter the spatial resolution of the input feature maps. Spatial resolution is changed via down-sampling layers by utilizing max-pooling layers of 2×2 kernel size with 2 pixel stride in the encoder side, and is conducted through transpose convolutions in the decoder side. The output block, which contains a single convolution operation of 1×1 filters with Sigmoid activation, receives the output of the last up-sampling layer, and yields an initial estimate for the vessel map.

The *Fine-tune Tail* sub-network is a very shallow CNN block, which is designed to fine-tune the initial estimates of the *Backbone Residual Dense* sub-network. The fine-tuning operation is conducted as follows: first, a single-layer of RDN and RSE neural block is applied to the input and output of *Backbone Residual Dense* sub-network; then, outputs are concatenated and sent to a 2-layer of RDN and RSE neural block; and finally, the output block, which has similar architecture as the output block of the backbone sub-network, is fed-forward by the previous layer. The vessel map is then extracted by thresholding.

4   Experiments

Datasets: Three publicly available datasets of colour retinal images have been used to evaluate the proposed network. The DRIVE[1] dataset [24] consists of 40 retinal images (resolution 565×584 pixels), which are divided into training and test sets, and each set contains 20 images. The CHASE DB[2] dataset [19] contains 28 retinal images with a resolution of 999×960 pixels, where they are acquired from both the left and right eye of 14 children. The STARE[3] dataset [9] consists of 20 retinal images with a resolution of 700×605 pixels. Each dataset provides expert annotations for the retinal vessels, and these annotations are used to train the network and to quantitatively evaluate the results.

Implementation Details and Training Procedure: Given a color retinal fundus image I, our algorithm starts with zero padding it in the four margins to a set size $H \times W$. Then, the zero padded images are fed-forward to the retinal vessel segmentation network in order to train the network in two phases:

1. In the first phase, we train the *Backbone Residual Dense* sub-network, using an initial learning rate of 10^{-3} that is divided by 10 at every 50 epochs, converging after 150 epochs.
2. In the subsequent phase, we train the full network by cascading the *Fine-tune Tail* sub-network to the backbone sub-network, using a similar learning rate strategy. In this phase the weights from *Backbone Residual Dense* sub-network are frozen, and the remaining weights in the *Fine-tune Tail* sub-network are learned in 100 epochs.

Our pipeline is implemented using Tensorflow, with a composite loss function that consists of a weighted sum between the binary cross-entropy L_b and the Dice loss L_d [16]:

$$\mathcal{L} = \lambda_1 \, L_b + \lambda_2 \, L_d, \tag{2}$$

---

[1] https://drive.grand-challenge.org/.
[2] https://www.kaggle.com/khoongweihao/chasedb1.
[3] https://cecas.clemson.edu/~ahoover/stare/.

where λ_1 and λ_2 are the weighting parameters for the loss functions. We used $\lambda_1 = 1$ and $\lambda_2 = 0.5$ for both training phases. The scaling ratio for all RSE blocks has been set to $r = 2$. As for training time, the convergence is accomplished less than 5 h on average for each dataset on a Tesla K40m NVidia GPU.

Data augmentation with random rotations, horizontal, vertical and diagonal flips are applied to all the training images of the three datasets. Adam optimizer is utilized with a batch size of 2 for DRIVE and STARE datasets and a batch size of 1 for CHASE DB. For the size adjustment, we use $H = W = 592$, $H = W = 1008$ and $H = W = 704$ for DRIVE, CHASE DB and STARE datasets respectively as in [6]. Finally, the datasets are partitioned as follows:

1. DRIVE, 90-10 % train-validation data separation is used from the training set of 20 images, and a testing set of 20 images are used for testing;
2. CHASE DB, first 20 images are utilized for training-validating (90-10) %, and the last 8 images are used for testing;
3. STARE, following the previous models [6,17], we adopt a 4-fold cross-validation strategy for training and testing.

The segmented vessel images (output of our pipeline) are cropped back to the original size, then a thresholding operation is applied, and finally the results are compared with the expert annotations provided with the datasets. More precisely, a vessel pixel at location x in the output image I_o is validated if the corresponding pixel location has a higher confidence value than a certain threshold T, i.e., if $T < I_o(x)$ (we have set $T = 0.5$). The code and results are shared online[4].

Quantitative Evaluation: Table 1(a), 1(b) and 1(c) summarize the average results of a multiple run of our proposed approach along with the standard error and competitive state of the art methods [6,17,26] on the aforementioned three datasets. The following metrics are reported: Specificity (Sp), Sensitivity (Se), Accuracy (Acc), Area Under the ROC Curve (AUC), and the G-mean ($G = \sqrt{Se \times Sp}$) to quantitatively compare our retinal vessel segmentation approach with other competitive methods.

We first illustrate the quantitative results for DRIVE dataset in Table 1(a). As it can be seen from the table, our approach achieves the highest sensitivity rate among the all other approaches (3.7 % better than the second best [6]), while keeping the other evaluation metrics at a promising level such as specificity, accuracy and AUC. Furthermore, our approach presents the highest G-mean score, which indicates that the proposed approach has a promising trade-off between specificity and sensitivity rates. Likewise the quantitative results for CHASE dataset in Table 1(b) shows that our proposed approach presents the best performance in terms of Sensitivity rate by presenting 6.8 % higher value than the second best [6] with a significant rise in G-mean score, while keeping the other metrics at a desired level among all competing methods. Notably, standard

---

[4] https://github.com/alikaraali/DR-VNet.

Table 1. Comparison with state of the art approaches (Vessel-Net [26], 2019; DDNet [17], 2020; CAR-UNet [6], 2021) on the three datasets: DRIVE (Table 1(a), CHASE DB (Table 1(b)) and STARE (Table 1(c)). Each result is reported as an average over 5 runs for DRIVE and CHASE DB datasets, and 4-Fold Cross Validation for STARE dataset along with the standard errors. Our pipeline outperforms significantly other approaches systematically for Sensitivity (Se) and G-mean scores, while maintaining excellent performances for Specificity (Sp), Accuracy (Acc) and Area Under the ROC Curve (AUC).

(a) Quantitative evaluations on the DRIVE dataset.

Method	Sp ↑	Se↑	Acc↑	AUC↑	G-mean↑
Vessel-Net [26]	0.9802	0.8038	0.9578	0.9821	0.8876
DDNet [17]	0.9788	0.8126	0.9594	0.9796	0.8918
CAR-UNet [6]	**0.9849**	0.8135	**0.9699**	**0.9852**	0.8951
DR-VNet	0.9795	**0.8512**	0.9682	0.9848	**0.9127**
stderr × 10⁻³	0.5	3.2	0.2	0.5	1.4

(b) Quantitative evaluations on the CHASE DB dataset.

Method	Sp ↑	Se↑	Acc↑	AUC↑	G-mean↑
Vessel-Net [26]	0.9814	0.8186	0.9661	0.986	0.8963
DDNet [17]	0.9773	0.8268	0.9637	0.9812	0.8989
CAR-UNet [6]	**0.9839**	0.8439	**0.9751**	**0.9898**	0.9112
DR-VNet	0.9733	**0.9120**	0.9694	0.9884	**0.9421**
stderr × 10⁻³	0.1	6.3	1.0	0.3	2.5

(c) Quantitative evaluations on the STARE dataset.

Method	Sp ↑	Se↑	Acc↑	AUC↑	G-mean↑
DDNet [17]	0.9769	0.8391	0.9685	0.9858	0.9053
CAR-UNet [6]	**0.9850**	0.8445	**0.9743**	**0.9911**	0.9097
DR-VNet	0.9841	**0.8572**	0.9744	0.9847	**0.9183**
stderr × 10⁻²	0.1	3.4	0.2	1.0	1.8

errors computed with training our approach 5 times highlight that our results are significant in showing that our approach provides improvements for these metrics for both datasets.

Finally, the quantitative results for the STARE dataset are summarized in Table 1(c). As it can be seen from the table, the SOTA methods present similar scores on this dataset in terms of used evaluation metrics. However, the proposed approach yields again a significantly higher sensitivity rate and the G-mean score on average when compared to the state of the art methods.

The average running times of our approach for a single retinal image at inference are 0.25 s on the DRIVE dataset, 0.25 s on the STARE dataset, and 0.32 s on the CHASE DB dataset. For comparison the average running time for Guo et al.'s

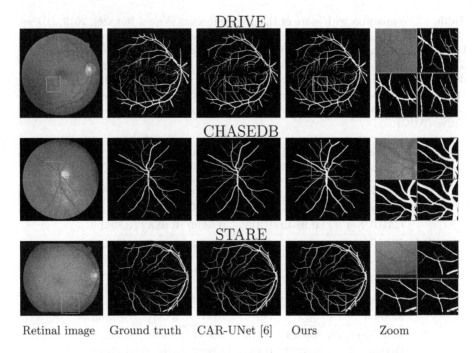

DRIVE

CHASEDB

STARE

Retinal image   Ground truth   CAR-UNet [6]   Ours   Zoom

Fig. 2. Retinal vessel segmentation results on three publicly available datasets. From left to right: Retinal image, ground truth, results of CAR-UNet [6], results of the proposed method (Ours), and zooms of patches for the corresponding images (to read from left to right as retinal image (green), ground truth (blue), and in second line, CAR-UNet [6] (red) and our proposed method (yellow)). (Color figure online)

approach [6] is 0.35 s on the DRIVE dataset, 0.35 s on the STARE dataset, and 0.45 s on the CHASE DB dataset and in [17], the average running time reported is 0.14 s for all datasets using a similar hardware configuration to ours.

Qualitative Evaluation: Figure 2 shows the original retinal vessel images, expert annotations for vessels (ground truth), results of the competitive method CAR-UNet [6], and results of the proposed method for the three datasets. Although visual analysis is very subjective, it can be observed from the figure that the proposed approach present visually coherent results by performing a clear segmentation not only of the thick vessels but also of around thin/tiny blood vessels, which can be better seen in the last column of Fig. 2, where the zoomed patches are shown for the original retinal image (upper left), ground truth annotation (upper right), result of the competitive method CAR-UNet [6] (bottom left), and result of the proposed method (bottom right).

Ablation Study

The binary cross-entropy is one of the most widely used loss functions, and works very well for many types of binary classification tasks. On the other hand,

Table 2. Effectiveness of the loss function and fine-tuning sub-block on DRIVE dataset. BC. and D. represent the binary cross-entropy and Dice losses respectively.

Method	Sp ↑	Se ↑	Acc ↑	AUC ↑	G-mean ↑
Backbone with BC	**0.9850**	0.8100	0.9696	0.9866	0.8932
Backbone with D	0.9802	0.8467	0.9685	0.9471	0.9110
Backbone with BC&D	0.9811	0.8417	**0.9689**	**0.9868**	0.9087
Full Net. with BC&D	0.9793	**0.8519**	0.9682	0.9855	**0.9134**

Table 3. Effectiveness fine-tuning sub-block on CHASE DB dataset. BC. and D. represent the binary cross-entropy and Dice losses respectively.

Method	Sp ↑	Se ↑	Acc ↑	AUC ↑	G-mean ↑
Backbone with BC&D	**0.9815**	0.8675	**0.9743**	**0.9899**	0.9227
Full Net. with BC&D	0.9723	**0.9160**	0.9688	0.9887	**0.9438**

the Dice loss [16] is a commonly used loss function for medical imaging related segmentation tasks, which has several advantages over binary cross-entropy loss function, such as that the loss information is evaluated both locally and globally. We have proposed a composite loss function (cf. Eq. 2) that combines the traditional binary cross-entropy loss function with the dice loss and we explore its effectiveness along with the contribution of the fine-tuning sub-network for the DRIVE (largest) dataset.

We conduct experiments by applying different configuration to the loss function to validate which one presents the best result. First, we train the backbone sub-network using only the binary cross-entropy (BC) loss function; second, using only the Dice (D) loss function; third, by combining the binary cross-entropy and Dice loss functions (BC&D); and finally, we trained the backbone and the fine-tuning sub-networks together (i.e. full network) using the proposed composite loss function. It worths noting that experiments are conducted over a single run.

Inference results on the test set are summarized in Table 2: the Dice loss provides a clear improvement for the sensitivity rate (compare the first and second row in Table 2), yet there is a trade-off with other metrics, especially with AUC. We also note that there is a significant improvement in performance when the composite loss function is used (see the sensitivity rate at the third row in Table 2), instead of using either one of them alone. Considering the provided trade-off between sensitivity rate and other evaluation metrics, we opt to use the composite loss function.

Finally, the results obtained by training the full network (freezing the weights of backbone network and training the entire network) are shown at the forth row in Table 2. It can be observed that there is a slight improvement in sensitivity rate when the fine-tuning sub-network is cascaded to the backbone sub-network. Although the other evaluation metrics remain at a similar level when the network is trained without fine-tuning, the proposed network (i.e. the full network) remarkably yields not only the best balance between the G-mean and AUC scores but also conceivable results with respect to the remaining evaluation metrics. The results of this ablation study are likewise confirmed on the CHASE DB dataset (cf. Table 3).

5   Conclusion

We have proposed a supervised CNN based pipeline for retinal vessel segmentation that is on par with state of the art approaches on three benchmark datasets for metrics such as accuracy, specificity and AUC, but that outperforms significantly on metrics such as G-mean and sensitivity. In practical terms our pipeline is performing better for not only segmenting the larger and thicker retinal blood vessel branches but also the more distal retinal blood vessel branches which are much smaller and thinner. Accurate image interpretation for both thick and thin vessels is important since subtle differences in vessel segmentation patterns may be linked with a specific systemic diseases or cardiovascular risk factors. Future work will look at combining information extracted from segmented images with other biological parameters using data from the Irish Longitudinal Study on Ageing (TILDA) [12] in an effort to develop novel prediction tools for cardiovascular disease and other important conditions.

Acknowledgments. This work was partly funded by the ADAPT Centre for Digital Content Technology, which is funded under the SFI Research Centres Programme (13/RC/2106_P2) and is cofunded by the European Regional Development Fund, and also partly supported by Department of Nephrology, St. James's Hospital, Dublin Ireland. Dr. Donal J. Sexton is funded by Health Research Board of Ireland: grant number ARPP-P-2018-011.

References

1. Bankhead, P., Scholfield, C.N., McGeown, J.G., Curtis, T.M.: Fast retinal vessel detection and measurement using wavelets and edge location refinement. PLOS ONE **7**(3), 1–12 (03 2012)
2. Câmara Neto, L., Ramalho, G.L., Rocha Neto, J.F., Veras, R.M., Medeiros, F.N.: An unsupervised coarse-to-fine algorithm for blood vessel segmentation in fundus images. Expert Syst. Appl. **78**, 182–192 (2017)
3. Farrah, T.E., Dhillon, B., Keane, P.A., Webb, D.J., Dhaun, N.: The eye, the kidney, and cardiovascular disease: old concepts, better tools, and new horizons. Kidney Int. **98**(2), 323–342 (2020)
4. Ghiasi, G., Lin, T.Y., Le, Q.V.: DropBlock: a regularization method for convolutional networks (2018)
5. Guo, C., Szemenyei, M., Yi, Y., Zhou, W., Bian, H.: Residual spatial attention network for retinal vessel segmentation. In: Yang, H., Pasupa, K., Leung, A.C.S., Kwok, J.T., Chan, J.H., King, I. (eds.) Neural Information Processing, pp. 509–519. Springer, Cham (2020). https://doi.org/10.1007/978-3-030-63830-6_43

6. Guo, C., Szemenyei, M., Hu, Y., Wang, W., Zhou, W., Yi, Y.: Channel attention residual U-Net for retinal vessel segmentation. In: ICASSP 2021–2021 IEEE International Conference on Acoustics, Speech and Signal Processing (ICASSP), pp. 1185–1189 (2021)

7. Guo, C., Szemenyei, M., Pei, Y., Yi, Y., Zhou, W.: SD-UNet: a structured dropout u-net for retinal vessel segmentation. In: 2019 IEEE 19th International Conference on Bioinformatics and Bioengineering (BIBE), pp. 439–444 (2019)

8. He, K., Zhang, X., Ren, S., Sun, J.: Deep residual learning for image recognition. In: 2016 IEEE Conference on Computer Vision and Pattern Recognition (CVPR), pp. 770–778 (2016)

9. Hoover, A., Kouznetsova, V., Goldbaum, M.: Locating blood vessels in retinal images by piecewise threshold probing of a matched filter response. IEEE Trans. Med. Imaging **19**(3), 203–210 (2000)

10. Hu, J., Shen, L., Sun, G.: Squeeze-and-excitation networks. In: 2018 IEEE/CVF Conference on Computer Vision and Pattern Recognition, pp. 7132–7141 (2018)

11. Huang, G., Liu, Z., Van Der Maaten, L., Weinberger, K.Q.: Densely connected convolutional networks. In: 2017 IEEE Conference on Computer Vision and Pattern Recognition (CVPR), pp. 2261–2269 (2017)

12. Kearney, P.M., et al.: Cohort profile: the Irish longitudinal study on ageing. Int. J. Epidemiol. **40**(4), 877–884 (2011)

13. Li, T., Comer, M., Zerubia, J.: A connected-tube MPP model for object detection with application to materials and remotely-sensed images. In: 2018 25th IEEE International Conference on Image Processing (ICIP), pp. 1323–1327 (2018)

14. Li, T., Comer, M., Zerubia, J.: An unsupervised retinal vessel extraction and segmentation method based on a tube marked point process model. In: ICASSP 2020–2020 IEEE International Conference on Acoustics, Speech and Signal Processing (ICASSP), pp. 1394–1398 (2020)

15. Liskowski, P., Krawiec, K.: Segmenting retinal blood vessels with deep neural networks. IEEE Trans. Med. Imaging **35**(11), 2369–2380 (2016)

16. Milletari, F., Navab, N., Ahmadi, S.A.: V-Net: fully convolutional neural networks for volumetric medical image segmentation (2016)

17. Mou, L., Chen, L., Cheng, J., Gu, Z., Zhao, Y., Liu, J.: Dense dilated network with probability regularized walk for vessel detection. IEEE Trans. Med. Imaging **39**(5), 1392–1403 (2020)

18. Nguyen, U.T., Bhuiyan, A., Park, L.A., Ramamohanarao, K.: An effective retinal blood vessel segmentation method using multi-scale line detection. Pattern Recogn. **46**(3), 703–715 (2013)

19. Owen, C.G., et al.: Measuring retinal vessel tortuosity in 10-year-old children: validation of the computer-assisted image analysis of the retina (CAIAR) program. Invest Ophthalmol. Vis. Sci. **50**, 2004–10 (2009)

20. Poplin, R., et al.: Prediction of cardiovascular risk factors from retinal fundus photographs via deep learning. Nat. Biomed. Eng. **2**(3), 158–164 (2018)

21. Ricci, E., Perfetti, R.: Retinal blood vessel segmentation using line operators and support vector classification. IEEE Trans. Med. Imaging **26**(10), 1357–1365 (2007)

22. Ronneberger, O., Fischer, P., Brox, T.: U-Net: convolutional networks for biomedical image segmentation. In: Navab, N., Hornegger, J., Wells, W.M., Frangi, A.F. (eds.) Medical Image Computing and Computer-Assisted Intervention – MICCAI 2015, pp. 234–241. Springer, Cham (2015). https://doi.org/10.1007/978-3-319-24574-4_28

23. Soares, J., Leandro, J., Cesar, R., Jelinek, H., Cree, M.: Retinal vessel segmentation using the 2-D Gabor wavelet and supervised classification. IEEE Trans. Med. Imaging **25**(9), 1214–1222 (2006)
24. Staal, J., Abramoff, M., Niemeijer, M., Viergever, M., van Ginneken, B.: Ridge-based vessel segmentation in color images of the retina. IEEE Trans. Med. Imaging **23**(4), 501–509 (2004)
25. Woo, S., Park, J., Lee, J.-Y., Kweon, I.S.: CBAM: convolutional block attention module. In: Ferrari, V., Hebert, M., Sminchisescu, C., Weiss, Y. (eds.) ECCV 2018. LNCS, vol. 11211, pp. 3–19. Springer, Cham (2018). https://doi.org/10.1007/978-3-030-01234-2_1
26. Wu, Y., et al.: Vessel-Net: retinal vessel segmentation under multi-path supervision. In: Shen, D., et al. (eds.) MICCAI 2019. LNCS, vol. 11764, pp. 264–272. Springer, Cham (2019). https://doi.org/10.1007/978-3-030-32239-7_30

Dealing with Incomplete Land-Cover Database Annotations Applied to Satellite Image Time Series Semantic Segmentation

Lucas Colomines[1], Camille Kurtz[1(✉)], Anne Puissant[2], and Nicole Vincent[1]

[1] Université Paris Cité, LIPADE, Paris, France
camille.kurtz@u-paris.fr
[2] Université de Strasbourg, LIVE – UMR, 7362 Strasbourg, France

Abstract. Machine learning is used in many supervised applications, nevertheless a learning process needs a sufficiently large amount of annotated data to build a model able to generalize. The lack of such annotated data is a bottleneck to the use of supervised methods in certain applications. Such data can be scarce or contain label errors. In this study, we are addressing both aspects in the context of a remote sensing application, for the task of segmentation. We aim to update the content of a database of vineyard plots, thanks to the analysis of satellite image time series (SITS). Such databases are far from being complete and constitute poor-quality training sets. After training a convolutional neural network for a categorization task, we then propose a segmentation-based methodology involving 2D spatio-temporal representations (STR), built from the content of the SITS and labeled thanks to a deep learning process. The semantic segmentation is achieved thanks to the retro projection of the STR in the geographical space. The experimental results highlight the efficiency of the method when focusing in searching for a specific crop, in this study vineyards, from high spatial resolution images. Starting from an initial labeling that fails to label 40% of the ground-truth, we are able to recall up to 96% of the searched vineyard pixels, increasing indirectly the quality of the initial annotations.

Keywords: Image segmentation · SITS · CNN · Annotation correction

1 Introduction

The lack of data in order to apply machine (deep) learning method is still a challenging problem even though data augmentation methods have been developed. This is particularly true in the field of video analysis and image time series. Another problem when using machine learning is the pure quality of the available annotated data. In this paper we are to tackle these two problems in the context of a remote sensing application. Remote sensing applications are numerous thanks to the variety of satellite sensors that produce images at a daily scale. Most of the time, a single image is acquired and then analyzed, but

© Springer Nature Switzerland AG 2022
M. El Yacoubi et al. (Eds.): ICPRAI 2022, LNCS 13363, pp. 211–222, 2022.
https://doi.org/10.1007/978-3-031-09037-0_18

recently, new sensors have been providing satellite image time series (SITS) over the same geographical areas at different dates all along the year. This enables to get more information about a sensed scene and to choose the most suited resolution according to the application. In the same time it is obvious the number of training samples cannot be large.

Land-cover mapping [1] is one of these applications. Two different aspects of the problem can be distinguished. It can be considered as a segmentation problem when the labeling is done without any *a priori* knowledge except the images. Or it can be considered as an updating problem when a labeling of the existing plots is already known in some database and needs to be checked or modified. In that case, a study of new image acquisitions can be done with some *a priori* information and some classification tasks can be considered. Actually, many geographic databases are available, particularly in the urban or agricultural landscapes. For the latter, they contain information at the plot scale for monitoring environmental changes or for agricultural crop type detection, as illustrated by the RPG database in France. The RPG database is mostly built and updated by annual declarations of farmers within the framework of the Common Agricultural Policy (CAP) in Europe. Because of their manual aspect, these declarations may contain errors or inaccuracies.

In this study, we are interested in the specific vineyard label, and our aim is not to deliver an up-to-date geographic vineyard database thanks to a satellite acquisition. Instead of that, we aim to correct the database in a timely/accurate manner via SITS. Of course, it is not just an update of the database that has to be performed, but the spatial domains outside the database plots have to be analyzed in order to find new or forgotten vineyard parcels. Indeed, in this particular domain it is known that the labeling in the RPG may be erroneous, since many plots are not recorded. However, the RPG is used as reference for monetary assistance delivered to winemakers by CAP aids. The errors could be automatically pointed out to get a more accurate monitoring system. Thanks to the increasing availability of high spatial resolution satellite imagery via European programs (e.g. Sentinel, Venµs), it becomes possible to use series of images to analyze this type of geographic database [2] or to check the consistency of the data through the analysis of the visual content of the images. In particular, SITS make it possible to study, from 2D+t imaging data, the spatio-temporal evolutions of the territory, which may for example indicate a change in management of the cropping system or an error in the actual labeling [3,4]. This, in fact is similar to improving the initial annotated data used in the learning process, in a region or an other, the representativity of the data being assumed.

Many studies in remote sensing have been focused on the use of images from Sentinel 2 satellites which produce optical data at high temporal frequency with a medium spatial resolution (10 to 20 m) [1]. It has already been proved that Sentinel 2 sensors do not provide images with spatial resolution high enough to distinguish for example between vineyards and orchards. The level of details is too low to make apparent the structure in tree or vine stock rows of these types of crops. In this project, we want to explore new data from the Venµs satellite, which also offers a good temporal frequency (3 days) but with a finer

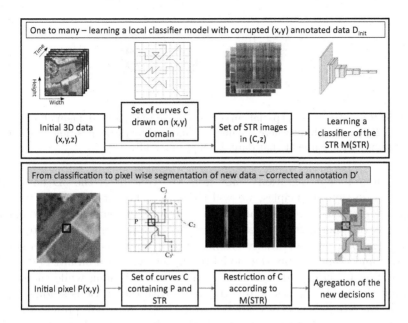

Fig. 1. Workflow of the proposed approach. The box at the top recalls the Deep-STaR principle [6], while the box at the bottom illustrates the innovation developed in this study, how a spatial segmentation can be performed.

spatial resolution (5 m). Such data were already considered in the literature for agricultural monitoring [5]. Here we want to take advantage of their spatial resolution to analyze the vineyards.

In this context, the aim of the paper is to propose an approach that enables to use a corrupted training set to achieve the update of the vineyard labeling in the RPG database (Sect. 2). The process is to achieve a semantic segmentation of the spatial data in two classes defining a multi-view approach, vineyard and non-vineyard. The basis of the approach is illustrated in the top part of Fig. 1. This allows us to recover the labeling at plot level as illustrated in the bottom part of Fig. 1. Furthermore, from a general point of view, we have developed a method that is able to partially uncorrupt badly annotated data. The main study area will be Alsace (France) where we have considered two geographical regions respectively around the cities of Obernai and Epfig (Sect. 3).

2   Proposed Method

SITS can be viewed as 3D data, with two spatial dimensions and one temporal one, linked to the acquisition date of the images. When considering a supervised approach, the number of training examples is an important issue.

We have already developed a methodology involving the Deep-STaR model [6] for the classification of agricultural plots according to their temporal behaviors and spatial configurations thanks to SITS. Deep-STaR takes as input, 2D

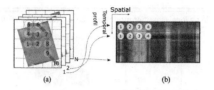

Fig. 2. STR construction: a spatial curve is drawn in the spatial domain of a SITS (a) and (b) a 2D image is built where the lines are indexed by the acquisition date and are the unfurling of the curve at that date, leading to a STR.

spatio-temporal representations built from the content of the 3D data cube. Based on the same principles, we will show here, how it is possible to use a similar approach to solve a semantic segmentation problem, enabling to extract all the vineyard pixels from a geographical area. More precisely, we intend first to use a training set (potentially erroneous) of plots to learn characteristics of vineyards and then to apply the model to segment vineyard on any region. The segmentation is performed regardless of the plot positioning while enabling us to rebuilt them. This makes quite a difference with the previous studies.

First, we recall the Deep-STaR principle (Fig. 1, top). We present then our contribution, how a spatial segmentation can be performed, starting with a coarse approach and then from a finer point of view (Fig. 1, bottom).

2.1 Deep-STaR Principle [6]

In a classification process, the labeling may be done at different levels: the pixels or regions, that can be plots in remote sensing applications. In our case, we consider another level, the curve segment level. We assume that, on short curve segments, the label of all pixels is the same. This assumption has led us to define 2D elements within the 3D data as an intermediate point of view. They are similar to temporal pixels but more complex and they carry more information, in particular spatial information. We name them spatio-temporal representations (STR). Such planar representations enable to take advantage of the 2D+t nature of the data, as well as to benefit from the efficiency of classical 2D convolutional neural networks (CNN) trained on large training data sets (e.g. ImageNet) and providing interesting initialization for CNN used on other problems.

STR carry more information than a temporal pixel that is only considering the evolution along time [7]. They are based on curves drawn in the spatial domain and unfurled in a straight-line segment, the new pixel index being the curvilinear abscissa of the pixel in the curve. The construction of such STR is illustrated in Fig. 2. The straight-line segments associated with each image of the STIS are structured as rows of a 2D image. Its lines are indexed by the dates associated with the images of the series and they contain the pixels of the unfurled curve in the image of the series at this time.

The curves that we have chosen to consider are defined by an initial point and they are built according to a random walk process according to an 8-connected topology. The length of the curves is a parameter of the method that has to be fixed according to the problem. It has to be linked to the size of the entities (e.g. the plots) to be considered in the spatial domain. Then, we can build and associate with an image (or a region of interest), as many STR as it is necessary, even more than the number of pixels of the region. Each STR contains spatial information as each pixel has two neighboring pixels that carry partial information on the local environment of the pixel. The random aspect in the construction of the curve contributes to the method invariance to rotation, as the behavior in all directions are equality represented. The width of the STR is the length of the curve and its height is the number of dates in the STIS (Fig. 2).

From the SITS, STR images are built either in vineyard plots or outside. The way the STR are built ensures to have all the pixels in the plot, some spatial constraints are added to the random walk to stay in the region of interest. The labeling of the STR is performed thanks to the learning of a classical 2D CNN designed for a two classes categorization task: vineyard and non-vineyard. The final labeling of the plots is achieved thanks to an aggregation of the decisions given by the CNN at the STR level in the plot to be labeled.

Now we are ready to use this approach to achieve a spatial semantic segmentation. This will be done by considering two steps (Fig. 1, box at the bottom). First, we describe the general principle of the method leading to a coarse segmentation and then we show how a finer result can be obtained thanks to an improvement of the curve analysis process.

2.2 From Classification to Segmentation

As already mentioned, our problem here is not a classification one. The input information is given as a set of agricultural plots labeled as vineyard. But the results on vineyard regions have to be presented as existing plots or new plots (the objective is not only to correct the given plots but also to find the ones missing from the input). It has also to be mentioned the plots are not raster regions but vectorial regions whereas we are working at the pixel level. Considering this information, we need to study the whole region covered by the RPG section we want to correct and not only existing plots. Segmentation is the best approach to the problem. Indeed, the training of the CNN classifier can be performed as in the case of Deep-STaR, as it is independent of the final decision making, but then, the decision can be done at pixel level. A post processing step is needed to rebuild some quasi-plots. In order to propose smooth contour to the new quasi-plots, we resorted to the agricultural land register that is public information available in any country. The land register plots are labeled thanks to the pixel labeling or they have to be partitioned to define homogeneous zones. We present hereinafter the segmentation principle.

The labeling has to be performed at the pixel level. From the labeling point of view, one pixel p is known both from its spatial coordinates (x, y) and through the index in the STR curves $C_i(p)$ it belongs to, where i is varying from 1 to n_p. This is illustrated in Fig. 1 (bottom, second box) where $n_p = 3$. The number of curves generated has to be sufficient so that, for each pixel p, several decisions at the STR level are available, their number is n_p. The available information is

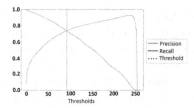

Fig. 3. Graph of the evolution of recall in red and precision in green with respect to the threshold value in the decision process of labeling pixels as vineyard or non-vineyard. The blue vertical line indicates the chosen threshold. (Color figure online)

given by the CNN classifier thanks to the confidence scores given in the output layer for both classes $(s_i(v), 1 - s_i(v))$, $s_i(v)$ being the score associated with the vineyard class. We do not apply a majority rule as it gives lower results than using the confidence scores through their mean value of the n_p values.

The decision rule for pixel p is involving a confidence score defined as: $S(p) = \frac{1}{n_p} \sum_{i=1}^{n_p} s_i(v)$. The pixel p, in first approximation, can be considered as a vineyard pixel if $S(p) > \frac{1}{2}$. Thanks to this approach based on S, it is possible to build a grey level map where the bright pixels are vineyard pixels. A binarization process is needed in order to take the final decision and it can be either local or global. In our case, we have chosen a global threshold, not fixed as the $\frac{1}{2}$ example, but it is learned on a training set through an exhaustive search. We choose the threshold associated with the equal error rate of vineyard pixel recognition rate computed in a region included in the training set. Figure 3 shows the evolution of recall and precision with respect to the threshold, allowing to choose the optimal value.

After this learning phase, a two-step system enables to study any region and to label the pixels of a specific area. Figure 4 illustrates a result on a geographical area distinct from the learning one. It can be observed, for example, that roads are not visible in this map and that small plots surrounded by other vegetation than vineyard are missing. The origin of the errors was analyzed to come from the labeling itself first performed at the STR level. All pixels of the curve are labeled in the same way but this may be wrong. A curve can pass through both a vineyard and a road (or a path). This was not happening in the classification process where the curves were drawn totally inside the plots to be labeled.

2.3 Pixel Classification Improvement

The non-homogeneous aspect of the STR is normal in the non-vineyard geographical zones, but in vineyard zone the STR should present a similar temporal evolution all over the pixels of the curve. When the curve is going through a vineyard but also comprises parts in a road or in a tree for example, the STR can be labeled as vineyard, nevertheless, all the pixels have not the same behavior along the year. This is illustrated in Fig. 5 where two behaviors can be observed, the blue vertical area in (b) is associated with a road that has the same aspect

Fig. 4. Example of a binary map obtained in the region of Obernai in Alsace (France). White pixels indicate vineyards.

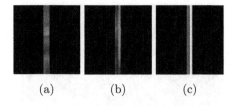

(a)   (b)   (c)

Fig. 5. (a, b) Example of two STR labeled as vineyard but associated in (a) with a curve entirely included in a vineyard plot and in (b) with a curve passing through a road (the blue area, its appearance is stable all over the year). (c) Example of a STR image shown in (b) split in two classes. Only pixels of the grey class will be labeled as vineyard. (Color figure online)

all over the year whereas for vineyard pixels, in the beginning of the year at the top of the STR, the blue color indicates no vegetation and the reddish aspect is increasing as chlorophyll is developing along the year.

The idea is then to post-process only the STR that are labeled as vineyard and for them to check whether several classes of behavior are present or not. If two types of columns (or more) are present, only the pixels associated with the largest one will be labeled as vineyard. We have opted for a process, transforming the color STR image in a grey level image, we consider the mean value of each column. Their number is equal to the length of the curves. The modes of this grey value population are assumed to correspond to different vegetation types and that the most important mode is corresponding to vineyard pixels. If more than one class appears, the curve can be segmented. The result of the segmentation is illustrated in Fig. 5(c). The confidence of curve C pixels in the vineyard class is the confidence associated with the STR $s_C(v)$ and for the other pixels the confidence in the vineyard class is $1 - s_C(v)$. The result of this process is presented in Fig. 6 that can be compared to Fig. 4. The plots are materialized by some limits, the paths between plots are visible, then at the pixel level the results seem satisfactory.

Of course, such pixel-level results are not usable for real applications requiring a plot-level segmentation. Small connected components are considered as noise, so they are removed. But here the size of the removed components is not fixed in an empirical way, it is learned from the data in the training region in order

Fig. 6. Process of the same zone as in Fig. 4. White pixels indicate vineyards. Paths and plot limits are visible.

Fig. 7. Results (same zone as in Fig. 4), superimposed on the satellite image: in blue (resp. green) the plots labeled vineyard with 90% (resp. between 70 and 90%) of vineyard pixels. (Color figure online)

to optimize the results at the pixel level. Furthermore, in order to make the results more easily usable and exploitable by end-users, the maps obtained at pixel level have to be transformed in vectorized form. For this, the agricultural land register is used, all its plots are polygons. We tag with a label both the plots in the RPG and the land register plot outside the labeled plot of the RPG. A plot is labeled vineyard when 90% of its pixels are labeled as vineyard. One can notice that for some end-user applications, the threshold of 90% can be modified to define confident labels and labels to be manually verified on an ortho-image. Most of the time, the land register plots are homogeneous with respect to our class decision, but sometimes a segmentation of the plot has to be performed. The result of the segmentation is illustrated in Fig. 7. Two colors have been used to indicate the confident conclusions in blue and in green the plots where only between 70% and 90% of the pixels are labeled as vineyard.

In this section, we have described the method illustrated thanks to qualitative results. Hereinafter, we precise the experiments and present quantitative results.

3   Experimental Study

First, we precise the data and the way the parameters of the system have been fixed, before to present two aspects of the results. One is the segmentation of an area that is ignored during the training, the other is the method ability to correct some poor-quality annotations without any other information.

3.1 Data

We have studied vineyard regions in Alsace (France). As satellite data, 39 Venμs images were available (Level 2A) through the Theia service, around the year 2019 without clouds. They are not uniformly distributed along the year.

Besides, because of the input nature of the considered CNN, SqueezeNet, that we use in the STR labeling, a linear interpolation is performed at two levels, one to fill the cloudy zones where no information is available and also to define 224 images equally distributed. The global data cube has a depth of 224 and the STR have 224 lines. To benefit from the ImageNet initialization of the CNN, we use 3 (near infrared, red and green channels) among the 12 spectral bands available in the Venμs images. They are the most often used for crop analysis. In order to avoid the effect of outliers in the raw data, a normalization is performed at the STIS level. A linear transformation is applied between minimum and maximum values in the STIS, where the min and max values are set respectively at 2 and 98 percentiles of the values.

We considered two geographical zones, one for training (Epfig region, $\approx$ 86 km^2) and one for testing (Obernai region, $\approx$ 62 km^2). But one originality of our work is that we do not know any ground-truth. The content of the RPG is actually used in the training phase but it cannot be considered as a ground-truth since it contains several errors. Nevertheless, a ground-truth is required to evaluate our methodology. Then we had to build one, in a manual way, looking at ortho images under the supervision of an experimented geographer scientist. Despite the ground-truth is built in a vectorial mode, we will have to use it at the pixel level. The ground-truth is built over the Obernai region where the evaluation will be done.

3.2 Parameter Values

The aim being to show the methodology associated with Deep-STaR enables to manage learning with very poor annotation, the learning of the classifier of STR in vineyard and non-vineyard is done using the RPG. An idea of the low quality of the annotation is given in Fig. 8 where most of red pixels are due to RPG errors. The length of the curves must be long enough to support information but not too long as their position with respect to vineyard is random. Considering the resolution of the images and the small size of vineyard plots, we have chosen a length of 20 pixels (100 m). In an automatic way, in the Epfig region, 100,000 STR are built in each class for the learning phase among which 20,000 are used as a validation set. The STR are 224 × 224 color images, but only 20 columns in them are significant and all other pixels are characterized by 0 values.

The number of STR that are used in the decision step is computed such that all pixels of the studied region are belonging to a curve and around 4 curves pass through all pixels. To set the threshold value in the binarization of the map, a zone in the studied region has been used and is never modified in the evaluations. The evaluation of this classification of the STR is achieved in the testing zone of Obernai, where a ground-truth has been manually constructed.

Fig. 8. Results in the same zone as in Fig. 4, superimposed on the satellite image where in white the plots labeled vineyard by both the RPG and our method, in red our prediction not present in the RPG and in green the elements we missed. (Color figure online)

3.3   Evaluation

We propose three types of evaluations. First, the evaluation of the STR classification; then the evaluation of the segmentation and vineyard plots proposition, and finally we evaluate the capacity of the method to correct an erroneous labeling used in the learning phase. The evaluation relies on recall and precision quality indexes computed at the pixel level.

STR Classification. It is achieved on 20,000 STR that have been randomly extracted in vineyard and non-vineyard areas. Table 1 presents the results. The precision is important and higher than the recall which means there is more false negatives than false positives, the system is then better in labeling non-vineyard. The recognition rate could be higher but, we must keep in mind the training set contains errors that must influence the global results. Besides, in the end, several STR will be used to make a decision at the pixel level, then if the philosophy of STR is good, the rate would increase.

Table 1. Evaluation of the STR classification on Obernai.

Recognition rate	Precision	Recall
0.88	0.92	0.83

Segmentation. It will be performed at the pixel level. As we have a manually checked ground-truth, it is also possible to compute the evaluation for the RPG, enabling a comparison with our proposal. Besides, for the chosen region, it exists for the East side of France a manually labeled topographic database OCS GE2 ⓒGeoGrandEst, 2019 containing landuse/cover map with plots of vineyards.

The three segmentations are then compared to our ground-truth and the results are provided in Table 2. If the STR classification was limited to 0.88 in Table 1, thanks to the several curves passing through the pixels, the segmentation results are increased to 0.97. We can observe that our precision is lower than in the other maps, but our recall is much larger than the recall of the RPG and the global recognition rate is higher. The level of our results, obtained in an automatic way, nearly reach the evaluation computed for the OCS GE2 that has been manually labeled by experts.

Table 2. Evaluation of the segmentation on Obernai at the pixel level.

Method	Recognition rate	Precision	Recall
RPG	0.95	0.94	0.59
OCS GE2	0.98	0.89	0.93
Our segmentation	0.97	0.87	0.90

Figure 8 illustrates the differences between our results and the RPG. In white are the joint label vineyard, in red is the vineyards we predict and is not contained in the RPG and in green the vineyard present in the RPG that we missed. Most of the new predicted vineyards are really vineyards.

RPG Correction. Until now, we have achieved the segmentation thanks to a system trained to differentiate vineyard from everything else. Then vineyards can be segmented in any region. In this new study, we take advantage of the RPG in the new region (Obernai) and we learn the CNN with supplementary epochs using STR from Obernai, before we apply the system on the same region. Results are reported in Table 3. The STR classification system has been updated with respect to the RPG in the region. No other hyperparameter has been changed. It can be observed that the recall has been increased, better than in the general case, but precision is decreased. As the aim is to recover the non-labeled vineyard plots, this new system is improved compared to previously.

Table 3. Correction of the RPG on the Obernai region at the pixel level.

Method	Recognition rate	Precision	Recall
RPG	0.95	0.94	0.59
Our segmentation	0.97	0.87	0.90
RPG correction	0.96	0.78	0.96

4 Conclusion

From this study, we can give several conclusions, either from a methodological point of view or from the applicative point of view. Through the use of 2D data representations that we can develop in large quantity, deep learning is made possible. These data contain both spatial and temporal information making possible to study crop classes that are characterized by structural texture and this is done in a rotation invariant way. We have showed that the Deep-STaR model built in a classification context can be extended to solve a semantic segmentation task. Here only two types of regions are considered but the number of types of regions can be extended to deal with the semantic segmentation of other types of agricultural crops. We have also highlighted that, thanks to a two-step process, a poor quality annotation can be improved or used in a learning process and a redundancy process introduced by the multi-view aspect.

Our methodology can be applied to other applications, for example in radiology where imaging modalities lead to 3D images. Video analysis in the context of the localization of violent areas is another perspective. Besides we think important to deeper analyze the filters leading to spatio-temporal features to better understand the properties of the model that is built.

Acknowledgments. Work co-supported by diiP, IdEx Univ. de Paris, ANR-18-IDEX-0001 and by the TIMES project, ANR-17-CE23-0015.

References

1. Phiri, D., Simwanda, M., Salekin, S., Nyirenda, V., Murayama, Y., Ranagalage, M.: Sentinel-2 data for land cover/use mapping: a review. Remote Sens. **12**(14), 2291 (2020). https://doi.org/10.3390/rs12142291
2. Stoian, A., Poulain, V., Inglada, J., Poughon, V., Derksen, D.: Land cover maps production with high resolution satellite image time series and convolutional neural networks: Adaptations and limits for operational systems. Remote Sens. **11**(17), 1986 (2019)
3. Interdonato, R., Ienco, D., Gaetano, R., Ose, K.: DuPLO: a DUal view Point deep Learning architecture for time series classificatiOn. ISPRS J. Photogramm. Remote Sens. **149**, 91–104 (2019)
4. Di Mauro, N., Vergari, A., Basile, T.M.A., Ventola, F.G., Esposito, F.: End-to-end learning of deep spatio-temporal representations for satellite image time series classification. In: DC@PKDD/ECML Proceedings, pp. 1–8 (2017)
5. Gao, F., Anderson, M., Daughtry, C., Karnieli, A., Hively, D., Kustas, W.: A within-season approach for detecting early growth stages in corn and soybean using high temporal and spatial resolution imagery. Remote Sens. Environ. **242**, 111752 (2020)
6. Chelali, M., Kurtz, C., Puissant, A., Vincent, N.: Deep-star: classification of image time series based on spatio-temporal representations. Comput. Vis. Image Underst. **208–209**, 103221 (2021)
7. Pelletier, C., Webb, G.I., Petitjean, F.: Temporal convolutional neural network for the classification of satellite image time series. Remote Sens. **11**(5), 523 (2019)

On the Feasibility and Generality of Patch-Based Adversarial Attacks on Semantic Segmentation Problems

Soma Kontár and András Horváth[✉]

Peter Pazmany Catholic University - Faculty of Information Technology and Bionics,
Práter u. 50/A, Budapest 1083, Hungary
{kontar.soma.gabor,horvath.andras}@itk.ppke.hu

Abstract. Deep neural networks were applied with success in a myriad of applications, but in safety critical use cases adversarial attacks still pose a significant threat. These attacks were demonstrated on various classification and detection tasks and are usually considered general in a sense that arbitrary network outputs can be generated by them.

In this paper we will demonstrate through simple case studies both in simulation and in real-life, that patch based attacks can be utilised to alter the output of segmentation networks. Through a few examples and the investigation of network complexity, we will also demonstrate that the number of possible output maps which can be generated via patch-based attacks of a given size is typically smaller than the area they effect or areas which should be attacked in case of practical applications.

We will prove that based on these results most patch-based attacks cannot be general in practice, namely they can not generate arbitrary output maps or if they could, they are spatially limited and this limit is significantly smaller than the receptive field of the patches.

1 Introduction

With the application of deep neural networks becoming mainstream in our everyday lives, questions and concerns about the robustness and reliability of these networks are also becoming ever more important. Adversarial attacks targeting the vulnerabilities of neural networks were investigated heavily in the past years. These attacks are considered general in the sense that with the proper optimization techniques arbitrary outputs can be generated by them, regardless of the input image, which means that these attacks pose a significant threat in practical applications.

Adversarial attacks were first introduced in [1] and they have revealed an important aspect of deep neural networks: although they generalise well and work properly not just on the typical input set, but also on similar inputs, they can be exploited by malevolent attackers, since inputs are high dimensional and one can easily generate non-real life samples, which fall extremely far from both human judgement and the expected outcome.

© Springer Nature Switzerland AG 2022
M. El Yacoubi et al. (Eds.): ICPRAI 2022, LNCS 13363, pp. 223–235, 2022.
https://doi.org/10.1007/978-3-031-09037-0_19

In the following years, the possibilities of exploiting adversarial attacks were investigated elaborately, building on the original authors' findings [2–5], devising new attack strategies improving the robustness of the generated attacks [6,7], enabling black-box attacks in which case the gradients of the network are not necessary [8–10]. Later, adversarial attacks were also presented on more complex tasks than classification, like detection and localisation problems [11], and on various network architectures (e.g.: Faster-RCNN [12]).

The first attacks in classification and detection problems applied minor, low-intensity perturbations over the whole image, just like in [2] for classification. It was later demonstrated that low-intensity attacks are not at all robust in the wild [13]. In practice this special additive noise is usually altered by perspective distortion and additive noise in the environment (e.g.: illumination changes) and also not life-like, since in practice the attacker needs to have access to the image processing system to modify all elements of the input, instead of modifying a real-world object.

Although real life and robust attacks were demonstrated for classification and detection problems, in case of segmentation problems, only low intensity attacks were investigated [14,15]. Segmentation problems are also more complex and their output depends on fine details of the input samples. In case of classification one expects that the output class should not depend at all from the pose of the investigated object and in case of detection problems only small changes should appear. If the object rotates slightly or changes its pose (e.g.: a person moves his arm) output classes should remain exactly the same and bounding-boxes should change slightly, meanwhile segmentation masks might change rather significantly. Based on this one could expect that segmentation networks are more robust toward real-life adversarial attacks.

It was demonstrated in [14] and [15] that networks trained for semantic segmentation problems can also be attacked with low-intensity noise and the authors could generate arbitrary output maps with the proper additive noise. Although it was never proven that these methods can generate arbitrary output maps, the authors have demonstrated that highly uncorrelated and randomly selected output maps could be achieved, which gave rise to the general belief in the scientific community that these low-intensity approaches can result in arbitrary output maps.

In [16] it is shown that state-of-the-art semantic segmentation networks are vulnerable to some indirect local adversarial attacks – in the attack scenario a patch is placed in the environment, creating "dead zones" for a particular class of objects. While this does show that some networks are vulnerable to patch-based adversarial attacks, the authors found that models with a bigger field of view are more sensitive to these kinds of attacks. In contrast, our method is closer to a real-life scenario, since we are only modifying the object the attack is targeting, thus not needing access to the environment we are performing our attack in.

The authors of this paper are not aware of any successful direct patch based attacks on semantic segmentation problems, which emphasises the difficulty of generating such samples.

In this paper we will demonstrate that patch based attacks are feasible on semantic segmentation problems. After demonstrating their feasibility we will analyze their generality. The number of possible output maps using a patch of limited size is typically fairly small, which means that these attacks – contrary to general belief – can not be used to generate arbitrary outputs, driving the conclusion that they cannot be general.

We also have to admit that the non-generality of patch based attacks on segmentation problems does not mean at all that they can not be applied in practice. This only means that arbitrary outputs can not be generated by them, but the question of which outputs can and can not be generated by an adversarial patch remains open which the authors plan to investigate in their future work.

2   Adversarial Attacks

The term *adversarial example* was coined by [1], where attacks on neural networks trained for image classification were generated via a very low intensity, specially formed additive noise, completely imperceptible to the human observer. The method used to generate these so-called adversarial examples was to maximize the networks response to a certain class by altering the input image.

The first attacks [2] were implemented by calculating the sign of the elements of the gradient of the cost function (J) with respect to the input (x) and expected output (y), multiplied by a constant to scale the intensity of the noise (formally $\epsilon \text{sign} \nabla_x J(\theta, x, y)$), where θ is the parameter vector of the model). This allows for much faster generation of attacks. This method is called the Fast Gradient Sign Method (FGSM).

An extension to FGSM by [3] was to use not only the sign of the raw gradient of the loss, but rather a scaled version of the gradient's raw value. This method is usually referred to as the Fast Gradient Value (FGV) method.

Another extension to the iterative version of FGSM by [4] was to incorporate momentum into the equation, theorizing that similarly to 'regular' optimization during training, it would help avoiding poor local minima and other non-convex patterns in the objective function's landscape.

[5] builds on the assumption that the robustness of a binary classifier f at point x_0, is equal to the distance of x_0 from the separating hyperplane $\Delta(x_0; f)$. Therefore the necessary smallest perturbation to change the sign of the output of f corresponds to the orthogonal projection of x_0 onto the separating hyperplane. They solve this in a closed-form formula, and apply these small perturbations to the image in an iterative manner until the decision of the classifier is changed. Later they extended it to multiclass classification problems as well.

Though these approaches were extremely important from a theoretical point of view and the generation methods are general, they pose no significant threat to practical applications of neural network, since they limit the amount of applied noise. The smallest perturbations beside the engineered additive noise, e.g.: perspective or illumination changes, lens distortion could completely upend the desired results. Hence, the application of these attacks in real life is unfeasible [13].

In [6, 7] robust and real-world attacks were presented against various classification networks. These methods create an adversarial patch, where instead of the global, but low-intensity approaches, distortions appear in a region with limited area, but intensity values are not bounded.[1] Successful attacks with adversarial patches were also demonstrated using black and white patches only [8], where not the intensities of the patch, but the locations and sizes of the stickers are optimized. These attacks, where the gradients of the networks are not necessarily used during optimization open space towards black-box attacks [9,10], where the attacker needs access only to the final responses, confidence values to generate attacks using evolutionary algorithms. Later these approaches were presented on detection and localization problems as well [11] using various network architectures (e.g.: Faster-RCNN [12]).

A general overview of adversarial attacks, containing a more detailed description of most of the previously mentioned methods can be found in the following survey paper [17]. The resilience of segmentation networks against adversarial attacks was investigated heavily in the past years [14,15,18,19]. But only global, low-intensity attacks were examined. The authors are not aware of any publication demonstrating patch based attacks on semantic segmentation.

3   Patch-Based Segmentation Attacks on a Simple Dataset

Since we were not able to find a simple segmentation dataset (like MNIST [20] for classification), where objects with various shapes can be found we have created a simple dataset based on CLEVR [21]. The original dataset did not contain segmentation masks but was used for visual question answering. We have modified the generator script and generated masks for semantic, amodal and instance segmentation.

The dataset contains 25200 colored images (of size 320×240) of simple objects along with their instance masks, amodal masks and pairwise occlusions and three-dimensional coordinates for each object. This results a simple dataset for various tasks, ranging from three-dimensional reconstruction and instance segmentation to amodal segmentation. The dataset contains objects of simple shapes, but also contains shadows, reflections and different illuminations, which make it relevant for the evaluation of segmentation algorithms.

The dataset along with the script and all our training codes belonging to later chapter is available at the following repository to help reproducibility and the detailed investigation of the applied parameters.

We have selected the U-net architecture [22] to be trained on our simple CLEVR inspired dataset. Our aim was to demonstrate adversarial attacks with architectures where classification and segmentation are handled in the same layers and not by different heads, as in case of Mask-RCNN [23], where the classifier head might be fooled by the attack, meanwhile the network provides a same or similar instance mask. We have used a U-NET like structure containing convolution blocks with 8, 16, 32, 64 channels, downscaling was accomplished by strided convolution, while upscaling was implemented by transposed convolution. 23400

---

[1] Apart from the global bounds of image values.

images were selected for training and 1800 images were left for validation. All the validation scenes were generated independently from the training scenes. Our selected task was semantic segmentation, where a four-channeled output image had to be generated by the network representing the probabilities, that a pixel belongs to a cube, sphere, cylinder or to the background.

We have selected 100 samples from our test set randomly and trained adversarial patches using the method published in [4]. We have tried scripted attacks where we have changed the expected output class of a selected object (in this case we did not change the shape of the mask), but even in this case the network has no advantage from the previously learned shapes or from the fact that objects in our database has consistent shapes, since here the aim was to segment spheres with shape of a cube or cylinder. But to prove that the network can create arbitrary shapes and segments, we have also created expected masks by hand and tested our approach on them. We have opted for the previously mentioned, scripted method in larger case experiments because class switching could be easily implemented by scripts. Sample attacks with the expected masks and network outputs before and after the attacks can be found on Fig. 1.

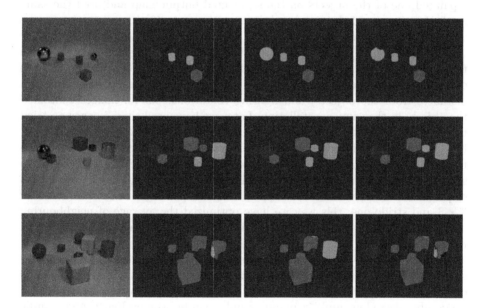

Fig. 1. This figure depicts segmentation attacks on the CLEVER dataset. The first column contains the attacked image, after the patch was optimized for this sample for 5000 iterations. The second column displays the expected outputs after the attacks, meanwhile the third and fourth columns show the network output before and after the attack. The first two rows contain samples where object classes were switched and the last row contains a sample, where the mask was drawn by hand. Please note that part of the output mask was deleted, to demonstrate that objects can not only be turned to other classes, but they can partially or completely disappear. We have to note that there is no theoretical difference between modifying an output pixel to belong to a desired class or to none of them.

As it can be seen from the previous examples, patch based attacks were possible on this simple segmentation task. The outcome of the network was close to the expected mask in almost all examined cases and even though they were not perfectly reconstructed every time, altogether 95% of the output pixels were modified as expected.

3.1   Real-Life Images of Simple Shapes

Once we have created successful attacks in simulation we gathered 100 real life samples (10 different setups from 10 different views) and tested our approach on them. We have applied our method without fine-tuning or further optimisation on real samples or without the application of any domain adaptation methods [24, 25]. Our network worked on an acceptable level on real-life samples. Although segmentation was noisy and many small objects have appeared in the background, segmentation of real objects was correct regarding shapes and classes, which are the most important to investigate possible attacks.

We have selected 10 images and changed their outputs by hand: we have repainted one of the objects on the segmented output map and used the same method as in case of the simulated data on these specific images to change the output of the network.

To demonstrate the robustness of the patches in this experiment we have followed the generation of the patches introduced in [6]. For training we have created new simulated data, with added variance on view-angles, scales (camera distances from the objects) and lighting conditions, but all images contained the objects in the same constellation. Later we have used these images an tried to generate one patch which works well on the selected object regardless of the previously listed variances. We have also added small random noise to the intensity values of the patch and changed the position of the patch on the image slightly to avoid the generation of a low-intensity attack. Additionally to random disposition of the patch we have applied average pooling on it with a kernel of 3×3 and stride one, this way we have optimized the average of neighbouring patch pixels in each kernel, instead of directly optimizing each pixel and we got more consistent and better results.

In all the previous cases patches were created and added to the image in simulation, in this case we have optimized a patch to turn a cylinder to a cube on our simulated dataset, but printed it out and tested it on real life samples. A randomly selected example from our samples can be seen on Fig. 2. As it can be seen the blue cylinder was segmented correctly without the patch, but when the patch was attached to it its segmentation turned red signifying its pixels belong to a cube. We have to note that a more thorough study on more samples and with more complex examples is needed to understand how patch based attack can be efficiently generated in real-life, but our experiments demonstrate that robust adversarial patches, which are applicable under multiple views and conditions, are feasible.

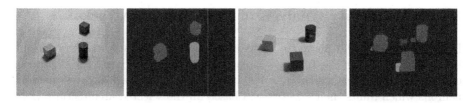

Fig. 2. This figure presents the effect of a printed patch in real life in segmentation. As it can be seen we have managed to train an adversarial patch in simulation which was able to turn a cylinder into a cube in a real life segmentation problem.

4   Patch-Based Segmentation Attacks on Cityscapes

For a more complex case study we have chosen the Cityscapes dataset [26] focusing on the semantic segmentation task of the dataset. Our models of choice were the Deeplab V3 [27] and MobileNet V3 architectures [28], in both of which a significant feature is that the mask prediction and the classification are calculated jointly, unlike in case of Mask-R-CNN [23].

In our experiments, we used a ResNet-18 backbone for the Deeplab V3 architecture and MobileNet V3 Large network, with 128 filters in the segmentation head. For both models, we utilized openly available pre-trained models, the Deeplab V3 model is available on Github, while the MobileNet V3 model is available via PyPi.

For the generation of the adversarial patch we have followed the method described in [6], in which the adversarial patch, which instead of modifying every pixel of the image with an additive noise completely replaces a small part of the image, is trained in a white-box setting by minimizing a loss between a (usually hand-crafted) target and the output of the network by only altering the values in the patch arbitrarily.[2] In our experiments, we have first selected a class and for the sake of reproducibility we used an algorithm to find the largest inscribable rectangle for a given binary object mask of this class, which can easily be extracted from the Cityscapes dataset's annotations. We then placed the patch in the middle of this target area to effectively quantize the area of effect of the adversarial patch. By this we aim to simulate the effect of real-life patches, where they can be found in the middle of objects instead of overstretching to multiple objects. Some sample attacks can be seen on Fig. 3.

As these results demonstrate patch based attacks are feasible in practice in case of segmentation problems. Based on this findings one can ask the question what kind of limitations are there for patch based attacks, can they generate arbitrary, general output maps?

---

[2] The values are of course bounded within the regular image values before preprocessing, e.g. [0, 255].

5   A Complexity Analysis of Patch Based Attacks

In this section we will prove that it is impossible to generate arbitrary output images by attacking the inputs with patches. Obviously patch based attacks can not modify pixels which fall outside of the receptive field of corresponding neurons which limits their effectiveness based on the selected architecture. Here we will demonstrate that if patch-based attacks could generate arbitrary outputs, than the size of these patches has to be limited to a much smaller region than their receptive field.

Our proof follows the following way: We investigate a number of total different segmentation maps that can be generated in a region and provide an upper-bound for them based on the network architecture. We consider two maps different if the winning class (the largest value after softmax normalisation) at least at one pixel is different. This can only happen if non-linear changes happen in the forward path of the network. If one considers an output map in one region of the image containing $W \times H$ pixels where W represents the width, H the

Fig. 3. Example attacks on the Cityscapes dataset. The top row depicts details of an attack on the DeeplabV3 architecture where the pixels of the car should be turned into arbitrary other classes. The first column contains the input image with a 2×2 patch on the left lamp of the parking car and the second column display original output of the trained network without the adversarial patch. The next image displays the output of the network for the patched image and the effect of the patch, those pixels are marked by white where the output class (after argmax) of a pixel have changed are marked on the last image. As it can be seen from this figure the effect of 2×2 patch is fairly large and it has changed the output class of 7461 pixels. The second row contains a similar example with the Mobilenet V3 architecture where an imaginary wall should be placed in the middle of the road. The last row depicts an other attack scenario where a pedestrian is completely removed from the network's output. The row's layout is the following left to right, by rows: original input, target mask, Deeplab V3 patched input, Deeplab V3 attack result, MobileNet V3 patched input and finally MobileNet V3 attack result. This not only demonstrates the vulnerability of neural networks that are used in mission-critical applications (i.e. self-driving), but also signifies that adversarial attacks pose a significant threat in security applications as well.

height of the region and the network used for semantic segmentation can differentiate between D number of classes one can generate: D^{WH} different output maps where at least one pixel is classified differently.

To allow an attack that can generate all these patterns the network has to contain at least this many distinct linear regions (separated by a non-linear change in network output), since changing the largest value at a selected output pixel can only be implemented by non-linear functions, hence it is a non-monotonic change. To simply put it, the network has to move the output to a different linear region to ensure that it generates a different output map. Also it is not necessary that every linear region generates a different output map and while many of these could be the same, we will demonstrate that even if each one of them would be different, they still can not cover all the possible output maps in practice.

For this we will calculate the maximal number of linear regions in which the patch is involved and we will demonstrate that it is significantly larger than D^{WH}, which shows that in practice it is not possible to generate arbitrary output maps in case of semantic segmentation using patch based attacks.

5.1   Upper Bound of Linear Regions

An upper bound for the number of liner regions in a fully connected layer using ReLus as non-linearities was first introduced in the paper of Montufar et al. in 2014 [29], which states that the number of linear regions R_n is upper bounded by the following expression:

$$R_{L_{FC}} \leq \sum_{i=0}^{n_0} \binom{n_1}{i} \tag{1}$$

where the layer contains n_0 number of input and n_1 number of output neurons.

In 2020 in the paper [30] this theorem was extended to convolutional networks where the authors proved that applying L number of consecutive convolutional layers cannot generate more separated linear regions than:

$$R_{Conv} \leq \prod_{l=1}^{L} \sum_{i=0}^{w_0 h_0 c_0} \binom{w_l h_l c_l}{i} \tag{2}$$

where in an L layered network w_k and h_k represent the spatial dimensions of the data in the k-th layer, meanwhile c_k represents the number of channels in the selected layer (e.g. w_0, h_0, c_0 note the dimensions of the input data).

This formula means that a convolutional layer working on an input data of 25×25 pixels containing 64 channels can multiply the number of linear regions by $3.29 * 10^{220}$, meanwhile in case of 128 channels this number is $5.3 * 10^{269}$.

In case of patch-based attacks the spatial dimensions are determined by the receptive field of the neurons in which the original patch is present, but these are typically small numbers, since the patch has to be small to ensure that it is hardly noticeable on the image by human perception. This means that a typical convolutional layer (containing 128 or 256 channels) where the size of a patch is around 25×25 pixels multiplies the number of linear regions by less than 10^{300}. This way five convolutional layers could generate (at most) 10^{1500} linear regions. In case of ten possible output classes this means that if this network could generate all possible output elements in a region, the region can not be larger than 10^{WH}, where WH has to be smaller than 1500. Otherwise the number of possible output maps would be larger and could not be generated by a network with such complexity. In this case for example it means that a 25×25 patch could only generate output maps with the area of 1500 pixels (38×38 pixels), if they are general and can yield arbitrary outputs.

Table 1 contains the maximal number of linear regions for networks which are typically applied on semantic segmentation problems. These data were calculated for different patch sizes along with the maximal patch size which can be generated with this complexity if we assume that patch generation is universal, namely arbitrary output maps can be created with an appropriate attack. The numbers were done considering the Cityscapes dataset as a case study, where each output pixel can belong to nineteen different classes.

Table 1. This table displays the maximal number of non-linear regions (R_N) for different network architectures (UNET [22], FCN8 [31], MobileNetv3-Large (MN_{V3}) [28] and DeeplabV3 with ResNet18 backbone (DL_{V3}) [27] and) and patch sizes (S_R) along with maximal number of pixels which could be changed by such a region if generic output maps can be created

	UNET	FCN8	MN_{V3}	DL_{V3}
R_N (2×2)	10^{219}	10^{168}	10^{229}	10^{584}
S_R (2×2)	13×13	11×11	13×13	21×21
R_N (5×5)	10^{1448}	10^{1203}	10^{1239}	10^{3421}
S_R (5×5)	33×33	30×30	31×31	51×51
R_N (10×10)	10^{5034}	10^{4646}	10^{3446}	10^{12725}
S_R (10×10)	62×62	60×60	51×51	99×99
R_N (20×20)	10^{16842}	10^{17864}	10^{9343}	10^{48151}
S_R (20×20)	114×114	118×118	85×85	194×194

We also have to mention that all the aforementioned calculations contain the upper bound of linear regions. This number can only be achieved if a new non-linearity intersects each earlier linear regions. It was demonstrated in [32] and [33] that the number of linear regions can also be measured or algorithmically approximated using sampling in a trained architecture. In all the investigated cases the number of linear regions were significantly smaller in practice than the upper bound provided by the theorem. (e.g. in case of the investigated seven and eight layered convolutional networks the upper bound was 356180 and 819115, meanwhile by sampling methods only 3398 and 4822 linear regions were identified in the trained networks). This means that in practice one can assume that the number of output maps which can be generated by a network is orders of magnitude smaller than the previously introduced upper bounds and this way the maximal sizes in which arbitrary output maps can be generated is significantly smaller. The exact measurement of linear regions is important in practice for trained networks, but the presented upper bounds are more general and depend only on the network architecture and not the training data or the weights of the network.

We have seen in the previous sections that adversarial patches affect larger regions than the number presented in Table 1. Based on these empirical results we can state that patch based attacks can not be general in practice and they can not produce arbitrary output maps. We also have to mention that this paper only shows that arbitrary output maps can not be generated. This does not mean that in practice a whole object could not be altered, non-existing objects could be hallucinated or one could not make a person disappear in semantic segmentation in practice using patches as camouflage, which can also be seen on some of our samples.

6   Conclusion

In this paper we have investigated the generality of patch based attacks in semantic segmentation problems. For our case study we have investigated a simple simulated dataset with the U-NET architecture and the commonly investigated Cityscapes datasets and two commonly used network architectures: DeepLab V3 and MobileNet V3. Our finding shows that patch based attacks are feasible in case of semantic segmentation in practice and even in case of small patches such as 2×2 they are able to change the output classes of the segmentation maps on a large area (in certain cases containing more than 5000 modified pixels). On the other hand the complexity analysis of these architectures revealed that these networks can generate a lower number of possible outputs maps. This deducts that semantic segmentation can only be attacked successfully under certain conditions with patch based attacks, which largely depend on the network architecture and patch based attacks can not results arbitrary output maps. There are certain output maps in these segmentation networks which can not be generated by any patches (with limited size) for a given input.

Acknowledgment. This research has been partially supported by the Hungarian Government by the following grant: 2018-1.2.1-NKP00008: Exploring the Mathematical Foundations of Artificial Intelligence and the support of the Alfréd Rényi Institute of Mathematics if also gratefully acknowledged.

References

1. Szegedy, C., et al.: Intriguing properties of neural networks. arXiv preprint arXiv:1312.6199 (2013)
2. Goodfellow, I.J., Shlens, J., Szegedy, C.: Explaining and harnessing adversarial examples. arXiv preprint arXiv:1412.6572 (2014)

3. Rozsa, A., Rudd, E.M., Boult, T.E.: Adversarial diversity and hard positive generation. In: Proceedings of the IEEE Conference on Computer Vision and Pattern Recognition Workshops, pp. 25–32 (2016)
4. Dong, Y., et al.: Boosting adversarial attacks with momentum. In: Proceedings of the IEEE Conference on Computer Vision and Pattern Recognition, pp. 9185–9193 (2018)
5. Moosavi-Dezfooli, S.-M., Fawzi, A., Frossard, P.: DeepFool: a simple and accurate method to fool deep neural networks. In: Proceedings of the IEEE Conference on Computer Vision and Pattern Recognition, pp. 2574–2582 (2016)
6. Brown, T.B., Mané, D., Roy, A., Abadi, M., Gilmer, J.: Adversarial patch. arXiv preprint arXiv:1712.09665 (2017)
7. Athalye, A., Engstrom, L., Ilyas, A., Kwok, K.: Synthesizing robust adversarial examples. arXiv preprint arXiv:1707.07397 (2017)
8. Eykholt, K., et al.: Robust physical-world attacks on deep learning models. arXiv preprint arXiv:1707.08945 (2017)
9. Alzantot, M., Sharma, Y., Chakraborty, S., Srivastava, M.: GenAttack: practical black-box attacks with gradient-free optimization. arXiv preprint arXiv:1805.11090 (2018)
10. Papernot, N., McDaniel, P., Goodfellow, I., Jha, S., Celik, Z.B., Swami, A.: Practical black-box attacks against machine learning. In: Proceedings of the 2017 ACM on Asia Conference on Computer and Communications Security, pp. 506–519. ACM (2017)
11. Thys, S., Van Ranst, W., Goedemé, T.: Fooling automated surveillance cameras: adversarial patches to attack person detection. arXiv preprint arXiv:1904.08653 (2019)
12. Chen, S.-T., Cornelius, C., Martin, J., Chau, D.H.P.: ShapeShifter: robust physical adversarial attack on faster R-CNN object detector. In: Berlingerio, M., Bonchi, F., Gärtner, T., Hurley, N., Ifrim, G. (eds.) ECML PKDD 2018. LNCS (LNAI), vol. 11051, pp. 52–68. Springer, Cham (2019). https://doi.org/10.1007/978-3-030-10925-7_4
13. Lu, J., Sibai, H., Fabry, E., Forsyth, D.: No need to worry about adversarial examples in object detection in autonomous vehicles. arXiv preprint arXiv:1707.03501 (2017)
14. Xie, C., Wang, J., Zhang, Z., Zhou, Y., Xie, L., Yuille, A.: Adversarial examples for semantic segmentation and object detection. In: Proceedings of the IEEE International Conference on Computer Vision, pp. 1369–1378 (2017)
15. Metzen, J.H., Kumar, M.C., Brox, T., Fischer, V.: Universal adversarial perturbations against semantic image segmentation. In: 2017 IEEE International Conference on Computer Vision (ICCV), pp. 2774–2783. IEEE (2017)
16. Nakka, K.K., Salzmann, M.: Indirect local attacks for context-aware semantic segmentation networks. In: Vedaldi, A., Bischof, H., Brox, T., Frahm, J.-M. (eds.) ECCV 2020. LNCS, vol. 12350, pp. 611–628. Springer, Cham (2020). https://doi.org/10.1007/978-3-030-58558-7_36
17. Akhtar, N., Mian, A.: Threat of adversarial attacks on deep learning in computer vision: a survey. IEEE Access 6, 14410–14430 (2018)
18. Arnab, A., Miksik, O., Torr, P.H.: On the robustness of semantic segmentation models to adversarial attacks. In: Proceedings of the IEEE Conference on Computer Vision and Pattern Recognition, pp. 888–897 (2018)
19. Al-afandi, J., András, H.: Class retrieval of detected adversarial attacks. Appl. Sci. 11(14), 6438 (2021)

20. LeCun, Y.: The MNIST database of handwritten digits (1998). http://yann.lecun. com/exdb/mnist/
21. Johnson, J., Hariharan, B., van der Maaten, L., Fei-Fei, L., Zitnick, C.L., Girshick, R.: CLEVR: a diagnostic dataset for compositional language and elementary visual reasoning. In: 2017 IEEE Conference on Computer Vision and Pattern Recognition (CVPR), pp. 1988–1997. IEEE (2017)
22. Ronneberger, O., Fischer, P., Brox, T.: U-Net: convolutional networks for biomedical image segmentation. In: Navab, N., Hornegger, J., Wells, W.M., Frangi, A.F. (eds.) MICCAI 2015. LNCS, vol. 9351, pp. 234–241. Springer, Cham (2015). https://doi.org/10.1007/978-3-319-24574-4_28
23. He, K., Gkioxari, G., Dollár, P., Girshick R.: Mask R-CNN. In: Proceedings of the IEEE International Conference on Computer Vision, pp. 2961–2969 (2017)
24. Ganin, Y., et al.: Domain-adversarial training of neural networks. J. Mach. Learn. Res. **17**(1), 2096–3030 (2016)
25. Tzeng, E., Burns, K., Saenko, K., Darrell, T.: SPLAT: semantic pixel-level adaptation transforms for detection. arXiv preprint arXiv:1812.00929 (2018)
26. Cordts, M., et al.: The cityscapes dataset for semantic urban scene understanding. In: Proceedings of the IEEE Conference on Computer Vision and Pattern Recognition (CVPR) (2016)
27. Chen, L.-C., Papandreou, G., Schroff, F., Adam, H.: Rethinking atrous convolution for semantic image segmentation. arXiv preprint arXiv:1706.05587 (2017)
28. Hu, J., Shen, L., Sun, G.: Squeeze-and-excitation networks. In: Proceedings of the IEEE Conference on Computer Vision and Pattern Recognition, pp. 7132–7141 (2018)
29. Montúfar, G., Pascanu, R., Cho, K., Bengio, Y.: On the number of linear regions of deep neural networks. arXiv preprint arXiv:1402.1869 (2014)
30. Xiong, H., Huang, L., Yu, M., Liu, L., Zhu, F., Shao, L.: On the number of linear regions of convolutional neural networks. In: International Conference on Machine Learning, pp. 10514–10523. PMLR (2020)
31. Long, J., Shelhamer, E., Darrell, T.: Fully convolutional networks for semantic segmentation. In: Proceedings of the IEEE Conference on Computer Vision and Pattern Recognition, pp. 3431–3440 (2015)
32. Serra, T., Tjandraatmadja, C., Ramalingam, S.: Bounding and counting linear regions of deep neural networks. In: International Conference on Machine Learning, pp. 4558–4566. PMLR (2018)
33. Trimmel, M., Petzka, H., Sminchisescu, C.: TropEx: an algorithm for extracting linear terms in deep neural networks. In: International Conference on Learning Representations (2021)

Unsupervised Cell Segmentation in Fluorescence Microscopy Images via Self-supervised Learning

Carola Krug[(✉)] and Karl Rohr

Biomedical Computer Vision Group, BioQuant, IPMB, Heidelberg University,
Heidelberg, Germany
carola.krug@bioquant.uni-heidelberg.de, k.rohr@uni-heidelberg.de

Abstract. Cell segmentation in microscopy images is challenging particularly when only few or no annotations available. Existing unsupervised deep learning-based segmentation methods rely on large data sets to train large networks, use synthetic training data, pre-trained networks for domain adaptation, or exploit labels to further train pre-trained networks. We propose an unsupervised deep learning method which is trained from scratch by self-supervised learning without requiring any segmentation labels. Our deep neural network generates an attention map and performs the auxiliary task in one network. The segmentation result is directly obtained from the network, and model selection is performed unsupervised based on the behavior of the loss function during training. We applied our approach to two different fluorescence microscopy data sets and achieved generally better or similar results than classical unsupervised segmentation methods. Furthermore, we compared our method to a supervised method trained with a different number of labels, as well as a semi-supervised version of our method where we select the model based on few annotations.

Keywords: Segmentation · Deep learning · Unsupervised learning · Self-supervised learning · Fluorescence microscopy

1 Introduction

Automatic segmentation of cells and cell nuclei in microscopy images is a central task in biological image analysis. In recent years, many *supervised* deep learning methods for cell segmentation were introduced (e.g., [5,17,20,24]). However, supervised methods often rely on manual annotations, which are time consuming to obtain, error-prone, and generally require expert knowledge. Alternatively, synthetic data is used for training, which requires prior knowledge of the real data, and generally does not well represent real data. A promising alternative are *unsupervised* and *self-supervised* methods which only need few or even no manual annotations (see [10] for a survey). Domain adaptation techniques (e.g., [22,28]) do not need manual annotations, but adapt the image data in such a

© Springer Nature Switzerland AG 2022
M. El Yacoubi et al. (Eds.): ICPRAI 2022, LNCS 13363, pp. 236–247, 2022.
https://doi.org/10.1007/978-3-031-09037-0_20

way that the segmentation can be performed by a network trained with other, labeled data in a supervised manner. *Self-supervised* methods perform network training using an auxiliary task (e.g., transformation prediction, solving a jigsaw puzzle, or image restoration) in a supervised way using self-created labels from the given data or by comparing feature embeddings. The result for the target task like segmentation is typically determined after further supervised network training with few manually annotated labels. Such approaches were previously mainly used for images of natural scenes (e.g., persons, cars) [2,9,11] or medical images (e.g., MR, CT) [26,27]. Although unsupervised methods do not depend on reference annotations, existing methods which are trained from scratch (e.g. [2, 3]) often need millions of images to train the network. Therefore, these methods are well applicable to large natural image data sets but not to microscopy data, as there are often only relatively few images available.

In previous work on cell segmentation in microscopy images, only few deep learning methods for *self-supervised* or *unsupervised* learning were proposed. Some work considers histopathological images [18,25], which are very different to fluorescence microscopy images. Liu et al. [12] as well as Haq et al. [7] propose unsupervised methods via domain adaptation for histopathological images. Though these methods do not require annotations for a target data set, they need a very well-trained model on another data set using annotations, thus these methods are not trained from scratch. Xie et al. [25] use feature embeddings of histopathological image patches for self-supervised pre-training of the encoder. However, for the decoder, supervised learning is employed. Sahasrabudhe et al. [18] developed a self-supervised method for segmentation of nuclei in histopathological images. The method uses an attention network and a network for the auxiliary task. However, manual segmentation labels are needed to select the best model for inference. Dunn et al. [4] as well as Liu et al. [13] consider fluorescence microscopy images and train their segmentation networks without manual annotations but using synthetic data. However, prior knowledge of the microscopy data is required for simulation, and synthetic data generally does not well represent real data, especially in case of non-regular object shapes and intensity structures. Wolf et al. [23] employ in-painting of fluorescence microscopy image regions as self-supervised auxiliary task to separate cells. However, subsequent supervised learning is required to determine the segmentation. Instead of using an auxiliary task, Horlava et al. [8] maximize mutual information between feature embeddings of fluorescence microscopy image pairs generated by different augmentations, and determine the segmentation by clustering the feature embeddings. Thus, the segmentation is not directly determined by the network but a subsequent clustering step is required which increases the computational costs. Robitaille et al. [16] applied self-supervised learning using temporal microscopy image sequences. Their method creates pixel-wise class labels of cells and background by employing optical flow. However, the method uses temporal information and is not applicable for single images.

In this work, we present a fully unsupervised segmentation method based on self-supervised learning to segment cells in fluorescence microscopy images. We propose a novel deep neural network architecture which generates an attention map and performs the auxiliary task by combining the attention map with the original image. Thus, only a single network is required for both the attention map and the auxiliary task. In contrast, [18] use separate networks for the attention map and the auxiliary task, which requires more model parameters. In contrast to [18,23,25], our method is completely unsupervised since we do not need manual segmentation labels for additional supervised learning or for model selection. Instead, model selection is based on the behavior of the loss function of the auxiliary task during training. We applied our method to two different fluorescence microscopy data sets and it turned out that our unsupervised method generally outperforms or performs similar as classical unsupervised approaches. Furthermore, a semi-supervised version of our method where we select the model based on few annotations performs as well as a supervised method trained with 30% of all labels.

2   Method

An overview of the proposed self-supervised deep neural network is provided in Fig. 1. A main characteristic compared to previous work is that we use a single encoder-decoder network to generate the attention map as well as to perform the auxiliary task. The auxiliary task classifies the scale of an image (factors of 1, 1.2, 1.5, or 2) and is integrated in the network by extending the encoder path by three fully connected layers with softmax as activation function for the last layer. We investigated different auxiliary tasks and found that determining the scale of an image yields the best result. Compared to the standard U-net [17], our network uses Batch Normalization (BN) after each convolutional layer. One Conv-Block consists of two convolutional layers with kernel size 3×3, each with ReLU and BN, and maxpooling in the encoder as well as upsampling in the decoder, respectively. The convolutional layers use 16, 32, 48, 64, 128 filters for the blocks in the encoder and decoder path and we apply symmetric padding. After the decoder path, there is one 1×1-convolutional layer followed by the sigmoid function $\sigma(a) = \frac{1}{1+\exp(a)}$. The attention map is obtained from this layer (see the black arrows) and is multiplied with the original image to weight the relevant structures for scale prediction in the original image. Then, the result is passed through the encoder with the auxiliary task as extension (pink arrows).

To determine the scale of an image by the auxiliary task, the network generates an attention map $A \in \mathbb{R}^{HxW}$ from an input image patch $P \in \mathbb{R}^{HxW}$ with height H and width W, and performs element-wise multiplication of A and P. The underlying assumption is that the image scale can be determined from the size of image structures like the cells. The threshold to obtain the segmentation from the attention map is determined automatically using Otsu's method [15].

The loss function consists of three terms which contribute equally and is defined by $\mathcal{L} = \mathcal{L}_{\text{scale}} + \mathcal{L}_{\text{smooth}} + \mathcal{L}_{\text{equiv}}$ as in [18]. The scaling loss $\mathcal{L}_{\text{scale}}$ represents the binary cross-entropy of the self-created scaling labels and the predictions. The smoothness regularizer for the attention map A

$$\mathcal{L}_{\text{smooth}} = c \sum_{i,j} ||A_{i+1,j} - A_{i,j}||_1 + ||A_{i,j+1} - A_{i,j}||_1 \qquad (1)$$

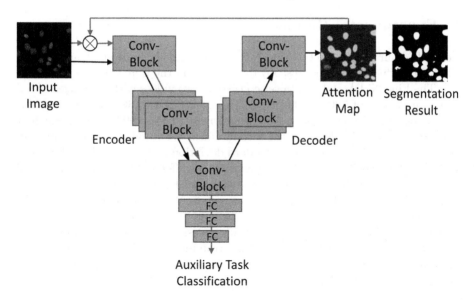

Fig. 1. Overview of the proposed network for attention map generation (black arrows) and auxiliary task classification (pink arrows). (Color figure online)

with $c = \frac{1}{(H-1)(W-1)}$, is used to focus on coherent regions such as cells instead of focusing on very small objects or single pixels. To improve semantic consistency between the input image and the attention map, we also include transformation equivariance of the network in the loss function. A network f_θ with parameters θ is transformation equivariant if $f_\theta(t(x)) = t(f_\theta(x))$ holds for a transformation t and input x. We sample a set of transformations $t \in \mathcal{T}$ for each image patch P in a batch and use a mean squared error loss

$$\mathcal{L}_{\text{equiv}} = \frac{1}{HW} ||\sigma(t(f_\theta(P))) - \sigma(f_\theta(t(P)))||_2^2 \tag{2}$$

to ensure transformation equivariance. The set of transformations $\mathcal{T}$ includes horizontal, vertical, and diagonal flipping as well as rotation by 90, 180, and 270 degrees.

To select the final network model, we take into account the behavior of the loss function during training. If the change in the loss function is below a certain threshold (we used $1e-5$) for a certain number of epochs (we used 5 epochs), we stop the training and use the current model to generate the segmentation result. This leads to a fully unsupervised method in contrast to [18], where the final model is selected from all models during training by computing the network's performance using segmentation labels. In addition, in our method no additional hyperparameter is needed for the attention map while in previous work two hyperparameters are required.

We trained the network using stochastic gradient descent optimization with a learning rate of 0.01 for at most 150 epochs with a batch size of 32.

3   Experimental Results

We applied our method to the Fluo-N2DL-HeLa and the more challenging Fluo-C2DL-MSC fluorescence microscopy data sets from the Cell Tracking Challenge [14]. The Fluo-N2DL-HeLa data set consists of two videos with 92 images of cell nuclei and a size of 700×1100 pixels. The Fluo-C2DL-MSC data set contains two videos with 48 images of whole cells and a size of 832×992 pixels for the first video and 782×1200 pixels for the second video. We standardized the intensity values per image using mean and standard deviation and extracted 10 patches of size 256×256 pixels per image. We investigated different auxiliary tasks as well as combinations of them: Predicting the image scale, the rotation, flipping, and the relative position of a second, smaller patch. We found that predicting the image scale yielded the best results in our experiments. Scaling of the patches (using bilinear interpolation) for the auxiliary task was performed randomly but uniformly for each batch to ensure robust training (Fig. 2). We chose one video for training and used images with complete ground truth of the other video for testing.

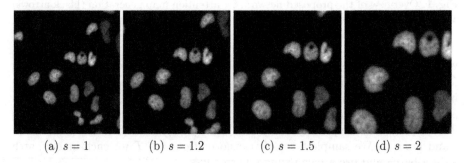

(a) $s = 1$ (b) $s = 1.2$ (c) $s = 1.5$ (d) $s = 2$

Fig. 2. Example image patch with different scaling factors s from the Fluo-N2DL-HeLa data set.

To quantify the segmentation performance, we used the Dice coefficient (DC), Jaccard Similarity Index (JI), and the segmentation accuracy (SEG) from [14]. DC is defined based on the intersection between the reference object R and the segmentation S as well as the number of pixels of R and S:

$$DC(S, R) = \frac{2|R \cap S|}{|R| + |S|} \tag{3}$$

JI is defined based on the intersection and union of R and S:

$$JI(S, R) = \frac{|R \cap S|}{|R \cup S|} \tag{4}$$

While DC and JI are pixel-wise metrics, SEG is defined object-wise based on the average JI. A segmentation S is considered to match a reference object R if

Table 1. Results for Fluo-C2DL-MSC data set.

	Video 1			Video 2		
	DC	JI	SEG	DC	JI	SEG
Otsu	0.237	0.134	**0.331**	0.478	0.321	0.182
Watershed	0.237	0.136	0.011	0.439	0.304	0.133
K-means	0.291	0.170	0.210	0.491	0.332	0.154
Chan-Vese	0.092	0.048	0.059	0.106	0.059	0.107
Ours	**0.609**	**0.439**	0.309	**0.810**	**0.685**	**0.589**

$|R \cap S| > 0.5 \cdot |R|$. Only one segmented object can match each reference object. If there is no match then JI for this object is zero.

We compare our method with the following classical unsupervised segmentation methods: Otsu [15], watershed algorithm [21], K-means [1], and Chan-Vese [6]. For our method we performed the training 10 times and determined the mean values for all metrics. For the challenging Fluo-C2DL-MSC data set the results are provided in Table 1. For both videos, our method outperforms the classical methods or performs similar for all three metrics. For the first video, our method achieves a DC of 0.609 ± 0.015, JI of 0.439 ± 0.045, and SEG of 0.309 ± 0.093. For the second video, we obtain a DC of 0.810 ± 0.011, a JI of 0.685 ± 0.016, and a SEG of 0.589 ± 0.024. Figure 3 shows an example attention map (visualized using a color map) as well as the segmentation result, which agrees well with the ground truth. The best classical method in terms of DC and JI is K-means while the best SEG score is obtained by Otsu's method. Classical methods lack performance on this data set due to the complex cell shape and strongly varying image contrast (see Fig. 5). Especially the SEG values are relatively low because the segmentation is not sufficient to fulfill the matching criterion of SEG for a number of cells.

For the first video of the Fluo-N2DL-HeLa data set (Table 2), our method outperforms all classical methods for all three metrics. We achieved a DC of 0.798 ± 0.065, a JI of 0.671 ± 0.084, and a SEG of 0.574 ± 0.108. For the Chan-Vese method the matching criterion of SEG is not fulfilled. Figure 4 shows the attention map and the segmentation result of our method for an example image. It can be seen that the segmentation agrees well with the ground truth. For the second video, the classical methods perform better than our method. The reason is probably that the images in this video partially contain very bright cells on which the network focuses and hardly takes into account the information of the darker cells to determine the scale for the auxiliary task.

Furthermore, we compare our method to a U-net trained supervised using the same network architecture as for our method. We did only little hyperparameter tuning to simulate a realistic application (e.g., by biologists) with time restrictions and without much computational resources, but we also report the results of specifically optimized supervised learning for a data set. We studied supervised learning with a different number of manual annotations for training.

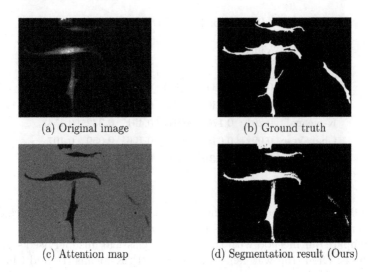

(a) Original image   (b) Ground truth

(c) Attention map   (d) Segmentation result (Ours)

Fig. 3. Result of our method for an example image from the Fluo-C2DL-MSC data set.

Table 2. Results for Fluo-N2DL-HeLa data set.

	Video 1			Video 2		
	DC	JI	SEG	DC	JI	SEG
Otsu	0.677	0.512	0.441	0.784	0.645	**0.534**
Watershed	0.644	0.476	0.417	0.801	0.668	0.533
K-means	0.672	0.506	0.431	0.774	0.632	0.524
Chan-Vese	0.417	0.259	0.000	**0.847**	**0.735**	0.498
Ours	**0.799**	**0.671**	**0.574**	0.759	0.615	0.471

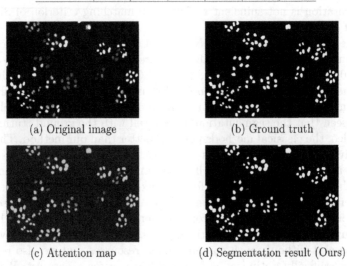

(a) Original image   (b) Ground truth

(c) Attention map   (d) Segmentation result (Ours)

Fig. 4. Result of our method for an example image from the Fluo-N2DL-HeLa data set.

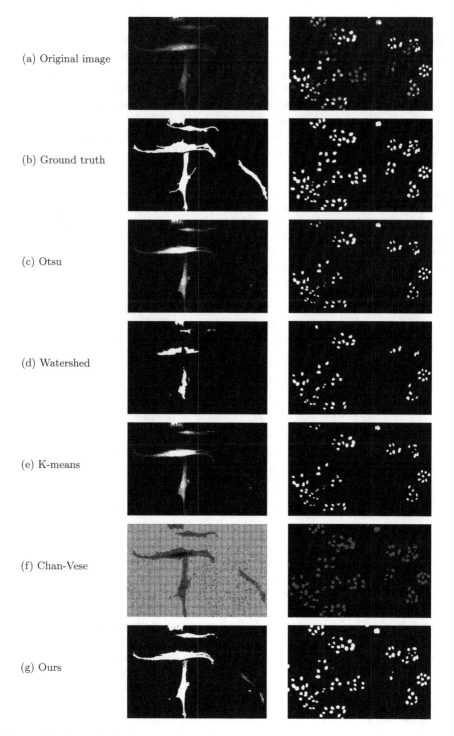

Fig. 5. Results of different methods. Left: Fluo-C2DL-MSC data set (Video 2), Right: Fluo-N2DL-HeLa data set (Video 1)

Since the number of available labels per image varies strongly, we reduce the overall number of labels per image instead of reducing the number of images. We considered 90%, 70%, 50%, 30%, and 10% of the labels. To generate the training data, we extract 10 patches of size 128×128 pixels from each image and restrict the crops to contain at least half of a labeled cell. We split the extracted patches from images of one video in 80% training data and 20% validation data. The images of the other video are used as test set. We train the network with a batch size of 64, use Adam optimizer with a learning rate of 0.001, and run every experiment five times for 1000 epochs.

Table 3. SEG score for supervised and unsupervised methods for different data sets. CTC [19] is a U-Net with hyperparameters specifically optimized for a data set. U-Net (Sup., %) is the standard U-net with little hyperparameter tuning and a different number of labels. Ours (Semi-sup.) is our method trained unsupervised, but model selection is performed based on annotations. Ours (Unsup.) is our fully unsupervised method. For all supervised method we report the best result while the result of our unsupervised method is the mean over all experiments.

	Fluo-C2DL-MSC		Fluo-N2DL-HeLa	
	Video 1 SEG	Video 2 SEG	Video 1 SEG	Video 2 SEG
CTC (Sup., [19])	0.633	0.636	0.827	0.846
U-net (Sup., 100%)	0.460	0.605	0.808	0.735
U-net (Sup., 90%)	0.416	0.639	0.734	0.714
U-net (Sup., 70%)	0.307	0.655	0.704	0.520
U-net (Sup., 50%)	0.309	0.689	0.787	0.265
U-net (Sup., 30%)	0.187	0.381	0.545	0.585
U-net (Sup., 10%)	0.256	0.531	0.679	0.581
Ours (Semi-sup.)	0.415	0.627	0.684	0.531
Ours (Unsup.)	0.309	0.589	0.574	0.471

Table 3 summarizes the results of our evaluation. As reference we used a fully supervised learning method by a U-net with hyperparameters specifically optimized for a data set from the CTC [19]. All reported values of the supervised methods are the best result of all experiments as we select the best model using ground truth. The performance of the supervised method generally decreases when reducing the number of labels, but since the labels are reduced by random selection and the optimization process is stochastic, experiments with fewer labels can also perform well in some cases. In contrast to the supervised method, for our fully unsupervised method we state the mean result over all experiments when the loss function converges as we assume no ground truth data to select a best model. In addition, we also investigated a semi-supervised version of our method, where the model is selected based on the validation data. In this case, we report the best value as for the supervised methods. For the Fluo-C2DL-MSC data set, our fully unsupervised method is as good as supervised training with 70% of the labels for the first video and better than supervised training with 30% of the labels for the second video. The semi-supervised version is as good as supervised training using 90% of the labels for the first video and better than using 30% of the labels for the second video. For the Fluo-N2DL-HeLa data set our semi-supervised version performs similar or better than the supervised method using 30% of the labels. The fully unsupervised method is somewhat worse than the semi-supervised method.

We also investigated the stability behavior during training by considering the validation SEG score. We considered the mean SEG score for each 5th training epoch over all experiments and fitted a logarithmic curve (see Fig. 6 (a)). For supervised training, the mean SEG score is related to the number of labels in most cases. For our unsupervised method the best curve is obtained since the method achieves stable training with low variance of the validation score over time. This is an advantage since we select the model after the loss converges (without using ground truth) instead of selecting the model based on the highest validation score as for the supervised method. Obviously, the final test score is higher using methods with model selection based on the validation score (supervised and semi-supervised methods). As can be seen in Fig. 6 (b), there are partially higher validation scores in the supervised case compared to the unsupervised method. This could also explain the higher test scores for the supervised method. The reason is that for the supervised method the training is more directed using the ground truth labels. However, the unsupervised method yields relatively high scores compared to the supervised method.

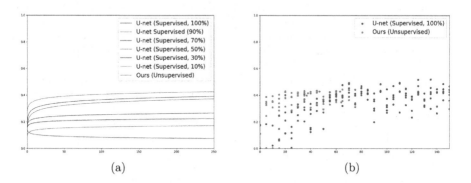

(a)   (b)

Fig. 6. Validation SEG scores during training (Fluo-C2DL-MSC data set, Video 1). Each experiment was performed five times. (a) Logarithmic curve fitted to the mean validation SEG values over all experiments for the U-net with a different number of labels as well as our unsupervised method (orange). (b) Single values of the SEG scores for the U-net with 100% of the labels (blue) and our unsupervised method (orange). (Color figure online)

4   Conclusion

We presented a novel fully unsupervised method for cell segmentation in fluorescence microscopy images using self-supervised learning. Our deep neural network performs attention map generation and the auxiliary task in one network, and the segmentation is directly determined from the network. The method generally outperforms or achieves similar results as classical unsupervised methods. Furthermore, we showed that the training is stable, so that model selection based on convergence of the loss function achieves reliable results. We can improve the result of our unsupervised method using few annotations for model selection and achieve similar results as the supervised method using 90% of the labels for the first video of the Fluo-C2DL-MSC data set and 30% of the labels for the second video as well as for both videos from the Fluo-N2DL-HeLa data set. The fully unsupervised method is somewhat worse than the semi-supervised method.

Acknowledgements. Support of the BMBF within de.NBI (031A537C, HD-HuB) and the DFG within the SFB 1129, project number 240245660, and the SPP 2202, project number 402733153, is gratefully acknowledged.

References

1. Achanta, R., et al.: SLIC superpixels compared to state-of-the-art superpixel methods. IEEE Trans. Pattern Anal. Mach. Intell. **34**(11), 2274–2282 (2012)
2. Caron, M., et al.: Emerging properties in self-supervised vision transformers. arXiv:2104.14294 (2021)
3. Cho, J.H., et al.: PiCIE: unsupervised semantic segmentation using invariance and equivariance in clustering. In: Proceedings of IEEE/CVF Conference on Computer Vision and Pattern Recognition, pp. 16794–16804 (2021)
4. Dunn, K.W., et al.: DeepSynth: three-dimensional nuclear segmentation of biological images using neural networks trained with synthetic data. Sci. Rep. **9**(1), 1–15 (2019)
5. Fujii, H., et al.: X-net with different loss functions for cell image segmentation. In: Proceedings of IEEE/CVF Conference on Computer Vision and Pattern Recognition, pp. 3793–3800 (2021)
6. Getreuer, P.: Chan-Vese segmentation. Image Process. On Line **2**, 214–224 (2012)
7. Haq, M.M., Huang, J.: Adversarial domain adaptation for cell segmentation. In: Proceedings of Medical Imaging with Deep Learning, pp. 277–287. PMLR (2020)
8. Horlava, N., et al.: A comparative study of semi-and self-supervised semantic segmentation of biomedical microscopy data. arXiv:2011.08076 (2020)
9. Ji, X., et al.: Invariant information clustering for unsupervised image classification and segmentation. In: Proceedings of IEEE/CVF International Conference on Computer Vision, pp. 9865–9874 (2019)
10. Jing, L., Tian, Y.: Self-supervised visual feature learning with deep neural networks: a survey. IEEE Trans. Pattern Anal. Mach. Intell. **43**, 4037–4058 (2020)
11. Larsson, G., et al.: Colorization as a proxy task for visual understanding. In: Proceedings of IEEE Conference on Computer Vision and Pattern Recognition, pp. 6874–6883 (2017)

12. Liu, D., et al.: Unsupervised instance segmentation in microscopy images via panoptic domain adaptation and task re-weighting. In: Proceedings of IEEE/CVF Conference on Computer Vision and Pattern Recognition, pp. 4243–4252 (2020)

13. Liu, Q., et al.: GAN based unsupervised segmentation: should we match the exact number of objects. In: Proceedings of Medical Imaging 2021: Image Processing, vol. 11596. International Society for Optics and Photonics (2021)

14. Maška, M., et al.: A benchmark for comparison of cell tracking algorithms. Bioinformatics **30**(11), 1609–1617 (2014)

15. Otsu, N.: A threshold selection method from gray-level histograms. IEEE Trans. Syst. Man Cybern. **9**(1), 62–66 (1979)

16. Robitaille, M.C., et al.: A self-supervised machine learning approach for objective live cell segmentation and analysis. bioRxiv:2021.01.07.425773 (2021)

17. Ronneberger, O., Fischer, P., Brox, T.: U-Net: convolutional networks for biomedical image segmentation. In: Navab, N., Hornegger, J., Wells, W.M., Frangi, A.F. (eds.) MICCAI 2015. LNCS, vol. 9351, pp. 234–241. Springer, Cham (2015). https://doi.org/10.1007/978-3-319-24574-4_28

18. Sahasrabudhe, M., et al.: Self-supervised nuclei segmentation in histopathological images using attention. In: Martel, A.L., et al. (eds.) MICCAI 2020. LNCS, vol. 12265, pp. 393–402. Springer, Cham (2020). https://doi.org/10.1007/978-3-030-59722-1_38

19. Ulman, V., et al.: An objective comparison of cell-tracking algorithms. Nat. Methods **14**(12), 1141–1152 (2017)

20. Van Valen, D.A., et al.: Deep learning automates the quantitative analysis of individual cells in live-cell imaging experiments. PLoS Comput. Biol. **12**(11), e1005177 (2016)

21. Vincent, L., Soille, P.: Watersheds in digital spaces: an efficient algorithm based on immersion simulations. IEEE TPAMI **13**(06), 583–598 (1991)

22. Wang, Z., et al.: Differential treatment for stuff and things: a simple unsupervised domain adaptation method for semantic segmentation. In: Proceedings of IEEE/CVF Conference on Computer Vision and Pattern Recognition, pp. 12635–12644 (2020)

23. Wolf, S., et al.: Inpainting networks learn to separate cells in microscopy images. In: Proceedings of BMVC (2020)

24. Wollmann, T., et al.: GRUU-Net: integrated convolutional and gated recurrent neural network for cell segmentation. Med. Image Anal. **56**, 68–79 (2019)

25. Xie, X., Chen, J., Li, Y., Shen, L., Ma, K., Zheng, Y.: Instance-aware self-supervised learning for nuclei segmentation. In: Martel, A.L., et al. (eds.) MICCAI 2020. LNCS, vol. 12265, pp. 341–350. Springer, Cham (2020). https://doi.org/10.1007/978-3-030-59722-1_33

26. Zhou, Z., et al.: Models genesis. Med. Image Anal. **67**, 101840 (2021)

27. Zhu, J., et al.: Rubik's cube+: a self-supervised feature learning framework for 3D medical image analysis. Med. Image Anal. **64**, 101746 (2020)

28. Zou, Y., et al.: Unsupervised domain adaptation for semantic segmentation via class-balanced self-training. In: Proceedings of European Conference on Computer Vision (ECCV), pp. 289–305 (2018)

Document

Hypercomplex Generative Adversarial Networks for Lightweight Semantic Labeling

Giorgos Sfikas[1,3,4(✉)], George Retsinas[2,4], Basilis Gatos[1], and Christophoros Nikou[4]

[1] Computational Intelligence Laboratory, Institute of Informatics and Telecommunications, National Center for Scientific Research "Demokritos", Athens, Greece
`bgat@iit.demokritos.gr`
[2] School of Electrical and Computer Engineering, National Technical University of Athens, Athens, Greece
`gretsinas@central.ntua.gr`
[3] Department of Surveying and Geoinformatics Engineering, University of West Attica, Athens, Greece
`gsfikas@uniwa.gr`
[4] Department of Computer Science and Engineering, University of Ioannina, Ioannina, Greece
`cnikou@cs.uoi.gr`

Abstract. Following recent advances on parameterized hypercomplex multiplication [21], we explore the usefulness of hypercomplex convolutions and deconvolutions in a document labeling task. We show that the proposed Hypercomplex Generative Adversarial Networks achieve excellent results while requiring significantly less independent parameters than real-valued models.

Keywords: Quaternions · Parameterized hypercomplex multiplication · Semantic labeling · Multiple labels · Document image processing · Generative Adversarial Networks

1 Introduction and Related Work

Quaternions are numbers that are part of the family that is known as hypercomplex numbers, and perhaps the better known member of this family. Regarding their applications, again the most well-known example concerns quaternions and their use in expressing rotations in 3D (and 4D) space [9,20]. Other applications in computer science are more or less unknown to the majority of researchers in the community, and at best seem exotic or of marginal use. One line of research involves quaternions, and to some extend other hypercomplex numbers, as a tool to generalize standard methods in signal and image processing. Notable examples are the Quaternion Fourier Transform [4], and Quaternion Singular Value Decomposition [10], or extensions of standard image filters like Sobel or the

© Springer Nature Switzerland AG 2022
M. El Yacoubi et al. (Eds.): ICPRAI 2022, LNCS 13363, pp. 251–262, 2022.
https://doi.org/10.1007/978-3-031-09037-0_21

Laplacian to $\mathbb{R}^3$ and colour image processing. In keypoint detection, a quaternionic variant of the Harris-Stephens detector has been recently described [17]. The advantage of a hypercomplex framework is, in a nutshell, that any methodology that assumes scalar values, signals or tensors can be extended to account for multiple values per number, as each hypercomplex number encapsulates in itself multiple (real) values in a holistic manner. On the downside, quaternions and other hypercomplex number systems involve various difficulties; quaternions define a non-commutative multiplication rule, which subsequently leads to problems in many facets of their use. For example, an immediate implication is that the problem $Ax = \lambda x$ is different than $Ax = x\lambda$, which means that there exist two different types of eigenvalues and eigenvectors [17,22]. A determinant is impossible to define for quaternion matrices [3] (at least, without dropping important defining properties of the classic determinant), and so on and so forth.

Another, more recent line of applications of hypercomplex numbers involves their use with neural networks. Networks with values, inputs, outputs, layers, parameters that are hypercomplex-valued have been proposed and successfully used in a variety of signal processing, vision, and pattern recognition tasks in general. In general, perhaps the most successful feature of these networks is that they lead to implementations that are not-as-demanding as real valued models in terms of storage space requirements, while achieving good results for most tasks where they were employed. The key to their being less resource demanding, lies with the definition of hypercomplex multiplication, which in the context of a neural network layer definition, leads naturally to extended parameter sharing. Quaternions have been the paradigm most prominently used in this respect [11–13,16]. Extensions to other high-dimensional number domains have been recently shown not only to be possible, but also very beneficial [21].

Parameterized Hypercomplex Multiplication is a technique that has recently been proposed as a means to extend the parameter sharing/sparsness benefits of quaternion neural networks to arbitrary, n-dimensional number systems [7,21]. Under this framework, quaternion networks are considered a special case for $n = 4$, and the multiplication is learnable.

The main points of contribution of this work are as follows: First, we explore the use of parameterized hypercomplex multiplication and Hamilton (quaternion) product to extend convolution and deconvolution layers. Previous work has addressed convolutions only, and in the context of very standard feed-forward models (VGG, ResNet [7]). The hypercomplex layer integration addressed in the current work is done in the context of a Generative Adversarial Network, with fully convolutional generator and discriminator components. Second, we apply the novel hypercomplex model in a document layout labeling task. Specifically, the task is to label each pixel of a document image according to the semantics of the pixel and its neighbourhood. The task is different than standard semantic segmentation, in that multiple labels are allowed per pixel. We show that a hypercomplex architecture can lead to a useful, lightweight model in terms of size, corroborating the results of recent related work [21].

The paper is structured as follows. In Sect. 2 we present the proposed model, after discussing theoretical preliminaries: we review elements of quaternion algebra, hypercomplex numbers, parameterized hypercomplex operations and describe the proposed model architecture. In Sect. 3 we apply the model on a document labeling task. In Sect. 4 we discuss our conclusions and envisage future work.

Fig. 1. Sample scanned pages from the PIOP-B dataset, used in our labeling experiments with the proposed Hypercomplex GANs.

2 Proposed Model

2.1 Hypercomplex Layers

Quaternions and Elements of Quaternionic Algebra. Quaternions have been introduced in the 19th century by Hamilton. Historically, Hamilton was initially trying to create a 3-dimensional algebra that would employ one real part and two imaginary components, all orthogonal to one another. He eventually found the undertaking to be impossible, which gave birth to the algebra of quaternions. The latter instead prescribes one real part and three imaginary components. This result has been subsequently codified and formalized in a theorem by Frobenius, which states that the only associative division algebras (up to an isomorphism) that are possible are the real numbers $\mathbb{R}$, the complex numbers $\mathbb{C}$, and quaternionic numbers $\mathbb{H}$ [5].

A quaternion can be formally defined as a number $q \in \mathbb{H}$:

$$q = a + b\boldsymbol{i} + c\boldsymbol{j} + d\boldsymbol{k}, \tag{1}$$

where $\boldsymbol{i}$, $\boldsymbol{j}$, $\boldsymbol{k}$ are independent unit "imaginary" components, and $a, b, c, d \in \mathbb{R}$ are respective coefficients to the real and the imaginary parts. From Eq. 1 it is straightforward that $\mathbb{H}$ is isomorphic to $\mathbb{R}^4$. Hence, quaternions can be understood as a four-dimensional generalization of complex numbers, with two extra imaginary components.

Analogous to what holds with numbers in $\mathbb{C}$, the square of the imaginary unit is -1, i.e. $\boldsymbol{i}^2 = \boldsymbol{j}^2 = \boldsymbol{k}^2 = -1$, where of course the relation holds for any of the three imaginary units. This leads to the interesting consequence that

$\mu^2 = -1$ has infinite solutions for $\mu \in \mathbb{H}$. For quaternion multiplication, we have the following rule:

$$pq = S(p)S(q) - V(p) \cdot V(q) + S(p)V(q) + S(q)V(p) + V(p) \times V(q), \qquad (2)$$

where $S(q)$ is the scalar (real) component of q and $V(q)$ is the "vector" component of q, $V(q) = [b \ c \ d]^T$ (hence $q = S(q) + V(q)$). Operands $\cdot$ and $\times$ denote the dot and cross product respectively. The rule Eq. 2 is occasionally referred to as a Hamilton product in the literature [11]. Another equivalent way to write the same rule is:

$$pq = (a_p a_q - b_p b_q - c_p c_q - d_p d_q) + \qquad (3)$$
$$(a_p b_q + b_p a_q + c_p d_q - d_p c_q)\boldsymbol{i} + \qquad (4)$$
$$(a_p c_q - b_p d_q + c_p a_q + d_p b_q)\boldsymbol{j} + \qquad (5)$$
$$(a_p d_q + b_p c_q - c_p b_q + d_p a_q)\boldsymbol{k}, \qquad (6)$$

where $p = a_p + b_p\boldsymbol{i} + c_p\boldsymbol{j} + d_p\boldsymbol{k}$ and $q = a_q + b_q\boldsymbol{i} + c_q\boldsymbol{j} + d_q\boldsymbol{k}$. Finally, we can also write the product rule using a matrix-vector notation:

$$\begin{pmatrix} a_{pq} \\ b_{pq} \\ c_{pq} \\ d_{pq} \end{pmatrix} = \begin{pmatrix} a_p & -b_p & -c_p & -d_p \\ b_p & a_p & -d_p & c_p \\ c_p & d_p & a_p & -b_p \\ d_p & -c_p & b_p & a_p \end{pmatrix} \begin{pmatrix} a_q \\ b_q \\ c_q \\ d_q \end{pmatrix}, \qquad (7)$$

where we write the product result as $pq = a_{pq} + b_{pq}\boldsymbol{i} + c_{pq}\boldsymbol{j} + d_{pq}\boldsymbol{k}$. We shall see in Sect. 2 that this way of writing the Hamilton product is useful in underpinning the relation of parameterized hypercomplex multiplication to quaternionic operations, also discussed in the same section.

A quaternion conjugate is defined analogously to the complex conjugate, as $\bar{q} = a - b\boldsymbol{i} - c\boldsymbol{j} - d\boldsymbol{k}$, and likewise a quaternion magnitude, as $|q| = \sqrt{q\bar{q}} = \sqrt{\bar{q}q} = \sqrt{a^2 + b^2 + c^2 + d^2}$. Generalizing the formula for $e^{i\theta}$, for any $\mu \in \mathbb{H}$ for which $\mu^2 = -1$ and $\theta \in \mathbb{R}$ it holds $e^{\mu\theta} = cos\theta + \mu\sin\theta$. Using the latter formula, a polar representation of quaternions is possible, as: $q = |q|e^{\mu\theta}$, where $\mu \in \mathbb{H}$ and $\theta \in \mathbb{R}$ are called eigenaxis and eigenangle [4].

Hypercomplex Numbers Beyond Quaternions. Historically, quickly after quaternions were introduced, it was understood that numbers of higher intrinsic dimensionality than that of quaternions (i.e., $d = 4$), were possible (where again, "possibility" should be understood as feasibility of construction of a field or field-like algebraic structure, based on those numbers). Eight-dimensional numbers, called *octonions*, and sixteen-dimensional numbers, called *sedenions*, were in introduced in this manner, as well as a multitude of other constructions [5,15]. These number systems came to be known collectively as hypercomplex numbers. In this work, numbers with dimensionality $d \geq 4$ are of interest as they are related to parameterized hypercomplex variations of "traditional" (i.e. real-valued) neural network operations [21]. Octonions and sedenions also define operations in an analogous manner to that described for quaternions in the previous paragraphs. In a nutshell, "movement" to a higher dimensionality comes at a cost of losing important algebraic structure properties. For example, octonion multiplication is non-commutative, like quaternions, however unlike the latter, it is furthermore non-associative.

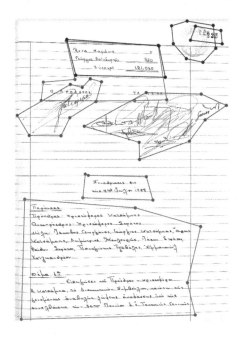

Fig. 2. Example of manual annotation. Polygon colours correspond to the following semantic labels: 1) Dark green: Handwritten text. 2) Blue: Stamp. 3) Olive green: Matrix. 4) Violet: Signature. 5) Brown: Page number. A single pixel may correspond to a number of labels ranging from none, up to multiple labels. (Color figure online)

Parameterized Hypercomplex Convolutional/Deconvolutional Layer.
As a building block in our architecture, we use convolutional and deconvolutional layers. The GAN generator uses a cascade of convolutions and deconvolutions; the GAN discriminator uses a cascade of convolutions (The specific architecture will be described in more detail in the following subsection). Models that make use of parameterized hypercomplex convolutions have been explored recently [7]. In our model, we also experiment with parameterized hypercomplex versions of deconvolutions. Generally, we can write a convolution or deconvolution, parameterized by its kernel H as:

$$y = H * x, \tag{8}$$

where x, y are the input and output tensors respectively, of dimensionality χ and ψ respectively. The operation kernel H is assumed to be rectangular with side equal to k. These operations are well-known to be linear, so we can equivalently write $y = C_H x$, where C_H is the respective Toeplitz or Circulant matrix, depending on the specifics of the operation [8]. Kernel H is in $\mathbb{R}^{\chi \times \psi \times k \times k}$, and the total number of *independent* parameters (or "degrees of freedom") involved is $\chi \times \psi \times k \times k$.

Following the parameterized hypercomplex construction introduced with [21], we can write the operation

$$y = \sum_{i=1}^{n} A_i \otimes F_i * x, \tag{9}$$

where the operation kernel is determined by the sum of kronecker products of matrices A_i and F_i, $i \in [1, n]$, and n is a operation hyperparameter that determines the characteristics of the operation. Matrices A_i are in $\mathbb{R}^{n \times n}$, independent of the input and output tensor dimensions. Matrices F_i are in $\mathbb{R}^{\frac{\chi}{n} \times \frac{\psi}{n} \times k \times k}$. The resulting kronecker products are in $\mathbb{R}^{\frac{\chi}{n} \times \frac{\psi}{n} \times k \times k}$, hence the sum $\sum_{i=1}^{n} A_i \otimes F_i$ of Eq. 9 is also of the same dimensionality. However, the important difference to standard convolution and deconvolution is here that the corresponding parameters are *not independent*; in fact, in this formulation the operation parameters form n-sized groups of shared parameters.

Interestingly, quaternion convolution and deconvolution [16] can be written in the form set in Eq. 9, with n equal to 4 and fixed matrices A_1, A_2, A_3, A_4. Specifically, for quaternion operations these matrices are:

$$A_1 = I_4, A_2 = \begin{pmatrix} 0 & -1 & 0 & 0 \\ 1 & 0 & 0 & 0 \\ 0 & 0 & 0 & -1 \\ 0 & 0 & 1 & 0 \end{pmatrix}, A_3 = \begin{pmatrix} 0 & 0 & -1 & 0 \\ 0 & 0 & 0 & 1 \\ 1 & 0 & 0 & 0 \\ 0 & -1 & 0 & 0 \end{pmatrix}, A_4 = \begin{pmatrix} 0 & 0 & 0 & -1 \\ 0 & 0 & -1 & 0 \\ 0 & 1 & 0 & 0 \\ 1 & 0 & 0 & 0 \end{pmatrix}$$

$$\tag{10}$$

Essentially, the matrices of Eq. 10 are determined by the Hamilton product rule (Eq. 2), and more specifically its matrix-vector version (Eq. 7).

For either quaternion or parameterized hypercomplex versions of the convolution and deconvolution operations, their degrees of freedom is much lower than the dimensionality of the tensor space where they are defined. In particular, a parametrized hypercomplex kernel has $\frac{\chi}{n} \times \frac{\psi}{n} \times k^2$ degrees of freedom for each matrix F_i, for a total of $\frac{\chi}{n} \times \psi \times k^2$ for all n matrices. The matrices A_i have $n \times n$ degrees of freedom each, for a total n^3 for all n matrices. Hence, a parameterized hypercomplex convolution or deconvolution has a total of $n^3 + \frac{\chi}{n} \times \psi \times k^2$ independent parameters. For the quaternionic case, we have to set $n = 4$ and disregard the A_i matrices since these are fixed, thus we have $\frac{\chi}{4} \times \psi \times k^2$ independent parameters. In most practical cases, these numbers should be understood as dominated by the parameters of the F_i matrices, or $\frac{\chi}{n} \times \psi \times \psi \times k^2 \gg n^3$. The degrees of freedom associated with each operation kernel version are summarized in Table 1.

Table 1. Degrees of freedom for each convolution/deconvolution kernel operation. Real, quaternion and parameterized hypercomplex variants are compared. n is a "user-defined" operation hyperparameter, k is the size of the kernel, χ and ψ are the input and output feature map dimensionalities.

Operation variant	Degrees of freedom
Standard (real-valued) variant	$\chi \times \psi \times k^2$
Quaternion variant	$\frac{\chi}{4} \times \psi \times k^2$
Parameterized Hypercomplex variant	$n^3 + \frac{\chi}{n} \times \psi \times k^2$

2.2 Model Architecture

A Generative Adversarial Network is composed of two networks: The generator and the discriminator network, denoted as functions $G(\cdot)$ and $D(\cdot)$ respectively. In this work, both networks are fully convolutional. The generator is structured as a U-Net [14], with skip connections used to bridge the corresponding "mirror" layers in the encoder and the decoder part. Both models use hypercomplex convolutions and deconvolutions in all cases, unless stated explicitly otherwise.

The generator is structured as follows: The input is first padded with as many zero channels as required, in order to match the PHM hyperparameter n. We set this padding to 16 channels, to match the maximum value for n that is considered in this work. This action is equivalent to zero-ing the imaginary components of the input. The padded input is passed to a series of convolutional layers, followed by deconvolutional layers, as is the standard structure of U-Net. Four convolutional layers, topped by batch normalization and split-activation leaky ReLU, are followed by an equal number of deconvolutional layers. The number of channels are: 64, 128, 128, 256, 128, 128, 64, 16 (these are real-valued channels; when hypercomplex layers are considered, channels are grouped in n-tuples, hence these numbers should be divided by n for a PHM/n convolution or deconvolution. For quaternion layers, $n = 4$). The first two deconvolutions are also followed by Dropout layers. The last convolutional output is processed by a real-valued 1×1 convolution in order to drop the number of channels to the number of classes $K = 5$. This K-depth map is essentially a stack of class-specific activation maps, with each one corresponding to a different class. This map is followed naturally by a sigmoid activation. Note that, a sigmoid activation is used as each pixel may correspond to zero, one, or more classes, i.e. classes are not mutually exclusive. Hence, the generator is structured so as to take a document image as input, and produce a K-level activation map.

The discriminator is structured as follows: A total of six convolutional blocks comprise the discriminator, each having a convolutional layer and batch normalization. Tensor (real-valued) depths for each block are 16, 64, 128, 256, 256, 16. Then follow a sum over channel values, topped by a sigmoid activation. The input of the discriminator is the document image with the (real or fake) annotation activation map, and the result is an estimate of the model whether the document with the provided annotation seem like an "authentic" pair or not.

Regarding situations where training and evaluation classes are not balanced, several strategies have been proposed, as proceeding with standard loss and/or no resampling or reweighting is non-optimal. Briefly, one major strategy is using resampling in order to prioritize classes that are initially under-represented, by sampling more augmented samples from low-volume classes. The other major strategy is to tweak the loss function, so that under-represented classes are artificially assigned a larger loss. In this manner, training can be implicity manipulated towards an optimum that classifies small classes as well the larger ones. In this work, we have used a reweighting strategy, and balanced each per-class loss term inverse proportionally to the number of "positives" of each class.

After taking into account the aforementioned considerations, the required penalties are combined to a single, multi-task term as $L_{\text{total}} = L_{\text{adversarial}} + \lambda L_{bce}$, where we have $L_{adversarial} = E_x[logD(y)] + E_x[log(1 - D(G(x)))]]$, and $L_{bce} = E_{x,y}BCE(G(x), y)$, where λ_{bce} is a hyperparameter that controls the relative importance of the BCE to the adversarial term on the generator. The BCE term considers inconsistency of the estimate map $G(x)$ to ground truth y, by accounting divergence w.r.t. all class separately.

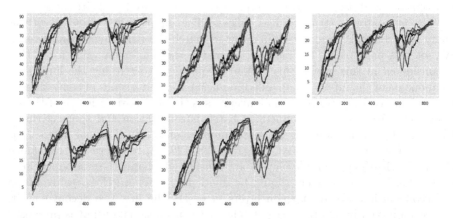

Fig. 3. Plots for resulting Intersection over Union (IoU) values. From top row to bottom row, in "reading order", plots correspond to classes: Handwritten text, Stamp, Matrix, Signature, Page number. Colours correspond to type of employed GAN: Vanilla/real-valued GAN (red), Quaternion GAN (blue), PHM/n = 2 (green), PHM/n = 4 (black), PHM/n = 8 (magenta), PHM/n = 16 (cyan). (Color figure online)

3 Experiments

The PIOP-B dataset consists of 203 manuscripts, scanned from the archives of the Greek *Peiraiki-Patraiki* bank. The dataset has been partitioned into a training and a test set with 162 and 41 document images respectively. All pages have been manually annotated with respect to 5 semantic classes (plus background). These classes are: 1. Handwritten text, 2. Stamp, 3. Matrix, 4. Signature, 5. Page

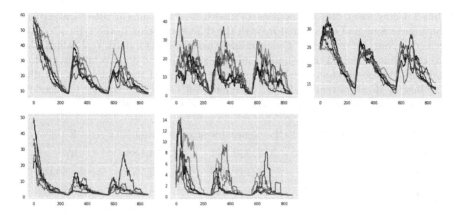

Fig. 4. Plots for resulting test binary cross entropy values. Lower values are better. From top row to bottom row, in "reading order", plots correspond to classes: Handwritten text, Stamp, Matrix, Signature, Page number. Colours correspond to type of employed GAN: Vanilla/real-valued GAN (red), Quaternion GAN (blue), PHM/n = 2 (green), PHM/n = 4 (black), PHM/n = 8 (magenta), PHM/n = 16 (cyan). (Color figure online)

number. Sample pages can be viewed in Fig. 1. An example manually annotated page can be examined in Fig. 2. Note that a single pixel may correspond to multiple labels.

The choices of hyperparameters for our model are as follows. We used a batch size equal to 14, multi-task hyperparameter equal $\lambda = 10$, learning rates for the generator and discriminator equal to 0.01 and 0.001 respectively. All convolutions and deconvolutions use a kernel size equal to 4×4 and stride equal to 2. Leaky ReLU split-activation uses parameter equal to 0.2, and Dropout uses probability parameter equal to 0.5. The Adam optimizer was used to train the models, with cosine annealing and restarts at every 300 epochs, with training for a total of 900 epochs for each case. Activation functions on the hypercomplex networks were "split-type", i.e. all activations treated their inputs as if they were sets of real numbers. Input document images have been sub-sampled to a fixed size, equal to 512×704. This resolution has been chosen with the consideration of preserving aspect ratio as much as possible, while easing computational burden and enabling batch processing during training. Furthermore, as the hypercomplex models treat channels as n-sized groups, care has been taken so as the input and intermediate processing tensors in the generator and discriminator are sized as multiples of the considered values for n, i.e. 2, 4, 8, 16. This was necessary in order to ensure a fair comparison between compared real-valued and hypercomplex models.

Numerical results comparing the vanilla (standard/real-valued) GAN model using the described architecture, against hypercomplex variants, are reported in detail in Table 2. The compared architectures are: vanilla GAN, i.e. a standard GAN with real-valued parameters; this is used as the baseline model. Quaternion GAN and the PHM/n models use hypercomplex layer, input values, intermediate

Table 2. Comparison of GAN models. All models bear the same architectural structure in both generator and discriminator, with the difference being in the type of convolution and deconvolution layers. The "vanilla" variant is a standard, real-valued GAN. The "quaternion" variant uses quaternionic convolutions and deconvolutions, while the PHM variants use parameterized hypercomplex versions of the same layers, for different values of the hyperparameter n. "Economy" denotes how smaller the model is, compared to the vanilla version (rounded up to a single decimal).

Model type	IoU	Test BCE	Generator size	Discriminator size	Economy
Vanilla	53.3	4.74	2, 280, 117	3, 886, 688	0%
PHM (n = 2)	55.5	4.42	1, 141, 493	1, 945, 232	−49.9%
Quaternion	53.0	4.92	572, 085	974, 432	−74.9%
PHM (n = 4)	53.9	4.86	572, 597	974, 816	−74.9%
PHM (n = 8)	52.5	4.96	291, 509	492, 128	−87.3%
PHM (n = 16)	52.3	5.82	177, 845	270, 944	−92.7%

network values, and split-type activations as described in Sect. 2. The difference between PHM/n models is in the choice of the hyperparameter n. Concerning PHM/n = 4 and Quaternion GAN, network values are grouped in quaternions in both cases, but in PHM/n = 4 the $\{A_i\}_{i=1}^4$ matrices are learnable, unlike the Quaternion GAN where they fixed w.r.t. the Hamilton product definition. Intersection over Union figures were computed after binarizing the sigmoid-activated map using threshold = 0.5. Additional plots are in Fig. 3 and Fig. 4, showing the progression of Intersection over Union (higher is better) and test Binary Cross Entropy (lower is better) per semantic class.

Perhaps the most straightforward conclusion is that all models attain evaluation measures that are comparable to each other. Concerning the attained IoU value of ∼55%, it is hampered chiefly by the results in the Matrix and Signature classes, which are perhaps objectively the hardest to detect correctly. The Matrix class for example, differs to Handwritten text only in terms of the way the content is structured, and table horizontal and vertical lines are not necessarily always present. The other classes – Handwritten text, Stamp, Page Number attain higher values. In particular, the final values attained in terms of IoU, per class, for the PHM/n = 2 model are: 88.7, 72.4, 27.2, 30.8, 58.4 for Handwritten text, Stamp, Matrix, Signature, Page number respectively.

The great advantage of the proposed PHM models is that they manage to attain results that are in the ballpark of the standard, real-valued model, by using only a fraction of the model's computational footprint, measured in terms of model size. All versions, including the most light one, PHM/n = 16, which uses only 7.3% of the vanilla model size, give similar, competitive end-results. Also, we note the slight improvement over the vanilla model attained IoU/loss values for the PHM/n = 2 model; while such a difference could be statistically insignificant, it is not inconsistent to similar comparisons in the literature [7, 16, 21]. In this respect, we believe that we must also take into account the size of each model with respect to it being a defining factor during model training. Indeed, in model training essentially we look for an optimal value in a search space; if this search space is significantly smaller than a baseline space, then attaining a good value should (all other factors being equal) be significantly easier for the smaller model. Apparently, PHM nets share this benefit while (crucially!) not leading to significant loss w.r.t. the model expressiveness.

4   Conclusion and Future Work

In this work, we have validated the usefulness of parameterized hypercomplex multiplications used in the context of a GAN architecture, comprised of convolutional and deconvolutional layers. Tested in a document labeling scenario, the proposed Hypercomplex GANs attain accuracy that is comparable to that of the GAN baseline, but using only a small fraction of the baseline cost, measured in terms of model size. As future work, we plan to extend the labeling model by considering more modern reweighting/class-balancing methods [1], exploring the use of Ising-like smoothness penalties [2,18,19], or experiment with using keyword spotting or shape [6] as a semantic content cue. In terms of hypercomplex components, we also plan to experiment with activation functions that are also fully hypercomplex (non "split-type"). Also, an interesting point would be whether imposing an orthogonality constraint on the PHM components (A_i matrices) could improve or accelerate learning.

Acknowledgments. This research has been partially co-financed by the EU and Greek national funds through the Operational Program Competitiveness, Entrepreneurship and Innovation, under the calls "OPEN INNOVATION IN CULTURE" (project *Bessarion* - T6YBΠ-00214) and "RESEARCH - CREATE - INNOVATE" (project *Culdile* - T1EΔK-03785).

References

1. Cui, Y., Jia, M., Lin, T.Y., Song, Y., Belongie, S.: Class-balanced loss based on effective number of samples. In: Proceedings of the IEEE International Conference on Computer Vision and Pattern Recognition (CVPR), pp. 9268–9277 (2019)
2. Dimitrakopoulos, P., Sfikas, G., Nikou, C.: ISING-GAN: annotated data augmentation with a spatially constrained generative adversarial network. In: 2020 IEEE 17th International Symposium on Biomedical Imaging (ISBI), pp. 1600–1603. IEEE (2020)
3. Dyson, F.J.: Quaternion determinants. Helv. Phys. Acta **45**(2), 289 (1972)
4. Ell, T.A., Sangwine, S.J.: Hypercomplex Fourier transforms of color images. IEEE Trans. Image Process. **16**(1), 22–35 (2007)
5. Fraleigh, J.B.: A First Course in Abstract Algebra, 7th edn. (2002)
6. Giotis, A.P., Sfikas, G., Nikou, C., Gatos, B.: Shape-based word spotting in handwritten document images. In: 13th International Conference on Document Analysis and Recognition (ICDAR), pp. 561–565. IEEE (2015)
7. Grassucci, E., Zhang, A., Comminiello, D.: Lightweight convolutional neural networks by hypercomplex parameterization. arXiv preprint arXiv:2110.04176 (2021)

8. Jain, A.K.: Fundamentals of Digital Image Processing. Prentice-Hall Inc., Hoboken (1989)
9. Kuipers, J.B.: Quaternions and Rotation Sequences: A Primer with Application to Orbits, Aerospace and Virtual Reality. Princeton University Press, Princeton (1999)
10. Le Bihan, N., Mars, J.: Singular value decomposition of quaternion matrices: a new tool for vector-sensor signal processing. Signal Process. **84**(7), 1177–1199 (2004)
11. Parcollet, T., Morchid, M., Linarès, G.: Quaternion convolutional neural networks for heterogeneous image processing. In: ICASSP 2019–2019 IEEE International Conference on Acoustics, Speech and Signal Processing (ICASSP), pp. 8514–8518. IEEE (2019)
12. Parcollet, T., Morchid, M., Linarès, G.: A survey of quaternion neural networks. Artif. Intell. Rev. **53**(4), 2957–2982 (2019). https://doi.org/10.1007/s10462-019-09752-1
13. Parcollet, T., et al.: Quaternion convolutional neural networks for end-to-end automatic speech recognition. arXiv preprint arXiv:1806.07789 (2018)
14. Ronneberger, O., Fischer, P., Brox, T.: U-Net: convolutional networks for biomedical image segmentation. In: Navab, N., Hornegger, J., Wells, W.M., Frangi, A.F. (eds.) MICCAI 2015. LNCS, vol. 9351, pp. 234–241. Springer, Cham (2015). https://doi.org/10.1007/978-3-319-24574-4_28
15. Sangwine, S.J.: Biquaternion (complexified quaternion) roots of- 1. Adv. Appl. Clifford Algebras **16**(1), 63–68 (2006). https://doi.org/10.1007/s00006-006-0005-8
16. Sfikas, G., Giotis, A.P., Retsinas, G., Nikou, C.: Quaternion generative adversarial networks for inscription detection in byzantine monuments. In: Del Bimbo, A., et al. (eds.) ICPR 2021. LNCS, vol. 12667, pp. 171–184. Springer, Cham (2021). https://doi.org/10.1007/978-3-030-68787-8_12
17. Sfikas, G., Ioannidis, D., Tzovaras, D.: Quaternion Harris for multispectral keypoint detection. In: 2020 IEEE International Conference on Image Processing (ICIP), pp. 11–15. IEEE (2020)
18. Sfikas, G., Nikou, C., Galatsanos, N., Heinrich, C.: MR brain tissue classification using an edge-preserving spatially variant Bayesian mixture model. In: Metaxas, D., Axel, L., Fichtinger, G., Székely, G. (eds.) MICCAI 2008. LNCS, vol. 5241, pp. 43–50. Springer, Heidelberg (2008). https://doi.org/10.1007/978-3-540-85988-8_6
19. Sfikas, G., Nikou, C., Galatsanos, N., Heinrich, C.: Majorization-minimization mixture model determination in image segmentation. In: CVPR 2011, pp. 2169–2176. IEEE (2011)
20. Vince, J.: Quaternions for Computer Graphics. Springer, Cham (2011). https://doi.org/10.1007/978-1-4471-7509-4
21. Zhang, A., et al.: Beyond fully-connected layers with quaternions: parameterization of hypercomplex multiplications with $1/n$ parameters. arXiv preprint arXiv:2102.08597 (2021)
22. Zhang, F.: Quaternions and matrices of quaternions. Linear Algebra Appl. **251**, 21–57 (1997)

Learning Document Graphs
with Attention for Image Manipulation
Detection

Hailey Joren, Otkrist Gupta$^{(\boxtimes)}$, and Dan Raviv

Lendbuzz, Boston, MA 02110, USA
{hailey.joren,otkrist.gupta}@lendbuzz.com

Abstract. Detecting manipulations in images is becoming increasingly important for combating misinformation and forgery. While recent advances in computer vision have lead to improved methods for detecting spliced images, most state-of-the-art methods fail when applied to images containing mostly text, such as images of documents. We propose a deep-learning method for detecting manipulations in images of documents which leverages the unique structured nature of these images in comparison with those of natural scenes. Specifically, we re-frame the classic image splice detection problem as a node classification problem, in which Optical Character Recognition (OCR) bounding boxes form nodes and edges are added according to a text-specific distance heuristic. We propose a Variational Autoencoder (VAE)-based embedding algorithm, which when combined with a graph neural network with attention, outperforms both a state-of-the-art image splice detection method and a document-specific method.

Keywords: Manipulation detection · Graph Neural Networks · Variational auto-encoders

1 Introduction

Identifying spliced images, or images in which content has been added during post-processing, has become an important area of research in computer vision. While spliced images of natural scenes can be used to propagate fake news, many real-world image splicing examples occur in images containing primarily text, or images of documents. Digital documents are commonly used to verify information in domains such as finance and administration, which creates a natural opportunity for forgery and manipulation. With a background of largely white space, images of digital documents pose a problem for most state-of-the-art image manipulation detection models, as they are traditionally trained to detect inconsistencies in texture and background features. In addition, the forged region of a document often looks very similar to the original image, as both often are simply black text on a white background.

The original version of this chapter was revised: error in the author name has been corrected. The correction to this chapter is available at
https://doi.org/10.1007/978-3-031-09037-0_57

© Springer Nature Switzerland AG 2022, corrected publication 2023
M. El Yacoubi et al. (Eds.): ICPRAI 2022, LNCS 13363, pp. 263–274, 2022.
https://doi.org/10.1007/978-3-031-09037-0_22

In this paper, we propose an image manipulation detection system designed for improved performance on digital documents. Unlike in natural scene images, forgery detection in digital documents allows us to use Optical Character Recognition (OCR) to narrow the search space of potential manipulations to the textual content of the image. As the number of text boxes on a given page varies and the existence of meaningful relationships between boxes can be inferred, the resulting OCR bounding boxes are natural candidates for learning with Graph Neural Networks (GNNs). Specifically, we can construct a graph G from a single image of a document in which the OCR bounding boxes form nodes $\mathbf{v} = \{v_1, v_2, v_3, ...v_{|V|}\}$ where $|V|$ is the number of detected OCR text boxes on the page. We can then re-frame the splice detection in digital documents as a node classification problem, in which text nodes are classified either spliced or genuine. The nodes are connected by edges using a document-specific distance heuristic, such that

$$e_{v_i,v_j} = \begin{cases} 1, & \text{if } d_{v_i,v_j} \leq T \\ 0, & \text{otherwise} \end{cases} \tag{1}$$

where d_{v_i,v_j} is the distance between nodes v_i and v_j, T is a numeric threshold tuned such that connected edges exist within the same paragraph or textual region on a page.

The primary challenge for this approach is initializing the node embeddings to effectively create feature vectors $\mathbf{h} = \{\vec{h_1}, \vec{h_2}...\vec{h_{|V|}}\}$ for effective splice manipulation detection. Most methods for learning text-based features from images (such as OCR) are designed to extract high-level features such as character values while ignoring low-level features such as text blur, spacing, or font properties. However, these are the exact properties which are most likely to be relevant for identifying a spliced box, while high-level features such as the character value or word are less likely to be discriminative. In the case of manipulation detection we are interested specifically in ignoring high-level features such as text content while extracting low-level character-based features.

To accomplish this task, we designed a feature extraction algorithm based on pre-training the embeddings using a Variational Autoencoder (VAE) on a set of input and output image pairs. In each image pair, the content varies while the low-level features (character weight, font, spacing, etc.) are held constant. This results in a latent space embedding that is sensitive to manipulation artifacts while agnostic to the text content. The encoder from this feature extraction model forms the first part of the manipulation detection model, with weights pre-trained on the specially-designed images pairs.

An additional challenge is to design a mechanism which leverages the context of a given block of text for improved classification. In the case of forgery detection, the relationships between text nodes are particularly important, as an anomalous node is most likely to be detected by comparing its features with those of its neighbors. We would expect to see subtle feature differences in spliced text, as it likely would have been spliced from another document or image with different character-level features.

Our solution involves adapting a graph attention layer [32], in which attention weights are trained to update the node embeddings according to the edges between nodes $\mathbf{h} = \{\vec{h}_1, \vec{h}_2...\vec{h}_{|V|}\} \rightarrow \mathbf{h}' = \{\vec{h}'_1, \vec{h}'_2...\vec{h}'_{|V|}\}$. This allows our model to appropriately update a node embedding by attending to its neighbors for binary classification (see Fig. 1).

We evaluate our method on programmatically-generated document splice dataset. Our proposed model outperforms both a state-of-the-art image splice detection method and a document-specific method, both of which are generally unable to differentiate the spliced text from the genuine text.

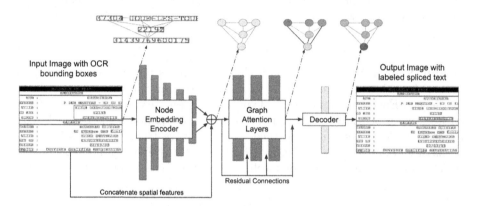

Fig. 1. Architecture overview. Our proposed system is designed to label text on an image of a document as original to the document or as spliced (copied and pasted from another image). Left to right: First Optical Character Recognition (OCR) bounding boxes are obtained, and a graph structure is formed by treating the text boxes as nodes and adding edges accordingly to a document-based distance heuristic. Each graph is passed through the pre-trained encoder, embedding each node based on low-level features (Sect. 2). The graph's spatial features are then concatenated with the encoder output, as represented by $\oplus$. Next, the node embeddings are updated by a trained graph attention layer, which implicitly weights edges between nodes to encode relational information. Finally, a decoder classifies each node as spliced or genuine, at which point they can be mapped back onto the input image.

2   Related Work

Image Splice Detection. Image splicing is a manipulation operation in which content is copied and pasted from a source image onto a destination image. Current methods for detecting splices in images can be broadly categorized as methods that search for local inconsistencies in the image background noise [22,26] or compression discrepancies [12,16,23], methods that leverage camera-based artifact inconsistencies [17,27,33], camera-based methods [9] or deep-learning based methods [2,9,11,18,34], with deep-learning based methods generally achieving the best performance. Several public datasets for benchmarking performance on image splice detection in natural scenes have been released [20]. In this paper, we compare our model with Self Consistency [18], a state-of-the-art image splice detection method with a publicly available trained model.

Document Manipulation Detection. Methods for detecting manipulations in documents often try to leverage document-specific features. Examples include methods that use intrinsic document elements, or portions of the document that can be matched against a template to gauge authenticity [1], font-based features [4,8,10], alignment or skew-based features [6] For images of physical documents, this has included printer identification [5,13,28,29]. [31] present findings from deploying manipulation techniques on real-world datasets.

Graph Neural Networks. Graph Neural Networks (GNNs) are intended to deal with arbitrarily structured data in order to generalize learning methods to the non-Euclidean domain [7]. Typically, Graph Neural Networks perform an iterative process of updating node states until equilibrium is reached. The resulting node states can be learned by consecutive trainable layers in order to classify nodes, graphs, or edges. [32] proposed a Graph Attention Networks (GATs) for learning an attention mechanism on the relationships between nodes.

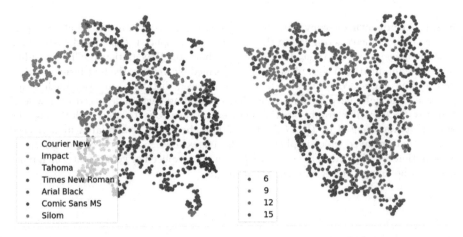

Fig. 2. Encoder embeddings capture low-level font features. UMAP [24] visualization of randomly-generated text node embeddings labeled by font (left) and font size (right). The VAE is able to separate text images based on these low level features. Notably, the embeddings reveal groups based on character size, despite each text box being scaled to a uniform height and cropped to a uniform width before being passed to the model.

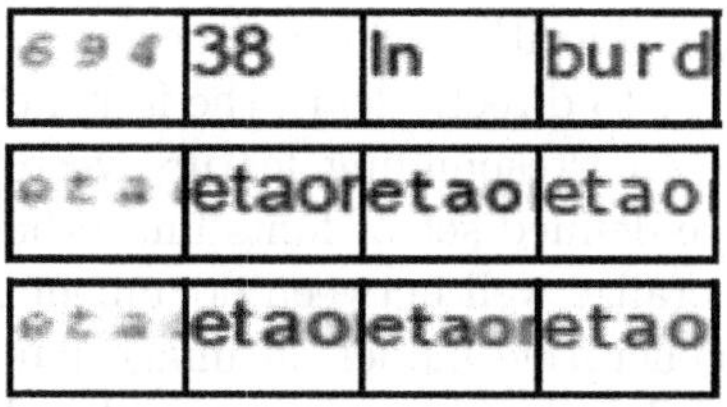

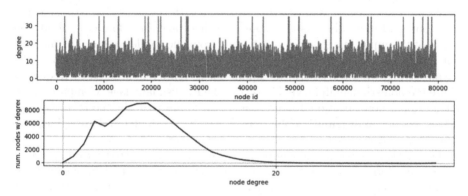

Fig. 3. Data used for pre-training the encoder. VAE inputs (top), VAE outputs (middle), and VAE reconstructions (bottom). The inputs are constructed by drawing random strings of text (not OCR text images) from OCR results on the training images. The input images are constructed by assigning the random string specific properties, and the outputs are always the same string ("etaonisrhldcmufpgwybvkjxqz") with matching properties to the input. This pairing enables the encoder to capture low-level manipulation artifacts while ignoring content-like character value or sequence patterns.

Fig. 4. Graph statistics on a sample of 256 images from the Auto-Splice Dataset. Top: Degree by number of nodes with that degree on a sample set. Bottom: Number of nodes by degree. The median degree is 8, which intuitively makes sense as the number of nearby words that might be examined to determine if a block of text has been spliced.

3 Methods

Node Embedding Initialization. One of the primary challenges in learning the document graph for forgery localization is initializing the node embeddings. The node embeddings must have uniform size and contain information that is likely to be useful for manipulation detection. While we can naïvely obtain OCR bounding boxes to represent each node, bounded regions of pixel values will be variable in size and obscure important information features. When text is spliced from one image to another, it is unlikely that features like the character size, font, spacing, and aspect ratio will be identical from the source to the destination. Thus while most learning methods using images of text seek to extract the high-level features such as character value or words (i.e. using OCR), we are interested in an embedding algorithm which can capture these low-level features. One option would be to try to directly learn the fonts, character spacing values, and font sizes and form a corresponding feature vector. However, this would require constructing a pre-defined set of fonts and other low-level features and would be unlikely to generalize well between document sets.

Instead, we train a generative model on image pairs in which the content (character values) change but low-level forgery related features are held constant (see Figs. 3 and 2. Ablation studies show improvements of a Variational Autoencoder (VAE) over a simple auto-encoder and no pretraining, indicating that a VAE architecture constrains our model to form smooth latent space representations that are conducive to interpolation when unseen data is encountered. In each image pair, the input is formed by sampling a random string from the text in the training images (as obtained through OCR) and creating an image formed from this text and a random character spacing, size, font, and level of Gaussian blur. The output image is formed by taking a fixed string (the same string for every output) and creating an image with the same character spacing, size, font, and blur values as the input. We then take a random crop of 30×50 pixels of the input image and a fixed crop (from the top left corner) of the output image of the same dimensions. While any fixed string could be used as the output string, we chose to use the alphabetical characters ordered by frequency of use ("etaonisrhldcmufpgwybvkjxqz") in the English language. Compared with a traditional non-variational autoencoder, we found that the model performed better on "out of distribution" data, or when the manipulated dataset included fonts or variations not found in the pre-training data.

Our VAE architecture is composed of four fully-connected encoding layers (sizes 1500, 1204, 908, and 612) with ReLU activation and four fully-connected decoding layers (size 612, 908, 1204, and 1500) with ReLU activation, with a latent dimension of size twenty. We use a final Sigmoid activation function, Xavier initialization, batch size 32, learning rate 0.0001. The loss function is composed of the reconstruction loss and a regularization term, the Kullback-Leibler (KL) divergence between the means and variances encoded in latent space and that of a unit Gaussian. To train our model, we adapt the approximation proposed in [19].

$$\sum_j KL(q_j(z|x) \parallel \mathcal{N}(0,1)) + \mathbf{L}(x, \hat{x})$$

where $\mathbf{L}$ is the reconstruction error, j is the latent space dimension, KL is the KL divergence, $q_j(z|x)$ is the encoded distribution, and $\mathcal{N}(0,1)$ is a unit Gaussian. To train our model, we adapt the approximation proposed in [19], or

$$\mathcal{L}(\theta; \hat{x}^{(i)}, x^{(i)}) \simeq \frac{1}{2} \sum_j (1 + \log((\sigma_j^{(i)})^2) - (\mu_j^{(i)})^2 - (\sigma_j^{(i)})^2)) + BCE_\theta(\hat{x}^{(i)}, x^{(i)})$$

where $\mathcal{L}$ is the loss given the parameters θ on a text image $x^{(i)}$ from the synthetic dataset, $\mu_j^{(i)}$ and $\sigma_j^{(i)}$ are the mean and variance of the distribution j on image i in the latent space, and $BCE_\theta(\hat{x}^{(i)}, x^{(i)})$ is the binary cross entropy loss between the output text image $x^{(i)}$ from image pair i and the reconstructed image $\hat{x}^{(i)}$.

Graph Learning and Classification. We construct the graph by adding edges between OCR bounding boxes given a document-based heuristic. Because boxes can vary significantly in size, considering a midpoint to midpoint euclidean distance d is not practical for adding edges, as larger boxes would be biased towards having a lower degree than smaller boxes. Instead, we propose an edge addition formula which adds edges based on a function of vertical and horizontal gaps between the bounding boxes and the respective widths and heights of each box. Specifically, edges are added when the vertical gap g_v between the boxes is less than three times the minimum height h_{min} and the horizontal gap g_h is less than four times the minimum height h_{min} (see Fig. 4).

The nature of text on a page means that, for the purpose of splice detection, not all edges can be considered equal. For example, a block of text that differs from the rest of the text on a horizontal line may be more likely to have been spliced than a block of text that differs from the text above or below. In order to learn these relationships and implicitly apply different weights to different edges, we developed a model based on graph attention layers, as proposed in [32]. The graph attention layer takes as input the set of node features, $\mathbf{h} = \{\vec{h}_1, \vec{h}_2...\vec{h}_{|V|}\}, \vec{h}_i \in \mathbb{R}^{F_n}$, where $|V|$ is the number of nodes in the graph and F_n is the node embedding dimension at the nth graph attention layer. In the first graph attention layer, the input is the encoder latent space embedding concatenated with the scaled bounding box coordinates of the text nodes, or $2 \times latent\ dim + 4$. The outputs of a graph attention layer are an updated set of node features, potentially with a new node embedding dimension, or $\mathbf{h}' = \{\vec{h}'_1, \vec{h}'_2...\vec{h}'_N\}, \vec{h}'_i \in \mathbb{R}^{F_{n+1}}$.

An attention weight matrix, $\mathbf{W} \in \mathbb{R}^{F_n \times F_{n+1}}$, performs self-attention on each of the nodes by sharing the attention mechanism a for coefficient computation. While the weight matrix is applied over all nodes in the graph, structural information is preserved by masking the attention to include only first-order neighbors of a node i. Attention is normalized across all edges by using the softmax function. In our proposed model, the attention mechanism is a single-layer neural network with Leaky ReLU activation.

$$\alpha_{ij} = \frac{\exp(a(\mathbf{W}\vec{h}_i, \mathbf{W}\vec{h}_j))}{\sum_{z \in N_x} \exp(a(\mathbf{W}\vec{h}_i, \mathbf{W}\vec{h}_k))}$$

The normalized attention coefficients serve to form a linear combination of input features, and form the final output node embeddings for the layer. We found that using multi-head attention and ELU activation improved training stability, consistent with results in [32]. The output features can thus be represented by

$$\vec{h}'_i = \|_{k=1}^{K} ELU(\sum_{j \in N_i} \alpha_{ij}^k \mathbf{W}^k \vec{h}_j)$$

where K represents the independent attention heads, and $\|$ denotes the concatenation of the K outputs, or averaging in the case of the final graph attention layer.

The model architecture is composed of four fully-connected encoding layers with 1500, 1204, 908 and 612 nodes respectively (Sect. 2). The encoder is followed by a three graph attention layers of sizes 36, 29 and 22 and with 4,4, and 6 attention heads respectively. Residual connection are added between graph attention layer. Finally the updated embeddings are classified by a decoder with a single fully connected layer of size 22. We use simple binary cross-entropy loss for training the model end to end. See Fig. 1 for a visualization of the model pipeline.

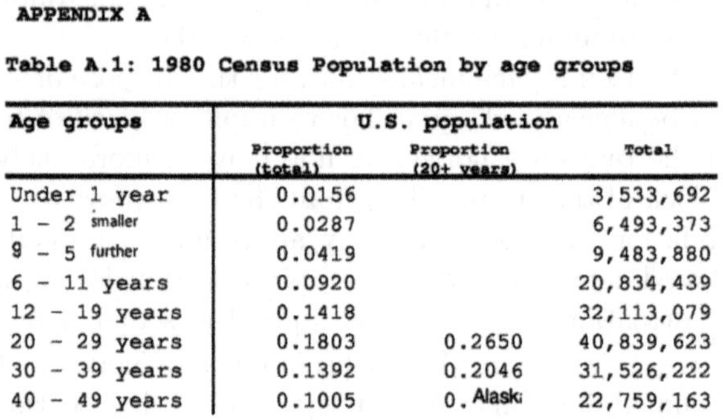

APPENDIX A

Table A.1: 1980 Census Population by age groups

Age groups	U.S. population		
	Proportion (total)	Proportion (20+ years)	Total
Under 1 year	0.0156		3,533,692
1 - 2 smaller	0.0287		6,493,373
9 - 5 further	0.0419		9,483,880
6 - 11 years	0.0920		20,834,439
12 - 19 years	0.1418		32,113,079
20 - 29 years	0.1803	0.2650	40,839,623
30 - 39 years	0.1392	0.2046	31,526,222
40 - 49 years	0.1005	0. Alaska	22,759,163

Fig. 5. An example image from the spliced image dataset with three splices ("smaller", "further" and "Alaska." In order to classify each block of text as spliced or genuine, the model is trained to recognize the subtle variations in font or character width in comparison to its surrounding text.

Auto-Splice Dataset. While many publicly available datasets exists for benchmarking image splice detection, there are few datasets designed for investigating manipulations in images of text-based documents. As a result, we have created and release for public use a dataset of spliced text in images of non-private documents. The original source of the documents is PDF files from the ICDAR 2013 Table Competition [14].[1] The original PDFs contain a wide variety of text types, ranging from paragraphs in articles to numeric tables. This property helps ensure a wide variety of character-level features both within and between documents. Although care was taken to design an automatic splicing process for realistic splices, it is possible that the automation process introduces biases compared with a dataset of hand-spliced text boxes. To account for this, we manually inspected the dataset and found that it contains a range of difficulty levels as judged by human detection ability. Figure 5 displays a "typical" easy/medium difficulty image based on visually inspecting a random subset of samples.

First, PDF-level word boxes are extracted from the PDF document directly. Importantly, the boxes are extracted directly from the PDFs and *not* using OCR, which would otherwise give our model an advantage by being able to

---

[1] The images in this dataset are images from PDFs from academic works. The PDFs include articles from sociology journals, some of which discuss violent content and may be upsetting to certain readers.

bound each potential spliced region with certainty. Each page is then converted to a PNG image to form a set of unmanipulated document images. To calculate the number of splices that will occur in the dataset, we multiply the number of PDF word boxes in the dataset by 0.05, such that in the dataset overall, 5% of the PDF boxes will be spliced. To perform each splice, a source image is chosen at random, from which a source box is drawn. A destination box and destination image are similarly drawn at random, and the source box is scaled and cropped in order to fit the dimensions of the destination box and pasted. This process is repeated until the specified number of splices have been performed, with the constraint that every document retains at least 85% of its original text boxes. Splicing does not occur between instances of the same document, and there is no constraint that enforces boxes to be spliced from a document with different character-level features (font, font size, etc.). From each of the 200 total PDF pages, we create 50 identical images to serve as an initial images. The required number of splicing operations is performed based on the percentage of splices – we created datasets of both 1% and 5% spliced text boxes, as is reported in Table 1. The resulting dataset has 10,000 unique images of size 1700×2200, complete with ground truth splice bounding boxes.

4   Experiments

To train our model, we use Tesseract OCR [30] to extract word-level bounding boxes, as the open-source version of the software yielded low-precision character-level bounding boxes. We experimented with a variety of architectures and ranges for the hyperparameters, including an encoder with up to 16 fully-connected layers, up to 5 graph attention layers, up to 4 fully-connected decoding layers, and the presence or absence of residual connections, and ablation studies for the VAE-based pretraining. We note that our architecture exploration was far from exhaustive and that further experimentation in architecture design could lead to improved performance.

Table 1. The results of our model compared with two other splice detection models on our dataset of digital document splices. The state-of-the-art image manipulation detection models are in effect unable to identify splices in documents, despite being far more computationally expensive than our proposed model. Each model was run on a single NVIDIA GeForce 29C RTX P8 GPU, which is reflected in the mean seconds per image.

	Auto-splice (5% Manip)	Auto-splice (1% Manip.)	Auto-splice
	Test F1		Mean seconds per image
Self Cons.	0.171	0.130	104.40 s
Intrin. Doc.	0.559	0.348	17.64 s
Proposed model	**0.904**	**0.653**	**8.01 s**

Comparison Models. We compare our proposed model with two state-of-the-art splice detection models, Intrin. Feats [3] and Self Consistency [18]. [3] is a model especially designed for detecting manipulations in images of documents. Similar to our proposed model, it starts from OCR bounding boxes obtained through Tesseract OCR. Following OCR extraction, a feature vector for each text bounding box is constructed using the character size, principal inertia axis, horizontal alignment, and Hu moments [15]. One of the main contributions of the method is the use of character-level features that are intrinsic to the document, in comparison with other methods which rely on the presence of extrinsic feature watermarks or a master template. [18] is a deep learning based method designed to search for inconsistencies in the low-level pixel information for the purpose of splice detection. It has achieved state-of-the-art performance on several challenging splice datasets of images of natural scenes, such as *Columbia* [25] and *Realistic Tampering* [21]. We made use of the publicly available code and pre-trained model for evaluation released by the authors to perform the comparison on the spliced document image datasets.

Results. While object detection methods often report a mean Average Precision (mAP) score, this would primarily measure the quality of the OCR engine rather than splice detection model performance. This is because the inputs to our model and [3] are OCR bounding boxes. Instead, to evaluate our proposed model's ability to detect splices in digital documents, we measure both the F1 score with respect to labeling boxes as manipulated or genuine. Because our model takes inputs already partitioned by OCR bounding boxes, it is straightforward to calculate the F1 score given the predicted labels and ground truth labels.

Discussion. We find our model compares favorably to both comparison models, both in Test F1 score and in Mean Seconds per Image. Future work could consider new graph construction methods, including methods which are trainable alongside the rest of the network. One example could include adding edges between blocks of text that are the same throughout the document. Additionally, we anticipate significant improvement could come from employing a more robust OCR method.

References

1. Ahmed, A.G.H., Shafait, F.: Forgery detection based on intrinsic document contents. In: 2014 11th IAPR International Workshop on Document Analysis Systems, pp. 252–256. IEEE (2014)
2. Bayar, B., Stamm, M.C.: A deep learning approach to universal image manipulation detection using a new convolutional layer. In: ACM Workshop on Information Hiding and Multimedia Security, pp. 5–10 (2016)
3. Bertrand, R., Gomez-Kramer, P., Terrades, O.R., Franco, P., Ogier, J.M.: A system based on intrinsic features for fraudulent document detection. In: ICDAR, pp. 106–110. IEEE (2013)

4. Bertrand, R., Terrades, O.R., Gomez-Kramer, P., Franco, P., Ogier, J.M.: A conditional random field model for font forgery detection. In: ICDAR, pp. 576–580. IEEE (2015)

5. van Beusekom, J., Shafait, F., Breuel, T.M.: Automatic authentication of color laser print-outs using machine identification codes. Pattern Anal. Appl. **16**(4), 663–678 (2012). https://doi.org/10.1007/s10044-012-0287-5

6. van Beusekom, J., Shafait, F., Breuel, T.M.: Text-line examination for document forgery detection. IJDAR **16**(2), 189–207 (2013)

7. Bronstein, M.M., Bruna, J., LeCun, Y., Szlam, A., Vandergheynst, P.: Geometric deep learning: going beyond Euclidean data. IEEE Signal Process. Mag. **34**(4), 18–42 (2017)

8. Chernyshova, Y.S., Aliev, M.A., Gushchanskaia, E.S., Sheshkus, A.V.: Optical font recognition in smartphone-captured images and its applicability for ID forgery detection. In: ICMV 2018, vol. 11041, p. 110411J (2019)

9. Cozzolino, D., Verdoliva, L.: Noiseprint: a CNN-based camera model fingerprint. IEEE Trans. Inf. Forensics Secur. **15**, 144–159 (2019)

10. Cruz, F., Sidere, N., Coustaty, M., D'Andecy, V.P., Ogier, J.M.: Local binary patterns for document forgery detection. In: ICDAR, vol. 1, pp. 1223–1228. IEEE (2017)

11. Ghosh, A., Zhong, Z., Boult, T.E., Singh, M.: SpliceRadar: a learned method for blind image forensics. In: CVPR Workshops, pp. 72–79 (2019)

12. Gupta, A., Saxena, N., Vasistha, S.: Detecting copy move forgery using DCT. Int. J. Sci. Res. Publ. **3**(5), 1 (2013)

13. Gupta, S., Kumar, M.: Forensic document examination system using boosting and bagging methodologies. Soft. Comput. **24**(7), 5409–5426 (2019). https://doi.org/10.1007/s00500-019-04297-5

14. Hassan, T.: ICDAR 2013 table competition dataset (2013)

15. Hu, M.K.: Visual pattern recognition by moment invariants. IRE Trans. Inf. Theory **8**(2), 179–187 (1962)

16. Hu, W.C., Chen, W.H.: Effective forgery detection using DCT+ SVD-based watermarking for region of interest in key frames of vision-based surveillance. Int. J. Comput. Sci. Eng. **8**(4), 297–305 (2013)

17. Hu, W.-C., Chen, W.-H., Huang, D.-Y., Yang, C.-Y.: Effective image forgery detection of tampered foreground or background image based on image watermarking and alpha mattes. Multimedia Tools Appl. **75**(6), 3495–3516 (2015). https://doi.org/10.1007/s11042-015-2449-0

18. Huh, M., Liu, A., Owens, A., Efros, A.A.: Fighting fake news: image splice detection via learned self-consistency. In: ECCV, pp. 101–117 (2018)

19. Kingma, D.P., Welling, M.: Auto-encoding variational Bayes. In: 2nd International Conference on Learning Representations, ICLR 2014, Conference Track Proceedings, Banff, AB, Canada, 14–16 April 2014 (2014)

20. Kniaz, V.V., Knyaz, V., Remondino, F.: The point where reality meets fantasy: mixed adversarial generators for image splice detection (2019)

21. Korus, P., Huang, J.: Evaluation of random field models in multi-modal unsupervised tampering localization. In: 2016 IEEE International Workshop on Information Forensics and Security (WIFS), pp. 1–6 (2016)

22. Liu, B., Pun, C.M.: Splicing forgery exposure in digital image by detecting noise discrepancies. Int. J. Comput. Commun. Eng. **4**(1), 33 (2015)

23. Mayer, O., Stamm, M.C.: Exposing fake images with forensic similarity graphs. IEEE J. Sel. Top. Signal Process. **14**(5), 1049–1064 (2020)

24. McInnes, L., Healy, J., Melville, J.: UMAP: uniform manifold approximation and projection for dimension reduction (2018). http://arxiv.org/abs/1802.03426. Comment: Reference implementation available at http://github.com/lmcinnes/umap

25. Ng, T.T., Chang, S.F., Sun, Q.: A data set of authentic and spliced image blocks. ADVENT Technical Report, Columbia University, pp. 203–2004 (2004)

26. Pun, C.M., Liu, B., Yuan, X.C.: Multi-scale noise estimation for image splicing forgery detection. J. Vis. Commun. Image Represent. **38**, 195–206 (2016)

27. Roy, A., Dixit, R., Naskar, R., Chakraborty, R.S.: Copy-move forgery detection with similar but genuine objects. In: Digital Image Forensics. SCI, vol. 755, pp. 65–77. Springer, Singapore (2020). https://doi.org/10.1007/978-981-10-7644-2_5

28. Shang, S., Kong, X., You, X.: Document forgery detection using distortion mutation of geometric parameters in characters. J. Electron. Imaging **24**, 023008 (2015)

29. Shang, S., Memon, N., Kong, X.: Detecting documents forged by printing and copying. EURASIP J. Adv. Signal Process. **2014**(1), 1–13 (2014). https://doi.org/10.1186/1687-6180-2014-140

30. Smith, R.: An overview of the Tesseract OCR engine. In: ICDAR 2007, vol. 2, pp. 629–633. IEEE (2007)

31. van Beusekom, J., Stahl, A., Shafait, F.: Lessons learned from automatic forgery detection in over 100,000 invoices. In: Garain, U., Shafait, F. (eds.) IWCF 2012/2014. LNCS, vol. 8915, pp. 130–142. Springer, Cham (2015). https://doi.org/10.1007/978-3-319-20125-2_12

32. Veličković, P., Cucurull, G., Casanova, A., Romero, A., Lio, P., Bengio, Y.: Graph attention networks. arXiv preprint arXiv:1710.10903 (2017)

33. Wen, L., Qi, H., Lyu, S.: Contrast enhancement estimation for digital image forensics. ACM Trans. Multimedia Comput. Commun. Appl. (TOMM) **14**(2), 1–21 (2018)

34. Wu, Y., AbdAlmageed, W., Natarajan, P.: ManTra-Net: Manipulation tracing network for detection and localization of image forgeries with anomalous features. In: CVPR, pp. 9543–9552 (2019)

Modular StoryGAN with Background and Theme Awareness for Story Visualization

Gábor Szűcs$^{(\boxtimes)}$ ⓘ and Modafar Al-Shouha ⓘ

Budapest University of Technology and Economics, Műegyetem rkp. 3, Budapest 1111, Hungary
{szucs,modafar.alshouha}@tmit.bme.hu

Abstract. Story visualization is a novel topic that intersects computer vision and natural language processing. In this task, given a series of natural language sentences that compose a story, a sequence of images should be generated that correspond to the sentences. Prior works have introduced recurrent generative models which outperform text-to-image models on this task; however, local and global consistency is a challenging attribute of these solutions. For the improvement, we proposed a new modular model architecture named Modular StoryGAN containing the best promising components of prior works. To measure the local and global consistency we introduced background and theme awareness, which are expected attributes of the solutions. Based on the human evaluation, the generated images demonstrate that Modular StoryGAN possesses background and theme awareness. Besides the subjective evaluation, the objective one also shows that our model outperforms the state-of-the-art CP-CSV and DuCo models.

Keywords: Background segmentation · GAN · Image generation · Story visualization · Text-to-image

1 Introduction

Story visualization is a recently proposed task [11, 26], where given a multi-sentence paragraph, the story is visualized by generating a sequence of images, one for each sentence. In this task, there are two subtasks. First, the sequence of images must consistently depict the whole story. This subtask is highly related to text-to-image (T2I) generation [17], but T2I does not consider the sequence of the sentences, thus the context can be missed. There are many methods in the T2I research, e.g. StackGAN [27], MirrorGAN [16], DM-GAN [28]. In the second subtask, the appearance of objects and background should evolve coherently as the story progresses. This is similar to video generation [7, 12, 15, 25] (e.g. text-to-video generation [4], but image-to-video [20] and image-to-image are also related topics [1]), however, the story visualization focuses less on the continuity in images, but more on the global consistency. The contribution of the paper is a proposed modular solution and two attributes related to the consistency: the background and theme awareness. Our paper is organized as follows. Section 2 discusses the related works, Sect. 3 introduces our Modular StoryGAN, Sect. 4, 5, and 6 describe the evaluation, the results, and the conclusion, respectively.

© Springer Nature Switzerland AG 2022
M. El Yacoubi et al. (Eds.): ICPRAI 2022, LNCS 13363, pp. 275–286, 2022.
https://doi.org/10.1007/978-3-031-09037-0_23

2 Related Works

Ian Goodfellow et al. [5] have introduced GAN (Generative Adversarial Networks) as a general-purpose solution to the image generation problem; GANs are used for different computer vision applications, for text-to-image synthesis as well. The StoryGAN method [11] solves the story visualization task by jointly considering the current input sentence with the contextual information. This is achieved by the Text2Gist component in the Context Encoder. StoryGAN uses a recurrent neural network (RNN) to incorporate the previously generated images into the image generation of the current sentence; this recurrent structure and two-level discriminator (story and image-level discriminator to enhance the image quality and the consistency of the generated sequences) help ensure the consistency across the generated images and the story. Contextual information is extracted by the Context Encoder module, including a stack of a GRU cell [3] and Text2Gist cell mentioned above. The Gist is a high-dimensional feature vector for further image generation, where Context Encoder transforms the current sentence and a story encoding vector into this Gist. As the story proceeds, the Gist is dynamically updated to reflect the change of objects and background in the story flow, thus the Context Encoder efficiently provides the image generator with conditional information.

Based on the baseline StoryGAN, the so-called Improved-StoryGAN method [10] was developed to improve the performance of generated sequential images. In this method dilated convolution [23] was used in the discriminators to expand the receptive field of the convolution kernel in the feature maps, thus enhancing the quality of the generated images. Bidirectional GRU (Bi-GRU) [2] stores the historical and future information of each sentence to effectively extract the textual features. There was a modification, gated convolution [24] was used to replace the original MLP (multilayer perceptron) in the Initial State Encoder to improve the consistency between the generated sequential images. There was another modification in the discriminators to provide a robust evaluation in view of the similarity between the generated images and the target story, which resulted in enhancement of the consistency between the images and the story. This was based on the WAD (Weighted Activation Degree) [21] considering that different features have different weighting coefficients according to the different dispersion degrees of the feature representations.

At the story visualization challenge, the Character-Preserving Coherent Story Visualization (CP-CSV) method [19] focuses on three critical modules. The first module is the story and context encoder, where the task is the story and sentence representation learning. The second module aims to solve the figure-ground segmentation, this is an auxiliary task to provide information for preserving the character and story consistency. The third is the figure-ground aware generation module with image sequence generation by incorporating figure-ground segmentation information layer by layer.

The majority of the researches deal with text-to-image synthesis, and some of them explore the usage of the linguistic structure of the input text and visuospatial information [13]. Besides visuospatial and linguistic information, Maharana et al. developed a new method, called DuCo-StoryGAN (briefly DuCo) for story visualization. DuCo method [14] is based on StoryGAN, but it consists of some improvements. The main idea was a dual learning framework that utilizes video captioning to reinforce the semantic alignment between the story and generated images; the generated images are passed to the story and image discriminators, and this dual learning video captioning model. Another improvement was a copy-transform mechanism, which copies features from the images generated in previous timesteps to the image in the current timestep for sequentially consistent story visualization. The copy-transform module performs attention-based semantic alignment by Attentional Generative Adversarial Network (AttnGAN) [22] between word features and image features. The third improvement was MART (Memory-Augmented Recurrent Transformer) [9] based transformers to model complex interactions between frames; the story encoder is used to initialize the memory module in this MART encoder, which encodes the captions for the image generator. While the existing works are focusing on only one side of the consistency, we have taken it into account from many sides, and the idea was a modular architecture.

3 Modular StoryGAN

3.1 Ideas for Background and Theme Awareness

The story visualization task visualizes a textual story S by a sequence of frames (images) $\widehat{X}$ based on a training set consisting of story-frames pairs. The story S consists of a sequence of sentences $S = [s_1, s_2, \ldots, s_T]$, and the generated visualization is a sequence of the corresponding images $\widehat{X} = [\hat{x}_1, \hat{x}_2, \ldots, \hat{x}_T]$, where s_k is the kth sentence in S and S is of length T. For training, ground truth images are denoted as $X = [x_1, x_2, \ldots, x_T]$. The aim of the task, as described in StoryGAN [11], is to generate $\widehat{X}$ which is consistent with S both locally and globally. $\widehat{X}$ is consistent if the generated image $\hat{x}_k$ is able to visualize the content of the sentence s_k (local consistency), while the full story coherence is preserved in $\widehat{X}$ and represents the content of the story S (global consistency).

The tasks of story visualization include visualizing the characters, their movements and interactions, and the background and the surrounding. Despite the overlap between these aspects of the visualization, "background" and "theme" awareness represents the ability of the model to preserve the "local" and "global" consistency in the background and surrounding in each frame and through the whole story.

A model which is aware of the "background" translates the content of each sentence s_k into a frame $\hat{x}_k$, and can switch backgrounds between the frames based on the story description. Therefore, "background awareness" represents the flexibility of the model to reflect the dynamicity of the surrounding through the frames. For instance, the movement between indoor and outdoor scenes or the change from dark to bright environments. On the other hand, in such short stories, i.e. five sentences/frames, the theme throughout the story is not changing usually, and the events happen in a relatively static surrounding. For example, the whole story takes place in a "spooky", "dreamy" or "bright" environment. This is what we consider as "theme awareness".

Being only aware of the "background" results in changing the task into "text2image" instead of the "story visualization" task, where the generated frames are not more than separate images which translate each sentence without considering the full picture of the story. Contrastingly, trying to be aware only of the "theme", or in other words, excluding individual sentence information and translating the full story, i.e. five sentences empties the "story visualization" task from its meaning and pushes it closer to the "video generation" task. Consequently, it is clear that "background" and "theme" awareness are two factors that play contradicting roles to some extent, and balancing between them is a challenge that a "story visualization" model has to tackle.

In real life, "background" and "theme" should reflect the story content, and the choice to prioritize one over the other is influenced by the individual/subjective decision of the creator. In our task, we looked for a possible solution that can balance those two aspects to create a proper visualization of the story.

For the solution, we examined the baseline approach, i.e. StoryGAN [11], and the improvements as possible components for our design architecture. The baseline approach solves the task by utilizing the recurrent neural network (RNN) to consider the previously generated images into the image generation of the current sentence. The sequence s_k is represented by o_k, which is passed to the image generator to generate the corresponding image $\hat{x}_k$. The result $\hat{x}_k$ is evaluated by image and story discriminators to update the network parameters in the next steps. One main improvement [19] focuses on solving the consistency across different frames challenge, by enhancing the learning process by the figure-ground components information, which is extracted from figure-ground segmentation and shared with the image generator. This improvement is a promising component, and another improvement is the dual learning framework [14] for more consistent alignment between S and $\hat{X}$, along with a copy-transform module to assist the functionality of the RNN by adding the attention mechanism and taking advantage of the continuity of the background through the story with respect to the other components, and lastly, the MART (Memory-Augmented Recurrent Transformer) [9] module to process the frames complex interactions. From these components, we proposed a new design architecture.

3.2 Proposed Design Architecture

In general, what makes the task of "story visualization" different from "video generation" is the emphasis on consistency and less on the continuity between the frames, considering the dynamicity of the scenes and characters.

While CP-CSV [19] enhancement aims to improve the consistency in the generated story by utilizing the information of the figure-ground to disentangle the background from the characters in the scene, as a consequence the "local consistency" is improved. DuCo [14] follows a different approach by taking advantage of the continuity of the background in between the frames to improve the "local consistency" and the "global consistency". Our proposed model fuses both improvements in order to exploit the strength of both.

The overall architecture of the proposed model is presented in (Fig. 1). As can be seen, the "Story Encoder" from the baseline produces a low-dimensional embedded vector from the given story, by learning a stochastic mapping from it, and is used to initialize the memory module in "MART". The recurrent nature of "MART" is vital in giving it the possibility of learning the story frames interactions considering the background and presence of the character, which improves the visualized story consistency. The contextualized embeddings which are generated from "MART" are passed as input to the following layer of GRU cells to produce an output vector g_k. Then, it is used to produce the output vector o_k, which carries the local sentence s_k and the global context embeddings on each step and is used in image generation. In addition to o_k, "Copy-Transform" influences the image generation step, it connects every two consecutive time steps, by sharing the most relevant features of the previously generated frame $\hat{x}_{k-1}$ with the current one $\hat{x}_k$, where attention-based semantic is performed between the features from $\hat{x}_{k-1}$ and the current time step word features. In parallel to the image generation step, "Figure-ground generator" uses the information that is based on o_k to generate a synthesized figure-ground segmentation map conditioned on it, by sharing this location information with the "Image generator", the characters in the foreground can be followed and synthesized with better quality. Altogether, the output of the "Copy-Transform", the context-encoder, and "Figure-ground generator" modules are passed to the "Image generator" to generate the current image $\hat{x}_k$. The generated images are evaluated by "Image, Figure-ground and Story Discriminators", while the general purpose is to align the generated output $\hat{x}_k$ with the ground truth x_k, "Image discriminator" performs character classification, and "Story discriminator" calculates the global consistency by performing element-wise product between the concatenated encoded features from the sequence of images and the multi-sentence story. Lastly, the "Dual learning" module is pretrained on the ground truth story captions and the frozen parameters are used later while training the generative model. The pretrained model receives a sequence of generated images $\hat{X}$ to generate the corresponding sequence of captions W_k during the generative model training process. This block also plays a role in measuring the generated visual stories and the captions' global semantic alignment. The network which is used for video captioning is a recurrent encoder-decoder network.

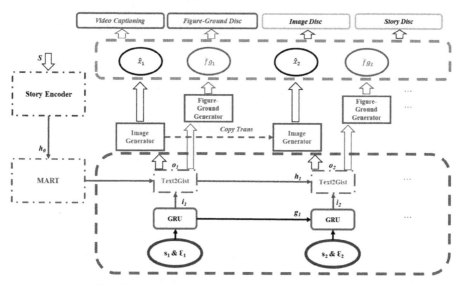

Fig. 1. Proposed model architecture: modular StoryGAN

3.3 The Objective Function for Learning

The objective function of the proposed design consists of the losses of the fused components. The objective function for the generative model is:

$$min_{\theta_G} \, max_{\theta_i \theta_{fg} \theta_s} \, L_{KL} + L_{img} + L_{fg} + L_{story} + L_{dual} \tag{1}$$

The parameters θ_G, θ_i, θ_{fg} and θ_s are for the generator, image, figure-ground, and story discriminators, respectively. We trained the model except for the "Dual learning" component, which was pretrained and frozen.

The first term of the function L_{KL} is for the "Story encoder", this term uses Kullback-Leibler (KL) divergence between the learned distribution from S and the standard Gaussian distribution. S is passed to $\mu(.)$ and $\sigma(.)$ to get the mean and the standard deviation of the distribution respectively, and $\sigma^2(S)$ is restricted as a diagonal matrix by $diag(.)$.

$$L_{KL} = KL\Big(N\Big(\mu(S), diag\big(\sigma^2(S)\big)\Big)||N(0, 1)\Big) \tag{2}$$

The following function is the conditional loss function for the generator consisting of two terms for the conditional loss of the image and the story discriminator, respectively, where $\hat{x}_i$ is the generated image sampled from the distribution $p_{\hat{x}_i}$ during the ith stage of generation:

$$L_G = -\frac{1}{2}E_{\hat{x}_{k,j} \sim p_{\hat{x}_{k,j}}}\big[log\big(D_{img}\big(\hat{x}_{k,j}, s\big)\big)\big]$$
$$-\frac{1}{2}E_{\hat{X}_j \sim p_{\hat{X}_j}}\Big[log\Big(D_{story}\big(\hat{X}_j, S\big)\Big)\Big] \tag{3}$$

The losses for the image, figure-ground and story discriminators are as the following:

$$L_{D_{img}} = -\frac{1}{2}E_{x_{k,j} \sim p_{x_{k,j}}}\big[log\big(D_{img}\big(x_{k,j}, s\big)\big)\big]$$
$$-\frac{1}{2}E_{\hat{x}_{k,j} \sim p_{\hat{x}_{k,j}}}\big[log\big(1 - D_{img}\big(\hat{x}_{k,j}, s\big)\big)\big] \tag{4}$$

$$L_{D_{fg}} = -\frac{1}{2}E_{x_{k,j} \sim p_{x_{i,j}}}\big[log\big(D_{fg}\big(x_{k,j}, s\big)\big)\big]$$
$$-\frac{1}{2}E_{\hat{x}_{k,j} \sim p_{\hat{x}_{k,j}}}\big[log\big(1 - D_{fg}\big(\hat{x}_{k,j}, s\big)\big)\big] \tag{5}$$

$$L_{D_{story}} = -\frac{1}{2}E_{X_j \sim p_{X_j}}\big[log\big(D_{story}\big(X_j, S\big)\big)\big]$$
$$-\frac{1}{2}E_{\hat{X}_j \sim p_{\hat{X}_j}}\Big[log\Big(1 - D_{story}\big(\hat{X}_j, S\big)\Big)\Big] \tag{6}$$

L_{dual} is the loss term for the "Dual learning" component. It is a cross-entropy loss on the predicted vocabulary probability distribution (p) over its vocabulary (w). As mentioned earlier, the model is trained after the freezing the pretrained parameters of the "Dual learning" component:

$$L_{dual} = \sum_{k=1}^{T}\sum_{i=1}^{L} log p_{k,i}\big(w_{k,i}\big) \tag{7}$$

4 Evaluation

4.1 PororoSV Dataset

PororoSV dataset is presented in the paper of the StoryGAN [11] as a modified version from Pororo dataset [8]. While the original dataset is originally used for video question answering, Pororo-SV is introduced to fit story visualization task. It contains the total of 15,336 description-story pairs (13,000 train and 2,336 test) and every five consecutive frames are considered as one story. In addition to this, and since a segmentation functionality is introduced to aid the image generation process, we used the segmented version of PororoSV dataset [14] as well.

There are nine main characters in the PororoSV dataset [11], however, the characters' appearance frequency is imbalanced (Fig. 2). This causes the model to learn their individual features with different degrees; for instance, "Pororo" character features can be identified more often compared to less frequent characters like "Harry". The other main attribute of PororoSV is the theme, where in addition to the default two themes, i.e. "outdoor snowy" and "indoor", there are other themes, which are also not presented equally (Fig. 2).

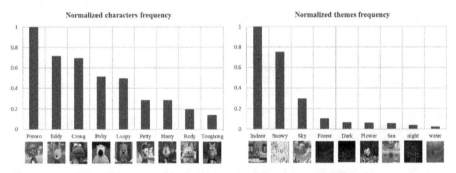

Fig. 2. Normalized characters and themes frequencies on the right and the left, respectively.

4.2 Quantitative Evaluation Metrics

Evaluating story visualization is a challenging task. The first question is how to measure the quality/goodness of the generated images sequence objectively. While there is no clear answer for this question, we try to use a combination of qualitative and quantitative metrics which could indicate the design performance on one hand and allow us to compare the results with other works. In the evaluation, we focus on comparing the relative improvement achieved by our design concerning CP-CSV [19] and DuCo [14], because our proposed design is a continuation of their improvements, and their results outperform the baseline results StoryGAN [11].

In order to identify the characters in the generated images, we follow DuCo [14] and use the pre-trained and fine-tuned Inception-v3 which is provided by DuCo [14] in their repo. We report the weighted-average F_1 score for character classification because of its ability to detect the model quality in including the desired characters in the generated image, i.e. more characters are visualized is better.

Another aspect of the evaluation is to report the bleu score [18] between the captions of the generated story and the ground truth captions as an indication of the global semantic alignment between them. The frames captioning is done using the pretrained MART module (which is explained above).

The third evaluation metric is the FID score (Fréchet Inception Distance) [6], which is commonly used to measure the image quality concerning a ground truth image. Although it does not cover the story visualization task evaluation solely, it is useful in expressing the descriptive nature of the generated image. It does so by comparing the similarity of the feature vectors between the generated and the corresponding ground truth images. In addition to the quantitative metrics, i.e. classification accuracy, bleu score, and FID score, we introduce two human-based metrics, i.e. background and theme awareness.

4.3   User Assessment: Background and Theme Awareness

The improvement achieved by our model appears clearly in maintaining consistency through the whole story and being aware of the background and the theme aspects. In the following part, we show some evidence by studying and analyzing several cases from both sides, i.e. background and theme awareness.

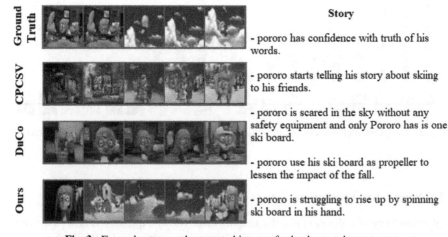

Fig. 3. Example story and generated images for background awareness

The results show that our proposed model is more aware of the background than the other two models, i.e. CP-CSV [19] and DuCo [14]. In generated images by CP-CSV, the transition appears to be noisy in-between frames. Checking the story in Fig. 3, it can be seen that there is a change in the scenes after the first frame. CP-CSV generates scenes that align partially with the story and the ground truth, but in the second frame, due to the sudden transition, there is a confusing scene without clear characters and objects. On the other hand, DuCo [14] sticks with the background from the first frame without being able to detect the dynamic change inside the story. Our model performs better than both, it clearly detects the change in the second frame as CP-CSV [19] with less confusion. In overall, our model generates a story that aligns with the ground truth and offers better and clearer visualization.

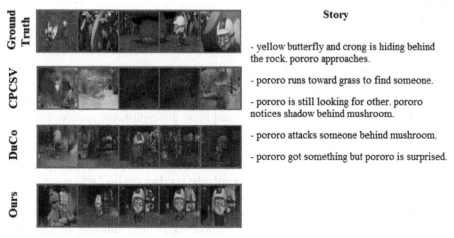

Story

- yellow butterfly and crong is hiding behind the rock. pororo approaches.

- pororo runs toward grass to find someone.

- pororo is still looking for other. pororo notices shadow behind mushroom.

- pororo attacks someone behind mushroom.

- pororo got something but pororo is surprised.

Fig. 4. Example story and generated images for theme awareness

Figure 4 is a good example to show our model's ability over CP-CSV [19] and DuCo [14] in detecting and preserving the theme through the whole story. Our model understands that the scene is an outdoor "forest" scene, without being confused or disturbed by the appearance of signs such as "run" in the second sentence, which is usually connected with outdoor scenes where the theme is snowy mostly in "PororoSV" dataset [11], or by "shadow" in the third sentence which has a "dark" theme by itself. CP-CSV [19] and DuCo [14] generated results show a lack of "theme awareness" due to these mixed signals present in the text. This also affects the visualization and the quality of the scenes drastically.

It seems that our model has more "theme awareness" than the others. It provides better visualization for the whole story in such cases, while DuCo [14] lacks the ability to detect the theme, and CP-CSV [19] appears to be confused and its results are noisy.

5   Results

The previous examples were only small samples, but the background and theme awareness quality in the test set were investigated by humans. Additionally, the ability to visualize the character-distinctive features, i.e. visualization quality, is investigated. Comparison of the methods based on human evaluations can be seen in Table 1, where the values present the average (mean) number of appropriate images in the stories, e.g. the second row contains the number of images that meet background awareness expectations (the 5 is the possible best value in the Table).

Table 1. Qualitative comparison of the methods based on human evaluations

Indicator	CPCSV	DuCo	Ours
Background awareness	1.6	2.5	**3.7**
Theme awareness	2.8	3.1	**4.2**
Visualization quality	1.2	2.1	**2.9**

Considering the goodness of the generated characters (weighted F_1 score in Table 2), our model achieved higher results with 22.5% and 11% improvement concerning CP-CSV [19] and DuCo [14], respectively. This suggests a better visual representation of the characters in the generated frames and more distinguishable features for them concerning the other two models.

Regarding the Bleu score, our model results exceed CP-CSV [19] results, but the best is the DuCo [14]. The Bleu score measures the word similarities between the textual story and the captions, so this indicates not only the goodness of the "goal process", i.e. the image generation, but the goodness of additional process as well, i.e. the captioning.

At the FID score (Table 2) the smaller the better, our model achieves 17% and 5% better results than CP-CSV and DuCo, respectively, when evaluating the generated images with the ground truth images. Although the FID score by itself might not carry much information, it shows that the generated stories by our model are more similar to the ground truth, and the model can learn the dataset features better than the other two.

Table 2. Quantitative comparison of our model with CP-CSV [19] and DuCo [14]

Metric	CPCSV	DuCo	Ours
Weighted F_1 score	0.173	0.191	**0.212**
BLEU1/BLEU2 score	0.127 / 0.037	**0.137/0.042**	0.131/0.040
FID score	119.4	104.7	**99.0**

6   Conclusion

For story visualization, we proposed a new modular model architecture named Modular StoryGAN containing the best promising components of prior works. The objective function of the proposed design consists of the losses of all components. We introduced background and theme awareness, which are expected attributes of the solutions. Our model was compared with the state-of-the-art CP-CSV and DuCo models based on human evaluation, and it can be concluded that the StoryGAN possesses the best background and theme awareness and the best visualization quality. Besides the subjective evaluation, the objective one also shows that our model outperforms the state-of-the-art methods. The model originality is limited by the PororoSV dataset [11]. Thus, it is unable to identify or visualize any characters and themes which do not appear in it. This limitation is not necessarily undesirable for some applications, but it makes it hard to generalize its performance on the story visualization task.

Acknowledgment. The work was supported by the Ministry of Innovation and Technology through the MEC_R_21 program of the National Research, Development and Innovation Office.

References

1. Babu, K.K., Dubey, S.R.: CDGAN: cyclic discriminative generative adversarial networks for image-to-image transformation. J. Vis. Commun. Image Represent. **82**(2022), 103382 (2021)
2. Bahdanau, D., Cho, K.H., Bengio, Y.: Neural machine translation by jointly learning to align and translate. In: 3rd International Conference on Learning Representations, ICLR 2015 (2015)
3. Chung, J., Gulcehre, C., Cho, K., Bengio, Y.: Empirical evaluation of gated recurrent neural networks on sequence modeling. In: NIPS 2014 Workshop on Deep Learning, December 2014
4. Deng, K., Fei, T., Huang, X., Peng, Y.: IRC-GAN: introspective recurrent convolutional GAN for text-to-video generation. In: IJCAI Proceedings of the 28th International Joint Conference on Artificial Intelligence (IJCAI), pp. 2216–2222 (2019). https://doi.org/10.24963/ijcai.201 9/307
5. Goodfellow, I., et al.: Generative adversarial nets. In: Advances in Neural Information Processing Systems, vol. 27 (2014)
6. Heusel, M., Ramsauer, H., Unterthiner, T., Nessler, B., Hochreiter, S.: GANs trained by a two time-scale update rule converge to a local Nash equilibrium. In: Advances in Neural Information Processing Systems, pp. 6626–6637 (2017)
7. Hu, Y., Luo, C., Chen, Z.: Make it move: controllable image-to-video generation with text descriptions. arXiv preprint arXiv:2112.02815 (2021)
8. Kim, K.M., Heo, M.O., Choi, S.H., Zhang, B.T.: DeepStory: video story qa by deep embedded memory networks. In: Proceedings of the 26th International Joint Conference on Artificial Intelligence, pp. 2016–2022 (2017)
9. Lei, J., Wang, L., Shen, Y., Yu, D., Berg, T., Bansal, M.: MART: memory-augmented recurrent transformer for coherent video paragraph captioning. In: the 58th Annual Meeting of the Association for Computational Linguistics, pp. 2603–2614 (2020)
10. Li, C., Kong, L., Zhou, Z.: Improved-StoryGAN for sequential images visualization. J. Vis. Commun. Image Represent. **73**, 102956 (2020)
11. Li, Y., et al.: StoryGAN: a sequential conditional GAN for story visualization. In: Proceedings of the IEEE/CVF Conference on Computer Vision and Pattern Recognition, pp. 6329–6338 (2019)
12. Li, Y., Min, M.R., Shen, D., Carlson, D., Carin, L.: Video generation from text. In: 32nd AAAI Conference on Artificial Intelligence, pp. 7065–7072. AAAI Press (2018)
13. Maharana, A., Bansal, M.: Integrating visuospatial, linguistic, and commonsense structure into story visualization. In: Proceedings of the 2021 Conference on Empirical Methods in Natural Language Processing, pp. 6772–6786 (2021)
14. Maharana, A., Hannan, D., Bansal, M.: Improving generation and evaluation of visual stories via semantic consistency. In: Proceedings of the 2021 Conference of the North American Chapter of the Association for Computational Linguistics: Human Language Technologies, pp. 2427–2442 (2021)

15. Marwah, T., Mittal, G., Balasubramanian, V.N.: Attentive semantic video generation using captions. In: IEEE International Conference on Computer Vision, pp. 1426–1434 (2017)

16. Qiao, T., Zhang, J., Xu, D., Tao, D.: MirrorGAN: learning text-to-image generation by redescription. In: Proceedings of the IEEE/CVF Conference on Computer Vision and Pattern Recognition, pp. 1505–1514 (2019)

17. Reed, S., Akata, Z., Yan, X., Logeswaran, L., Schiele, B., Lee, H.: Generative adversarial text to image synthesis. In: International Conference on Machine Learning, pp. 1060–1069. PMLR (2016)

18. Sharma, S., Asri, L.E., Schulz, H., Zumer, J.: Relevance of unsupervised metrics in task-oriented dialogue for evaluating natural language generation. arXiv preprint arXiv:1706. 09799 (2017)

19. Song, Y.-Z., Rui Tam, Z., Chen, H.-J., Lu, H.-H., Shuai, H.-H.: Character-preserving coherent story visualization. In: Vedaldi, A., Bischof, H., Brox, T., Frahm, J.-M. (eds.) ECCV 2020. LNCS, vol. 12362, pp. 18–33. Springer, Cham (2020). https://doi.org/10.1007/978-3-030-58520-4_2

20. Tulyakov, S., Liu, M.Y., Yang, X., Kautz, J.: MocoGAN: decomposing motion and content for video generation. In: Proceedings of the IEEE Conference on Computer Vision and Pattern Recognition, pp. 1526–1535 (2018)

21. Wen, Z., Xie, L., Feng, H., Tan, Y.: Robust fusion algorithm based on RBF neural network with TS fuzzy model and its application to infrared flame detection problem. Appl. Soft Comput. **76**, 251–264 (2019)

22. Xu, T., et al.: AttnGAN: fine-grained text to image generation with attentional generative adversarial networks. In: Proceedings of the IEEE Conference on Computer Vision and Pattern Recognition, pp. 1316–1324 (2018)

23. Yu, F., Koltun, V.: Multi-scale context aggregation by dilated convolutions. arXiv preprint arXiv:1511.07122 (2015)

24. Yu, J., Lin, Z., Yang, J., Shen, X., Lu, X., Huang, T.S.: Free-form image inpainting with gated convolution. In: Proceedings of the IEEE/CVF International Conference on Computer Vision, pp. 4471–4480 (2019)

25. Yu, Y., Tu, Z., Lu, L., Chen, X., Zhan, H., Sun, Z.: Text2Video: automatic video generation based on text scripts. In: Proceedings of the 29th ACM International Conference on Multimedia, pp. 2753–2755 (2021)

26. Zeng, G., Li, Z., Zhang, Y.: PororoGAN: an improved story visualization model on Pororo-SV dataset. In: Proceedings of the 2019 3rd International Conference on Computer Science and Artificial Intelligence, pp. 155–159 (2019)

27. Zhang, H., et al.: StackGAN: text to photo-realistic image synthesis with stacked generative adversarial networks. In: IEEE International Conference on Computer Vision (ICCV), vol. 1, pp. 5908–5916 (2017). https://doi.org/10.1109/ICCV.2017.629

28. Zhu, M., Pan, P., Chen, W., Yang, Y.: DM-GAN: dynamic memory generative adversarial networks for text-to-image synthesis. In: Proceedings of the IEEE/CVF Conference on Computer Vision and Pattern Recognition, pp. 5802–5810 (2019)

Is On-Line Handwriting Gender-Sensitive? What Tells us a Combination of Statistical and Machine Learning Approaches

Laurence Likforman-Sulem[1]([⊠]), Gennaro Cordasco[2,3], and Anna Esposito[2,3]

[1] Telecom Paris/Institut Polytechnique de Paris, Palaiseau, France
likforman@telecom-paris.fr
[2] Department of Psychology, Università degli Studi della Campania "L. Vanvitelli", Caserta, Italy
[3] International Institute for Advanced Scientific Studies (IIASS), Vietri sul Mare, Italy

Abstract. Handwriting is an everyday life human activity. It can be collected off-line by scanning sheets of paper. The resulting images can then be processed by a computer-based system. Thanks to digitizing tablets, handwriting can also be collected on-line. From the collected raw signals (pen position, pressure over time), the dynamics of the writing can be recovered. Since handwriting is unique for each individual, it can be considered as a biometric modality. Biometric systems predicting gender from off-line handwriting, have thus been recently proposed. However we observe that, in contrast to other modalities such as speech, it is not straightforward for a human being (even expert) to predict gender. In this study we explore the limits of automatic gender prediction from on-line handwriting collected from a young adults population, homogeneous in terms of age and education. Statistical analysis of on-line dynamic features can highlight differences between male and female groups [6]. In the present study, we focus on a sentence copying task, and provide statistically significant features to a classifier, based on a machine learning approach (SVMs). Since the dataset is relatively small (240 subjects), several evaluation frameworks are explored: cross validation (CV), bootstrap, and fixed train/test partitions. Accuracies obtained from fixed partitions range from 37% to 79%, while those estimated by CV and bootstrap are around 65%. This shows to our opinion the limits of the gender recognition task for our young adult population dataset.

Keywords: Gender recognition · Handwriting · Statistical analysis

1 Introduction

Handwriting is an everyday life human activity used from centuries for registering counts, communicating ideas, writing/copying books, sending letters or encrypted messages [10]. Many skills are involved in handwriting: gross and fine

© Springer Nature Switzerland AG 2022
M. El Yacoubi et al. (Eds.): ICPRAI 2022, LNCS 13363, pp. 287–298, 2022.
https://doi.org/10.1007/978-3-031-09037-0_24

motor skills, ability to plan, eye-hand coordination [18]. Character models, learnt at school and related to an era and a geographical location, are also influencing the writer. Personal motor characteristics combined with the character models the writer has in mind, result in an unique handwriting [14].

In order to be processed by a computer-based system, handwriting must first be digitized, off-line or on-line. Off-line handwriting is collected by scanning sheets of paper. This results into images that can be processed automatically for tasks such as recognition or authentication. On-line handwriting is collected thanks to digitizing tablets. Applications range from creating/correcting documents, authenticating signatures, education (learning to write) [13] but also to detect health issues: neurological disorders, or upcoming strikes [11,17].

Systems that use off-line handwriting for predicting gender, have been recently proposed [3,4,8]. These can be useful for various domains and tasks such as author profiling [16], forensics, and biometry. However we observe that, in contrast to other modalities such as speech, it is not straightforward for a human being (even expert) to predict gender from off-line handwriting [2,5].

In our collective culture, women are assumed to write more legibly, with embellishments, using round shapes. Men are assumed to put more pressure and to use spiky shapes [9]. More often samples displayed as "male" and "female" are not so convincing (see for instance [3,15] and our own samples in Fig. 3). Indeed explanations on gender differences in handwriting, change and are related to the ideas promoted in an era, about the social condition of women. In our era, in countries such as Italy, girls and boys are taught to write together. One can hardly find an argument that would justify a difference due to gender.

However, at school, girls are known to be more proficient in writing, than boys [12]. Writing speed, less time spent in air, are signs of writing proficiency. Features related to speed may thus be proposed for gender prediction. Indeed a statistical analysis of features extracted from handwriting can highlight differences between male and female groups [6]. The feature means are found distinct for each group, but feature distributions may overlap so that one can hardly predict gender, from a machine learning point of view. To cope with overlapping distributions, we use a combination of several features selected by a statistical analysis and feed them as input to an SVM classifier.

In the literature, gender recognition systems provide accuracies ranging from 60% to 80% for fixed train/test partitions. A common train/test partition consists in taking 70% of the samples for training, the remaining ones for testing. For small sets, using fixed train/test partitions may over or under-estimate performance. More robust frameworks exist to evaluate performance, such as cross validation and bootstrap.

In the following, data collection and extracted features are described in Sects. 2.1 and 2.2. Statistical analyses such as ANOVA [6] and Logistic Regression have been conducted in order to select the most discriminant features with respect to female and male groups (Sect. 2.3). In Sect. 3, gender recognition experiments are conducted with the SVM classifier and selected features. We compare the accuracies obtained according to the evaluation framework (cross validation, bootstrapping, fixed train/test partition). We conclude this study in

Sect. 4 on the possibility of distinguishing gender for the observed population, from handwriting dynamics.

2 Data Collection and Extracted Features

2.1 Data Collection

Handwriting samples are collected by a digitizing INTUOS WACOM series 4 tablet associated with a dedicated writing pen named Intuos Inkpen. Participants write on a sheet of paper (normal paper) laid on the tablet. The tablet records each 8 ms (125 Hz) the following values; (x, y) positions of the pen, pen inclinations (azimuth, altitude), pressure of the pen on paper, time in milliseconds since the UNIX epoch (January 1, 1970 00:00:00 UTC), and the pen status (on paper = 1 or in-air = 0). It also records these values when the pen is in-air, close to the tablet. The tablet thus collects seven raw signals, one for each type of values. Figure 1 shows recorded signals. The null values in the pressure signal correspond to in air movements.

The dataset includes the handwriting samples of 240 subjects. The two groups (male, female) are balanced by age, and level of education: 126 males (mean age 24.65 years old, SD = 2.45) and 114 females (mean age = 24.51 years old, SD = 2.50), SD being the Standard Deviation. The subjects were volunteers recruited at University of Campania "Luigi Vanvitelli" in Caserta (south Italy). All subjects are right-handed and were asked to perform seven handwriting tasks: (1) drawing of two-pentagons (2) drawing of a house (3) writing of the following four Italian words in capital letters (BIODEGRADABILE, FLIPSTRIM, SMINUZZAVANO, CHIUNQUE); (4) drawing loops with left hand (5) drawing loops with right hand; (6) drawing a clock (7) writing the following Italian sentence in cursive letters (*I pazzi chiedono fiori viola, acqua da bere, tempo per sognare* meaning Crazy people are seeeking for purple flowers, drinking water and dreaming time).

Figure 2 shows the pen position (x, y) on paper (black points) and in air (red points). The positions of the pen when the tablet is too far are not recorded. But the time spent far from the tablet can be recovered through the time-stamp raw signal. Henceforth, we will name this pen status as idle.

Figure 3 shows four samples of the copy task (task 7). It can be noted that guessing gender is not straightforward[1,2].

2.2 Extracted Features

From the raw signals collected by the tablet, features can be extracted in order to represent the samples in a concise way, adapted to a machine learning approach. For each task, 17 features were computed at global level, grouped in 5 categories. These are [6]:

---

[1] Gender ground truth: the first and third samples are from women, the other ones from men.

[2] (From top to bottom).

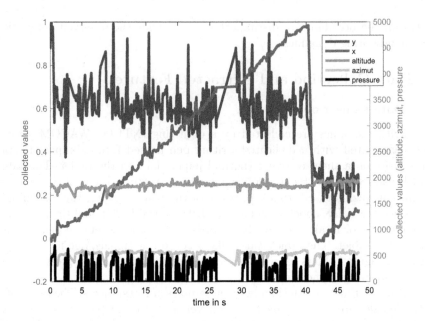

Fig. 1. Raw signals captured by the Wacom digitizing tablet when copying the task7 sentence (Fig. 2). The x and y curves have been rescaled to better fit the figure.

- time: the total time elapsed for the task, the total time spent in each pen status: in air, on paper, and idle[3] (Total#, tUp#, tDown#, tIdle#)
- pressure: statistics about pressure, minimum (Pmin#), maximum (Pmax#), mean (Pavg#), standard deviation (Psd#), lower 10th (P_{10}#) and 90th (P_{90}#) percentiles),
- ductus: the number of strokes in each pen status, number of in-air strokes, number of on-paper strokes, number of idle strokes (nbUp#, nbDown#, nbIdle#).
- slope: the average inclination of the straight lines passing through the diagonals of the axis-aligned bounding boxes containing the strokes (slopeA#).
- space: based on the area occupied by axis-aligned bounding boxes containing the strokes (spaceA) and the distance between consecutive strokes (spaceT#). Only on-paper traits are considered.

Considering the seven tasks, 119 features have been extracted. In the following, we focus on the seventh task which consists in copying a sentence. This is the only task that is done in cursive writing.

2.3   Feature Selection

Starting with 17 features extracted from task7, a small number were found significant according to gender, by two statistical approaches. The first one was

---

[3] # denotes the task number.

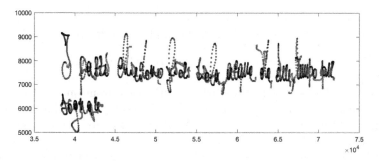

Fig. 2. Sample ink trace from the sentence copy task (task7). The red points correspond to in air movements close to the tablet area. (Color figure online)

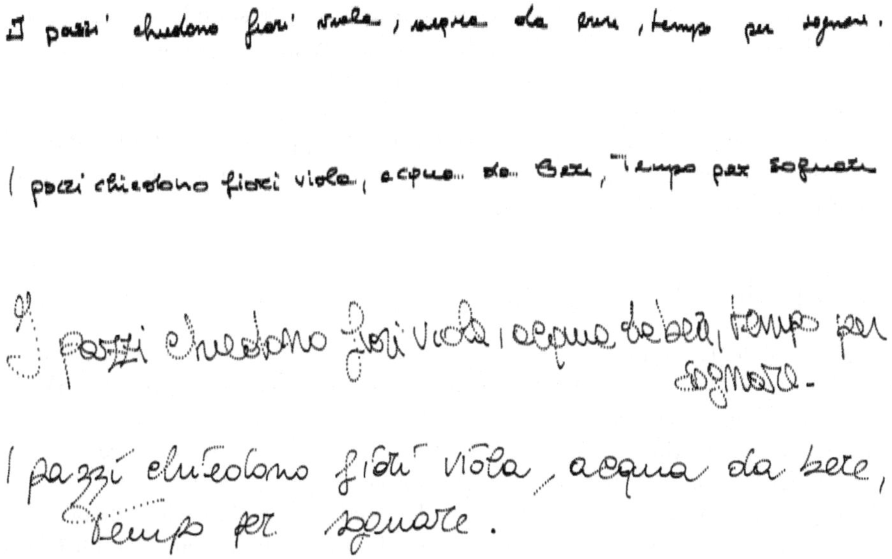

Fig. 3. Four task7 samples from subjects 16, 1, 20 and 141. Guessing gender is not straightforward.

ANOVA, the second one Logistic Regression [1]. For selected features, a difference in the means of each group (men/women), could be observed with a significant level measured by a p-value smaller than 0.05. Considering task7, 6 features were selected by ANOVA analysis: nbDown7, nbUp7, nbIdle7, Total7, tUp7, tDown7. The ANOVA analysis was performed on the whole set of subjects (240 samples). Similarly a logical regression analysis was conducted with all samples. Four features were selected: nbDown7, nbUp7, nbIdle7, Pmax7. It can be noted that this second set has a large overlap with the ANOVA set, and that a pressure-based feature (maximum pressure during the task) has been added. In the following we will consider several sets of features:

- the whole set of 17 features (no selection)
- the union of features selected by ANOVA+Logistic Regression (7 features)

The features presented above are selected on the whole set of 240 samples. In our experiments (Sect. 3) we will also consider selecting the features on the training samples only. The set of features will slightly vary from one fold to another (cross validation), or from one train partition to another. According to the folds, 3 to 7 features among the whole set of 17 extracted features, may be selected by Logistic Regression.

In Fig. 4, are shown the boxplots of the total time spent to complete task 7 (Total7), and the number of on paper strokes (nbDown7). Total7 is the whole time spent (on-paper, in-air or idle) when completing the seventh task. According to the means: men would write the given sentence more slowly in average (37s) than women (28s). For both features, the boxplots corresponding to men and women largely overlap so that a classifier can hardly predict gender from one of these features alone. However, one can generally expect prediction improvements by combining several features (see Fig. 5).

In the following, we will use a machine learning approach, and build an SVM classifier from features that are considered significant according to gender, by statistical analyses.

3   Experiments

A subset of features presented above, have been selected to build classifiers based on the SVM (Support Vector Machines) machine learning approach. SVMs are popular since they are suitable for datasets limited in size. The selected features are those which are found statistically different according to gender by an ANOVA [6] and a logistic regression approach.

To evaluate SVM classifiers for the gender prediction task, we use the popular accuracy metric. Accuracy is the proportion of correct predictions, computed on a test set. We propose several frameworks to compute accuracy, which differ in the way of choosing training and test data. These are:

- fixed train/test partitions. The training and test sets do not vary. A common partition is 70% training/30% test.
- Cross validation (CV): train/test set are cycling according to K folds (K-1 folds for training, the Kth for test). The mean of the K accuracies is provided.
- Bootstrap: random train/test partitions (f.i. 70% training/ 30% test) are repeated N times (f.i. N = 100). Accuracy of each repetition is collected, and the mean is provided.

Each instance of bootstrap, as well as each cycle of CV correspond to a fixed train/test partition. Thus, results corresponding to the fixed train/test partition framework, may be grasped through max and min values of Tables 1 and 2 (4th column).

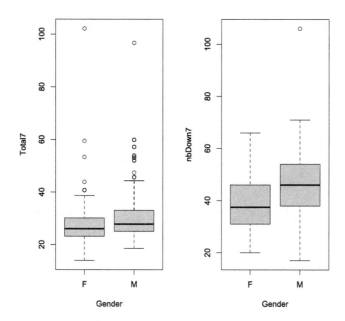

Fig. 4. Boxplots of Total7 and nbDown7 features, according to gender. a) Total7 feature is equal to the total time in seconds spent for completing the copy of the cursive sentence (task7). b) nbDown7 feature is equal to the number of strokes performed when writing the same sentence. Whiskers denote quartiles.

The accuracies provided by these frameworks may largely differ, especially when dealing with small-size datasets (several hundred of subjects). Publicly available datasets often provide fixed train and test partitions. This is practical in order to compare approaches. However the actual accuracy may not correspond to this particular partition, especially for small datasets. Second, the test partition is often released, in contrast to keep it apart by the dataset designers who evaluate themselves the test accuracy. As a consequence, hyper-parameters may be tuned including test data, as well as feature selection. Accuracy may thus be over-estimated.

Figure 6 shows the interest of using cross validation, in contrast to fixed partitions. The mean CV accuracy is equal to 63.3% while the accuracy of one fold partition is much lower, equal to 37.5%, and that of another partition is much higher, and equal to 79.1%. Indeed the actual accuracy is around 60% which differs from a 79% accuracy provided by one particular partition.

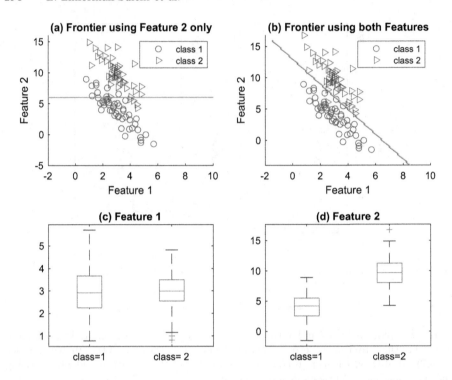

Fig. 5. (c) Feature 1 alone is inefficient for making class predictions in this two-class problem since whisker boxes largely overlap). (a) Feature 2 alone is more efficient but the resulting classifier is weak (many misclassifications). (b) An efficient classifier can be obtained by combining both features 1 and 2 (few misclassifications). Inspired from [7].

The accuracies shown in CV (with $K = 10$) and Bootstrap (100 repetitions with 168 training samples and 72 test samples) results (see Tables 1 and 2) are rather low: 64.8% for bootstrap, 66.2% for cross-validation. However these accuracies may be still over-estimated since the selection of features was conducted with all samples (240 subjects), thus including the samples of the testing folds. A fairer approach consists in clearly separating training data from test data. Thus an alternate feature selection approach for the CV framework consists in:

1. start with all samples divided in K folds and the set of extracted features
2. select the more efficient features from the K-1 training folds by a statistical approach
3. from the selected features, and the samples of the K-1 folds, build a gender prediction model
4. use the model to predict gender for the samples of the Kth fold.

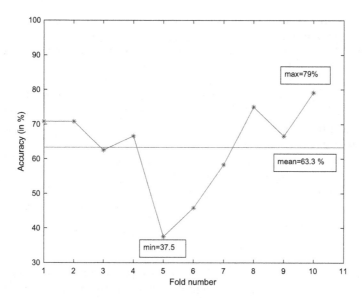

Fig. 6. Cross validation accuracies are varying according to the folds. The so-called CV accuracy is the mean accuracy equal to 63.3%. The train/test partition corresponding to test the 10th fold and train on the remaining ones, reaches a maximum accuracy equal to 79%.

This approach can directly be extended to the bootstrapping framework, by selecting features, at each repetition, on the current training partition.

The set of features selected may vary from one training set to another. In the experiment conducted with the CV approach, the features selected by logistic regression in all training folds were: nbDown7, nbUp7, nbIdle7. For a few folds, feature max7 was also considered as a significant feature. Similarly in Table 2 several features may be added according to the train partition (max7, min7, slopeA7, spaceA7). We observe with CV (see Table 1) that selecting features from all samples (240) performs better than selecting features from the training set only: 66.2% accuracy versus 63.3%. Thus using test data for feature selection may provide an over-estimation of the classifier accuracy.

Results show that mean accuracies obtained by cross validation or boot-strapping, are rather low. Selecting features, even found as important by statistical analysis, does not bring much improvement. An estimated accuracy of 66% (Bootstrap with feature selection) is slightly greater than an estimated accuracy of 64.8% (no selection of features). However these accuracies can be considered as equivalent since standard deviations are large.

Our results are consistent with those obtained in the literature for predicting gender from on-line handwriting [8] where accuracies range from 60% to 80%. Our results show that an accuracy of 76% or even 79% can be obtained for a number of train/test partitions (see Max column in Tables 1 and 2). However a reliable estimation of the accuracy is around 65%, using CV or bootstrap. To our

Table 1. Accuracies (in %) obtained by Cross Validation (K = 10 folds). Standard deviations, min and max fold accuracies are provided. Feature selection is performed from whole set (240 samples) or from the training folds (216 samples), by Anova and Logistic Regression (LR).

Approach	Features	Accuracy (in %)	Min/Max
CV & feat select. ANOVA+LR on whole set	max7, tUp7, tDown7, Total7 nbDown7, nbUp7, nbIdle7	66.2 [11.6]	45.8/79.2
CV & feat select. LR on training folds	[max7] nbDown7, nbUp7, nbIdle7	63.3 [12.9]	37.5/79.1
CV no feature selection	17 features	66.2 [8.9]	54.1/79.1

Table 2. Accuracies (in %) obtained by Bootstrapping (100 repetitions) with 168 training samples/72 test samples resampled at each repetition). Standard deviations, min and max accuracies are provided. Feature selection is performed on all samples or on the training set built at each repetition, by Anova and Logistic Regression (LR).

Approach	Features	Accuracy (in %)	Min-Max
Bootstrap & feat select. ANOVA+LR on whole set	Total7, tDown7, tUp7, max7 nbDown7, nbUp7, nbIdle7	64.8 [4.5]	52.7/76.4
Bootstrap & feat select. LR on 168 training samples	[max7, spaceA7, min7, slopeA7] nbDown7, nbUp7, nbIdle7	66 [4.3]	55.6/76.4
Bootstrap & no selection	17 features	64.2 [4.7]	54.1/76.4

opinion, these low accuracies show that gender has a weak influence on on-line handwriting for the observed population (an accuracy of 50% would be obtained just with random guess).

4　Conclusion

Handwriting results from the combination of motor programs and social and environmental conditions. In this study, global features linked to hand movements and writing speed were extracted. First, features were selected according to statistical analysis (Anova and Logistic Regression). These features were found distinct according to gender, but they could not be used in isolation because of large overlaps in the feature female/male distributions. Thus, selected features were combined through a machine learning based classifier (SVM).

Low accuracies (around 65%) were obtained, estimated by cross validation and bootstrapping, while higher ones were obtained with fixed train/test partitions (79%). Such differences are observed due to the small dataset-size (several hundreds of subjects). However, to our opinion, the actual low accuracies (around 65%) corroborate the fact that the dynamics of handwriting may not be gender-based among the european young adult population in our dataset.

The handwriting tasks performed by young adults are impersonal, and as mentioned before, there is no reason to find in the samples a difference due to gender. This could be different in another cultural context. In such case, experts should be able to illustrate and justify gender differences, if any.

Future work may consist in testing dynamic features such as jerk and acceleration, and design features linked to writing fluidity. Future work may also consist in exploiting the remaining tasks, individually or in combination.

References

1. Kabacoff, R.I.: Generalized linear models. https://www.statmethods.net/advstats/glm.html
2. Akbari, Y., Nouri, K., Sadri, J., Djeddi, C., Siddiqi, I.: Wavelet-based gender detection on off-line handwritten documents using probabilistic finite state automata. Image Vis. Comput. **59**, 17–30 (2017)
3. AL-Qawasmeh, N., Suen, C.Y.: Gender detection from handwritten documents using concept of transfer-learning. In: Lu, Y., Vincent, N., Yuen, P.C., Zheng, W.-S., Cheriet, F., Suen, C.Y. (eds.) ICPRAI 2020. LNCS, vol. 12068, pp. 3–13. Springer, Cham (2020). https://doi.org/10.1007/978-3-030-59830-3_1
4. Alaei, F., Alaei, A.: Gender detection based on spatial pyramid matching. In: Lladós, J., Lopresti, D., Uchida, S. (eds.) ICDAR 2021. LNCS, vol. 12824, pp. 305–317. Springer, Cham (2021). https://doi.org/10.1007/978-3-030-86337-1_21
5. Berrichon-Seyden, M.J.: Personal communication, July 2021
6. Cordasco, G., Buonanno, M., Faundez-Zanuy, M., Riviello, M., Likforman-Sulem, L., Esposito, A.: Gender identification through handwriting: an online approach. In: 11th IEEE International Conference on Cognitive Infocommunications, CogInfoCom 2020, pp. 197–202 (2020)
7. Guyon, I., Elisseeff, A.: An introduction to variable and feature selection. J. Mach. Learn. Res. **3**(7–8), 1157–1182 (2003). https://doi.org/10.1162/153244303322753616
8. Liwicki, M., Schlapbach, A., Bunke, H.: Automatic gender detection using on-line and off-line information. Pattern Anal. Appl. **14**(1), 87–92 (2011)
9. Maken, P., Gupta, A.: A method for automatic classification of gender, based on text-independent handwriting. Multimedia Tools Appl. **80**, 24573–24602 (2021)
10. Megyesi, B., et al.: Decryption of historical manuscripts: the decrypt project. Cryptologia **44**(6), 545–559 (2020)
11. Plamondon, R., O'Reilly, C., Ouellet-Plamondon, C.: Strokes against stroke - strokes for strides. Pattern Recognit. **47**(3), 929–944 (2014). https://doi.org/10.1016/j.patcog.2013.05.004
12. Rosenblum, S.: Development, reliability, and validity of the handwriting proficiency screening questionnaire (HPSQ). Am. J. Occup. Therapy **62**, 298–307 (2008)

13. Simonnet, D., Girard, N., Anquetil, E., Renault, M., Thomas, S.: Evaluation of children cursive handwritten words for e-education. Pattern Recognit. Lett. **121**, 133–139 (2019). https://doi.org/10.1016/j.patrec.2018.07.021
14. Sirat, C., Irigoin, J., Poulle, E.: L'écriture: le cerveau, l'oeil et la main. In: Colloque International du CNRS, IRHT Paris, pp. 1–6 (1990)
15. Sokic, E., Salihbegovic, A., Ahic-Djokic, M.: Analysis of off-line handwritten text samples of different gender using shape descriptors. In: IX International Symposium on Telecommunications (BIHTEL), pp. 1–6 (2012)
16. Sotelo, A.F., Gómez-Adorno, H., Esquivel-Flores, O., Bel-Enguix, G.: Gender identification in social media using transfer learning. In: Figueroa Mora, K.M., Anzurez Marín, J., Cerda, J., Carrasco-Ochoa, J.A., Martínez-Trinidad, J.F., Olvera-López, J.A. (eds.) MCPR 2020. LNCS, vol. 12088, pp. 293–303. Springer, Cham (2020). https://doi.org/10.1007/978-3-030-49076-8_28
17. Taleb, C., Likforman-Sulem, L., Mokbel, C., Khachab, M.: Detection of Parkinson's disease from handwriting using deep learning: a comparative study. Evol. Intell. (2020). https://doi.org/10.1007/s12065-020-00470-0
18. Therapist team: The Handwriting Book. https://www.yourtherapysource.com/blog1/2016/01/20/gross-motor-skills-and-handwriting-3/

Using Convolutional Neural Network to Handle Word Shape Similarities in Handwritten Cursive Arabic Scripts of Pashto Language

Muhammad Ismail Shah[✉] and Ching Y. Suen

CENPARMI (Center for Pattern Recognition and Machine Intelligence), Computer Science and Software Engineering Department, Concordia University, Montreal, QC H3G 1M8, Canada
ismail_csit@yahoo.com, suen@encs.concordia.ca

Abstract. The Inter-Class Word Similarities in combination with Intra-Class Variations make it a difficult task for an OCR or any other machine learning system to recognize the handwritten characters and words with high accuracy, especially in the domain of cursive Arabic scripts. Convolutional Neural Network was originally designed to handle the problems of shape resemblance, position shift and distortion in the domain of handwritten characters and digit recognition. In this paper, we have used Convolutional Neural Network (CNN) to recognize multi class handwritten words written in cursive Arabic scripts of Pashto Language. The handwritten word images in Pashto Database [3] contain a high level of shape resemblance, and position shift in terms of diacritic marks. Hence it has been proved to be a good source for properly analyzing the performance of any CNN based recognition system. The model has successfully handled the problem and has not been affected by the level of complexity of Inter-class resemblances. The CNN model has been well tested on three sub data sets of Pashto Database. In each data set the number of classes and level of complexity, i.e., Shape Similarity, increase from one data set to another, i.e., 25, 40 and 68 classes of handwritten words. The average accuracies for the three Data Sets are 97.26%, 96.25% and 95.84%, respectively.

Keywords: Arabic scripts · Pashto language · Convolutional Neural Network · Shape similarity · Handwritten word recognition

1 Introduction

In 1980, Fukushima et al. [1] presented a basic Neural Network for image recognition known as Neocognitron. The goal was to develop a pattern recognition system that could recognize various patterns without being affected by shift in position, small distortion as well as resemblance with other patterns. The main concepts presented were Feature Extraction, the use of Convolution and Pooling Layers in Neural Network. The proposed system successfully handled the shape resemblance of patterns such as "X", "Y", "T" and "Z".

© Springer Nature Switzerland AG 2022
M. El Yacoubi et al. (Eds.): ICPRAI 2022, LNCS 13363, pp. 299–310, 2022.
https://doi.org/10.1007/978-3-031-09037-0_25

Inspired by the work of Fukushima [1], LeCun et al. [2] developed a pattern recognition system called LeNet-5, by combining three architectural ideas, i.e., *local receptive fields, shared weights and temporal sub-sampling*. The main goal was to make the resulting pattern recognition system invariant to scale, distortion and position shift, especially, in the domain of handwritten digit and character recognition. They used the term "Convolutional Neural Network" for the network architecture of LeNet-5 which has been adopted by the research community as a standard name for such kind of network architectures commonly represented as CNN or ConvNet. A general conceptual model of a simple CNN is shown in Fig. 1.

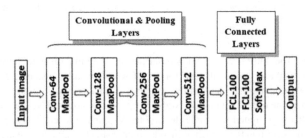

Fig. 1. Conceptual model of a simple convolutional neural network

Though primarily designed for solving the variation problems in handwritten document analysis [2], Convolutional Neural Networks have been widely adopted by the research community for the recognition of any kind of images. Several advanced architectures have been produced and applied for research and commercial purposes. Kumar, B [10] has given a comprehensive review of these architectures, for example AlexNet [11], VGGNet [12], **GoogLeNet** [13] and **ResNet** [14].

As mentioned earlier, the main goal behind the design of Convolutional Networks, by both Fukushima et al. [1] and LeCun et al. [2], was to handle the problem of *resemblance*, (i.e., the Inter-class similarities among various handwritten images) *distortion* and *position shift* in the domain of handwriting documents. This ability of CNN has made it a good choice for recognition of handwritten Arabic scripts. Because these scripts have high level of shape similarity at character level as well as word level. There is always a need for a good machine learning model which can effectively classify and recognize the handwritten documents in Arabic scripts.

Like Arabic and Farsi languages, Pashto is a well-known language of the South-Central Region of Asia. There are approximately 60 million Pashto speakers, who are mainly living in Pakistan and Afghanistan [8]. Pashto is the official language of Afghanistan as well as the provincial language of two provinces in Pakistan, i.e., North West Frontier Province (N.W.F.P) and Balochistan. In Northwest India, there are also some Pashtun communities.

The scripts generally used for Pashto writings are called 'Naskh', which are the modified Arabic scripts [8]. In addition, Pashto language has several unique letters which do not appear in any other Arabic script [8]. The shape similarity in Pashto language becomes more challenging because in addition to the 28 Arabic characters there are 21 more modified characters based on the position of diacritic marks/points, as shown in Fig. 2. We can see that the characters in first three rows share the same body shape.

This problem becomes more complicated in the domain of handwritten documents where these characters adopt different shapes at different positions within a word, i.e., beginning, middle, and end. For example, in Fig. 3 we have shown five groups of words, selected from CENPARMI Pashto Database [3], which show higher shape similarities to each other among the corresponding group. This shape similarity problem makes it very difficult for any OCR system to correctly recognize such handwritten words or isolated characters of Pashto language.

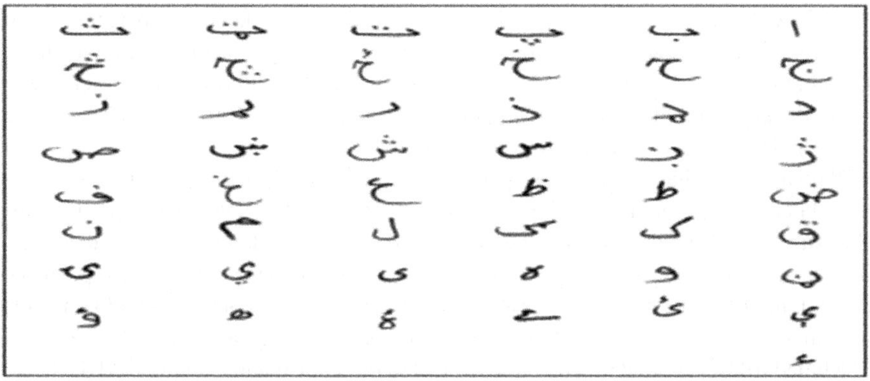

Fig. 2. Handwritten samples of 49 characters in the Pashto alphabets.

Group 1		Group 2		Group 3		Group 4		Group 5	
Word	Label	Word	Label	Word	Label	Word	Label	Word	Label
	Expire		Number		Liter		Price		Nine
	Volume		Amount		Meter		Period		Inch
	Article		Cash		One		Eighty		Five

Fig. 3. Shape similarities among different word classes

In this paper, we have applied Convolutional Neural Networks, for the first time, to recognize these challenging scripts at *Word Level*. The goal of this work is to demonstrate how effectively the CNN can handle the challenge of *Inter-Class Similarities* as well as *Intra-Class Variations*. To test if CNN can achieve this goal we need a good source of handwritten data which contains all or most of these problems. Fortunately, the CENPARMI Pashto Database [3] contains such a challenging handwritten data. Hence, we have used handwritten Pashto words presented in the CENPARMI Pashto Database [3].

The rest of the paper has been organized in such a way that Sect. 2 gives an overview of the related work, Sect. 3 provides information about the target data as well as the experimental setup. In Sect. 4 we have given an analysis of the experimental results. In the last we have given the concluded remarks.

2 Background

Several efforts have been made by the research community to show the effectiveness of CNN in the domain of handwriting recognition of Arabic Scripts at the level of *Isolated Characters* which show high level of shape similarity to each other.

El-Sawy et al. [4] have used CNN for recognition of isolated handwritten Arabic characters. Their data set contain 16,800 character level images comprising of 28 classes of Arabic characters, written by 60 people. They have reported that the resemblance among the character classes negatively affected the overall performance of the resulted classifier. The average accuracy rate achieved was 94.9%.

Najwa et al. [5] have reported the performance of the CNN in the domain of handwritten isolated Arabic characters. They used the 29 classes of Arabic characters including "Hamza" as an isolated character. The data set they used contains the original shape of each isolated character as well as the shapes of some characters at different positions, i.e., start, middle and end position. Their data set, called Hijja, contains 47,434 character level images written by 591 writers. They achieved an average accuracy of 88%.

Khaled [6] has applied a CNN based model to the same database, called AHCD, used by El-Sawy et al. [4]. In addition, a second database containing 8,738 Arabic letters, written by 107 people was also used. The average accuracies achieved, using all the 28 classes for both the data sets, were 94.7% and 94.8% respectively.

Khaled [6] also conducted a second set of experiments on 16 classes of distinct characters, i.e., removing other characters that have shape resemblance. On this distinct set of characters the average accuracy achieved was 98.22%. The difference between the results of the two sets of experiments indicate that the character shape resemblance in Arabic scripts negatively affect the overall performance of recognition system.

Mohamed et al. [7] used CNN for the recognition of handwritten Arabic characters. They trained and tested their model on a database called HACDB [9] which contain 6,600 images of Arabic characters written by 50 people. The data in this database has been divided into 66 classes based on the isolated character shape as well as their corresponding shapes at three possible positions within a word, i.e., beginning, middle and end. Using 24 classes they got an error rate of 2.09%, whereas for using 66 classes together the error rate increased to 5.83%.

All the research works mentioned above have shown that despite *Intra-Class Variations* as well as *Inter-Class Shape Similarities* of *Isolated Characters,* the overall accuracy of CNN is satisfactory. In this paper, we are going to analyze how effectively CNN can handle these two major problems at *Word Level* in cursive Arabic scripts of Pashto language.

3 Procedure

In this section we are going to describe the architecture of our CNN model as well as the nature of data and associated challenges in the Database used.

3.1 Experimental Setup

We have used 'Python 3.7.4', an open source, data science programming language. The libraries we used for machine learning are Tensor-Flow 2.0 as a back-end library whereas the Keras as an interface for Python. The overall model used in our experiments is shown in Fig. 4.

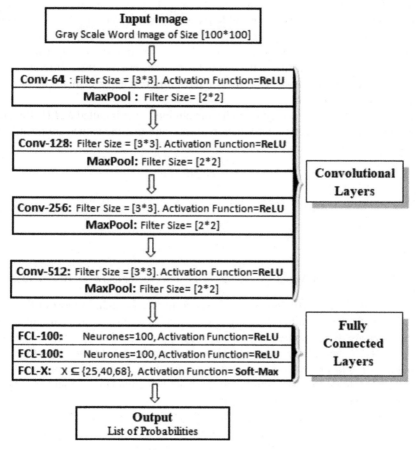

Fig. 4. CNN-model used in experiments

We use a gray scale word image of size 100 * 100 pixels as an input image. The word images have already been preprocessed for noise removal and have good quality [3]. The only preprocessing steps that we take in this work are the removal of white margins around the word images and then resizing them to 100 * 100 pixels. Removing the extra white spaces is advantageous because it makes the target word area more centralized and helps the Convolutional process effective in feature mappings.

In Convolutional Neural Networks we do not have to explicitly extract features from images in the form of a feature vector. Instead, the whole image is given as an input and the model detects and learns the various discriminative features by itself using the convolution and pooling layers.

We have used four Convolutional Layers with 64, 128, 256 and 512 filters respectively, with filter size of [3 * 3] each. Every Convolution layer is followed by a MaxPool Layer with filter size of [2 * 2]. As we can see that the number of filters in the convolution layers increases from previous layer to the next layer which enables the detection and extraction of fine features relevant to a given class of target image. The filters in MaxPool layers select the maximum values in each of the corresponding feature maps. Once the processing of Convolution and MaxPooling is completed the resulting feature maps are then joined together and passed to the fully connected layers (FCL).

In the Fully Connected Layers the two inner layers contain 100 neurons each, whereas the third layer which is considered the output layer has been given three different values based on the number of word classes used in three different experiments which we will describe in the next section.

The Activation Function used in each Convolution Layer is called **_ReLU_** (Rectified Liner Unit). The ReLU activation function makes sure that the values are positive by using the definition as given;

$$f(a) = max(0, a)$$

given

$$a = W^T x + b$$

where

$$W^T = \text{Transposed Weight Vector}, x = \text{Feature Vector and } b = \text{Bias value.}$$

In this way, all the negative values are converted to '0'. Though, in most of the cases ReLU is beneficial by creating 'Sparsity', in some cases it can also create trouble called 'Dying Neurons' where some neurons may stay inactive all the time. In our case this function has done well, hence we have chosen to use it as an Activation Function.

In the output layer we have used **_SoftMax_** Activation Function which creates a list of valid probabilities, that is, the probabilities of all the output labels should be between 0 and 1 and the total sum should be equal to 1.

For Optimization Function we have used SGD (Stochastic Gradient Descend) with _Learning Rate_ = 0.01 and _Momentum_ = 0.9. We have chosen these parameters after a series of experiments which showed that these are the best parameters in the current context. We have kept the _Batch Size_ = 32 for all the experiments, because this is an optimal number and has given comparatively good results. This size is also the default batch size of TensorFlow 2.0.

The number of _Epochs (i.e., Iterations)_ used in all the experiments is 20. We have kept _Epochs_ = 20 constant throughout the experiments, because the _Accuracy_ for each of the 21 experiments had reached its maximum for both Training and Validation in *Epochs* 10–12 and did not improve afterward, as shown in Fig. 5.a.

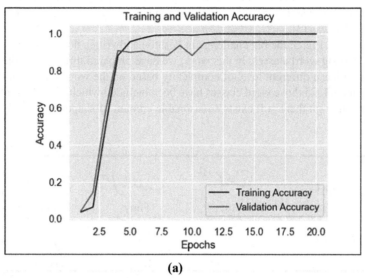

(a)

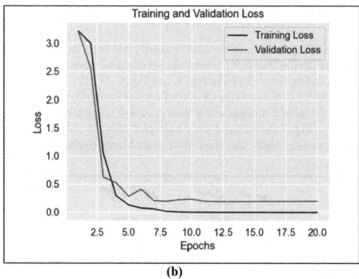

(b)

Fig. 5. a. Training and validation accuracy for 20 Epochs **b.** Training and validation loss for 20 Epochs

Similarly, the **Loss** for both Training and Validation reached its minimum in Epochs 10–12 and did not decrease afterward, as shown in Fig. 5.b. Due to this fact we have not increased the number of Epochs as it would have no effect on improvement of the results.

3.2 Data Base

We have used the *Handwritten Pashto Words* taken from CENPARMI Pashto Database [3]. This database contains 14,859 word images belonging to 68 different word classes written by 219 writers belonging to different genders, age groups, educational level as well as handedness [3].

As shown in Fig. 3, the big challenge in Pashto handwritten documents is the shape similarity among word classes. In this work, we have prepared three sets of data where each data set has a different level of complexity based on the word shape similarity. In the first Data Set, 25 those word classes have been included which show less inter-class similarities, though there still exists a reasonable amount of shape similarity as shown in Fig. 6.

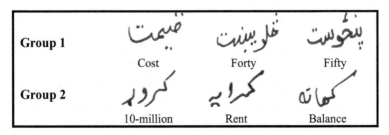

Fig. 6. Shape similarity among word classes in Data Set 1.

In the second Data Set, the Inter-Class similarity has been increased by adding 15 more word classes to the Data Set 1. This Data Set contains more number of resembled word classes including those shown in Fig. 3, and Fig. 6.

The third Data Set contains all the 68 word classes of Pashto Database [3]. In addition to Figs. 3 and 6, Data Set 3 contains many more groups of classes that show resemblance among them, e.g., Fig. 7 shows some more examples of word classes, along with their corresponding meaning labels, that show more resemblance to each other.

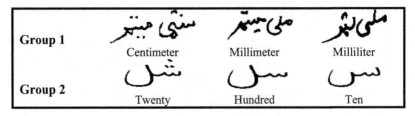

Fig. 7. Shape similarity among additional word classes present in Data Set 3

In addition to the Shape Similarity Problem (i.e., *Inter-Class Similarity*), in the domain of handwriting recognition, there is another problem of *Inter-Class Variations*. These variations are usually caused by non-uniform inter/intra word spacing, slanted characters, skewed lines, non-uniform inter-line spaces, uneven ink distribution, overlapping and touching characters, multiple writers, stylistic variations, corrections, cutting lines, and ink bleeds etc. Figure 8 shows some examples of Intra-Class Word variations of the Pashto words belonging to 8 classes.

Fig. 8. Intra-class word variations of the classes shown in Fig. 3.

The combination of visual similarities and handwriting variations, as described above, make it an uphill task to correctly recognize and analyze handwritten documents of cursive Arabic scripts, especially Pashto language. In the next section, we are going to describe how effectively CNN has handled the problem of shape similarity as well as *Inter-Class Variations*.

4   Analysis

The word images in each Data Set have been exclusively divided into three parts, i.e., Training, Testing and Validation, as shown in Table 1. The three Data Sets have been selected in such a way that;

$$Data\ Set\ 1 \subseteq Data\ Set\ 2 \subseteq Data\ Set\ 3$$

For all the three Data Sets the number of writers is the same, i.e., 219 people. The main goal of using three levels of Data Set, based on level of visual similarities, is to analyze how effectively a CNN model can overcome these challenges.

Table 1. Statistics of the three Data Sets used in experiments

Data set	Number of classes	Number of words			
		Testing	*Validation*	*Training*	*Total*
1	25	750	750	3962	5462
2	40	1200	1200	6341	8741
3	68	2040	2040	10779	14859

We have conducted our experiments using *Seven Fold Cross Validation* for each of the three Data Sets. In order to make the analysis more transparent, we have presented the Accuracy, of both Validation and Testing, for each of the Cross Validation Experiments individually, as shown in Table 2.

Table 2. Validation and testing accuracies for the three Data Sets

Cross validation	Data Set 1 (*25 Classes of words*)		Data Set 2 (*40 Classes of words*)		Data Set 3 (*68 Classes of words*)	
	Validation	Testing	Validation	Testing	Validation	Testing
1	97.73%	96.13%	97.42%	94.75%	96.81%	93.08%
2	95.87%	98.53%	94.17%	97.33%	97.11%	96.62%
3	97.87%	98.27%	96.92%	97.58%	93.00%	97.40%
4	98.27%	97.07%	97.92%	97.58%	95.78%	95.78%
5	95.87%	96.93%	96.26%	96.66%	96.03%	95.88%
6	96.80%	96.40%	97.00%	97.08%	95.93%	95.44%
7	96.67%	97.47%	96.82%	97.00%	96.42%	96.71%
Average	**97.01%**	**97.26%**	**96.64%**	**96.85%**	**95.87%**	**95.84%**

The *Minimum Test Accuracy* achieved for Data Sets 1, Data Set 2 and Data Set 3 are **96.13%**, **94.75%** and **93.08%** respectively. Similarly, the *Minimum Validation Accuracies* for the concerned three data sets are **95.87%**, **94.17%** and **93.00%** respectively.

The *Maximum Test Accuracies* for Data Sets 1, Data Set 2 and Data Set 3 are **98.53%**, **97.58%** and **97.40%**, respectively. The *Maximum Validation Accuracies* for the concerned three data sets are **98.27%**, **97.92%** and **97.11%**, respectively.

The *Average Test Accuracy* for Data Sets 1, Data Set 2 and Data Set 3 are **97.26%**, **96.85%** and **95.84%**, respectively. The *Average Validation Accuracies* for the concerned three data sets are **97.01%**, **96.64%** and **95.87%**, respectively.

It is evident from Table 2, that *Convolutional Neural Network* (CNN) has given satisfactory results for all the three Data Sets. Though, in the three Data Sets the number of classes and level of complexity increases from one Data Set to another, the difference between their average accuracies is not very significant. For example, Data Set 2 contains 40 different classes of words and Data Set 1 contains 25 different classes which give a difference of 15 classes. In other words, Data Set 2 is more complex, in terms of Shape Similarity, as compared to Data Set 1. However, the difference between average Accuracies of Data Set 1 and Data Set 2 is just **0.41%** which is not a big difference.

More interesting aspect is the differences between average the Accuracies of Data Set 3 and its sub-sets, i.e., Data Set 1 and Data Set 2 which are just 1.42% and 1.01% respectively. As mentioned earlier, Data Set 3 contains all the challenging word classes present in its sub-sets plus 28 additional classes which also have high resemblance among a few example of which are as shown in Fig. 7.

Apart from this, for all the three data sets, the Testing and Validation Accuracies of the seven Cross Validation Experiments are either very close or above the average value. Looking at the results, we can observe that the Accuracies for all the three data sets are very close to each other. This shows that the CNN model has performed consistently well in handling the challenges of handwriting variations as well as shape similarities in the given problem domain.

In Table 3, we have presented a summarized comparison of the Data Sets and the Accuracies of the CNN based models presented by other researchers as described in Sect. 2.

Table 3. Comparison to other CNN based research works based on Data Sets and accuracies

References	Target Data Sets					Accuracy
	Language	Level	Images	Classes	Writers	
El-Sawy et al. [4]	Arabic	Characters	16,800	28	60	94.90%
Najwa et al. [5]	Arabic	Characters	47,434	29	591	88.00%
Khaled [6]	Arabic	Characters	8,738	28	107	94.80%
Mohamed et al. [7]	Arabic	Characters	6,600	66	50	94.17%
This paper	Pashto	Words	5,462	25	219	97.26%
This paper	Pashto	Words	8,741	40	219	96.85%
This paper	Pashto	Words	14,859	68	219	95.84%

5 Conclusion

A 7-Layers model of Convolutional Neural Network has been applied to recognize handwritten *Pashto Words* which have high level of Shape Similarity. In addition, these words also contain Intra-Class Variations due to hundreds of different writers. The model has been well tested on three data sets which contain different level of complexity in terms of Shape Similarity and Number of Classes. *The main goal of using three data sets, based on level of shape similarities, was to analyze how much the performance of the CNN model is affected when the shape similarity is increased from one data set to the other.* The results show that the differences among the average accuracies for the three data sets are not very significant. Hence, the CNN is very robust to handle *Shape Similarity* problem in the challenging Arabic scripts of Pashto language, especially, at Word Level.

Acknowledgment. We are really grateful to the entire team of Google Brain the developers of TensorFlow 2.0 as well as the developers of Keras who have designed and developed such powerful machine learning libraries and have made them available for free. In last but not least, we really appreciate the entire community of Python as well as Eclips developers for their devoted work for the open source Data Science platforms.

References

1. Fukushima, K., Miyake, S.: Neocognitron: a self-organizing neural network model for a mechanism of visual pattern recognition. In: Amari, Si., Arbib, M.A. (eds.) Competition and Cooperation in Neural Nets. LNBM, vol. 45, pp, 267–285. Springer, Heidelberg (1982). https://doi.org/10.1007/978-3-642-46466-9_18
2. LeCun, Y., Bottou, L., Bengio, Y., Haffner, P.: Gradient-based learning applied to document recognition. Proc. IEEE **86**(11), 2278–2324 (1998)
3. Shah, M.I., He, C.L., Nobile, N., Suen, C.Y.: A Handwritten pashto database with multi-aspects for handwriting recognition. In: Proceedings of 14th Conference of the International Graphonomics Society, Dijon, France, pp. 157–161 (2009)
4. El-Sawy, A., Loey, M., El-Bakry, H.: Arabic Handwritten characters recognition using convolutional neural network. WSEAS Trans. Comput. Res. **5**, 11–19 (2017)
5. Altwaijry, N., Al-Turaiki, I.: Arabic handwriting recognition system using convolutional neural network. Neural Comput. Appl. **33**(7), 2249–2261 (2020). https://doi.org/10.1007/s00521-020-05070-8
6. Khaled, S.Y.: Arabic handwritten character recognition based on deep convolutional neural network. Jourdanian J. Comput. Inf. Technol. **3**(3), 188–199 (2017)
7. Muhammad, E., Maalej, R., Kherallah, M.: A new design based-SVM of the CNN classifier architecture with dropout for offline Arabic handwritten recognition. Procedia Comput. Sci. **80**, 1712–1723 (2016)
8. Pashto Language. http://en.wikipedia.org/wiki/Pashto_language. Current 5 January 2022
9. Lawgali, A., Angelova, M., Bouridane, A.: HACDB: handwritten Arabic characters database for automatic character recognition. In: European Workshop on Visual Information Processing (EUVIP), pp. 255–259 (2013)
10. Brajesh Kumar | AppyHigh Blog | Medium. https://medium.com/appyhigh-technology-blog/convolutional-neural-networks-a-brief-history-of-their-evolution-ee3405568597
11. Krizhevsky, A., Sutskever, I., Hinton, G.E.: ImageNet classification with deep convolutional neural networks. Commun. ACM, **60**(6), 84–90 (2017)
12. Simonyan, K., Zisserman, A.: Very deep convolutional networks for large-scale image recognition. arXiv preprint arXiv:1409.1556 (2014)
13. Christian, S., et al.: Going deeper with convolutions. In: IEEE Conference on Computer Vision and Pattern Recognition (CVPR), pp. 1–9 (2015)
14. He, K., Zhang, X., Ren, S., Sun, J.: Deep residual learning for image recognition. In: Proceedings of the IEEE Conference on Computer Vision and Pattern Recognition, pp. 770–778 (2016)

Discriminatory Expressions to Improve Model Comprehensibility in Short Documents

Manuel Francisco$^{(\boxtimes)}$ and Juan Luis Castro$^{(\boxtimes)}$

Department of Computer Science and Artificial Intelligence, University of Granada, Granada, Spain
{francisco,castro}@decsai.ugr.es

Abstract. Microblogging sites are being used as analysis avenues due to their peculiarities (promptness, short texts...). Lately, researchers have focused mainly in classification performance rather than interpretability. When the problem requires transparency, it is necessary to build interpretable pipelines, and even though, resulting models are too complex to be considered comprehensible, making it impossible for humans to understand the actual decisions. This paper presents a feature selection mechanism that is able to improve comprehensibility by using less but more meaningful features. Results show that our proposal is better and the most stable one in terms of accuracy, generalisation and comprehensibility in microblogging context.

Keywords: Interpretability · Text mining · Feature selection · Microblogging

1 Introduction

Social Networking Sites (SNS) constitute an analysis avenue of interest and opinion trends worldwide. Twitter is the most popular microblogging site, with 126 million daily active users as of 2018 and almost 6000 tweets being sent per second [13,25]. However, short documents present clear handicaps when using machine learning (ML) techniques (lack of context, abundance of misspelled words, contractions...). Thus, most widely used techniques do not yield as good results as expected.

Moreover, there are domains where interpretability is required due to decisions that may have a social impact, e.g. censor algorithms [23] and recommendation systems [20]. Lately, ML research has focused mostly in performance metrics. State-of-the-art language models (such as ELMo, BERT and/or GPT-3 [4,8,22]) are based on *deep* techniques and thus they are not interpretable. There is a growing

This work was financially supported by the Spanish Ministry of Economy and Competitiveness (MINECO), project FFI2016-79748-R, and cofinanced by the European Social Fund (ESF). Manuel Francisco Aparicio was supported by the FPI 2017 predoctoral programme, from the Spanish Ministry of Economy and Competitiveness (MINECO), grant reference BES-2017-081202.

M. El Yacoubi et al. (Eds.): ICPRAI 2022, LNCS 13363, pp. 311–322, 2022.
https://doi.org/10.1007/978-3-031-09037-0_26

tendency to *explain* current black-box models with subordinated ones; this approach may preserve bad practices over time that can lead to potential harm [24].

Even though there are interpretable algorithms, resulting models are sometimes far too complex to be understandable. In 1956, [16] showed that 7 ± 2
is the number of chunks that a person can remember for a short time. Further
research proved that this number could be smaller [6].

Model performance is not necessarily related to its complexity [24]. Therefore, we propose the use of expressions biased towards a class as classifier-agnostic
features in order to (1) improve classification performance, (2) improve generalisation capacity, and (3) improve comprehensibility, all three targets in the
context of a reduced dimensionality. [19] tried a similar approach with success,
although in a different domain.

The rest of this paper is organised as follows. Section 2 revise other works in
the field. Section 3 introduces our proposal and its formulation. Section 4 present
conducted evaluation and Sect. 5 discuss the obtained results. We present our
conclusions in Sect. 6.

2 Related Work

2.1 Dimensionality Reduction

Text mining research in Social Media has become very relevant [1,3,21]. Natural
language models produce highly-dimensional and very sparse feature matrices
[29]. It is required to select and/or recombine them to decrease complexity and
to improve classification performance [26].

There are several classes of feature selection (FS) methods that are, generally,
grouped into three categories [28]: (1) Filtering methods. Given a set of features,
they apply an evaluation function and select the k best, where k is an hyperparameter; (2) Wrapper methods. Given a set of features, they select different
subsets of them to train a classifier and check out how good its performance
is. Since selected features are tested directly within the classifier, they normally
achieve better performance than filters; (3) Hybrid methods. They combine both
techniques: first, they perform a filter to reduce the number of features; then,
optimal subset is computed by feeding a classifier.

There are loads of filtering methods available and backed by the scientific
community, and we have selected a few of them based on relevance and performance metrics: χ^2, Information Gain (IG), Mutal Information (MI), Odds
Ratio (OR), Expected Cross Entropy (ECE), ANOVA F-value, and Galavotti-
Sebastiani-Simi coefficient (GSS) [5,7,10,11,18,27,30].

All these filters present similar drawbacks: features are selected regardless of
the classifier, so the selected feature subset may not be ideal for every classification stage. Wrappers try to overcome this by assessing the relevance of each
subset of features within the context of a given classifier [12,14]. However, the
evaluation is complex and classifier-dependant. Hybrids methods are a combination of them.

Since 2012, *state-of-the-art* is abandoning these *handcrafted* methods in favour of auto-encoded features [17]. Yet, we cannot consider these approaches since they behave as black-box models and cannot be interpreted. Nevertheless, we include one in our experiments for comparative purposes.

2.2 Interpretability Measures

There is no general consensus on how to measure interpretability. This concept, along with similar ones like *comprehensibility* and *understandability*, are usually synonyms [2]. However, there is kind of a distinction between those related to the ability to read the model (*interpretability*) and those related to the human capacity to understand it (*comprehensibility*) [15].

[9] defined *interpretability* as "*the ability to explain or to present in understandable terms to a human*". They elaborated a taxonomy on how to evaluate interpretability: (1) application level (consisting in an expert evaluation of the model itself); (2) Human metrics (where any human can perform such evaluation without the need of being a domain expert. It is normally performed by comparison with other models/explanations); (3) Proxy tasks (when we make the assumption that the user understands the model and we only compare parameters within it, e.g. depth of a decision tree). Our proposal focuses in a functional evaluation (proxy task).

3 Discriminatory Expressions

We present in this section our proposal to obtain significant feature sets that improve model comprehensibility in microblogging contexts.

Let $X = \{d_1, d_2, ..., d_n\}$ be a set of documents where each document $d \in X$ belongs to a class C. We consider S as the set of *stop words*.

Definition 1 (Expression). *Given a document $d \in X$ as a sequence of words $d = (t_1, t_2, ..., t_n)$, e is said to be an expression of the document, noted as $e\ expr\ x$, iff: (1) It is not composed strictly by stop words; (2) All words of the expression can be found in the document and the order is preserved (e is a regular expression that matches the document).*

$$e\ expr\ d \longleftrightarrow \begin{cases} \exists t_i \in e : t_i \notin S \\ \wedge \\ /t_1 * t_2 * ... * t_n/\ matches\ d \end{cases} \tag{1}$$

Definition 2 (Discriminatory expression). *Given r (minimum relevance or recall) and p (minimum precision), an expression e is said to be (r, p)-discriminatory for the class C, noted as $e\ dexpr_{r,p}\ C$ iff: (1) Recall of e for the class C is over a given threshold r; (2) Precision of e for the class C is at least p (Table 1).*

$$e\ dexpr_{r,p}\ C \longleftrightarrow \begin{cases} \frac{|e\ expr\ d_i : d_i \in C|}{|C|} > r \\ \wedge \\ \frac{|e\ expr\ d_i : d_i \in C|}{|e\ expr\ d_i' : d_i' \in X|} > p \end{cases} \tag{2}$$

Table 1. Examples of discriminatory expressions

Discriminatory expression	Description
*recortes*ministro*	Expression extracted from the Spanish dataset that makes reference to the budget cuts and associated with *negative sentiment*
*well*man*	Expression extracted from the Twitter Gender Dataset associated with *male gender class*

Despite expressions may be an intuitive way to look at *microblogging* documents, the search space is too complex to be explored completely. There are several ways to obtain suboptimal solutions to this problem (metaheuristic techniques). We used a greedy approach with a custom ranking function based on TF-IDF (see Sect. 3.1).

The algorithm we propose for feature extraction will compute a set of discriminatory expressions D taking into consideration that each expression needs to meet some frequency and distinguishability criteria with respect to a class. In other words, each expression e should be skewed towards a class, such that the frequency in which that expression appears in the class exceeds a certain threshold (r) meanwhile the ratio between the matches in the class and the total number of matches is above a given boundary (p). Once we have the set of discriminatory features, we can transform each document to a binary vector (v_i) where each component v_i stands for the appearance of the i-th discriminatory expression in the document.

Our python proof-of-concept implementation can be found in our project's repository[1].

3.1   Ranking Method: *CF-ICF*

We build discriminatory expressions from the words that are present in the documents of a class. Usually, there are several expressions that can accomplish our criteria, but a few of them are more useful than the rest. As we want to maximise statistical relevance and discriminatory performance, we propose a ranking method based on *TF-IDF* that takes into consideration the class whose expression we are looking for.

Let X be a set of documents $X = \{d_0, d_1, ..., d_n\}$ where $n = |X|$. L is a binary property that can be present (or not) in each document, such that for a given document $d_i \in X$, $L(d_i) \in \{0, 1\}$. We will now define the sets $X_L^+ \subseteq X, X_L^+ = \{d \in X : L(d) = 1\}$ and $X_L^- \subseteq X, X_L^- = \{d \in X : L(d) = 0\}$, where n_L^+ and n_L^- stand for $|X_L^+|$ and $|X_L^-|$, respectively.

---

[1] https://github.com/nutcrackerugr/discriminatory-expressions.

Table 2. Datasets used to conduct our experiments.

Dataset	Size	Classes	Balanced
Twitter US Airlines	15k	Negative, Neutral, Positive	No
Twitter Gender Classification	25k	Brand, Female, Male	Yes
Sentiment140	1.6M	Negative, Neutral, Positive	Yes
SLS (imdb subset)	3k	Negative, Positive	Yes
TASS2017	7k	Negative, Neutral, Positive	Yes

The function $f(t, d)$ yields the number of times that a word t appears in the document d. From here, we can define classic *TF-IDF* as follows:

$$tf(t, d, X) = \frac{f(t, d)}{\max\{f(t, d'), \forall d' \in X\}} \tag{3}$$

$$df(t, X) = |\{d \in X : t \text{ in } d\}| \tag{4}$$

$$idf(t, X) = \log \frac{n}{df(t, X)} \tag{5}$$

$$tfidf(t, d, X) = tf(t, d, X)idf(t, X) \tag{6}$$

Now, let $cf(t, L)$ be a function that returns the number of times that the word t appears in the documents of X_L^+ and let $d_L = \bigcup_{d \in X_L^+} d$ (meaning that d_L is the result of concatenating all the documents in X_L^+). We can define cf as a function of tf using the concatenated d_L as follows:

$$cf(t, L) = \sum_{d \in X_L^+} f(t, d) = tf(t, d_L) \tag{7}$$

In the same way, let $n_L^-(t) = |\{d \in X_L^- : t \text{ in } d\}|$ and $n_L^+(t) = |\{d \in X_L^+ : t \text{ in } d\}|$. We can also express *IDF* as follows:

$$idf(t, X) = \log \frac{n}{n_L^-(t) + n_L^+(t)} \tag{8}$$

Now, *idf* can be modified to define *icf*, as shown below:

$$icf(t, L, X) = \log \frac{n}{n_L^-(t) + 1} \tag{9}$$

$$cficf(t, L, X) = cf(t, L)icf(t, L, X) \tag{10}$$

4   Experiments

We performed exhaustive experiments with four different purposes: (1) In order to evaluate mean classification performance of the different methods; (2) In order to evaluate generalisation capacity; (3) In order to check how comprehensible the resulting models are. We measured all three aspects in terms of mean values and dispersion rate. All experiments were run using python 3.8.1 with sklearn 0.22, using the datasets described in Table 2. Tweet classes were binarised following a one-vs-rest approach. We used four classifiers that are widely considered interpretable. k-nearest neighbours (kNN), Decision Trees (DT), Random Forest (RF) and Logistic Regression (LR). We did not perform hyperparameter tuning on any of them. With the exception of those tests that explicitly evaluate some variable against the number of features, we conducted our experiments using 9 features (see Sect. 1).

Performance and comprehensibility test were conducted following a 5-fold cross-validation scheme on four datasets. For the generalisation test, we used a 100-fold cross-validation reversed approach on the Sentiment140 dataset to replicate real-world scenarios where available supervised datasets are small.

Additionally, we wanted to quantify baseline performance loss when using interpretable models. We include results for ELMo in a comparative perspective despite that deep neural networks (DNNs) are not interpretable. Experiments were run using Tensorflow Hub ELMo v3 model. We did not restrict the number of features used by the model.

5   Results and Discussion

We evaluated classification performance, stability across experiments, generalisation capacity and comprehensibility.

5.1   Classification Performance

Table 3 shows accuracy, precision, recall, $f1$-score and area under the curve ROC. Presented values correspond to the mean between cross-validation folds, datasets and classifiers. Figure 1 shows $f1$-score evolution against the number of features. Features selected by Discriminatory Expressions (DE) are more useful to train a classifier with a reduced feature space. As the number of features increases, the rest of methods get closer and even surpass DE in some cases. This happens when the number of features is higher than the amount that we can consider feasible to be managed by humans (see Sect. 1). DNN model does not show a significant improvement of the classification performance. DE dispersion is the lowest among the rest. Figure 2 depicts the dispersion of the performance for each feature selection method while varying the number of features.

5.2   Generalisation Capacity

In order to measure how good a method models reality when training with small datasets, we used a reversed 100-fold cross-validation scheme. We considered mean and dispersion rates for accuracy, precision, recall, $f1$-score and area under the curve ROC. Table 5 shows the behaviour of the feature selection method for our biggest dataset (Sentiment140). Results show that our proposal not only has the best mean generalisation capacity but also the lowest deviation (Table 4).

Table 3. Classification performance of our proposal (DE) against the rest of the selected methods measured with accuracy, precision, recall, f1-score and area-under-curve ROC when training with 9 features. *The number of features used by ELMo was not restricted.

FS method	Accuracy		Precision		Recall		f1-score		ROC AUC	
	mean	std	mean	std	mean	std	mean	std	mean	std
CHI2	0.6692	0.1273	0.6763	0.1461	0.4979	0.2845	0.5030	0.1472	0.6226	0.0720
DE	0.6869	0.1156	0.6309	0.0955	0.5367	0.1472	**0.5610**	**0.0624**	0.6370	0.0540
ECE	0.6353	0.1267	0.5872	0.1196	0.3950	0.2485	0.4228	0.1525	0.5714	0.0607
f-ANOVA	0.6787	0.1198	0.6829	0.1370	0.5282	0.2754	0.5295	0.1306	0.6306	0.0680
GSS	0.6608	0.1311	0.6691	0.1168	0.3869	0.2189	0.4449	0.1322	0.6102	0.0743
IG	0.6793	0.1194	0.7006	0.1350	0.4756	0.2637	0.5040	0.1335	0.6286	0.0695
MI	0.6784	0.1223	0.7014	0.1456	0.4797	0.2698	0.5044	0.1379	0.6280	0.0694
OR	0.6500	0.1229	0.6033	0.1079	0.4214	0.2200	0.4591	0.1330	0.5927	0.0649
ELMo*	0.6811	0.1480	0.6908	0.1460	0.5403	0.3074	0.5285	0.2076	0.6405	0.0995

Table 4. Further measurements of performance dispersion for our proposal (DE) against the rest of the selected methods measured with range, interquartile range (IQR), standard deviation (STD) and coefficient of variation (CV) when training with 9 features. *The number of features used by ELMo was not restricted.

FS method	Range	IQR	STD	CV (%)
CHI2	0.6730	0.1732	0.1472	29.2623
DE	**0.2977**	**0.1008**	**0.0624**	**11.1313**
ECE	0.5772	0.2161	0.1525	36.0694
f-ANOVA	0.6276	0.1829	0.1306	24.6674
GSS	0.4964	0.1330	0.1322	29.7014
IG	0.5860	0.2020	0.1335	26.4790
MI	0.6420	0.1625	0.1379	27.3400
OR	0.5174	0.1801	0.1330	28.9810
ELMo*	0.7904	0.2368	0.2076	39.2822

Table 5. Mean generalisation capacity and its deviation for a reversed 100-fcv using 9 features with Sentiment140 dataset. Results are the mean between folds and classifiers.

FS method	Accuracy		Precision		Recall		f1-score		ROC AUC	
	mean	std	mean	std	mean	std	mean	std	mean	std
CHI2	0.5781	0.0071	0.5672	0.0672	0.8805	0.2320	0.6553	0.1218	0.5781	0.0071
DE	0.6526	0.0161	0.6313	0.0198	0.7446	0.0988	**0.6784**	**0.0456**	0.6526	0.0161
ECE	0.5370	0.0068	0.5790	0.0553	0.4557	0.2946	0.4437	0.1674	0.5371	0.0068
f-ANOVA	0.5776	0.0097	0.5684	0.0702	0.8750	0.2378	0.6517	0.1312	0.5776	0.0097
GSS	0.5865	0.0208	0.7009	0.0438	0.3324	0.1274	0.4367	0.0509	0.5865	0.0208
IG	0.5784	0.0085	0.5605	0.0606	0.9092	0.1936	0.6682	0.1092	0.5784	0.0085
MI	0.5784	0.0086	0.5650	0.0670	0.8941	0.2176	0.6607	0.1203	0.5784	0.0086
OR	0.5549	0.0155	0.6559	0.0645	0.3059	0.1941	0.3819	0.0944	0.5549	0.0155

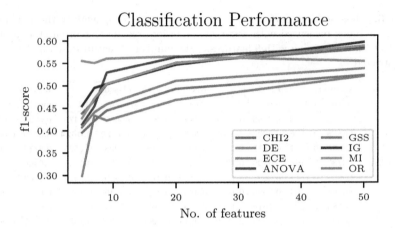

Fig. 1. Classification performance measured with $f1$-score when varying the number of features. Results shown are aggregated by dataset and classifier. Our proposal has a better performance under 20 features.

5.3 Comprehensibility

In this section, we will perform an analysis on the practical interpretability of the models that result from each feature selection method.

k-nearest neighbours (kNN) get the k most similar neighbours to the one that is being classified and outputs the majority class. The interpretation is straightforward, since it is a mere comparison. Hence, the fewer neighbours you need to consider, the better. Figure 3 shows different dispersion measures between folds and datasets for $f1$-score values with respect to the number of considered neighbours. Discriminatory Expressions (DE) method has its better comprehensibility rate grouped under 9 neighbours, without significant difference than when using 5 of them.

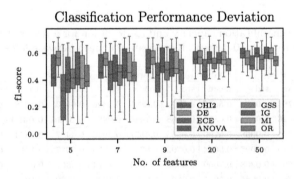

Fig. 2. $f1$-score dispersion between iterations for each fold, classifier and dataset while varying the number of features. Our proposal shows a lower dispersion and, generally, better performance while working with a low number of features.

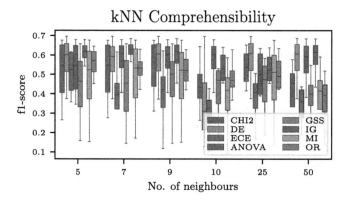

Fig. 3. Performance comparison between kNN models generated using different feature sets. The plot shows the number of neighbours considered (less is better) against $f1$-score.

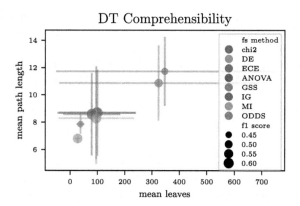

Fig. 4. Complexity measures comparison between DT models generated using different feature sets. The size of each marker stands for the $f1$-score and the error bars represent the dispersion (standard deviation) for each dimension.

Decision Trees (DT) interpretation relies not only in the number of features selected but also in (1) the number of leaves (equivalent to number of rules) and (2) the length of the path from the root to each leaf node. In both cases, less is better.

Figure 4 shows centrality and dispersion measurements on the number of rules and their length. It also shows the classification performance. It is possible to notice that Discriminatory Expressions method is (1) the feature set that produces the simpler trees (the closer to the bottom left corner, the better), (2) the most stable in both dimensions (shortest whiskers) and (3) the feature set that produces one of the best performing models (dot size).

Table 6. Performance and complexity measures of RF-based models when training with 5 trees.

FS method	f1-score		Leaves		Length	
	mean	std	mean	std	mean	std
CHI2	0.6039	0.08	105.3000	126.73	9.2564	3.18
DE	0.5707	0.14	**41.9000**	19.93	**7.4953**	0.62
ECE	0.4681	0.13	368.9000	377.17	11.7672	2.82
F-ANOVA	0.5954	0.10	98.3000	104.34	9.1386	2.47
GSS	0.4485	0.18	58.6500	28.79	8.4637	0.82
IG	0.6102	0.08	111.2000	118.40	9.4097	2.30
MI	0.5937	0.09	109.8500	124.97	9.4794	3.01
OR	0.5309	0.13	341.1000	349.87	11.5126	2.68

Finally, Random Forests (RF) are collections of DTs. Their complexity can be evaluated in the same way than decision trees, but it is necessary to consider the number of trees in the forest (fewer is better). Table 6 shows centrality and dispersion measurements for each feature set, including model complexity, for a fixed number of trees. Our proposal has the best behaviour among the tested methods.

6   Conclusions

We developed a feature selection algorithm for microblogging contexts focused in obtaining a well-structured set of significant features in order to improve the comprehensibility of the model while offering good classification performance. We used expressions (sequences of words) that are biased towards specific classes, inspired in linguists procedures when analysing text. In order to assemble those expressions, we introduced a word ranking method that we have called *CF-ICF*.

We compared eight different feature selection methods using five different popular datasets. Results showed that our algorithm achieves a good baseline performance while being the most stable method regardless of the context and classifier used (even agains deep neural networks). It is also noticeable that classification performance does not improve significantly with the number of features, that suggests that our feature set is quite relevant from the beginning. As for comprehensibility, our proposal managed to score among the best for every case. When combined with decision trees or random forests, we achieve the best overall results.

References

1. Alharbi, A., de Doncker, E.: Twitter sentiment analysis with a deep neural network: an enhanced approach using user behavioral information. Cognit. Syst. Res. **54**, 50–61 (2019). https://doi.org/10.1016/j.cogsys.2018.10.001

2. Alonso, J.M., Magdalena, L., González-Rodríguez, G.: Looking for a good fuzzy system interpretability index: an experimental approach. Int. J. Approx. Reasoning **51**(1), 115–134 (2009). https://doi.org/10.1016/j.ijar.2009.09.004. https://www.sciencedirect.com/science/article/pii/S0888613X09001418

3. Alsaig, A., Alsaig, A., Alsadun, M., Barghi, S.: Context based algorithm for social influence measurement on Twitter. In: Cong Vinh, P., Alagar, V. (eds.) ICCASA/ICTCC -2018. LNICST, vol. 266, pp. 136–149. Springer, Cham (2019). https://doi.org/10.1007/978-3-030-06152-4_12

4. Brown, T.B., et al.: Language models are few-shot learners. arXiv:2005.14165 [cs], July 2020

5. Caropreso, M.F., Matwin, S., Sebastiani, F.: A learner-independent evaluation of the usefulness of statistical phrases for automated text categorization (2001)

6. Cowan, N.: The magical number 4 in short-term memory: a reconsideration of mental storage capacity. Behav. Brain Sci. **24**(1), 87–114 (2001). Discussion 114–185

7. Deng, X., Li, Y., Weng, J., Zhang, J.: Feature selection for text classification: a review. Multimedia Tools Appl. **78**(3), 3797–3816 (2019). https://doi.org/10.1007/s11042-018-6083-5

8. Devlin, J., Chang, M.W., Lee, K., Toutanova, K.: BERT: pre-training of deep bidirectional transformers for language understanding. arXiv:1810.04805 [cs], October 2018

9. Doshi-Velez, F., Kim, B.: Towards a rigorous science of interpretable machine learning. arXiv:1702.08608 [cs, stat], February 2017

10. Forman, G.: An extensive empirical study of feature selection metrics for text classification. J. Mach. Learn. Res. JMLR **3**, 1289–1305 (2003)

11. Galavotti, L., Sebastiani, F., Simi, M.: Experiments on the use of feature selection and negative evidence in automated text categorization. In: Borbinha, J., Baker, T. (eds.) ECDL 2000. LNCS, vol. 1923, pp. 59–68. Springer, Heidelberg (2000). https://doi.org/10.1007/3-540-45268-0_6

12. Hans, C., Dobra, A., West, M.: Shotgun stochastic search for "Large p" regression. J. Am. Stat. Assoc. **102** (2005). https://doi.org/10.2307/27639881

13. Internet Live Stats: Twitter usage statistics - internet live stats (2020). https://www.internetlivestats.com/twitter-statistics/

14. Meiri, R., Zahavi, J.: Using simulated annealing to optimize the feature selection problem in marketing applications. Eur. J. Oper. Res. **171**(3), 842–858 (2006). https://doi.org/10.1016/j.ejor.2004.09.010. http://www.sciencedirect.com/science/article/pii/S0377221704005892

15. Mencar, C., Fanelli, A.M.: Interpretability constraints for fuzzy information granulation. Inf. Sci. **178**(24), 4585–4618 (2008). https://doi.org/10.1016/j.ins.2008.08.015. https://www.sciencedirect.com/science/article/pii/S0020025508003484

16. Miller, G.A.: The magical number seven, plus or minus two: some limits on our capacity for processing information. Psychol. Rev. **63**(2), 81–97 (1956). https://doi.org/10.1037/h0043158

17. Minaee, S., et al.: Deep learning based text classification: a comprehensive review. arXiv:2004.03705 [cs, stat], April 2020, version: 1

18. Misangyi, V.F., LePine, J.A., Algina, J., Francis Goeddeke, J.: The adequacy of repeated-measures regression for multilevel research: comparisons with repeated-measures ANOVA, multivariate repeated-measures anova, and multilevel modeling across various multilevel research designs. Organ. Res. Methods (2016). https://doi.org/10.1177/1094428105283190. https://journals.sagepub.com/doi/10.1177/1094428105283190

19. Moreo, A., Navarro, M., Castro, J.L., Zurita, J.M.: A high-performance FAQ retrieval method using minimal differentiator expressions. Knowl. Based Syst. **36**, 9–20 (2012). https://doi.org/10.1016/j.knosys.2012.05.015. http://www.sciencedirect.com/science/article/pii/S0950705112001657

20. O'Dair, M., Fry, A.: Beyond the black box in music streaming: the impact of recommendation systems upon artists. Pop. Commun. (2019). https://doi.org/10.1080/15405702.2019.1627548

21. Periñán-Pascual, C., Arcas-Túnez, F.: Detecting environmentally-related problems on Twitter. Biosyst. Eng. **177**, 31–48 (2019). https://doi.org/10.1016/j.biosystemseng.2018.10.001

22. Peters, M.E., et al.: Deep contextualized word representations. arXiv:1802.05365 [cs], February 2018

23. Phillips, A.: The Moral Dilemma of Algorithmic Censorship, August 2018. https://becominghuman.ai/the-moral-dilemma-of-algorithmic-censorship-6d7b6faefe7

24. Rudin, C.: Please stop explaining black box models for high stakes decisions. arXiv:1811.10154 [cs, stat], November 2018

25. Twitter Inc.: Q1 2019 earning report. Technical report, Twitter Inc. (2019). https://s22.q4cdn.com/826641620/files/doc_financials/2019/q1/Q1-2019-Slide-Presentation.pdf

26. Wang, H., Hong, M.: Supervised Hebb rule based feature selection for text classification. Inf. Process. Manag. **56**(1), 167–191 (2019). https://doi.org/10.1016/j.ipm.2018.09.004. http://www.sciencedirect.com/science/article/pii/S0306457318305752

27. Wu, G., Wang, L., Zhao, N., Lin, H.: Improved expected cross entropy method for text feature selection. In: 2015 International Conference on Computer Science and Mechanical Automation (CSMA), pp. 49–54, October 2015. https://doi.org/10.1109/CSMA.2015.17. ISSN: null

28. Xue, B., Zhang, M., Browne, W.: Particle swarm optimization for feature selection in classification: a multi-objective approach. IEEE Trans. Cybern. **43**, 1656–1671 (2013). https://doi.org/10.1109/TSMCB.2012.2227469

29. Zheng, H.T., et al.: Learning-based topic detection using multiple features. Concurr. Comput. Pract. Exp. **30**(15), e4444 (2018). https://doi.org/10.1002/cpe.4444. wOS:000438339700001

30. Zheng, Z., Wu, X., Srihari, R.: Feature selection for text categorization on imbalanced data. ACM SIGKDD Explor. Newsl. **6**(1), 80–89 (2004). https://doi.org/10.1145/1007730.1007741

Scene Text Recognition: An Overview

Shiqi Liang[1] , Ning Bi[1,2] , and Jun Tan[1,2(✉)]

[1] School of Mathematics and Computational Science, Sun Yat-Senen University,
Guangzhou 510275, People's Republic of China
`liangshq7@mail2.sysu.edu.cn`, `{mcsbn,mcstj}@mail.sysu.edu.cn`
[2] Guangdong Province Key Laboratory of Computational Science, Sun Yat-Senen University,
Guangzhou 510275, People's Republic of China

Abstract. Recent years have witnessed increasing interest in recognizing text in natural scenes in both academia and industry due to the rich semantic information carried by text. With the rapid development of deep learning technology, text recognition in natural scene, also known as scene text recognition (STR), has also made breakthrough progress. However, noise interference in natural scene such as extreme illumination and occlusion, as well as other factors, lead huge challenges to it. Recent research has shown promising in terms of accuracy and efficiency. In order to present the entire picture of the field of STR, this paper try to: 1) summarize the fundamental problems of STR and the progress of representative STR algorithms in recent years; 2) analyze and compare the advantages and disadvantages of them; 3) point out directions for future work to inspire future research.

Keywords: Deep learning · Scene text recognition · Scene text detection

1 Introduction

Scene text is one of the most general visual objects in natural scenes. The rich text information in natural scenes is very useful for vision-based applications such as industrial automation and image-based geo-location. Therefore, text recognition in natural scene, also known as scene text recognition (STR), has become an active research field in computer vision and natural language processing.

Generally, there are two tasks in STR: text detection and text recognition. The former is aimed at finding the text region in the image as accurately as possible, while the latter is aimed to identify the characters and get the final text sequence based on text detection. However, detecting and recognizing text in natural scenes is a very difficult task. The challenges can be roughly divided into three parts: 1) Compared with the text in the document image, the color, the orientation, and the size of the scene text show more diversity. 2) The background of the natural scene may be very complicated, and the texture on the background is difficult to distinguish from the real text, leading to confusion and errors. 3) There are various interference factors in the natural scene, such as noise, distortion and unbalanced illumination, etc., all of which increase the difficulty

© Springer Nature Switzerland AG 2022
M. El Yacoubi et al. (Eds.): ICPRAI 2022, LNCS 13363, pp. 323–334, 2022.
https://doi.org/10.1007/978-3-031-09037-0_27

of scene text detection and recognition. Figure 1 shows some failure examples in [1], which illustrate the complexity of scene text detection.

To address these challenges, a large amount of approaches have been proposed and promising progress has been made in recent years. These approaches can be roughly divided into two-step approaches and end-to-end approaches, the architecture of which is shown in Fig. 2. As shown in Fig. 2, two-step approaches complete text detection and recognition separately, while end-to-end approaches simultaneously optimize the two modules which share the same feature map.

Fig. 1. Some failure examples in [1]. Green bounding boxes: correct detections; Red solid boxes: false detections; Red dashed boxes: missed ground truths. (Color figure online)

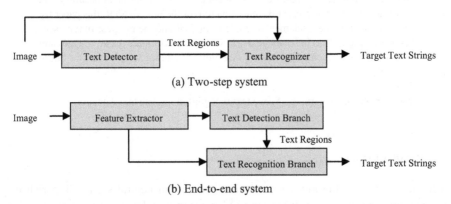

Fig. 2. Illustration of two-step system and end-to-end system.

The major contributions of this paper are as follows:

1) We summarize the existing representative research of scene text detection based on regression and segmentation respectively, scene text recognition based on Connectionist Temporal Classification (CTC) and attention mechanism respectively, as well as end-to end scene text recognition, also known as scene text spotting.
2) We compare the advantages and disadvantages of each algorithm;
3) We predict the trend of scene text recognition development and point out the direction of future work.

2   Scene Text Detection Based on Deep Learning

Compared to general objects, text tends to have large aspect ratios, so the axis-aligned rectangular box in general object detection methods is not suitable for text detection. In addition, text has rich global and local semantic information while objects only have visual information. Therefore, researchers have improved the traditional object detection model based on the characteristics of text detection, and proposed many excellent text detection models.

Different from traditional sliding window-based methods and connected component-based methods, text detection methods based on deep learning make use of higher-level semantic features with more training data, resulting to a more robust model. Generally, they can be roughly classified into regression-based methods, segmentation-based methods and hybrid-based methods combining the previous two methods.

2.1   Regression-Based Scene Text Detection

Faster R-CNN-Based Methods. Tian et al. [2] proposed a vertical anchor-based method, Connectionist Text Proposal Network (CTPN). Different from the region proposal in Faster R-CNN, CTPN detects a text line in a sequence of fine-scale text proposals, and in order to improve the robustness, it adds a Bidirectional Long Short-Term Memory (BLSTM) to capture the context information. However, CTPN shows bad performance in arbitrary-oriented text detection. Therefore, Ma et al. [3] designed a Rotation Region Proposal Networks (RRPN) that generated multi-directional proposals and a Rotation Region-of-Interest (RRoI) pooling for feature projection.

SSD-Based Methods. Liao et al. [4] proposed TextBoxes, adding a text-box layer with irregular 1 * 5 convolutional filters. TextBoxes++ [1] improved TextBoxes by predicting oriented text represented by quadrilaterals or oriented rectangles rather than default boxes. For elongated default boxes in TextBoxes which are sparse vertically, TextBoxes++ also proposed to densify default boxes with vertical offsets.

Shi et al. [5] proposed a bottom-up Segment Linking (SegLink), where improved SSD was used to detect the boundary of segments and the links between segments, after which segments belonging to the same text line are merged together according to the scores of links. ReLaText [6] improved SegLink by using contextual information to modify the predicted wrong links by Graph Convolutional Network (GCN).

YOLO-Based Methods. YOLOv4-based R-YOLO [7] added a 4th scale detection branch into the architecture of YOLO v4 to extract shallow features and fuse them with deep features. YOLO v3-based MDA [8] proposed a new nine-parameter sliding vertex box definition method to better adapt to multi-directional text detection and a corresponding position bounding box loss function MD-CLoss.

2.2   Segmentation-Based Scene Text Detection

Compared with regression-based methods, segmentation-based methods show superior performance and advantages of detecting arbitrary-shape text. Recent years have witnessed attempts to improve the performance of segmentation-based scene text detection methods under the following two conditions:

Irregular and Multi-oriented Text Instances. To improve the detection performance of irregular text, Long et al. [9] proposed TextSnake, where the representation for text instances are a series of ordered overlapping disks, each of which have learnable radius and positions. Xie et al. [10] proposed Supervised Pyramid Context Network which produced text segmentation using contextual feature, enhancing instance segmentation performance of the following Mask R-CNN [11] branch.

Dense Text Instances. Compared to semantic segmentation-based methods, instance segmentation-based methods show better performance when it comes to dense text detection. Wang et al. [12] proposed Progressive Scale Expansion Network (PSENet) based on instance segmentation, where segmentation with different kernel scales are produced. The prediction can be carried out by gradually expanding kernel from minimal scale to maximal one. However, PSENet is inefficient since it has a complex structure with cumbersome post-processing. To tackle this issue, Wang et al. [13] proposed Pixel Aggregation algorithm (PA), clustering pixels with high similarity which were learned from the semantic feature. Similar to PA, Tian et al. [14] proposed Learning Shape-aware Embedding (LSAE), which projects pixels into the embedded space to make pixels belonging to the same instance closer and vise versa.

Xu et al. [15] argued that relative position of pixels in the corresponding text is useful for separating adjacent text instances and detecting multi-oriented text instances. Therefore, they proposed text direction field, which points away from the nearest text bounder to each text point. Similarly, Zhu et al. [16] proposed TextMountain, based on the idea that text center-border probability (TCBP) is just like a mountain whose top is text center and foot is text border. TextMountain separates dense text instances by searching a road to mountaintop for each pixel from the mountain foot. However, post-processing of traditional segmentation-based text detection method requires manual setting of binarization threshold. To simplify the post-processing, Liao et al. [17] proposed a Differentiable Binarization Network (DBNet), which adaptively learns robust binarization thresholds for each pixel point.

2.3   Hybrid-Based Scene Text Detection

Efficient and Accurate Scene Text Detector (EAST) [18] proposed in 2017 is well-known model with simple structure that only contained two stages: generating the text regions from Full Convolutional Network (FCN) and filtering them by locality-aware Non-Maximum Suppression (NMS). However, due to its small receptive field, it cannot perform well when it comes to sheared scene text detection and long text detection. To tackle the first issue, Ghosh et al. [19] proposed a lightweight M-EAST with a rotation and shearing module. For the second issue, Zhang et al. [20] proposed a scene text detector LOMO with an Iterative Refinement Module, which learns the coordinate offsets of each corner of the predicted box iteratively by corner attention mechanism and perceives the entire long text progressively. However, the iteration process of LOMO is tedious. Therefore, He et al. [21] proposed a Multi-Oriented Scene Text Detector with Localization Refinement (MOST), adopting Deformable Convolutional Network to dynamically adjust the receptive fields of feature. It solves the problem of imprecise geometry prediction of long text instances in EAST and LOMO.

Table 1 shows the performance comparison of some algorithms mentioned above.

Table 1. Performance comparison of detection algorithms on benchmark datasets including Total-Text dataset, CTW1500 dataset and ICDAR 2015 dataset. 'P', 'R', 'F' indicate precision, recall and F-measure respectively. The **bold** represents the best results.

Methods	Total-text			CTW1500			ICDAR 2015		
	P	R	F	P	R	F	P	R	F
CTPN [2]	48.0	38.0	42.0	60.4	53.8	56.9	74.2	51.6	60.9
SegLink [5]	30.3	23.8	26.7	42.3	40.0	40.8	76.8	73.1	75.0
EAST [18]	50.0	36.2	42.0	78.7	49.2	60.4	83.6	73.5	78.2
TextSnake [9]	82.7	74.5	78.4	67.9	**85.3**	75.6	84.9	80.4	82.6
PSENet [12]	84.0	78.0	80.9	84.5	79.7	82.2	**96.9**	**84.5**	85.7
TextField [15]	81.2	79.9	80.6	83.0	79.8	81.4	84.3	83.9	84.1
LOMO [20]	**87.6**	79.3	83.3	**89.2**	69.6	78.4	91.3	83.5	87.2
DBNet [17]	87.1	**82.5**	**84.7**	86.9	80.2	**83.4**	91.8	83.2	**87.3**

3   Scene Text Recognition Based on Deep Learning

After being detected and extracted from the image, scene text needs to be identified to obtain the final text sequence in recognition module. Through the efforts of researchers, there have been many text recognition models based on deep learning, which can be generally divided into CTC-based methods, attention-based methods and hybrid-based methods combining both CTC and attention mechanism.

3.1   CTC-Based Scene Text Recognition

CTC converts the features from CNN or RNN into string sequences by maximizing the cumulative conditional probability of all input-output matching sequences. It effectively handles sequences in arbitrary lengths, involving no character segmentation or prior alignment between the input and target sequences.

Shi et al. [22] first applied CTC to STR and proposed Convolutional Recurrent Neural Network (CRNN), which consists of the convolutional layers for feature extraction, the recurrent layers for per-frame predictions of the feature sequence, and a transcription layer for translating the per-frame predictions into a label sequence. To weaken the signal that comes from unrelated context, Wang et al. [23] improved CRNN by adding a gate to the recurrent layer of CRNN, which balances the feed-forward information and the recurrent information. In addition, since CRNN cannot recognize text with considerable distortions accurately, Liu et al. [24] proposed SpaTial Attention Residue Network (STAR-Net), which employs a spatial transformer to remove the distortions of text in natural images and obtain the rectified text region.

Although CTC enjoys remarkable transcription performance and stability, it tends to produce highly peaky and overconfident distributions, which may lead to local optimal solution. Therefore, Liu et al. [25] proposed a regularization for CTC (EnCTC) based on maximum conditional entropy, in order to enhance the exploration for CTC training. In addition, most CTC-based models are based on RNN, which are are time-consuming without parallel calculation and may suffer from gradient disappearance and gradient explosion in the training process. To handle these problems, Yin et al. [26] proposed an implicit segmentation-based model without RNN, comprising a sliding window layer to extract local features, a classification layer to predict label distributions from the input window image, and a CTC-based transcription layer. Gao et al. [27] modified the traditional CRNN by adopting the stacked convolutional layers instead of RNN to capture the contextual dependencies of input sequence, leading to lower computational complexity.

3.2 Attention-Based Scene Text Recognition

Most mainstream STR models are based on encoder-decoder framework. Traditional methods only take the ultimate output of encoder as the decoder's input, thus resulting to poor performance for long text recognition. Thanks to attention mechanism, decoder can make good use of the encoder's hidden states and the historical characters output, which helps to learn the alignment between the input and output. For STR, the attention mechanism is often combined with the RNN structure as a prediction module. In recent years, attempts have been made to improve the attention-based STR from different perspectives and Table 2 gives a comprehensive list and categorization of these attention-based scene text recognition methods.

Building Model More Robust to Irregular Text. Aimed for recognition of irregular scene text, Shi et al. [28] proposed Robust text recognizer with Automatic REctification (RARE), based on which Shi et al. [29] reduced the number of model's parameters and speed up the convergence during training. Other approaches [30, 31] also successfully built models more robust to arbitrary-shaped text.

Addressing Attention Drift. The attention drift phenomenon, common for images with low-quality, means that the attention model cannot accurately associate each feature vector with the corresponding target region in the input image. Various approaches [32–34] have been proposed to address this issue.

Improving Language Model. Fang et al. [37] argued that the limitation of language models comes from unidirectional feature representation, implicit language model and noise input, so they correspondingly proposed a model to alleviate this three problems. Compared to SRN [39] which is non-differentiable, Bhunia et al. [38] proposed a differentiable attention-based decoder with a Gumbel-Softmax operator.

Hybrid-based Scene Text Recognition. Compared with attention-based methods, CTC decoder has a much shorter inference time, yet a lower accuracy. Therefore, recent approaches combine CTC with attention mechanism to obtain efficient and effective models.

Litman et al. [40] employed CTC-based decoding to refine visual features extracted from CNN and a two-step 1D attention mechanism to refine contextual features extracted from each BLSTM. Hu et al. [41] proposed a model named guided training of CTC (GTC), where the STN and the feature extractor are first trained by cross-entropy loss of the attention branch and the decoder is trained by the CTC loss of the CTC branch. In order to further improve the accuracy, GCN was added to CTC branch to learn the local correlations of extracted features.

Table 2. Summary of some attention-based scene text recognition approaches. "1", "2" and "3" indicate building model more robust to irregular text, addressing attention drift and improving language model respectively.

Method	Challenge	Solutions
Shi et al. [28]	1	Using Spatial Transformer Network(STN) with Thin Plate-Spline (TPS) for automatic rectification
Shi et al. [29]	1	Improving [28] by: Using images of different down-sampled size in localization network; Dropping the non-linear activation function
Luo et al. [30]	1	Using the predicted offset of each pixel for rectification
Lin et al. [31]	1	Applying STN on divided image patches instead of the whole image
Cheng et al. [32]	2	Using proposed Focusing Network with focusing-mechanism to rectify the drifted attention
Lu et al. [33]	2	Using proposed Multi-Aspect Global Context Attention based encoder to different aspects of spatial 2D attention
Wang et al. [34]	2	Decoupling the alignment operation in attention module from historical decoding results
Yan et al. [35]	2	Applying GCNs [36] to use the global visual information
Fang et al. [37]	3	Using proposed bidirectional cloze network and an execution manner of iterative correction for language model; Blocking gradient flow between vision and language model
Bhunia et al. [38]	3	Combining visual and semantic information by a differentiable multi-stage multi-scale attention decoder

4   End-to-End Scene Text Spotting

The advantage of the two-stage scene text recognition method is that we can pick and combine suitable detection and recognition algorithms for different tasks. However, its disadvantages are also obvious: 1) these two modules cannot share the parameters of convolution layers, which reduce the robustness of the model; 2) the model is complex and inefficient since it needs two independent forward-backward propagations; 3) the recognition performance highly relies on the accuracy of detected text proposals. Recent years have witnessed a great amount of research on end-to-end scene text spotting, which optimize the detection and recognition modules jointly to improve the accuracy and efficiency, summarized in Table 3.

Those existing end-to-end methods are aimed to solve the following problems:

Arbitrary-Shaped Text and Occluded Text. Inspired by Mask R-CNN, Mask Textpotter [42] was designed with a mask branch, comprising an instance-segmentation based detector and a character-segmentation based recognizer, and the mask-loss is made up of the loss of these two modules. Instead of using segmentation mask, Wang et al. [46] used a set of boundary points to represent the text region by refining the predefined boundary points with the learned offsets. Liu et al. [47] introduced a parametric representation of curved scene text using Bezier curves, which is suitable for real-time applications. To deal with the problem of missing text information caused by occlusion, Mittal et al. [47] adopts Bayesian classifier for text detection and natural language processing for text predicting.

Sampling Methods for Accurate Feature Alignment. RoI Pooling and RoI Align are not suitable for RoI of text which is not axis-aligned rectangle. To address this problem, Liu et al. [43] introduced RoIRotate, adding a parameter for the orientation representation compared to RoI Align and using bilinear interpolation instead of max-pooling. However, RoIRotate shows bad performance for curved text feature alignment. RoISlide was proposed in TextDragon [44] with a Local Transformer Network (LTN). It transformed feature of each quadrangle, the output of detection branch, into axis-aligned feature in a sliding manner. BezierAlign was proposed in [48] as an extension of RoIAlign, where each column of the oriented or curved grid is orthogonal to the Bezier curve boundary of the text.

Limitations of Character-Level Segmentation. There are three limitations of character-level segmentation: 1) character-level annotations are too expensive to afford; 2) complex post-processing is required to integrate characters into complete text; 3) character sequence cannot be obtained from the character segmentation graph. To mitigate the above-mentioned issues, Mask Textpotter v2 [45], integrated a Spatial Attention Module (SAM) in the recognizer, which can globally predict the label sequence of each word with a spatial attention mechanism, using only word-level annotations for training. Inspired by TextSnake [9], Feng et al. [44] proposed TextDragon, where the shape of text is described by a serious of quadrangles rather than disks. Wang et al. [49] proposed Point Gathering CTC (PG-CTC) loss to learn the pixel-level character classification map, which alleviates the expensive cost of obtaining character-level annotations and gets free from non-negligible computational overhead of NMS and RoI operations such as RoISlide and BezierAlign.

Limitations of Predefined Text Reading Direction. TextDragon [44] and Mask Textpotter [42] make a strong assumption that the reading direction of text regions is either from left to right or from up to down, which precludes correct recognition of more challenging text. In order to handle this problem, Wang et al. [49] proposed fully convolutional Point Gathering Network (PGNet), where a FCN was used to learn the text center line (TCL), text border offset (TBO), text direction offset (TDO), and text character classification map (TCC) of text regions simultaneously, with which to restore the reading order of characters in each text instance.

Table 3. Summary of some scene text spotting approaches. "word" and "character" represent word-level and character-level annotations, respectively. "Quad", "Quad-Pixel", "Kernel" and "Bezier" are different text representations shown in Fig. 3.

Method	Year	Annotation	Detection	Recognition	Result
Lyu et al. [42]	2018	Char	Quad-Pixel	Attention	Arbitrary-shaped
Liu et al. [43]	2018	Word	Quad	CTC	Multi-oriented
Feng et al. [44]	2019	Word	Quad-Pixel	CTC	Arbitrary-shaped
Liao et al. [45]	2019	Char	Quad-Pixel	Attention	Arbitrary-shaped
Wang et al. [46]	2020	Word	Quad	Attention	Arbitrary-shaped
Liu et al. [48]	2020	Word	Bezier	CTC	Arbitrary-shaped
Wang et al. [49]	2021	Word	Kernel	CTC	Arbitrary-shaped

(a) Quad   (b) Quad-Pixel   (c) Kernel   (d) Bezier

Fig. 3. Comparisons of different scene text representations [48, 50].

5   Future Direction

Although scene text recognition has made great progress in terms of accuracy and efficiency in recent years, there is ample room remaining for future research: 1) Generalization ability. Although the present scene text recognition models show great performance on synthetic datasets, diversity and complexity of text in natural scenes require more robust models to adapt to complex real text instances. 2) End-to-end architecture. Compared with the end-to-end models for document text recognition, end-to-end scene text recognition models' performance still needs to be improved in terms of both efficiency and accuracy. 3) Multi-language scenes. The demand for multi-language text recognition technology is increasing day by day. Therefore, building models that can be applied to multi-language scenes is still a very meaningful research direction at present and in the future. 4) Semantics information of text. How to make good use of semantic information is the key to further improving the recognition accuracy. We see a trend that more and more researchers devote themselves to exploiting models using both visual information and semantic information.

Acknowledgments. This work was supported by Guangdong Province Key Laboratory of Computational Science at the Sun Yat-sen University (2020B1212060032), the National Natural Science Foundation of China (Grant no. 11971491, 11471012).

References

1. Liao, M., Shi, B., Bai, X.: Textboxes++: a single-shot oriented scene text detector. IEEE Trans. Image Process. **27**(8), 3676–3690 (2018)
2. Tian, Z., Huang, W., He, T., He, P., Qiao, Y.: Detecting text in natural image with connectionist text proposal network. In: Leibe, B., Matas, J., Sebe, N., Welling, M. (eds.) ECCV 2016. LNCS, vol. 9912, pp. 56–72. Springer, Cham (2016). https://doi.org/10.1007/978-3-319-464 84-8_4
3. Ma, J., et al.: Arbitrary-oriented scene text detection via rotation proposals. IEEE Trans. Multimedia **20**(11), 3111–3122 (2018)
4. Liao, M., Shi, B., Bai, X., Wang, X., Liu, W.: Textboxes: a fast text detector with a single deep neural network. In: Thirty-first AAAI Conference on Artificial Intelligence (2017)
5. Shi, B., Bai, X., Belongie, S.: Detecting oriented text in natural images by linking segments. In: Proceedings of the IEEE Conference on Computer Vision and Pattern Recognition, pp. 2550–2558 (2017)
6. Ma, C., Sun, L., Zhong, Z., Huo, Q.: ReLaText: exploiting visual relationships for arbitrary-shaped scene text detection with graph convolutional networks. Pattern Recogn. **111**, 107684 (2021)
7. Wang, X., Zheng, S., Zhang, C., Li, R., Gui, L.: R-YOLO: a real-time text detector for natural scenes with arbitrary rotation. Sensors **21**(3), 888 (2021)
8. Xiao, L., Zhou, P., Xu, K., Zhao, X.: Multi-directional scene text detection based on improved YOLOv3. Sensors **21**(14), 4870 (2021)
9. Long, S., et al.: TextSnake: a flexible representation for detecting text of arbitrary shapes. In: Ferrari, V., Hebert, M., Sminchisescu, C., Weiss, Y. (eds.) ECCV 2018. LNCS, vol. 11206, pp. 19–35. Springer, Cham (2018). https://doi.org/10.1007/978-3-030-01216-8_2
10. Xie, E., et al.: Scene text detection with supervised pyramid context network. In: Proceedings of the AAAI Conference on Artificial Intelligence, vol. 33, no. 01, pp. 9038–9045 (2019)
11. He, K., Gkioxari, G., Dollár, P., Girshick, R.: Mask R-CNN. In: Proceedings of the IEEE International Conference on Computer Vision, pp. 2961–2969 (2017)
12. Wang, W., et al.: Shape robust text detection with progressive scale expansion network. In: Proceedings of the IEEE/CVF Conference on Computer Vision and Pattern Recognition, pp. 9336–9345 (2019)
13. Wang, W., et al.: Efficient and accurate arbitrary-shaped text detection with pixel aggregation network. In: Proceedings of the IEEE/CVF International Conference on Computer Vision, pp. 8440–8449 (2019)
14. Tian, Z., et al.: Learning shape-aware embedding for scene text detection. In: Proceedings of the IEEE/CVF Conference on Computer Vision and Pattern Recognition, pp. 4234–4243 (2019)
15. Xu, Y., Wang, Y., Zhou, W., Wang, Y., Yang, Z., Bai, X.: TextField: learning a deep direction field for irregular scene text detection. IEEE Trans. Image Process. **28**(11), 5566–5579 (2019)

16. Zhu, Y., Du, J.: Textmountain: accurate scene text detection via instance segmentation. Pattern Recogn. **110**, 107336 (2021)
17. Liao, M., Wan, Z., Yao, C., Chen, K., Bai, X.: Real-time scene text detection with differentiable binarization. In: Proceedings of the AAAI Conference on Artificial Intelligence, vol. 34, no. 07, pp. 11474–11481 (2020)
18. Zhou, X., et al.: East: an efficient and accurate scene text detector. In: Proceedings of the IEEE conference on Computer Vision and Pattern Recognition, pp. 5551–5560 (2017)
19. Ghosh, M., et al.: Movie title extraction and script separation using shallow convolution neural network. IEEE Access **9**, 125184–125201 (2021)
20. Zhang, C., et al.: Look more than once: an accurate detector for text of arbitrary shapes. In: Proceedings of the IEEE/CVF Conference on Computer Vision and Pattern Recognition, pp. 10552–10561 (2019)
21. He, M., et al.: MOST: a multi-oriented scene text detector with localization refinement. In: Proceedings of the IEEE/CVF Conference on Computer Vision and Pattern Recognition, pp. 8813–8822 (2021)
22. Shi, B., Bai, X., Yao, C.: An end-to-end trainable neural network for image-based sequence recognition and its application to scene text recognition. IEEE Trans. Pattern Anal. Mach. Intell. **39**(11), 2298–2304 (2016)
23. Wang, J., Hu, X.: Gated recurrent convolution neural network for OCR. In: Proceedings of the 31st International Conference on Neural Information Processing Systems, pp. 334–343 (2017)
24. Liu, W., Chen, C., Wong, K.Y.K., Su, Z., Han, J.: STAR-Net: a spatial attention residue network for scene text recognition. In: BMVC, vol. 2, p. 7 (2016)
25. Liu, H., Jin, S., Zhang, C.: Connectionist temporal classification with maximum entropy regularization. Adv. Neural. Inf. Process. Syst. **31**, 831–841 (2018)
26. Yin, F., Wu, Y.C., Zhang, X.Y., Liu, C.L.: Scene text recognition with sliding convolutional character models. arXiv preprint arXiv:1709.01727(2017)
27. Gao, Y., Chen, Y., Wang, J., Tang, M., Lu, H.: Reading scene text with fully convolutional sequence modeling. Neurocomputing **339**, 161–170 (2019)
28. Shi, B., Wang, X., Lyu, P., Yao, C., Bai, X.: Robust scene text recognition with automatic rectification. In: Proceedings of the IEEE Conference on Computer Vision and Pattern Recognition, pp. 4168–4176 (2016)
29. Shi, B., et al.: ASTER: an attentional scene text recognizer with flexible rectification. IEEE Trans. Pattern Anal. Mach. Intell. **41**(9), 2035–2048 (2018)
30. Luo, C., Jin, L., Sun, Z.: MORAN: a multi-object rectified attention network for scene text recognition. Pattern Recognt. **90**, 109–118 (2019)
31. Lin, Q., Luo, C., Jin, L., Lai, S.: STAN: a sequential transformation attention-based network for scene text recognition. Pattern Recognt. **111**, 107692 (2021)
32. Cheng, Z., et al.: Focusing attention: towards accurate text recognition in natural images. In: Proceedings of the IEEE International Conference on Computer Vision, pp. 5076–5084 (2017)
33. Lu, N., et al.: MASTER: multi-aspect non-local network for scene text recognition. Pattern Recognt. **117**, 107980 (2021)
34. Wang, T., et al.: Decoupled attention network for text recognition. In: Proceedings of the AAAI Conference on Artificial Intelligence, vol. 34, no. 07, pp. 12216–12224 (2020)
35. Yan, R., Peng, L., Xiao, S., Yao, G.: Primitive representation learning for scene text recognition. In: Proceedings of the IEEE/CVF Conference on Computer Vision and Pattern Recognition, pp. 284–293 (2021)
36. Chen, Y., et al.: Graph-based global reasoning networks. In: Proceedings of the IEEE/CVF Conference on Computer Vision and Pattern Recognition, pp. 433–442 (2019)

37. Fang, S., Xie, H., Wang, Y., Mao, Z., Zhang, Y.: Read like humans: autonomous, bidirectional and iterative language modeling for scene text recognition. In: Proceedings of the IEEE/CVF Conference on Computer Vision and Pattern Recognition, pp. 7098–7107 (2021)

38. Bhunia, A. K., et al.: Joint visual semantic reasoning: Multi-stage decoder for text recognition. In: Proceedings of the IEEE/CVF International Conference on Computer Vision, pp. 14940–14949 (2021)

39. Yu, D., et al.: Towards accurate scene text recognition with semantic reasoning networks. In: Proceedings of the IEEE/CVF Conference on Computer Vision and Pattern Recognition, pp. 12113–12122 (2020)

40. Litman, R., et al.: SCATTER: selective context attentional scene text recognizer. In: Proceedings of the IEEE/CVF Conference on Computer Vision and Pattern Recognition, pp. 11962–11972 (2020)

41. Hu, W., Cai, X., Hou, J., Yi, S., Lin, Z.: GTC: guided training of CTC towards efficient and accurate scene text recognition. In: Proceedings of the AAAI Conference on Artificial Intelligence, vol. 34, no. 07, pp. 11005–11012 (2020)

42. Lyu, P., Liao, M., Yao, C., Wu, W., Bai, X.: Mask TextSpotter: an end-to-end trainable neural network for spotting text with arbitrary shapes. In: Ferrari, V., Hebert, M., Sminchisescu, C., Weiss, Y. (eds) ECCV 2018. LNCS, vol. 11218, pp. 67–83. Springer, Cham (2018). https://doi.org/10.1007/978-3-030-01264-9_5

43. Liu, X., et al.: FOTS: fast oriented text spotting with a unified network. In: Proceedings of the IEEE Conference on Computer Vision and Pattern Recognition, pp. 5676–5685 (2018)

44. Feng, W., He, W., Yin, F., Zhang, X.Y., Liu, C.L.: TextDragon: an end-to-end framework for arbitrary shaped text spotting. In: Proceedings of the IEEE/CVF International Conference on Computer Vision, pp. 9076–9085 (2019)

45. Liao, M., et al.: Mask TextSpotter: an end-to-end trainable neural network for spotting text with arbitrary shapes. IEEE Trans. Pattern Anal. Mach. Intell. (2019)

46. Wang, H., et al.: All you need is boundary: toward arbitrary-shaped text spotting. In: Proceedings of the AAAI Conference on Artificial Intelligence, vol. 34, no. 07, pp. 12160–12167 (2020)

47. Mittal, A., Shivakumara, P., Pal, U., Lu, T., Blumenstein, M.: A new method for detection and prediction of occluded text in natural scene images. Signal Process. Image Commun. **100**, 116512 (2022)

48. Liu, Y., et al.: ABCNet: real-time scene text spotting with adaptive Bezier-curve network. In: Proceedings of the IEEE/CVF Conference on Computer Vision and Pattern Recognition, pp. 9809–9818 (2020)

49. Wang, P., et al.: PGNet: real-time arbitrarily-shaped text spotting with point gathering network. arXiv preprint arXiv:2104.05458(2021)

50. Wang, W., et al.: PAN++: towards efficient and accurate end-to-end spotting of arbitrarily-shaped text. IEEE Trans. Pattern Anal. Machi. Intell. (2021)

An Encoder-Decoder Approach to Offline Handwritten Mathematical Expression Recognition with Residual Attention

Qiqiang Lin[1] [ID], Chunyi Wang[1] [ID], Ning Bi[1,2] [ID], Ching Y. Suen[3] [ID],
and Jun Tan[1,2(✉)] [ID]

[1] School of Mathematics, Sun Yat-Sen University, Guangzhou 510275,
People's Republic of China
{linqq9,wangchy53}@mail2.sysu.edu.cn, {mcsbn,
mcstj}@mail.sysu.edu.cn
[2] Guangdong Province Key Laboratory of Computational Science, Sun Yat-Sen University,
Guangzhou 510275, People's Republic of China
[3] Centre for Pattern Recognition and Machine Intelligence, Concordia University, Montreal,
QC H3G 1M8, Canada
suen@encs.concordia.ca

Abstract. Unlike handwritten numeral recognition and handwritten text recognition, the recognition of handwritten mathematical expressions is more difficult because of their complex two-dimensional spatial structure. Since the "watch, attend and parse (WAP)" method was proposed in 2017, encoder-decoder models have made significant progress on handwritten mathematical expression recognition. Our model is improved based on the WAP [1] model. In this paper, the attention module is reasonably added to the encoder to make the extracted features are more informative. The new network is called Dense Attention Network (DATNet), which allows for an adequate extraction of the structural information from handwritten mathematical expressions. To prevent the model from overfitting during the training process, we use label smoothing [2] as the loss. Experiments showed that our model (DATWAP) improved WAP expression recognition from 48.4%/46.8%/45.1% to 54.72%/52.83%/52.54% on the CROHME 2014/2016/2019 test sets.

Keywords: Handwritten · Encoder-decoder · Attention

1 Introduction

1.1 Handwritten Mathematical Expression Recognition

There are currently two main types of handwritten mathematical expression recognition systems, the online recognition system and the offline recognition system. The main difference between these two systems is in the input data. This paper focuses on the offline recognition system.

© Springer Nature Switzerland AG 2022
M. El Yacoubi et al. (Eds.): ICPRAI 2022, LNCS 13363, pp. 335–345, 2022.
https://doi.org/10.1007/978-3-031-09037-0_28

Handwritten mathematical expression recognition (HMER) is more complicated than recognizing one-dimensional handwriting (handwritten numbers, hand-written text). Because one-dimensional handwriting often has the same symbol size and the symbols are clearly spaced apart, symbol segmentation and recognition is easier. Mathematical expressions, on the other hand, are two-dimensional structures made up of mathematical symbols. To recognize mathematical expressions correctly, not only do the mathematical symbols contained within them need to be recognized accurately, but also the two-dimensional relationships between the symbols need to be resolved accurately, any tiny errors in these two processes will lead to a failure.

Zhang et al. [1] first proposed an end-to-end offline recognition method, referred to as the WAP model. The WAP model uses a full convolutional network (FCN) as the encoder and a gated recurrent unit (GRU) as the decoder and applies a time-space hybrid attention mechanism in the decoding process to convert mathematical expression images directly into latex command sequences. Later, Zhang et al. improved the WAP model [3] by using a tightly connected convolutional network on the encoder, while proposing a multi-scale attention model to solve the recognition problem of mathematical symbols, and the results were well improved. In addition to the encoder-decoder method above, there are some other methods. For example, in order to improve the robustness of the model, Wu et al. [4] proposed a method based on adversarial learning, which also achieved good results.

The current mainstream models are built on an encoder-decoder framework, such as replacing the encoder with a transformer, which has recently become popular in natural language processing [5] or using a multi-headed attention mechanism in the decoder instead of the traditional spatial attention mechanism [6], or building models based on sequences of relations [7], all of which are based on improving the decoder or the form of the output sequence.

1.2 Our Main Work

The encoder is the start of the encoder-decoder framework and if it is poor then it is difficult to get good results even if the decoder is nice. Therefore, we keep the decoder of the WAP model unchanged and investigate how to improve the encoder to make the extracted features more informative. Firstly, we innovatively add residual attention modules at reasonable locations in the encoder, which greatly improves the performance of the encoder and hence the recognition accuracy. We also use the label smoothing method to change the original one-hot label into a soft label to assist the training, which enhances the generalization and calibration ability of the model. Finally, we conduct ablation experiments to compare the performance of different types and numbers of non-local attention modules in the handwritten expression recognition model. Our best model improved the accuracy by 6.32%/6.03%/7.44% over the original model (WAP) on the CROHME2014/2016/2019 test sets.

2   Related Studies

There are currently two HMER methods, the grammar-based recognition method and the end-to-end deep learning method. In this section, we will focus on the end-to-end deep learning method and related attention modules.

2.1   HMER Method

The mainstream deep learning framework is the encoder-decoder framework. The most typical model is the WAP model. In recent years, many models have been enhanced mainly by optimizing the decoder or the output sequence.

Improved WAP. Improved WAP uses DenseNet as an encoder to extract features, and two layers of unidirectional GRU network in the decoder to decode them, with attention modules added to boost decoding. The decoder in this paper is the same as WAP.

2.2   Attention

Convolutional neural networks have certain limitations. The reason is that when we use convolution, the size of the convolution kernel is fixed, which leads to the lack of global information in the extracted features. Therefore, we add attention modules to the DenseNet as an encoder to achieve sufficient extraction of structural information from handwritten mathematical expressions. In this paper, two types of attention modules are considered: criss-cross attention [9] and coordinate attention [10]. The following section will explain these two attention models.

Criss-Cross Attention. For feature vectors, the general non-local attention module calculates the interrelationship between the target pixel and all other points in the feature map, and uses this interrelationship to weight the features of the target pixel to obtain a more efficient target feature.

In contrast, the criss-cross attention module only calculates the relationship between the target pixel and the pixel in the row and column in which it is located. A global contextual feature vector can be obtained after two identical criss-cross attention modules, which have a smaller number of parameters and are less computationally intensive than the usual non-local attention modules, but yield more effective contextual information, maintaining long-range spatial dependence.

Coordinate Attention. Coordinate attention is an improved version of channel attention Senet [11], in which global pooling is typically used to globally encode spatial information, but it compresses global spatial information into channel descriptors, making it difficult to retain positional information, which is crucial for capturing spatial structure in visual tasks. To encourage the attention module to capture remote interactions spatially with precise location information, coordinate attention decomposes global pooling into X-directional averaged pooling and Y-directional averaged pooling, and finally fuses them to obtain global attention.

3   Methodology

This paper is based on a multi-scale attention mechanism coding and decoding network for the recognition of offline handwritten mathematical expressions, starting with the encoding of the expressions using DenseNet and adding residual attention modules at appropriate locations.

3.1   DenseNet Encoder

In the encoder section, DenseNet is used as a feature extractor for HME images, as DenseNet has a densely connected structure that allows for significant compression of the parameters that need to be trained, thus greatly reducing the complexity of model training and the time required. The subsequent experimental part of this paper uses the DenseNet structure to encode expressions, producing better model results by adding residual attention modules to DenseNet.

3.2   Residual Attention Modules

A limitation of CNN networks is the lack of global information in the extracted features. In this paper, we refer to the residual attention network [12] to construct simple residual attention modules suitable for DenseNet (Fig. 1).

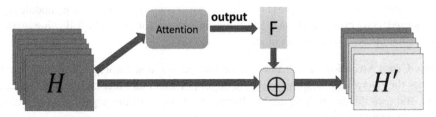

Fig. 1. Diagram of the residual attention network

For a feature map $H \in R^{C \times W \times H}$, an attention feature map $F \in R^{C \times W \times H}$ is obtained after the attention module.

$$F = Attention(H) \tag{1}$$

Similar to ResNet, the attention feature map F is directly added to the feature map H to obtain a new feature map H':

$$H'(c, x, y) = H(c, x, y) + F(c, x, y) \tag{2}$$

The residual attention module enables the model to retain important features without destroying the properties of the original features, and the individual feature points of the resulting new feature map contain both local and global information to facilitate the decoder.

Table 1. DenseNet architectures for WAP and DenseNet architectures with attention (DAT) for our model.

Layers	Input size	Output size	DenseNet-B	DAT Net
Convolutions	$H \times W \times 1$	$\frac{H}{2} \times \frac{W}{2} \times 48$	7×7 conv, stride 2	
Pooling	$\frac{H}{2} \times \frac{W}{2} \times 48$	$\frac{H}{4} \times \frac{W}{4} \times 48$	Max pool, stride 2	
Dense block (1)	$\frac{H}{4} \times \frac{W}{4} \times 48$	$\frac{H}{4} \times \frac{W}{4} \times 432$	$\begin{bmatrix} 1 \times 1 \ conv \\ 3 \times 3 \ conv \end{bmatrix} \times 16$	
Transition (1)	$\frac{H}{4} \times \frac{W}{4} \times 432$	$\frac{H}{4} \times \frac{W}{4} \times 216$	$1 \times 1conv$	
	$\frac{H}{4} \times \frac{W}{4} \times 216$	$\frac{H}{8} \times \frac{W}{8} \times 216$	2×2 average pool, stride 2	
Dense block (2)	$\frac{H}{8} \times \frac{W}{8} \times 216$	$\frac{H}{8} \times \frac{W}{8} \times 600$	$\begin{bmatrix} 1 \times 1 \ conv \\ 3 \times 3 \ conv \end{bmatrix} \times 16$	
Transition (2)	$\frac{H}{8} \times \frac{W}{8} \times 600$	$\frac{H}{8} \times \frac{W}{8} \times 300$	$1 \times 1conv$	
	$\frac{H}{8} \times \frac{W}{8} \times 300$	$\frac{H}{16} \times \frac{W}{16} \times 300$	2×2 average pool, stride 2	
Attention (1)	$\frac{H}{16} \times \frac{W}{16} \times 300$	$\frac{H}{16} \times \frac{W}{16} \times 300$	--	Residual attention
Dense block (3)	$\frac{H}{16} \times \frac{W}{16} \times 300$	$\frac{H}{16} \times \frac{W}{16} \times 684$	$\begin{bmatrix} 1 \times 1 \ conv \\ 3 \times 3 \ conv \end{bmatrix} \times 16$	
Attention (2)	$\frac{H}{16} \times \frac{W}{16} \times 684$	$\frac{H}{16} \times \frac{W}{16} \times 684$	--	Residual attention

3.3 DATWAP Architecture

Encoder

The design of the DAT network is relatively simple: the residual attention module is added after Transition (2) and Dense Block (3) respectively.

In this paper, the residual attention module is built using the criss-cross attention module and the coordinate attention module, respectively (Fig. 2).

Decoder. Given an input mathematical expression image, let $X \in R^{D \times H \times W}$ denote extracted DATNet feature maps, where D, H and W represent channel number, height and width, respectively. We consider these feature maps as a sequence of feature vectors $x = \{x_1, x_2, ..x_L\}$, where $x_i \in R^D$ and $L = H \times W$. Let $y = \{y_1, y_2, \ldots y_T\}$ denote the target output sequence, where y_T represents a special end-of-sentence (EOS) symbol. The decoder uses two unidirectional GRU layers and an attention with cover vector mechanism. The specific calculation formula is as follows:

$$h_t^{(0)} = GRU^{(0)}\left(y'_{t-1}, h_{t-1}^{(1)}\right) \tag{3}$$

$$c_t = f_{att}\left(h_t^{(0)}, x\right) \tag{4}$$

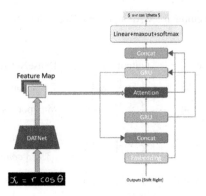

Fig. 2. Diagram of the overall architecture of DATWAP.

$$h_t^{(1)} = GRU^{(1)}\left(c_t, h_t^{(0)}\right) \tag{5}$$

Previous step's y'_{t-1}, which is a trainable embedding of y_{t-1}, and output $h_{t-1}^{(1)}$ are used as inputs in the first GRU layer to produce $h_t^{(0)} \in R^{d_{GRU}}$, which works as the query of the attention mechanism. Then, the attention with cover vector mechanism uses x as key and value to produce context $c_t \in R^{d_{out}}$. Finally, the second GRU layer uses c_t and $h_t^{(0)}$ as input and produces $h_t^{(1)} \in R^{d_{GRU}}$.

3.4 Label Smoothing

Label smoothing combines uniform distribution, replacing the traditional one-hot label vector y with a soft label vector y^{SL}:

$$y_i^{SL} = \begin{cases} 1 - \alpha, & i = target \\ \alpha/K, & i \neq target \end{cases} \tag{6}$$

where K is the number of latex characters predicted, and α is a small hyperparameter.

Deep neural networks tend to overfit during training, which can reduce their generalization ability. In addition, large datasets often contain mislabeled data, meaning that neural networks should inherently be skeptical of the 'right answer'. Using label smoothing can produce a better-calibrated network, which will generalize better and ultimately produce more accurate predictions on the test data. In particular, in seq2seq tasks where beam search is taken for decoding, training with smooth loss gives a good boost.

4   Experiments

4.1   Experimental Setup

We evaluated our method on the CROHME dataset [13–15]. The training set chosen for this paper is the CROHME2014 training set, containing a total of 8836 handwritten

InkML files of mathematical expressions, which we converted into the corresponding 8836 offline images as the training set. The CROHME2014 test set with 986 images was chosen as the validation set. The CROHME2016 test set containing 1147 images and the CROHME2019 test set containing 1199 images were used as the test sets.

The experiments were run on an Ubuntu server with Pytorch version 1.7.1 and python version 3.7.9. The loss function used in the experiments was smooth loss, label smoothing adjustment $\varepsilon = 0.1$ The model is trained using the AdaDelta optimizer with an initial learning rate of 1 and weight decay of 0.0001, patience $= 15$, and the learning rate is reduced when the error rate does not decrease after 15 epochs. After the learning rate has been reduced twice, the training is terminated early to prevent overfitting if the results do not improve on the validation set. Gradient clipping is performed during training to prevent gradient explosion, and the clipping value is set to 100. Beam search is used for prediction, and the beam width is set to 10.

4.2 Ablation Experiment

Different Types of Residual Attention Modules. We first evaluated the performance of the DATWAP model based on criss-cross attention and coordinate attention.

DATWAP model based on criss-cross attention: attention (1) and attention (2) are criss-cross residual attentions.

DATWAP model based on coordinate attention: attention (1) and attention (2) are coordinate residual attention (Table 2).

Table 2. Performance comparison of DATWAP with criss-cross attention and DATWAP with coordinate attention on CROHME 2014, CROHME 2016 and CROHME 2019.

Model	CROHME 2014 ExpRate (%)	CROHME 2016 ExpRate (%)	CROHME 2019 ExpRate (%)
WAP (Our implementation)	48.4%	46.8%	45.1%
DATWAP with criss-cross	**54.72**	**52.83**	**52.54**
DATWAP with coordinate	54.11	49.26	48.62

From the above table, it can be seen that DATWAP works better with criss-cross residual attention. It may be that the criss-cross attention module learns the connections between images at the pixel level, similar to learning the structural relationships between expression characters. Therefore, the model performs better.

Different Layers of Residual Attention Modules. We try to add different layers of residual attention modules to DenseNet-B.

Add two layers of residual attention modules: Residual attention module is added after Transition (2) and Dense Block (3) in Table 1 respectively.

Add three layers of residual attention modules: Residual attention module is added after Transition (1), Transition (2) and Dense Block (3) in Table 1 respectively.

Table 3. Performance comparison of residual attention modules in different layers of the DATWAP with on CROHME 2014, CROHME 2016 and CROHME 2019.

Residual attention module layers	CROHME 2014 ExpRate (%)	CROHME 2016 ExpRate (%)	CROHME 2019 ExpRate (%)
2	**54.72**	**52.83**	**52.54**
3	53.4	50.39	50.04

As can be seen from Table 3, the use of two layers of residual attention modules works best, which is another reflection of the fact that more attention modules are not better, and that the location and number of layers of attention modules used are important.

4.3   Comparison with Other HMER Systems and Case Study

In Tables 5 and 6, we compare our models with other offline HMER systems on the CROHME2016 and CROHME2019 test sets, respectively. Performance comparison of a single model on the CROHME2016/2019 test set (%), where the "ExpRate", " ≤ 1 error" and " ≤ 2 error" columns indicate the expression recognition rate when 0, 1 and 2 structural or symbolic errors can be tolerated.

Table 4. Performance comparison of HMER systems on CROHME 2016

Model	ExpRate (%)	≤ 1 error (%)	≤ 2 error (%)
Wiris [14]	49.61	60.42	64.69
PGS [16]	45.60	62.25	70.44
WAP [17]	46.82	64.64	65.48
WS-WAP [18]	48.91	57.63	60.33
PAL-v2 [4]	49.61	64.08	70.27
BTTR [5]	52.31	63.90	68.61
Relation-based Rec-wsl [7]	52.14	63.21	69.40
DATWAP (our)	**52.83**	**65.65**	**70.96**

As can be seen from Table 4 and Table 5, adding two layers of residual attention modules at the appropriate locations in Dense-B while training the model using smooth loss does result in good recognition. The experiments demonstrate that our model (DATWAP) improves the recognition rate of WAP expressions from 48.4%/46.8%/45.1% to 54.72%/52.83%/52.54% on the CROHME2014/2016/2019 test sets (Fig. 3).

Table 5. Performance comparison of HMER systems on CROHME 2019

Model	ExpRate (%)	≤1 error (%)	≤2error (%)
Univ. Linz [15]	41.29	54.13	58.88
DenseWAP [8]	41.7	55.5	59.3
DenseWAP-TD [8]	51.4	**66.1**	69.1
BTTR [5]	52.96	65.97	69.14
Relation-based Rec-wsl [7]	**53.12**	63.89	68.47
DATWAP (our)	52.54	65.72	**70.81**

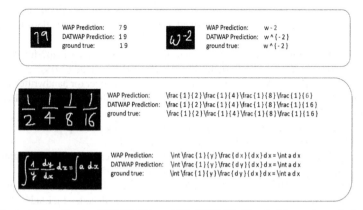

Fig. 3. Case studies for the "WAP" [1] and "DATWAP" (Ours). The red symbols represent incorrect predictions. (Color figure online)

As can be seen from the above examples, the accuracy is greatly improved relative to WAP as the encoder used by DATWAP extracts features with richer global information, facilitating the decoder.

5 Conclusion

This paper is based on an improvement of the WAP model. Using the decoder of WAP, the model performs better in recognizing handwritten mathematical expressions by introducing a residual attention module into the encoder. Because the CNN focuses on local information, while the residual attention module focuses on global information, the addition of the residual attention module can make full use of the long-distance correlation and alleviate the problem that the dependency information between the captured current symbol and the previous symbol diminishes with increasing distance. The model is also trained using smoothing losses, which is similar to adding noise to the original label, effectively preventing overfitting. Experiments conducted on the CROHME dataset show that our model (DATWAP) improves the recognition rate of WAP expressions from 48.4%/46.8%/45.1% to 54.72%/52.83%/52.54% on the CROHME 2014/2016/2019 test sets.

Acknowledgments. This work was supported by the Guangdong Provincial Government of China through the Computational Science Innovative Research Team" program and Guangdong Province Key Laboratory of Computational Science at the Sun Yat-sen University, and the National Science Foundation of China (11971491, 11471012).

References

1. Zhang, J., Du, J., Zhang, S., et al.: Watch, attend and parse: an end-to-end neural network based approach to handwritten mathematical expression recognition. Pattern Recognit. **71**, 196–206 (2017)
2. Müller, R., Kornblith, S., Hinton, G.: When does label smoothing help? In: Advances in Neural Information Processing Systems 32 (NeurIPS 2019), vol. 32 (2019)
3. Zhang, J., Du, J., Dai, L:. Multi-scale attention with dense encoder for handwritten mathematical expression recognition. In: 2018 24th International Conference on Pattern Recognition (ICPR), pp. 2245–2250. IEEE (2018)
4. Wu, J.W., Yin, F., Zhang, Y.M., et al.: Handwritten mathematical expression recognition via paired adversarial learning. Int. J. Comput. Vis., 1–16 (2020)
5. Zhao, W., Gao, L., Yan, Z., et al.: Handwritten mathematical expression recognition with bidirectionally trained transformer. arXiv preprint arXiv:2105.02412 (2021)
6. Ding, H., Chen, K., Huo, Q.: An encoder-decoder approach to handwritten mathematical expression recognition with multi-head attention and stacked decoder. In: Lladós, J., Lopresti, D., Uchida, S. (eds.) ICDAR 2021. LNCS, vol. 12822, pp. 602–616. Springer, Cham (2021). https://doi.org/10.1007/978-3-030-86331-9_39
7. Truong, TN., Ung, H.Q., Nguyen, H.T., Nguyen, C.T., Nakagawa, M.: Relation-based representation for handwritten mathematical expression recognition. In: Barney Smith, E.H., Pal, U. (eds.) ICDAR 2021. LNCS, vol. 12916, pp. 7–19. Springer, Cham (2021). https://doi.org/10.1007/978-3-030-86198-8_1
8. Zhang, J., Du, J., Yang, Y., et al.: A tree-structured decoder for image-to-markup generation. In: International Conference on Machine Learning. PMLR, pp. 11076–11085 (2020)
9. Huang, Z., Wang, X., Huang, L., et al.: CCNET: criss-cross attention for semantic segmentation. In: Proceedings of the IEEE/CVF International Conference on Computer Vision, pp. 603–612 (2019)
10. Hou, Q., Zhou, D., Feng, J.: Coordinate attention for efficient mobile network design. In: Proceedings of the IEEE/CVF Conference on Computer Vision and Pattern Recognition, pp. 13713–13722 (2021)
11. Hu, J., Shen, L., Sun, G.: Squeeze-and-excitation networks. In: Proceedings of the IEEE Conference on Computer Vision and Pattern Recognition, pp. 7132–7141 (2018)
12. Wang, F., Jiang, M., Qian, C., et al.: Residual attention network for image classification. In: Proceedings of the IEEE Conference on Computer Vision and Pattern Recognition, pp. 3156–3164 (2017)
13. Mouchere, H., Viard-Gaudin, C., Zanibbi, R., et al.: ICFHR 2014 competition on recognition of on-line handwritten mathematical expressions (CROHME 2014). In: 2014 14th International Conference on Frontiers in Handwriting Recognition, pp. 791–796. IEEE (2014)

14. Mouchère, H., Viard-Gaudin, C., Zanibbi, R., et al.: ICFHR2016 CROHME: competition on recognition of online handwritten mathematical expressions. In: 2016 15th International Conference on Frontiers in Handwriting Recognition (ICFHR), pp. 607–612. IEEE (2016)
15. Mahdavi, M., Zanibbi, R., Mouchere, H., et al.: ICDAR 2019 CROHME+ TFD: competition on recognition of handwritten mathematical expressions and typeset formula detection. In: 2019 International Conference on Document Analysis and Recognition (ICDAR), pp. 1533–1538. IEEE (2019)
16. Le, A.D., Indurkhya, B., Nakagawa, M.: Pattern generation strategies for improving recognition of handwritten mathematical expressions. Pattern Recognit. Lett. **128**, 255–262 (2019)
17. Wang, J., Du, J., Zhang, J., et al.: Multi-modal attention network for handwritten mathematical expression recognition. In: 2019 International Conference on Document Analysis and Recognition (ICDAR), pp. 1181–1186. IEEE (2019)
18. Truong, T.N., Nguyen, C.T., Phan, K.M., et al.: Improvement of end-to-end offline handwritten mathematical expression recognition by weakly supervised learning. In: 2020 17th International Conference on Frontiers in Handwriting Recognition (ICFHR), pp. 181–186. IEEE (2020)

Hologram Detection for Identity Document Authentication

Oumayma Kada[1], Camille Kurtz[1(✉)], Cuong van Kieu[2], and Nicole Vincent[1]

[1] Université Paris Cité, LIPADE, Paris, France
`camille.kurtz@u-paris.fr`
[2] IMDS Software Inc., Montréal, Canada

Abstract. Authentication of person is a challenging security problem that becomes more and more important, as identity of user has to be checked in a remote way through web exchanges between two partners. Identity documents are exchanged but how to be sure they are authentic? To prevent fake identity documents, they are designed with many details that are very complex to reproduce. In this article, we address the case of holograms that are embedded in passports, the presence of which is to be detected. Unlike most of the methods in the literature tackling this problem, our image analysis approach is looking for any hologram on any part of a document and relies on the acquisition of a video with a smartphone in natural light conditions, indoor or outdoor. From a first selection of pixels in each frame of the video, based on pixel properties such as saturation and value, shape and hues of the selection set are then studied. The whole hologram is reconstructed by an accumulation of parts extracted on each frame. The method has been evaluated on a database of 85 identity documents comprising authentic ones as well as fakes.

Keywords: Hologram · Identity documents · Image and video analysis · Authentication

1 Introduction

The ways of sharing information are constantly evolving. People exchange via the Internet using speech, but they also have to share certain documents. Then it is more and more important to be able to check the identities through the Internet. Identity of a person is supposed to be given thanks to an identity card (ID) or to a passport. Through the Internet, only a photo of the identity document (conveyed as a digital image) can be exchanged. Then, the problem of person authentication has evolved and not only the person has to be identified but also the document, that is supposed to precise the identity, has to be assessed, through the digital image representing it, in order to detect fake documents. The identity documents are built so that a fake document is difficult to be produced. Many elements are added (and/or hidden) in the background of the information, within the paper and the ink. Another element is RFID tags added in the document, or holograms. Among the added elements, some can be verified in a remote way but others obviously cannot.

© Springer Nature Switzerland AG 2022
M. El Yacoubi et al. (Eds.): ICPRAI 2022, LNCS 13363, pp. 346–357, 2022.
https://doi.org/10.1007/978-3-031-09037-0_29

Fig. 1. Illustration of a French passport where a part of a hologram is visible.

In an airport, the checking of the identity documents is done by an accredited person who takes the document and manipulates it as needed in order to detect all the different elements that must be checked. Their number is depending on the degree of confidence that is needed for the person and the document. When the checking has to be operated in a remote way, things are quite different. The tactile aspect is no more available. The visual inspection can be done only thanks to a camera that is managed by the end-user. The current smartphones are good candidates to be used in this context since they enable to capture easily photos as well as videos.

In this paper, we address the problem of document rather than person authentication. We do not consider the person who makes the transaction, but we are more concerned by the document that is produced to justify the identity. More specifically, we propose to study the holograms often present in passports (Fig. 1), identity or consular cards, etc. Holograms are elements added in identity documents because the production of such elements in a document is very specific. By the nature itself of such an element, the aspect of a hologram is changing according to the view point [1]. Then a simple photo of a document is not enough to test the presence of the whole hologram. In each view, only parts of the hologram are visible. In a remote context, authentication has to be based on the images provided by the end-user. Here, the aim is to reconstitute the largest part of the hologram, in some cases two figures are superimposed, viewed according to the vision angle.

The first problem to be solved is the acquisition protocol. It cannot be the same as in most studies taking advantage of the nature of the hologram. The acquisition is based on the use of specific light, a set of fixed well positioned LED that can be operated in a specific way to organize images and lighting as in the case of a portable ring-light illumination module proposed by Soukup [2] or mobile support of the identity document that is moved in front of a fixed

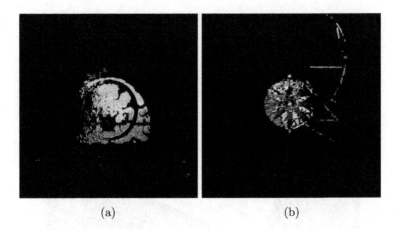

(a)   (b)

Fig. 2. Parts of a hologram with flashy colors.

camera as proposed by Pramila [3]. Of course, such *ad hoc* solutions cannot be used in our case. End-users have not specialized light sources; they cannot be asked to have several LEDs to be used in a sophisticated manner or to organize the acquisition with fixed camera and a moving device on which the document is positioned. The users have to deal with some usual camera, and nowadays the smartphones are the mostly available camera with several acquisition possibilities such as still images, videos with flash (enabled or disabled). We will discuss this in the following.

Most studies in the literature or existing commercial systems are focusing on small holograms embedded in cards or notes. The considered methods often take advantage of the *a priori* on the size and the precise position of the hologram in the document to be authenticated and rely on traditional image processing techniques with (un-)supervised learning phases [4,5]. In this paper we are dealing with passports that include very large and diverse holograms on their whole surfaces. Then the process cannot be a verification but really a detection. We propose an approach allowing simultaneously the extraction of all the content of a hologram and its detection, taking advantage of the partial presence of the hologram depending on the point of view considered in the successive images of a video acquired by a smartphone. The experimental results obtained on a private database of authentic identity documents coupled with a public database of fake documents (without holograms) highlight the interest of this approach for the considered task.

2   Single Image Analysis

Looking at a passport or at an image of a passport, it is obvious the human vision does not see the entire hologram embedded in the document. Then it is not possible to study only an image of a document. Nevertheless, on a single

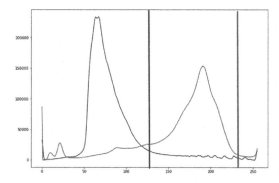

Fig. 3. Example of a saturation histogram in blue and a value histogram in red for an image with hologram. The respective blue and red vertical lines materialize the ideal value of a threshold in order to select the hologram pixels. (Color figure online)

image some parts of the hologram are visible. Then, first of all, we focus on the detection of hologram parts on a single image, before addressing the whole document hologram and getting the conclusion of the presence of a hologram. Furthermore, the study is performed at the pixel level before local and global approaches. A selection of pixels is carried out thanks to a color histogram analysis, leading to hologram part candidate, then the connected components of such pixels are analyzed both from their shapes and colors properties.

2.1   Pixel Level

In this first part, the aim is not to find exactly the hologram pixels but to exploit general properties of such pixels without missing too much true visible hologram pixels and introducing too much false hologram pixels. When looking at a hologram it is obvious the colors are flashy colors (Fig. 2); then, we could consider pixels with high values in one of the three colors highlighted in the RGB color space. But these three colors have no specificity with respect to a hologram presence. All hues are equally concerned in hologram and whatever the colors are, a hologram contains a wide variety of hues. That means the hologram pixel color, hue, is not so important but saturation and value are the most salient elements to be considered in order to characterize hologram pixels. Based on this observation, the usual RGB color space is not the most suited for the study and the HSV color space has been preferred.

A pixel P of spatial coordinates (x, y) will be characterized in a two dimensional space (c_s, c_v) considering respectively the saturation and value of the pixel expressed in the HSV space. The potential hologram pixels are those with high saturation (S) and value (V), thresholds have to be chosen and of course have to be adapted to each image content and illumination context. The thresholds are considered as global to an image. They are computed thanks to the analysis of two histograms, the saturation and value pixel histograms. As a matter of fact, in the image, the part of the hologram that is visible in natural illumination is

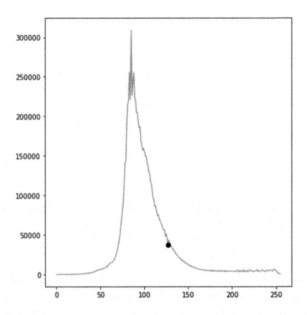

Fig. 4. Example of a saturation histogram with the position of the threshold defining a constraint for hologram pixels. (Color figure online)

very small with respect to the image domain, then the presence of such pixels is not materialized by a peak in the histogram as can be seen in Fig. 3 where histograms of saturation and value of pixels in an image are built. The values of the best thresholds manually fixed, designed by the blue and red vertical lines are not associated with a very significant valley or peak in the histogram curve.

The threshold for one image is fixed so that the maximum number of hologram pixels is obtained. It is chosen at a minimum of the histogram, the significant minimum higher than the mean value of the histogram or more precisely the first maximum after the mean value to limit the number of false positive hologram pixels. The significance of the minimum and maximum are measured thanks to morphological operations. The position of such a threshold is indicated by the blue dot on Fig. 4.

The same process is applied on the saturation and value channels leading to two thresholds T_s and T_v. The retained pixels in an image I are those for which the two constraints are holding. They constitute a set M defined as

$$M = \{P(x, y) \in I \mid c_s > T_s \text{ and } c_v > T_v\} \qquad (1)$$

Let us have some comments. A white high luminance zone is not selected in M as potential hologram; Indeed, the saturation in such zone is not high enough to be selected in the thresholding phase. This can be seen in Fig. 5 where light coming from a bright white screen turned on in the right of the image is not selected as hologram pixels, only the contour of the screen is selected and it will be easy to eliminate them in a second phase.

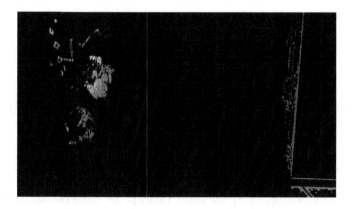

Fig. 5. A hologram part detected in an image where a display device can be seen in the right part of the image. Only the edges of the screen are selected.

Of course, as already indicated, in M are some false hologram pixels and the next objective is to eliminate them as they are considered as noise for our problem, nevertheless true hologram pixels must be preserved.

2.2   Local Level

To achieve this, a more local approach is considered. In M each connected component is studied independently. Two aspects are considered, on the one hand, the shape of the candidate zones is analyzed and on the other hand, the hues of the components are analyzed. To be more precise, we are to compare the behavior of M and of a dilation of M using a square structuring element of radius 1, the result of the dilation will be a set noted M_d.

Shape Analysis. Here, the aim is to characterize zones in M according to their texture in zones different from line drawings or flat zones. It can be noticed that when a hologram zone is concerned, the edges of the zone are quite smooth whereas when some glint is present, the zone is not so coherent and appears most often as blobs that are near one from the other but spread on the zone. This effect can be seen in Fig. 6 where some non-hologram pixels are shown, they are associated with a glint in the initial image. We want to detect such pixels and eliminate them from M.

Due to the porous aspect in some parts of M, the connected components of M are not all significant with respect of the extraction of a hologram. M_d has been built in order to consider a smaller number of connected components and we consider the connected components of M_d. The connected components in M are embedded in one of the connected components of M_d:

$$M_d = \bigcup_{i=1}^{N} C_i \tag{2}$$

Fig. 6. A noisy part selected in the first step of the process. The selected pixels have a porous structure figured by small neighboring components.

The analysis is done for each connected component C_i in M_d. This local observation level is a good comprise between the pixel study and a global study. The zones that are looked for in M are zones that appear quite porous. In that case, some connected components in M, thanks to the dilation, become connected in M_d.

This evolution is measured by the number of connected components in M included in one component of M_d. Each time the number of connected components of M in C_i is too high, it can be concluded the C_i part is porous and cannot be considered as a potential hologram zone. So, it will be suppressed from M. The suppressed part S_s in M is obtained from the study of all connected components of M_d:

$$S_s = \bigcup \{ C_i \cap M \mid T(C_i \cap M) \geq n_0 \text{ for } i = 1 \text{ to } N \} \tag{3}$$

where $T(X)$ is the number of connected components in X and n_0 is a constant that has been fixed during training, using a set of images.

Color Analysis. Another characteristic of the holograms is the distribution of hues that distinguishes a hologram from any glittering surface. Globally but also locally, the number of hues contained in a hologram is high whereas a glint has generally an only global color. So, locally, on each part of M limited by a connected component of M_d, the number of hues is computed and normalized according to the size of the component evaluated. Here, we consider the area as the size of the component. This enables to define a set of pixels S_c that can be assumed not to be in a hologram:

$$S_c = \bigcup \{ C_i \cap M \mid \frac{C(C_i \cap M)}{|C_i \cap M|} \leq c \text{ for } i = 1 \text{ to } N \} \tag{4}$$

where $C(X)$ gives the number of different hues contained in a set X of pixels, $|X|$ gives the area of X and c is a constant that has been fixed during training, using a set of images.

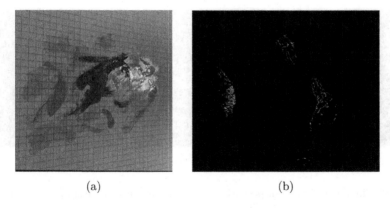

(a)   (b)

Fig. 7. In (a) an image I (a document covered in varnish) without any hologram and in (b) a zoom on a part of $H(I)$ associated with the white part on the right part of I.

At this stage of the process, in the image I, the hologram pixels extracted $H(I)$ are those with high saturation and value but that do not form a porous region and are locally with several hues:

$$H(I) = M \setminus (S_s \cup S_c) \tag{5}$$

Of course, $H(I)$ should be empty if the image I does not contain hologram, this happens most often but some images can contain pixels that are selected in the process of a single image. The case is illustrated in Fig. 7 with a document covered in varnish.

This last example highlights that the study of a single image is not enough to extract with high confidence only hologram pixels. Then, at least two images are necessary to decide whether a document contains or not a hologram. Furthermore, to extract and reconstruct the hologram it is necessary to analyze a larger number of images acquired with several points of view so that each part can be aggregated to reconstitute the whole hologram. We have decided to use a video that is obtained from an acquisition by the end-user using a smartphone as a camera for example.

3   Video Analysis

The main objective of the paper is to authenticate the identity document thanks to the presence of an authentic hologram. This can be done in two steps, first the document must contain a hologram and this hologram must be authentic. The passports of different countries do not contain the same hologram. The aim of this section is first to assert a document D contains or not a hologram. The material studied is now a video we consider as a series of images $(I_i)_{i=1}^{T}$. Then, the extraction of the potential hologram will be performed thanks to the study of each frame of the video.

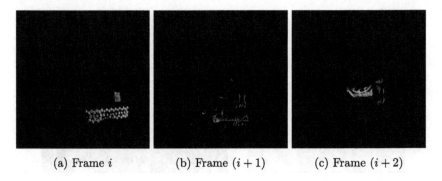

(a) Frame i (b) Frame $(i+1)$ (c) Frame $(i+2)$

Fig. 8. Three extractions of potential histogram in consecutive frames of a video.

3.1 Two Images Analysis

When looking at a hologram, the visual aspect of the image is varying according to the angle between the document surface orthogonal axis and the axis of the camera. This can be observed in Fig. 8 where are displayed the results of the process described in Sect. 2, applied to three adjacent frames in a video. We assume this is characteristic of an authentic hologram. In the video without any hologram, the elements mistaken in $H(I)$ as part of a potential hologram are seen in the same way in all the frames of the video and the difference visible in $H(I_i)$, $H(I_{i+1})$ is just linked to a change in perspective in the two frames. The method we developed is then relying on the computation of the difference between the contents of the different $H(I_i)$. The difference is quantitatively measured as:

$$d(H(I_i), H(I_j)) = \frac{1}{|H(I_i) \cup H(I_j)|} \sum_{P \in H(I_i) \cup H(I_j)} ||I_i(P) - I_j(P)||^2 \qquad (6)$$

where $|X|$ indicates the cardinal of a set X. Here the difference between the color features of P pixels that we used is linked to the usual Euclidean norm in the RGB space. The highest $d(H(I_i), H(I_j))$ is, the highest the probability of the document to contain an authentic hologram is.

To emphasize the difference between documents with and without a hologram, this computation can be done on all pairs of consecutive frames or considering a set J of pairs of distant frames. Then, we define the score of a document D as:

$$Score(D) = \frac{1}{|J|} \sum_{(i,j) \in J} d(H(I_i), H(I_j)) \qquad (7)$$

where $|X|$ indicates the cardinal of a set X. When a hologram is present, the score must be high. In order to make a decision, a threshold has to be fixed according to a representative training set. The threshold is depending on the number and nature of frame pairs involved in the computation of the score.

In case of a positive presence of a hologram in the document, it is possible to rebuild the hologram or part of the hologram from the study of each frame.

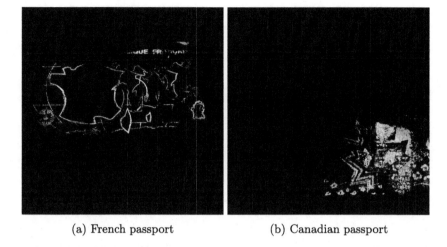

(a) French passport   (b) Canadian passport

Fig. 9. Extraction of hologram pixels from passports thanks to videos.

3.2 Hologram Extraction

On each frame I of the video some part of the hologram has been detected and extracted, associated with $H(I)$. Nevertheless, it is not sufficient to consider the union of the $H(I_i)$. Indeed, maybe the document is hold by the user in a non-stable position or the camera is hold in hand and is mobile with respect to the document or both document and camera are moving. Before the aggregation of the different parts, a registration process has to be performed between consecutive frames, or, depending on the acquisition protocol, all frames can be registered on a single frame of the video.

Let us note R_I the transform of frame I during the registration with a fixed frame of the video. Then the hologram of the document can be recovered by following process:

$$\bigcup_{i=1}^{T} R_{I_i}(H(I_i)) \tag{8}$$

Figure 9 illustrates the extraction of holograms from a French passport and a Canadian one. All the pixels in the holograms are not recovered, but enough is extracted so that the origins of the documents can be deduced. The omitted parts are linked to the way the videos are acquired. The length of the videos can be too short to make all parts of the holograms visible in normal light. Some parts can be seen as blurred when two different patterns of the hologram are superimposed.

4 Experimental Study

The method that we have described is suited for any type of document containing a hologram and it is not the verification of the presence of a hologram that

(a)   (b)

Fig. 10. Two fake identity documents (no hologram) from MIDV-500 [6].

is supposed to be present in the document but it really is an analysis of the document representation with no *a priori* information.

Of course, as for any project involving identity document and fake ones, it is difficult to constitute a database of authentic identity documents. Quite rightly, no one wants to share this kind of documents and it is too difficult to build true false documents. The availability of true fake documents is in same way difficult to find. Extra from the passports that have been used to fix the thresholds involved in the process, the experiments have been performed on a set of 37 videos of true passports of three different nationalities and on 48 videos of documents without hologram (Fig. 10) including the videos of the public database MIDV-500 of identity documents, introduced in [6]. Indeed, in this database, images of true identity documents have been printed and coated with plastic. These still documents do not contain any more any true hologram.

For each video of our database, the aim is to determine whether the document contains or not a hologram. The evaluation is then performed with respect to precision, recall and F1-measure. Precision here evaluates how false documents have been authenticated, recall evaluates how true documents have not been authenticated and F1-measure gives the harmonic mean of the previous two. Table 1 gathers together the three values.

Table 1. Evaluation of the method.

Precision	Recall	F1-measure
97.22	92.11	94.60

The values in Table 1 mean only one of the holograms in the 37 videos containing one has not been detected. In this case the distance (during acquisition) between the camera and the document was too large and explains the results. Some registration at detection level would be needed. The false positives are linked with the instability of the acquisition mode of the different videos. To improve such false positives, as well as for false negatives a registration would be needed in the detection phase whereas we have only performed it in the hologram extraction but not in the detection process.

The confidence on the presence of the hologram is linked to the score value that is computed in Eq. 7 and more precisely on the position of the score value and the threshold. We have observed that the confidence is larger when the acquisition is performed with a rather small distance between the document and the camera.

5   Conclusion

In this paper we have proved it is possible to detect a hologram in a remote way, that is to say thanks to images of the document acquired with common smartphone and lighting conditions. The acquisition is then possible by the end-user. One image is not enough to make a conclusion and for very large holograms, a video is the best way with a relative movement between the document and the camera. A suited protocol is easy to define to improve the results and make the method more robust, in particular the distance between the document and the camera or the way the smartphone or the passport is mobile.

Next possible improvement of the retrieval of the hologram would be to manage the different superimposed elements. Continuity in the appearance of the pattern can help to discriminate between the multishape of the hologram. Furthermore, from the hologram extracted some recognition of the identity document could be achieved and would confirm the authentication of the document.

References

1. Hartl, A., Grubert, J., Schmalstieg, D., Reitmayr, G.: Mobile interactive hologram verification. In: ISMAR, pp. 75–82 (2013)
2. Soukup, D., Huber-Mörk, R.: Mobile hologram verification with deep learning. IPSJ Trans. Comput. Vis. Appl. 9(1), 1–6 (2017). https://doi.org/10.1186/s41074-017-0022-7
3. Pramila, A., Keskinarkaus, A., Rahtu, E., Seppänen, T.: Watermark recovery from a dual layer hologram with a digital camera. In: Heyden, A., Kahl, F. (eds.) SCIA 2011. LNCS, vol. 6688, pp. 146–155. Springer, Heidelberg (2011). https://doi.org/10.1007/978-3-642-21227-7_14
4. Hartl, A., Arth, C., Schmalstieg, D.: AR-based hologram detection on security documents using a mobile phone. In: Bebis, G., et al. (eds.) ISVC 2014. LNCS, vol. 8888, pp. 335–346. Springer, Cham (2014). https://doi.org/10.1007/978-3-319-14364-4_32
5. Hartl, A.D., Arth, C., Grubert, J., Schmalstieg, D.: Efficient verification of holograms using mobile augmented reality. IEEE Trans. Vis. Comput. Graph. 22(7), 1843–1851 (2016)
6. Arlazarov, V.V., Bulatov, K.B., Chernov, T.S.: MIDV-500: a dataset for identity documents analysis and recognition on mobile devices in video stream. CoRR, abs/1807.05786 (2018)

A New Deep Fuzzy Based MSER Model for Multiple Document Images Classification

Kunal Biswas[1], Palaiahnakote Shivakumara[2(✉)], Sittravell Sivanthi[2], Umapada Pal[1], Yue Lu[3], Cheng-Lin Liu[4,5], and Mohamad Nizam Bin Ayub[1]

[1] Computer Vision and Pattern Recognition Unit, Indian Statistical Institute, Kolkata, India
umapada@isical.ac.in, nizam_ayub@um.edu.my
[2] Faculty of Computer Science and Information Technology, University of Malaya,
Kuala Lumpur, Malaysia
shiva@um.edu.my
[3] Shanghai Key Laboratory of Multidimensional Information Processing,
East China Normal University, Shanghai, China
ylu@cs.ecnu.edu.cn
[4] National Laboratory of Pattern Recognition, Institute of Automation of Chinese Academy
of Sciences, Beijing, China
liucl@nlpr.ia.ac.cn
[5] School of Artificial Intelligence, University of Chinese Academy, Beijing, China

Abstract. Understanding document images uploaded on social media is challenging because of multiple types like handwritten, printed and scene text images. This study presents a new model called Deep Fuzzy based MSER for classification of multiple document images (like handwritten, printed and scene text). The proposed model detects candidate components that represent dominant information irrespective of the type of document images by combining fuzzy and MSER in a novel way. For every candidate component, the proposed model extracts distance-based features which result in proximity matrix (feature matrix). Further, the deep learning model is proposed for classification by feeding input images and feature matrix as input. To evaluate the proposed model, we create our own dataset and to show effectiveness, the proposed model is tested on standard datasets. The results show that the proposed approach outperforms the existing methods in terms of average classification rate.

Keywords: Document image analysis · Document image understanding · Handwritten documents understanding · Scene text recognition · Document classification

1 Introduction

Since the use of social media, such as Facebook, Twitter, Instagram is part of human activities for communication, creating awareness, sharing information, broadcasting news etc., uploading images, videos and texts by users is common and it has become day to

M. El Yacoubi et al. (Eds.): ICPRAI 2022, LNCS 13363, pp. 358–370, 2022.
https://doi.org/10.1007/978-3-031-09037-0_30

day activities [1]. But at the same time, users use the social media platform for spreading fake news, threatening blackmailing, abusing by uploading fake information such as manipulated images, videos and documents etc. [2]. Therefore, there is a need to detect whether the images/documents uploaded on social media are genuine or fake. To solve the above challenge, it is necessary to separate images uploaded on social media as printed, handwritten and scene text document images. This is because each document type behaves differently in terms of background, appearance of text, text style and shapes of characters. Therefore, this work aims at classifying given document images into printed handwritten and scene text images such that the complexity of image understanding can be reduced. In addition, an appropriate method can be chosen for understanding different types of document images.

Several approaches have been developed for document image classification [3]. For example, classification of printed, handwritten documents, different degraded documents, documents containing picture and text, only text, email, forms, news and reports etc. [4, 5]. The past methods explored deep learning approaches for successful classification. However, it is noted from the past that most methods focus on particular category like different types of printed documents, handwritten documents and complex documents but none of the methods considered different categories of documents, namely, printed, handwritten and scene text images. Therefore, the existing methods may not be effective for the above-mentioned documents and report poor results. The reason is that all the three types of documents have distinct and unique nature and characteristics. It is evident from the illustration shown in Fig. 1, where for the texts of three categories shown in (a), the OCR (printed text) and HCR (handwritten text), and SCR (scene text), which are GOOGLE API [6] available online report inconsistent results as shown in Fig. 1(b). Therefore, this illustration infers that the existing OCR may not have the ability to recognize documents of different categories.

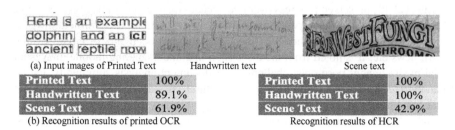

(a) Input images of Printed Text   Handwritten text   Scene text

Printed Text	100%		Printed Text	100%
Handwritten Text	89.1%		Handwritten Text	100%
Scene Text	61.9%		Scene Text	42.9%

(b) Recognition results of printed OCR   Recognition results of HCR

Fig. 1. Recognition performance of different OCRs for different document types.

Thus, this observation motivated us to propose a new Deep Fuzzy based MSER Model for Multiple Document Images Classification. It can be seen from a sample image of three categories shown in Fig. 1(a) that the spacing between character and words is almost uniform in the case of printed text, while the spacing between the character words is non-uniform in the case of handwritten and scene text images. This makes sense because the aspect ratio of character for printed text is almost similar compared to handwritten text and scene text due to size and font variations. In addition, when we compare scene text with other two document images (printed and handwritten), scene text images have complex backgrounds with many non-text components and other two documents have homogeneous background without non-text components. To extract these observations, we propose a new Fuzzy based Maximally Stable Extremal Regions (MSER), which outputs candidate components including characters (printed document), words (handwritten document) and characters and words (scene text document). The proposed approach finds a relationship between every candidate component by estimating distances using colors, spatial information, and alignments. This results in a proximity matrix for each input image, and it is considered as a feature matrix. Motivated by the success of deep learning models for classification, we propose an AlexNet based deep learning model for classification of three type of documents by feeding input images and feature matrix.

The contribution of the proposed work is as follows. (i) Proposing a fuzzy based MSER for detecting accurate candidate components is new compared to conventional MSER. (ii) Extracting distance-based features using color values, spatial information and alignment of components is new for document type classification. (iii) The way the proposed approach integrates features and deep learning model for successful classification is one more key contribution compared to the past methods.

The rest of the paper is organized as follows. Critical analysis of existing methods related to document image classification is presented in Sect. 2. Section 3 describes the proposed method including candidate component detection, feature extraction and classification. Experimental analysis is presented in Sect. 4. Section 5 concludes the summary of the proposed work.

2   Related Work

We review the methods related to document image classification, which includes printed, handwritten and degraded document images and scene text images classifications.

Liu et al. [3] presented progress over two decades on document image classification. The survey discusses four types of methods, namely, textual based, structural based, visual based and hybrid methods for the classification documents of email, resume, report, news etc. It is noted from the discussion that understanding mobile images and social media images pose open challenges for document analysis community. Pal and Chaudhuri [7] proposed a method based on structural and statistical features for machine printed and handwritten document classification.

Bakkali et al. [4] proposed a method for document image classification using cross-model deep networks. The approach uses textual and visual features for classifying the document of email, news forms and reports. Bakkali et al. [8] developed a method based on visual clues and textual deep features fusion for different document image classification. The proposed deep learning model fuses both textual and image features for successful classification. Bhowmik et al. [9] developed a method for classifying text region in the document based on analyzing connected components. The aim of the approach is to detect text, picture and graphics in the images by extracting connected component-based features. Fu et al. [10] explored transductive transfer learning based on genetic algorithm for the classification of balanced and unbalanced document types.

Jadli et al. [11] prosed a data augmentation-based method for classification of documents. The technique classifies a given document as an electronic invoice, handwritten invoice, checks and receipts. The method generates fake documents that are similar to input documents to improve the performance of the method. Raghunandan et al. [12] proposed an approach for fraud handwritten document classification using Fourier coefficients. Rani et al. [5] used a variational denoising auto encoder for classifying degraded photographed document images. The approach focuses on image enhancement to improve document image classification performance. Saddami et al. [13] explore deep neural networks for classifying degraded ancient documents. The technique considers bleed through, faint text, low contrast, spot and uniform degraded documents for classification. Nandanwar et al. [14] explored local gradient difference features for the classification of 2D and 3D scene text images. The technique focuses on 2D and 3D scene text in the natural scene images for improving text detection and recognition performances.

It is observed from the above review that most of the methods target for the classification of a particular category of documents, but not multiple categories of different documents considered in this work. Therefore, this work aims at developing a new model for the classification of documents of printed, handwritten and scene text images.

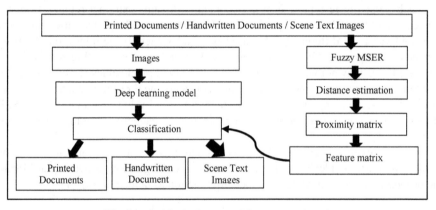

Fig. 2. The block diagram of the proposed work

3   The Proposed Method

The aim of the proposed work is to classify the given document images into printed, handwritten and scene text images such that an appropriate method can be chosen for improving the performance of respective methods. It is observed from three types of documents that due to variation in handwritten text, complex background in the case of scene text and plain background of printed document images, the number of connected components, their shapes and spatial relationship changes from one document type to another document type. This observation motivated us to extract connected components from the input images. For extracting connected components irrespective of background complexity, most of the existing methods use Maximally Stable Extremal Regions (MSER) [15]. Based on experimental study, it is noted that MSER is sensitive to background complexity. This led to introduce Fuzzy to avoid a confusion to define connected components irrespective of background complexity [16]. To the best of our knowledge, this is the first work that combines fuzzy and conventional MSER for detecting components. This step outputs a candidate component which represents text as well as a few components in the background of scene text images. To extract the spatial relationship between candidate components, similarity and dissimilarity between the candidate components, the proposed method calculates distance between the candidate components using color, spatial information and alignment information [17]. This step outputs a proximity matrix for the input images, which is considered as a feature matrix for classification of three document types.

Inspired by the success of the deep learning model for classification [18], we explore CNN based models to combine feature extraction from the input images and feature extraction from the proximity matrix of the input image. The steps of the proposed method are presented in Fig. 2.

3.1 Candidate Component Detection

For each input image type, the proposed method obtains extremal regions from the conventional MSER. When conventional MSER finds extremal regions, it uses automatic threshold values at different levels based on pixel values for defining granularity of connected components. For the complex background images, the threshold value at different levels may not work well due to uncertainty at pixel values. To overcome this problem, we propose a fuzzy concept which considers the threshold values of different levels of the same components to find a stable threshold value such that fuzzy-MSER obtains proper connected components irrespective of background complexity in this work.

For each extremal reason, which is considered as connected component (α) and thresholds at different levels of the same component (T_i) given by conventional MSER, the proposed method calculates membership function as defined in Eq. (1).

$$\mu(T_i) = \frac{|Ar(\alpha)T_{i+1} - Ar(\alpha)T_{i-1}|}{|Ar(\alpha)T_i|} \tag{1}$$

where $Ar(\alpha)T_i$ denotes the Area of Extremal Region (component) and T_i denotes intensity threshold value at 'i'. While calculating $\mu(T_i)$ where 'i' is 0 and maximum the previous and next threshold do not exist and therefore we consider the $Ar(\alpha)T_{i+1}$ & $Ar(\alpha)T_{i-1}$ as zero.

After calculating all the membership values, $\mu(T_i)$, the proposed method performs intersection operation as defined in Eq. (2), which outputs stable threshold value for different situations.

$$\mu(T_1 \cap T_2 \cap \cdots \cap T_{max}) = \min\{\mu(T_1), \mu(T_2), \ldots, \mu(T_{max})\} \tag{2}$$

where Max denotes the number of thresholds at different levels in each component. The effect of Fuzzy-MSER for candidate component detection for three different document type images is shown in Fig. 3, where one can see that the conventional MSER lose many components as shown in Fig. 3(a), while the proposed Fuzzy-MSER detects almost all the text components properly in all the three categories as shown in Fig. 3(b). This shows that threshold values used in conventional MSER are not robust to defect caused by complexities of different categories. On the other hand, the proposed fuzzy-MSER combination is capable of handling challenges of different types of documents. This is the advantage of the Fuzzy-MSER over conventional MSER for detecting candidate components.

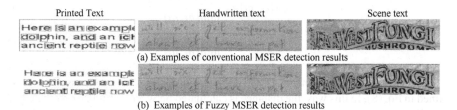

Printed Text	Handwritten text	Scene text

(a) Examples of conventional MSER detection results

(b) Examples of Fuzzy MSER detection results

Fig. 3. Performance of conventional MSER and the proposed Fuzzy-MSER on different type of documents

3.2 Distance Feature Extraction from Candidate Components

It is observed from the results shown in Fig. 3 that the size, shape and spatial information between the components vary from one type to another type of document images. In addition, these observations are unique feature for classifying three document types successfully. Therefore, the proposed method extracts the following distance-based features for each component in the images as defined in Eq. (3)–Eq. (8).

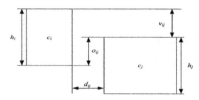

Fig. 4. The spatial measurement between two components

For each candidate component given by Fuzzy-MSER,

- **Color difference feature:**

$$\varphi_1(c_i, c_j) = \sqrt{(r_i - r_j)^2 + (g_i - g_j)^2 + (b_i - b_j)^2} \tag{3}$$

where r_i, r_j, g_i, g_j, b_i and b_j are the mean intensity of RGB channel of candidate components, i and j.

- **Spatial distance feature:**

$$\varphi_2(c_i, c_j) = \frac{v_{ij}}{\min(h_i, h_j)} \tag{4}$$

$$\varphi_3(c_i, c_j) = \frac{d_{ij}}{\min(h_i, h_j)} \tag{5}$$

where c_i, c_j, v_{ij}, h_i, h_j, d_{ij} are represented in Fig. 4, where all the variables are defined using candidate component, c_i and candidate component, c_j.

- **Alignment features**:

$$\varphi_4(c_i, c_j) = \frac{|h_i - h_j|}{\min(h_i, h_j)} \tag{6}$$

$$\varphi_5(c_i, c_j) = \frac{o_{ij}}{\min(h_i, h_j)} \tag{7}$$

For the candidate components, c_i and c_j, the proposed method estimates distance as defined in Eq. (8). In this way, the distance is calculated between candidate component-1 with all other candidate components and candidate component-2 with all other candidate components and so on. This results in a proximity matrix for each input image, which is considered as a feature matrix for the classification of three document types. We extract Color, Spatial and Alignment features to calculate the distance/proximity between components. Some features may or may not be more important than others but for the sake of simplicity, the proposed work considers each to be equally important.

$$D(c_i, c_j) = \sum_{k=1}^{5} \varphi_{i,j,k} \tag{8}$$

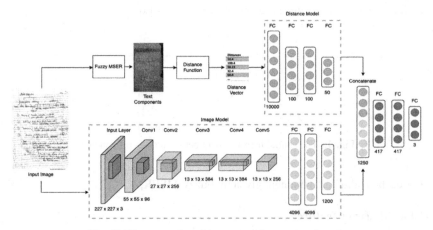

Fig. 5. The network architecture of the proposed work

3.3 Deep CNN for Classification of Multiple Documents

To exploit the strength of a deep learning model that requires image information, the proposed work feeds original image as input for feature extraction and then the proposed model integrates features extracted from the input image and the feature extracted from the candidate components (distance features) for classification. The complete architecture of the proposed deep learning model is shown in Fig. 5, where the steps to combine both the features are presented.

The image model is an architecture derived from AlexNet as shown in Fig. 5. The input layer requires the image to be $227 \times 227 \times 3$. The size of different input images is resized to a standard size to make implementation simple. The CNN layer uses filters/kernels to convolve the image. Filters are small units that we apply across the data through a sliding window. This process involves taking the element-wise product of the filters in the image and then summing those specific values for every sliding action. The stride is how many features the sliding window skips along the width and height. The output is a 3D matrix of different sizes representing the image features. This layer is repeated at least 4 times. The Batch Normalization is a process to make neural networks faster and more stable by adding extra layers in deep neural network. It standardizes the distribution of layer inputs to combat the internal covariance shift. This layer is only applied once. Max Pooling is a process of downsampling the features. This is done using a filter with a fixed size and stride. The filter would return the max value within the region. This layer is applied every time after a CNN layer. The Fully Connected Layer (FC) behaves like feed forward neural networks for classification. The output from Max Pooling is flattened (3D matrix converted to 1D matrix) and fed to the FC. The final FC layer produces an output with the size of 1×1200 and this is the feature dimension. The feature matrix is reduced to a standard size of 10000 dimensions by padding or trimming as needed. This is then fed to a FC layer which produces an output of 1×50. Both these outputs are then concatenated to form 1250 dimensions and a final FCNN classifies the input to predicted a class.

4 Experimental Results

For evaluating the proposed classification method, we create our own dataset, which consists of three classes, namely, class of printed document image, class of handwritten document images, and the class of natural scene text images. It is noted that the images of printed and handwritten document images have homogeneous background without non-text components, while the images of scene text have complex background with non-text components as shown in the sample images in Fig. 6. Our dataset provides 3008 images. Out of which, 1001 images for the class of printed document images, 995 images for the class of handwritten document images and 1012 images for the class of scene text images. To show the objectiveness of the proposed method, we choose 1000 handwritten images from standard datasets of IAM and KHATT for handwritten image class randomly [19], and 1000 images from ICDAR 2019 MLT dataset for scene text class [20], and 1001 printed document images of our dataset for printed image class. We prefer 1000 images per class to avoid skewed data. Since the images are collected from standard dataset of IAM, KHATT and ICDAR 2019 MLT, the dataset is considered as a standard dataset for evaluating the proposed method.

In the same way, to show the robustness of the proposed method, we compare the results of the proposed method with the results of existing methods that use a cross-model proposed by [4] using NASNet and BERT and the method developed by [8], which explores the combination of visual and textual features for document images classification. The reason to consider these two methods for the comparative study is that these two are state-of-the-art methods and explored deep learning models for successful classification of document images. For measuring the performance of the proposed and existing methods, we use the standard metrics, namely, Accuracy, Precision, Recall and F1-score as defined in Eq. (9)–Eq. (12). In addition, we also calculate Average Classification Rate (ACR) through a confusion matrix. For validating the usefulness of classification, we estimate character recognition rate before and after classification. Before classification experiments, we consider the images of all the classes as input while after classification we consider images of each class as input. It is expected that the results of before classification should report poor results compared to the results of after classification. This is due to the reduction in complexity of the classification problem.

$$Accuracy = \frac{TP + TN}{TP + FP + TN + FN} \tag{9}$$

$$Precision = \frac{TP}{TP + FP} \tag{10}$$

$$Recall = \frac{TP}{TP + FN} \tag{11}$$

$$F1 - Score = \frac{2(Recall) \times (Precision)}{Recall + Precision} \tag{12}$$

where TP, TN, FP, FN are True Positive, True Negative, False Positive and False Negative, respectively. For a 3-class problem the only the correct class is labelled as 'True' and the other two classes are labelled as 'False', on the other hand, the correctly predicted will be labelled 'Positive' and predicted as any of the other 2 classes would be labelled 'Negative'.

4.1 Ablation Study

To solve the complex classification problem, there are key steps explored in the proposed methodology section for successful classification and these steps are fuzzy based MSER for detecting candidate components, the features based on distance measures, and deep CNN model for classification. For assessing the effectiveness of the above key steps, we conduct the following experiments listed in Table 1 for calculating Accuracy, Precision, Recall and F-score using our dataset. (i) Applying the deep learning model (Image model) directly on input images for classification, which is considered as a baseline experiment. (ii) This experiment uses text candidates detected by fuzzy-MSER and features extracted from distance measures (Text model) for classification. (iii) This experiment uses the image model for extracting features, detecting text candidates using Fuzzy-MSER, considers edge components given by Canny edge operator and distance-based features and finally text model for classification. (iv) This experiment uses the same steps of (iii) except by replacing edge components given by Canny edge operator with the text candidates given by conventional MSER. (v) This is the proposed method which includes the steps of fuzzy-MSER for candidate components detection, distance-based features and deep CNN for classification.

The results of the above experiments reported in Table 1 show that the results achieved by the proposed method are the best compared to the results of all the steps and the baseline method. It is also observed from Table 1 that the key steps proposed (fuzzy-MSER, distance-based features and deep CNN) in the work are effective and contribute equally for obtaining the high results for classification.

Table 1. Evaluating the effectiveness of the key steps of the proposed method on our dataset

#	Steps	Accuracy	Precision	Recall	F1-score
(i)	Baseline: Image Model	0.95	0.92	0.92	0.92
(ii)	Fuzzy MSER + Text Model	0.60	0.40	0.40	0.40
(iii)	Image Model + Canny Edge + Distance-Based Feature + Text Model	0.89	0.84	0.84	0.84
(iv)	Image Model + MSER + Distance-Based Feature + Text Model	0.96	0.93	0.93	0.93
(v)	Proposed Method: Image Model + Fuzzy MSER + Distance-Based Feature + Text Model	**0.98**	**0.98**	**0.98**	**0.98**

4.2 Experiments on Classification of Multiple Documents

Sample images of successful and unsuccessful classification of the proposed method on our dataset are shown in Fig. 6, where it can be seen that the proposed model work well for images of different types, at the same time, when the images are sparse and affected by illumination effect, blur and degradations, the proposed model misclassifies the images. The results of the proposed and existing methods for our and standard datasets reported in Table 2 and Table 3, respectively, show that the proposed method outperforms compared to the existing methods in terms of average classification rate. This shows that the proposed method is capable of classifying different types of document as well as scene text images. Since the existing methods were developed for only document types with a plain background, when the classification includes the images of scene text, the performance of the existing methods degrades. On the other hand, because of the effectiveness of the key steps proposed in this work, the proposed model is successful in classification of different types of document images including scene text images.

4.3 Experiments for Validating Classification Method

To validate the results of the proposed classification, as mentioned earlier we calculate recognition rate before and after classification for both our and standard datasets using HCR (Handwritten OCR), OCR (Printed document OCR) and SCR (Scene text OCR). It is noted that the above-mentioned OCRs are powerful and work for documents affected

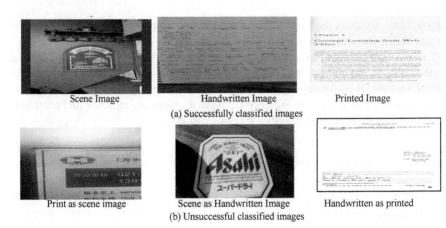

(a) Successfully classified images

Print as scene image   Scene as Handwritten Image   Handwritten as printed

(b) Unsuccessful classified images

Fig. 6. Examples of successful and unsuccessful classification of the proposed method

Table 2. Average Classification Rate (ACR) of proposed and existing methods on our dataset

Classes	Proposed method			Bakkali et al. [4]			Bakkali et al. [8]		
	Scene	Hand	Print	Scene	Hand	Print	Scene	Hand	Print
Scene	1.00	0.00	0.00	0.98	0.02	0.00	1.00	0.00	0.00
Handwriting	0.00	0.97	0.03	0.02	0.93	0.05	0.00	0.95	0.05
Printed	0.00	0.04	0.96	0.00	0.10	0.90	0.00	0.09	0.91
ACR	**0.976**			0.936			0.953		

Table 3. Average Classification Rate (ACR) of proposed and existing methods on standard dataset

Classes	Proposed method			Bakkali et al. [4]			Bakkali et al. [8]		
	Scene	Hand	Print	Scene	Hand	Print	Scene	Hand	Print
Scene	0.98	0.00	0.02	0.93	0.07	0.00	0.95	0.02	0.03
Handwriting	0.05	0.92	0.03	0.10	0.90	0.00	0.02	0.93	0.05
Printed	0.02	0.04	0.94	0.00	0.09	0.91	0.08	0.01	0.91
ACR	**0.946**			0.913			0.930		

by different complexities. This reason led to test the OCR on different types of documents in this work. Before classification, experiments consider the images of all the classes as input for recognition while after classification experiments consider images of each class as input for recognition. The results of the HCR, OCR and SCR before and after classification on our standard dataset reported in Table 4 show that the OCRs reports poor recognition rate for all the classes while for after classification, the same OCRs report a very high recognition rates for respective classes compared to the results of before classification. Therefore, we can conclude that the classification is necessary for achieving a high recognition result for different types of documents. In addition, we can also infer that single OCR for different types of documents is still an open challenge for the researchers.

Table 4. Recognition performance before and after classification using our and standard datasets.

OCR	Our dataset				Standard dataset (IAM + KHATT + ICDAR 2019)			
	Before classification	After classification			Before classification	After classification		
	All the classes	Handwritten	Printed	Scene text	All the classes	Handwritten	Printed	Scene text
HCR [6]	0.87	0.98	0.84	0.80	0.88	0.95	0.82	0.86
OCR [6]	0.79	0.67	0.98	0.73	0.80	0.70	0.96	0.75
SCR [6]	0.92	0.84	0.91	1.00	0.88	0.72	0.92	0.99

5 Conclusion and Future Work

This work proposes a novel method for classifying three different types of document images. The proposed work involves fuzzy based MSER step for candidate components detection from the input images. The distance features are estimated using color, spatial and alignment information of candidate components, which results in a feature matrix. The input image is fed to the proposed AlexNet deep learning model for feature extraction. The proposed architecture integrates the features extracted from the input images and features extracted from the distances for the classification of three different document types. Experimental results on our own dataset and standard datasets show that the proposed method is effective and superior to existing methods in terms of classification rate. The recognition results show that the proposed classification is useful, and it improves the recognition performance of the methods. However, when we include a greater number of complex document images for classification, the performance of the proposed method degrades. Therefore, there is a scope for extending the proposed method for a larger number of classes in the near future.

Acknowledgement. Yue Lu's work is supported by the National Key Research and Development Program of China under Grant No. 2020AAA0107903, the National Natural Science Foundation of China under Grant No. 62176091, and the Shanghai Natural Science Foundation under Grant No. 19ZR1415900. And also, partially supported by TIH, ISI, Kolkata.

References

1. Krishnani, D., et al.: A new context-based features for classification of emotions in photographs. Multimedia Tools Appl. **80**, 15589–15618 (2021)
2. Nandanwar, L., et al.: Chebyshev-Harmonic-Fourier-Moments and deep CNNs for detecting forged handwriting. In: Proceedings of the ICPR, pp. 6562–6569 (2021)
3. Liu, L., et al.: Document image classification: progress over decades. Neurocomputing **453**, 223–240 (2021)
4. Bakkali, S., Ming, Z., Coustaty, M., Rusinol, M.: Cross-modal deep networks for document image classification. In: Proceedings of the ICIP, pp. 2556–2560 (2020)
5. Rani, N.S., Nair, B.J.B., Karthik, S.K., Srinidi, A.: Binarization of degraded photographed document images-a variational denoising auto encoder. In: Proceedings of the ICIRCA, pp. 119–124 (2021)
6. Vision AI | Derive Image Insights via ML | Cloud Vision API. https://cloud.google.com/vision. Accessed 28 Jan 2022
7. Pal, U., Chaudhuri, B.B.: Machine-printed and hand-written text lines identification. Pattern Recognit. Lett. **22**(3/4), 431–441 (2001)
8. Bakkali, S., Ming, Z., Coustaty, M., Rusinol, M.: Visual and textual deep feature fusion for document image classification. In: Proceedings of the CVPRW, pp. 2394–2403 (2020)
9. Bhowmic, S., Sarkar, R.: Classification of text regions in a document image by analyzing the properties of connected components. In: Proceedings of the ASPCON, pp. 36–40 (2020)
10. Fu, W., Xue, B., Gao, X., Zhang, M.: Transductive transfer learning based genetic programming for balanced and unbalanced document classification using different types of features. Appl. Soft Comput. J. **103**, 107172 (2021)
11. Jadli, A., Hain, M., Chergui, A., Jaize, A.: DCGAN-based data augmentation for document classification. In: Proceedings of the ICECOCS (2020)
12. Raghunandan, K.S., et al.: Fourier coefficients for fraud handwritten document classification through age analysis. In: Proceedings of the ICFHR, pp. 25–30 (2016)
13. Saddami, K., Munadi, K., Arnia, F.: Degradation classification on ancient document image based on deep neural networks. In: Proceedings of the ICOIACT, pp. 405–410 (2020)
14. Nandanwar, L., et al.: Local gradient difference features for classification of 2D-3D natural scene text images. In: Proceedings of the ICPR, pp. 1112–1119 (2021)
15. Xue, M., et al.: Arbitrarily-oriented text detection in low light natural scene images. IEEE Trans. MM, 2706–2719 (2021)
16. Fuzzy logic - membership function. https://www.tutorialspoint.com/fuzzy_logic/fuzzy_logic_membership_function.htm. Accessed 16 Jan 2022
17. Liu, J., Su, H., Yi, Y., Hu, W.: Robust text detection via multi-degree of sharpening and blurring. Signal Process., 259–265 (2016)
18. Krizhevsky, A., Sutskever, I., Hinton, G.E.: ImageNet classification with deep convolutional neural networks. Commun. ACM, 84–90 (2017)
19. Basavaraj, V., et al.: Age estimation using disconnectedness features in handwriting. In: Proceedings of the ICDAR, pp. 1131–1136 (2019)
20. Nayef, N., et al.: ICDAR2019 robust reading challenge on multi-lingual scene text detection and recognition—RRC-MLT-2019. In: Proceedings of the ICDAR, pp. 1582–1587 (2019)

Video – 3D

Multi-view Monocular Depth and Uncertainty Prediction with Deep SfM in Dynamic Environments

Christian Homeyer[1,2]([envelope]) [ORCID], Oliver Lange[1] [ORCID], and Christoph Schnörr[2] [ORCID]

[1] Robert Bosch GmbH, Hildesheim, Germany
christian.homeyer@bosch.com
[2] IPA Group, Heidelberg University, Heidelberg, Germany

Abstract. 3D reconstruction of depth and motion from monocular video in dynamic environments is a highly ill-posed problem due to scale ambiguities when projecting to the 2D image domain. In this work, we investigate the performance of the current State-of-the-Art (SotA) deep multi-view systems in such environments. We find that current supervised methods work surprisingly well despite not modelling individual object motions, but make systematic errors due to a lack of dense ground truth data. To detect such errors during usage, we extend the cost volume based Deep Video to Depth (DeepV2D) framework [26] with a learned uncertainty. Our resulting Deep Video to certain Depth (DeepV2cD) model allows (i) to perform en par or better with current SotA and (ii) achieve a better uncertainty measure than the naive Shannon entropy. Our experiments show that we can significantly reduce systematic errors by taking the uncertainty into account. This results in more accurate reconstructions both on static and dynamic parts of the scene.

Keywords: Deep learning · Structure-from-motion · Uncertainty prediction · Depth prediction · Visual odometry · Monocular video · Supervised learning

1 Introduction

Reconstruction of scene geometry and camera motion is an important task for autonomous driving and related downstream tasks, e.g. collision avoidance and path planning. In particular, reconstruction from *monocular* videos has become an important research direction, due to the possibility of low-cost realizations in concrete autonomous systems.

Traditional non-learning algorithms [24] either fail to resolve the inherent ambiguities resulting from moving objects or do not scale well for dense predictions [19]. *Deep learning* based systems can resolve these shortcomings, but their accuracy is dependent on architecture and learning strategy. Depth reconstruction from a single image [8,11,13] is an even more challenging problem, as no motion cues can act as input. *Single-view* networks may not generalize well from one dataset to another [6] or need to be trained on massive datasets [20]. Using a true *multi-view* learning approach

---

Supported by Robert Bosch GmbH.

M. El Yacoubi et al. (Eds.): ICPRAI 2022, LNCS 13363, pp. 373–385, 2022.
https://doi.org/10.1007/978-3-031-09037-0_31

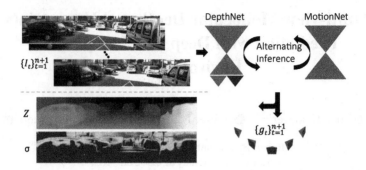

Fig. 1. We predict camera pose graph $\{\mathbf{g}_t\}_{t=1}^{2n+1}$, depth Z and uncertainty σ from an image sequence $\{\mathbf{I}_t\}_{t=1}^{2n+1}$. Warm colors indicate high uncertainty. The uncertainty prediction helps to identify falsely reconstructed regions, which typically occur due to missing lidar supervision.

[12,25–27,29] turns out to be favorable in terms of performance. An *unsupervised* learning strategy can leverage large-scale datasets without gathering expensive depth groundtruth. While impressive progress has been made [11–13,29], accurate depth on dynamic objects cannot be learned when objects move colinear to the camera, since the photometric loss cannot resolve the underlying ambiguity [32]. *Supervised* training can leverage a signal for these cases, which is why we base our work on a supervised multi-view framework.

Recent developments show that modeling scene geometry explicitly inside the architecture [12,25,26] leads to better reconstruction results than loosely coupling neural networks with a common training loss. Inside this paradigm, learned features are aligned temporally and spatially based on scene geometry and camera motion. Our evaluation in Sect. 5 indicates that depth prediction works surprisingly well for dynamic objects, even though a static scene is assumed during this explicit modelling. However, we demonstrate quantitatively and qualitatively that reconstructions of dynamic objects are systematically worse than the static scene on real world autonomous driving data. Our findings show, that the root cause is mostly a lack of supervision from the lidar ground truth.

We extend the supervised DeepV2D framework [26] by learning an additional uncertainty and show how this can identify gross outliers in these regions. An overview can be seen in Fig. 1: based on a sequence of images we compute i) a camera pose graph ii) the key frame depth and iii) an uncertainty estimate. Because the depth network utilizes a cost volume based architecture, this extension comes with no additional overhead. In fact, any cost volume based approach maintains a probability volume, such that an uncertainty measure can be readily computed [17,33]. However, our experiments indicate that by adding a separate uncertainty head to our network and learning a measure, we achieve superior performance compared to the Shannon entropy as done in related work [17,31]. Training this uncertainty head requires an additional loss term, which we adapt from [33]. Our training strategy results in slightly better final accuracy and has the benefit of an additional uncertainty.

An alternative approach to dealing with missing groundtruth in real data, is the use of synthetic data. Advances in datasets [1] allow training with a dense and accurate ground truth before finetuning unsupervised on sparse real data. As a final contribution we show that the DeepV2D networks generalize well to the real world, even when only trained on virtual data. The domain gap can be further reduced by finetuning with a semi-supervised loss on the real data without the need for expensive depth ground truth. We make a comparison of current unsupervised, weakly supervised and supervised SotA on the KITTI [9, 18] and Cityscapes [5] dataset.

2   Related Work

Reconstruction from monocular image sequences has a large body of literature. We refer interested readers to an in-depth survey with focus on dynamic scenes [23] and more background information that is beyond the scope of this paper. Non-learning techniques cannot resolve the arising ambiguities for dynamic scenes [24] or do not scale well [19]. Other works assume a piecewise-planar scene and perform reconstruction based on optical flow [21]. Still, especially colinearly moving objects cannot be distinguished from observed background and result in wrong reconstructions [32]. We therefore focus on learning based approaches and highlight only few selected works.

Learning Geometry and Motion. With the advances of deep neural networks, the single-view reconstruction problem can be effectively approached with Convolutional Neural Networks (CNN's) [7,8] or Transformers [20]. Accurate camera trajectories can be learned from whole image sequences [28]. Self-supervised learning objectives allow learning both geometry and motion without expensive 3D ground truth data [11,13]. In this context, dynamic objects were for example addressed with semantics [2]. However, self-supervised training cannot fully resolve the inherent ambiguities in dynamic scenes. Furthermore, they rely on single-view reconstruction networks, which may not generalize well from one dataset to another [6] or create the need for massive datasets [20]. Finally, the accuracy is still behind multi-view approaches. Multi-view stereo approaches [17,30] learn geometry from multi-view information based on cost volumes, but assume known camera poses.

Deep SfM. A series of recent frameworks combine multi-view image information for inferring camera motion and scene geometry [4,12,25,26,29]. [4,25,26] go one step further and combine learning with a traditional geometric optimization. We base our model on DeepV2D [26], which couples supervised training of depth based on a cost volume architecture with geometric pose graph optimization. These choices seem to result in stronger cross-dataset generalization, as seen from the results in [26] and our experiments. The Manydepth framework [29] focuses on training unsupervised multi-view cost volumes and DRO [12] leverages a fully recurrent architecture both for structure and motion estimation. DRO achieves SotA accuracy, but cannot detect model errors inherent to the sparse supervision. While it collapses the cost volume in order to achieve a lightweight architecture, we exploit the uncertainty information that is maintained inside the volume. We focus on depth prediction, but results could be leveraged for e.g. mapping/fusion [17].

Uncertainty Estimation. Uncertainty can be distinguished into *aleatoric* and *epistemic* uncertainty [14]. As related work [14,17,31], we estimate an aleatoric uncertainty. The idea of using cost volumes for depth reconstruction originates from stereo disparity estimation [3,16,33]. In this context, we investigate uncertainty estimation for a recent deep SfM-framework in the multi-view setting. We realize, that using the Shannon entropy naively [17,31] within our framework does not result in optimal estimates. We instead follow a similar strategy as [33], and introduce a separate uncertainty head into the network.

3   Approach

Problem Statement. Given an ordered sequence of images $\{\mathbf{I}_t\}_{t=1}^{2n+1}$ from a calibrated camera with intrinsics $\mathbf{K}$, compute the set of extrinsic camera parameters $\{\mathbf{g}_t\}_{t=1}^{2n+1}$ and scene depth Z_{n+1}. This can be considered as windowed bundle adjustment problem. For ease of notation, we use simply Z to denote the key frame depth.

Notation. Based on a pinhole camera model, projection and backprojection are defined as:

$$\pi\left(\mathbf{X}\right) = \left[f_x \frac{X}{Z} + c_x, f_y \frac{Y}{Z} + c_y\right] \quad \pi^{-1}\left(\mathbf{x},\ Z\right) = \left[Z \frac{u-c_x}{f_x}, Z \frac{v-c_y}{f_y}, Z, 1\right]^T \quad (1)$$

with camera coordinates $\mathbf{x} = [u,\ v,\ 1]$, 3D coordinates $\mathbf{X} = [X,\ Y,\ Z,\ 1]^T$ and camera intrinsics $[f_x,\ f_y,\ c_x,\ c_y]$. The camera motion is modeled using the rigid body motion $\mathbf{g}_{ij} \in SE_3$. Given two views i and j, the relative coordinate transformation is defined as:

$$\mathbf{x}^j = \pi\left(\mathbf{g}_{ij}\mathbf{X}^i\right) = \pi\left(\mathbf{g}_j \mathbf{g}_i^{-1} \pi^{-1}\left(\mathbf{x}^i,\ Z\right)\right) = \Psi\left(\mathbf{g}_{ij},\ \mathbf{x}^i,\ Z\right), \quad (2)$$

where Ψ is the reprojection operator that transforms a pixel coordinate from camera i into camera j. Given an element of the Lie group $\mathbf{g}$, the logarithm map $\xi = \log \mathbf{g} \in se_3$ maps to the Lie algebra. Vice versa the exponential map is defined as $\mathbf{g} = e^\xi \in SE_3$.

3.1   Networks

This section introduces the DeepV2cD framework. We shortly restate the base networks [26], then introduce our uncertainty head and the explored learning strategies. As the two networks are functions partially dependent on the output of each other, it is alternated between them during inference. They converge to a final optimum after few iterations as shown in [26]. At the start of the inference, the depth is initialized to a constant depth map for all of our experiments, thus requiring no warm start.

Motion Network. We leave the motion architecture design from [26] fixed. This recurrent network takes as input geometry Z and images $\{\mathbf{I}_t\}_{t=1}^{2n+1}$ and outputs the camera pose graph $\{\mathbf{g}_t\}_{t=1}^{2n+1}$. Inside the architecture, $\{\mathbf{g}_t\}_{t=1}^{n+1}$ act as state variables that determine the geometric alignment of learned features $F_t \in \mathbb{R}^{\frac{H}{4} \times \frac{W}{4} \times 32}$ based on the input scene geometry Z. Each recurrence, misalignment $\mathbf{R}$ and confidence $\mathbf{W}$ are estimated.

An unrolled Gauss-Newton optimization produces updates ξ that minimize misalignment in the pose graph. Since it is a recurrent network, it makes a sequence of m predictions $[\{\mathbf{g}\}_1, \{\mathbf{g}\}_2, \ldots, \{\mathbf{g}\}_m]$.

Depth Network. We extend the depth architecture with an additional prediction head and restate the core principles in the following. An overview of the depth network can be seen in Fig. 2. The network design is conceptually similar to PSMNet [3], but gives only two instead of three intermediate predictions due to memory constraints in our setting. This network predicts a dense depth map Z based on $\{\mathbf{I}_t\}_{t=1}^{2n+1}$ and $\{\mathbf{g}_t\}_{t=1}^{2n+1}$. The motion of dynamic objects is not given as input to the network.

For each image $I^i \in \mathbb{R}^{H \times W \times 3}$, learned 2D features $F^i \in \mathbb{R}^{\frac{H}{4} \times \frac{W}{4} \times 32}$ are backprojected into 3D over a discrete 1D depth interval with $\tilde{Z} = [z_1, z_2, \ldots, z_D]$. The 3D points are reprojected based *only on camera motion* $\mathbf{g}_{ij}$ and aligned in the key frame as canonical coordinate frame j. Features should be matched well for the correct depth Z^* and motion $\{\mathbf{g}_t^*\}_{t=1}^{2n+1}$ as long as the scene is static. For each point $\mathbf{x}_k^i$ in frame i and depth $z_d \in \tilde{Z}$ we can define $C_{kd}^j = \Psi\left(\mathbf{g}_{ij}, \mathbf{x}_k^i, z_d\right)$. Concatenating the non-keyframe and keyframe features gives a pairwise cost volume $\mathbf{C}^{ij}$. Matching is learned with a series of 3D convolutions and a final cost volume $\mathbf{C} \in \mathbb{R}^{\frac{H}{4} \times \frac{W}{4} \times D \times 32}$ is globally pooled over view pairs. The cost volume is then regularized by a series of 3D hourglass modules. This step is commonly referred to as cost volume regularization in the stereo literature [3,16] and we believe it is crucial to achieve good performance in dynamic environments.

Each intermediate regularized cost volume is run through a depth head to give a final depth estimate $Z_i \in \mathbb{R}^{\frac{H}{4} \times \frac{W}{4} \times 1}$. The depth head produces a probability volume by a series of $1 \times 1 \times 1$ convolutions and a softmax operator over the depth dimension. The prediction is estimated using the differentiable argmax function [16], thus giving the expected depth of the probability distribution. All predictions are upsampled to final resolution $H \times W$ with naive bilinear upsampling. Similar to related work [17, 31], we can estimate an uncertainty based on the maintained probability volume. Given the probability distribution P over $\tilde{Z}$ for a point $\mathbf{x}_k$, we can compute the Shannon

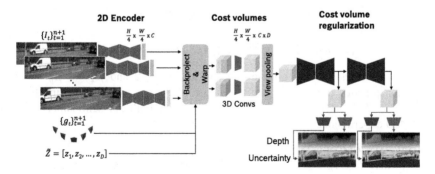

Fig. 2. Depth network of DeepV2cD. Based on $\{I_t\}_{t=1}^{t=n+1}$ and camera poses $\{g_t\}_{t=1}^{t=n+1}$ the network builds a cost volume with learned features. After learned regularization two separate heads infer depth Z and uncertainty σ for each intermediate volume.

entropy $H_k = \sum_{d=1}^{D} P_k(z_d) \log P_k(z_d)$ as a measure of uncertainty [31]. However, due to the limited discrete depth hypothesis space and the soft-argmax operation, the network does not necessarily learn to estimate uni-modal distributions since an infinite number of distributions can produce the same expected depth value. The entropy is not necessarily a good measure of uncertainty. Instead of taking the entropy naively, we learn a confidence $f \in [0, 1]^{H \times W \times 1}$ with a separate network head similar to [33]. This head performs a series of $3 \times 3 \times 3$ convolutions on the regularized cost volume to check for hard-to-match pixels; we use 4 convolution layers. The uncertainty σ is then defined as the linearly scaled $\sigma = s \cdot (1 - f) + \epsilon$, which avoids numerical issues; we set $s = 2$ and $\epsilon = 0.25$ empirically. For training the uncertainty head we adopt the regularization loss from [33] and define an unimodal groundtruth distribution:

$$P^*(z_d) = \text{softmax}\left(-\frac{|z_d - Z^*|}{\sigma}\right) \tag{3}$$

over all values in the depth hypothesis space z_d and with the estimated uncertainty σ from the uncertainty head.

4   Training

We follow the training protocol of [26]. Each network outputs a sequence of predictions, resulting in $\mathbf{Z}_s$ and $\{\mathbf{g}\}_s$. Since the model output is a sequence of m predictions, the final loss is defined as the weighted sum $L = \sum_{s=1}^{m} \gamma^{m-s} L_s$ with $\gamma = 0.5$. Depth supervision on real data is costly to obtain, but camera poses are often readily available. We experiment with a supervised and semi-supervised setting.

Supervised Losses. We supervise depth with l_1, smoothness and focal loss [33] and motion with a reprojection loss $L_{spvd} = \lambda_1 L_1 + \lambda_2 L_{smooth} + \lambda_3 L_{focal} + \lambda_4 L_{flow}$:

$$
\begin{aligned}
L_{spvd} = \frac{1}{HW} \sum_k & \lambda_1 |Z(\mathbf{x}_k) - Z^*(\mathbf{x}_k)| + \lambda_2 M \odot |\mu_x \cdot \partial_x Z(\mathbf{x}_k) + \mu_y \cdot \partial_y Z(\mathbf{x}_k)| \\
& + \lambda_3 \sum_{d=1}^{D} (1 - P_k^*(z_d))^{-\delta} \cdot (-P_k(z_d) \cdot \log P_k^*(z_d)) \\
& + \lambda_4 ||\Psi(\{\mathbf{g}\}, \mathbf{x}_k, Z(\mathbf{x}_k)) - \Psi(\{\mathbf{g}^*\}, \mathbf{x}_k, Z(\mathbf{x}_k))||_1,
\end{aligned}
\tag{4}
$$

where M indicates missing groundtruth; we set $\delta = 2$ and $\mu_x = \mu_y = 1$. It is common practice in unsupervised learning to use edge-aware smoothing [10,12], i.e. $\mu_x = e^{-|\partial_x I|}$ and $\mu_y = e^{-|\partial_y I|}$. We use this for both our semi-supervised and DeepV2cD experiments.

Semi-supervised Losses. We use $L_{semi} = \hat{\lambda}_1 L_{d, photo} + \hat{\lambda}_2 L_{smooth} + \hat{\lambda}_3 L_{m, photo} + \hat{\lambda}_4 L_{se3}$, where $L_{se3}(\mathbf{g}^*, \mathbf{g}) = d(\mathbf{T}^*, \mathbf{T}) + d(\mathbf{R}^*, \mathbf{R})$ is the geodesic distance of camera poses [15] averaged over the pose graph. For self-supervision, we use the photometric loss of [11,13] for both depth and motion predictions by synthesizing an image I' with Ψ and compare it to the reference I. We use edge-aware smoothness with M being all in-view pixels and use the minimum fusion strategy of [11].

Implementation Details. We extend on the published code of Teed et al. [26], but upgrade their implementation to *Tensorflow 2*. We follow the same augmentation [12,26] and two stage training protocol as [26]. We adopt hyperparameters for balancing the loss terms from [26] and determine others empirically. For our results, we set $\lambda = [1.0, 0.02, 0.002, 1.0]$ and $\hat{\lambda} = [10.0, 0.02, 10.0, 1.0]$. Our input and output resolution is 192×1088, which is reasonable for the limited lidar coverage. We use $n = 5$ frames as input for optimal performance [26]. We train for approx. $[5, 15]$ epochs with batch sizes $[12, 3]$ for the respective stages like the baseline from [26] if not stated otherwise. During inference we run 5 instead of 8 iterations compared to [26], because we found that this already matches the reported performance.

5   Experiments

We test DeepV2cD and our own DeepV2D implementation on multiple automotive datasets that include dynamic objects. Our primary focus lies on the depth prediction performance and we include both multi-view and single-view comparisons. As common in deep monocular multi-view SfM we report results for the ground truth scale aligned depth [25–27]. We compare with current SotA multi-view frameworks and report results for their publicly available models.

Datasets. The *KITTI* dataset [9] contains image and lidar sequences from a moving car and is widely established for evaluating depth estimation. We follow the Eigen train/test split and evaluation protocol [7] with the official ground truth maps. The original dataset has only sparse depth ground truth and misses moving object labels. To address these shortcomings, the KITTI 2015 dataset was published [18]. We evaluate on the KITTI 2015 training split to distinguish between static scene and dynamic objects.

Virtual KITTI [1] is a synthetic dataset that imitates several scenes from the KITTI dataset. We use it to investigate the zero-shot generalization performance of DeepV2D and improve performance for our supervised DeepV2cD model. We noticed, that some frames have misaligned ground planes, objects that appear/vanish in the middle of the scene and no camera motion. After dataset cleaning, we achieve a split of approx. 14.3k and 754 train/test frames. We train for $[9, 20]$ epochs.

The *Cityscapes* dataset [5] is an autonomous driving dataset collected from various cities in Germany. The dataset contains many moving object classes, such as cars and pedestrians. It is mainly used for object detection, but also contains 1500 frames with depth ground truth. We evaluate on this dataset to test zero-shot generalization performance and follow the evaluation protocol of [2,29].

Accuracy of Multi-view Networks. Table 1 shows the current SotA for monocular depth prediction on the KITTI Eigen split. It can be seen that DeepV2D and DeepV2cD achieve the best reconstruction accuracy in the 5-view setting on the KITTI Eigen split. All multi-view frameworks achieve better results than single-view ones. While DRO [12] and Manydepth [29] are significantly faster than DeepV2D and DeepV2cD, they are less accurate in a 5-view setting. Depending on the training, not all multi-view models achieve higher accuracy with more views added compared to the 2-view setting. Our cost volume regularization and uncertainty strategy gives better results than

Table 1. Results on KITTI Eigen split with improved ground truth.

Method	Views	Supervised	$W \times H$	Abs Rel ↓	Sq Rel ↓	RMSE ↓	RMSE log ↓	$\delta < 1.25$ ↑
MonoDepth2 [11]	1	✗	1024×320	0.091	0.531	3.742	0.135	0.916
Packnet-SfM [13]	1	(✓)	640×192	0.078	0.420	3.485	0.121	0.931
DORN [8]	1	✓	513×385	0.069	0.300	2.857	0.112	0.945
BANet [25]	5	✓	–	0.083	–	3.640	0.134	–
Manydpepth [29]	2	✗	1024×320	0.055	0.313	3.035	0.094	0.958
Manydpepth [29]	5	✗	1024×320	0.055	0.312	3.034	0.094	0.958
DRO [12]	2	✗	960×320	0.057	0.342	3.201	0.123	0.952
DRO [12]	5	✗	960×320	0.064	0.381	3.262	0.120	0.951
DRO [12]	2	✓	960×320	0.046	0.210	2.674	0.083	0.969
DRO [12]	5	✓	960×320	0.047	0.212	2.711	0.084	0.968
DeepV2D (ours) (VK)	5	✗	1088×192	0.060	0.423	3.302	0.110	0.950
DeepV2D (ours) (VK + K)	5	(✓)	1088×192	0.058	0.669	3.246	0.100	0.960
DeepV2D [26]	2	✓	1088×192	0.064	0.350	2.946	0.120	0.946
DeepV2D [26]	5	✓	1088×192	_0.037_	0.174	2.005	0.074	0.977
DeepV2cD (ours)	5	✓	1088×192	_0.037_	_0.167_	_1.984_	_0.073_	_0.978_
DeepV2cD* (ours) (K + VK)	5	✓	1088×192	**0.035**	**0.158**	**1.877**	**0.071**	**0.980**

the DeepV2D baseline [26] while needing fewer inference iterations due to an improved learning strategy. We achieve best results by training with more data.

Table 2 shows results on the KITTI 2015 training split to emphasize the difference between static and dynamic scene. In Fig. 3, we show some qualitative examples. DeepV2cD achieves the best reconstruction of the static scene. All frameworks perform systematically worse on moving objects. Unsupervised training cannot resolve the inherent ambiguity resulting from the independent object motion and thus results in gross errors when not taking care of regularization. Manydepth resolves this problem partially by regularizing their network with a single-view teacher network compared to the self-supervised DRO during training. We observe, that even though no supervised framework addresses the object motion directly in their reprojection operator, the reconstruction errors are low in most cases.

We believe that this is due to cost volume regularization in DeepV2D and DeepV2cD and the temporal information of the recurrent network in DRO. Because we could not observe the increased errors on virtual data, we believe that they are due to missing supervision with the sparse lidar. While the systematic model errors of DeepV2cD and DRO on the dynamic parts look qualitatively similar, DRO has a significantly lower gap to the static reconstruction. We observe that DeepV2cD sometimes does not reconstruct the car shapes as well and produces more gross outliers. A possible explanation for this is the longer training time of DRO compared to DeepV2cD (50 epochs compared to 15) and the pre-trained ImageNet [22] weights. Pretraining on Virtual KITTI does not resolve this issue completely.

Table 2. Results on KITTI 2015 train split.

Method	Supervised	ARE Dyn. ↓	ARE Static ↓	ARE All ↓	$\delta < 1.25$ ↑
DRO [12]	✗	449.1	0.081	0.276	0.795
Manydpepth	✗	0.177	0.0641	0.090	0.914
DRO [12]	✓	**0.069**	0.050	**0.056**	0.953
DeepV2D (ours)	✓	0.152	0.042	0.071	0.959
DeepV2cD* (ours)	✓	0.127	**0.039**	0.062	**0.965**

Fig. 3. Qualitative results on dense KITTI 2015 training split for 5-frame predictions. Error maps are capped at 10%. Self-supervised training struggles with objects moving colinear to the camera. While supervised frameworks do not suffer from this, they have error patterns due to sparse lidar groundtruth (e.g. cars and windows). Moving objects are usually not fully covered.

Table 3 shows the zero-shot cross-dataset generalization performance of current SotA multi-view frameworks. DeepV2D and DeepV2cD can generalize well to other datasets. We generalize best from KITTI to Cityscapes and outperform unsupervised single-view networks trained on the target. This could be explained with the explicit geometric pose graph optimization for motion estimation and the cost volume. The learned uncertainty transfers well to Cityscapes. When keeping the 80% most certain pixels, we effectively reach 50% of the error of other frameworks in this setting.

Table 3. Zero shot cross-dataset generalization of multi-view frameworks. We evaluate models trained on KITTI (K) on Cityscapes (CS).

Method	Supervised	Dataset	Abs Rel ↓	Sq Rel ↓	RMSE ↓	RMSE log ↓	$\delta < 1.25$ ↑	$\delta < 1.25^2$ ↑	$\delta < 1.25^3$ ↑
Manydpepth [29]	✗	CS	0.114	1.193	6.223	0.170	0.875	0.967	0.989
DRO [12]	✗	K → CS	0.328	7.348	11.656	0.597	0.548	0.747	0.822
DRO [12]	✓	K → CS	0.157	2.228	10.306	0.299	0.777	0.900	0.948
Manydpepth [29]	✗	K → CS	0.162	1.697	8.230	0.229	0.764	0.935	**0.979**
DeepV2D	✓	K → CS	0.109	1.479	6.7633	0.1842	0.876	0.952	0.978
DeepV2cD*	✓	K + VK → CS	**0.104**	**1.325**	**6.7328**	**0.1792**	**0.883**	**0.955**	**0.979**
DeepV2cD* filtered 80%	✓	K + VK → CS	0.070	0.559	4.188	0.124	0.930	0.975	0.989

Uncertainty. The previous experiments have shown that with an uncertainty head and an improved regularization strategy, DeepV2cD achieves SotA depth prediction accuracy on 5-frame videos on KITTI. In Fig. 4, we show qualitative examples of our learned uncertainty on the KITTI dataset. It correlates with hard to match pixels, occlusions, reflective surfaces and areas of missing ground truth. In general it is higher at far away pixels in the scene. Since the uncertainty head can be run in parallel to the depth prediction head, this does not come with an additional computational overhead.

In the next experiments, we investigate the quality of the learned uncertainty for identifying errors made by the model. This implicates, that sorting the pixels by uncertainty results in the same ordering as when we sort by errors. We use sparsification plots [31,33] and compare the learned uncertainty with three baselines: 1. Shannon entropy 2. Random filtering 3. Oracle. Furthermore, we compare DeepV2cD to the inherent Shannon entropy of DeepV2D and DRO [12], which cannot estimate an uncertainty.

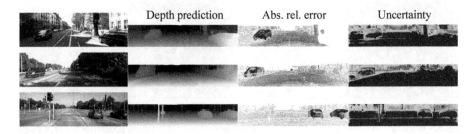

Depth prediction   Abs. rel. error   Uncertainty

Fig. 4. Qualitative results on three samples of KITTI 2015 training split. Warm colors indicate high error (capped at 10%) and uncertainty.

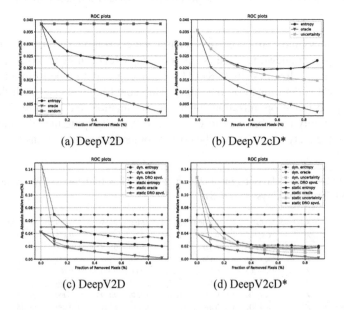

(a) DeepV2D   (b) DeepV2cD*

(c) DeepV2D   (d) DeepV2cD*

Fig. 5. Sparsification plots on KITTI Eigen split (top) and KITTI 2015 (bottom).

Figure 5 shows that DeepV2cD can learn a reliable aleatoric uncertainty while achieving SotA accuracy. We beat all baselines and can achieve cleaner reconstructions after filtering with no significant overhead. When throwing away 20% of the pixels, the avg. abs. rel. error is below 2.5% and similar on both static and dynamic parts of the scene.

6 Conclusion

In this paper, we investigated the performance of recent deep SfM frameworks on several autonomous driving datasets. We show improved results for a cost volume based architecture due to better loss supervision and an additional uncertainty head. Our results indicate that supervised models make errors on real datasets mainly due to a lack of supervision and that they are able to learn more accurate depths when provided with dense virtual data. Missing supervision can be compensated by considering the aleatoric uncertainty. Instead of taking the Shannon entropy inside the cost volume, a learned uncertainty showed better performance at identifying outliers.

Acknowledgement. Research presented here has been supported by the Robert Bosch GmbH. We thank our colleauges Jan Fabian Schmidt, Annika Hagemann and Holger Janssen for fruitful discussions and proof reading.

References

1. Cabon, Y., Murray, N., Humenberger, M.: Virtual kitti 2. arXiv preprint arXiv:2001.10773 (2020)
2. Casser, V., Pirk, S., Mahjourian, R., Angelova, A.: Unsupervised monocular depth and ego-motion learning with structure and semantics. In: Proceedings of the IEEE Conference on Computer Vision and Pattern Recognition Workshops (2019)
3. Chang, J.R., Chen, Y.S.: Pyramid stereo matching network. In: Proceedings of the IEEE Conference on Computer Vision and Pattern Recognition, pp. 5410–5418 (2018)
4. Clark, R., Bloesch, M., Czarnowski, J., Leutenegger, S., Davison, A.J.: Learning to solve nonlinear least squares for monocular stereo. In: Ferrari, V., Hebert, M., Sminchisescu, C., Weiss, Y. (eds.) ECCV 2018. LNCS, vol. 11212, pp. 291–306. Springer, Cham (2018). https://doi.org/10.1007/978-3-030-01237-3_18
5. Cordts, M., et al.: The cityscapes dataset for semantic urban scene understanding. In: Proceedings of the IEEE Conference on Computer Vision and Pattern Recognition, pp. 3213–3223 (2016)
6. Dijk, T.V., Croon, G.D.: How do neural networks see depth in single images? In: Proceedings of the IEEE/CVF International Conference on Computer Vision, pp. 2183–2191 (2019)
7. Eigen, D., Puhrsch, C., Fergus, R.: Depth map prediction from a single image using a multi-scale deep network. arXiv preprint arXiv:1406.2283 (2014)
8. Fu, H., Gong, M., Wang, C., Batmanghelich, K., Tao, D.: Deep ordinal regression network for monocular depth estimation. In: Proceedings of the IEEE Conference on Computer Vision and Pattern Recognition, pp. 2002–2011 (2018)
9. Geiger, A., Lenz, P., Urtasun, R.: Are we ready for autonomous driving? the KITTI vision benchmark suite. In: 2012 IEEE Conference on Computer Vision and Pattern Recognition, pp. 3354–3361. IEEE (2012)

10. Godard, C., Mac Aodha, O., Brostow, G.J.: Unsupervised monocular depth estimation with left-right consistency. In: Proceedings of the IEEE Conference on Computer Vision and Pattern Recognition, pp. 270–279 (2017)

11. Godard, C., Mac Aodha, O., Firman, M., Brostow, G.J.: Digging into self-supervised monocular depth estimation. In: Proceedings of the IEEE/CVF International Conference on Computer Vision, pp. 3828–3838 (2019)

12. Gu, X., Yuan, W., Dai, Z., Tang, C., Zhu, S., Tan, P.: DRO: deep recurrent optimizer for structure-from-motion. arXiv preprint arXiv:2103.13201 (2021)

13. Guizilini, V., Ambrus, R., Pillai, S., Raventos, A., Gaidon, A.: 3D packing for self-supervised monocular depth estimation. In: Proceedings of the IEEE/CVF Conference on Computer Vision and Pattern Recognition, pp. 2485–2494 (2020)

14. Kendall, A., Gal, Y.: What uncertainties do we need in Bayesian deep learning for computer vision? arXiv preprint arXiv:1703.04977 (2017)

15. Kendall, A., Grimes, M., Cipolla, R.: PoseNet: a convolutional network for real-time 6-dof camera relocalization. In: Proceedings of the IEEE International Conference on Computer Vision, pp. 2938–2946 (2015)

16. Kendall, A., et al.: End-to-end learning of geometry and context for deep stereo regression. In: Proceedings of the IEEE International Conference on Computer Vision, pp. 66–75 (2017)

17. Liu, C., Gu, J., Kim, K., Narasimhan, S.G., Kautz, J.: Neural RGB (r) D sensing: depth and uncertainty from a video camera. In: Proceedings of the IEEE/CVF Conference on Computer Vision and Pattern Recognition, pp. 10986–10995 (2019)

18. Menze, M., Geiger, A.: Object scene flow for autonomous vehicles. In: Proceedings of the IEEE Conference on Computer Vision and Pattern Recognition, pp. 3061–3070 (2015)

19. Park, H.S., Shiratori, T., Matthews, I., Sheikh, Y.: 3D trajectory reconstruction under perspective projection. Int. J. Comput. Vision 115(2), 115–135 (2015)

20. Ranftl, R., Bochkovskiy, A., Koltun, V.: Vision transformers for dense prediction. In: Proceedings of the IEEE/CVF International Conference on Computer Vision, pp. 12179–12188 (2021)

21. Ranftl, R., Vineet, V., Chen, Q., Koltun, V.: Dense monocular depth estimation in complex dynamic scenes. In: Proceedings of the IEEE Conference on Computer Vision and Pattern Recognition, pp. 4058–4066 (2016)

22. Russakovsky, O., et al.: ImageNet large scale visual recognition challenge. Int. J. Comput. Vision 115(3), 211–252 (2015)

23. Saputra, M.R.U., Markham, A., Trigoni, N.: Visual slam and structure from motion in dynamic environments: a survey. ACM Comput. Surv. (CSUR) 51(2), 1–36 (2018)

24. Schonberger, J.L., Frahm, J.M.: Structure-from-motion revisited. In: Proceedings of the IEEE Conference on Computer Vision and Pattern Recognition, pp. 4104–4113 (2016)

25. Tang, C., Tan, P.: BA-Net: dense bundle adjustment network. arXiv preprint arXiv:1806.04807 (2018)

26. Teed, Z., Deng, J.: Deepv2d: video to depth with differentiable structure from motion. arXiv preprint arXiv:1812.04605 (2018)

27. Ummenhofer, B., et al.: Demon: depth and motion network for learning monocular stereo. In: Proceedings of the IEEE Conference on Computer Vision and Pattern Recognition, pp. 5038–5047 (2017)

28. Wang, S., Clark, R., Wen, H., Trigoni, N.: DeepVO: towards end-to-end visual odometry with deep recurrent convolutional neural networks. In: 2017 IEEE International Conference on Robotics and Automation (ICRA), pp. 2043–2050. IEEE (2017)

29. Watson, J., Mac Aodha, O., Prisacariu, V., Brostow, G., Firman, M.: The temporal opportunist: self-supervised multi-frame monocular depth. In: Proceedings of the IEEE/CVF Conference on Computer Vision and Pattern Recognition, pp. 1164–1174 (2021)

30. Wimbauer, F., Yang, N., von Stumberg, L., Zeller, N., Cremers, D.: MonoRec: semi-supervised dense reconstruction in dynamic environments from a single moving camera. arXiv preprint arXiv:2011.11814 (2020)

31. Yang, G., Hu, P., Ramanan, D.: Inferring distributions over depth from a single image. In: 2019 IEEE/RSJ International Conference on Intelligent Robots and Systems (IROS), pp. 6090–6096. IEEE (2019)

32. Yuan, C., Medioni, G., Kang, J., Cohen, I.: Detecting motion regions in the presence of a strong parallax from a moving camera by multiview geometric constraints. IEEE Trans. Pattern Anal. Mach. Intell. **29**(9), 1627–1641 (2007)

33. Zhang, Y., et al.: Adaptive unimodal cost volume filtering for deep stereo matching. In: Proceedings of the AAAI Conference on Artificial Intelligence, vol. 34, pp. 12926–12934 (2020)

Fourier Domain CT Reconstruction with Complex Valued Neural Networks

Zoltán Domokos[✉] [iD] and László G. Varga[iD]

Department of Image Processing and Computer Graphics, University of Szeged,
Árpád tér 2., Szeged 6720, Hungary
{domokos,vargalg}@inf.u-szeged.hu

Abstract. In computed tomography, several well-known techniques exist that can reconstruct a cross section of an object from a finite set of it's projections, the sinogram. This task – the numerical inversion of the Radon transform – is well understood, with state of the art algorithms mostly relying on back-projection. Even though back-projection has a significant computational burden compared to the family of direct Fourier reconstruction based methods, the latter class of algorithms is less popular due to the complications related to frequency space resampling. Moreover, interpolation errors in resampling in frequency domain can lead to artifacts in the reconstructed image. Here, we present a novel neural-network assisted reconstruction method, that intends to reconstruct the object in frequency space, while taking the well-understood Fourier slice theorem into account as well. In our case, the details of approximated resampling is learned by the network for peak performance. We show that with this method it is possible to achieve comparable, and in some cases better reconstruction quality than with another state of the art algorithm also working in frequency domain.

Keywords: Computed tomography · Machine learning · Neural networks

1 Introduction

The computed tomography community has seen an emerging trend in the application of machine learning methods recently. Learning based models thriving to enhance reconstruction quality range from early applications of the Hopfield network [1] to deep convolutional neural networks (CNN) that approach artifact removal by residual learning [2,3]. An example of a solution which is computationally similar to analytical methods is presented in [4]. This network can merge the results of multiple filtered back-projection steps to increase reconstruction quality. Alternatively, [5] employs a convolutional network to fuse the results of different reconstructions. Most of the proposals mentioned above post-process the reconstructed image. However a few alternatives exist, like [6] where CT-specific noise pattern removal is performed on the wavelet transform coefficients

© Springer Nature Switzerland AG 2022
M. El Yacoubi et al. (Eds.): ICPRAI 2022, LNCS 13363, pp. 386–397, 2022.
https://doi.org/10.1007/978-3-031-09037-0_32

of low-dose images. Although [18] is rather an iterative method than a machine learning assisted solution, it is still a connected approach worth mentioning. Here local approximation is carried out using a linear combination of Gaussian functions. Due to the fact that our approach is based on the same core ideas that enable local approximation, this work is a relevant antecedent of the current proposal.

Using complex valued neural networks for enhancing reconstruction quality was mainly pioneered by the magnetic resonance imaging community. In MRI, several recent articles (e.g. [7–9]) reported novel reconstruction techniques using complex valued CNNs. An important advantage of complex valued networks is their ability to preserve phase information as data propagates through network layers, a feature that makes them perfectly suitable for complex valued regression tasks. Due to the nature of MRI data, the advantages of the complex valued representation can be more convincing, nevertheless there are some applications in other sub-domains of medical image processing. As an example [10] applies complex valued CNNs combined with a residual learning approach to denoising chest X-ray images. Finally, [20] should also be mentioned as a deep neural network solution that is capable of learning reconstruction in various data acquisition settings, while having the ability to learn to reconstruct phase information, when complex valued sensor data is given.

In this article, we present a complex valued neural network architecture that is capable of reconstructing an image in the Fourier domain, assuming equidistant parallel beam projection geometry. Our custom network topology – that is based on the initial knowledge incorporated in the Fourier slice theorem – enables us to perform reconstruction with superior time complexity compared to backprojection based methods. We show that even a relatively shallow network is capable of providing comparable, or slightly better results than Gridrec [11], a classical Fourier domain-based reconstruction algorithm.

2   Projections and the Fourier Slice Theorem

In tomography we intend to reconstruct an unknown function $f(x, y)$ (i.e., a representation of a cross section of the object) from a set of it's projections. A projection corresponding to angle φ can be defined as the result of integration along all the lines subtending this angle with the coordinate system's vertical axis:

$$p(\varphi, t) = \int_{-\infty}^{+\infty} f(t\cos(\varphi) - s\sin(\varphi), t\sin(\varphi) + s\cos(\varphi))\, ds \qquad (1)$$

where t denotes the distance between a line and the origin, and s is the integration parameter of the line integral.

Let $F(u, v)$ and $S(\varphi, \omega)$ be the two dimensional Fourier transform of $f(x, y)$ and the one dimensional Fourier transform of $p(\varphi, t)$ along axis t respectively. In order to solve the inversion problem in frequency domain, $F(u, v)$ has to be found given the set of projections. Then the object function's image domain representation can be retrieved by two dimensional inverse Fourier transform:

$$f(x, y) = \int\limits_{-\infty}^{+\infty} \int\limits_{-\infty}^{+\infty} F(u, v) e^{i2\pi(ux+vy)} du dv \tag{2}$$

This means that a connection between $S(\varphi, \omega)$ and $F(u, v)$ has to be established.

Theorem 1. *The parallel projection of a function f(x, y) taken at angle φ_0, and Fourier transformed in dimension t, equals to the two-dimensional Fourier transform F(u, v) along a line that subtends an angle φ_0 with the u axis.*

The Fourier slice theorem is stated above similarly as in [22]. It suggests that in case the one dimensional Fourier transforms of the projections are known, $F(u, v)$ can be recovered as:

$$F(\omega \cos(\varphi_0), \omega \sin(\varphi_0)) = S(\varphi_0, \omega) \ , \tag{3}$$

Even though (3) could provide perfect reconstruction, if we had all the continuously many samples, in practice only a finite subset is available. Furthermore sampling happens over a polar grid, which leads to the problem that an efficient approximation of resampling to the Cartesian grid is necessary (see, Fig. 1).

3   Problem Statement

As it has already been mentioned, direct application of the Fourier slice theorem is not feasible in practice, because one has a finite number of samples. Furthermore, a resampling with regular spacing should take place in frequency domain. Even though this operation can not be carried out perfectly, we seek the best possible approximation.

Let R be a complex valued multi-output regression, that takes the regular sampling of an arbitrary $S(\varphi, \omega)$, and maps the corresponding estimation of a regularly sampled $F(u, v)$ to it. Note that a regular sampling of $S(\varphi, \omega)$ exhibits circular and radial symmetry when represented in a Cartesian coordinate system (see Fig. 1). For the sake of simplicity we will denote these sample values by one dimensional indices, assuming row-major conversion. Therefore $F_n = F(u_i, v_j)$ and $S_m = S(\varphi_i, \omega_j)$. Also, let $\Omega = \{S_0, S_1, \ldots, S_n, \ldots\}$ be the set of all S_n values. To a given ground truth F_n the estimate will be $\hat{F}_n$. Note, that the estimation is calculated as the regression from the S_n values, therefore $\hat{F} = R(\Omega)$. Taking into account that samples are generated by a distribution D, our problem statement can be made as follows:

$$\min_R E_D \left(\left\| F_n^{(b)} - \hat{F}_n^{(b)} \right\|^2 \right) , \tag{4}$$

where b is the index of a given observation, label, and estimate triplet. We seek a regression that minimizes the expected value of the squared error. In our case this will be implemented as a neural network.

Although (4) helps defining our goal, it is rather formal, since in practice D is unknown. As a consequence a neural-network regressor, with pre-defined topology and weights acquired by stochastic optimization, can only demonstrate it's capability of efficient generalization empirically. For this purpose several metrics exist, and our selection will be discussed later. As a loss function for the optimization problem yielding the weights, we will use the mean squared error (MSE) metric

$$L = \frac{1}{BN^2} \sum_b \sum_n \left\| F_n^{(b)} - \hat{F}_n^{(b)} \right\|^2 \, , \tag{5}$$

where size of the Cartesian square grid is assumed to be $N \times N$, and we have samples from B observations.

4 Reconstruction with Complex Valued Neural Networks

The optimisation problem formulated in (4) suggests that our neural network should be able to operate with complex values, because it's input samples and the estimation results are represented as complex numbers. Complex valued neural networks have been studied extensively since the 1970's [14], and several proposals can be found - see [12,23] for examples - regarding the adaptation of the error backpropagation algorithm and gradient descent based weight optimisation methods.

In this section a custom feed-forward complex valued network architecture will be proposed to approximate the ground truth F_n values. We rely on the generalization of error backpropagation for complex values presented in [12], however restricting discussion to only those details that are specific to our model.

4.1 The Complex Valued Regression Model

Output of a neuron n of layer l will be $X_n^{(l)}$, connection weights between neuron m and n are denoted by $W_{nm}^{(l)}$, and the error terms by $E_n^{(l)}$. All these values are complex numbers. The relation between our samples and network inputs can be written as $X_n^{(0)} = S_n$. The second layer shall output approximations of the F_n values, i.e., $X_n^{(2)} = \hat{F}_n$. Consequentially, layer indices are included in the $[0, 2]$ range.

We would like to describe a network that is not fully connected. In order to do this conveniently, connectivity between neurons of consecutive layers will be defined by sets that contain indices of all those neurons which are connected to a given neuron m of the preceding layer. Let R_n be a rectangle of unit area centered at a node of the regular grid, where F_n shall be approximated (for an illustration, see the right side of Fig. 1). Furthermore, we define a p_m point as a pair of coordinates $u\left(\omega_j \cos\left(\varphi_i\right)\right)$ and $v\left(\omega_j \sin\left(\varphi_i\right)\right)$, that represents an $X_m^{(0)} = S_m$ sample's location in the Cartesian coordinate system. Now the set containing indices of all those input neurons which are connected to a given neuron n of the first layer can be defined as

$$\Gamma_n^{(1)} := \{m \mid \exists X_m^{(0)} \;\; : \; p_m \in R_n\} \;. \tag{6}$$

Our second layer serves the purpose of local post-processing within a small window around each F_n value. A locally connected layer, similar to the one defined in [24] is suitable. Therefore, we implemented a complex-valued variant of this layer. Connectivity is expressed by sets of indices, just like in the $l = 1$ case. A straightforward derivation of a set definition can be done by the reader.

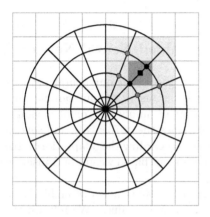 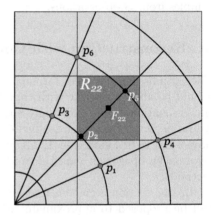

Fig. 1. Resampling the Polar Grid to the Cartesian in Frequency Space. Full image (left) and a magnified part (right). A black rectangle marks F_n, around which the dark grey zone is the unit rectangle R_n. Some Cartesian images of our sampling locations, p_m points, are represented by black and light grey dots. Black ones are within the boundaries of the unit rectangle, therefore their indices will be in $\Gamma_n^{(1)}$, while grey dots fall out of bounds and are ignored.

Our intention is to build a regression model and we use a relatively shallow network, therefore linear activation functions will be a good choice for our layers. According to Eq. (13) defined in [12] and considering activation linearity, we can write a layer's prediction phase output as

$$X_n^{(l)} = \sum_{m \in \Gamma_n^{(l)}} W_{nm}^{(l)} X_m^{(l-1)} \;. \tag{7}$$

Here we used (6) to restrict the sum to only those neurons that are connected. We provide an algorithmic description (see Algorithm 1) to explain how the elements of these sets are identified.

Let us denote the number of projections by M and the number of detectors by N. Furthermore we assume that $M \le c \cdot N$ for some c constant value. Taking into account the fact that to a given S_n element of the input a single R_n is

---

Algorithm 1. Define Connectivity of the First Layer

---

for u in $[0, N]$ **do**
    for v in $[0, N]$ **do**
        $n \leftarrow RowMajorConversion\,(u, v)$
        $Corners \leftarrow RectangleCorners\,(u, v)$
        $[a_{min}, a_{max}] \leftarrow AngleRange\,(Corners)$
        $[r_{min}, r_{max}] \leftarrow RadiusRange\,(Corners)$
        $i \leftarrow 0$
        for a in $[a_{min}, a_{max}]$ **do**
            for r in $[r_{min}, r_{max}]$ **do**
                $(w, z) \leftarrow PolarToCartesian\,(r, a)$
                $[u_{min}, u_{max}] \leftarrow VerticalRange\,(u, v)$
                $[v_{min}, v_{max}] \leftarrow HorizontalRange\,(u, v)$
                if $w \in [u_{min}, u_{max}] \wedge z \in [v_{min}, v_{max}]$ **then**
                    $\Gamma_n^{(1)}[i] \leftarrow RowMajorConversion\,(r, a)$
                end if
            end for
        end for
    end for
end for

---

mapped, it is easy to prove based on (7) and Algorithm 1 that a prediction with our model can be done in $O(NM) \sim O(N^2)$ time. As a consequence, the most expensive operation during reconstruction is the two dimensional (inverse) fast Fourier transform. The same is true for the second layer, therefore total time complexity of our algorithm scales with the $O(N^2 \cdot \log N^2)$ cost of a two dimensional (inverse) fast Fourier transform opposed to the $O(N^2 \cdot M) \sim O(N^3)$ complexity of back-projection-based methods.

4.2 The Training Phase

In order to comply with any gradient descent based optimizer, we have to calculate gradients of a loss function L with respect to the weights. With definition (4) we have already selected the Mean Squared Error as a loss function. Applying (22) and (16) from [12], while keeping in mind that our activation is linear, gradients can be acquired as

$$\nabla_{W_{nm}^{(l)}}(L) = -2E_n^{(l)} X_m^{*(l-1)}, \quad m \in \Gamma_n^{(l)}. \tag{8}$$

Here the error term associated to neuron n of layer l is multiplied with the conjugate of another m neuron's output value. This latter neuron resides in the preceding layer and has a connection with n.

As it can be seen in (8), gradient computation requires a recursion to resolve the error terms. For any hidden layer a sum of the error terms multiplied by the conjugate of connection weights shall be taken for all connected neurons of the consecutive layer

$$E_n^{(l)} = \sum_{q \in \Lambda} E_q^{(l+1)} W_{qn}^{*(l+1)} \ , \quad \Lambda = \left\{ r \mid n \in \Gamma_r^{(l+1)} \right\} \ . \tag{9}$$

In case of the output layer ($l = 2$) the error term is simply the difference between a ground truth F_n value and the outputted estimate: $E_n^{(l)} = F_n - X_n^{(l)}$.

Weight updates are done by the Adam optimizer [13], with the restriction that second moments of gradients with respect to complex weights are not considered. Squared coefficients of the real and imaginary parts of the gradients are used instead. Although empirical evaluation was promising, it is an open question if this simplification has any adverse effects.

5   Evaluation and Results

We measured the performance of our proposed neural network on a set of artificial monochrome phantom images. These 24 samples (including a Shepp-Logan head phantom [21]) were selected to show high structural variability. We also performed reconstruction based on data from real-world measurements to demonstrate that our method is capable of handling these scenarios.

Normalized root mean squared error (NRMSE) and mean structural similarity ratio (MSSIM) were used to quantify reconstruction quality while performing tests on the artificial data sets. We calculated these metrics for each sample, then averaged over the whole test set. Parametrization of MSSIM was done according to [15], therefore we selected a Gaussian weighting function with $\sigma = 1.5$ and covariances were normalized by the number of pixels covered by the sliding window.

Our proposed solution was compared to Gridrec [11], a well-known frequency domain algorithm that has a similar approach as the solution proposed in this article. We used an implementation of Gridrec that is available in Tomopy [19], a popular tomographic imaging library.

5.1   Training Data and Hyperparameters

We collected 3600 artificial binary images to generate our training data set. Image size was 256 pixels in both dimensions, which we padded to 366×366 in order to properly cover the hypotenus of the image during projection acquisition. Intensity values were handled as 32 bit floating point numbers, initially scaled to the $[0.0, 1.0]$ range.

Every input-output pair in the training set was generated starting from a linear combination of three randomly selected artificial phantoms, with coefficients sampled from a uniform distribution. We applied the projection acquisition formulas to the combined images, followed by a one dimensional fast Fourier transform, in order to acquire the training inputs. As a ground truth, we took the two dimensional fast Fourier transforms of the combined phantoms.

For all the different projection counts a unique model had to be trained, running 250 epochs in each case, with a batch size of 16. Learning rate was set to 0.0005, which is a bit lower then usual. This choice can be justified by the linearity of our activation functions. Parameters for the first and second order momentum were defined as 0.9 and 0.99 respectively.

5.2   Results

Testing of our own method was carried out with sinograms of the same size and padding that we used for training. In case of the reference reconstructions with Gridrec, an extra zero padding was applied to the sinograms to avoid inter-period interference, as suggested in [17]. Therefore, Gridrec processed double sized sinograms, while size of the region of interest stayed the same. With this padding strategy an increased structural similarity could be observed. Tomopy offers various filters for Gridrec, from which we selected the default Shepp-Logan filter and the cosine filter. The latter was chosen due to it's performance surpassing other filters in most of our test cases.

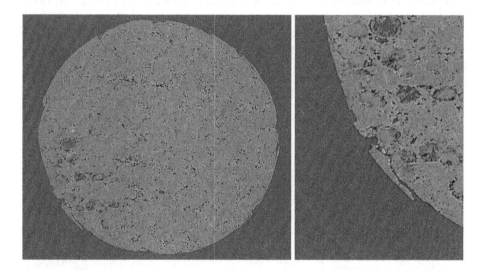

Fig. 2. Reconstruction of a Slice from the AlSiC Data Set with the Proposed Method. Region of Interest of the selected slice (left) and it's enlarged lower left section (right) is shown. The 1440 × 1440 image was reconstructed from a 1016 × 1200 sinogram. The same padding strategy was applied as in case of the artificial images.

Calculation of image quality metrics was focused on a 128 × 128 pixels sized central section within the region of interest of the original phantoms. We performed two rounds of measurements to study the effect of decreasing angular sampling and additive Gaussian noise. In the first round, four different projection counts - 90, 180, 366, and 600 - were taken, without the presence of noise.

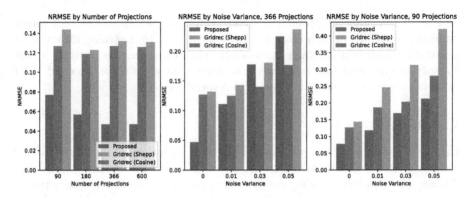

Fig. 3. Normalized Root Mean Squared Error Results. Measurements of noiseless artificial phantoms with decreasing projection count (left), a combination of varying levels of additive Gaussian noise and balanced angular sampling (mid), finally angular undersampling combined with the same noise levels.

Gradually increasing Gaussian noise was combined with 366 and 90 projections. For both projection counts, noise variance was between 0.01 and 0.05 which corresponds to a peak signal to noise ratio (PSNR) decrease from ~68 dB to ~61 dB. (Note that results with zero variance noise, which means a noiseless input in our case, were included in each subplot for the sake of convenient comparison.) (Fig. 4)

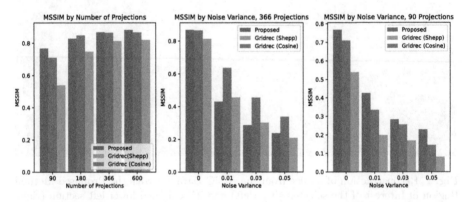

Fig. 4. Mean Structural Similarity Results. Measurements of noiseless test phantoms with varying angular sampling density (right), additive Gaussian noise combined with balanced angular sampling (mid), and undersampling (right).

Although in the noiseless case our method outperformed Gridrec in terms of NRMSE regardless of the selected filter (see Fig. 3), we found that adding Gaussian noise can abruptly close this quality gap between the proposed method and Gridrec with a Shepp-Logan filter when the peak signal to noise ratio (PSNR) is below 68 dB. Moreover with a cosine filter the classical method was more tolerant to all noise levels. In the other hand, decreasing angular sampling density does not have an excessively negative effect on our proposal's reconstruction quality. As a consequence our method was slightly more accurate when insufficient angular sampling was combined with noise (Fig. 5).

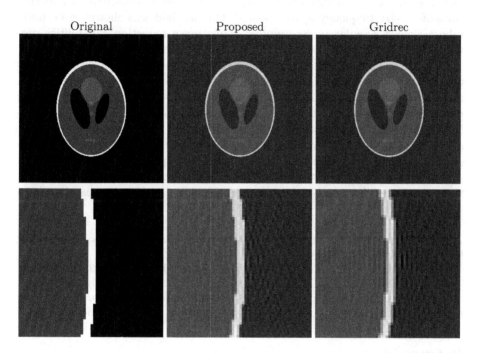

Fig. 5. Comparison of the Reconstructions of a Shepp-Logan Head Phantom. In the top row, complete 366 × 366 phantoms can be seen with a 256 × 256 sized region of interest. The second row shows a zoomed 58 × 58 section of the right edge.

We found less explicit difference in mean structural similarity, which suggests similar reconstruction quality for most of the noiseless cases with projection counts 366 and above. Regarding MSSIM the same tendency can be observed as in case of NRMSE, namely that our method is more robust against undersampling, while it's susceptibility to noise is clearly a disadvantage when noise is combined with balanced angular sampling. Nevertheless, in all the tests, the results of the two methods were comparable in regard of the quality.

Our real-world data set was recorded using a cylindrical AlSiC sample. This metal matrix composite material is widely used in the semiconductor industry. It contains silicon-carbide particles embraced by an aluminum matrix. A set of radiographs, taken from 1200 projection angles, had to be converted to sinograms of 2032 separate object slices. Initial corrections were done based on averaging 50 and 30 flat and dark field images. Results (see Fig. 2) show well preserved structural traits and clean edges.

6 Conclusion

In the preceding section we demonstrated that it is possible to achieve encouraging results in terms of reconstruction quality, if frequency space reconstruction is enhanced with a complex valued neural network. We proposed a method that managed to achieve slightly better quality reconstructions compared to another state-of-the-art frequency space method. Our method was shown to be fairly robust against angular undersampling, while noise reduction capabilities provide a room for improvement.

A remarkable advantage is that these results can be achieved with a shallow network of relatively sparse connectivity, while it is not necessary to apply additional zero-padding to the sinogram. Moreover it also worth mentioning, that our model enables other users to train and test it easily, without the need for a carefully assembled and populous data set. Unfortunately, it is required to implement a custom network topology in order to reproduce our results, which can complicate the implementation process. Nevertheless, we expect that extensions of our proposed network architecture can provide light-weight machine-learning solutions for several frequently occurring reconstruction artifacts in parallel beam tomography.

Acknowledgments. The authors would like to thank Rajmund Mokso for supplying the real test dataset for the studies.

This research was supported by Project no. TKP2021-NVA-09. Project no. TKP2021-NVA-09 has been implemented with the support provided by the Ministry of Innovation and Technology of Hungary from the National Research, Development and Innovation Fund, financed under the TKP2021-NVA funding scheme.

References

1. Srinivasan, V., Han, Y.K., Ong, S.H.: Image reconstruction by a Hopfield neural network. Image Vis. Comput. **11**(5), 278–282 (1993)
2. Jin, K.H., McCann, M.T., Froustey, E., Unser, M.: Deep convolutional neural network for inverse problems in imaging. IEEE Trans. Image Process. **26**(9), 4509–4522 (2017)
3. Han, Y.S., Yoo, J., Ye, J.C.: Deep residual learning for compressed sensing CT reconstruction via persistent homology analysis. arXiv preprint arXiv:1611.06391 (2016)
4. Pelt, D.M., Batenburg, K.J.: Fast tomographic reconstruction from limited data using artificial neural networks. IEEE Trans. Image Process. **22**(12), 5238–5251 (2013)
5. Boublil, D., Elad, M., Shtok, J., Zibulevsky, M.: Spatially-adaptive reconstruction in computed tomography using neural networks. IEEE Trans. Med. Imaging **34**(7), 1474–1485 (2015)
6. Kang, E., Junhong, M., Ye, J.C.: A deep convolutional neural network using directional wavelets for low-dose X-ray CT reconstruction. Med. Phys. **44**(10), 360–375 (2017)

7. Xiao, L., et al.: Partial Fourier reconstruction of complex MR images using complex-valued convolutional neural networks. Magn. Reson. Med. **87**(2), 999–1014 (2022)
8. El-Rewaidy, H., et al.: Deep complex convolutional network for fast reconstruction of 3D late gadolinium enhancement cardiac MRI. NMR Biomed. **33**(7), e4312 (2020)
9. Cole, E.K., et al.: Analysis of deep complex-valued convolutional neural networks for MRI reconstruction. arXiv preprint arXiv:2004.01738 (2020)
10. Rawat, S., Rana, K.P.S., Kumar, V.: A novel complex-valued convolutional neural network for medical image denoising. Biomed. Sig. Process. Control **69**, 102859 (2021)
11. Dowd, B.A., et al.: Developments in synchrotron x-ray computed microtomography at the National Synchrotron Light Source. In: Developments in X-ray Tomography II, vol. 3772, pp. 224–236. International Society for Optics and Photonics, Denver (1999)
12. Benvenuto, N., Piazza, F.: On the complex backpropagation algorithm. IEEE Trans. Sig. Process. **40**(4), 967–969 (1992)
13. Kingma, D.P., Ba, J.: Adam: a method for stochastic optimization. arXiv preprint arXiv:1412.6980 (2014)
14. Widrow, B., McCool, J., Ball, M.: The complex LMS algorithm. Proc. IEEE **63**(4), 719–720 (1975)
15. Wang, Z., Bovik, A.C., Sheikh, H.R., Simoncelli, E.P.: Image quality assessment: from error visibility to structural similarity. IEEE Trans. Image Process. **13**(4), 600–612 (2004)
16. Cooley, J.W., Lewis, P.A.W., Welch, P.D.: The fast Fourier transform and its applications. IEEE Trans. Educ. **12**(1), 27–34 (1969)
17. Marone, F., Stampanoni, M.: Regridding reconstruction algorithm for real-time tomographic imaging. J. Synchrotron Radiat. **19**(6), 1029–1037 (2012)
18. Paleo, P., Desvignes, M., Mirone, A.: A practical local tomography reconstruction algorithm based on a known sub-region. J. Synchrotron Radiat. **24**(1), 257–268 (2017)
19. Gürsoy, D., et al.: TomoPy: a framework for the analysis of synchrotron tomographic data. J. Synchrotron Radiat. **21**(5), 1188–1193 (2014)
20. Zhu, B., Liu, J., Cauley, S., et al.: Image reconstruction by domain-transform manifold learning. Nature **555**, 487–492 (2018)
21. Shepp, L.A., Logan, B.F.: The Fourier reconstruction of a head section. IEEE Trans. Nucl. Sci. **21**(3), 21–43 (1974)
22. Kak, A.C., Slaney, M.: Principles of Computerized Tomographic Imaging, pp. 21–43. Society for Industrial and Applied Mathematics (2001)
23. Hirose, A.: Complex-Valued Neural Networks: Theories and Applications, vol. 5. World Scientific (2003)
24. Keras API Reference. https://keras.io/api/layers. Accessed 11 Jan 2022

Seeking Attention: Using Full Context Transformers for Better Disparity Estimation

Nadir Bengana[✉], Janne Mustaniemi, and Janne Heikkilä

University of Oulu, Oulu, Finland
mohamed.bengana@oulu.fi

Abstract. Until recently, convolutional neural networks have dominated various machine vision fields-including stereo disparity estimation-with little to no competition. Vision transformers have shaken up this domination with the introduction of multiple models achieving state of art results in fields such as semantic segmentation and object detection. In this paper, we explore the viability of stereo transformers, which are attention-based models inspired from NLP applications, by designing a transformer-based stereo disparity estimation as well as an end-to-end transformer architectures for both feature extraction and feature matching. Our solution is not limited by a pre-set maximum disparity and manages to achieve state of the art on SceneFlow dataset.

Keywords: Stereo disparity · Depth estimation · Vision transformer

1 Introduction

What is the next step for stereo disparity estimation? Until recently, convolutional neural networks (CNN) dominated computer vision applications. However, a novel method called transformers has proved to be effective in various fields including but not limited to classification [2], semantic segmentation [14], image inpainting [15], and super-resolution [18].

Unlike Convolutional Neural Networks, transformers are attention based models. The term attention was used to refer to how we pay attention to specific areas of an image or words in a sentence. In machine learning context, attention [1] was born to address an issue in sequence to sequence problems where only the output of the decoder was considered. Attention, on the other hand, takes the output at each step and assigns a weight to it, allowing the decoder to focus on the most important parts of the sequence.

Unlike early attention based models, transformers rely exclusively on attention to draw global dependencies between the input and output [6]. Transformers revolutionized the field of Natural Language Processing (NLP) with models such as GPT [17], and BERT [16] vastly outperforming their recurrent neural network counterparts.

© Springer Nature Switzerland AG 2022
M. El Yacoubi et al. (Eds.): ICPRAI 2022, LNCS 13363, pp. 398–409, 2022.
https://doi.org/10.1007/978-3-031-09037-0_33

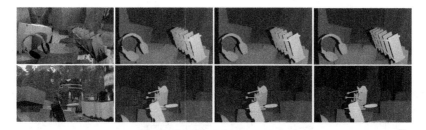

Fig. 1. Samples from SceneFlow Dataset. From left to right: left images, STTR output, output of our model, Ground Truth (GT) disparity.

Shortly after transformers became mainstream in NLP applications, transformer based models for machine vision began to appear. Some of the early examples tried to incorporate transformer concepts into convolution [20], however, these solutions did not provide the substantial jump in accuracy seen in NLP. Recently, more pure transformer based machine vision models were developed. Vision Transformer (ViT) [2] is an example model that tries to be as close as possible to the original transformer. The equivalent for words is patches in the image. However, these solutions still need to be creative to successfully include transformers. For example, most semantic segmentation models use CNN decoders.

In the field of stereo matching and disparity estimation, CNNs reign supreme with most models following the same pipeline of feature extraction, cost volume generation, feature matching, and disparity refinement. All of these steps heavily rely on CNNs, notably the feature matching step which uses 3D CNNs. Therefore, to incorporate transformers, a new feature matching approach must be used. Stereo Transformer (STTR) [11] is one of very few transformer based disparity estimation models. In STTR, the feature matching is done using a dynamic programming method introduced in by Ohta *et al.* [12] which relies only on the epipolar lines thus making the model blind to any context outside those lines. The solution they came up with is adding a CNN post processing method to regain some global context.

In this paper, we introduce a method to have global context while still keeping the computational complexity low. We also introduce an end to end transformer based model for stereo disparity estimation. The flowcharts are shown in Fig. 2. We achieve state of the art results on the SceneFlow dataset. Samples are shown in Fig. 1.

2   Related Work

2.1   Vision Transformers

Since their inception, transformers became very successful in NLP applications. Models such as BERT [16] and GPT-3 [17] substantially improved the performance of various NLP tasks. In the original paper [6], transformers are described

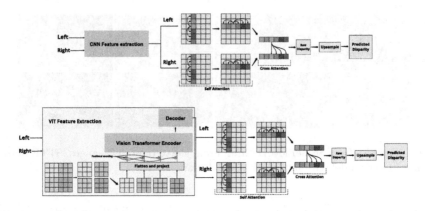

Fig. 2. Architectures of our models. *Top* CNN based model. *Bottom* ViT based model.

to use self-attention to compute representations of its input and output without the use of RNNs or CNNs. Self-attention allows the transformer to learn long-range dependencies in a more effective way compared to RNNs. Therefore, efforts have been made to port this success to computer vision tasks.

In their early form, transformers were used alongside convolution or as a way to tackle the downsides of convolution. Examples of these early methods include deformable convolutions [20] which use self-attention to allow convolution kernels to change shape, and Squeeze-and-Excitation networks [21] which address channel-wise feature responses by selecting information features to emphasise on.

To fully replace convolutional layers, transformers needed to be adapted to image data. Equating pixels to words would result in large memory consumption and a computation complexity of $O(h^2w^2)$ where h and w are the height and with of the image respectively. There are various ways this issue has been handled. Methods applied by Han *et al.* [22], Zheng *et al.*, [14] and Strudel *et al.* [19] among others, tackled this issue by dividing the image into patches essentially mimicking the behaviour of convolutional kernels, however, unlike convolution, these patches do not rely on fixed pattern matching but instead attentively determine aggregation weights, i.e., something akin to a dynamic kernel. Another method called Axial DeepLab introduced by the DeepLab team [7] chose the patches to be 1 pixel wide vectors along the x and y axis consecutively to build full context. However, this method is a hybrid between convolution and self-attention.

2.2 Stereo Disparity Estimation

In a stereo image setup, finding the stereo disparity relies on finding a match across these two images for every pixel. Classical methods such as semi-global matching [8] relied on finding differences between patches along the epipolar lines from both images. However, these methods are not reliable when it comes to un-textured objects and noisy images. Deep Learning (DL) methods brought a substantial improvement over previous methods where a CNN learn to extract features from both images followed by concatenation and finally passing through fully connected layers which learn to find the disparity [9]. Subsequently, CNN based methods advanced further using a cost volume and cost aggregation where a 4D vector is build out of the feature maps where the 4th dimension is the candidate disparities and using a 3D CNN to find the best match. These methods follow a similar pipeline of feature extraction, calculating matching cost, cost aggregation, and disparity refinement [3,5,10].

To translate stereo disparity estimation to transformers a new approach needed to be followed. Although transformers have not been used much in the subject of disparity estimation, some works have explored and proved its feasibility. Wang et al. [25] proposed a generic parallax-attention mechanism (PAM), which does not rely on self-attention, but only on cross-attention across epipolar lines as a way to match features.

Li et al. [11] (STTR) introduced a full ViT approach to stereo matching where both self and cross-attention are used. STTR relies on finding self and cross-attention across the horizontal lines. The matching is obtained using the dynamic programming method introduced in 1985 [12], where similarities between pixel intensities were used to find the equivalent match. The pixel intensities are replaced in STTR with attention which gives better contextual information for each pixel and long range associations. Since the transformer can only attend to epipolar lines, it misses the context across the $y - axis$ of the feature map. To tackle that issue a post processing convolutional network has been introduced which aims at capturing context from the original image.

3 Methods

Stereo disparity estimation methods that rely on DNN follow a pipeline consisting of feature extraction, cost volume generation, stereo matching, and disparity calculation. However, using transformers the pipeline is slightly different, where the cost volume steps are omitted in favor of direct matching.

3.1 Feature Extraction

To test various options for feature extraction we designed multiple feature extraction models based on both CNNs and ViT. This variation serves to perform an extensive ablation study on what works best for a transformer feature matching.

For our CNN based model, the feature extraction network consists of 42 layers in an encoder-decoder architecture as shown in Fig. 3. Our model is slightly inspired by PSMNet [3]. It is meant to be lightweight keeping the runtime and memory consumption low as well as the resolution of the feature map consistently at $\frac{1}{4}H, \frac{1}{4}W, C$ where H and W are the height and weight of the input images consecutively, and C is the depth of the feature map.

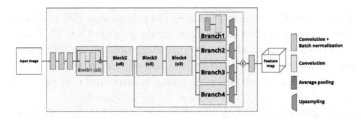

Fig. 3. Architecture of Feature extraction network.

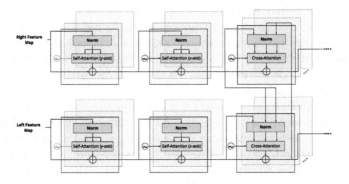

Fig. 4. Architecture of attention layers. The sine sign represents the positional encoding.

Transformers are notorious for requiring huge datasets for pretraining. Therefore, to select an option for our transformer based feature extraction, we chose Visual Transformer (ViT) since it is pretrained on various large datasets on the task of classification. We use a model pretrained on ImageNet21K [4], which contains over 16 million samples. According to Alexey *et al.* [2], Larger datasets yield better results, in fact, their in house JFT 300M which contains over 300 million samples, outperformed ImageNet 21K by consistently improving the classification accuracy by up to 5%. We chose ImageNet21K due to its open availability. We modified the ViT model to fit to the task of feature extraction by introducing an encoder-decoder architecture. The model architecture is shown in Fig. 2. The output of the ViT feature extraction is set to match the same output stride and feature depth as the CNN feature extraction. Additionally, we tested the feature extraction network introduced in STTR [11].

3.2 Full Context Stereo Transformers

In CNN based stereo matching, a cost volume is constructed containing all the candidate disparities. However, the model cannot attain to disparities outside the preset maximum disparity. Most CNN models set this maximum value to be 192 or 384. However, even the mainstream datasets, the maximum disparity can surpass 384 pixels. The main reasons why the cost volume is limited are memory consumption and complexity. Therefore, most models try to find a balance that would achieve the best test results, which would not necessarily translate well to situations where the disparity is higher than the preset limit.

With transformers, the cost volume generation step is avoided in favor of attention layers. Transformers contain 4 main sub-components: the self-attention layers, the cross-attention layers, the positional encoding, and the feed forward layers [6]. STTR [11], replaced the cost volume with dynamic programming [12], which originally relies on comparing the intensity of pixels. Using self-attention, weights are associated with each pixel, giving it richer information than simply its intensity. This extra information may be its relative distance to a landmark or how color changes in nearby pixels. Subsequently, cross-attention layers are used to compare these weighted pixels in the stereo views.

In previous transformer based methods, either local context [25] or epipolar only context is used [11]. Therefore, a lot of information that can be useful in stereo matching is omitted. The perfect scenario would be to include the whole feature map, that is, however, not feasible due to memory and computation constraint. Hence, we developed a method that can leverage the information from not only the epipolar lines $(x - axis)$, but also from the vertical lines $(y - axis)$. Our method illustrated in Fig. 4 is based on and improves upon the Stereo Transformer (STTR) [11]. As shown in Fig. 4, the feature maps go through self-attention along the vertical $y - axis$ before the horizontal $x - axis$ as shown in Fig. 2. This setup allows the self-attention layers to have information regarding the whole vertical $y - axis$ at each point in the epipolar lines. The intuition is that each pixel in the feature map would first be enhanced with weights from the vertical $y - axis$ before being matched along the epipolar lines.

The attention layers take 3 inputs called the Key, $Query$, and $Value$. These are obtained by passing the feature map through a linear feed forward layer. These terms are borrowed from retrieval systems. The query is what we are searching for, the key is a unique identifier and the value is the main data. The attention layer aims at finding weights to be associated with the values. These weights, as we will see, are obtained by selecting from a set of keys using a query.

The linear equation used in the attention is presented as follows:

$$F(x, W, b) = Wx + b \tag{1}$$

where x is the input, W contains the weights, and b is the bias.

In the case of self-attention layers, the Key, $Query$, and $Value$ are obtained using the output of the previous cross-attention layer or the feature maps in the first layer. For the cross-attention layers, while $Value$ is similarly obtained from the previous self-attention layers, the Key, and $Query$ of the left transformer are obtained from the previous self-attention output of the right transformer and vice-versa.

Each attention layer is divided into 8 heads which take a portion of the feature map. The Key, $Query$, and $Value$ are obtained using the following equations:

$$K_i = F(f, W_K, b_K)_i$$
$$Q_i = F(f, W_Q, b_Q)_i \qquad (2)$$
$$V_i = F(f, W_V, b_V)_i$$

where $f = o + PE$ with o representing the output of the feature extraction network in the case of the first layer or the output of the previous attention layers. PE is the positional encoding. K_i, Q_i, and V_i are the Key, $Query$, and $Value$ of the ith head, respectively. Therefore, the selection of the $Keys$, $Querys$, and $Values$ is done by the model in the learning phase. The Positional Encoding (PE) is an important part of transformers. The goal of PE is to add information regarding the position of each pixel. For the feature matching network, we used sinusoidal positional encoding similar to the one used in the original Transformer paper [6]:

$$PE_{(pos, 2i)} = sin(pos/10000^{2i/d})$$
$$PE_{(pos, 2i+1)} = cos(pos/10000^{2i/d}) \qquad (3)$$

where pos is the position, i is the dimension, and d is the dimension of the model. Multiple forms of positional encoding can be used. The two requirements for the positional encoding are the ability to represent PE_{pos+k} as a linear function of PE_{pos}, and unambiguity, that is, no two positions have the same encoding. In the feature extraction ViT network, the positional encoding is done using standard learnable 1D position embedding similar to what was introduced in the original ViT paper [2].

The attention layers first extract the attention weights using the following equation:

$$\alpha_i = \frac{Q_i^T K_i}{\sqrt{C_i}} \qquad (4)$$

where α_i is the attention weight of the ith head, and C_i is the depth of the ith $value$. The output value V is obtained with the following equation:

$$V = Concat(\alpha_1 V_i, ..., \alpha_H V_H) \qquad (5)$$

Finally, the output of each layer is obtained as follows:

$$O = F(V, W_o, b_o) \qquad (6)$$

4   Experiments and Results

4.1   Datasets and Metrics

SceneFlow: The SceneFlow dataset [23] comprises of more than 39000 stereo frames in 960×540 pixel resolution. The dataset is divided into 3 subsets. Like most previous works, we use the FlyingThings3D subset with the default training, validation, and test subsets.

KITTI: KITTI dataset [24] consists of 200 training scenes and 200 test scenes obtained from a moving vehicle.

Metrics. The metrics used are the percentage of errors larger than 3 pixels, known as 3px error, and Expected Prediction Error (EPE).

4.2   Training

The optimizer used is AdamW, with $1e^{-4}$ as weight decay and a learning rate of $1e^{-4}$. The pretraining is done with a fixed learning rate on SceneFlow for 15 epochs while finetunning is done with a learning rate decay of 0.99 for up to 400 epochs. The training was performed on multiple Nvidia GPUs. The feature extraction transformer has 12 self-attention layers with the output depth being 128 with an output stride of 4. The feature matching has 6 self and cross-attention layers. The output stride for the CNN feature extraction is 4. The image size is the default for SceneFlow and KITTI.

4.3   Experiments

In our ablation studies, we test 3 feature extraction models and 3 feature matching models. This would result in 9 experiments, but, we only test the new attention models with the best performing feature extraction models.

4.4   Results and Comparison

Comparison with Other Methods. We compare our method with prior stereo disparity estimation methods, notably, works holding the state of the arts in the datasets we are studying. The architecture of our method is based on CNN feature extraction with 42 layer and feature matching with transformers using self-attention across the vertical $y - axis$, then self-attention across horizontal $x - axis$ followed by cross-attention across the epipolar lines from both views. The results are shown in Table 1.

In the SceneFlow dataset, our method holds the SOA 3px results. The current epe SOA holder is HITNet [27] which-unlike most CNN based methods-does not rely on 3D convolutions. Instead, it employs a fast multi-resolution step followed by geometric propagation. The SOA method for KITTI 2015 is LEAStereo [5], which uses a classical cost volume and 3D convolution for matching. However, it uses Neural Architectural Search (NAS) to find the optimal model within the search space they employed. Our method fails to achieve similar outstanding results with KITTI. The reason, we theorize is the size of the dataset. Although, we pretrained the models on SceneFlow, KITTI still is different enough and does not have as many samples. Therefore, the transformers could not learn enough to overcome CNNs.

Table 1. Results with SceneFlow pretraining

	KITTI 2015			SceneFlow	
	bg	fg	all	epe	3px
STTR [11]	1.70	3.61	2.01	0.45	1.26
PSMNet [3]	1.71	4.31	2.14	1.03	3.60
AANet [26]	1.80	4.93	2.32	0.87	2.38
LEAStereo [5]	**1.29**	**2.65**	**1.51**	0.78	2.60
HITNet [27]	1.74	3.20	1.98	**0.36**	2.21
Ours	2.00	4.20	2.38	0.38	**1.10**

Feature Extraction Results. We tested the feature extraction methods explained previously. We refer to the feature extraction used in STTR as Dense FE, the ViT based feature extraction as ViT FE, and our convolution based feature extraction model as Conv FE. The feature matching architecture used in this section uses self-attention on horizontal $x - axis$ only. Table 2 shows the results obtained using different feature extraction methods.

Table 2. SceneFlow results using different feature extraction networks

Experiment	3px error	EPE	Runtime (s)	Training time (1epoch)
Dense FE	1.26	0.45	0.79	11 h 28 m 12 s
Conv FE	1.20	0.40	0.52	6 h 54 m 40 s
ViT FE	1.86	0.52	0.41	2 h 14 m 40 s

From these results, we can deduce that a very deep CNN feature extraction method with an output stride of 0 is not necessary. Previous works using NAS showed that shallower DNNs can perform better than their deeper counterparts [13].

Transformer Matching Results. We tested multiple transformer architectures. $xSAxCA$ refers to attention across $x - axis$ only in both self and cross-attention. $xySAxCA$ refers to attention across $x - axis$ and $y - axis$ in self-attention and rows only in cross-attention. $xySAxyCA$ refers to attention across $x - axis$ and $y - axis$ in both self and cross-attention.

Intuitively, objects in the $y - axis$ might not seem to be very useful since they change position depending on their disparity. However, we are not trying to match across both views using the y-axis, instead, we are trying to add more data to pixels especially in difficult regions such as textureless ones. To know whether it helps to include the vertical $y - axis$ self-attention prior to the horizontal $x - axis$ self-attention, we visualize the self and cross final attention weights

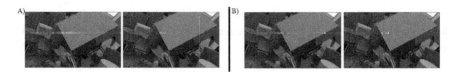

Fig. 5. Self attention of a single pixel (marked with red x). *A)*: Self attention of pixel from STTR. *B)*: Self attention from out model. Self-attention of pixel in the first and last self-attention layer respectively. (Color figure online)

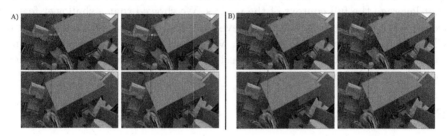

Fig. 6. Cross attention of a single pixel (marked with red x). *A)*: Cross attention of pixel from STTR. *B)*: Cross attention from our model. *Top*: cross-attention of pixel in the first and last cross-attention layer respectively. *Bottom*:right image with the GT location of the pixel in the left image marked as an x and a line going through the left image for reference. (Color figure online)

at a certain point in the left image in all the layers in Fig. 5, and Fig. 6. These figures show the weights with the highest values. They give us an idea as to what the transformer is seeing as important landmarks to identify to corresponding pixel in the right view. We can see that with out method, the output in each layer is sharper. That is, the model finds it easier to select landmarks in self attention and finding corresponding pixels in the cross attention. In the cross-attention figure (Fig. 6), we can observe that the STTR algorithm fails to select the correct corresponding pixel while our method is more accurate. The feature extraction used in this section is the Conv FE.

The dataset used for this ablation study is SceneFlow. The results are displayed in Table 3.

Table 3. SceneFlow results using different transformer architecture

Experiment	3px error	EPE
xSAxCA	1.20	0.40
xySAxCA	**1.10**	**0.38**
xySAxyCA	1.15	0.41

We observe that the results improve with the inclusion of a self-attention on the $y - axis$. However, no such improvement is obtained with the inclusion of cross-attention along the $y - axis$.

5 Conclusion

We demonstrated a method that rivals CNNs in stereo matching achieving state of the art in SceneFlow dataset. We introduced a feature matching architecture that leverage the full context of the images. We showed that a shallower feature extraction method is sufficient to achieve good results. Our solution still relies on CNN for feature extraction. However, ViT based feature extraction performed well especially considering it is the fastest configuration which would be beneficial for time critical applications.

References

1. Dzmitry, B., Cho, K., Bengio, Y.: Neural machine translation by jointly learning to align and translate. CoRR arXiv:1409.0473 (2015). n. pag
2. Dosovitskiy, A., et al.: An image is worth 16x16 words: transformers for image recognition at scale. CoRR, arXiv (2020)
3. Chang, J., Chen, Y.: Pyramid stereo matching network. In: 2018 IEEE/CVF Conference on Computer Vision and Pattern Recognition (CVPR), Salt Lake City, UT, USA, pp. 5410–5418 (2018)
4. Russakovsky, O., et al.: ImageNet large scale visual recognition challenge. Int. J. Comput. Vision **115**(3), 211–252 (2015). https://doi.org/10.1007/s11263-015-0816-y
5. Yang, G., Manela, J., Happold, M., Ramanan, D.: Hierarchical deep stereo matching on high-resolution images. In: 2019 IEEE/CVF Conference on Computer Vision and Pattern Recognition (CVPR), Long Beach, CA, USA, pp. 5510–5519 (2019)
6. Vaswani, A., et al.: Attention is all you need. In: Proceedings of the 31st International Conference on Neural Information Processing Systems (NIPS 2017), pp. 6000–6010. Curran Associates Inc., Red Hook (2017)
7. Wang, H., Zhu, Y., Green, B., Adam, H., Yuille, A., Chen, L.-C.: Axial-DeepLab: stand-alone axial-attention for panoptic segmentation. In: Vedaldi, A., Bischof, H., Brox, T., Frahm, J.-M. (eds.) ECCV 2020. LNCS, vol. 12349, pp. 108–126. Springer, Cham (2020). https://doi.org/10.1007/978-3-030-58548-8_7
8. Hirschmuller, H.: Accurate and efficient stereo processing by semi-global matching and mutual information. In: 2005 IEEE Computer Society Conference on Computer Vision and Pattern Recognition (CVPR 2005), vol. 2, pp. 807–814 (2005)
9. Herb, M.: Computing the Stereo Matching Cost with a Convolutional Neural Network Seminar Recent Trends in 3D Computer Vision (2015)
10. Khamis, S., Fanello, S., Rhemann, C., Kowdle, A., Valentin, J.P.C., Izadi, S.: StereoNet: guided hierarchical refinement for real-time edge-aware depth prediction. In: ECCV (2018)
11. Li, Z., et al.: Revisiting stereo depth estimation from a sequence-to-sequence perspective with transformers. In: IEEE/CVF International Conference on Computer Vision (ICCV), vol. 2021, pp. 6177–6186 (2021). https://doi.org/10.1109/ICCV48922.2021.00614

12. Ohta, Y., Kanade, T.: Stereo by intra- and inter-scanline search using dynamic programming. IEEE Trans. Pattern Anal. Mach. Intell. **7**(2), 139–154 (1985)

13. Cheng, X., et al.: Hierarchical neural architecture search for deep stereo matching. In: Lorochelle, H., Ranzato, M., Hadsell, R., Balcan, M.F., Lin, H. (eds.) Advances in Neural Information Processing Systems (NeurIPS 2020), December 2020, vol. 33. Neural Information Processing Systems (NIPS) (2020)

14. Zheng, S., et al.: Rethinking semantic segmentation from a sequence-to-sequence perspective with transformers. In: Proceedings of the 2021 IEEE/CVF Conference on Computer Vision and Pattern Recognition (CVPR), pp. 6877–6886. IEEE (2021)

15. Zhou, Y., Barnes, C., Shechtman, E., Amirghodsi, S.: TransFill: reference-guided image inpainting by merging multiple color and spatial transformations. In: Proceedings of the IEEE/CVF Conference on Computer Vision and Pattern Recognition (CVPR), pp. 2266–2276. IEEE (2021)

16. Devlin, J., Chang, M.W., Lee, K., Toutanova, K.: BERT: pre-training of deep bidirectional transformers for language understanding. NAACL (2019)

17. Brown, T., et al.: Language Models are Few-Shot Learners (2020)

18. Fuzhi, Y., Yang, H., Fu, J., Lu, H., Guo, B.: Learning texture transformer network for image super-resolution. In: 2020 IEEE/CVF Conference on Computer Vision and Pattern Recognition (CVPR), pp. 5790–5799 (2020)

19. Strudel, R., Garcia, R., Laptev, I., Schmid, C.: Segmenter: transformer for semantic segmentation. In: 2021 IEEE/CVF International Conference on Computer Vision (ICCV), Montreal, QC, Canada, pp. 7242–7252 (2021)

20. Dai, J., et al.: Deformable convolutional networks. In: IEEE International Conference on Computer Vision (ICCV), vol. 2017, pp. 764–773 (2017)

21. Hu, J., Shen, L., Sun, G.: Squeeze-and-excitation networks. In: IEEE/CVF Conference on Computer Vision and Pattern Recognition, vol. 2018, pp. 7132–7141 (2018)

22. Hu, H., Zhang, Z., Xie, Z., Lin, S.: Local relation networks for image recognition. In: IEEE/CVF International Conference on Computer Vision (ICCV), vol. 2019, pp. 3463–3472 (2019)

23. Mayer, N., et al.: A large dataset to train convolutional networks for disparity, optical flow, and scene flow estimation. In: 2016 IEEE Conference on Computer Vision and Pattern Recognition (CVPR), Las Vegas, NV, USA, pp. 4040–4048 (2016)

24. Moritz, M., Heipke, C., Geiger, A.: Joint 3D estimation of vehicles and scene flow. ISPRS Ann. Photogramm. Remote Sens. Spat. Inf. Sci. **2**, 427–434 (2015)

25. Wang, L., et al.: Parallax attention for unsupervised stereo correspondence learning. IEEE Trans. Pattern Anal. Mach. Intell. (2020). https://doi.org/10.1109/TPAMI.2020.3026899

26. Xu, H., Zhang, J.: AANet: adaptive aggregation network for efficient stereo matching. In: 2020 IEEE/CVF Conference on Computer Vision and Pattern Recognition (CVPR), Seattle, WA, USA, pp. 1956–1965 (2020)

27. Tankovich, V., Häne, C., Zhang, Y., Kowdle, A., Fanello, S., Bouaziz, S.: HITNet: hierarchical iterative tile refinement network for real-time stereo matching. In: IEEE/CVF Conference on Computer Vision and Pattern Recognition (CVPR), vol. 2021, pp. 14357–14367 (2021)

Inpainting Applied to Facade Images: A Comparison of Algorithms

Willy Fritzsche, Steffen Goebbels$^{(\boxtimes)}$ [ID], Simon Hensel, Marco Rußinski, and Nils Schuch

Faculty of Electrical Engineering and Computer Science, iPattern Institute, Niederrhein University of Applied Sciences, 47805 Krefeld, Germany
{willy.fritzsche,marco.russinski,nils.schuch}@stud.hn.de,
{steffen.goebbels,simon.hensel}@hsnr.de

Abstract. Many municipalities provide textured 3D city models for planning and simulation purposes. Usually, the textures are automatically taken from oblique aerial images. In these images, walls may be occluded by building parts, vegetation and other objects such as cars, traffic signs, etc. To obtain high quality models, these objects have to be segmented and then removed from facade textures. In this study, we investigate the ability of different non-specialized inpainting algorithms to continue facade patterns in occluded facade areas. To this end, non-occluded facade textures of a 3D city model are equipped with various masks simulating occlusions. Then, the performance of the algorithms is evaluated by comparing their results with the original images. In particular, very useful results are obtained with the neural network "DeepFill v2" trained with transfer learning on freely available facade datasets and the "Shift-Map" algorithm.

Keywords: Inpainting · 3D city models · Facade textures

1 Introduction

During the last decades, various image inpainting techniques have been developed that fill absent regions in images. In [15], an extensive survey is given. Inpainting is an ill-assorted problem because there is no hard criterion how missing information has to look like. However, generated edges and texture patterns should somehow fit with the given data. Such reconstruction of missing information is often required for optical remote sensing data, see the overview paper [19]. Our goal is to restore areas on facade images that are occluded, e.g., by vegetation or other buildings. These facade images are used as textures in 3D city models, cf. Fig. 1, and they are typically obtained from oblique aerial images. Occluded facade regions can be segmented by detecting objects like trees and vehicles as well as by drawing the 3D model from the camera perspective. The 3D model then helps to identify regions hidden by other buildings, cf. [7]. There exist specialized inpainting algorithms for building facades, see Sect. 2.

© Springer Nature Switzerland AG 2022
M. El Yacoubi et al. (Eds.): ICPRAI 2022, LNCS 13363, pp. 410–422, 2022.
https://doi.org/10.1007/978-3-031-09037-0_34

However, the contribution of this paper is to investigate whether readily available general methods can be used instead of specialized algorithms. The occluded regions are usually so large that realistic results are difficult to obtain by merely considering only local data from the region boundary. Nevertheless, we consider the boundary-based Navier-Stokes and the Telea diffusion algorithms [1, 21] (see Sect. 3.1) to compare the results with global inpainting, i.e., with texture synthesis approaches. Facade images often show a repetitive pattern due to a regular arrangement of windows. Such patterns can be described by grammars and they are the reason why the continuation of global texture properties can work sufficiently for facades. We compare the results of both explicitly implemented algorithms and deep neural networks, see Sect. 3.3 for the two convolution based deep neural networks DeepFill v2 [27] and GMCNN [23] as well as Sect. 3.2 for other algorithms.

It turns out that global texture synthesis works better than local inpainting algorithms. Due to technical problems, Frequency Selective Reconstruction [5, 18] operates only very well on downscaled images. Without adjusting the scale, the best results are gained with transfer learning applied to DeepFill v2 and the example-based Shift-Map inpainting algorithm, see Sect. 5.

2   Related Work

Whereas we discuss the application of general purpose algorithms, various papers have treated the specialization of inpainting techniques to facade images. A selection of these algorithms is briefly described in this section.

Facades of large buildings often have a regular pattern of windows that can be expressed with an Irregular Rectangular Lattice (IRL). This is a grid of lines that extend the boundaries of semantically labeled facade objects like windows and doors. Based on an IRL, a recurrent neural network was used in [9] to propose positions and sizes of occluded windows. In the context of 3D city models, the algorithm in [3] synthesizes photorealistic facade images using example-based inpainting. To this end, textured tiles are defined by the rectangles of the IRL obtained from a random forest. The IRL is then extrapolated to occluded regions. A genetic algorithm is applied to optimize a labeling of the rectangular tiles. The algorithm decides which rectangles show the same textures. These textures are taken from non-occluded rectangle instances. Such tile based synthesis was also discussed and applied to facades in [25]. In [13], information about detected facade objects was combined with example-based inpainting, and in [28], instance segmentation of unwanted objects was combined with a generative adversarial network (GAN) to fill regions occupied by the objects.

The EdgeConnect GAN [16] was slightly improved for facade images in [14] by applying semantic segmentation. It was extended to a three-stage model that uses three GANs to reconstruct an edge image, a label image, and a texture image.

Another approach to reconstruct missing facade regions is to apply split grammars, see [24]. These grammars are a collection of rules that describe the placement of facade objects. With their help, missing facade objects can be added and even complete facades can be generated procedurally. Often, facades show symmetry. This is utilized in the algorithm [2].

Facade regions can be also reconstructed with the inpainting algorithm in [10]. After detecting line segments of edges, the segments are classified according to vanishing points of corresponding lines. Then image regions covered by line segments that belong to two classes are likely to describe a plane in 3D. Textures are continued by considering these planes.

Often, facades are visible in multiple oblique aerial images belonging to different camera positions and directions. Algorithms like the one in [12] address facade texture generation based on images taken from a moving camera.

3   Algorithms

For this study, we have selected algorithms that are freely available via the computer vision library OpenCV[1] or via open code repositories.

3.1   Local, Diffusion-Based Inpainting Algorithms

OpenCV offers traditional inpainting algorithms that locally continue patterns from the boundary of a region to its interior. They require a source image and a separate 8-bit, one channel mask to define occluded areas. These algorithms are also classified as structure-based.

Navier-Stokes (NS) Algorithm. The Navier-Stokes equations are partial differential equations that model the motion of viscous fluids. Applied to image inpainting, the equations can be used to continue isophotes (curves connecting points of equal gray value) while matching gradient vectors at the boundary of inpainted regions, see [1]. Due to the diffusion process, some blur is visible if the algorithm is applied to fill a larger region.

Inpainting Based on the Fast Marching Method (Telea Algorithm). In [21], Alexandru Telea presented an inpainting algorithm that is easier to implement than the NS algorithm. It iteratively propagates boundary information to the interior of occluded regions by computing weighted means of pixel values that are estimated with a linear Taylor approximation. Thus, as with many algorithms, the region is synthesized from the outside inward.

3.2   Global Inpainting Algorithms Not Relying on Deep Learning

With the Shift-Map and the Frequency Selective Reconstruction methods, we take into account two algorithms that are provided by the "xphoto" package[2] of OpenCV. These algorithms do not only consider the boundary of occluded regions but the whole image. They are also called texture-based.

---

[1] https://opencv.org (all websites accessed on January 12, 2022).

[2] https://docs.opencv.org/5.x/de/daa/group_xphoto.html.

Shift-Map Algorithm. A shift-map consists of offsets that describe how pixels are moved (shifted, transformed) from a source to a target image region. Shift maps can be optimized with respect to certain smoothness and consistency requirements by solving a graph labeling problem, see [17]. The cited paper also introduced shift-map-based inpainting: By choosing an occluded area as a source, inpainting can be viewed as finding an optimized shift-map. The xphoto-implementation is based on [8] where a sparsely distributed statistics of patch offsets was utilized to implement example-based inpainting. This algorithm can be seen as a generalized variant of example-based synthesis of facade patterns proposed with algorithms mentioned in Sect. 2.

Frequency Selective Reconstruction (FSR). In contrast to local inpainting techniques based on boundary information, Fourier analysis is a means for global approximation due to the global support of basis functions. When Fourier coefficients are determined based on known image areas, the Fourier partial sums also provide data for unknown areas. This is the idea behind Frequency Selective Inpainting, see [11], which is based on the discrete Fourier transform. Discrete Fourier coefficients are estimated from the given, incomplete sample data. The coefficients can be seen as factors in a linear combination of Fourier basis functions to represent the given discrete data. Since the given information is incomplete, the corresponding system of linear equations is underdetermined, and there are infinitely many solutions for the coefficients. Therefore, the method applies a heuristics called Matching Pursuit. It iteratively selects a basis function that best approximates the given data. In each iteration, this best approximation is subtracted from the given data (residual vector). Thus, rather than calculating all the coefficients at once, iterations are performed by selecting the most important frequencies. Once the discrete coefficients are estimated, the data can be reconstructed by the inverse discrete Fourier transform. The xphoto-implementation follows [5] and [18].

3.3   Deep Learning-Based Global Inpainting Algorithms

DeepFill V2. The "Free-Form Image Inpainting with Gated Convolution" network, "DeepFill v2" for short, is based on gated convolution, see [26,27]. In contrast to the application of partial convolution, gated convolution allows the network to learn how to apply convolution kernels to incomplete data. While the features are based on general convolution, the algorithm uses an adaptive dynamic feature selection mechanism (known as gating mechanism) for each channel at each spatial position. When applied, the network consists of two separate encoder-decoder sub-networks, the coarse network and the refinement network which implements contextual attention. An input mask defines the regions to be filled. In these regions, the output of the coarse network looks like a blurred image. The contextual attention stage adds the missing details such as contours. In the training phase, a third sub-network is attached to compute an adversarial loss that is linearly combined with a pixel-wise l_1 reconstruction loss.

Fig. 1. Textured city model of Krefeld

GMCNN. The Generative Multi-column Convolutional Neural Network (GMCNN) uses local as well as global information to predict pixels in regions that are specified by a mask, see [23]. In total, the network consists of three sub-networks. The inpainting is done with the first sub-network, the generator. The second sub-network implements local and global discriminators for adversarial training and the third sub-network is a pre-trained VGG network [20] that provides features to calculate the implicit diversified Markov random fields (ID-MRF) loss introduced in [23]. With respect to the feature space, this loss minimizes the distance between the generator output and a nearest neighbor in the set of ground truth images. Only the first sub-network is used for testing. This generator consists of three parallel encoder-decoders, which help to determine features on multiple scales, and a shared decoder module to reconstruct the image.

4   Ground Truth, Training Data, and Network Training

Our aim is to improve facade textures obtained from oblique aerial images. Thus, we generated a realistic set of test images from a textured 3D city model of the area around our institute. We previously computed this model with the method described in [6] based on airborne laser scanning point clouds and cadastral footprints (available from the state cadastral office of the German state North Rhine-Westphalia[3]) and textured it with oblique aerial images provided by the city of Krefeld, see Fig. 1. The obtained facade images had a resolution of about 15×15 pixels per square meter and were free of perspective distortions. For this study, we considered only rectangular images that were completely covered with facades and did not show a background like the sky. To define a ground truth, we manually selected 120 images that were free of occlusions. This proved to be no easy task since most facade textures showed occlusions (mostly vegetation) of different sizes. We increased the number of images to 206 by mirroring and periodic repetition. Together with automatically generated occlusion masks, we tested all algorithms on these images. The masks were assembled from filled

---

[3] https://www.bezreg-koeln.nrw.de/brk_internet/geobasis/hoehenmodelle/3d-messd aten/index.html.

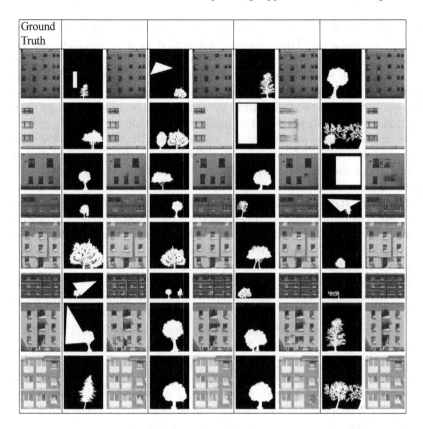

Fig. 2. Results of the DeepFill v2 scenario (S2) with regard to different masks

triangles, rectangles, circles and higher level shapes like trees, see Fig. 2. Additionally, these objects were scaled, mirrored and rotated slightly. The shape templates were taken from a dataset that has been published on the internet[4], cf. Fig. 2.

Our dataset is too small to train the two neural networks. Therefore, we worked with pre-trained models of DeepFill v2 and GMCNN. In both cases, the pre-training was based on images of the "places2"[5] [29] dataset that had a resolution of 256 × 256 pixels. In this model as well as in Figs. 2 and 4, all pixels with the color white (RGB (255, 255, 255)) define a mask. Masks can represent more than one freely shaped object. We also worked with GMCNN pre-trained on "Paris streetview" data [4] but observed artifacts along the boundaries of occluded regions so that we went on only with the "places2" model. Since only part of the images in "places2" show facades, we applied transfer learning with

---

[4] https://www.etsy.com/de/listing/726267122/baum-silhouette-svg-bundle.
[5] http://places2.csail.mit.edu/download.html.

images from the "Ecole Centrale Paris Facades Database"[6], "FaSyn13"[7] [3], and "CMP"[8] [22] datasets. These images were scaled to have the same number of 512 rows. If the number of columns exceeded 512, an image was cut into several frames. If a width was less than 512 columns, the image was expanded by means of mirroring. We also tried transfer-learning with images having 256 columns and rows, but, at least with DeepFill v2, transfer-learning with images having a resolution of 512 × 512 pixels led to much better results.

The training dataset contained 1,600 images divided into 1,440 training images and 160 images for validation. Whereas the three source datasets are widely used to compare the performance of facade related algorithms (e.g., for instance segmentation), their images do not origin from oblique aerial imaging such that, e.g., their resolution is higher and background like the sky is visible.

To train DeepFill v2, we equipped the training and validation images with the automatically generated occlusion masks. GMCNN allows for automatic training with randomly chosen rectangles as occluded areas. For simplicity, we did not change the code but used this training option.

Both neural networks ran on an NVIDIA P6000 GPU. DeepFill v2 was trained with a batch size of eleven due to hardware limitations. As proposed in [27], the adversarial loss and the l_1 reconstruction loss were equally weighted in one test scenario, denoted with (S1). For this scenario, 74,000 training steps were executed in 18.5 epochs in 90 h. Since we compare inpainted images with ground truth images in an l_2 norm that is equivalent to the l_1 norm in a finite dimensional space, we did a second test in which we chose a higher weight factor for the l_1 loss by multiplying this loss with 1.1 whereas the adversarial loss was only weighted with 0.9. This scenario is denoted with (S2). To train the scenario, 134,000 training steps were executed in 33.5 epochs in 160 h.

GMCNN was trained with a batch size of 32 and 60,000 training steps were executed in 60 epochs in 120 h.

5   Results

Figure 4 shows the inpainting results for several facade images and occlusion masks. The Navier-Stokes and Telea algorithms were applied with a circular neighborhood having a radius of 128 pixels. Unfortunately, the openCV xphoto beta version of the FSR algorithm had memory allocation problems and failed to compute results for some images. In contrast to the other algorithms, we therefore tested FSR with reduced image sizes. First, we trained both DeepFill v2 scenarios (S1) and (S2) for 90 h. Since the results of (S2) were visually better than those of (S1), we extended (S2) training to 160 h as described before.

We compared the output images with the corresponding ground truth images by simply applying an l_2-norm, for other metrics cf. [16]. Let $G, A \in \{0, 1, \ldots, 255\}^{m \times n \times 3}$ be a ground truth image G and an inpainted image A with

---

[6] http://vision.mas.ecp.fr/Personnel/teboul/data.php.

[7] http://people.ee.ethz.ch/~daid/FacadeSyn/.

[8] https://cmp.felk.cvut.cz/~tylecr1/facade/.

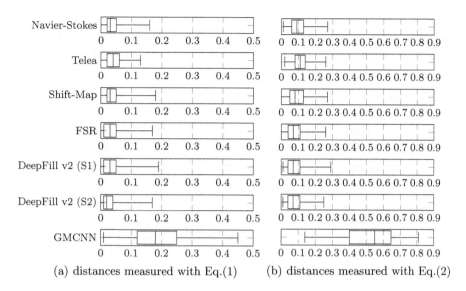

(a) distances measured with Eq.(1)   (b) distances measured with Eq.(2)

Fig. 3. Distribution of distances between ground truth and inpainted images of the entire test dataset; DeepFill v2 (S1) relates to equally weighted loss components and DeepFill v2 (S2) shows the result for a higher weighted l_1 loss

m rows, n columns and three channels. Let M be the set of coordinates of all masked pixels with $|M|$ elements. Then we measured the distance between A and G via two distance metrics

$$\text{dist}_{\text{all}}(A, G) := \sqrt{\frac{\sum_{i=1}^{m} \sum_{j=1}^{n} \sum_{k=1}^{3} (A_{i,j,k} - G_{i,j,k})^2}{m \cdot n \cdot 3 \cdot 255^2}}, \tag{1}$$

$$\text{dist}_{\text{mask}}(A, G) := \sqrt{\frac{\sum_{(i,j) \in M} \sum_{k=1}^{3} (A_{i,j,k} - G_{i,j,k})^2}{|M| \cdot 3 \cdot 255^2}}. \tag{2}$$

These distances are normed to be in the interval $[0, 1]$. The box plots in Fig. 3 show how the distances are distributed for each algorithm. A high distance value might indicate a bad inpainting result but a pixel-wise comparison might also lead to significant distances although the images appear similar. Instead of using more sophisticated metrics to measure similarity, the quantitative evaluation can be accompanied by a visual qualitative inspection. For example, the Shift-Map algorithm copies rectangular structures that appear consistent even if they do not fit. But a blurred region attracts attention even if it is closer to the ground truth. For the images in Fig. 4, distances dist_{all} are listed in Table 1 and distances $\text{dist}_{\text{mask}}$ are shown in Table 2. While $\text{dist}_{\text{mask}}$ only measures how well mask regions can be reconstructed, dist_{all} also takes into account changes outside the mask region, e.g., along its border. The data show that the algorithms focus the changes to the mask regions. Although the distance measures are normalized with respect to the image size, a comparison of the FSR values calculated

Table 1. Distance between ground truth images and inpainted images, see Eq. (1); the image numbers refer to Fig. 4. Bold and underlined numbers indicate best and second best results

Image	Navier-Stokes	Telea	Shift-Map	FSR	DeepFill v2 (S1)	DeepFill v2 (S2)	GMCNN
1	0.026	0.05	0.024	**0.007**	0.013	<u>0.012</u>	0.255
2	0.022	0.023	0.033	**0.019**	<u>0.02</u>	0.022	0.257
3	0.043	0.045	0.077	0.037	<u>0.032</u>	**0.028**	0.096
4	0.027	0.03	0.028	0.018	<u>0.016</u>	**0.014**	0.168
5	0.071	0.066	<u>0.057</u>	**0.05**	0.073	0.061	0.194
6	0.097	0.088	0.134	0.121	<u>0.084</u>	**0.079**	0.211
7	0.038	0.044	0.051	**0.025**	0.027	<u>0.026</u>	0.15
8	0.035	0.036	0.034	**0.025**	0.031	<u>0.03</u>	0.163
9	0.094	0.088	**0.077**	0.097	0.089	<u>0.086</u>	0.26
10	0.081	0.079	0.083	**0.073**	0.077	**0.073**	0.198
11	0.093	0.087	0.108	**0.075**	0.099	<u>0.08</u>	0.259
12	0.047	0.044	**0.025**	0.05	0.034	<u>0.031</u>	0.127
13	<u>0.005</u>	0.009	<u>0.005</u>	**0.003**	0.006	0.006	0.262

Table 2. Mask-specific distance between ground truth images and inpainted images corresponding to Table 1, see Eq. (2)

Image	Navier-Stokes	Telea	Shift-Map	FSR	DeepFill v2 (S1)	DeepFill v2 (S2)	GMCNN
1	0.06	0.117	0.051	**0.014**	0.029	<u>0.027</u>	0.589
2	0.059	0.061	0.086	**0.047**	<u>0.054</u>	0.059	0.696
3	0.126	0.133	0.215	0.097	<u>0.094</u>	**0.082**	0.283
4	0.09	0.107	0.089	0.055	<u>0.053</u>	**0.049**	0.574
5	0.168	0.157	<u>0.13</u>	**0.108**	0.174	0.146	0.463
6	0.194	0.175	0.263	0.228	<u>0.168</u>	**0.157**	0.42
7	0.123	0.143	0.155	**0.073**	0.09	<u>0.086</u>	0.492
8	0.115	0.119	0.107	**0.073**	0.102	<u>0.101</u>	0.542
9	0.18	0.17	**0.145**	0.178	0.17	<u>0.166</u>	0.5
10	0.219	0.213	0.222	**0.19**	0.211	<u>0.198</u>	0.537
11	0.175	0.164	0.2	**0.136**	0.185	<u>0.149</u>	0.485
12	0.136	0.128	**0.069**	0.13	0.098	<u>0.089</u>	0.365
13	0.016	0.026	<u>0.013</u>	**0.006**	0.017	0.018	0.795

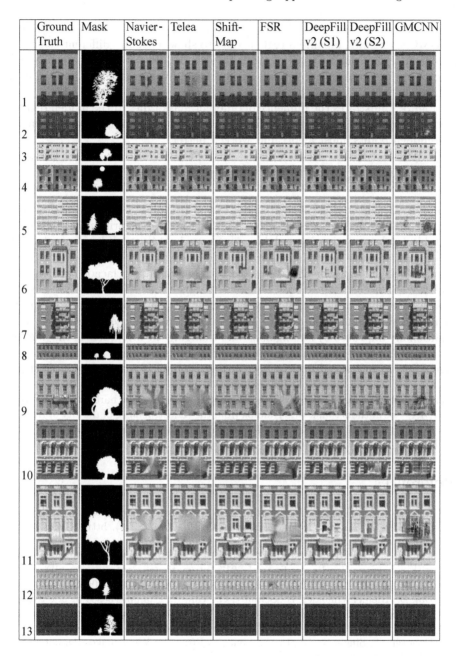

Fig. 4. Comparison of inpainting algorithms; DeepFill v2 was trained with equal weighted loss functions (S1) and with l_1 loss weighted higher than GAN loss (S2)

on downscaled images with those of the other algorithms is somewhat limited. In GMCNN results, inpainted regions tend to show a slightly different color distribution. This leads to large distance values. We did not investigate if better results can be obtained with a different choice of hyperparameters and training data.

Figure 2 illustrates the influence of different mask types. If the hidden regions were not described by completely filled contours but were interrupted by many non-hidden points, most algorithms worked better.

6   Conclusions

DeepFill v2 delivered excellent results, but also the Shift-Map algorithm performed well. This is expected to be true for the FSR algorithm as well, once a stable implementation is available. As shown in [14], the EdgeConnect GAN [16] also is suitable for facade inpainting. The algorithms can be used without problem specific adjustments. We tested with low resolution facade textures of a real city model but trained with datasets of higher resolution images. It may be possible to enhance the neural network output further by adding low-resolution images to the training dataset. To achieve better results, the datasets could be additionally improved by adding noise and changing the brightness of the images.

There seems to be no longer a need for highly specialized facade inpainting algorithms as referenced in Sect. 2, so a direct comparison would be interesting.

Acknowledgements. This work was supported by a generous hardware grant from NVIDIA. The authors thank Udo Hannok from the cadastral office of the city of Krefeld for providing the oblique aerial images. The authors are also grateful to Regina Pohle-Fröhlich for valuable comments.

References

1. Bertalmio, M., Bertozzi, A., Shapiro, G.: Navier-Stokes, fluid dynamics, and image and video inpainting. In: Proceedings of CVPR 2001 (2001). https://doi.org/10.1109/CVPR.2001.990497
2. Cohen, A., Oswald, M.R., Liu, Y., Pollefeys, M.: Symmetry-aware façade parsing with occlusions. In: Proceedings of 2017 International Conference on 3D Vision (3DV), pp. 393–401 (2017). https://doi.org/10.1109/3DV.2017.00052
3. Dai, D., Riemenschneider, H., Schmitt, G., Van, L.: Example-based facade texture synthesis. In: Proceedings of 2013 IEEE International Conference on Computer Vision (ICCV), pp. 1065–1072. IEEE Computer Society, Los Alamitos, CA (2013)
4. Doersch, C., Singh, S., Gupta, A., Sivic, J., Efros, A.: What makes Paris look like Paris? ACM Trans. Graph. **31**(4:101), 1–9 (2012)
5. Genser, N., Seiler, J., Schilling, F., Kaup, A.: Signal and loss geometry aware frequency selective extrapolation for error concealment. In: Proceedings of 2018 Picture Coding Symposium (PCS), pp. 159–163 (2018)
6. Goebbels, S., Pohle-Fröhlich, R.: Roof reconstruction from airborne laser scanning data based on image processing methods. ISPRS Ann. Photogramm. Remote Sens. Spatial Inf. Sci. **III-3**, 407–414 (2016)

7. Goebbels, S., Pohle-Fröhlich, R.: Automatic unfolding of CityGML buildings to paper models. Geographies **1**(3), 333–345 (2021)
8. He, K., Sun, J.: Statistics of patch offsets for image completion. In: Fitzgibbon, A., Lazebnik, S., Perona, P., Sato, Y., Schmid, C. (eds.) ECCV 2012. LNCS, vol. 7573, pp. 16–29. Springer, Heidelberg (2012). https://doi.org/10.1007/978-3-642-33709-3_2
9. Hensel, S., Goebbels, S., Kada, M.: LSTM architectures for facade structure completion. In: Proceedings of GRAPP 2021, pp. 15–24 (2021)
10. Huang, J.B., Kang, S.B., Ahuja, N., Kopf, J.: Image completion using planar structure guidance. ACM Trans. Graph. **33**(4), 1–10 (2014)
11. Kaup, A., Meisinger, K., Aach, T.: Frequency selective signal extrapolation with applications to error concealment in image communication. AEUE - Int. J. Electron. Commun. **59**, 147–156 (2005)
12. Korah, T., Rasmussen, C.: Spatiotemporal inpainting for recovering texture maps of occluded building facades. IEEE Trans. Image Process. **16**(9), 2262–2271 (2007)
13. Kottler, B., Bulatov, D., Zhang, X.: Context-aware patch-based method for façade inpainting. In: Proceedings of GRAPP 2020, pp. 210–218 (2020)
14. Kottler, B., List, L., Bulatov, D., Weinmann, M.: 3GAN: a three-GAN-based approach for image inpainting applied to the reconstruction of occluded parts of building walls. In: Proceedings of VISAPP 2022 (2022)
15. Mehra, S., Dogra, A., Goyal, B., Sharma, A.M., Chandra, R.: From textural inpainting to deep generative models: an extensive survey of image inpainting techniques. J. Comput. Sci. **16**(1), 35–49 (2020)
16. Nazeri, K., Ng, E., Joseph, T., Qureshi, F.Z., Ebrahimi, M.: EdgeConnect: generative image inpainting with adversarial edge learning. arXiv Preprint: arXiv: 1901.00212 (2019)
17. Pritch, Y., Kav-Venaki, E., Peleg, S.: Shift-map image editing. In: Proceedings of 2009 IEEE International Conference on Computer Vision (ICCV), pp. 151–158. IEEE Computer Society, Los Alamitos, CA (2009)
18. Seiler, J., Jonscher, M., Schöberl, M., Kaup, A.: Resampling images to a regular grid from a non-regular subset of pixel positions using frequency selective reconstruction. IEEE Trans. Image Process. **24**(11), 4540–4555 (2015)
19. Shen, H., et al.: Missing information reconstruction of remote sensing data: a technical review. IEEE Geosci. Remote Sens. Mag. **3**(3), 61–85 (2015)
20. Simonyan, K., Zisserman, A.: Very deep convolutional networks for large-scale image recognition. In: Proceedings of 3rd International Conference on Learning Representations (ICLR) 2015, San Diego, CA, USA (2015)
21. Telea, A.: An image inpainting technique based on the fast marching method. J. Graph. Tools **9**(1), 23–34 (2004)
22. Tyleček, R., Šára, R.: Spatial pattern templates for recognition of objects with regular structure. In: Weickert, J., Hein, M., Schiele, B. (eds.) GCPR 2013. LNCS, vol. 8142, pp. 364–374. Springer, Heidelberg (2013). https://doi.org/10.1007/978-3-642-40602-7_39
23. Wang, Y., Tao, X., Qi, X., Shen, X., Jia, J.: Image inpainting via generative multi-column convolutional neural networks. In: Proceedings of 32nd International Conference on Neural Information Processing Systems, pp. 329–338. NIPS 2018. Curran Associates Inc., Red Hook, NY (2018)
24. Wonka, P., Wimmer, M., Sillion, F., Ribarsky, W.: Instant architecture. ACM Trans. Graph. **22**(3), 669–677 (2003)
25. Yeh, Y.T., Breeden, K., Yang, L., Fisher, M., Hanrahan, P.: Synthesis of tiled patterns using factor graphs. ACM Trans. Graph. **32**(1), 1–13 (2013)

26. Yu, J., Lin, Z., Yang, J., Shen, X., Lu, X., Huang, T.: Generative image inpainting with contextual attention. In: Proceedings of CVPR 2018, arXiv preprint arXiv:1801.07892 (2018)
27. Yu, J., Lin, Z., Yang, J., Shen, X., Lu, X., Huang, T.: Free-form image inpainting with gated convolution. In: Proceedings of CVPR 2019, arXiv preprint arXiv:1806.03589 (2019)
28. Zhang, J., Fukuda, T., Yabuki, N.: Automatic object removal with obstructed façades completion using semantic segmentation and generative adversarial inpainting. IEEE Access **9**, 117486–117495 (2021)
29. Zhou, B., Lapedriza, A., Khosla, A., Oliva, A., Torralba, A.: A 10 million image database for scene recognition. IEEE Trans. Pattern Anal. Mach. Intell. (TPAMI) **40**(6), 1452–14649 (2018)

Self-distilled Self-supervised Depth Estimation in Monocular Videos

Julio Mendoza[ID] and Helio Pedrini[(✉)][ID]

University of Campinas, Institute of Computing, Campinas, SP 13083-852, Brazil
`helio@ic.unicamp.br`

Abstract. In this work, we investigate approaches to leverage self-distillation via predictions consistency on self-supervised monocular depth estimation models. Since per-pixel depth predictions are not equally accurate, we propose a mechanism to filter out unreliable predictions. Moreover, we study representative strategies to enforce consistency between predictions. Our results show that choosing proper filtering and consistency enforcement approaches are key to obtain larger improvements on monocular depth estimation. Our method achieves competitive performance on the KITTI benchmark.

Keywords: Depth estimation · Self-distillation · Monocular videos

1 Introduction

Depth estimation is an essential task used in a wide range of applications in computer vision, for instance, 3D modeling, virtual and augmented reality, and robot navigation. Depth information can be obtained using sensors such as LIDAR or RGB-D cameras. However, in some scenarios, we cannot rely solely on them due to their limited range and operating conditions. Thus, alternative approaches such as estimating depth from images become more appealing. Supervised deep learning methods for depth estimation have shown impressive results. However, these approaches depend on the expensive acquisition of high-quality ground-truth depth data for training.

In contrast, self-supervised depth estimation approaches do not require ground-truth. Since the only inputs required are stereo images or monocular sequences, they can be trained on diverse data sets without depth labels. Self-supervised methods leverage geometric priors to learn image reconstruction as an auxiliary task. Depth maps are obtained as an intermediary result of the image reconstruction process.

Several works have shown that self-supervised depth estimation can be benefited from learning additional auxiliary tasks, for example, self-distillation. Self-distillation methods aim to improve a model performance by distilling knowledge from the model itself. An interesting strategy for performing self-distillation consists in extracting information from distorted versions of the input data by enforcing consistency between their predictions [26]. In this work,

© Springer Nature Switzerland AG 2022
M. El Yacoubi et al. (Eds.): ICPRAI 2022, LNCS 13363, pp. 423–434, 2022.
https://doi.org/10.1007/978-3-031-09037-0_35

we propose a self-distillation approach via prediction consistency to improve self-supervised depth estimation from monocular videos. Since enforcing consistency between predictions that are unrealiable cannot provide useful knowledge, we propose an strategy to filter out unreliable predictions. Moreover, the idea of enforcing consistency between predictions has been widely explored in self-distillation [8,18,27] and semi-supervised learning [1,13,20–22,24]. In order to explore the space of consistency enforcement strategies, we adapt and evaluate representative approaches on the self-supervised depth estimation task.

In summary, the main contributions of our work are the following: (i) the proposition of a multi-scale self-distillation method based on prediction consistency, (ii) the design of an approach to filter unreliable per-pixel predictions on the pseudo-labels used in self-distillation, and (iii) the exploration and adaptation of several consistency enforcement strategies for self-distillation. To validate our method, we show a detailed evaluation and a comparison against state-of-the-art methods on the KITTI benchmark. Our code is available at https://github.com/jmendozais/SDSSDepth.

2   Related Work

Self-supervised Depth Estimation. The main intuition of self-supervised depth estimation methods is to leverage multi-view geometry relations computed from depth and camera motion predictions to reconstruct one view with the pixel values from another view. Depth and camera motion can be obtained from deep networks that are trained by minimizing the reconstruction error. Garg et al. [9] used this intuition to train a depth network using stereo pairs as views. Similarly, Zhou et al. [29] proposed a method to obtain the views from monocular sequences and used deep networks to estimate relative pose and depth maps. Several works addressed limitations of these methods such as inaccurate prediction in occluded regions [16] and regions with moving objects [2,12]. Other works aim to improve the learning signal by enforcing consistency between several representations of the scene [3,16,17] or by using auxiliary tasks such as semantic segmentation or self-distillation [14,15]. Similarly to [14], our method leverages self-distillation to improve depth estimation. Unlike prior work, we focus on exploring representative strategies to distill knowledge from the predictions of our model.

Pseudo-labeling Approaches for Self-supervised Depth Estimation. Many self-supervised methods trained from stereo images [23,25] or monocular sequences [4,5,14,15,23] rely on pseudo-labels to provide additional supervision for training their depth networks. These methods can use state-of-the-art classical stereo matching algorithms [23], external deep learning methods [4,5], or their own predictions [25] to obtain pseudo-labels. Since the quality of the pseudo-labels is not always guaranteed, methods filter out unreliable per-pixel predictions based on external confidence estimates [4,5,23] or uncertainty estimates that are a result of the method itself [25]. Additionally, some methods leverage multi-scale predictions for creating pseudo-labels by using the predictions at the highest-resolution as pseudo-labels to supervise predictions at lower resolutions [28] or by selecting, per pixel, the prediction with the lowest reconstruction error among the multi-scale predictions [19].

We focus on methods that use their own prediction as pseudo-labels. For example, Kaushik et al. [14] augmented a self-supervised method by performing a second forward pass with strongly perturbed inputs. The predictions from the second pass are supervised with predictions of the first pass. Liu et al. [15] proposed to leverage the observation depth maps predicted from day-time images are more accurate than predictions from night-time images. They used predictions from day-time images as pseudo-labels and train a specialized network with night-time images synthesized using a conditional generative model.

Self-distillation. These methods let the target model leverage information from itself to improve its performance. An approach is to transfer knowledge from an instance of the model, previously trained, via predictions [8,18,27] and/or features to a new instance of the model. This procedure could be repeated iteratively. Self-distillation has a regularization effect on neural networks. It was shown that, at earlier iterations, self-distillation reduces overfitting and increases test accuracy, however, after too many iterations, the test accuracy declines and the model underfits [18].

Self-distillation has been extensively explored, mainly in image classification problems. An approach performs distillation by training instances of a model sequentially such that a model trained on a previous iteration is used as a teacher for the model trained in the current iteration [8]. Similarly, Yang et al. [27] proposed to train a model in a single training generation imitating multiple training generations using a cyclic learning rate scheduler and using the snapshots obtained at the end of the previous learning rate cycle as a teacher. Our work explores the idea of leveraging multiple snapshots in a single training generation on the self-supervised depth estimation problem.

Consistency Regularization. Enforcing consistency between predictions obtained from perturbed views of input examples is one of the main principles behind consistency regularization approaches on deep semi-supervised works. An early method [20] used this principle doing several forward passes on perturbed versions of the input data. Furthermore, other methods showed that the usage of advanced data augmentation perturbations [24] or a combination of a weak and strong data augmentation perturbation in a teacher-student training scheme [21] can be helpful to improve the resulting models.

Existing works showed that average models, i.e., models whose weights are the average of the model being trained at different training steps, can be more accurate [1,13,22]. Average models can be used, as teachers, to obtain more accurate pseudo-labels [1,22]. Moreover, the use of cyclic learning rate schedulers can improve the quality of the models that are averaged and the resulting model at accuracy and generalization [13], as well as it can be adapted to the consistency regularization framework [1]. Similarly to [1], our method uses a cyclic cosine annealing learning rate schedule to obtain a better teacher model.

3   Depth Estimation Method in Monocular Videos

3.1   Preliminaries

Our method is built on self-supervised depth estimation approaches that use view reconstruction as main supervisory signal [29]. These approaches require to find correspondences between pixel coordinates on frames that represent views of the same scene. We represent this correspondences in Eq. 1.

$$x_s \sim \mathbf{K}\mathbf{T_{t \to s}}\mathbf{D_t}(x_t)\mathbf{K}^{-1}x_t \tag{1}$$

We reconstruct the target frame using the correspondences and the pixel intensities in the source frame $\mathbf{\hat{I}_{s \to t}}(x_t) = \mathbf{I_s}(x_s)$. This process is known as image warping. This approach requires the dense depth map $\mathbf{D_t}$ of the target image, which we aim to reconstruct, the Euclidean transformation $\mathbf{T_{t \to s}}$, and camera intrinsics $\mathbf{K}$. Our model used to convolutional neural network to predict the depth maps and the Euclidean transformation, and assumes that the camera intrinsics are given. The networks are trained using the adaptive consistency loss $\mathcal{L}_{ac}$. We refer the reader to [17] for a detailed explanation.

3.2   Self-distillation via Prediction Consistency

The core idea of self-distillation based on prediction consistency is to provide additional supervision to the model by enforcing consistency between the depth map predictions obtained from different perturbed views of an input image. Our self-distillation approach applies two different data augmentation perturbations to an input snippet. To use less computational resources, we use snippets of two frames $\mathcal{I} = \{\mathbf{I_t}, \mathbf{I_{t+1}}\}$. The model predicts the depth maps for all images in the input snippet. Since we need to apply two data augmentation perturbations, we have two depth maps for each frame in the snippet. Then, we enforce consistency by minimizing the difference between the predicted depth maps for each frame.

There are several approaches to enforce consistency between prediction. The simplest variation of our method use the pseudo-label approach. It considers one of depth maps as pseudo-label $\mathbf{D}^{(\mathbf{pl})}$, which implies that gradients are not back-propagated through it, and the other depth map as prediction $\mathbf{D}^{(\mathbf{pred})}$. In Sect. 3.4, we improve our method considering other consistency enforcement strategies. Moreover, we enforce prediction consistency using the mean squared error (MSE) as difference measure. In addition, we filter the unreliable depth values on the pseudo-label using a composite mask. Equation 2 shows the self-distillation loss term for a snippet $\mathcal{I}$.

$$\mathcal{L}_{sd} = \frac{1}{|\mathcal{I}|} \sum_{\mathbf{I_k} \in \mathcal{I}} \frac{1}{|\mathbf{M_k^{(c)}}|} \sum_{x \in \Omega(\mathbf{I_k})} \mathbf{M_k^{(c)}}(x)\Big(\mathbf{D_k^{(pl)}}(x) - \mathbf{D_k^{(pred)}}(x)\Big)^2 \tag{2}$$

where $\mathbf{I_k}$ is a frame in the snippet and $\mathbf{M_k^{(c)}}$ is its composite mask, $\Omega(\mathbf{I_k})$ is the set of pixel coordinates, and $\mathbf{D_k^{(pl)}}$ and $\mathbf{D_k^{(pred)}}$ represent the pseudo-label and predicted depth maps, respectively.

Since our model predicts the depth maps at multiple scales, we compute the self-distillation loss for each scale. We assume that the pseudo-label at the finest scale is more accurate than the pseudo-labels at coarser scales. Thus, we only use the finest pseudo-label. We upscale the predictions to the finest scale to match the pseudo-label scale. Finally, we compute the self-distillation loss for each scale. Figure 1 depicts our self-distillation approach.

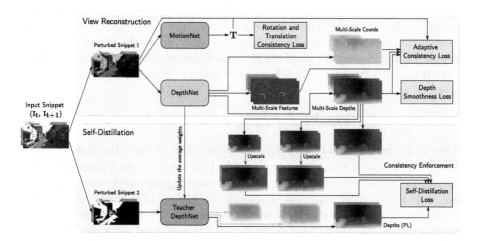

Fig. 1. Overview of our method. The self-distillation component leverages the multi-scale predictions obtained from the view reconstruction component. The predictions are upscaled to the finest resolution. More accurate predictions are obtained from the teacher model. The teacher predictions at the finest resolution are used as pseudo-labels to improve the predictions obtained from view reconstruction.

3.3 Filtering Pseudo-labels

We noticed empirically that unreliable depth prediction produces very large differences between pseudo-labels and predictions. These very large differences make training unstable and do not allow the model to converge randomly. We address this problem by excluding pixels with very large differences using a threshold value. In this section, we present two schemes to determine the threshold.

In the first scheme, we compute the threshold as a percentile P on the pseudo-label and prediction differences for all pixels in a batch of snippets. Then, we create valid mask considering as valid all the pixels with differences smaller than the threshold, as shown in Eq. 3.

$$\mathbf{M}^{(p)}(x) = \left[\left(\mathbf{D}^{(pl)}(x) - \mathbf{D}^{(pred)}(x) \right)^2 < P \right] \tag{3}$$

where [.] denotes the Iverson bracket operator. The final mask is obtained combining the latter mask with the compound mask. The final mask could be expressed as $\mathbf{M} = \mathbf{M}^{(p)} \odot \mathbf{M}^{(c)}$, where $\odot$ represents the element-wise product. Finally, we replace $\mathbf{M}^{(c)}$ with $\mathbf{M}$ in Eq. 3.

We believe that the idea of using a threshold obtained from the distribution of differences by batch might be detrimental because we do not take into consideration that batches with reliable predictions should have thresholds that exclude less pixels than the threshold used on batches with more unreliable predictions.

In the second scheme, we address this limitation by approximating a global threshold $P^{(\mathrm{EMA})}$ using the exponential moving average (EMA) of the percentile values for each batch during training. Another advantage of using a moving average is that we take into consideration that the distribution of depth differences change during training. This means that, when the depth differences become smaller during training, the threshold changes by increasing the weight of the percentiles from latter batches on the average. Equation 4 shows our global threshold approximation.

$$P_t^{(\mathrm{EMA})} = P_{t-1}^{(\mathrm{EMA})} \cdot \beta + P_t \cdot (1 - \beta) \tag{4}$$

where P_t is the threshold computed from the batch at the t training iteration, $P_t^{(\mathrm{EMA})}$ is threshold obtained using the EMA at the t training iteration, and β controls the influence of the previous moving average percentile and the current percentile into the computation of the current threshold. Similarly to the first scheme, we compute a valid mask $\mathbf{M}^{(\mathrm{EMA})}$ using $P^{(\mathrm{EMA})}$, we combine this mask with the compound mask $\mathbf{M} = \mathbf{M}^{(\mathrm{EMA})} \odot \mathbf{M}^{(c)}$ and, finally, we use $\mathbf{M}$ instead of $\mathbf{M}^{(c)}$ in Eq. 2.

3.4   Consistency Enforcement Strategies

In previous sections, we used a pseudo-label strategy to enforce consistency between depth predictions. Here, we describe representative consistency enforcement strategies adapted to our self-distillation approach. Figure 2 depicts these consistency enforcement strategies. We named each strategy similarly to the methods that introduced the key idea into external domains [1,13,20,22]. Similarly to the pseudo-label strategy, variants of our method that use the strategies described in this section also adopt the second scheme described in Sect. 3.3 to filter out unreliable per-pixel predictions before computing the predictions difference.

Π-Model. Similarly to the pseudo-label approach, this strategy consists in enforcing consistency between prediction from two perturbed views of the same input. In contrast with the pseudo-label approach, the gradients are back-propagated through both predictions.

Mean Teacher. Instead of using the same depth network to generate the pseudo-labels and the predictions, we can introduce a teacher network that can

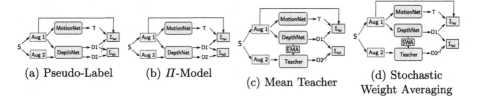

(a) Pseudo-Label   (b) Π-Model   (c) Mean Teacher   (d) Stochastic Weight Averaging

Fig. 2. Simplified views of the consistency enforcement strategies. S denotes the input snippet, $Aug\ 1$ and $Aug\ 2$ denote two perturbed views of the input snippet, T denotes the camera motion transformation, $D1$ and $D2$ denote depth maps predictions, L_{ac} denotes the adaptive consistency loss, L_{sd} denotes the self-distillation loss, and red lines —— mark connections where the gradients are not back-propagated. (Color figure online).

potentially predict more accurate pseudo-labels, and provide better supervisory signal to the model currently being trained, the student network. In this approach, the teacher depth network weights are the EMA of the depth network weights in equally spaced training iterations.

Stochastic Weight Averaging. Similarly to the mean teacher strategy, we set the teacher depth network weights as the EMA of the depth network weights. In contrast, the training process is split into several cycles. At each cycle, the learning rate decreases and the teacher depth network is updated with the weights of depth network at the end of the last epoch of each training cycle, where the learning rate reaches its lowest value.

In the first generation of the training process, we use the student network to predict pseudo-label. Once the model has converged to a proper local optimum, we use its weights to initialize the teacher network. Then, in the following cycles, the training process mimics multiple training generations using a cyclic cosine annealing learning rate. At the end of each cycle, when the learning rate reaches its lowest value, and model likely converged to a good local optimum, we update the weights the teacher network using EMA with the student network weights.

3.5   Additional Considerations

Final Loss. The overall loss is a weighted sum of our self-distillation loss $\mathcal{L}_{sd}$, adaptive consistency loss $\mathcal{L}_{ac}$ [17], depth smoothness loss $\mathcal{L}_{ds}$, translation consistency loss $\mathcal{L}_{tc}$, and rotation consistency loss $\mathcal{L}_{rc}$. The rotation and translation consistency losses are similar to the cyclic consistency loss defined in [12]. In contrast, our translation consistency loss only considers camera motion. Equation 5 shows our final loss.

$$\mathcal{L} = \sum_{i \in \mathcal{S}} \frac{1}{2^i} \left(\mathcal{L}_{ac}^{(i)} + \lambda_{ds} \mathcal{L}_{ds}^{(i)} + \lambda_{sd} \mathcal{L}_{sd}^{(i)} \right) + \lambda_{rc} \mathcal{L}_{rc} + \lambda_{tc} \mathcal{L}_{tc} \tag{5}$$

where $\mathcal{S}$ is the set of scales and λ_{sd}, λ_{ds} λ_{rc}, λ_{tc} is the weight of the self-distillation, depth smoothness, rotation consistency, and translation consistency loss terms, respectively.

4   Evaluation

4.1   Experimental Setup

Dataset. We use the KITTI benchmark [10]. It is composed of video sequences with 93 thousand images acquired through high-quality RGB cameras captured by driving on rural areas and highways of a city.

We used the Eigen split [6] with 45023 images for training and 687 for testing. Moreover, we partitioned the training set on 40441 for training, 4582 for validation. For result evaluation, we used the standard metrics.

Training. Our networks are trained using ADAM optimization algorithm using $\beta_1 = 0.9$, $\beta_2 = 0.999$. We used the batch size of 4 snippets. We use 2-frame snippets unless otherwise specified. We resize the frames to resolutions of 416×128 pixels unless otherwise specified.

The training process is divided into three stages. In the first stage, we train the model with the self-distillation loss disabled. The model is trained using a learning rate of $1e-4$ during 15 epochs, and then its reduced to $1e-5$ during 10 additional epochs. In the second stage, we train the model with self-distillation term enabled. The model is trained with a learning rate of $1e-5$ during 10 additional epochs. Finally, in the third stage, we train the model enabling SWA teacher for the depth network with a cyclical cosine learning rate schedule with an upper bound of $1e-4$, a lower bound of $1e-5$, and using 4 cycles of 6 epochs each, unless otherwise specified.

4.2   Self-distillation via Prediction Consistency

Table 1 shows the results with the simplest variant of our self-distillation approach. The results show a consistent improvement when self-distillation loss is used. The model trained with self-distillation loss outperforms the baseline at all error metrics and almost all accuracy metrics.

When searching for the optimal weight λ_{sd} for the self-distillation term, we noticed that large λ_{sd} values allow to obtain good results. However, due to large depth differences, the model diverges on some executions. Due to this instability, we use a smaller $\lambda_{sd} = 1e2$. This observation motivated us to explore approaches to filter unreliable predictions.

4.3   Filtering Pseudo-labels

Table 2 shows that our two filtering strategies outperform that variation of our method does not use any additional filtering approach other than the composite

Table 1. Comparison of the baseline model and the variation of our method that uses the *pseudo-label* strategy.

Method	↓ Lower is better				↑ Higher is better		
	Abs Rel	Sq Rel	RMSE	LRMSE	$\delta < 1.25$	$\delta < 1.25^2$	$\delta < 1.25^3$
Baseline	0.128	1.005	5.152	0.204	**0.848**	**0.951**	0.979
PL	**0.126**	**0.907**	**5.068**	**0.202**	0.847	**0.951**	**0.980**

mask in the majority of error and accuracy metrics. Moreover, the results show that the approach that uses the EMA of the percentiles to estimate the threshold is better than using only the percentile of each batch.

Table 2. Comparison of variants of our method with and without filtering strategies. P denotes that we filtered pseudo-labels using a percentile by batch as thresholds, and $P^{(\text{EMA})}$ denotes that we filtered pseudo-labels using a threshold that is the EMA computed from percentiles of the batches during training iterations.

Method	↓ Lower is better				↑ Higher is better		
	Abs Rel	Sq Rel	RMSE	LRMSE	$\delta < 1.25$	$\delta < 1.25^2$	$\delta < 1.25^3$
PL (w/o filtering)	**0.126**	0.907	5.068	**0.202**	**0.847**	0.951	**0.980**
PL + P	**0.126**	0.911	5.033	0.203	**0.847**	**0.952**	**0.980**
PL + $P^{(\text{EMA})}$	**0.126**	0.904	**5.024**	**0.202**	**0.847**	**0.952**	**0.980**

4.4   Consistency Enforcement Strategies

Table 3 shows that, regardless the consistency enforcement strategy, self-distillation via prediction consistency can improve the performance of our baseline model. Moreover, the results show that the variant that uses SWA strategy outperforms the other consistency enforcement strategies in most of the error and accuracy metrics. This variant is used as our final model. Some qualitative results are illustrated in Fig. 3.

Fig. 3. Qualitative results. Depths maps obtained using our final model.

Table 3. Comparison of the representative consistency enforcement strategies. PL denotes the pseudo-label, Π M denotes the Π-Model, MT denotes the mean teacher, and SWA denotes the stochastic weight averaging strategy.

Method	↓ Lower is better				↑ Higher is better		
	Abs Rel	Sq Rel	RMSE	LRMSE	$\delta < 1.25$	$\delta < 1.25^2$	$\delta < 1.25^3$
Baseline	0.128	1.005	5.152	0.204	**0.848**	0.951	0.979
PL + $P^{(EMA)}$	0.126	0.904	**5.024**	0.202	0.847	**0.952**	0.980
Π-M + $P^{(EMA)}$	0.126	0.902	5.041	0.202	0.847	**0.952**	0.980
MT + $P^{(EMA)}$	0.126	0.898	5.061	**0.201**	0.846	**0.952**	**0.981**
SWA + $P^{(EMA)}$	**0.125**	**0.881**	5.056	0.202	**0.848**	**0.952**	0.980

4.5 State-of-the-Art Comparison

Table 4 shows a quantitative comparison with state-of-the-art methods. Our method outperforms methods that explicitly address moving objects such as [2,3,12]. Fang et al. [7] obtained better results due to the usage of VGG16 as encoder, which has 138 million parameters. In contrast, our method uses a smaller encoder ResNet-18, which has 11 million parameters. The results show that our method achieves competitive performance when compared to state-of-the-art methods.

Table 4. Results of depth estimation on the Eigen split of the KITTI dataset. We compared our results against several methods of the literature. To allow a fair comparison, we report the results of competitive methods trained with a resolution of 416 × 128 pixels. N.F. denotes the number of frames in the input snippet (*) indicates newly results obtained from an official repository. (-ref.) indicates that the online refinement component is disabled.

Method	N.F.	↓ Lower is better				↑ Higher is better		
		Abs Rel	Sq Rel	RMSE	Log RMSE	$\delta < 1.25$	$\delta < 1.25^2$	$\delta < 1.25^3$
Gordon et al. [12]	2	0.129	0.959	5.230	0.213	0.840	0.945	0.976
Our method	2	**0.125**	**0.881**	**5.056**	0.202	**0.848**	**0.952**	**0.980**
Zhou et al. [29]*	3	0.183	1.595	6.709	0.270	0.734	0.902	0.959
Mahjourian et al. [16]	3	0.163	1.240	6.220	0.250	0.762	0.916	0.967
Casser et al. [2] (-ref)	3	0.141	1.026	5.290	0.215	0.816	0.945	0.979
Chen et al. [3] (-ref)	3	0.135	1.070	5.230	0.210	0.841	0.948	0.980
Godard et al. [11]	3	0.128	1.087	5.171	0.204	0.855	0.953	0.978
Our method	3	0.123	**0.906**	5.083	0.200	0.856	0.953	0.980
Fang [7]	3	**0.116**	–	**4.850**	**0.192**	**0.871**	**0.959**	**0.982**

5 Conclusions

We showed that to take full advantage of self-distillation, we need to consider additional strategies, such as the filtering approaches we proposed in this work, to deal with unreliable predictions. We demonstrated that choosing a proper consistency enforcement strategy in self-distillation is important. Our results suggest that the features of consistency enforcement strategies, such as (i) enforcing teacher quality and (ii) enforcing difference between teacher and student network weights, which are embedded in the SWA strategy, are important to obtain larger improvements. We explored various strategies to benefit from self-distillation for self-supervised depth estimation when the input are monocular sequences. Moreover, we believe that our findings can provide useful insights to leverage self-distillation in methods that use stereo sequences as input, as well as semi-supervised and supervised methods.

References

1. Athiwaratkun, B., Finzi, M., Izmailov, P., Wilson, A.G.: There are many consistent explanations of unlabeled data: why you should average. In: International Conference on Learning Representations (2019)
2. Casser, V., Pirk, S., Mahjourian, R., Angelova, A.: Depth prediction without the sensors: leveraging structure for unsupervised learning from monocular videos. In: AAAI Conference on Artificial Intelligence, vol. 33, pp. 8001–8008 (2019)
3. Chen, Y., Schmid, C., Sminchisescu, C.: Self-supervised learning with geometric constraints in monocular video: connecting flow, depth, and camera. In: IEEE International Conference on Computer Vision, pp. 7063–7072 (2019)
4. Cho, J., Min, D., Kim, Y., Sohn, K.: Deep monocular depth estimation leveraging a large-scale outdoor stereo dataset. Expert Syst. Appl. **178**, 114877 (2021)
5. Choi, H., et al.: Adaptive confidence thresholding for monocular depth estimation. In: IEEE/CVF International Conference on Computer Vision, pp. 12808–12818 (2021)
6. Eigen, D., Puhrsch, C., Fergus, R.: Depth map prediction from a single image using a multi-scale deep network. In: Advances in Neural Information Processing Systems, pp. 2366–2374 (2014)
7. Fang, Z., Chen, X., Chen, Y., Gool, L.V.: Towards good practice for CNN-based monocular depth estimation. In: IEEE/CVF Winter Conference on Applications of Computer Vision, pp. 1091–1100 (2020)
8. Furlanello, T., Lipton, Z., Tschannen, M., Itti, L., Anandkumar, A.: Born again neural networks. In: International Conference on Machine Learning, pp. 1607–1616. PMLR (2018)
9. Garg, R., Bg, V.K., Carneiro, G., Reid, I.: Unsupervised CNN for single view depth estimation: geometry to the rescue. In: Leibe, B., Matas, J., Sebe, N., Welling, M. (eds.) ECCV 2016. LNCS, vol. 9912, pp. 740–756. Springer, Cham (2016). https://doi.org/10.1007/978-3-319-46484-8_45
10. Geiger, A., Lenz, P., Stiller, C., Urtasun, R.: Vision meets robotics: the KITTI dataset. Int. J. Robot. Res. **32**(11), 1231–1237 (2013)
11. Godard, C., Mac Aodha, O., Firman, M., Brostow, G.J.: Digging into self-supervised monocular depth prediction. In: International Conference on Computer Vision, October 2019
12. Gordon, A., Li, H., Jonschkowski, R., Angelova, A.: Depth from videos in the wild: unsupervised monocular depth learning from unknown cameras. arXiv preprint arXiv:1904.04998 (2019)
13. Izmailov, P., Podoprikhin, D., Garipov, T., Vetrov, D., Wilson, A.G.: Averaging weights leads to wider optima and better generalization. arXiv preprint arXiv:1803.05407 (2018)

14. Kaushik, V., Jindgar, K., Lall, B.: ADAADepth: adapting data augmentation and attention for self-supervised monocular depth estimation. arXiv preprint arXiv:2103.00853 (2021)

15. Liu, L., Song, X., Wang, M., Liu, Y., Zhang, L.: Self-supervised monocular depth estimation for all day images using domain separation. In: IEEE/CVF International Conference on Computer Vision, pp. 12737–12746 (2021)

16. Mahjourian, R., Wicke, M., Angelova, A.: Unsupervised learning of depth and ego-motion from monocular video using 3D geometric constraints. In: IEEE Conference on Computer Vision and Pattern Recognition, pp. 5667–5675 (2018)

17. Mendoza, J., Pedrini, H.: Adaptive self-supervised depth estimation in monocular videos. In: Peng, Y., Hu, S.-M., Gabbouj, M., Zhou, K., Elad, M., Xu, K. (eds.) ICIG 2021. LNCS, vol. 12890, pp. 687–699. Springer, Cham (2021). https://doi.org/10.1007/978-3-030-87361-5_56

18. Mobahi, H., Farajtabar, M., Bartlett, P.: Self-distillation amplifies regularization in Hilbert space. In: Larochelle, H., Ranzato, M., Hadsell, R., Balcan, M.F., Lin, H. (eds.) Advances in Neural Information Processing Systems, vol. 33, pp. 3351–3361. Curran Associates, Inc. (2020)

19. Peng, R., Wang, R., Lai, Y., Tang, L., Cai, Y.: Excavating the potential capacity of self-supervised monocular depth estimation. In: IEEE International Conference on Computer Vision (2021)

20. Sajjadi, M., Javanmardi, M., Tasdizen, T.: Regularization with stochastic transformations and perturbations for deep semi-supervised learning. In: Advances in Neural Information Processing Systems, vol. 29, pp. 1163–1171 (2016)

21. Sohn, K., et al.: FixMatch: simplifying semi-supervised learning with consistency and confidence. In: Advances in Neural Information Processing Systems, vol. 33 (2020)

22. Tarvainen, A., Valpola, H.: Mean teachers are better role models: weight-averaged consistency targets improve semi-supervised deep learning results. In: Guyon, I., et al. (eds.) Advances in Neural Information Processing Systems, vol. 30. Curran Associates, Inc. (2017)

23. Tonioni, A., Poggi, M., Mattoccia, S., Di Stefano, L.: Unsupervised domain adaptation for depth prediction from images. IEEE Trans. Pattern Anal. Mach. Intell. **42**(10), 2396–2409 (2019)

24. Xie, Q., Dai, Z., Hovy, E., Luong, T., Le, Q.: Unsupervised data augmentation for consistency training. In: Advances in Neural Information Processing Systems, vol. 33 (2020)

25. Xu, H., et al.: Digging into uncertainty in self-supervised multi-view stereo. In: IEEE/CVF International Conference on Computer Vision, pp. 6078–6087 (2021)

26. Xu, T.B., Liu, C.L.: Data-distortion guided self-distillation for deep neural networks. In: AAAI Conference on Artificial Intelligence, vol. 33, pp. 5565–5572 (2019)

27. Yang, C., Xie, L., Su, C., Yuille, A.L.: Snapshot distillation: teacher-student optimization in one generation. In: IEEE/CVF Conference on Computer Vision and Pattern Recognition, pp. 2859–2868 (2019)

28. Yang, J., Alvarez, J.M., Liu, M.: Self-supervised learning of depth inference for multi-view stereo. In: IEEE/CVF Conference on Computer Vision and Pattern Recognition, pp. 7526–7534 (2021)

29. Zhou, T., Brown, M., Snavely, N., Lowe, D.G.: Unsupervised learning of depth and ego-motion from video. In: IEEE Conference on Computer Vision and Pattern Recognition, pp. 1851–1858 (2017)

Improving UWB Image Reconstruction for Breast Cancer Diagnosis by Doing an Iterative Analysis of Radar Signals

Henrry Adrian Torres-Quispe(✉) and Raquel Esperanza Patino-Escarcina(✉) (iD)

Universidad Católica San Pablo, Arequipa, Peru
{henrry.torres,rpatino}@ucsp.edu.pe

Abstract. UWB (Ultra-Wideband) radar technology is based on the general principle that an antenna transmits an electromagnetic signal and the echo of the reflected signal is detected. This technology is used in different applications, such as medical monitoring or imaging applications for a more precise diagnosis as breast cancer. The diagnostic process of it consists of detecting any lesion or abnormality in the breast tissue, for this, imaging techniques of the breast are used. This UWB technology has given good results compared to traditional methods that lack effectiveness, producing false positives. The images obtained by microwave signals have electrical properties according to the different tissues. Comparing healthy tissues with malignant tissues, a contrast of 8% in permittivity and 10% in conductivity was found in research on the dielectric properties of breast tissue. Previous research proposed reconstruction algorithms for the detection of breast tumors based on a maximum likelihood expectation maximization (MLEM) algorithm. This work proposes an iterative algorithm for imaging based on traditional delay-and-sum (DAS) and delay-multiply-and-sum (DMAS) methods. The main characteristic of this work is the elaboration of an algorithm based on MLEM for a bistatic radar system, to reconstruct an enhanced image where possible tumors with a diameter of up to 1 cm are better distinguished. In a bistatic system, signal processing and reconstruction algorithm differs from a monostatic system, because 2 antennas are considered (emitter and receiver). The MLEM algorithm reduces statistical noise over conventional back-projection algorithms. Experiments were performed with data taken in the laboratory with simulated tumors inside a breast phantom. The results show the images where the tumors are highlighted with 4 iterations.

Keywords: UWB radar technology · Breast cancer · Enhanced image

1 Introduction

A general principle of radar is that an antenna transmits an electromagnetic signal and the echo of the reflected signal is detected. This technology was used

This research was funded by CONCYTEC-PROCIENCIA under grant agreement No. 03-2020-FONDECYT-BM.

M. El Yacoubi et al. (Eds.): ICPRAI 2022, LNCS 13363, pp. 435–446, 2022.
https://doi.org/10.1007/978-3-031-09037-0_36

in World War II for the detection of suspicious objects [22]. UWB technology was a better proposal than radar technology due to the wide bandwidth (from 1 GHZ to 10 GHZ) that allows the visualization of objects, since they have low frequencies. UWB has good resolution for high magnitude frequencies. Another important feature is robustness to noise [6,17,22]. UWB radar technology has various applications, among which medical applications predominate, especially in the detection of breast cancer, which is where most of the research has focused [4,14]. Breast cancer is a very common disease in women, being the second with the highest number of cases in both sexes. It is characterized by being the most lethal in women, and according to the American Cancer Society, one in eight women will suffer from breast cancer, which implies that adult women should have an annual check-up [6]. The main advantage of UWB radar technology compared to traditional imaging technologies is portability, low cost and that it is non-ionizing microwave radiation. The MABIS (Microwave Analyzer for breast imaging system) project aims to prevent breast cancer by making this technology more accessible to hard-to-reach areas. Breast cancer in Peru is more dense in urban areas and has a higher population, but it also has an incidence in rural areas, specifically in remote areas. The process of imaging from UWB signals it consists of the process of data acquisition, preprocessing, and interpretation. So you have a transmission signal that is frequency modulated. Given that in this case there is a tumor inside a phantom, ideally a receiving antenna is expected to receive the signal reflected from it. More reflected signals will be obtained when considering skin tissue. With two objects that are reflected, the delays of the two propagations are considered, and the receiving antenna obtains what would be the sum of the 2 reflections. In the case of the phantoms made by the research group, in addition to the simulated tumor and skin, the breast phantom is filled with a mixture with permittivity similar to fatty breast tissue. In order to have the correct permittivity measurements, they were checked with a precision dielectric measurement system (DAK 3.5 probe). Then for different obstacles P and having n antennas positioned, the propagation delays change being the round trip propagation delay between the transmitting and receiving antenna n-th location (L_n) and a target p be represented by $\tau_{n,p}$ where p is the number of targets, then the acquired signal, explained in detail in [22], is:

$$I(L_n, f_m) = \sum_{k=1}^{P} A_p e^{-j(2\pi f_m(t+\tau_2))} \tag{1}$$

where A_p is the amplitude of each received signal that depends on the target position respect to the receiver, such as the material and the target size, f_m is the step frequency (in the data acquired for this research 501 points are considered in the frequency of 2 to 7 GHz). Signal represented by Eq. 1 it does not change to the 2-dimensional or 3-dimensional reconstruction. The image area is divided up into a plane of pixels in the case of two dimensions, in three dimensions the image volume is divided up into a pixels in the 3-dimensional space, the intensity is processed for each pixel at a time.

1.1   Breast Cancer Diagnosis

Breast cancer is a disease with a high incidence in the female population after lung cancer. In 2012, 1.7 million cases were diagnosed, of which more than 500 thousand ended in death [6,14,15,23]. The diagnostic process consists of detecting any lesion or abnormality in the tissue using breast imaging techniques (X-ray or MRI). The best way to be able to overcome the disease more effectively is through early detection, because the procedures are of lower risk, and the probability of survival is greater; this requires an effective diagnosis and a correct technique [6,14,16]. The most popular techniques lack effectiveness, producing false positives, this can harm those who suffer from cancer. That's why sensitivity is important in detecting lesions that turn out to be cancer. According to [12], from 1977 to 1998, up to 34% of false negatives were detected, that is, lesions that were diagnosed with X-rays as benign but turned out to be harmful. Another disadvantage of X-rays is that it can only be used at most twice per patient in a year. Compared with other technology, ultrasound is the second most used technology for cancer detection, which, like X-rays, has poor resolution and its implementation can be painful. For these reasons, microwave technology is an alternative because benign breast tissue differs in conductivity and permittivity from malignant tissues, producing a high contrast in imaging. UWB technology is not ionizing radiation [14,16]. This technology has been relevant, because clinical applications in real patients are already being considered [13]. From the signals obtained from the UWB antennas, these signals can be enhanced or conditioned and then imaging algorithms are applied to obtain visualization of the breast. These images may require feature enhancement for better diagnosis or classification [13,14,16]. UWB (UltraWideband) is one of the newest technologies applied to imaging. This technology is based on using radar technology for medical applications using ultra-narrow pulses in the time domain to contrast and detect between malignant and normal tissues [5,6,14,21]. Basically an antenna transmits signals which are collected on its radar return in order to detect an object. The images obtained from microwave signals are analyzed to find differences in the electrical properties of different tissues [5,16]. Comparing healthy tissues with malignant tissues, a contrast of 8% in permittivity and 10% in conductivity was found [4,15]. A radar system has a transmitter that emits electromagnetic waves (called radar signals) in viewing directions. When these waves come into contact with an object, they are usually reflected or scattered in many directions. Receivers (usually, but not always, in the same location as the transmitter) are used to receive the echoes. Through the processing of echoes, the radar can determine the range, angle or speed of objects of interest [6,14,16,22].

2   Breast Cancer Detection by UWB Imaging

Systems implementing UWB imaging technology are expected to have 5 characteristics [4]:

1. Significant contrast of dielectric properties
2. Breast compression to be avoided, low power signals
3. The computational challenges for imaging, can be in 2D or 3D.
4. A precision of less than 0.5 cm.
5. The detection of a lesion and classify it if it is benign or malignant.

Research is mainly focused on the development of algorithms for imaging and microwave electronics. So to apply this UWB radar technology to detect tissue abnormalities, the process is based on the contrast between benign and malignant tissue at microwave frequencies. As mentioned, this is one of the main reasons why research is dedicated to microwave imaging [6,14,16,21]. There is a difference between the permittivity and conductivity of malignant and benign tissue [6,7,10,14,16]. This is seen in Fig. 1, in which a difference in electrical characteristics of healthy breast tissue with malignant tissue is observed, and that at high frequencies, the permittivity decreases and the conductivity increases. Indicators of conductivity and dielectric constant can associate a malignant lesion with other physiological characteristics such as blood flow rate or temperature. In obtaining signals, it is required that the breast be crossed with a UWB pulse, the lesion tissue will provide backscattered energy; this energy is produced by the difference in dielectric properties of malignant tissue with normal. This is used to find the location. An energy record is created, the areas that present high energy suggest the presence of a tumor [3,6,14,20]. Other studies on dielectric properties were made in various works. The work of [6] consists of dielectric properties of normal tissue, where it was shown that adipose tissue has lower dielectric properties, benign tissue has higher dielectric properties. The paper [21] had the objective of finding differences between malignant, normal and benign tumors in a frequency range of 0.5 to 20 GHz; from this work it was concluded that the fibroglandular tissue are false positives [6,21].

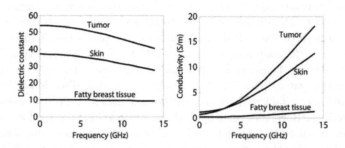

Fig. 1. Dielectric constant and conductivity as a function of frequency of skin, breast tissue, and tumor. (Image in [4])

3   Iterative Method Adopting Form of MLEM (Maximum-Likelihood Expectation-Maximization) Algorithm

An iterative structure can be developed based on the maximum expectation algorithm, this is derived from the Poisson statistic of emission and detection events that is characteristic of imaging based on tomography [18]. A relationship is sought between a reconstruction technique based on radar and one based on tomography, because the iterative structure will be applied to DAS and DMAS. A basic structure of the maximum expectation algorithms is given by the Eq. 2 where the new estimate is multiplied from the current (or last estimate) with the back-projection operator.

$$
new\,estimate = current\,estimation \times B_p \left[\frac{measured\,projections}{F_p[current\,estimation]} \right] \quad (2)
$$

First, the B_p (back-projection operator) of the initial measurements in the time domain is done, the measurements are divided by the F_p (forward projection operator) of the last or current estimate, in this each update involves B_p and F_p for all projections. From this iterative form is that an algorithm is proposed in [18] to achieve what is proposed in this paper, the equation is

$$
E^{k+1} = \frac{E^k}{Bp[U]} \times Bp \left[\frac{I \cdot Fp[U]}{Fp[E^k]} \right] \quad (3)
$$

in which E^{k+1} is the new estimate, this must coincide with the number of rows of the last or current estimate E^k, I is the data that was obtained after processing all the signals, a reconstruction algorithm was not applied. U is a unitary matrix to which an operator is applied, this only serves to calibrate the new estimate. The multiplications in the Eq. 3 are position by position, not a matrix multiplication, and when multiplying the data with the forward projection, NaN values are obtained, so these should be replaced by 0 as [23] indicates. For the back-projection operator, the DAS beamformer will be used, which is represented by the Eq. 4. DAS method is the basic and the best known for breast reconstruction, characterized by its short execution time, robustness and simplicity [13]. In this method all backscattered time domain signals acquired by a radar system, are time-shifted and summed to a synthetic focal point [3,10,14].

$$
I_{DAS}(r) = \left[\sum_{k=1}^{N} s_k(\Delta t_k(r)) \right]^4 \quad (4)
$$

where $I_{DAS}(r)$ is the intensity of certain pixel, N is the number of reflected waves, k is iterated antenna pair, s_k is the signal contribution detected by element k, the corresponding time delay is $\Delta t_k(r)$. For better contrast, it is raised to the fourth. The iterative algorithm can also be executed having the DMAS beamformer as back-projection operator, which is represented in Eq. 5. DMAS method is based on DAS, the difference is that after the time shifted of backscattered signals, these are multiplied in pair, this is before the summation. There are derivatives of DAS beamformer that can be used which can be used as backprojection operator, these can be found in the review [1]

$$I_{DMAS}(r) = \left[\sum_{k=1}^{N} \sum_{m=k+1}^{N} s_k(\Delta t_k(r)) \times s_m(\Delta t_m(r)) \right]^4 \tag{5}$$

A radar signal modeling function from an image is used as a forward projection operator, will be considered the one used in [18]. For a specific pixel, it is necessary to find the round trip distance of each antenna with respect to that pixel. Using an average of the phantom permittivity ε_r over the indicated frequency range, time-of-flight Δt can be computed using Eq. 6.

$$\Delta t = \frac{(d_1 + d_2) \times \sqrt{\varepsilon_r}}{c_0} \tag{6}$$

where d_1 is the distance from emitter antenna to certain pixel, d_2 is the distance from receiver antenna to certain pixel, and c_0 is the speed of light in vacuum. The propagation speed that is used in reconstruction methods was the average permittivity in the scan region, this includes air, skin and simulated fatty breast tissue. We are assuming that at certain height of the breast phantom, in plane xy is formed a breast circle.

4   Experiments and Simulations

To perform experimental scans is necessary a radar-based system which was developed in MABIS project[1]. The MABIS system uses a VNA model S5085 (Copper Mountain Technologies) to generate a chirp signal in a range of 2–7 GHz at 501 frequency points. The signal is supplied for a flexible monopole microstrip antenna, antenna details are described in [2]. This system operates in air, without the use of a coupling medium. Previous experiments were done with the cross configuration in which good results were not obtained, so the research group developed a ring configuration. As concluded in the research of [11], the ring-type configuration improves the electromagnetic scattering at the tumor location. In summary, the MABIS system uses 16 antennas that illuminates a phantom or a breast with a microwave signal, the tissues within the breast scatter this signal, in which the information about the distribution of spatial permittivity could be obtained, and it is this result of the area measured by the transmitting antenna or another receiving antenna [18,21]. A bistatic configuration will be used for the measurement, in total are used 120 recorded signals, not all S_{21} scatter parameters will be used. The S_{21} measurements will be recorded in frequency domain, in this case the inverse chirp z-transform from

---

[1] https://ucsp.edu.pe/video-mabis-brasier-ayudara-masificar-deteccion-temprana-cancer-de-mama/.

[18] was used to convert data to time domain using 1400 points between 0 ns and 5 ns. Then all the signals in the time domain are aligned, in microwave imaging via space-time beamforming (MIST) apply this to precluding phase compensation [7]. For the elaboration of mammary cell simulations, it is only necessary to make fluids based on mixtures of Triton X-100 (TX-100 a non-ionic surfactant), salt and water, as well as in research of [9]. A disadvantage is that at high frequencies there are limitations for the simulation of the behavior, which is why salt is added to simulate values of permittivity and conductivity similar to those of mammary cells. All this information was provided by the university's chemistry department. The research group developed three breast phantoms, the simulate skin has an approximate thickness of 0.3 cm, the permittivity considered for the simulated skin is $\epsilon_r = 38$. The breast phantom was filled with an elaborate mixture that simulates fatty breast tissue, the average permittivity in the indicated frequency range that was measured with the DAK is $\epsilon_r = 10$. The simulated tumors were developed by the research group, and three tumors were considered for the experiments, two tumors with a radius of 1 cm and another of 1.5 cm, one for each breast phantom.

4.1   Calibration

For calibration we use rotate subtraction calibration, which is one of the basic calibration technique, this technique don't suppress the early-stage artifacts efficiently and are not very efficient as shown in [8]. The first set of measurements is scanned with ring antenna configuration within the breast in one position, and a second set of signals is scanned after the breast phantom has been rotated at a certain angle in horizontal plane, but depending on the radar system used, you can rotate the antenna array. Then the subtraction is done as follows:

$$s_i[n] = v_i[n] - v_r[n] \tag{7}$$

where $v_r[n]$ is the vector containing initial scan, $v_r[n]$ is the vector containing the signals scanned after the breast phantom was rotated.

4.2   Results of DAS, DMAS. Iterative DAS and Iterative DMAS

DAS, DMAS, iterative DAS and iterative DMAS were used to reconstruct images of breast phantoms scans. Considering that the phantom will be nipple up, so that it fits in the dome that is upside down, a 1 cm tumor was placed at a height of 1.2 cm in breast phantom I, another 1 cm tumor was placed at a height of 3.6 cm in breast phantom II, and the 1.5 cm tumor was placed at a height of 6.6 cm in breast phantom III. At each height of the phantom, a circular shape of the breast phantom is considered, the diameter of breast phantom I at the indicated height of the tumor is 7.98 cm, of breast phantom II is 6.8 cm, and of breast phantom III is 5.57 cm. The location of the tumor was given at the edges of its respective phantom, very close to the simulated skin. Since the dome is in the shape of a hemisphere, and considering the point of origin to be the center of the dome,

Breast phantom I reconstruction in two positions at z=1.2 cm

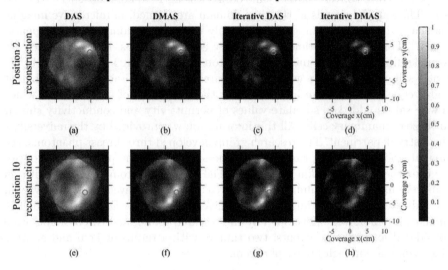

Fig. 2. Reconstructed breast phantom in two different position using the four reconstruction algorithms, with a tumor radius of approximately 1 cm

increasing on the z-axis causes the diameter of the dome to decrease. So for the height of the tumor in breast phantom I, the diameter of the dome is approximately 15.2 cm, for the height of the tumor in breast phantom II, the diameter of the dome is 14.26 cm, and for the height of the tumor in breast phantom III, the diameter of the dome is 10.31 cm. The reconstruction are in 2D in xy plane at a specified height, as the dome has a hemispherical shape upside down, the region of interest for reconstruction in iterative methods is a circle, rejecting unimportant results. The region of interest is part of the F_p function, this will influence the resulting image. Depending of the antenna array, the region of interest could be a circle, it also depends on the type of antenna, In the elaborate code, must be specified the radius of the dome (antenna array) at a certain height, the radius does not consider the distance of the antenna with the dome and the thickness of the dome. The center of the array is the point of origin, as it is an upside down dome as shown in [11]. Considering that the dome is a hemisphere, the point of origin is the center of what would be considered a complete sphere of the dome. Each image is normalized to its maximum intensity. The dotted green circle in the reconstructions are the estimated position of the tumor. The number of iterations are 4. The reconstruction of breast phantom I is shown in Fig. 2, the breast phantom was rotated in the xy plane so that the tumor points to antenna 2, for this reason the reconstructions using four methods (DAS, DMAS, Iterative DAS and Iterative DMAS) of Fig. 2a–d are considered "Position 2 reconstruction". The coordinates of antenna 2 are ($x = 6.6$ cm, $y = 2.9$ cm, $z = 1.75$ cm), In this experiment, the breast phantom was not placed in the center of the dome, the center of the phantom is placed approximately 2 cm more on the positive x-axis

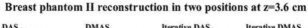

Breast phantom II reconstruction in two positions at z=3.6 cm

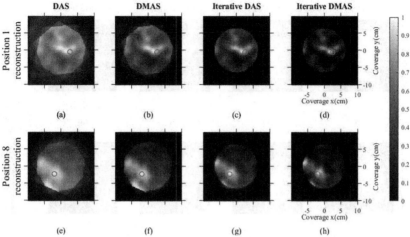

Fig. 3. Reconstructed breast phantom in two different position using the four reconstruction algorithms, with a tumor radius of approximately 1 cm

and 2 cm more on the positive y-axis, with respect to the point of origin. So in Fig. 2e–h, the scan were performed when the tumor is oriented to the antenna 10, which coordinates are ($x = 4.7$ cm, $y = 5.3$ cm, $z = 1.65$ cm). The iterative methods significantly reduced the high intensity clutter response near the tumor location compared to non-iterative methods. In DAS method, the pixels with the highest intensities are already displayed in the estimated location of the tumor, but with significant clutter around it. With iterative beamformers, the clutter intensity is significantly reduced and maintain the tumor response, this can be seen in Fig. 2d. In Fig. 2e–g, the tumor response is maintained, but there is high-intensity clutter around tumor location. In Fig. 2h, it seems that the reconstruction with the iterative DMAS the tumor response is not significantly greater then the highest clutter response. The high-intensity clutter is present near to the antenna 3. Breast phantom II this time is placed so that its center coincides with the point of origin, is rotated so that the tumor is oriented to antenna 1 and antenna 8, "Position 1 reconstruction" and "Position 8 reconstruction", respectively. Antenna 1 coordinates are ($x = 6.95$ cm, $y = -1.5$ cm, $z = 1.7$ cm) and antenna 8 coordinates are ($x = -3.6$ cm, $y = 6$ cm, $z = 1.55$ cm). As seen in the Fig. 3, now the position of the tumor tends to be closer to the origin because the phantom is located in the center and its diameter at that height is 6.8 cm. Again the reconstructions produced by iterative methods reduce clutter, both high intensity and low intensity. In Fig. 3a–d, highest intensities are close to the tumor response, with Iterative DMAS highest intensities are in or near the tumor location and clutter responses near the tumor are reduced, obtaining improved results. It is in the Fig. 3e–h where the non-interactive methods are producing high intensity outside the tumor location, with iterative

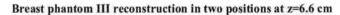

Breast phantom III reconstruction in two positions at z=6.6 cm

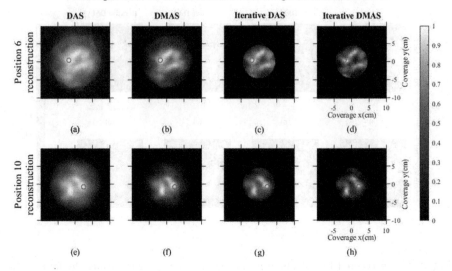

Fig. 4. Reconstructed breast phantom in two different position using the four reconstruction algorithms, with a tumor radius of approximately 1.5 cm

methods again clutter is reduced, both high intensity and low intensity, and highest intensities are now located in the tumor location. But tumor response is not significantly than high-intensity clutter responses, notoriously in iterative DMAS method. In the case of Fig. 4, breast phantom III was positioned so that the center of the phantom coincides with the point of origin, and was rotated so that the tumor is oriented to antenna 6 and antenna 10, "Position 6 reconstruction" and "Position 10 reconstruction", The coordinates of antenna 6 are $(x = -6.8\,\text{cm},\ y = 1.6\,\text{cm},\ z = 1.55\,\text{cm})$. Although it seems that highest intensities are at the location of the tumor in Fig. 4a–d, high-intensity clutter responses are not low enough to distinguish from tumor response, is in iterative methods that high-intensity clutter responses are reduced, and the tumor response is maintained. A similar description of the results is given in Fig. 4e–h, in which iterative methods displayed shown that tumor response is not significantly greater than the high-intensity clutter responses, the position of the tumor we could not say is clear. With iterative methods this does not happen, it is observed that high-intensity clutter responses are reduced and tumor response is improved, this is most noticeable in iterative DMAS.

5   Conclusions

The iterative method used in [18] can be applied to bistatic radar system with the correct modifications, with bistatic signals the reconstructions can be more accurate, because more signals can be processed, The iterative method applies the functional form of the MLEM algorithm from [19] to DAS and DMAS recon-struction algorithm, DAS and DMAS beamformer as the back-projection oper-ator is used, and a radar signal model as the forward projection operator. DAS, DMAS and their respective Iterative methods were used to reconstruct images of experimental brest phantoms. All beamformers produced 24 reconstructions that had identifiable tumor responses, high-intensity and low-intensity clutter responses are reduced and generally the clutter response is improved. The algo-rithms described were used to reconstruct images of 3 phantoms, with different orientation of the tumor, in total were performed 34 scans considering only bistatic signals. In the vast majority of cases, it was reduced high-intensity and low-intensity responses clutter, but in some cases the tumor response was not in the expected location, this may be due to the artifact removal technique. It is necessary a realistic result of the non-iterative method such as DAS or DMAS, without this the iterative method are useless. For future work, better calibra-tion methods will be applied, according to [8] the entropy-based time window is the most outstanding calibration technique, and this or Wiener filter could be implemented. In future work can investigate the impact of using other back-projection operator in the iterative structure, could be DAS-derivatives methods or alternatives can be explored. The implementation of better forward projection operator can be investigated, because in this work are using a basic radar signal model.

References

1. Aldhaeebi, M.A., Alzoubi, K., Almoneef, T.S., Bamatraf, S.M., Attia, H., Ramahi, O.M.: Review of microwaves techniques for breast cancer detection. Sensors **20**(8), 2390 (2020)
2. Bahramiabarghouei, H., Porter, E., Santorelli, A., Gosselin, B., Popovic, M., Rusch, L.A.: Flexible 16 antenna array for microwave breast cancer detection. IEEE Trans. Biomed. Eng. **62**(10), 2516–2525 (2015)
3. Been Lim, H., Thi Tuyet Nhung, N., Li, E.P., Duc Thang, N.: Confocal microwave imaging for breast cancer detection: delay-multiply-and-sum image reconstruction algorithm. IEEE Trans. Biomed. Eng. **55**(6), 1697–1704 (2008)
4. Bidhendi, H.K., Jafari, H.M., Genov, R.: Ultra-wideband imaging systems for breast cancer detection. In: Yuce, M.R. (ed.) Ultra-Wideband and 60 GHz Com-munications for Biomedical Applications, pp. 83–103. Springer, Boston (2014). https://doi.org/10.1007/978-1-4614-8896-5_5
5. Bond, E., Xu, L., Hagness, S., Van Veen, B.: Microwave imaging via space-time beamforming for early detection of breast cancer. IEEE Trans. Antennas Propag. **51**(8), 1690–1705 (2003)
6. Conceicao, R., Byrne, D., O'Halloran, M., Glavin, M., Jones, E.: Classification of suspicious regions within ultrawideband radar images of the breast. In: IET Irish Signals and Systems Conference (ISSC 2008), Galway, Ireland, pp. 60–65. IEE (2008)
7. Curtis, C.: Factors Affecting Image Quality in Near-field Ultra-wideband Radar Imaging for Biomedical Applications. University of Calgary (2015)
8. Elahi, M.A., Glavin, M., Jones, E., O'Halloran, M.: Artifact removal algorithms for microwave imaging of the breast. Prog. Electromagn. Res. **141**, 185–200 (2013)

9. Fear, E., Hagness, S., Meaney, P., Okoniewski, M., Stuchly, M.: Enhancing breast tumor detection with near-field imaging. IEEE Microw. Mag. **3**(1), 48–56 (2002)
10. Hagness, S., Taflove, A., Bridges, J.: Two-dimensional FDTD analysis of a pulsed microwave confocal system for breast cancer detection: fixed-focus and antenna-array sensors. IEEE Trans. Biomed. Eng. **45**(12), 1470–1479 (1998)
11. Kranold, L., Hazarika, P., Popovic, M.: Investigation of antenna array configurations for dispersive breast models. In: 2017 11th European Conference on Antennas and Propagation (EUCAP), Paris, France. pp. 2737–2741. IEEE, March 2017
12. Misilmani, H.M.E., Naous, T., Khatib, S.K.A., Kabalan, K.Y.: A survey on antenna designs for breast cancer detection using microwave imaging. IEEE Access **8**, 102570–102594 (2020)
13. Nikolova, N.: Microwave imaging for breast cancer. IEEE Microw. Mag. **12**(7), 78–94 (2011)
14. Oliveira, B.: Towards improved breast cancer diagnosis using microwave technology and machine learning. Ph.D. thesis, NUI Galway, September 2018
15. Oloumi, D., Bevilacqua, A., Bassi, M.: UWB radar for high resolution breast cancer scanning: system, architectures, and challenges. In: 2019 IEEE International Conference on Microwaves, Antennas, Communications and Electronic Systems (COMCAS), Tel-Aviv, Israel, pp. 1–4. IEEE, November 2019
16. Oloumi, D.: Ultra-wideband synthetic aperture radar imaging theory and applications. Ph.D. thesis, University of Alberta (2016)
17. Pan, J.: Medical applications of ultra-wideband (UWB). Technical Report, Washington University, October 2007
18. Reimer, T., Solis-Nepote, M., Pistorius, S.: The application of an iterative structure to the delay-and-sum and the delay-multiply-and-sum beamformers in breast microwave imaging. Diagnostics **10**(6), 411 (2020)
19. Shepp, L.A., Vardi, Y.: Maximum likelihood reconstruction for emission tomography. IEEE Trans. Med. Imaging **1**(2), 113–122 (1982)
20. Solis-Nepote, M., Reimer, T., Pistorius, S.: An air-operated bistatic system for breast microwave radar imaging: pre-clinical validation. In: 2019 41st Annual International Conference of the IEEE Engineering in Medicine and Biology Society (EMBC), Berlin, Germany, pp. 1859–1862. IEEE, July 2019
21. Töpfer, F., Oberhammer, J.: Microwave cancer diagnosis. In: Principles and Applications of RF/Microwave in Healthcare and Biosensing, pp. 103–149. Elsevier (2017)
22. Vargas, J.M.M.: Signal processing techniques for radar based subsurface and through wall imaging, p. 130 (2012)
23. Yin, T., Ali, F.H., Reyes-Aldasoro, C.C.: A robust and artifact resistant algorithm of ultrawideband imaging system for breast cancer detection. IEEE Trans. Biomed. Eng. **62**(6), 1514–1525 (2015)

Personalized Frame-Level Facial Expression Recognition in Video

Andrey V. Savchenko[(⊠)]

Laboratory of Algorithms and Technologies for Network Analysis,
HSE University, Nizhny Novgorod, Russia
avsavchenko@hse.ru

Abstract. In this paper, the personalization of the video-based frame-level facial expression recognition is studied for multi-user systems if a small amount of short videos are available for each user. At first, embeddings of each video frame are computed using deep convolutional neural network pre-trained on a large emotional dataset of static images. Next, a dataset of videos is used to train a subject-independent emotion classifier, such as feed-forward neural network or frame attention network. Finally, it is proposed to fine-tune this neural classifier on the videos of each user of interest. As a result, every user is associated with his or her own emotional model. The classifier in a multi-user system is chosen by an appropriate video-based face recognition method. The experimental study with the RAMAS dataset demonstrates the significant (up to 25%) increase in accuracy of the proposed approach when compared to a subject-independent facial expression recognition.

Keywords: Facial expression recognition · Face recognition · Video processing · RAMAS dataset

1 Introduction

One of the most acute tasks in pattern recognition and image analysis is a development of emotional intelligence [1] and, in particular, real-time facial expression recognition (FER) [2,3]. Emotion recognition is a crucial step toward more natural and intelligent man-machine interaction [4]. Unfortunately, the usage of even the state-of-the-art FER methods in practical applications is still limited. In contrast to the availability of very large facial datasets for in-the-wild face recognition [5], the datasets used to train FER models are much smaller and noisier [6]. Indeed, annotation of emotions on visual data is a challenging task [7] as perception of emotions varies from person to person [8]. Moreover, static images usually do not contain enough information about dynamical changes of emotions [9]. Facial (macro) expressions usually last for between 0.5 and 4 s, and are made using underlying facial movements that cover a large facial area [10]. Hence, the image sequence should be analyzed, which causes the need for labeling of the beginning and end positions of each facial expression at frame level [11].

© Springer Nature Switzerland AG 2022
M. El Yacoubi et al. (Eds.): ICPRAI 2022, LNCS 13363, pp. 447–458, 2022.
https://doi.org/10.1007/978-3-031-09037-0_37

Though the video-based FER task is still far from maturity, it has been widely studied in literature. The usage of facial landmarks for fast emotion analysis is discussed in [4]. Computing the video emotional descriptor using statistical (STAT) features (average, minimum, maximum, standard deviation) is discussed in [12]. Pre-training of deep convolutional neural networks (CNN) for face recognition and FER on static images from our previous article [3] lead to the state-of-the-art performance of single models for several video datasets. The paper [13] introduced the frame-attention network to extract the most important frames and aggregate the embeddings extracted from each frame. The concatenation of frame embeddings with average descriptor of the whole video significant increased the accuracy of recurrent and attention models [14]. The usage of audio and visual modality [15] and the factorized bi-linear pooling in the attention cross-modal feature fusion mechanisms highlighted important emotion features [16]. The baseline of the frame-level emotion recognition for the RAMAS (Russian Acted Multimodal Affective Set) [7] has been established by training of several CNN architectures to classify emotions of each video frame [8]. Though it is typical to train a model for face recognition and fine-tune it on FER [3], the paper [17] studied the link between these tasks in opposite direction when the biases introduced by facial expressions are observed in face recognition.

Unfortunately, due to the above-mentioned difficulties of the video-based FER problem, the recent studies have reported low recognition accuracy for basic emotions from several datasets [8,18]. Hence, in this paper, we examine the possibility to drastically increase the accuracy by borrowing the ideas of speaker adaptation from speech processing [19–21] to video FER. We propose to develop a personalized engine by fine-tuning a general subject-independent neural network-based classifier of frame-level visual features. Several subject-specific models are trained in the multi-user systems, one of which is chosen using contemporary face identification methods [22]. If the identity of a subject in a single-user system, e.g., personal mobile device, is unknown, the face verification may be implemented to either choose the subject-dependent model or a subject-independent classifier.

It is worth noting that the ideas of personalization of FER systems have recently appeared. For example, the authors of the paper [18] proposed to use the output of the first part of the face recognition network as an attention map for the FER model. However, their model has not been trained on the subject-specific emotional data. It is also typical to train a single model on videos of several subjects [8,23], so that the same persons are presented in both training and test sets. Such an approach is also not personal because it is not guaranteed that it works excellent for every concrete user because his or her videos may be imbalanced, and the number of training examples from a subject may be much lower when compared to the size of the whole training set [20]. Moreover, it needs to retrain the whole model when data from new subject is gathered.

The remaining part of the paper is structured as follows. The proposed approach to the video-based FER task is presented in Sect. 2. Section 3 contains experimental results for the RAMAS dataset. Conclusion and future work are discussed in Sect. 4.

2 Methodology

2.1 Facial Expression Recognition in Videos

The frame-level (or frame-based [11]) FER task is formulated as follows. Let a set of $M \geq 1$ subjects (users) is available. Given an input sequence of facial video frames $\{X(t)\}, t = 1, 2, ..., T$ from one of these subjects, it is required to predict the class label $c(t) \in \{1, ..., C\}$ of emotions represented in this frame. Here C is the total number of different emotions, t is the frame number and T is the number of frames with facial regions in the input video. We deal with the supervised learning scenario, where the training set of $N > 1$ video samples is denoted as $\{X_n\}, n \in \{1, 2, ..., N\}$ from other users with known emotions $c_n(t) \in \{1, ..., C\}$ of each video sequence $X_n = \{X_n(t)\}$. For simplicity, we assume that only one facial image has been preliminary extracted from each frame by using appropriate face detection technique [24].

In order to solve this task, a CNN is pre-trained on a large dataset with static facial images, such as AffectNet [6]. Next, the last (softmax) layer of this CNN is removed, and the $D \gg 1$ outputs of the penultimate layer are used as visual features (embeddings) [3]. The facial images $X(t)$ and $X_n(t)$ are fed into this CNN to extract the D-dimensional feature vectors $\mathbf{x}(t)$ and $\mathbf{x}_n(t)$, respectively. Finally, the emotions of each frame are predicted. Let us discuss several techniques to implement this step in the next subsection.

2.2 Classification of the Frame-Level Features

The simplest approach is a training of an arbitrary classifier, such as RF (Random Forest) or MLP (Multi-Layer Perceptron), on the set of extracted feature vectors with corresponding class label $\{(\mathbf{x}_n(t), c_n(t))\}$. However, one can notice that emotions of sequential frames are identical in most cases, so that it is possible to use the context of the t-th frame in order to increase the classification accuracy. In this paper, the frame-level feature vector is computed by concatenation of the frame embedding $\mathbf{x}(t)$ and a descriptor of embeddings $\overline{\mathbf{x}}(t)$ from the neighborhood $t' \in \{t - \Delta, ..., t + \Delta\}$ of the t-th frame, where $\Delta \geq 0$ defines the range of the neighborhood. Two aggregation techniques have been studied, namely:

1. Computing STAT features [12]. Only the average pooling will be used in this paper:

$$\overline{\mathbf{x}}_{avg}(t) = \frac{1}{2\Delta + 1} \sum_{t'=t-\Delta}^{t+\Delta} \mathbf{x}(t'), \tag{1}$$

2. Using frame attention network with a softmax activation function and a fully connected (FC) layer to estimate the attention weights for frame features [13].

In the latter case, the attention weight of each frame in a neighborhood t' is defined as follows [14, 25]:

$$\alpha(t') = \text{softmax}(\mathbf{x}(t')\mathbf{q}), \qquad (2)$$

where $\mathbf{q}$ is a D-dimensional vector of weights in the FC layer. As a result, one can obtain the following neighborhood descriptor

$$\overline{\mathbf{x}}_{attn}(t) = \sum_{t'=t-\Delta}^{t+\Delta} \alpha(t')\mathbf{x}(t'). \qquad (3)$$

It is also possible to combine both aggregation techniques [14] and learn the attention weights for concatenation of the frame embeddings $\mathbf{x}(t)$ and $\overline{\mathbf{x}}_{avg}(t)$ (1):

$$\alpha^{(1)}(t') = \text{softmax}([\mathbf{x}(t'); \overline{\mathbf{x}}_{avg}(t)]\mathbf{q}^{(1)}), \qquad (4)$$

where $\mathbf{q}^{(1)}$ is a $2D$-dimensional vector of weights in the FC layer. In this case, the final descriptor is computed as follows:

$$\overline{\mathbf{x}}_{attn;avg}(t) = \sum_{t'=t-\Delta}^{t+\Delta} \alpha^{(1)}(t')[\mathbf{x}(t'); \overline{\mathbf{x}}_{avg}(t)]. \qquad (5)$$

Finally, the FC layer with C outputs and softmax activation is attached on top of the aggregated features (3) or (5), and the FER neural classifier is trained using the subsets of frames from the training videos.

2.3   Proposed Approach

In this paper, we examine the possibility to increase the overall accuracy based on adaptation of the FER model from Subsect. 2.2 to a particular user by using additional subject-dependent dataset. Let us assume that a small set of $N_m \geq C$ videos $\{X_{m;n}(t)\}, n \in \{1, ..., N_m\}$ with different emotions $c_{m;n} \in \{1, ..., C\}$ was gathered for every m-th user ($m \in \{1, ..., M\}$. The novel pipeline for solving this task is shown in Fig. 1.

During training procedure, the subject-independent neural classifier from previous subsection is used. Next, it is proposed to perform an adaptation of a FER model on the data of each user [20]. A neural network is fine-tuned using only subsets of frames from the subject-specific training set $\{X_{m;n}(t)\}$. In particular, a neural network with the same architectures, but different weights for each user have been initialized by the weights of the subject-independent classifier, so that the subject-specific data is used for fine-tuning only. As this classifier is represented as a neural network, e.g., MLP or attention network, this initialization is implemented by simple copying of the pre-trained neural network.

The inference stage for an observed video starts from face detection using MTCNN (multi-task cascaded CNN) [24] and includes two parts. Firstly,

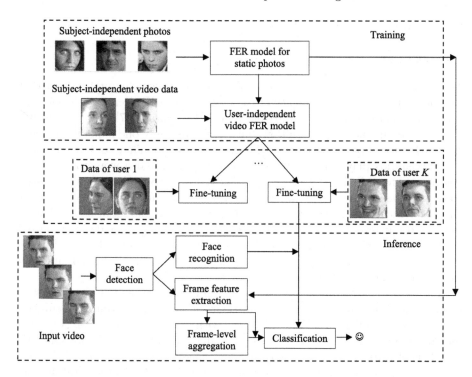

Fig. 1. Proposed pipeline

the video embeddings suitable for face identification are extracted by using VGGFace2 SENet [5], ArcFace [22] or our MobileNet/EfficientNet [3]. These embeddings are used in the open-set recognition scenario with k-NN to predict the user identifier and obtain the fine-tuned FER model associated with this user. In practice, the base subject-independent classifier may be used if the confidence of the decision is low.

Secondly, the frame-level emotions are recognized by using the subject-dependent model. Every frame of the input video is fed into a FER CNN [3] trained on AffectNet to extract emotional embeddings $\mathbf{x}(t)$. The descriptor of the neighborhood frames is computed for every t-th frame in the frame-level aggregation unit according to the previous Subsection (Eq. 1, 3 and 5). Decision about current emotional state of the frame is computed in the FC layer of a classifier network.

This algorithm may be modified if only one user is available, so that it is possible to completely ignore the face recognition step and use the fine-tuned classifier in all cases. An example of such a system is the emotion recognition on a personal device like mobile phone, which should work only for a specific user. However, it is possible to check by using *face verification* that a user has not been replaced by someone else [26]. Otherwise, the base subject-independent classifier may be used, or the emotion recognition engine is completely turned off.

3   Experimental Study

3.1   Dataset

Most publicly available datasets have labels for the video clip only, so that they cannot be used to test the quality of the frame-level FER. Hence, we decided to carry out experiments in this study on the RAMAS dataset [7]. It was developed for multimodal emotion recognition, but we will use only one modality, namely, $K = 564$ video clips captured from the close-up camera. They contain the interactive scenarios played by 10 Russian actors (5 men and 5 women). Six basic emotions (Anger, Sadness, Disgust, Happiness, Fear or Surprise) and the Neutral state are labeled. At least 5 annotations are available for each video clip. Each annotator marked the beginning and the end of each emotional expression, so that the frame-level labeling become available. In this paper, we decided to work with the most difficult technique to choose the ground-truth labels, namely, took all frames marked by at least one annotator, and select all emotional labels for each frame (multi-label classification).

The actor-based split of the dataset was implemented as follows. At first, 5 actors were randomly selected, and all their videos were put into the subject-independent training set $\{X_n = \{X_n(t)\}\}$ with $N = 315$ video clips. Next, the remaining $K - N = 249$ videos of the 5 testing actors were randomly split into two disjoint parts. The subject-independent classifier is fine-tuned on the first part with $N_m = \delta K_m$ videos of every m-th user. Here K_m is the total number of videos for the m-th user from the dataset, and split factor $\delta \in (0, 1)$ is the parameter that determines the relative size of the subject-specific training set. The second part with the remaining $K_m - N_m$ video clips is used to test the accuracy of the proposed approach.

3.2   Training Details

The code with the implementation of the proposed approach and experimental study is publicly available[1]. Two lightweight CNN were used to extract features, namely, MobileNet V1 and EfficientNet B0. They have been pre-trained on the VGGFace2 dataset [5] for face identification and further fine-tunes on the Affect-Net dataset [6]. The details about the training of these models are available in our previous paper [3].

As the multi-label classification task should be solved for the RAMAS dataset, the last FC layer in our models include sigmoid activation, and the binary cross-entropy was optimized. The attention-based subject-independent classifiers have been learned during 10 epochs using Adam optimizer with learning rate 0.0001 and batch size 256. We follow the recommendation from original paper [13] and randomly chose 3 frames from each video. In addition to attention networks, we trained the recurrent model based on 128 GRUs (gated recurrent

---

[1] https://github.com/HSE-asavchenko/face-emotion-recognition/blob/main/src/ train_ramas.ipynb.

Table 1. Weighted recall (%) of video-based facial expression recognition, $\delta = 0.5$

Method	MobileNet		EfficientNet	
	Embeddings	Embeddings+mean	Embeddings	Embeddings+mean
RF	59.97	60.33	54.62	65.58
GRU	43.57	50.74	47.69	55.03
Single attention	53.14	63.05	55.09	57.66
MLP	50.77	55.99	51.49	53.97
Proposed approach (attention)	67.41	70.49	68.53	65.66
Proposed approach (MLP)	64.83	75.18	66.31	75.87

unit). The MLP classifiers have been trained similarly, but the number of epochs was equal to 25, and the original training set with frame-level labeling was used. The whole video was used to compute average descriptor for each classifier (1). Moreover, RF with 1000 trees was trained on the frame-level set. The fine-tuning in the proposed approach is implemented by fitting the model during 5 epochs using Adam optimizer with learning rate 0.0001.

3.3   Results

The weighted average recall of subject-dependent and subject-independent classifiers computed on the testing sets of 5 actors with split factor $\delta = 0.5$ is shown in Table 1.

Here, first, the proposed adaptation (Fig. 1) leads to 7–20% greater accuracy when compared to the subject-independent models. Second, concatenation of mean features to the frame-level embeddings [14] lead to higher accuracy in the majority of cases except the attention-based adapted classifier with EfficientNet embeddings. This gain is especially noticeable (up to 9%) for our adaptation of the simple MLP classifier. It is interesting to emphasize that the MobileNet-based embeddings with dimensionality $D = 1024$ are classified more accurately when compared to 1280-dimensional embeddings from EfficientNet, though the latter are much more accurate in several other FER tasks [3].

In the second experiment, the efficiency of the proposed method was studied depending on the size of the subject-specific training set defined by the train/test split ratio δ. The average recall of the MLP classifier for the MobileNet emotional embeddings concatenated with the mean video descriptor (1) are presented in Fig. 2.

Here we additionally implemented the training from scratch of the neural classifier using data only from subject without fine-tuning of the subject-independent model. Though this techniques works rather accurately if a user have plenty of data, it is much worse than the conventional classifier for the small size of the training sample ($\delta = 0.1$). However, our approach has 2%

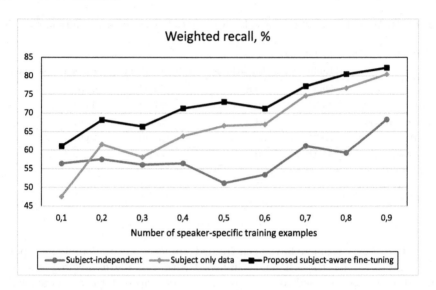

Fig. 2. Dependence of average accuracy on the size of the subject-specific training set, MobileNet features concatenated with their mean (1), MLP classifier

greater recall even if $\delta = 0.9$. And the usage of fine-tuning for the small subject-specific dataset ($\delta = 0.1$) leads to 14% more accurate decisions when compared to simple training of a classifier from scratch.

As it was expected, recall of the subject-independent model practically does not depend on δ and is approximately identical to the recall reported in Table 1. On the contrary, recall of the proposed adaptation is increased with the growth of the size of the subject-specific training set. Figure 3 highlights this difference by demonstrating the confusion matrices estimated for a test set of one actor using the subject-independent mode and our approach. The usage of the subject-specific data in our pipeline (Fig. 1) is preferable in all cases over subject-independent model. Even if the amount of the subject-specific training data is very small ($\delta = 0.1$), then our approach is still 5% more accurate.

Unfortunately, the RAMAS dataset is not very popular, and only few studies have previously deal with it. The authors of this dataset reported in their poster that achieved 52.5% weighted accuracy with stacked bidirectional long short-term memory recurrent neural network and decision-level feature fusion for the multimodal scenario [27]. The visual features have been classified by fine-tuned VGGFace2 (ResNet-50) and EfficientNet-B0 convolutional networks in [8]. These models reached recall 42.96% and 45.25% for the level of agreement of at least 1 annotator and 90–10% train-test split. As one can notice, even our subject-independent models are more accurate (Table 1), while the best classifier reaches recall 82.21% for $\delta = 0.9$ (Fig. 2).

Finally, the face identification quality was estimated using the same training and testing sets of 5 actors. The MobileNet model pre-trained on VGGFace2 [28] extracted $D = 1024$ features from each frame. The average of L_2-normalized

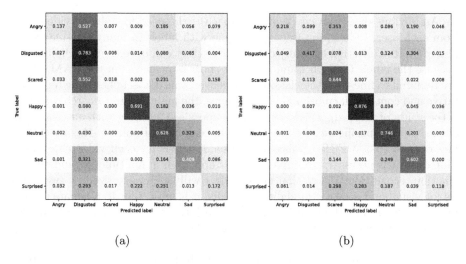

(a)   (b)

Fig. 3. Confusion matrix, MobileNet features, $\delta = 0.5$, actor 'Rodion Tolokonnikov': (a) subject-independent FER; (b) proposed personalized FER.

features extracted from the subject-dependent video clips $\{X_{m;n}(t)\}$ was used to train LinearSVC classifier from the scikit-learn library. The face recognition task here is very easy, because only 5 different actors should be identified, and the recording conditions are rather good. As a result, this task was perfectly solved with accuracy 100% even if the train-test split ratio was equal to $\delta = 0.1$.

4   Conclusion

In this paper we analyzed the possibility to develop a personalized emotion recognition engine if labeled video data from particular user is available. This fine-tuning of the subject-independent emotional classifier (Fig. 1) was implemented in either simple MLP or attention-based network (Subsect. 2.2). Only one dataset (RAMAS) was used in the experimental study because it is the only one publicly available FER dataset with frame-level annotations and known actors from a limited set of speakers. Nevertheless, it was demonstrated that such an adaptation significantly increased the recognition accuracy even if small amount of training data was available (Fig. 2).

It is important to emphasize that face recognition can be used for an observed video to select the proper classifier of particular subject from a pre-defined list of users. Hence, our method has great potential in any video-based recognition task even for the multi-user systems. If a system should work also for new users, a subject-independent model will be used. However, if the previous videos of a user are stored and labeled, there will be a great possibility to improve the quality of man-machine interaction using our personalized approach. It is extremely important that this paper deals with the frame-level recognition, so that our approach predicts dynamical changes of emotions.

An obvious disadvantage of our approach is the need for labeled video data from each user. Indeed, data does not come with labels in many real-life examples of FER. Collecting the subject-specific dataset can be extremely challenging because the labels for each frame (or their short sequence as in the RAMAS [7]) are required to fine-tune the classifier. Moreover, this dataset should be representative and contain all emotional labels. Hence, the main future research direction is the study of semi-supervised or weakly-supervised learning with auto-labeling of the subject-specific facial expressions. One can use the state-of-the-art ensembles of video-based FER to obtain the pseudo-labels for each video clip [2,12]. Moreover, it is necessary to implement our approach in multimodal/audiovisual emotion recognition [15], so that each subject will be characterized by two models for visual and acoustic modalities. Finally, it is important to estimate performance of the proposed technique combined with the state-of-the-art FER models for other datasets with frame-level emotional labels [29].

Acknowledgements. The work is supported by RSF (Russian Science Foundation) grant 20-71-10010.

References

1. Pietikäinen, M., Silven, O.: Challenges of artificial intelligence-from machine learning and computer vision to emotional intelligence. arXiv preprint arXiv:2201.01466 (2022)
2. Li, S., Deng, W.: Deep facial expression recognition: a survey. IEEE Trans. Affect. Comput. (2020). https://doi.org/10.1109/TAFFC.2020.2981446
3. Savchenko, A.V.: Facial expression and attributes recognition based on multi-task learning of lightweight neural networks. In: Proceedings of 19th International Symposium on Intelligent Systems and Informatics (SISY), pp. 119–124. IEEE (2021)
4. Cerezo, E., et al.: Real-time facial expression recognition for natural interaction. In: Martí, J., Benedí, J.M., Mendonça, A.M., Serrat, J. (eds.) IbPRIA 2007. LNCS, vol. 4478, pp. 40–47. Springer, Heidelberg (2007). https://doi.org/10.1007/978-3-540-72849-8_6
5. Cao, Q., Shen, L., Xie, W., Parkhi, O.M., Zisserman, A.: Vggface2: a dataset for recognising faces across pose and age. In: Proceedings of 13th International Conference on Automatic Face & Gesture Recognition (FG), pp. 67–74. IEEE (2018)
6. Mollahosseini, A., Hasani, B., Mahoor, M.H.: AffectNet: a database for facial expression, valence, and arousal computing in the wild. IEEE Trans. Affect. Comput. **10**(1), 18–31 (2017)
7. Perepelkina, O., Kazimirova, E., Konstantinova, M.: RAMAS: Russian multimodal corpus of dyadic interaction for affective computing. In: Karpov, A., Jokisch, O., Potapova, R. (eds.) SPECOM 2018. LNCS (LNAI), vol. 11096, pp. 501–510. Springer, Cham (2018). https://doi.org/10.1007/978-3-319-99579-3_52
8. Ryumina, E., Verkholyak, O., Karpov, A.: Annotation confidence vs. training sample size: trade-off solution for partially-continuous categorical emotion recognition. In: Proceedings of Interspeech 2021, pp. 3690–3694 (2021). https://doi.org/10.21437/Interspeech.2021-1636

9. Saleem, S.M., Zeebaree, S.R., Abdulrazzaq, M.B.: Real-life dynamic facial expression recognition: a review. J. Phys. Conf. Ser. **1963**, 012010 (2021). IOP Publishing
10. Ben, X., et al.: Video-based facial micro-expression analysis: a survey of datasets, features and algorithms. IEEE Trans. Pattern Anal. Mach. Intell. (2021)
11. Saeed, A., Al-Hamadi, A., Niese, R., Elzobi, M.: Frame-based facial expression recognition using geometrical features. In: Advances in Human-Computer Interaction 2014 (2014)
12. Bargal, S.A., Barsoum, E., Ferrer, C.C., Zhang, C.: Emotion recognition in the wild from videos using images. In: Proceedings of the 18th International Conference on Multimodal Interaction (ICMI), pp. 433–436. ACM (2016)
13. Meng, D., Peng, X., Wang, K., Qiao, Y.: Frame attention networks for facial expression recognition in videos. In: Proceedings of the International Conference on Image Processing (ICIP), pp. 3866–3870. IEEE (2019)
14. Demochkina, P., Savchenko, A.V.: Neural network model for video-based facial expression recognition in-the-wild on mobile devices. In: Proceedings of International Conference on Information Technology and Nanotechnology (ITNT), pp. 1–5. IEEE (2021)
15. Savchenko, A.V., Khokhlova, Y.I.: About neural-network algorithms application in viseme classification problem with face video in audiovisual speech recognition systems. Optical Memory Neural Netw. **23**(1), 34–42 (2014). https://doi.org/10.3103/S1060992X14010068
16. Zhou, H., et al.: Exploring emotion features and fusion strategies for audio-video emotion recognition. In: Proceedings of International Conference on Multimodal Interaction (ICMI), pp. 562–566. ACM (2019)
17. Peña, A., Morales, A., Serna, I., Fierrez, J., Lapedriza, A.: Facial expressions as a vulnerability in face recognition. In: Proceedings of International Conference on Image Processing (ICIP), pp. 2988–2992. IEEE (2021)
18. Shahabinejad, M., Wang, Y., Yu, Y., Tang, J., Li, J.: Toward personalized emotion recognition: a face recognition based attention method for facial emotion recognition. In: Proceedings of 16th International Conference on Automatic Face and Gesture Recognition (FG), pp. 1–5. IEEE (2021)
19. Zhao, Y., Li, J., Zhang, S., Chen, L., Gong, Y.: Domain and speaker adaptation for Cortana speech recognition. In: Proceedings of International Conference on Acoustics, Speech and Signal Processing (ICASSP), pp. 5984–5988. IEEE (2018)
20. Savchenko, L.V., Savchenko, A.V.: Speaker-aware training of speech emotion classifier with speaker recognition. In: Karpov, A., Potapova, R. (eds.) SPECOM 2021. LNCS (LNAI), vol. 12997, pp. 614–625. Springer, Cham (2021). https://doi.org/10.1007/978-3-030-87802-3_55
21. Savchenko, A.V.: Phonetic words decoding software in the problem of Russian speech recognition. Autom. Remote. Control. **74**(7), 1225–1232 (2013)
22. Deng, J., Guo, J., Xue, N., Zafeiriou, S.: Arcface: additive angular margin loss for deep face recognition. In: Proceedings of the Conference on Computer Vision and Pattern Recognition (CVPR), pp. 4690–4699. IEEE (2019)
23. Naas, S.A., Sigg, S.: Real-time emotion recognition for sales. In: Proceedings of 16th International Conference on Mobility, Sensing and Networking (MSN), pp. 584–591. IEEE (2020)
24. Zhang, K., Zhang, Z., Li, Z., Qiao, Y.: Joint face detection and alignment using multitask cascaded convolutional networks. IEEE Signal Process. Lett. **23**(10), 1499–1503 (2016)

25. Makarov, I., Bakhanova, M., Nikolenko, S., Gerasimova, O.: Self-supervised recurrent depth estimation with attention mechanisms. PeerJ Comput. Sci. **8**, e865 (2022)

26. Sokolova, A.D., Kharchevnikova, A.S., Savchenko, A.V.: Organizing multimedia data in video surveillance systems based on face verification with convolutional neural networks. In: van der Aalst, W.M.P., et al. (eds.) AIST 2017. LNCS, vol. 10716, pp. 223–230. Springer, Cham (2018). https://doi.org/10.1007/978-3-319-73013-4_20

27. Perepelkina, O., Sterling, G., Konstantinova, M., Kazimirova, E.: RAMAS: the Russian acted multimodal affective set for affective computing and emotion recognition studies. In: Proceedings of European Society for Cognitive and Affective Neuroscience (ESCAN), pp. 86–86 (2018)

28. Savchenko, A.V.: Efficient facial representations for age, gender and identity recognition in organizing photo albums using multi-output convnet. PeerJ Comput. Sci. **5**, e197 (2019)

29. Kollias, D., Zafeiriou, S.: Analysing affective behavior in the second ABAW2 competition. In: Proceedings of the International Conference on Computer Vision (ICCV), pp. 3652–3660. IEEE (2021)

3D Reconstruction of Medical Image Based on Improved Ray Casting Algorithm

Wang Yu[✉] and Gong Ning

School of Artificial Intelligence, Beijing Technology and Business University,
Beijing 100048, China
wangyu@btbu.edu.cn

Abstract. Although the traditional volume rendering ray casting algorithm has become one of the mainstream methods of medical image three-dimensional (3D) reconstruction, the 3D image quality and rendering speed still can not meet the requirements of high-definition and real-time in clinical medical diagnosis. In this paper, a fusion ray casting algorithm is proposed, which uses the improved resampling interpolation algorithm and the improved bounding box algorithm to improve the image rendering speed, and the improved data synthesis of sampling points is used to improve image quality in ray casting algorithm. The experimental results show that the method proposed in this paper can not only improve the speed of reconstruction, but also greatly improve the image quality of 3D reconstruction.

Keywords: Volume rendering · Ray casting algorithm · 3D reconstruction · Resampling interpolation · Bounding box · Data synthesis

1 Introduction

In the 1970s, the birth of Computed Tomography (CT) provided technical support for early detection, early diagnosis and early treatment of diseases [1, 2]. However, with the improvement of living standards, doctors and patients have higher requirements for disease diagnosis. Accurate and real-time diagnosis is an important trend in the development of medical equipment. With the continuous progress of medical image imaging technology, three-dimensional (3D) display of two-dimensional image sequences has become a reality [3, 4]. Because of the uncertain human tissue and the its complex spatial position, it is difficult to diagnose the focus tissue accurately if the clinician does not have rich basic medical knowledge. Moreover, if doctors only observe and analyze two-dimensional (2D) medical images, the shape characteristics and spatial location information of human tissue can not be fully understood [5]. In order to enable doctors to observe the tissue structure from any angle and avoid misdiagnosis or missed diagnosis, it is necessary to reconstruct the 2D image into a 3D model to directly display the complex internal structure of human tissue, and the lesions can be diagnosed objectively. The application of medical image 3D reconstruction technology to detect and judge diseases has become a research hotspot in recent years [6].

© Springer Nature Switzerland AG 2022
M. El Yacoubi et al. (Eds.): ICPRAI 2022, LNCS 13363, pp. 459–476, 2022.
https://doi.org/10.1007/978-3-031-09037-0_38

At present, the volume rendering of medical image has become one of the mainstream methods of medical image 3D reconstruction technology, and the ray casting algorithm is a better imaging method in volume rendering technology [7]. Although the principle of ray casting algorithm is simple to implement, in clinical application and basic research the traditional ray casting volume rendering algorithm may have poor image quality and slow rendering speed if it is directly applied to clinical treatment. This can not meet the requirements of high-definition accurate and real-time interaction in medicine [8]. At present, computer hardware and software can be considered to optimize the image quality of medical 3D reconstruction, but in practical application, the improvement of computer hardware is often limited because of the high cost. Therefore, the optimization of traditional 3D reconstruction algorithms has become the main method. For example, a parallel volume rendering method was proposed by Jiamin Wang [9], which could optimize image quality through the hybrid parallelization of image-based spatial partition and octree-based data spatial partition. An approximate image space multi-directional occlusion shadow model was proposed by JangYun et al. [10], which could realize interactive transfer function operation and light position change, and enhance the visual effect of the image. YonghaShin [11] proposed a method of high-quality MIP volume rendering accelerated by cubic interpolation, and also proposed an efficient parallel method of volume rendering using GPU, which improved the rendering speed and realizes high-quality MIP volume rendering. A visualization algorithm for isosurface 3D reconstruction based on seven-direction box splines was proposed by Liu Xiao [12], which improved the calculation method of gradient and interpolation, and combined various volume data attribute values and gradient amplitudes to form a new color mapping transfer function, increased the reliability and rendering accuracy of the algorithm. In order to improve the stereoscopic sense and depth of volume rendering images, a method of volume rendering using Blinn-Phong local illumination model was proposed by Li Zhixiang [13], and in order to increase the difference between classified volume data, a method of fusion of different transfer functions was proposed to improve the rendering effect of the image. Yin Zhe [14] adopted the MPR multi-plane reconstruction technology that could provide multiple orientation medical image sequences, and combined with the auxiliary segmentation technology of the 3D reconstruction of medical images, and the method could improve the fineness of the image. Inspired by the above methods, we come up with a ray casting fusion method which combines improved sampling data point synthesis, improved bounding box technique and improved resampling interpolation. The overall structure of this paper is as follows: (1) In the Sect. 2.1, an improved traditional resampling interpolation algorithm is proposed, which can reduce the complexity of interpolation algorithm, improve the operation efficiency of resampling interpolation algorithm, and achieve the purpose of speeding up the operation speed of ray casting algorithm. (2) In the Sect. 2.2, the improved bounding box is proposed, which is aimed to skip the empty voxels. The method can achieve the purpose of speeding up the operation speed of ray casting algorithm. (3) In the Sect. 2.3, the improved data synthesis of sampling points is used to improve image quality in ray casting algorithm. (4) In the Sect. 2.4, a fusion method is proposed, which uses the improved resampling interpolation algorithm and the improved bounding box algorithm to improve the image rendering speed, and the improved data synthesis of sampling points is used to improve image quality.

2 Method

As the most commonly used method in volume rendering technology, ray casting algorithm is one of the best rendering quality algorithms among all 3D reconstruction algorithms [15, 16]. It is a direct volume rendering algorithm based on a 2D image sequence, which reproduces the 3D features of the 2D image data. The basic principle [17] is that starting from each pixel on the screen, a ray along the line of sight is emitted. When it passes through the medical volume data, it will first be equidistantly sampled with a preset step size, and then the color value and opacity value of each sampling point calculated in advance through the interpolation method will be in accordance with the traditional ray projection algorithm. The front-to-back or back-to-front method is used for synthesis, and finally the color value of the pixels on the screen corresponding to all the rays is calculated to obtain a complete 3D image. The algorithm can be divided into four parts in the process [18]: data classification, color value and opacity value assignment, resampling interpolation calculation and image synthesis. A ray casting fusion method proposed by us, which combines improved sampling data point synthesis, improved bounding box technique and improved resampling interpolation.

2.1 Resampling Interpolation Algorithm

Traditional Resampling Interpolation Algorithm. The proportion of time-consuming, during resampling interpolation, is much higher than the other three steps. Therefore, speeding up the calculation speed of the resampling interpolation method under the premise of ensuring the image quality is an important way to improve the volume rendering speed.

The traditional resampling interpolation algorithm emits a ray through the 3D data field through each pixel on the screen along the direction of the viewpoint, and samples equidistant on each ray. Generally, one voxel is taken as the sampling step of equidistant sampling. Because the new sampling point is generally not on the original data point, the new sampling point is called resampling point. The data values of resampling points are obtained by trilinear interpolation of the color values and opacity values of the eight original data points closest to the resampling points [19]. The schematic diagram of the traditional resampling interpolation algorithm is shown in Fig. 1.

Assuming that dx, dy and dz are the offset values of point P relative to the vertex P the x, y and z axes, respectively, the coordinate position of the resampled point P is $P(x, y, z)$. Other adjacent original data points are $V_0(i, j, k)$, $V_1(i + 1, j, k)$, $V_2(i + 1, j, k + 1)$, $V_3(i, j, k+1)$, $V_4(i, j+1, k)$, $V_5(i+1, j+1, k)$, $V_6(i+1, j+1, k+1)$, $V_7(i, j+1, k+1)$. Use Δx, Δy, Δz to represent the resampling interval in the x, y, z directions respectively, then $i = [x/\Delta x]$, $j = [y/\Delta y]$, $i = [z/\Delta z]$. The symbol [.] represents the largest integer not greater than the value in the brackets. Then the operation process of trilinear interpolation is divided into the following three steps:

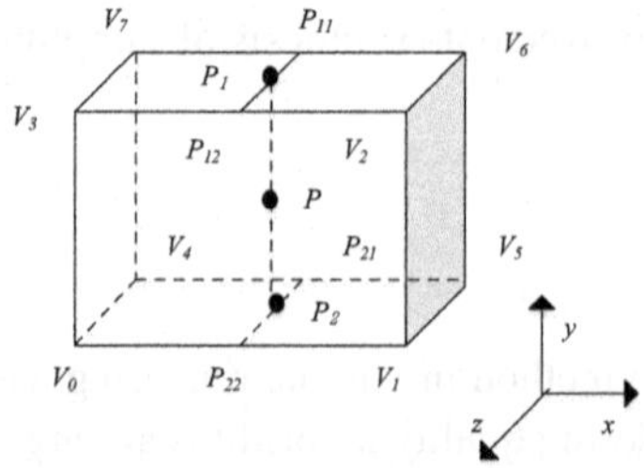

Fig. 1. Resampling interpolation diagram

(1) The values of P_{11}, P_{12}, P_{21} and P_{22} are obtained by interpolation in direction.

$$
\begin{aligned}
P_{11} &= V_7 + dx(V_6 - V_7) \\
P_{12} &= V_3 + dx(V_2 - V_3) \\
P_{21} &= V_4 + dx(V_5 - V_4) \\
P_{22} &= V_0 + dx(V_1 - V_0)
\end{aligned} \tag{1}
$$

(2) The values of P_1, P_2 are obtained by interpolation in direction from P_{11}, P_{12}, P_{21} and P_{22}.

$$
\begin{aligned}
P_1 &= P_{11} + dz(P_{12} - P_{11}) \\
P_2 &= P_{21} + dz(P_{22} - P_{21})
\end{aligned} \tag{2}
$$

(3) The values of P are obtained by interpolation in y direction from P_1, P_2.

$$
P = P_2 + dy(P_1 - P_2) \tag{3}
$$

Incorporate formula (1) and formula (2) into formula (3), and expand as follows,

$$
\begin{aligned}
P(x, y, z) =\ & V_0(i, j, k) * (1 - u) * (1 - v) * (1 - w) + V_1(i + 1, j, k) * u * (1 - v) * (1 - w) \\
& + V_2(i + 1, j, k + 1) * u * (1 - v) * w + V_3(i, j, k + 1) * (1 - u) * (1 - v) * w \\
& + V_4(i, j + 1, k) * (1 - u) * v * (1 - w) + V_5(i + 1, j + 1, k) * u * v * (1 - w) \\
& + V_6(i + 1, j + 1, k + 1) * u * v * w + V_7(i, j + 1, k + 1) * (1 - u) * v * w
\end{aligned} \tag{4}
$$

In formula (4), $u = x/\Delta x - i$, $v = y/\Delta y - j$, $w = z/\Delta z - k$. Because the trilinear interpolation formula is complex, and the data value of each resampling point needs to be calculated by using the trilinear interpolation formula, the resampling interpolation process in the ray casting algorithm consumes most of the operation time. The method proposed in this paper improves the traditional resampling interpolation algorithm, reduces the complexity of trilinear interpolation algorithm, improves the operation efficiency of resampling interpolation algorithm, and achieves the purpose of speeding up the operation speed of ray casting algorithm.

Improved Resampling Interpolation Algorithm. The data value of the original data point is obtained by assigning the color value and the opacity value in the previous step, and its value may be 0. In formula (5), the traditional trilinear interpolation formula consists of eight summations. If one of the data values in a sum is 0, the trilinear interpolation formula becomes composed of only seven sums. Therefore, according to whether the data value from V_0 to V_7 is equal to 0, this chapter uses the mathematical permutation and combination method to derive formula (5) into $2^8 = 256$ forms [20]. For example, if the data value of V_0 is 0, the trilinear interpolation of the final P point is:

$$
\begin{aligned}
P(x, y, z) &= V_1(i+1, j, k) * u * (1-v) * (1-w) + V_2(i+1, j, k+1) * u * (1-v) * w \\
&+ V_3(i, j, k+1) * (1-u) * (1-v) * w + V_4(i, j+1, k) * (1-u) * v * (1-w) \\
&+ V_5(i+1, j+1, k) * u * v * (1-w) + V_6(i+1, j+1, k+1) * u * v * w \\
&+ V_7(i, j+1, k+1) * (1-u) * v * w
\end{aligned}
\tag{5}
$$

Finally, four addition operations and three multiplication operations are missing, which reduces the amount of trilinear interpolation of the original resampling points. If $V_n = 0$ $(n = 0, 1, 2, 3, 4, 5, 6, 7)$, the corresponding binary bit is 0. When the data values of V_1, V_4 and V_7 are 0, the corresponding A is 1101101. In the form of binary number A, the corresponding trilinear interpolation formula is:

$$
\begin{aligned}
P(x, y, z) &= V_0(i, j, k) * (1-u) * (1-v) * (1-w) + V_2(i+1, j, k+1) * u * (1-v) * w \\
&+ V_3(i, j, k+1) * (1-u) * (1-v) * w + V_5(i+1, j+1, k) * u * v * (1-w) \\
&+ V_6(i+1, j+1, k+1) * u * v * w
\end{aligned}
\tag{6}
$$

To sum up, compared with formula (5), formula (6) reduces 12 addition operations and 9 multiplication operations, and reduces the amount of trilinear interpolation for resampling points. Figure 2 is a flow chart of the improved resampling interpolation algorithm in this chapter.In the resampling trilinear interpolation operation, the data values from V_0 to V_7 are first detected, and then the binary number A is obtained according to the detection results, and different simplified forms of the trilinear interpolation formula are selected in the form of A. Finally, the simplified trilinear interpolation formula is used to calculate the data values of resampling points, so as to reduce the amount of operation in the process of interpolation.

2.2   The Bounding Box in 3D Reconstruction

Traditional Bounding Box. When the ray is projected to the 3D volume data field, the 3D volume data field is wrapped by selecting the appropriate bounding box. First, the bounding box technology is used to determine whether the ray intersects the bounding box of the inclusion data [21, 22]. If not, it means that the voxels on the ray do not contribute to the image synthesis on the screen, and all voxels on this ray are not sampled, and then the next ray is detected. But if it intersects, the box-in point and the box-out point at which the ray intersects the bounding box will be found, and sampling calculations will be performed in the bounding box until the ray is out of the bounding box or the opacity value of the light composition reaches the preset value, then the image synthesis of the ray is ended. Simply skipping the data outside the bounding box and only performing the 3D reconstruction of coronary angiography images within the bounding box, and the method can significantly improve the image rendering speed of the 3D reconstruction

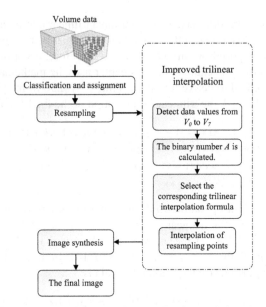

Fig. 2. Flow chart of improved resampling interpolation algorithm

algorithm. This is the principle of the bounding box technology. Bounding box includes Axis Aligned bounding boxes (AABB), Aphere, Oriented Bounding Box (OBB) and so on.

Compared with other bounding box, the OBB has good wrapping properties and can be close to the 3D data field [24]. OBB is a parallelepiped like AABB, but OBB does not need to be aligned with the axis of the coordinate system like AABB, and its direction can be arbitrary. The OBB is the smallest box in which the direction of the coordinate axis can be arbitrary, which leads to the OBB being able to adapt to different 3D data fields and better wrap the 3D data field.

The key to constructing the OBB is to find the best direction and determine the smallest OBB size in this direction [25]. Therefore, the calculation of OBB is more complicated, and its direction, size, and center position need to be calculated. Among them, the direction and center position of the bounding box are calculated using the covariance matrix and the mean value. First of all, a 3D object can be regarded as a collection of triangular faces. When calculating OBB, the vertex vector of the *i-th* triangle of the triangle set is p^i, q^i and r^i, and the number of triangular faces of the 3D object is n. The position m of the center of the OBB:

$$m = \frac{1}{3n} \sum_{i=1}^{n} (p^i + q^i + r^i) \tag{7}$$

Covariance matrix elements:

$$C_{jk} = \frac{1}{3n} \sum_{i=1}^{n} (\overline{p_j^i p_k^i} + \overline{q_j^i q_k^i} + \overline{r_j^i r_k^i}) \tag{8}$$

Among them, $p^i = p^i - m$, $q^i = q^i - m$, $r^i = r^i - m$, The covariance matrix is solved by numerical method to solve the eigenvector, and the eigenvector is unitized. Because C_{jk} is a real symmetric matrix, the eigenvectors are orthogonal to each other and can be used as the direction axis of the OBB. Finally, the geometric vertices of the 3D data field that need to be wrapped are projected to the direction axis, and the projection interval on each direction axis is recorded, so that the length of the projection interval is the size of the OBB. Figure 3 is a 2D diagram of the three bounding boxes.

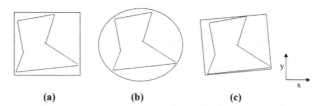

(a)   (b)   (c)

Fig. 3. 2D diagram of the three bounding boxes. (a)AABB, (b)Aphere, (c)OBB

Compared with AABB and aphere, OBB has better compactness. It can effectively reduce the number of projected light and the computational complexity of 3D reconstruction algorithm. However, although the number of projected light is reduced, the traditional image 3D reconstruction algorithm is still used for image synthesis in OBB, resulting in a large number of empty voxels participating in the operation, which greatly reduces the acceleration effect of bounding box technology. The rendering time is increased, so how to skip empty voxels in OBB and only sample and calculate non-empty voxels has become the focus of this section.

Improved Bounding Box. In the traditional 3D reconstruction algorithms, a lot of time is spent on the calculation of empty voxels. In order to improve the acceleration performance of the bounding box technology and make up for the defects of the bounding box technology, this paper combines the empty voxel skip method in the bounding box, so that the empty voxels in the bounding box do not participate in the calculation. The basic principle of the empty voxel skip method is that when sampling in 3D reconstruction algorithm, record the distance between each empty voxel and its nearest non-empty voxel, and then use this distance as the step of sampling data synthesis for data synthesis, so that the empty voxel does not participate in the calculation of data synthesis and greatly improve the efficiency of image rendering. The empty voxel skip method is mainly divided into two steps: establishing the distance field and empty voxel skip. The two processes are described in detail below.

Establish the Distance Field. It is assumed that the discrete 3D data field consists of two different point sets, the feature point set S and the non-feature point set P. The features of the feature point set can be specific points, regions of interest, edge contours and so on. Then the set of minimum values in the distance from each point in the non-feature point set P to all the points in the feature point set S becomes a distance field:

$$F_{dist}[P] = \min(d(p, S[i])) \tag{9}$$

The distance between the two spatial points is calculated by the block distance. If $M(x_1, y_1, z_1)$ and $N(x_2, y_2, z_2)$ are two points in the space, the distance L is

$$L = |x_2 - x_1| + |y_2 - y_1| + |z_2 - z_1| \tag{10}$$

Assuming that the spatial coordinate of any empty voxel is (i, j, k) and the spatial coordinate of the nearest non-empty voxel is (u, v, w) the distance value of the empty voxel is

$$D(i, j, k) = L((i, j, k), (u, v, w)) \tag{11}$$

Then the distance values obtained above are stored in the distance field to be used for empty voxel skipping.

Empty Voxel Jump. After obtaining the distance field, each empty voxel will obtain a distance value. In the step of sampling data synthesis, the traditional unit step is no longer used as the sampling unit, but the distance value is used as the sampling step. For any empty voxel $V(x,y,z)$, assuming that its distance value is D_v, and the projected ray direction vector is $I = (x_l, y_l, z_l)$, then the unit step is

$$d = |x_l| + |y_l| + |z_l| \tag{12}$$

Then when the sampling data is synthesized to the empty voxel, the actual step size through the empty voxel skip method is

$$s = D_v/d = \frac{D_v}{|x_l| + |y_l| + |z_l|} \tag{13}$$

The coordinate (x_2, y_2, z_2) of the next voxel reached by skipping the s step is

$$\begin{aligned}
x_2 &= x + ix * s = x + \frac{ix}{|x_l| + |y_l| + |z_l|} \times D_v \\
y_2 &= y + iy * s = y + \frac{iy}{|x_l| + |y_l| + |z_l|} \times D_v \\
z_2 &= z + iz * s = z + \frac{iz}{|x_l| + |y_l| + |z_l|} \times D_v
\end{aligned} \tag{14}$$

When the sampling data is synthesized, the non-empty voxels are sampled according to the original unit step, but when the empty voxels are encountered, the distance D between the nearest non-empty voxels in the ray direction is calculated first, and the sampling is carried out according to the distance value as the step size, skipping the empty voxels that have no contribution to the final drawing image, and saving the time of drawing. As shown in Fig. 4, the voxels from V_1 to V_{n-1} are all empty voxels, then when the data synthesis reaches V_1, the sampling step temporarily becomes s, and at this time, it can skip $n-2$ voxels at one time., To accelerate the speed of sampled data synthesis.

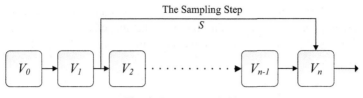

Fig. 4. Empty voxel skip

In this chapter, by combining the empty voxel skip method in the bounding box technology, Fig. 5 is a 2D diagram of the improved bounding box technology, so that when the ray carries out the sampling data synthesis processing inside the bounding box, the opacity value of the voxel is judged first. If the opacity value is 0, the empty voxel is skipped without sampling data synthesis. On the contrary, if the opacity value is 1, keep the voxel point and continue sampling. Figure 6 is a flow chart of the application of the improved bounding box technique.

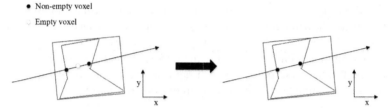

Fig. 5. 2D schematic diagram of improved bounding box

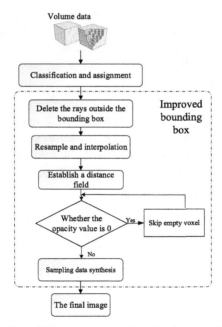

Fig. 6. Flow chart of 3D reconstruction based on improved bounding box

In the Sect. 2.1 and Sect. 2.2, the methods are proposed to improve the speed of the 3D reconstruction, and it make no contribution to the image quality. In order to improve the image quality, the method of improved data synthesis of sampling points is proposed in the Sect. 2.3.

2.3 Data Synthesis of Sampling Points

Traditional Data Synthesis of Sampling Points.   Sampling point data synthesis is the last step of the ray casting algorithm. After resampling and interpolation, the color value and opacity value of each sampling point on each ray are obtained. At this time, the sampling points on each ray have their own data values. Then the color value and opacity value of the sampled points on each ray are synthesized, and each pixel point generates the final color value. Using the above steps, the color value of each pixel on the screen is calculated to form a 3D image[27]. In practical applications, the sampling frequency may not meet the Nyquist sampling law, resulting in incomplete images. Therefore, by improving the sampling data synthesis method, we will improve the sampling frequency without affecting the operation speed of the algorithm, which is the main way to improve the quality of coronary artery 3D image. At present, there are two methods to synthesize the data of sampling points based on the light emission and absorption model, one is to synthesize the sampling points on each ray from back to front, and the other is to synthesize the sampling points on each ray from front to back[28].

Sampling Points are Synthesized from Front to Back.   The algorithm accumulates the color value and opacity value of each sampling point according to the distance from the viewpoint and in the order from far to near to get the final color of the pixel. Assuming that the color value and opacity value of the *i-th* sampling point on the ray are C_{now} and a_{now} respectively. Before synthesizing a sampling point on the ray, supposing the color value of the ray is C_i and the opacity value is a_i. After synthesis, the color values of the rays are C_{out} and a_{out} respectively, then:

$$C_{out} = C_i(1 - a_{now}) + C_{now}a_{now} \tag{15}$$

Assuming that the initial color value is C_0, the color value of the final screen pixel is C, and the color value and opacity value of the *i-th* sampling point along the ray propagation direction are C_i and a_i respectively. In addition, assuming that β_i is the transparency value, and $\beta_i = 1 - a_i$. Figure 7 is a schematic diagram of the synthesis of sampled data from back to front.

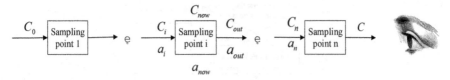

Fig. 7. Schematic diagram of sampling data synthesis from back to front

When the number of sampling points on the ray is n, the color of the screen pixels can be obtained,

$$C = C_0\beta_1\beta_2\cdots\beta_n + C_1a_1\beta_2\cdots\beta_n + \cdots + C_{n-1}a_{n-1}\beta_n\cdots C_na_n$$

$$= C_0\prod_{i=1}^{n}\beta_i + \sum_{i=1}^{n}C_ia_i\prod_{j=i+1}^{n}\beta_j \tag{16}$$

Sampling Points are Synthesized from Back to Front. This synthesis algorithm accumulates the color value and opacity value of each sampling point according to the distance from the viewpoint, from near to far, to obtain the final color of the pixel. Figure 8 shows a schematic diagram of the synthesis of sampled data from front to back. And the formulas for color value synthesis and opacity value synthesis are

$$C_{out}a_{out} = C_{in}a_i + C_{now}a_{now}(1 - a_i) \tag{17}$$

$$a_{out} = a_i + a_{now}(1 - a_i) \tag{18}$$

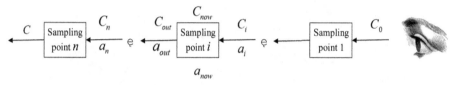

Fig. 8. Schematic diagram of sampling data synthesis from front to back

In the process of data synthesis from front to back sampling points, formula (23) sequentially synthesizes the opacity value a. When the a is close to 1, it means that the accumulated image is opaque. It is not necessary to continue the color value synthesis of the sampling points on this ray. At this time, it can be combined with the early ray termination algorithm to stop the data synthesis and reduce Computing overhead. The back to front sampling data synthesis needs to perform synthesis operations on all sampling points on the ray, and the ray can not be terminated, so this chapter chooses to improve the front to back sampling data synthesis algorithm.

According to the Nyquist sampling law, only the sampling frequency exceeds twice the highest frequency of the original signal, the original signal can be completely reconstructed. However, the sampling frequency of the two sampling data synthesis methods may not meet the Nyquist sampling law in practical applications, resulting in poor quality of the final drawn image.

Improved Data Synthesis of Sampling Points. In this chapter, the data synthesis method of front to back sampling points is improved. As shown in Fig. 9, the average values of the color values C_a and C_b and the opacity values a_a and a_b of the two adjacent sampling points are calculated, and the average values are stored in a new sampling point and inserted between the two sampling points. In this way, the color values $C_{\frac{a+b}{2}}$ and opacity values $a_{\frac{a+b}{2}}$ of the new sampling points are obtained:

$$C_{\frac{a+b}{2}} = \frac{C_a + C_b}{2} \tag{19}$$

$$a_{\frac{a+b}{2}} = \frac{a_a + a_b}{2} \tag{20}$$

By increasing the intermediate sampling points, the sampling frequency during the synthesis operation is increased to meet the Nyquist sampling law. This method improves the final image quality. However, due to the increase in the number of sampling points, the amount of calculation during the synthesis operation is increased, resulting in a slower speed during the synthesis of the sampling data. Therefore, this chapter combines the early ray termination algorithm to synthesize the sampling points from front to back. When the opacity value of the sampled points on a ray reaches 1, the operation on the ray is terminated, and the color value is taken as the final color. On the contrary, all the sampling points on the ray are synthesized. Figure 10 is a flow chart of the improved sampling point data synthesis in this chapter.

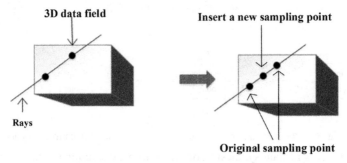

Fig. 9. Improved front to back sampling data synthesis method

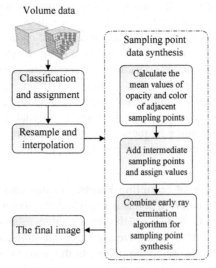

Fig. 10. Flow chart of 3D reconstruction based on improved sampling point data synthesis algorithm

2.4 The Fusion Algorithm

Based on the above three improved methods, a ray casting fusion method is proposed, which combined improved sampling data point synthesis, improved bounding box technology and improved resampling interpolation. The speed of 3D reconstruction is increased by improved the bounding box technology and resampling interpolation algorithm, and the image quality is improved by improved synthesis of sampled data points. The flow chart of the algorithm proposed in this paper is shown in Fig. 11.

This method firstly classifies and assigns volume data, and deletes the light outside the bounding box. Subsequently, in the process of data resampling and interpolation, this method selects the corresponding trilinear interpolation formula by detecting the type of the data value to speed up the speed of resampling and interpolation. Next, the algorithm establishes a data field for the bounding box technology and performs sampling point data synthesis. In this process, the algorithm improves the image quality by increasing the intermediate sampling points, and skips the empty voxels that do not contribute to the image synthesis in the data synthesis process. Finally, we get a better 3D model.

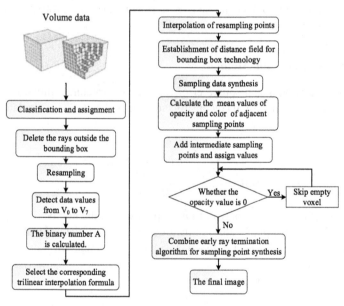

Fig. 11. Flow chart of the fusion method

3   Result

3.1   Experimental Equipment and Environment

The hardware and software environment of this experiment: CPU is Intel Core i5-9300H 2.40 GHz, memory is 8 GB, video card is NVDIA GeForce GTX 1660 Ti, video memory is 6 GB, programming environment is Visual Studio 2019 under Windows 10.

3.2   Data

The heart CT images and the hip joint images of real patients were selected in the database. And the CT images of the real patient's coronary were obtained from Peking Union Medical College Hospital with a total of 215 slices. The size of each image was 512*512 pixels, and the interval between layers was 0.5 mm. The hip joint images of real patient were obtained from Beijing An Zhen Hospital with a total of 411 slices. The size of each image was 512*512 pixels, and the interval between layers was 0.5 mm.

In order to objectively evaluate the effectiveness of the proposed algorithm, we artificially synthesized 20 3D cone images, each with a size of 1100*850 pixels, and a layer spacing of 0.7 mm.

3.3   Objective Evaluation Method

In this experiment, the mean square error (MSE) and structural similarity (SSIM) are used to evaluate the quality of 3D reconstructed images. The MSE is calculated as shown in formula (21).

$$MSE = \frac{\sum_{x=1}^{M} \sum_{y=1}^{N} (f_1(x, y) - f_2(x, y))^2}{M * N} \qquad (21)$$

where M is the number of columns of image pixels, N is the number of rows of image pixels, f_1 and f_2 are the pixel values of the three channels of the original 3D image and the reconstructed image at a certain viewing angle. The smaller the value, the better the reconstruction quality.

The SSIM calculation is shown in formula (22).

$$SSIM = \frac{(2\mu_x\mu_y + C_1)(2\sigma_{xy} + C_2)}{(\mu_x^2 + \mu_y^2 + C_1)(\sigma_x^2 + \sigma_y^2 + C_2)} \qquad (22)$$

where μ_x and μ_y represent the mean of the pixel values of the three channels of the reconstructed image, σ_x and σ_y represent the variance of the original 3D image and the reconstructed image, σ_{xy} represents the covariance, $C_1 = (K_1 L)^2$ and $C_2 = (K_2 L)^2$ are constants used to maintain stability. Generally, $K_1 = 0.01$, $K_2 = 0.03$, $L = 255$. SSIM ranges from 0 to 1, and the larger the value, the better the reconstruction quality.

3.4   Experimental Results and Analysis

In the experiment, the results of coronary 3D reconstruction are shown in Fig. 12, the results of hip joint 3D reconstruction are shown in Fig. 13. The results of cone 3D reconstruction are shown in Fig. 14. All results are also obtained in the same angle of view and scale. The coronary and the hip joint experimental results are shown in Table 1, as well as the cone experimental results in Table 2, and the average drawing time is the average time of 10 reconstructed images. This experiment also demonstrates *SSIM* and *MSE* to objectively evaluate the 3D reconstruction effect.

From the comparison results in Fig. 13 and Fig. 14, it can be seen that the fusion algorithm in this paper is better than the traditional ray casting algorithm, and eliminates the fault and mosaic caused by the sampling frequency in the traditional algorithm that may not satisfy the Nyquist sampling theorem. From Table 1, the coronary modeling speed of the improved algorithm in this paper is 1.45 times faster than the traditional ray casting algorithm, and the hip joint modeling speed of the improved algorithm is 1.35 times faster than the traditional ray casting algorithm, which effectively improves the rapidity in medical diagnosis. From Table 2, the cone modeling speed of the improved algorithm in this paper is 1.24 times faster that in the traditional ray casting algorithm. According to the objective evaluation method, the *SSIM* and *MSE* of the improved sampling point data synthesis method and the fusion method are better than other methods, which proves the effectiveness of the improved sampling point data synthesis method.

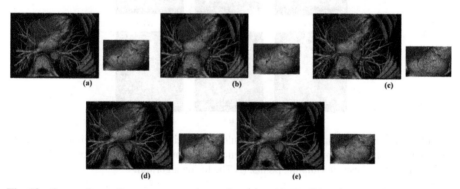

Fig. 12. Comparison of coronary experimental results. (a) Traditional ray casting algorithms. (b) Improved resampling interpolation algorithm. (c) Improved bounding box. (d) Improved data synthesis of sampling points. (e) The fusion algorithm

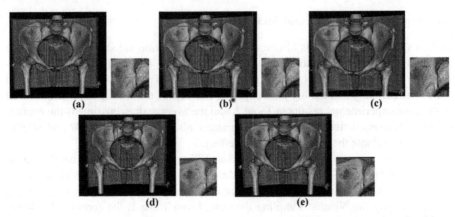

Fig. 13. Comparison of hip joint experimental results. (a) Traditional ray casting algorithms. (b) Improved resampling interpolation algorithm. (c) Improved bounding box. (d) Improved data synthesis of sampling points. (e) The fusion algorithm

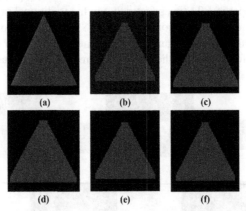

Fig. 14. Comparison of cone experimental results. (a) Original cone. (b) Traditional ray casting algorithms. (c) Improved resampling interpolation algorithm. (d) Improved bounding box. (e) Improved data synthesis of sampling points. (f) The fusion algorithm

Table 1. Comparison of 3D reconstruction

Algorithm	Average time of coronary	Average time of Hip joint
Traditional ray casting algorithms	17.41 s	31.52 s
Improved resampling interpolation algorithm	10.33 s	21.68 s
Improved bounding box	11.78 s	23.94 s
Improved data synthesis of sampling points	18.97 s	34.45 s
The fusion algorithm	9.54 s	20.50 s

Table 2. Comparison of 3D cone reconstruction

Algorithm	Average time	*SSIM*	*MSE*
Traditional ray casting algorithms	2.13 s	0.7242	137.12
Improved resampling interpolation algorithm	1.86 s	0.7105	137.53
Improved bounding box	1.65 s	0.7165	141.34
Improved data synthesis of sampling points	2.24 s	0.7891	114.58
The fusion algorithm	1.60 s	0.7714	115.60

3.5 Summary

The fusion algorithm proposed in this paper takes the improved bounding box technology and the improved resampling interpolation algorithm to increase the drawing speed, and the improved sampling point data synthesis algorithm is used to improve the image quality. Experiments show that, when performing 3D of coronary arteries, the image quality of this fusion algorithm is better than the traditional ray casting algorithm and the reconstruction software RadiAnt DICOM Viewer. In addition, the speed of the improved algorithm is 1.24 times faster than that in the traditional ray casting algorithm, which improves the real-time performance and clarity in clinical medical diagnosis. In summary, the research in this article has great application value.

Acknowledgments . This work is supported by Joint Project of Beijing Natural Science Foundation and Beijing Municipal Education Commission (No. KZ202110011015) and Beijing Technology and Business University graduate research capacity improvement plan project funding in 2022.

Conflicts of Interest. The authors declare that there are no conflicts of interest regarding the publication of this paper.

References

1. Choi, G., Kim, G., Lee, S., et al.: A study on the analysis of risk factors and correlations of coronary artery disease of the examinee taking coronary computed tomography angiography in a comprehensive health improvement center. J. Korean Soc. Radiol. **13**(7), 127–131 (2019)
2. Salim, S., Virani, A.A., et al.: Heart disease and stroke statistics— 2021 update: a report from the American heart association. Circulation **131**(01), 29 (2021)
3. Yi, H.: Discuss the diagnostic methods of coronary heart disease in detail. Jiangsu Health Care **12**(07), 19 (2018)
4. Rajani, R., Modi, B., Ntalas, I., Curzen, N.: Non-invasive fractional flow reserve using computed tomographic angiography: where are we now and where are we going? Heart (British Cardiac Society) **103**(15), 311029 (2017)
5. Ma, L.: Three-dimensional reconstruction of coronary artery and evaluation of coronary artery stenosis. Nanchang University (2020)
6. Zhang, Q., Zhang, X.: Application of coronary artery CTA in clinical diagnosis of coronary heart disease. Clin. Med. Res. Pract. **2**(16), 152–153 (2017)

7. Lecron, F., Jonathan, B., Hubert, L.: Three-dimensional spine model reconstruction using one-class SVM regularization. IEEE Trans. Biomed. Eng. **60**(11), 3256–3264 (2013)
8. Aydin, H., et al.: Importance of three-dimensional modeling in Cranioplasty. J. Craniofacial Surgery **30**(3) (2019)
9. Jiamin, W., Chongke, B., Liang, D., Fang, W., Yang, L., Yueqing, W.: A composition-free parallel volume rendering method. J. Visualizat. **24**(1), 531–544 (2021)
10. Jang, Y., Kim, S.: Approximate image-space multidirectional occlusion shading model for direct volume rendering. Appl. Sci. **11**(12), 5717 (2021)
11. Yongha, S., Bong-Soo, S.: Acceleration techniques for cubic interpolation MIP volume rendering. Multimedia Tools Appl. **4**(80), 20971–20989 (2021)
12. Liu, X.: Visualization of 3D Volume data field based on ray casting technology. Hangzhou University of Electronic Science and Technology (2015)
13. Li, Z.: Real-time volume rendering of medical images based on intelligent optimization algorithm. Huazhong University of Science and Technology (2017)
14. Yin, Z.: Design and implementation of medical image 3D reconstruction system. University of Electronic Science and Technology (2018)
15. Palak, C., Shivani, S., Purvi, R.: Different ray-casting algorithm implementations for volume rendering. Int. J. Innovat. Technol. Exploring Eng. (IJITEE) **9**(7s), 112–117 (2020)
16. Ji, J., Wang, Y.: Volume data display based on improved ray casting algorithm. Comput. Syst. Applicat. **26**(9), 205 (2017)
17. Shkarin, R., Shkarina, S., Weinhardt, V., Surmenev, R., Surmeneva, M., et al.: GPU-accelerated ray-casting for 3D fiber orientation analysis. **15**(7), 1–6 (2020)
18. Wang, M.: Design and implementation of vertebral CT image 3D reconstruction system based on improved RayCasting. Harbin University of Technology (2020)
19. Lu, K.: Research and implementation of medical image 3D reconstruction system. University of Electronic Science and Technology of China, Chengdu (2016)
20. Wang, Y., Wang, Y., Xing, S., et al.: 3D Reconstruction of Coronary artery Image based on improved Ray casting method. Chin. J. Med. Phys. **38**(04), 431–435 (2021)
21. Li, H., Sun, J.: Research on 3D reconstruction algorithm of maximum entropy threshold segmentation and bounding box partition. Mech. Des. Manuf. **12**, 187190 (2017)
22. Wang, R., Chen, C., Liu, G., et al.: Research on volume rendering acceleration method based on adaptive bounding box partition. J. Instrument. Meters **35**(11), 2560–2566 (2014)
23. Wang, W., An, W., Wang, H.: Roadway intersection modeling based on cylinder-axial bounding box detection. Comput. Appl. **35**(12), 3592–3596 (2015)
24. Shi, X., Qiao, L., Zhu, A.: Collision detection algorithm based on improved OBB bounding box. J. Hunan Univ. (Natural Science Edition) **41**(05), 26–31 (2014)
25. Qin, Q., Hu, Z.: Minimum directed bounding box generation algorithm based on convex hull. Minicomput. Syst. **39**(11), 2518–2522 (2018)
26. Zeng, Y., Pei, Q., Li, B.: Ray casting algorithm based on adaptive compound interpolation. J. Syst. Simulat. **30**(11), 4187–4194 (2018)
27. Zhang, P.: Research and implementation of ray casting volume rendering acceleration algorithm based on GPU. Beijing University of Technology (2018)
28. Bozorgi, M., Lindseth, F.: GPU-based multi-volume ray casting within VTK for medical applications. Int. J. Comput. Assist. Radiol. Surg. **10**(3), 293–300 (2015)

Lateral Ego-Vehicle Control Without Supervision Using Point Clouds

Florian Müller, Qadeer Khan$^{(\boxtimes)}$, and Daniel Cremers

Technical University of Munich, Munich, Germany
{f.r.mueller,qadeer.khan,cremers}@tum.de

Abstract. Existing vision based supervised approaches to lateral vehicle control are capable of directly mapping RGB images to the appropriate steering commands. However, they are prone to suffering from inadequate robustness in real world scenarios due to a lack of failure cases in the training data. In this paper, a framework for training a more robust and scalable model for lateral vehicle control is proposed. The framework only requires an unlabeled sequence of RGB images. The trained model takes a point cloud as input and predicts the lateral offset to a subsequent frame from which the steering angle is inferred. The frame poses are in turn obtained from visual odometry. The point cloud is conceived by projecting dense depth maps into 3D. An arbitrary number of additional trajectories from this point cloud can be generated during training. This is to increase the robustness of the model. Online experiments conducted on a driving simulator show that the performance of our model is superior to that of a supervised model trained on the same initial data set and comparable to the same model but trained on data collected with noise injection.

Keywords: Point cloud · Vehicle control · Deep learning

1 Introduction and Related Work

The autonomous driving stack can be segregated into 2 fundamental components. The first being the high level planning which calculates the optimal path that the driving agent ought to take to reach its destination. The second is the low level steering controls that the ego-vehicle should execute based on data being received from its immediate surroundings. [16,19] demonstrated path planning methods for generating safe vehicle trajectories. However, this work is focused on the latter. It uses a trained network for predicting low level lateral vehicle commands.

In recent years, deep learning approaches have shown a promising trend in the context of sensorimotor control [4,20,25]. The trained network can directly map input data to the steering commands [1,5]. Labeled training data is usually acquired by recording the raw sensory input and the corresponding steering commands executed by an expert driver traversing a reference trajectory. One of the main challenges of this approach is the lack of failure cases in the training data, caused by the driver's obligation to follow traffic rules and to remain within its own driving lane. Without failure cases in the

This work was supported by the Munich Center for Machine Learning.
F. Müller and Q. Khan—Contributed equally.

M. El Yacoubi et al. (Eds.): ICPRAI 2022, LNCS 13363, pp. 477–488, 2022.
https://doi.org/10.1007/978-3-031-09037-0_39

training data, the model has no way of learning to recover from a divergence from the reference trajectory [15]. This is a common issue with deep learning that models tend to fail at inference time when encountering images that are out-of-distribution from the training set [13]. Previous works have attempted to solve this problem by generating training images with lateral displacement and adjusted steering label [1, 12, 25]. However, due to limitations in the maximum lateral offset they can generate, the learned driving policy tends to be not robust enough [6].

In contrast to supervised approaches, Reinforcement Learning (RL) can be used to learn a driving policy for lateral control [17, 30]. RL does not require explicit data-label pairs for training. Rather, the model learns a suitable policy by randomly exploring the environment in a hit and trial method using a pre-defined reward function [24]. However, in the context of self-driving, random exploration of the driving environment is not a feasible solution as it may involve dangerous traffic violation, potentially causing crashes. This is why [13], have an expert driver that assumes control whenever the car starts to deviates off-course.

As depicted in Fig. 1, we propose a scalable framework that neither requires supervised labels nor needs data collected in violation of traffic rules. The model learns to predict the lateral offset to subsequent frames from an unlabeled sequence of RGB images, captured with a single front facing camera. Internally, the input images are converted to 3D point clouds, which enables the generation of an arbitrary number of realistic synthetic trajectories parallel to the reference trajectory. The labels for each frame are generated from camera poses using visual odometry. This removes the requirement of labeled training data.

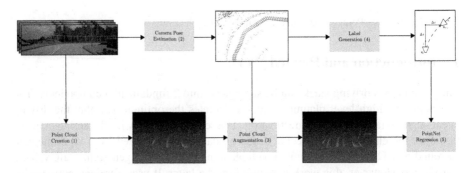

Fig. 1. This figure describes the high level overview of the proposed framework (1) Point clouds are generated from RGB images (Fig. 2, Sect. 2.1). (2) The camera pose of each frame is estimated using visual odometry (Sect. 2.2). (3) New camera frames are generated by aligning, shifting and cropping point clouds from existing frames (Sect. 2.3). (4) Labels representing the offset to a subsequent frame in lateral direction are generated from the camera poses (Sect. 2.4). (5) The resulting point clouds and labels are used to train a deep learning model to predict the lateral offset of the next frame given a point cloud (Sect. 2.5).

The primary contributions of our work are summarized below:

1. We demonstrate how a model for lateral vehicle control can be trained from only an unlabeled sequence of images.
2. We show how generating additional training data leads to enhanced robustness of the model at inference time.

2   Method

In this section the individual components of the self-supervised framework depicted in Fig. 1 are described in further detail. The framework trains a deep learning model for the task of lateral ego-vehicle control from an unlabeled sequence of RGB images.

2.1   Point Cloud Generation

Note that the point cloud for a corresponding RGB image is needed for 2 purposes:

1. As an input to the model for predicting the steering angle for lateral vehicle control
2. It is used for synthesizing additional training trajectories. Hence, the data collection along trajectories which would otherwise violate traffic rules can be avoided.

Figure 2 shows an example of a point cloud projected into 3D using the dense depth map of a corresponding RGB image. The depth map is obtained from a depth estimation network which takes an RGB image as input and can be trained in an entirely self-supervised manner [11]. The training only requires a monocular sequence of RGB images by synthesizing a target image in the sequence from the perspective of a different image. The predicted depth is used as the intermediary variable for this synthesis. Note that the depth produced is normalized. Hence, calibration is done to find the appropriate factor to scale the normalized depth map to the world scale.

In the point clouds generated from dense depth maps, it may be hard to recognize relevant high-level features like road markings, traffic poles etc. These high level features tend to be important for the model to take the appropriate steering decisions [14]. Moreover, having redundant points in the point cloud which do not yield useful information for the vehicle control model would impose an unnecessary computational burden. To counteract both issues, an edge filter [2] is applied on the RGB image used to predict the depth map. The resulting point cloud is then filtered to only include points on the detected edges. The edges can further be dilated by a small amount to prevent losing finer details. Additionally, points beyond a certain distance from the camera are discarded. This increases the concentration of points in the relevant areas closer to the camera. Points closer to the camera are more important for the control model for immediate decision making.

2.2   Camera Pose Estimation

The monocular sequence of RGB images contains no explicit information about the camera poses. The poses serve two purposes:

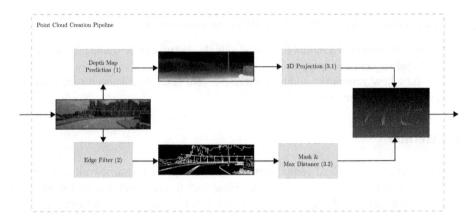

Fig. 2. The figure describes the high level overview of the point cloud creation pipeline. An (inverse) depth map is predicted from an input RGB image, which in turn is projected to a 3D point cloud. Additionally an edge filter is applied to filter the point cloud by removing points beyond a certain threshold distance

1. To determine the target labels when training the network for lateral ego-vehicle control. The input to this network is the filtered point cloud.
2. For aligning point clouds when additional trajectories are generated.

The camera poses in the global frame of reference can be obtained from the image sequence using a general-purpose visual odometry pipeline such as [18, 22, 23]. They produce the 6DoF camera pose and a sparse 3D representation of the scene. The camera pose can be expressed as a transformation matrix belonging to the special Euclidean group SE(3) representing a rigid body motion.

The path traversed by a sequence of these camera poses is referred to as the *reference trajectory*. However, note that the camera poses obtained from a monocular sequence of images does not necessarily reflect the actual scale. As was the case in Sect. 2.1, calibration is done to determine the appropriate scaling factor.

2.3   Point Cloud Augmentation

After obtaining the camera poses and point clouds for each camera frame, we finally have all prerequisites to generate additional trajectories needed to train the vehicle control model. Additional trajectories can be generated by laterally translating the point clouds from the base frame in the reference trajectory to a new frame position. Note that the reference trajectory's point cloud does not necessarily contain all the points encompassed by the field of view (FOV) of the new frame position. Those missing points are included from frames in the reference trajectory preceding the base frame. Conversely, points that do not fall within the field of view of the new camera frame position are discarded. The process is illustrated in Fig. 3, wherein Camera B is the base frame in the reference trajectory, while Camera A is a preceding frame also in the reference trajectory. We show how a point cloud at the new position represented by Camera C can be synthesized. The process can be split into the following steps:

1. Align the point cloud of a preceding frame in the reference trajectory with that of the base frame.
2. Shift the aligned point cloud from the base frame of reference to the new frame position
3. Remove all points outside the field of view of the new frame position.

Further details of each step can be found in Section II-C of a prior draft version of this work here: https://arxiv.org/abs/2203.10662.

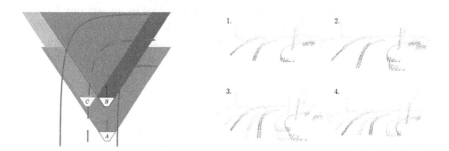

Fig. 3. Generation of a new camera frame. Left: Visualization of the fields of view of different camera frames. Camera C's field of view contains points not included in camera B's field of view. These points are added by aligning a previous camera frame A. **Right: 1.)** Point cloud of camera B (blue). **2.)** Aligning A's point cloud (red) to add missing points. We chose A to be far enough in the back to cover the field of view of C. **3.)** Changing the points' reference frame from B to C. (The faded points represent the points with reference frame B.) **4.)** Finalizing the point cloud creation by removing all points outside the field of view of C. (Color figure online)

2.4   Label Generation

We have already discussed the process of preparing the training data and generating additional trajectories. The next step is to generate the target labels for this data in order to be able to train a model for lateral vehicle control. Note that the camera is rigidly attached to the car, therefore the camera pose for any frame can also be used to determine the pose of the car at the corresponding timestep. For each car pose, we would like to find the appropriate steering angle to be executed such that a subsequent car pose is attained. We model the dynamics of front wheeled driven car using the bicycle model [26]. We assume the no-slip condition between the front and rear wheels [21]. This holds true when the car is moving straight or making turns at low/moderate speeds. Then the steering angle(δ) of the car is described by the equation [15]:

$$\delta = \tan^{-1}(\Delta x \cdot \alpha) \tag{1}$$

where Δx is the lateral distance between 2 frames. This can be determined from the camera poses. The 2 frames are chosen such that they are a fixed longitudinal distance (Δz) apart. This is to cater for the car moving at variable speed or in case of dropped camera frames during data collection. α is a constant that can be calibrated at inference time depending on the car.

2.5   Model Architecture

Using the generated point clouds and labels, a deep learning model is trained to predict the lateral deviation (Δx) between the current frame and a subsequent frame. The
model can be considered as comprising of 2 main components. The first takes raw point
clouds of the current frame as input and produces a global feature vector to furnish a
latent representation of the scene as seen by the ego-vehicle. We adapt the PointNet
architecture [3] prior to the classification head for this. The next component consists of
multi-layer perceptions which map this global feature vector to furnish the output. A
hyperbolic tangent function forms the last layer. It is scaled by an arbitrary fixed value
a to allow predictions in the range of $-a$ and a. The loss function chosen to train the
model is *mean squared error* of the lateral deviation (Δx) between the 2 frames and
that predicted by the model. Figure 4 shows a visualization of the model architecture.

Fig. 4. Shows the architecture of the model which takes a point cloud as input and predicts the
lateral deviation (Δx) to a subsequent frame. [3] is used as the base architecture to produce a
feature vector with length 1024 from the point cloud with n points. Meanwhile,"mlp" represents
a multi-layer-perceptron, with the numbers in brackets representing layer sizes. "tanh" is a hyperbolic tangent function. It is scaled by a fixed value a to allow predictions in the range of $-a$ to a.

3   Experiments

Embodied Agent Evaluation: Our task of sensorimotor control involves online interaction of the driving agent with its environment. There are many real world benchmarks
such as [8,10,29] etc. These datasets allow for evaluation of various driving algorithms
meant for tasks such as object detection ,visual odometry, semantic/instance segmentation etc. However, one severe limitation of these real world datasets is that they do not
facilitate online interaction with the environment. This interaction is necessary to quantitatively evaluate our approach for vehicle control. Therefore, simulation engines have
been used to evaluate driving performance in contemporary vehicle control research
[27,28,30]. They allow online interaction of the agent with its driving environment.
Hence, we also test our approach in simulation. In particular we use the CARLA (CAR
Learning to Act) [9] simulator (stable version 0.8.2). It can be used to evaluate both
perception and control algorithms. This provides the ability to quantitatively evaluate
the performance of embodied agents which is otherwise not possible with real world
datasets. We also make comparison with the supervised approach adapted in [6] and
demonstrate that our approach is at par despite being trained with an unlabeled sequence
of images. Another reason for online evaluation of driving agents in simulation is that
offline metrics that entail evaluation on static data would not necessarily reflect the true

performance of driving algorithms. In a realistic setting, even small divergences may accumulate causing the car to drift off course. In such a scenario, an offline evaluation provides no meaningful information about the model's capacity to counteract accumulated divergences to correct the car's trajectory. In fact, [7] have shown that offline evaluation metrics are not directly correlated with the actual driving performance. This is another reason to validate our approach in an online setting using a simulation engine. Online methods can simulate realistic scenarios thereby facilitating evaluation of actual driving quality. The unit of measurement we use in our experiments is the *ratio on lane* metric adapted from [14]. It gives the ratio of frames the ego-vehicle remains within its own driving lane to the total number of frames. The ego-vehicle is considered driving within its own lane if no part of the bounding box of the car is on the other lane or off the road and the car is not stopped due to a collision with other traffic.

Data Collection: Image data is collected at a fixed frame rate by traversing the ego-vehicle in auto-pilot mode in Town 01 of the CARLA simulator under the *CloudyNoon* weather condition. Images of size 640×192 ($90°$ FOV) are used to train the depth estimation network using [11]. Meanwhile, [22] determines the camera poses. The depth is used to generate a 3D point cloud which in turn produce additional shifted point clouds at off course trajectories.We generate ten additional point cloud trajectories at uniform lateral distances in the range of $[-2,2]$ meters from the single reference trajectory. The missing points at shifted point clouds can be compensated for by aligning preceding point clouds using the camera poses. Only the missing points from the preceding frames are added. This is because imperfect camera poses may result in duplication of objects thereby confusing the model. The camera poses additionally allow to determine the target labels to train the network. The number of points input to the network are fixed to 4096. This is done by filtering the point cloud to retain only the high level edge features, while points beyond 20m are discarded. This is followed by farthest point sampling.

Quantitative Evaluation: The evaluation at inference time is done for natural turns at different starting positions in the town that are unseen during training. Each episode is executed for 135 frames at fixed throttle and the mean *ratio on lane* metric is reported across all unseen episodes. Results of our method are reported in Fig. 5. Moreover, comparison with different point cloud configurations is done to see the impact of the various components of our framework on the overall driving performance. Configurations explored are training with a single trajectory rather than with multiple generated trajectories, aligning preceding point clouds to generate a new trajectory versus only shifting, limiting the maximum depth distance and using an edge filter to filter the point cloud. We additionally compare with supervised RGB model baselines. Therein, we demonstrate that the performance of our framework is superior to the supervised model and at par with the supervised model trained with noise injection[6] which we explain in Sect. 4. Lastly, we also report the performance of this supervised model and our method when evaluated on the *WetCloudyNoon* condition.

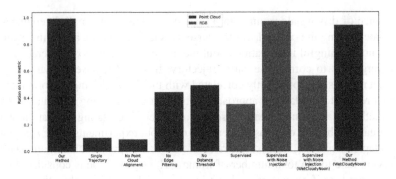

Fig. 5. Average ratio of frames the ego-vehicle remains within its driving lane for different model configurations across different starting positions unseen during training. Higher value is better. Unless specified, the evaluation is done on the *CloudyNoon* condition. Details of the various testing configurations are given in Sect. 4.

4   Discussion

In this section, an explanation of the various configurations given in Fig. 5 are described. The consequence of these configurations on the online driving performance are also discussed.

Single Trajectory v. Multiple Generated Trajectories: The core of our proposed method revolves around the capability of generating additional trajectories from a single reference trajectory, as described in Sect. 2.3. We therefore evaluate the impact of this by comparing with the single trajectory model trained only on the reference trajectory. It can be seen that the *ratio on lane* metric for the single trajectory is far inferior in comparison to our multi trajectory model. One plausible explanation is that when the model deviates off course, it cannot make the appropriate correction, since the reference trajectory data does not capture such scenarios during training.

Aligning Point Clouds when Generating new Trajectories: Section 2.3 described the process of generating point clouds in new trajectories by aligning point clouds from a preceding frame and then shifting. To examine the necessity of aligning previous point clouds we train another model whose point clouds were generated without aligning previous point clouds but instead only shifting and cropping the reference trajectory. Shifting the point cloud will yield empty regions that cannot be captured within the FOV of the source camera in the reference trajectory. This is particularly true of trajectories that are generated at farther distances away from the reference. It is further exacerbated for source images captured when the car is executing turns. As can be observed, the performance of such a model trained with partially observable point clouds drops dramatically.

Edge Filtered v. Full Point Cloud: The authors of [14] alluded to high level features such as lane markings, sidewalk/road intersections, barriers etc. being important for the vehicle control model to hold its driving lane. However, in uncolored point clouds those features are clearly less visible than in RGB images. This is why it is important to make them more prominent to the model and increase the density of relevant information in the point cloud. This is done by filtering seemingly irrelevant points from the point cloud by applying an edge filter as described in Sect. 2.1. To evaluate the benefit of edge filtering, another model was trained on the full, unfiltered point clouds. The *ratio on lane* performance of this model drops, thereby advocating in favor of our edge filtering approach.

Limiting the Distance: Section 2.1 also mentioned limiting the distance of points to the camera as part of an approach to increase concentration of points in relevant areas closer to the camera. If a model is trained without a maximum point distance, its performance drops. One tenable explanation for this is that at larger distances, the depth prediction is less certain. This imperfect depth could result in object duplication at farther distances when aligning point clouds. This can be observed in the top right region of the 2nd point cloud in Fig. 3. Hence, when such anomalies at farther depths are removed from the point cloud by limiting the maximum distance, the performance of the model is enhanced. Moreover, points in the immediate vicinity of the ego-vehicle are more important for executing the appropriate steering command rather than the points farther away that have imprecise depths.

Supervised RGB model: We additionally train a supervised convolutional model to compare with our framework using point clouds. This new model takes in an RGB image as input and directly predicts the appropriate steering command for vehicle control. In contrast to our method this RGB model is supervised and uses the ground truth steering commands as labels during training. The performance of this model is lower than our method. This is despite the fact that our model was not trained with any ground truth steering labels. Therefore, the superior performance of our method can be attributed to the ability to generate additional off trajectory training data from a single traversal of the ego-vehicle causing it to be more robust.

Affect of Perturbations: To further compare the robustness of our method with the supervised RGB model, we add perturbation of varying degree into the steering command predicted by the model at each time step. The amount of perturbation is sampled from a uniform random distribution. Figure 6 shows that as magnitude of perturbation is enhanced our model maintains a fairly consistent performance. In contrast, the supervised RGB model has a steep performance drop. This is because when perturbations are introduced the ego-vehilce may drive off-course for which the supervised model is not capable of counteracting such situations. In contrast, our model is accustomed to handling such situations as it was fed additional off trajectory point clouds during training.

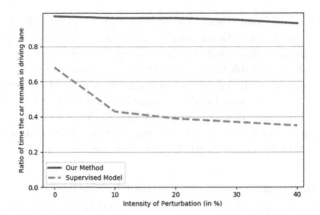

Fig. 6. Average *ratio on lane* metric for different levels of perturbation on the training trajectories. The performance of both the supervised RGB model (orange) and Our method (blue) decreases with higher intensity of perturbations, but the descent is more dramatic for the supervised model (Color figure online)

Supervised model with noise injection: We additionally compare our approach with the supervised RGB model proposed by [6]. It is similar to the supervised model described above except that during data collection, noise is injected into the steering command. This causes the vehicle to diverge from its normal path. The corrective steering maneuver taken by the expert driver to limit this divergence and bring the vehicle back on course is recorded. Performance of such a model is comparable to our approach. This is because the data used in training such a model contains off-trajectory images and corresponding labels. However, executing such a strategy for data collection with traffic participants may be extremely dangerous and may even involve violation of traffic rules. Moreover, it involves having an expert driver capable of handling dramatic maneuvers resulting from this noise injection. Most importantly, since our approach does not require any noise injection, it does not run the risk of violating traffic rules during data collection.

Different Weather/Lighting: Unless specified, the numbers reported in Fig. 5, are for models trained and evaluated on the *CloudyNoon* condition. We also did testing on a different *WetCloudyNoon* condition to see how the performance compares to the original condition. The test performance of our model drops slightly. Meanwhile, it drops significantly for the supervised RGB model with noise injection. We allude to the reasons in the next 2 points. 1) *Coloured Point Clouds*: Our model's performance does not drop as much as the one for the supervised RGB model. This is because we are only using the x, y, z points which tend to remain the same irrespective of the weather/lighting conditions. Hence, appending r, g, b values to create a coloured point cloud would rather be counterproductive due to domain shift between the training and testing distributions. In fact, the supervised RGB model shows a dramatic drop for precisely this reason. Please also see Fig. 7 for the depth maps. We would however like to highlight that the depth predicted by our model for far away objects is certainly much worse at the new weather condition. But since we are clipping the point clouds beyond a certain depth, this affect is mitigated. 2) *Edge Detection*: We find that even in the training condition, the edge detection is quite noisy. Items which are not necessary for decision making are also detected as edges. For e.g. road fissures, patchworks, potholes etc. We argue, that this noise in the point cloud additionally serves as data augmentation. This is because the model is then forced to implicitly filter out the essential points from the noise before predicting the correct steering command. Therefore, when testing on a different condition which contain for e.g. water puddles, the model is already aware of what are the essential points for decision making. Hence, we see that the performance of our model does not drop significantly on the *WetCloudyNoon* condition.

CLOUDYNOON IMAGE   CLOUDYNOON DEPTH   WETCLOUDYNOON IMAGE WETCLOUDYNOON DEPTH

Fig. 7. Shows the depth maps for the *CloudyNoon* and *WetCloudyNoon* weathers

5   Conclusion

In this paper, we put forth a framework to train a point cloud based deep learning model for the task of lateral control of an autonomous vehicle. The model is capable of learning a robust driving policy from merely an unlabeled sequence of RGB images, captured with a single front facing camera on a single reference trajectory. The efficacy of our approach comes from the capability of generating additional data from the same sequence. The additional data appears as if it emerges from an off course trajectory. This counteracts the limitations of imitation learning which suffer from insufficient robustness in the real world due to a lack of failure cases in the training data. Online experiments on the driving simulator showed that its performance is superior to a supervised baseline CNN trained on the same initial data set. Given no labels are required for the training data, the approach is scalable to large quantities of data. This makes it a more robust alternative to current supervised end-to-end lateral control methods.

References

1. Bojarski, M., et al.: End to end learning for self-driving cars. arXiv e-prints arXiv:1604.07316, April 2016
2. Canny, J.: A computational approach to edge detection. IEEE Trans. PAMI (1986)
3. Charles, R., et al.: Pointnet: deep learning on point sets for 3D classification and segmentation. In: CVPR 2017, pp. 77–85 (2017)
4. Chen, C., et al.: Deepdriving: learning affordance for direct perception in autonomous driving. In: ICCV 2015, pp. 2722–2730 (2015)
5. Chen, Z., Huang, X.: End-to-end learning for lane keeping of self-driving cars. In: 2017 IEEE Intelligent Vehicles Symposium (IV), pp. 1856–1860 (2017)
6. Codevilla, F., et al.: End-to-end driving via conditional imitation learning. In: ICRA (2018)
7. Codevilla, F., et al.: On offline evaluation of vision-based driving models. In: ECCV (2018)

8. Cordts, M., et al.: The cityscapes dataset for semantic urban scene understanding. In: CVPR (2016)
9. Dosovitskiy, A., et al.: CARLA: an open urban driving simulator. In: CoRL (2017)
10. Geiger, A., et al.: Are we ready for autonomous driving? The Kitti vision benchmark suite. In: CVPR (2012)
11. Godard, C., Aodha, O.M., Firman, M., Brostow, G.: Digging into self-supervised monocular depth estimation. In: ICCV (2019)
12. Hubschneider, C., et al.: Adding navigation to the equation: turning decisions for end-to-end vehicle control. In: ITSC (2017)
13. Kendall, A., et al.: Learning to drive in a day. In: ICRA (2019)
14. Khan, Q., et al.: Towards generalizing sensorimotor control across weather conditions. In: IROS (2019)
15. Khan, Q., et al.: Self-supervised steering angle prediction for vehicle control using visual odometry. In: AISTATS (2021)
16. Li, C., et al.: A model based path planning algorithm for self-driving cars in dynamic environment. In: Chinese Automation Congress (CAC) (2015)
17. Li, D., Zhao, D., Zhang, Q., Chen, Y.: Reinforcement learning and deep learning based lateral control for autonomous driving. IEEE Comput. Intell. Mag. **14**, 83 (2019)
18. Mur-Artal, R., et al.: ORB-SLAM: a versatile and accurate monocular SLAM system. IEEE Trans. Robot. **31**, 1147–1163 (2015)
19. Oliveira, R., Lima, P.F., Collares Pereira, G., Mårtensson, J., Wahlberg, B.: Path planning for autonomous bus driving in highly constrained environments. In: ITSC (2019)
20. Pomerleau, D.: Alvinn: an autonomous land vehicle in a neural network. In: NIPS (1988)
21. Rajamani, R.: Vehicle Dynamics and Control. 2nd edn., Springer, Cham (2012). https://doi.org/10.1007/978-1-4614-1433-9
22. Schönberger, J.L., Frahm, J.M.: Structure-from-motion revisited. In: Conference on Computer Vision and Pattern Recognition (CVPR) (2016)
23. Schönberger, J.L., Zheng, E., Frahm, J.-M., Pollefeys, M.: Pixelwise view selection for unstructured multi-view stereo. In: Leibe, B., Matas, J., Sebe, N., Welling, M. (eds.) ECCV 2016. LNCS, vol. 9907, pp. 501–518. Springer, Cham (2016). https://doi.org/10.1007/978-3-319-46487-9_31
24. Sutton, R.S., Barto, A.G.: Reinforcement Learning: An Introduction. MIT Press, Cambridge (2018)
25. Toromanoff, M., Wirbel, E., Wilhelm, F., Vejarano, C., Perrotton, X., Moutarde, F.: End to end vehicle lateral control using a single fisheye camera. In: IROS (2018)
26. Wang, D., Qi, F.: Trajectory planning for a four-wheel-steering vehicle. In: IEEE International Conference on Robotics and Automation (ICRA) (2001)
27. Wang, T., Chang, D.E.: Improved reinforcement learning through imitation learning pretraining towards image-based autonomous driving. In: ICCAS (2019)
28. Wenzel, P., et al.: Vision-based mobile robotics obstacle avoidance with deep reinforcement learning. In: ICRA (2021)
29. Wenzel, P., et al.: 4Seasons: a cross-season dataset for multi-weather SLAM in autonomous driving. In: GCPR (2020)
30. Zhang, Q., et al.: Model-free reinforcement learning based lateral control for lane keeping. In: 2019 International Joint Conference on Neural Networks (IJCNN) (2019)

RDMMLND: A New Robust Deep Model for Multiple License Plate Number Detection in Video

Amish Kumar[1], Palaiahnakote Shivakumara[2(✉)], and Umapada Pal[1]

[1] Computer Vision and Pattern Recognition Unit, Indian Statistical Institute, Kolkata, India
umapada@isical.ac.in
[2] Faculty of Computer Science and Information Technology, University of Malaya,
Kuala Lumpur, Malaysia
shiva@um.edu.my

Abstract. Accurate multiple license plate detection without affecting speed, occlusion, low contrast and resolution, uneven illumination effect and poor quality is an open challenge. This study presents a new Robust Deep Model for Multiple License Plate Number Detection (RDMMLND). To cope with the above-mentioned challenges, the proposed work explores YOLOv5 for detecting vehicles irrespective of type to reduce background complexity in the images. For detected vehicle regions, we propose a new combination of Wavelet Decomposition and Phase Congruency Model (WD-PCM), which enhances the license plate number region such that the license plate number detection step fixes correct bounding boxes for each vehicle of the input images. The proposed model is tested on our own dataset containing video images and standard dataset of license plate number detection to show that the proposed model is useful and effective for multiple license plate number detection. Furthermore, the proposed method is tested on natural scene text datasets to show that the proposed method can be extended to address the challenges of natural scene text detection.

Keywords: Vehicle detection · YOLO model · Wavelet decomposition · Phase congruency · License plate detection

1 Introduction

Tracing vehicles when many vehicles are moving is still considered as an open challenge due to variation in speed, occlusion, distance between camera and vehicles, non-uniform illumination, background effect and weather conditions [1]. It is expected that the video frames (images) are severely degraded by poor quality, low resolution and effect of perspective distortion and finally occlusion [2]. In this situation, it is difficult to trace the vehicle in a real environment. In order to trace vehicle and vehicle re-identification, the method should be able to recognize the license plate number accurately. It is noted that the recognition performance depends on the success of license plate number detection as it is a pre-processing step for recognition [3]. Therefore, an accurate license plate number

© Springer Nature Switzerland AG 2022
M. El Yacoubi et al. (Eds.): ICPRAI 2022, LNCS 13363, pp. 489–501, 2022.
https://doi.org/10.1007/978-3-031-09037-0_40

detection irrespective of afore-mentioned challenges is essential. There are methods developed for addressing challenges of license plate number detection and recognition in the past [4]. However, most of the methods target images containing single vehicles, high resolution. These constraints are not necessarily true for real time environment where one can expect multiple vehicles with different speed and variation in distances between camera and vehicles. In addition, when images are extracted from video, it is obvious that images suffer from low resolution and poor quality. Therefore, the existing methods are not effective for detecting license plate numbers for the images containing multiple vehicles. It is evident from the results shown in Fig. 1, where for image containing multiple vehicles, the existing method Yolov5, which is a state-of-the-art method for license plate number detection, does not perform well, while the proposed model detects license plate number of most of vehicles in the images including the license plate number of farthest vehicles. Therefore, this work aims at developing a new Robust Deep Model for Multiple License Plate Number Detection (RDMMLND).

(a) YOLOv5 [4] for license plate number detection in different situations

(b) Proposed model for license plate number detectio n at different situations

Fig. 1. Performance of the proposed and existing methods for multiple license plate number detection in video images

It is noted that when a video frame contains many, the region of license plate number has become tiny region and hence it loses quality. However, we can see the vehicles in the same images clearly. Motivated by this observation, the proposed work introduces vehicle detection to detect the region where license plate number exists rather than detecting license plate number directly. This step reduces background complexity and overcomes the influences of multiple vehicles. To reduce the effect of low resolution, poor quality and degradations, inspired the combination of Wavelet Decomposition and Phase Congruency Model (WD-PCM), which can preserve spatial information of fine details in the degraded images, we explore the same combination to enhance the fine details (edges), which represent license plate number in this work. Furthermore, the enhanced vehicle region is supplied to the detection step for detecting license plate number.

The key contributions of the proposed work are as follows. (i) Addressing challenges of license plate number detection in the images of multiple vehicles extracted from video is new compared to the existing methods. (ii) Use of vehicle detection to localize license plate number region to improve the performance of license plate number detection is new. (iii) The combination of wavelet decomposition and phase congruency for license plate number detection is new compared to the existing methods.

The rest of the paper is organized as follows. A review of existing methods related to license plate number detection is presented in Sect. 2. Section 3 describes the approach for vehicle detection and the combination of wavelet decomposition and phase congruency model for enhancing image and detection. Different experiments are conducted for evaluating the proposed method in Experimental Sect. 4 and Sect. 5 summarizes findings of the proposed method.

2   Related Work

In this work, we review the methods of scene text detection and license plate number detection. Since license plate number is a similar kind of scene text, scene text detection methods are considered as related work for license plate number detection.

For text detection in natural scene images, there are several elegant models developed recently for addressing challenges of scene text detection [6, 7]. Most methods used different deep learning models to cope with the challenges of scene text detection. It is noted from the recent methods that the key basis for the success of these models is defining context information and deriving semantic information between characters and words because every character in the words contributes to extract exact meaning of the whole words. This is not true in the case of license plate number detection because one cannot expect semantic similarity between alphanumeric characters. To our knowledge, each character exhibits independent characteristics. Therefore, one can infer that the recent scene text detection methods may not be effective for license plate number detection especially for the images containing multiple vehicles and affected by low resolution, poor quality and other degradations influenced by environmental factors.

We review the methods of license plate number detection. Chowdhury et al. [1] proposed graph attention model for license plate number detection in crowded street scenes. This approach is limited to still images with good quality but not the images where we can see vehicle with long distance. Chowdhury et al. [2] developed a method for detecting license plate number in low light images. It uses fractal series expansion for enhancing license plate region before recognition. However, the scope of the method is limited to enhancement but not license plate number detection. Jamtsho et al. [5] used YOLOv2 model for detecting license plate number of helmeted motorcyclists. The method considers video frames for detection. Kadam et al. [8] developed number plate detection and detection of bikers with no helmet. The method is confined to images of motorbikes. It also explored the YOLO model for detection. Maulana et al. [9] used region and point based method for detecting vehicle number plate. Menon et al. [10] developed a model for the detection and recognition of multiple license plates in the still images. Hsu et al. [11] proposed application-oriented license plate recognition. This work focuses on analyzing the results of license plate detection and recognition on different applications. Li et al. [12] used deep convolutional neural networks and LSTM for recognizing license plate number. Moreno et al. [13] developed an efficient scale-adaptive license plate detection system. It uses a constrained deformation model for extracting local features to achieve better results. Polishetty et al. [14] proposed cloud based deep learning license plate recognition for smart cities. The method is not robust because it uses handcrafted features and it follows conventional ways for detection and recognition.

Mokayed et al. [15] proposed a model for license plate detection in drone images. The approach explores the combination of DCT and phase congruency model for enhancing the fine details in the images. However, the method is not robust to severe degradations. Peng et al. [16] developed end-to-end model for vehicle license plate detection. The approach explores ES-YOLOv3-tiny model for achieving the results. Slimani et al. [17] proposed a wavelet decomposition-based model for license plate number detection and recognition. The approach combines wavelet decomposition and CNN for achieving the results. However, the method is limited to images of single vehicles. Thumthong et al. [18] proposed a model for Thai vehicle license plate number detection. The method uses the YOLOv4 model for detection. However, the main focus of the method is images of Thai script but not images of multiple vehicles. Zhang et al. [19] developed a unified model for license plate number detection in real world traffic videos. The method is suitable for videos but not still images or individual frames because the temporal information is explored for detection.

It is observed from the above review that most methods target images containing single vehicle with good quality. A few methods considered image containing multiple vehicles for license plate number detection. However, those methods are not robust for the images where we can see long distanced vehicles from the camera. Therefore, this study aims at proposing a new Robust Deep Model for Multiple License Plate Number Detection (RDMMLND).

3   The Proposed Method

This work aims to develop a robust model for multiple license plate detection in the images extracted from video where many vehicles are present in the same image. In this situation, a few vehicles are close to the camera and a few vehicles are away from the camera. As a result, the image contains vehicles affected by focus and defocus. In the case of vehicles affected by defocus (far from the camera), the license plate number appears small and hence it is difficult to notice and detect it. But the vehicle can be seen as larger than the license plate number. This observation motivated us to introduce the step of vehicle detection before license plate number detection [23]. The vehicle detection step helps us to reduce background complexity of the image, at the same time, it localizes the license plate number region. To improve the quality of the license plate number region, we propose the combination of Wavelet Decomposition (LH, HL and

HH) and Phase Congruency Model (WD-PCM). This is because wavelet decomposition has the ability to preserve spatial information of the edges [20], while phase congruency model can enhance the fine details called edges of the text information [15]. Since the WD-PCM enhances the quality of the license plate number region, we propose a CNN based model for license plate number detection in this work. The block diagram of the proposed model can be seen in Fig. 2.

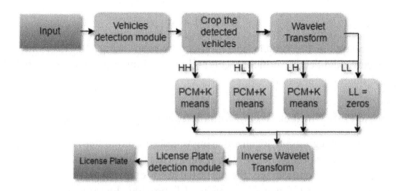

Fig. 2. Block diagram of the proposed work

Input image containing multiple vehicles   Vehicle detection

Fig. 3. The results of the proposed vehicle detection step

3.1 Vehicle Detection

For vehicle detection in the video image containing multiple vehicles, we explore CNN architecture through YOLOv5 based on Yolo-v1-yolo-v4. The motivation to explore YOLOv5 is that it involves a one-stage object detector, and it is computationally efficient compared to existing object detectors. Yolov5 consists of three parts: backbone, neck, and Yolo layers. The Backbone architecture involves Spatial Pyramidal Pooling (SPP) and Cross Stage Partial (CSP) Network, while the neck includes path aggregation network (PANET). Similarly, the CSPNet maps the features from the beginning and end of a network stage, and it extracts gradient variability. The PANet uses bottom-up path augmentation to strengthen extracted features. Furthermore, the Yolo layers generate three different feature maps at a different scale to detect vehicles. To use yolov5 CNN architecture, we need to change the numbers of filters in the last layers. Yolov5 uses an anchor box to predict each bounding box with 4 corresponding coordinates (x, y, w, h), confidence, and class probability. Here, we have selected only 9 classes $(nc = 9)$ (*Bus, Truck, Auto, Motorbike, Car, Person, caravan, bicycle, rider*) and anchors $(A = 3)$, so the number of filters in the last layers will be represented by (1).

$$(nc + 5) \times A. \tag{1}$$

Sample results of the vehicle detection can be seen in Fig. 3, where one can see the proposed model detects vehicles accurately for the images which suffer from poor quality and other degradations.

3.2 License Plate Number Region Enhancement

When license plate regions are localized using vehicle detection step, this step focuses on improving the quality of the license plate region in the vehicle region. For each detected vehicle region in the input image, the proposed work employs wavelet decomposition to obtain low and high frequency sub-bands, LL provides low frequency coefficients, LH highlights fine details in vertical direction, HL highlights the fine details in horizontal direction and HH highlights the fine details in diagonal direction as shown in Fig. 4. Wavelet decomposition of an input signal X can be mathematically represented as Eq. (2)–(5).

$$X_{LL}^{t} = h_{\psi}(-n) * \left(h_{\psi}(-m) * X_{LL}^{t-1} 2 \downarrow \right) 2 \downarrow \tag{2}$$

$$X_{LH}^{t} = h_{\psi}(-n) * \left(h_{\varphi}(-m) * X_{LL}^{t-1} 2 \downarrow \right) 2 \downarrow \tag{3}$$

$$X_{HL}^{t} = h_{\varphi}(-n) * \left(h_{\psi}(-m) * X_{LL}^{t-1} 2 \downarrow \right) 2 \downarrow \tag{4}$$

$$X_{HH}^{t} = h_{\varphi}(-n) * \left(h_{\varphi}(-m) * X_{LL}^{t-1} 2 \downarrow \right) 2 \downarrow \tag{5}$$

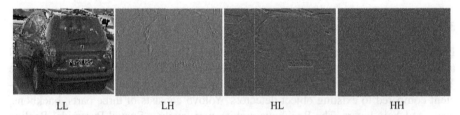

LL   LH   HL   HH

Fig. 4. The effect of wavelet decomposition for license plate number detection

where $h_{\varphi}(-n)$ and $h_{\psi}(-n)$ represents the high pass and low pass 1D filter coefficient and $2 \downarrow$ represents the down sampling. After one stage of wavelet transform dimension of an image will be reduced from $M \times N$ to $\frac{M}{4} \times \frac{N}{4}$ and four component will be generated X_{HH}, X_{HL}, X_{LH}, and X_{LL} for diagonal, vertical, horizontal and approximation band. In Fig. 5, it is noted that vertical, horizontal and diagonal edges information including edges of license plate regions are enhanced. However, due to severe low resolution and low contrast, edges in the license plate number region are still not visible.

To reduce the effect of low resolution, low contrast and poor quality, the proposed work performs inverse wavelet transform to reconstruct LH, HL and HH images and then the proposed work employs Phase Congruency Model (PCM) as defined in Eq. (6)-Eq. (8) for enhancing edges of license plate regions. Since PCM involves orientation and magnitudes of pixels values, it enhances edge pixels by suppressing its background information even the image is affected by distortion to some extent. To separate the pixels with high and low PCM values, we use K-means clustering with K = 2, which outputs two clusters. The cluster that gives high mean value is considered as candidate cluster. The effect to PCM through K-means clustering can be seen in Fig. 5, where we can see the license plate region clearly in LH, HL and HH sub-bands images. The proposed method performs the union operation as defined in Eq. (10) for the cluster of LH, HL and HH, which outputs better information for the license plate number region as shown in Fig. 5(a). For corresponding to pixels in the union image, the proposed method extracts color information from the input image as shown in Fig. 5(b), where we can clearly read the license plate number. The formal steps for computing PCM are as follows.

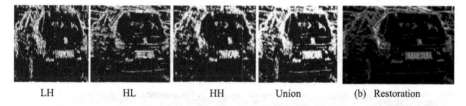

| LH | HL | HH | Union | (b) Restoration |

Fig. 5. The result of enhancement step for license plate number detection

The Phase congruency represents the behavior of signal in frequency domains. Phase congruency of an input 2D image X is calculated as defined in Eq. (6).

$$PC(x) = max_{\emptyset(x)\in[0,2\pi]} \frac{\sum_n A_n \cos\left(\emptyset(x)_n - \overline{\emptyset(x)}\right)}{\sum_n A_n} \tag{6}$$

where A_n represents the amplitude, and $\emptyset(x)_n$ represents the local phase of the Cosine component at position x, which can be calculated by using Eq. (7) and (8). The $\overline{\emptyset(x)}$ maximizes the value of Eq. (8) as it is the weighted mean of local phase angles.

$$\emptyset(u, v)_n = \tan^{-1} \frac{F_I(u, v)}{F_r(u, v)} \tag{7}$$

$$A_n(u, v) = \sqrt{F_I(u, v)^2 + F_r(u, v)^2} \tag{8}$$

where $F_r(u, v)$ and $F_I(u, v)$ represent the real and imaginary component of the Fourier transform $F(u, v)$. Fourier transform of a 2D image X can be represented as:

$$F(u, v) = \frac{1}{M}\frac{1}{N}\sum_{j=0}^{M-1}\sum_{k=0}^{N-1} X(j, k)exp^{-\frac{i2\pi ju}{M}}exp^{-\frac{i2\pi kv}{N}} \tag{9}$$

where u, v represent the frequency component, j, k represent the index of X, and M, N represents the dimensions of X.

$$X_{text}(i, j) = \begin{cases} X(i, j) & C(i, j) = 1 \\ 0 & C(i, j) \neq 1 \end{cases} \tag{10}$$

where $C = C_h \cup C_v \cup C_d$, and C_h, C_v, C_d represent horizontal, vertical and diagonal clusters of each sub-band in binary form, respectively. $C(i, j)$ represents the cluster values at i^{th} and j^{th} index of combined cluster C.

3.3 Multiple License Plate Number Detection

For the enhanced image given by the previous step, the proposed method modifies the architecture presented for vehicle detection (Sect. 3.1) for license plate region detection. The complete steps for the proposed multiple license plate number detection are presented in Algorithm 1. The final results of the proposed method are shown in Fig. 6, where for the image containing multiple vehicles, the enhancement step improves the quality of license plate region, and the detection step detects license plate number accurately for all the enhanced images shown in Fig. 6(a) and Fig. 6(b). Note that the green color in Fig. 6(b) indicates the license plate number detection.

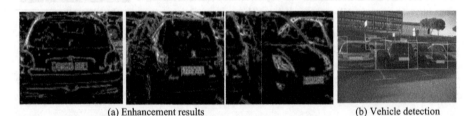

(a) Enhancement results   (b) Vehicle detection

Fig. 6. Illustrating the proposed model for multiple license plate detection

Algorithm 1: Multiple License Plate Number Detection
Input: 2D input image X
Output: License Plate bounding box
1.   Pass the input images (X) to CNN vehicles detection architecture to detect the vehicle.
2.   Crop each detected vehicle, Let number of vehicle present in the given X is N. Each vehicle can be represented as X_i.
3.   Apply wavelet decomposition for each vehicle X_i. Four Sub-band will be generated, represented as $(X_{iLL}, X_{iLH}, X_{iHL}, X_{iHH})$
4.   Apply inverse wavelet transform on $X_{iLH}, X_{iHL}, X_{iHH}$. Three different features images will be generated for horizontal, vertical and diagonal features, represented as $X_{iLH}^f, X_{iHL}^f, X_{iHH}^f$.
5.   Apply K-means clustering on three generated features ($X_{iLH}^f, X_{iHL}^f, X_{iHH}^f$), independently, with the number of clusters = 2. Each cluster is represented ($C_{i1}, C_{i2}, and\ C_{i3}$) for each sub-band (horizontal, vertical and diagonal) in binary form.
6.   Combine all three cluster $C_i = C_{i1} \cup C_{i2} \cup C_{i3}$ for each vehicles.
7.   Map the pixel values presents in X_i in such a way that $X_{i\_text} = X_i \times C_i$.
8.   Send X_{i_text} for number plate detection.

For training the proposed model for license plate number detection, we use the Kaggle number plate detection dataset (https://www.kaggle.com/andrewmvd/car-plate-detection), which provides 433 images with bounding boxes.

4 Experimental Results

We create our own dataset for experimentation in this work because there are no standard dataset that provides the images containing the license plate number of multiple vehicles. In addition, most of the standard datasets available provide images containing license plate number of particular vehicle but not multiple vehicles. Our dataset is named as **Multiple License Plate Number Detection** (MLPD), which comprises 761 images and the same number of images are used for testing. Out of 761 images, 651 images contain single vehicles (single license plate number) and 110 images contain multiple vehicles (multiple license plate numbers). For training the proposed system, we use the samples provided by Kaggle license plate dataset, consisting of 433 images.

To show the effectiveness of the proposed method, we also use the standard dataset called **Application-Oriented License Plate Recognition (AOLP)** [11] for experimentation. This dataset provides 2049 images that are categorized into three different sunset access control (AC), law enforcement (LE), and road patrol (RP). Out of 2049 images, 387 images are used for training and 1662 image are used for testing. To show the robustness and generic ability of the proposed method, we use the standard dataset of natural scene text detection [21]. This dataset provides 10000 images containing different text complexities, 2000 for validation, and 10000 images for testing. For measuring the performance of the proposed method, we use the standard measures as defined in Eq. (11)-Eq. (13). We follow the instructions stated in [12] for calculating measures. The reason to choose the above three measures is that these are standard measures and widely used for evaluating license plate number detection. Precision, Recall, and F1-score mathematically represented as:

$$Precision = \frac{TP}{TP + FP} \tag{11}$$

$$Recall = \frac{TP}{TP + FN} \tag{12}$$

$$F - Score = \frac{2 * Precision * Recall}{Precision + Recall} \tag{13}$$

where TP, FP, and FN represent true positive, False positive and False Negative respectively. For training the proposed vehicle detection step, we use INSAAN Indian Driving Dataset (IDD), which provides 13744 samples for training and 5197 samples for testing. (https://idd.insaan.iiit.ac.in/).

4.1 Ablation Study

The proposed method involves the steps of vehicle detection, image enhancement and license plate number detection for tackling challenges of multiple license plate number detection. Therefore, to access the contribution and effectiveness of the key steps, we conduct the following experiments using our dataset and the results are reported in Table 2. (i) the YOLOv5 [22] is employed on the input image without vehicle detection and image enhancement for license plate number detection, which is considered as baseline experiment. (ii) For this experiment we use the image enhancement step for license plate number detection using YOLOv5 without vehicle detection. (iii) In this experiment we use vehicle detection and then license plate number detection without image enhancement and (iv) This experiment uses all the steps, including vehicle detection, image enhancement and YOLOv5 for license plate detection. This is considered as the proposed method. The results reported in Table 1 show that the F-score improves progressively as the experiment changes. Therefore, one can infer that the key steps are effective in achieving the best results for license plate number detection. It is also noted from Table 1 that the experiments (ii)-(iv) are better than the baseline experiment (i). This shows that the proposed key steps are effective and contributes equally for achieving the results.

Table 1. Analyzing the contribution of the key steps of the proposed method using our dataset.

#	Key steps	F-score
(i)	Baseline: License plate detection	98.23
(ii)	Image enhancement + License plate detection	98.44
(iii)	Vehicle Detection + License plate detection	98.60
(iv)	Vehicle Detection + Image enhancement + License plate detection	**98.72**

4.2 Experiments on Multiple License Plate Number Detection

Qualitative results of the proposed method on our dataset and standard datasets are shown in Fig. 7(a), where it is noted that the proposed method detects license plate numbers in all the images accurately. In addition, Fig. 7(a) also shows that the proposed approach has the ability to detect multiple license plate numbers in the images. The same conclusions can be drawn from the results reported for our and standard datasets in Table 2 and Table 3. It is observed from Table 2 and Table 3 that the F-score of the proposed method is the best compared to the existing methods. This shows that the proposed method is independent of the number of license plate numbers in the image, and it works well for the defocused images. The reason for the poor results of the existing methods is that the existing methods do not have the ability to handle the challenges of the images which contain multiple license plate numbers, especially the images of our dataset. In addition, the existing methods suffer from their own constraints like high resolution and good quality images and this is not necessarily true for different situations. On the other hand, because of the key steps of vehicle detection, image enhancement and YOLOv5 [22], the proposed method achieves the best results for both the datasets compared to the existing methods.

(a) License plate number detection by the proposed method for our dataset and AOLP dataset

(b) Text detection performance on natural scene text images of ICDAR 2019 MLT [21]

Fig. 7. Performance of the proposed method on license plate and natural scene text datasets

Table 2. License plate number detection performance of the proposed method on our dataset

Methods	Single license plate images			Multiple license plate images		
	Precision	Recall	F-Score	Precision	Recall	F-Score
YOLOv5 [22]	92.94	95.85	94.85	90.33	93.45	91.85
Proposed	**93.37**	**98.11**	**95.68**	**91.07**	**97.52**	**94.18**

Table 3. Performance of the proposed and the existing methods on AOLP [11] dataset

Methods	Moreno et al. [12]	Hsu et al. [11]	Li et al. [13]	Polishetty et al. [14]	Proposed method
F-score	98.98	92.97	97.27	97.80	**98.72**

4.3 Experiments on Natural Scene Text Detection

When we look at scene text in the natural scene images and number plate in the license plate images, both the text shares the same text properties. Therefore, to demonstrate the effectiveness of the proposed method, we test the proposed method on scene text images for experimentation. Qualitative results of the proposed method on scene text images are shown in Fig. 7(b) for ICDAR 2019 MLT dataset, where it can be observed that the proposed method detects scene text well in the images of different cases. Therefore, one can conclude that the proposed method can detect license plate number and natural scene text in the images.

5   Conclusion and Future Work

In this work, we have proposed a novel model for detecting license plate numbers in the images (frames) extracted from video, which contain multiple vehicles. For reducing background complexity and localize the license plate region, the proposed work introduces vehicle detection step based on modified YOLOv5 architecture. The detected vehicle regions are supplied to the enhancement step which combines wavelet decomposition and phase congruency model. This step enhances the license plate number region irrespective of quality variations. The proposed work modifies YOLOv5 for detecting license plate number from enhanced image. Experimental results demonstrate the effectiveness of the proposed method for license plate number detection from the images of different situations. In addition, the results on scene text detection show that the proposed method is generic and it has the ability to extend to scene text detection in natural scene images. However, when the images are affected by many adverse factors, such as low resolution, blur and noise, the performance of the method degrades. To address this challenge, our future work aims at developing a unified deep learning model.

Acknowledgement. This work is partially supported by the Technology Innovation Hub, ISI, Kolkata, India.

References

1. Chowdhury, P.N., et al.: Graph attention network for detecting license plates in crowded street scenes. Pattern Recogn. Lett. 18–25 (2020)
2. Chowdhury, P.N., Shivakumara, P., Jalab, H.A., Ibrahim, R.W., Pal, U., Lu, T.: A new fractal series expansion-based enhancement model for license plate recognition. Signal Process. Image Commun. (2020)

3. Khare, V.: A novel character segmentation-reconstruction approach for license plate recognition. Expert Syst. Applicat. 219–239 (2019)
4. Shashirangana, J., Padmasiri, H., Meedeniya, D., Perera, C.: automated license plate recognition: a survey on methods and techniques. IEEE Access 11203–11225 (2020)
5. Jamtsho, Y., Riyamongkol, P., Waranusast, R.: Real-time license plate detection for non-helmeted motorcyclist using YOLO. ICT Press, pp. 104–109 (2021)
6. Jain, T., Palaiahnakote, S., Pal, U., Liu, C.L.: Deformable scene text detection using harmonic features and modified pixel aggregation network. Pattern Recognit. Lett. 135–142 (2021)
7. Chowdhury, T., Shivakumara, P., Pal, U., Lu, T., Raghavendra, R., Chanda, S.: DCINN: deformable convolution and inception based neural network for tattoo text detection through skin region. In: Proceedings of ICDAR, pp. 335–350 (2021)
8. Kadam, S., Hirve, R., Kawle, N., Shah, P.: Automatic detection of bikers with no helmet and number plate detection. In: Proceedings ICCNT (2021)
9. Maulana, H., Kartika, D.S.Y., Saputra, W.S., Alit, R.: Combining region-based and point based algorithm to detect vehicle plate location. In: Proceedings ITIS, pp. 183–187 (2020)
10. Menon, A., Omman, B.: Detection and recognition of multiple license plate from still images. In: Proceedings ICCSDET (2018)
11. Hsu, G.S., Chen, J.C., Chung, Y.Z.: Application-oriented license plate recognition. IEEE Trans. VT 552–561 (2012)
12. Moreno, M.M., Gonzalez-Diaz, I., Diaz-de-Maria, F.: Efficient scale-adaptive license plate detection system. IEEE Trans. ITS 2109–2121 (2018)
13. Li, H., Shen, C.: Reading car license plates using deep convolutional neural networks and LSTMs. arXiv preprint arXiv:1601.05610 (2016)
14. Polishetty, R., Roopaei, M., Rad, P.: A next-generation secure cloud-based deep learning license plate recognition for smart cities. In: Proceedings ICMLA, pp. 286–293 (2016)
15. Mokayed, H., Shivakumara, P., Woon, H.H., Kankanhalli, M., Lu, T., Pal, U.: A new DCT-PCM method for license plate number detection in drone images. Pattern Recogn. Lett. 45–53 (2021)
16. Peng, Y., Li, H., Qian, Z.: A new end-to-end secondary network for high efficient vehicles and license plates detection. In: Proceedings ICSGEA, pp. 6–9 (2019)
17. Slimani, I., Zaarane, A., Okaishi, W.A., Atoug, I., Hamdoun, A.: An automated license plate detection and recognition system based on wavelet decomposition and CNN. Array (2020)
18. Thumthong, W., Meesud, P., Jarupunphol, P.: Automatic detection and recognition of Thai vehicle license plate from CCTV images. In: Proceedings ICTEE, pp. 142–146 (2021)
19. Zhang, C., Wang, Q., Li, X.: V-LPDR: towards a unified framework for license plate detection, tracking and recognition in real-world traffic videos. Neurocomputing 189–206 (2021)
20. Liang, G., Shivakumara, P., Lu, T., Tan, C.L.: Multi-spectral fusion-based approach for arbitrarily oriented scene text detection in video images. IEEE Trans. Image Process. 4488–4501 (2015)
21. Nayef, N., et al.: ICDAR2019 robust reading challenge on multi-lingual scene text detection and recognition—RRC-MLT-2019. In: Proceedings of ICDAR, pp. 1582–1587, September 2019
22. Ultralytics-Yolov5. https://github.com/ultralytics/yolov5. Accessed 30 Nov 2021
23. Shivakumara, P., Tang, D., Asadzadehkaljahi, M., Lu, T., Pal, U., Anisi, M.H.: CNN-RNN based method for license plate recognition. CAAI Trans. Intell. Technol. 3(3), 169–175

Generative Target Update for Adaptive Siamese Tracking

Madhu Kiran[1(✉)], Le Thanh Nguyen-Meidine[1], Rajat Sahay[2],
Rafael Menelau Oliveira E Cruz[1], Louis-Antoine Blais-Morin[3], and Eric Granger[1]

[1] Laboratoire d'imagerie, de vision et d'intelligence artificielle (LIVIA), École de technologie supérieure, Montreal, Canada
madhu_sajc@hotmail.com
[2] Vellore Institute of Technology, Vellore, India
[3] Genetec Inc., Montreal, Canada

Abstract. Siamese trackers perform similarity matching with templates (i.e., target models) to recursively localize objects within a search region. Several strategies have been proposed in the literature to update a template based on the tracker output, typically extracted from the target search region in the current frame, and thereby mitigate the effects of target drift. However, this may lead to corrupted templates, limiting the potential benefits of a template update strategy. This paper proposes a model adaptation method for Siamese trackers that uses a generative model to produce a synthetic template from the object search regions of several previous frames, rather than directly using the tracker output. Since the search region encompasses the target, attention from the search region is used for robust model adaptation. In particular, our approach relies on an auto-encoder trained through adversarial learning to detect changes in a target object's appearance, and predict a future target template, using a set of target templates localized from tracker outputs at previous frames. To prevent template corruption during the update, the proposed tracker also performs change detection using the generative model to suspend updates until the tracker stabilizes, and robust matching can resume through dynamic template fusion. Extensive experiments conducted on VOT-16, VOT-17, OTB-50, and OTB-100 datasets highlight the effectiveness of our method, along with the impact of its key components. Results indicate that our proposed approach can outperform state-of-the-art trackers, and its overall robustness allows tracking for a longer time before failure.
Code: https://github.com/madhukiranets/AdaptiveSiamese.

1 Introduction

Many video analytics, monitoring, and surveillance applications rely on visual object tracking (VOT) to locate targets appearing in a camera viewpoint over time, scene understanding, action and event recognition, video summarizing, person re-identification. In real-world video surveillance applications, VOT is challenging due to real-time computational constraints, changes and deformation in target appearance, rapid motions, occlusion, motion blur, and complex backgrounds. The time required to capture and identify various events in real-time video surveillance applications is a significant constraint.

© Springer Nature Switzerland AG 2022
M. El Yacoubi et al. (Eds.): ICPRAI 2022, LNCS 13363, pp. 502–513, 2022.
https://doi.org/10.1007/978-3-031-09037-0_41

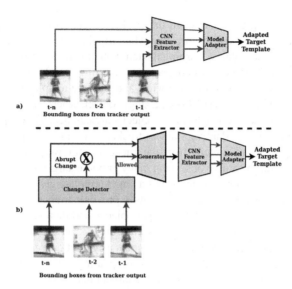

Fig. 1. Approaches to select templates for adaptive Siamese tracking. (a) Conventional approaches select templates from previous tracker outputs. (b) Our approach generates templates from previous ones using a generative model, and filters noisy templates via change detection.

Techniques for VOT may be categorized according to the target model or template construction mechanism, as either generative or discriminative. Generative appearance models represent target appearance without considering the background, while discriminative trackers learn a representation to distinguish between a target and background [21]. The trackers can be further classified based on their image representation techniques, ranging from conventional hand-crafted descriptors [10,12,20,27] to more recent deep learning models, like Siamese trackers [1,8,17,18,33,34,37] (Fig. 1).

One of the initial Siamese trackers – the Fully Convolutional Siamese tracker (SiameseFC) [1] – uses a single feature representation extracted at the beginning of a trajectory, and does not update the target features during tracking. Although this strategy can provide computational efficiency, SiameseFC trackers suffer from target drift over time. Target drift is defined as a situation when the tracker slowly starts focusing on distractive backgrounds (rather than the target), and eventually looses the target. Such drift causes broken tracklets, a potential problem in video surveillance applications such as loitering detection, video person re-identification, face recognition, and other related applications. When the object's appearance changes abruptly, or the object is occluded or partially leaves the search region, the SiameseFC tracker temporarily drifts to a location with a high response map score [31]. Some adaptive Siamese trackers have been proposed that allow for template updates. Most early trackers sought to update target features as a moving average based on localizations from the current frame output. Other trackers apply strategies to address drifting objects by storing an array of templates, or combining features from various tracker outputs [29,31]. However, these trackers face issues when updating templates on every frame based on tracker output.

In particular, they integrate noise from the tracker output templates, especially in the present image occlusion or drift. Moreover, when training a Siamese tracker for matching based on multiple templates, learning the template update function in addition to the conventional search-template pair may lead to over-fitting [31]. Hence, to avoid corrupting templates, it is important to manage when and how the templates are updated.

In this paper, we focus robust VOT of a single object, where the template is updated dynamically in response to changes in the object's appearance. This paper introduces a method that applied to any adaptive Siamese trackers for real-time applications. Instead of using the samples mined directly from the tracker output, we propose to use a generative model to generate a sample observing many previous target template. This generative model predicts the future appearance of a target template given a set of consecutive target templates localized from tracker outputs at previous frames. It also allows detecting abrupt changes in the appearance of target objects, and thereby preventing template corruption by suspending template updates until the tracker stabilizes. In the absence of an abrupt change, our generative model outputs a synthetic target template for robust matching through dynamic template fusion, and updating the target template.

In contrast with [31], our method learns the target update itself, using cross-attention between search region and template features. This allows selecting channels among the target features that are most useful for target update. The cross-attention approach relies on attention from the target's current appearance in the search region to update the existing target template. The proposed generative model is designed by adversarial training a video autoencoder to produce a future frame. The discrepancy between the generated future frame, and the target's appearance from tracker output helps detect appearance changes using a change detection mechanism. We summarise our contribution as follows. We propose a method for adaptation of Siamese trackers based generative model update. The generative model produces a future template by observing the the past templates. Additionally, change detection is proposed using the generative model to suspend model update during target drifting. Finally, the method relies on the difference between a simple average and a learned fusion templates to define an inequality constraint during learning of model adaptation. It uses attention from the search region to attend to salient regions in the tracker localised template. For proof-of-concept validation, the proposed method is integrated into state-of-art SiamFC+ and SiamRPN trackers [17,33], and compared to different conventional and state-of-art trackers from deep Siamese family [1,33] on videos from the OTB [28] and VOT [14,15] evaluations datasets. We also perform ablation studies on different modules to study the effectiveness of the proposed method.

2   Related Work

Pioneered by SINT [25] and SiamFC [1], the Siamese family of trackers evolved from Siamese networks trained offline with similarity metrics. These networks were trained on a large dataset to learn generic features for object tracking. SiamRPN [17] further improves on this work by employing region proposals to produce a target-specific anchor-based detector. Then, the following Siamese trackers mainly involved designing more powerful backbones [18,33] or proposal networks, like in [7]. ATOM [3] and

DIMP [2] are robust online trackers that differ from the general offline Siamese track-ers by their ability to update model online during tracking. Other paradigms of Siamese trackers are distractor-aware training, domain-specific tracking [11,37].

In [36], an LSTM is incorporated to learn long-term relationships during tracking and turns the VOT problem into a consecutive decision-making process of selecting the best model for tracking via reinforcement learning [6]. In [26] and [37], models are updated online by a moving average based learning. These methods integrate the target region extracted from tracker output into the initial target. In [22], a generative model is learned via adversarial learning to generate random masks that produce shifted versions of target templates from the original template. Then, an adversarial function is used to decide whether or not the generated template is from the same distribution and if they will be used as templates for tracking. In [29], an LSTM is employed to estimate the current template by storing previous templates in a memory bank. In [9], authors propose to compute transformation matrix with reference to the initial template, with a regularised linear regression in the Fourier domain. Finally, in [30], authors propose to learn the updating co-efficient of a correlation filter-based tracker using SGD online. All these methods use the tracker output as the reference template while updating on top of the initial template. [2,4] propose a model where an adaptive discriminative model is generated online by the steepest gradient descent method. They differ from another online learned method like [19] due to their real-time performance. Similarly [34] introduce online model prediction but employ a fast conjugate gradient algorithm for model prediction. Foreground score maps are estimated online, and the classification branch is combined by weighted addition.

Several methods follow the standard strategy of updating target template features, such as simple averaging, where the template is updated as a running average with exponentially decaying weights over time. This yields a template update defined by:

$$\widetilde{\varphi}^n = (1 - \gamma)\widetilde{\varphi}^{n-1} + \gamma\varphi^n, \tag{1}$$

where n denotes the time step, $\widetilde{\varphi}^n$ the predicted template, and γ the learning rate.

This strategy has several issues, most notably the possibility of integrating noise and corruption into templates during the update process. Therefore, authors in [31] proposed a network which, when given an input of past template features, the template extracted from current tracker output produces a new representation that can be added to the orig-inal ground truth template (obtained during tracker initialization). This approach further suffers from the following issues. (1) A future template for the tracker is unseen at the time of template update, and the model is updated solely based on the tracker output in the past frame output. (2) The model is updated every frame making it still susceptible to the integration of noise over time. (3) Network training is a tedious task since it must be trained continuously offline by running the tracker on the training dataset. It must produce a previous frame feature representation that needs to be stored and used for the next training iteration. Further developments in this direction are challenging.

3   Proposed Adaptive Siamese Tracker

Given the initial object location, a ground truth-object template image T is extracted, along with the corresponding deep CNN features φ_{gt}. A tracker seeks to produce object localization $BBox$ at a given time step by matching φ_{gt} with search region features φ_s. The objective is to produce a trajectory by recursively extracting search regions from tracker output, and matching them with a given template over each input video frame.

a) Template Prediction and Change Detection: Inspired from [24], We employ a video autoencoder that is trained through adversarial learning for template generation. Given an set of past templates T^n where $n = t, t - 1, t - 2, t - 3...$ we aim to predict a future template for time step t. As described below, our template generation method consists of a generator G and a discriminator D.

Generator (G): It consists of an encoder-decoder architecture (see Fig. 2) together represented by G. The encoder compresses an input video clip into a small bottleneck with a set of CNN layers and Conv-LSTM based recurrent network to model the temporal relationship between the frames. The decoder consists of some layers of transposed CNN to obtain the predicted video frame. Hence given an input video clip of $T^{t-k}, ..., T^{t-2}, T^{t-1}$, the generator produces the estimated future video frame $\hat{T}$. The generator is trained according to the Mean Squared Error ($L_{mse}(T, \hat{T})$) between predicted image $\hat{T}$ and ground truth image T along with adversarial loss $L_{adv}^G(\hat{T})$ (Fig. 3):

$$L_{mse}(T, \hat{T}) = \|T - \hat{T}\|_2 \qquad (2)$$

$$L_{adv}^G(\hat{T}) = \frac{1}{2}(D(\hat{T}) - 1)^2 \qquad (3)$$

Discriminator (D): It comprises of several CNN layers to compete with the generator to differentiate between the ground truth and generated frames. The discriminator distinguishes a real-world image from a fake image, promoting the generator to produce good quality images. Since training the autoencoder on MSE loss alone will cause the output to be blurry, we leverage the discriminator to help produce higher-quality images.

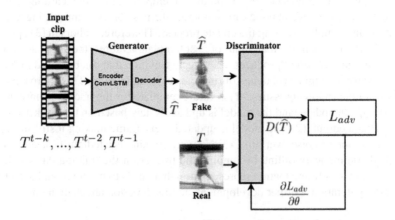

Fig. 2. Our generator model is a video autoencoder that is trained adversarially. A future target template is reconstructed from a sequence of input target templates. The discriminator D processed the reconstructed template as fake, and the ground truth template input as real.

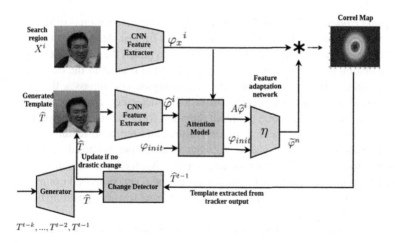

Fig. 3. Block diagram of our proposed generic template update system for Siamese trackers that adapts the model of the target template with a generative model and change detection. Our attention based dynamic ensemble of targets adapts the model to the current representation of the target with attention from search region. The change detection system disables template update during anomalies such as occlusion and severe target drift.

The labels are set to 0 for fake images (obtained from the autoencoder's reconstruction) and 1 for real (ground truth template image). The discriminator D is trained with an adversarial loss:

$$L_{adv}^{D}(T, \widehat{T}) = \frac{1}{2}(D(T) - 1)^2 + \frac{1}{2}(D(\widehat{T}) - 0)^2 \qquad (4)$$

Change Detection: Once the adversarial auto-encoder has been trained, the average MSE error between the reconstructed template and search regions from each input frame in the video clip is computed to produce the reconstruction error. Similar to previous methods such as [6,35], we adopt the regularity score to detect abrupt changes in template clips. Let $e(T)$ be the reconstruction error. Reconstruction error should be normalized from the sequences of the same video with:

$$s(x) = 1 - \frac{e(T) - \min_T e(T)}{\max_T e(T)} \qquad (5)$$

In practice it is difficult to set $\min_T e(T)$ and $\max_T e(T)$ as the future frames are not observable. Hence, we set $\min_T e(T)$ and $\max_T e(T)$ experimentally using a validation set. The regularity score $s(x)$ serves as the measure for regular templates. Hence a score of less than a threshold τ is considered an abrupt change. The length of the input template sequence is kept fixed, and new templates are updated into the sequence by pushing the oldest template out of the stack. When a change is detected, the template that was last pushed into the stack is rejected and considered a possible source of corruption, and the template update eventually stalled for that particular time step.

b) Template Update with Cross Attention: Target model adaptation is often based on the last known appearance of the object from previous frames. At the start of the tracking, the initial target feature φ_{init} needs to be adapted to match the latest object appearance. Such adaptation is not possible without predicting the tracker in the current frame. At the same time, it is to be noted that the search region encompasses the target in the current frame, given that the change detector has detected no drastic change. Therefore we propose to use this cue to obtain attention from the search region to adapt the model. In addition to this, search region features and template features are of different sizes. This difference in feature size has inspired our proposal of using channel attention across the search and template stream. We follow a similar model adaptation paradigm as [31] along with our attention model and proposed optimization with inequality constraints.[31] consider adapting the target feature by adding new information to the initial target feature φ_{init}.

Let $\widehat{\varphi}^t$ be the feature vector extracted from the generated template $\widehat{T}^t$. The generated template is the predicted target appearance. In comparison to $\widehat{\varphi}^t$, φ_{init} is the most reliable target feature vector, as it is obtained during track initialization, using ground truth information. The model adaptation mechanism considers both φ_{init} and $\widehat{\varphi}^t$ to predict the adapted features $\widetilde{\varphi}^t$. As discussed earlier, the first step is to obtain attention from the search region to select important channels in $\widehat{\varphi}^t$. Let $\varphi_z{}^t$ be the features extracted from search region. Although these are spatial features, they have different sizes for the search and template features. Hence the attention is obtained only on the channels using Global Average Pooling (GAP) of the features. An MLP with sigmoid activation was used on GAP features to select channels based on importance. The attention obtained from $\varphi_z{}^t$, φ_{init} and $\widehat{\varphi}^t$ are averaged to obtain channel attention A. Then, A is multiplied with $\widehat{\varphi}^t$. Therefore the channels of $\widehat{\varphi}^t$ are re-weighed, a common saliency across search region and target template are encompassed into the attention by the averaging of feature vectors described above.

The attended feature $A\widehat{\varphi}^t$ and $\widetilde{\varphi}^{t-1}$ (obtained from the prior frame after model adaptation) are then concatenating in the channel dimension as follows 6:

$$\varphi_{concat} = [\widetilde{\varphi}^{t-1}; A\widehat{\varphi}^t] \tag{6}$$

The concatenated feature φ_{concat} is passed through a two layer CNN with 1×1 convolution layer, followed by a TanH activation function to obtain adapted feature in:

$$\widetilde{\varphi}^t = \eta(\varphi_{concat}), \tag{7}$$

where η is the model adaptation network discussed above, and $\widetilde{\varphi}^t$ is the adapted target template for tracking.

c) Model Adaptation: During training, target samples are generated from the training data keeping the chronological order of the image frame in a video to obtain features $\varphi_{init}, \varphi_{GT}$. The ground truth video data generated these two, i.e., initial and template from future frames. To obtain the generated template, n consecutive templates are used from the same video to generate $\widehat{\varphi}^t$ by using the pre-trained generator that was previously discussed. To enable the system, learn to generate an adapted feature to resemble a target template from the next frame, we employ MSE loss:

$$L_{mdl-mse} = \|\varphi_{GT} - \widetilde{\varphi}^t\|_2, \tag{8}$$

where φ_{GT} are the ground truth target features which are chronologically the latest template. We expect the adapted template $\widetilde{\varphi}^t$ obtained by adapting previously seen target templates to resemble the future ground truth template.

Optimizing the MSE loss in our case is a difficult task since the model is being forced to learn to produce an unseen representation from future frames given two different previously seen frames. In [31], the tracker is recursively train on several training cycles, which is a tedious task. Template update can also be performed by simply averaging features that would suffer from noisy updates and feature smoothing due to averaging both leading to information loss. Such simple averaging can be used as a cue to introduce a constraint to optimize the template update.

Let φ_{avg} be the averaged template obtained by averaging φ_{init} and φ^{t-1}. Let D_E denote the Euclidean distance function. It is reasonable to assume that simple template averaging is a trivial solution and therefore the distance between learnt template $\widetilde{\varphi}^t$ and φ_{GT}(the future template) must be less than φ_{avg} and φ_{GT}. Constrained loss given by,

$$L_{const-mse} = \|\varphi_{GT} - \widetilde{\varphi}^t\|_2 + \lambda \, ReLU((D_E(\varphi_{GT}, \widetilde{\varphi}) - D_E(\varphi_{GT}, \varphi_{avg})) \quad (9)$$

where ReLU ensures that the gradients are passed for the constraint only when the constraint is not respected. λ is set to a value $\gg 1$ and is determined experimentally.

4   Results and Discussion

a) Experimental Methodology: A ResNet22 CNN similar to the SiamDW tracker [23, 33] is used for fair comparison. We use the GOT-10K dataset [13] to train our video autoencoder, as well as a tracking network similar to [23] for direct comparison, since they use a similar baseline to ours. GOT-10K contains about 10,000 video sequences with 1.5 million labeled bounding boxes to train our tracking network and autoencoder. In particular, give the large number of training sequences, the autoencoder overall motion model for objects in generic videos to predict frames in the future. We used the official training set of GOT10-K to train the networks. We use the same data augmentation techniques as [23,33], which includes shift and scale, and random cropping. The autoencoder was pre-trained adversarially with the discriminator. The Siamese tracker is pre-trained without the autoencoder by selecting random samples in a specific video, one for the template, and the other for the search region.

The standard tracking benchmarks, OTB-50, OTB-100 [28], and VOT2017 [14] video datasets, are used to evaluate trackers.The OTB [28] dataset consists of sets OTB-50 and OTB100, with 50 and 100 real-world tracking videos, respectively. VOT2017 dataset has 60 public test videos with a total of 21,356 frames. The VOT protocol re-initializes the tracker when the tracker fails with a delay of 5 frames. Evaluation measures used with VOT are EAO (Expected Average Overlap), a combination of accuracy and robustness. Robustness refers to the number of times a tracker needs to be initialized. To define EAO, let Φ_{N_s} be the average overlap of the tracking bounding box and ground truth over an N_s frame sequences. EAO is, $\hat{\Phi} = \frac{1}{N_{hi} - N_{lo}} \sum_{N_s = N_{lo}:N_{hi}} \hat{\Phi}_{N_s}$, where $\hat{\Phi}$ is the average computed over an interval of $[N_{lo}, N_{hi}]$ typical short term sequence lengths.

Table 1. EAO and robustness associated with different components of our proposed tracker on the VOT2017 dataset.

Sl	Ablation	Remark	EAO↑	Robustness↓
· Template update				
1	Only SiamFC+	Baseline	0.23	0.49
2	SiamFC+ and UpdateNet	Baseline and Update	0.26	0.40
3	SiamFC+ and Moving Average	Baseline and Linear	0.25	0.44
4	SiamFC+ and Dynamic Update	Ours without Constraint	0.27	0.41
5	SiamFC+ and Dynamic Constr	Ours with INQ. Constraint	0.29	0.38
· Generative modelling				
6	Generated Template Update	5) + Generated Template	0.29	0.37
7	Generated Model and Blend	6) + Tracker Output Blend	0.30	0.37
· Change detection				
8	Change Detection	7) + No Update on Drastic Change	0.31	0.34

b) Ablation Study: We study the contribution of different components of our proposed method on the VOT2017 dataset. In the first part of Table 1, "Template update," demonstrates our contribution to model adaptation. The second part, "Generative Model," evaluates the contribution of the generative model in the template update. Finally, the "Change Detection" part shows the effect of change detection on tracking EAO. In order to evaluate the template update part, we compare the results of the baseline [33] which is also our backbone. The template update mechanism uses the output from tracker instead of the generative model instead of $\hat{\varphi}^t$ in the template update network. We implement [31] based model adaptation for the baseline [33] and moving average based linear update as in [37] is compared with our proposed update method "Dynamic Update" (with attention), which refers to training without the inequality constraint discussed above. Number 5) in the table refers to the experiment where template update is used with inequality constraints. It can be seen that using the inequality constraint alone and our template update mechanism has improved the overall Robustness of the tracker as indicated by the robustness score(lower the score more robust the tracker is). 6) and 7) in the Table 1 uses the output from generative model to feed $\hat{\varphi}^t$. Since the generative model's output is a bit blurry in 7) we blend it with tracker output extracted target template image to obtain a sharper image. Such blending has been shown to improve the result further. We detect drastic changes in the model via the regularity score of the tracker. The change detection will help prevent noisy updates during drift or occlusion; this is shown in 8) where no updates were made during drastic changes.

c) Comparison with State-of-Art: We compare our proposed template update method implemented on SiamFC+ [33] back-end against popular Siamese methods bench marked on OTB-50,OTB-100,VOT16,17 datasets. Similar to the benchmarking method in SE-SiamFC [23] we have selected the Siamese trackers for direct comparison with

Table 2. Accuracy of the proposed and state-of-the-art trackers on the OTB-50, OTB-100, VOT2016 and VOT2017 datasets.

Tracker	OTB-50		OTB-100		VOT2016			VOT2017		
	AUC↑	Prec↑	AUC↑	Prec↑	EAO↑	A↑	R↓	EAO↑	A↑	R↓
SINT, CVPR-16 [25]	0.64	0.85	–	–	–			–	–	–
SiamFC, ECCV-16 [1]	0.61	0.81	0.58	0.77	0.24	0.53	0.46	0.19	0.5	0.59
DSiam, ECCV-17 [37]	0.64	0.81	0.64	0.81	–			–	–	–
StructSiam, ECCV-18 [32]	0.64	0.88	0.62	0.85		–	–	–	-	–
TriSiam, ECCV-18, [5]	0.62	0.82	0.59	0.78	–	–	–	0.2		–
SiamRPN, CVPR-18 [17]	–	–	0.64	0.85	0.34	0.56	0.26	0.24	0.49	0.46
SE-Siam, WACV-21 [23]	0.68	0.90	0.66	0.88	0.36	0.59	0.24	0.27	0.54	0.38
SiamFC+, CVPR-19 [33]	0.67	0.88	–	–	0.30	0.54	0.26	0.24	0.49	0.46
SiamRPN++, CVPR-19 [16]	–	–	0.69	0.89	0.46	0.64	0.20	0.41	0.60	0.23
Adaptive SiamFC+ (ours)	0.68	0.89	0.67	**0.89**	**0.39**	0.56	0.21	**0.31**	0.52	**0.34**
Adaptive SiamRPN++ (ours)	–	–	**0.71**	0.87	0.47	0.61	**0.19**	**0.44**	0.58	**0.21**

ours. It is important to note that our back-end Siamese tracker, training procedure, sample selection, Etc., are the same as [23]. OTB benchmark uses AUC, which signifies the average overlap over the dataset, and Precision (Prec) signifies the center distance error between object and tracker bounding box. We can see that our method performs competitively with [23] on OTB dataset shown in Table 2. It is important to note that OTB does not re-initialize the tracker on failure, and in addition, OTB does not consider track failures into the final evaluation.

On the other hand, the VOT dataset uses Expected average Overlap (EAO), Robustness (R), and Accuracy (A) as metrics. Particularly Robustness is interesting as it indicates some measure on tracker drift in a given dataset. EAO combines tracking accuracy and Robustness, and hence it is a better indicator of tracker performance than just AUC. We can see from the Table 2 our method outperforms state-of-the-art by 4% and outperforms the baseline SiamFC+ [33] by 7% on EAO. The results show that our proposed method would enable the tracker to track for longer periods before complete failure compared to the other methods we compare.

To show drastic changes during tracking, we plot the IOU "overlap" (intersection over union for tracking bounding box over ground truth) and the regularity score produced by our change detector. In Fig. 4 blue line indicates IOU for our proposed tracker. The thumbnails at the bottom indicate cutouts of the ground truth bounding box around the object being tracked. The video example is from "basketball" of the VOT17 dataset. It can be observed that the regularity score produced by our change detector is low during frames that have partial occlusion and during clutter around the background.

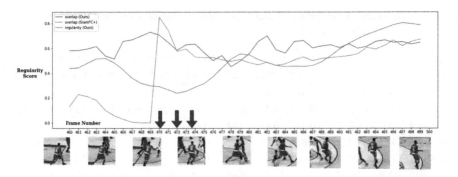

Fig. 4. Visualization of tracker accuracy in terms of IOU vs the frame number on x axis. From the figure, proposed method has larger overlap. Red arrow indicates points of drastic changes. (Color figure online)

5 Conclusion

Adaptive Siamese trackers commonly rely on the tracker's output to update the target model. In this paper, we have identified shortcomings with this approach, and proposed a generative model to predict a synthetic target template based on the appearance of several templates from previous time steps. Since the generative model learns the future template from the distribution over past time steps, it suppresses stochastic noise. We also propose a change detection mechanism to avoid noisy updates during abrupt changes in target appearance. Our proposed method can be integrated into any Siamese tracker, and results achieved on VOT16, VOT17, OTB-50, and OTB-100 datasets indicate that it can provide a high level of robustness (can track for a longer period before drifting) compared to state-of-the-art adaptive and baseline trackers.

References

1. Bertinetto, L., Valmadre, J., Henriques, J.F., Vedaldi, A., Torr, P.H.: Fully-convolutional Siamese networks for object tracking. arXiv:1606.09549 (2016)
2. Bhat, G., Danelljan, M., Gool, L.V., Timofte, R.: Learning discriminative model prediction for tracking. In: ICCV 2019
3. Danelljan, M., Bhat, G., Khan, F.S., Felsberg, M.: Atom: accurate tracking by overlap maximization. In: CVPR (2019)
4. Danelljan, M., Gool, L.V., Timofte, R.: Probabilistic regression for visual tracking. In: CVPR (2020)
5. Dong, X., Shen, J.: Triplet loss in Siamese network for object tracking. In: ECCV (2018)
6. Duman, E., Erdem, O.A.: Anomaly detection in videos using optical flow and convolutional autoencoder. IEEE Access **7**, 183914–183923 (2019)
7. Fan, H., Ling, H.: Siamese cascaded region proposal networks for real-time visual tracking. In: CVPR (2019)
8. Guo, D., Wang, J., Cui, Y., Wang, Z., Chen, S.: Siamcar: Siamese fully convolutional classification and regression for visual tracking. In: CVPR (2020)
9. Guo, Q., Feng, W., Zhou, C., Huang, R., Wan, L., Wang, S.: Learning dynamic Siamese network for visual object tracking. In: ICCV (2017)

10. Hare, S., et al.: Struck: Structured output tracking with kernels. IEEE Trans. Pattern Anal. Mach. Intell. **38**(10), 2096–2109 (2016)
11. He, A., Luo, C., Tian, X., Zeng, W.: A twofold Siamese network for real-time object tracking. In: CVPR 2018
12. Henriques, J.F., Caseiro, R., Martins, P., Batista, J.: High-speed tracking with kernelized correlation filters. IEEE Trans. Pattern Anal. Mach. Int. **37**(3), 583–596 (2015)
13. Huang, L., Zhao, X., Huang, K.: Got-10k: a large high-diversity benchmark for generic object tracking in the wild. IEEE Trans. Pattern Anal. Mach. Intell. **43**, 1562–1577 (2019)
14. Kristan, M., et al.: The visual object tracking vot2017 challenge results. In: ICCVW (2017)
15. Kristan, M., et al.: The sixth visual object tracking vot2018 challenge results (2018)
16. Li, B., Wu, W., Wang, Q., Zhang, F., Xing, J., Yan, J.S.: Evolution of Siamese visual tracking with very deep networks. In: CVPR (2019)
17. Li, B., Yan, J., Wu, W., Zhu, Z., Hu, X.: High performance visual tracking with Siamese region proposal network. In: CVPR (2018)
18. Li, Y., Zhang, X.: Siamvgg: visual tracking using deeper Siamese networks (2019)
19. Nam, H., Han, B.: Learning multi-domain convolutional neural networks for visual tracking. In: CVPR (2016)
20. Nebehay, G., Pflugfelder, R.: Consensus-based matching and tracking of keypoints for object tracking. In: WACV (2014)
21. Salti, S., Cavallaro, A., Stefano, L.D.: Adaptive appearance modeling for video tracking: Survey and evaluation. IEEE Trans. Image Process. **21**(10), 4334–4348 (2012)
22. Song, Y., et al.: Vital: visual tracking via adversarial learning. In: CVPR (2018)
23. Sosnovik, I., Moskalev, A., Smeulders, A.W.: Scale equivariance improves Siamese tracking. In: WACV (2021)
24. Tang, Y., Zhao, L., Zhang, S., Gong, C., Li, G., Yang, J.: Integrating prediction and reconstruction for anomaly detection. Pattern Recogn. Lett. **129**, 123–130 (2020)
25. Tao, R., Gavves, E., Smeulders, A.W.: Siamese instance search for tracking. In: CVPR (2016)
26. Valmadre, J., Bertinetto, L., Henriques, J., Vedaldi, A., Torr, P.H.: End-to-end representation learning for correlation filter based tracking. In: CVPR (2017)
27. Wang, X., O'Brien, M., Xiang, C., Xu, B., Najjaran, H.: Real-time visual tracking via robust kernelized correlation filter. In: ICRA (2017)
28. Wu, Y., Lim, J., Yang, M.H.: Online object tracking: a benchmark. In: CVPR (2013)
29. Yang, T., Chan, A.B.: Learning dynamic memory nets for object tracking. In: ECCV (2018)
30. Yao, Y., Wu, X., Zhang, L., Shan, S., Zuo, W.: Joint representation and truncated inference learning for correlation filter based tracking. In: ECCV (2018)
31. Zhang, L., Gonzalez-Garcia, A., Weijer, J.V.D., Danelljan, M., Khan, F.S.: Learning the model update for Siamese trackers. In: ICCV (2019)
32. Zhang, Y., Wang, L., Qi, J., Wang, D., Feng, M., Lu, H.: Structured Siamese network for real-time visual tracking. In: ECCV (2018)
33. Zhang, Z., Peng, H.: Deeper and wider Siamese networks for real-time visual tracking. In: CVPR (2019)
34. Zhang, Z., Peng, H., Fu, J., Li, B., Hu, W.: Ocean: Object-aware anchor-free tracking. In: ECCV (2020)
35. Zhao, Y., Deng, B., Shen, C., Liu, Y., Lu, H., Hua, X.S.: Spatio-temporal autoencoder for video anomaly detection. In: ICM (2017)
36. Zhong, B., Bai, B., Li, J., Zhang, Y., Fu, Y.: Hierarchical tracking by reinforcement learning-based searching and coarse-to-fine verifying. IEEE Trans. Image Process. **28**, 2331–2341 (2018)
37. Zhu, Z., Wang, Q., Bo, L., Wu, W., Yan, J., Hu, W.: Distractor-aware Siamese networks for visual object tracking. In: ECCV (2018)

From Synthetic to One-Shot Regression of Camera-Agnostic Human Performances

Julian Habekost[1]([✉]), Kunkun Pang[1], Takaaki Shiratori[2], and Taku Komura[1]

[1] School of Informatics, University of Edinburgh, Edinburgh, UK
{julian.habekost,k.pang,tkomura}@ed.ac.uk
[2] Facebook Reality Labs, Pittsburgh, USA
tshiratori@fb.com

Abstract. Capturing accurate 3D human performances in global space from a static monocular video is an ill-posed problem. It requires solving various depth ambiguities and information about the camera's intrinsics and extrinsics. Therefore, most methods either learn on given cameras or require to know the camera's parameters. We instead show that a camera's extrinsics and intrinsics can be regressed jointly with human's position in global space, joint angles and body shape only from long sequences of 2D motion estimates. We exploit a static camera's constant parameters by training a model that can be applied to sequences with arbitrary length with only a single forward pass while allowing full bidirectional information flow. We show that full temporal information flow is especially necessary when improving consistency through an adversarial network. Our training dataset is exclusively synthetic, and no domain adaptation is used. We achieve one of the best Human3.6M joint's error performances for models that do not use the Human3.6M training data.

Keywords: Human performance · Monocular video · Synthetic data

1 Introduction

3D human performance estimation from monocular videos is a challenging topic that attracts researchers attention from various areas such as computer animation, virtual reality, surveillance, health-care etc. One major problem is that this task is entangled with the camera: If a person is lying or standing straight on the floor can either be judged through a high level of visual understanding of the surroundings or other information about the camera angle and position. This is why the early human pose estimation task is only concerned with camera-relative body poses [15,16]. But the difference between laying and standing matters for performance capture, so subsequent work started to assume the camera intrinsics and extrinsics as given [25,27].

We instead propose a method that learns to regress the extrinsics and intrinsics implicitly and explicitly together with the 3D performance from 2D human

---

Supported by Facebook Reality Labs.

M. El Yacoubi et al. (Eds.): ICPRAI 2022, LNCS 13363, pp. 514–525, 2022.
https://doi.org/10.1007/978-3-031-09037-0_42

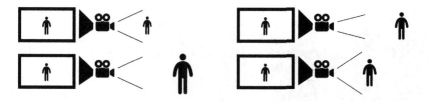

Fig. 1. Depth ambiguities of unknown monocular cameras. For all the depicted cases the person appears similar sized at the camera's viewfinder. We cannot differentiate between smaller people close and taller people further away (A.). Second, the field of view (FoV) influences how near or far objects and people appear (B.).

motion. The camera is unknown but static throughout one motion sequence and the motion is performed on a ground plane. Apart from the illustrated rotation ambiguity, this also is supposed to solve the FoV (field of view) depth ambiguity depicted in Fig. 1 B. That is possible just from 2D motion can be understood when imaging a person coming towards the camera with a constant walking speed: A large FoV will make the person's projected 2D size increase quicker. Further, we can learn the ground plane implicitly through foot contacts and other types of interaction of the subject with the ground plane. To achieve this Our method uses

- a synthetic dataset that renders minute-long videos with various settings of the body shape, camera parameters, occluders and backgrounds,
- DensePose [24] to obtain an intermediate 2D motion representation,
- and a model that is able to do one-shot regressions on arbitrarily large sequences with global temporal information flow.

We show that global motion estimation and explicit camera estimation is possible with our method. Further, our method is the only domain generalization approach to the popular Human3.6M [7] dataset known to us. We also beat all Human3.6M domain adaptation tasks in local pose performance.

2   Related Work

Local Pose Estimation. This is the task of estimating a human's pose rotated relative to the camera and with the hip centered at the origin. Martinez et al. [15] regress 2D keypoint detections [2,18] to 3D joint positions. Zhou et al. [28] directly incorporate a depth regression into a formerly 2D-only keypoint regressor. They use an adversarial pose prior when only 2D supervision is available. Kanazawa et al. [8] estimate both 3D pose and body shape based on SMPL [12], a parametric model of human shape and pose. Pavllo et al. [20] introduce a temporal model with dilated convolutions.

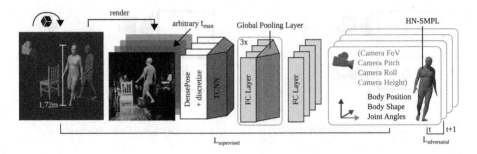

Fig. 2. We render differently body shaped subjects scaled to a body height of 172 cm together with small occlusions in front of a random background. DensePose [24] gives us projected UV maps that we then discretize for training feasibility. The global pooling enables bidirectional information flow without temporal limits. The HN-SMPL is a height normalized PCA-based subspace of SMPL.

Apart from our focus on the harder task of estimating global motion rotated relative to the world, another contrast is that these methods assume the camera intrinsics or field of view as known; in most cases [8,10,15,16,19,20,28] implicitly through training and evaluating on the same cameras in Human3.6M [7].

Global Pose Estimation. Here the estimated human poses are rotated and translated relative to the world's ground plane. Mehta et al.[17] use procrustes alignment style post-processing on per frame estimations with a given camera to obtain a temporally consistent real time global pose from a local pose estimator. Shimada et al. [25] establish a baseline by optimizing 2D and 3D keypoints from a local pose estimator [9] to match a reprojection loss given the camera extrinsics and intrinsics. This shows that with known camera and 2D keypoints the task of local and global pose estimation are equivalent up to a classic test-time optimization problem. It has been extended [25,27] by including temporal physical simulations and constraints into this projection based optimization loop. Rempe et al. [22] use the same optimization loop with a motion VAE instead of a physics simulation. All of these methods need camera intrinsics and extrinsics to be known, which our work explicitly does not rely on. Further all of these global pose works are based on some kind of test-time optimization; only ours is a purely one shot regression.

Domain Adaptation. Theoretically, training a deep model with fewer data could lead to worse generalisation performance [1,5]. This problem becomes more prominent if there is insufficient data on the target domain. To overcome this, researchers proposed to reformalise the pose estimation as a domain adaptation problem. Chen et al. [3] adapted the trained model to Human3.6M by fine-tuning in a supervised manner, whereas Chen et al. [4] and Habekost et al. [6] applied domain adversarial learning without using ground truth. Although these models can learn the dataset-specific intrinsics (i.e. same for training and testing), they may not be suitable for the task without a training set. Apart from this,

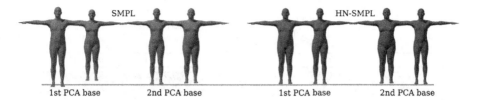

Fig. 3. HN-SMPL (Height-Normalized-SMPL) expresses all body shape variation except total body height through the bases of a PCA. The pairs show +1 and −1 of the noted PCA-basis. Note that even though less visible, height variation also does occur on other than the 1st SMPL PCA-base.

some works such as [9,10,23] use unpaired or unlabeled data, they use it to complement the supervised learning on Human3.6M.

Here, we go one step further and train the system without collecting the training data or any testing data except for the specific example of interest from the target dataset. The system will be trained on a synthetic dataset and generalize to an unseen Human3.6M dataset. This makes our work unique from existing works.

3 Synthetic Training Data Generation

Height Normalization. Due to the scale ambiguity of monocular video, it is impossible to estimate the height of a subject without reference or calibration (see Fig. 1A). We, therefore, assume that every subject has the height of 1.72 m, which is the average human height implied by the SMPL model. We circumvent the same scaling ambiguity for translation estimates by this assumption. Consequentially we predict the subject's body-height-normalized body shape and the subject's body-height-normalized translation. If the subject's real body height is known, the normalized translation can easily be scaled by the ratio between known and normalized body height to obtain a translation that adheres to scale.

The PCA-based SMPL body shape space implicitly and non-trivially embeds the total height. We propose a similar body shape space but with a fixed height. We sample the SMPL with random body shapes and T-pose angles, normalize the vertices by scaling the height difference between the top and bottom vertices to 1.72 m. These samples of scaled SMPL meshes are used to fit a new PCA, which then embeds a body space that is independent of the absolute body height (see 3). We only take the eight principal components. In order to be able to map back to the SMPL shape space, we fit the SMPL model to our height normalized body mesh by iterative gradient descent. We then learn a mapping from the new space to the SMPL body shape space with a simple neural network Θ with two layers and 16 hidden units each. To infer the mesh or joint positions from an HN-SMPL body shape β_{HN}, the SMPL body shape $\beta = \Theta(\beta^{HN})$ can be calculated.

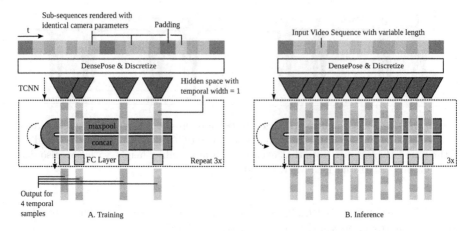

Fig. 4. The neural network regression model in detail. Input, output and hidden space are depicted in green. Processing steps and network functions have black borders around them. Similarly shaped and colored network functions share their weights. The forward pass direction is depicted through dotted lines. (Colour figure online)

Synthetic Sequence Rendering. For each video sequence S to render we sample a body shape $\beta_S^{HN} \sim \mathcal{N}(\mathbf{1}_{10}, \mathbf{0}_{10})$ and retarget all motions in S to this shape. We, therefore, randomly sample motion clips from the AMASS dataset. After retargeting, we randomly rotate the motion clip perpendicular to the ground plane and randomly translate it by $T_{xy} \sim \mathcal{N}(\mathbf{3}_2, \mathbf{0}_2)$ parallel to the ground plane. Each sequence has a uniquely random camera with a different pitch, roll, height and field of view. Only the yaw is kept such that the camera looks down the Z-axis because the camera's yaw is arbitrary and not inferable. Our random distributions cover most reasonable settings to capture human performances, from extremely close to exceptionally far away, from slightly up-looking to almost from above.

We simply concatenate the motion clips until a minimum of 60 s or 600 frames at 10fps is reached. Because we don't truncate sequences, the total length is variable and effectively a Poisson distribution starting at frame 600. Most sequences have a total length of around 700, but some rare examples of up to 2000 frame lengths exist.

Note that we do not transition between motion clips within a video sequence and account for this later in the model. If we only use long, continuous motion clips, the dataset size and variety would be reduced. Further, long motion clips often revolve around similar and repetitive actions, yielding global predictability that we want to avoid as our model could overfit it.

IUV Discretization. We choose IUV-Maps obtained with DensePose as an intermediate representation. This aims to leave the domain gap between simulated and real data to DensePose. This also reduces the data dimensionality while

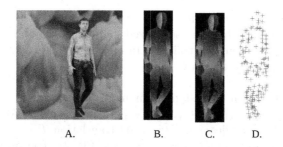

A.   B.   C.   D.

Fig. 5. The process of UV discretization visualized. DensePose [24] (B.) gives a dense map of the UV coordinates in image space. There are 178 discrete points (D.) in the final set.

keeping most of the useful information. We further reduce and adapt it to our sequence model by discretizing the dense IUV maps.

DensPose gives a three-channeled dense representation $D(x,y) \in \mathbb{N} \times \mathbb{R}^2$ containing the part index $D(x,y)_i$ with the highest posterior probability $P(i = p|x,y)$ and the part-specific projected U- and V-coordinates $D(x,y)_{uv}$ at the image pixels x, y. We heuristically choose a set of 178 IUV-coordinates based on their distance to each other. For each predefined IUV-coordinate C we exhaustively search in the image's pixel space x, y:

$$D(x,y)_i = C_i \tag{1}$$

$$d_{uv} = \|D(x,y)_{uv} - C_{uv}\|_2 \tag{2}$$

$$\min_{x,y} d_{uv}. \tag{3}$$

We don't specify a threshold for the part-specific UV-distance d_{uv}. As long as the part p is visible, all $C, C_i = p$ for that part will be found. As a result some C lie on the boundary of the part's segmentation mask, which gives a rough indication of the body part's shape.

4   Model

Network Design. Similar to [6], our model Φ is composed of a temporal convolutional neural network (TCNN). The TCNN aggregates local features of a 32 frame wide neighborhood. Each 1D convolutional layer down-samples the temporal space by half with stride 2. Five convolutional layers are necessary to arrive at a hidden space with a temporal width of one. In Fig. 4, the max-pooling is applied on the hidden units over the entire temporal channel so that the model can extract a sequence-level information flow. This method is inspired by Point-Net [21] and allows scaling the amount of temporal samples to an arbitrary length in a single regression. The max-pooling results are concatenated and a feed-forward layer is applied. These steps of max-pooling, concatenation, and fully-connected layer are repeated three times. The last fully-connected layer produces the model's output for every temporal step that the regression has originally been applied to. We use a fixed number of temporal neighborhoods sampled from the sequence in training. In inference, our model can regress the whole input sequence in one shot.

Network Loss. For each time step t, our network Φ maps the discretized IUV coordinates $c = \{\{c_{xi}, c_{yi}\}_1, ...\{c_{xi}, c_{yi}\}_{178}\} \in \mathbb{R}^{356}$ to a HN-SMPL body shape $\beta^{HN} \in \mathbb{R}^8$, 24 joint angles $\theta \in \mathbb{R}^{72}$, a 3D translation $T \in \mathbb{R}^3$ and a camera view $V = \{pitch, roll, height, fov\} \in \mathbb{R}^4$ (see Fig. 2). The objective function consists of an adversarial loss, and a weighted L1-loss between those mentioned components $X = \{\beta^{HN}, \theta, T, V\}$ and the network prediction $\Phi(c)$:

$$\ell = \sum_t (\sum_X l_X \cdot L_1(X, \Phi(c_t)) + L_{adversarial}$$ (4)

Table 1. Errors of camera estimation on the CP dataset, compared to methods that use images for camera parameter estimation.

Method	FoV (°)	Pitch (°)	Height (mm)
ScaleNet [29]	3.63	2.11	–
CamCalib [11]	3.14	1.80	–
Ours (linear)	3.84	2.95	32.8
Ours (adversarial + pooling)	3.92	3.21	36.1

5   Experiments

Datasets. Our synthetic training dataset uses motion sequences from **AMASS** [14] rendered with textures from **SURREAL** [26] and random CC0-licensed images as background. The horizontal field of view is drawn from [80°, 34°] for each sequence. We chose square 1000 × 1000 pixel images, which results in the vertical field of view being the same.

For evaluation we use subjects 9 and 11 of **Human3.6M** [7]. The other subjects are not used in this work. Note that the Human3.6M field of view is 46.4°. We report the mean per joint error (MPJE) and procrustes-aligned mean per joint error (PA-MPJE). We also make our own evaluation dataset where people walk in circles from different perspectives (**CP**, see Fig. 8). Each of the 25 sequences produced by one of the five different subjects has a different camera angle and focal length in a distribution similar to the training dataset. We only obtain the motion starting position as the ground truth and only report the translation error to this starting position.

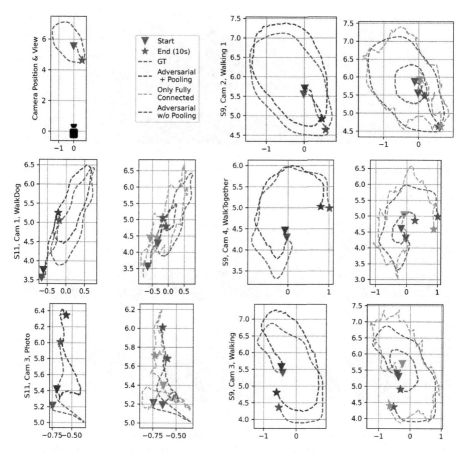

Fig. 6. Translation results on the first 10 s of Human3.6M sequences viewed from above. After the overview and legend, each two plots next to each other belong to the same sequence.

Training. We train on synthetic dataset sizes of 10 k, 20 k and 70 k sequences until the performance of the identical 1 k validation sequences cannot be further improved. We report our model's results with the 70 k training sample size, except when stated otherwise. In training, we sample 16 temporal neighborhoods from each sequence. The neural network has 6 linear layers with 2048 hidden units and concatenate 512 max-pooled hidden units, Adam [13] as the optimizer and a learning rate of $1e^{-4}$. We set $l_\theta = 1000, l_\beta = 10, l_T = 100$ and $l_V = 1$. We report results with the 70 k training set model, except when stated otherwise.

Results. Table 3 shows our local pose performance on Human3.6M. We are only beaten by methods that integrate supervised training into their model. Besides, we beat all domain adaptation methods on Human3.6M. This result is reasonable. The supervised learning approaches learn the dataset-specific camera

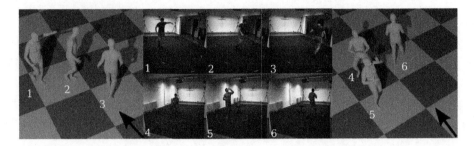

Fig. 7. Qualitative results of two Human3.6m test sequences. Both the pose and the translations are depicted. The camera is out of the rendered frame but its direction is shown with a black arrow.

Fig. 8. Our **CP** evaluation dataset. For different field of views, the camera is first calibrated (A). A marker on the floor (B) is used to infer the ground truth motion starting position.

intrinsics and have no domain gap, whereas our approach does not have domain knowledge and intrinsics.

Figure 6 shows a qualitative evaluation of the translation. It shows that the adversarial network pushes the model towards a more stable, smoother and more realistic overall motion shape. But without global pooling, the adversarial network's regime seems too strong; the model cannot infer the overall motion shape with only local temporal knowledge and collapses into a smaller motion.

As shown in the Table 2, the fully connected layer with the TCNN seems to deliver a slightly better performance than our adversarial approach on the 70k dataset. The gap becomes more extensive when a smaller training dataset is used, which is also reflected in the differences between training and validation data. This gap cannot be explained via a domain gap but simply because the training set is too small for enabling the model to learn the synthetic domain perfectly and not overfit to the training set. This is the reason why we believe

Table 2. Translation errors (in mm, non-procrustes) for different training set sizes. Both train and val are synthetic datasets.

Method	10 k				20 k				70 k			
	Train	val	H36	CP	Train	val	H36	CP	Train	val	H36	CP
Only FC	248	482	500	843	293	395	426	683	294	380	406	531
Advers. + Pool.	308	694	915	1072	323	476	721	882	315	414	421	539

Table 3. Evaluation results on Human3.6M sorted by MPJPE. Domain adaptation (DA) methods use Human3.6M training videos together with a non-GT based supervision. Supervised (S) papers directly train on the Human3.6M training set. Methods with implicit camera have seen the Human3.6M cameras, which are identical for training and testing. Domain generalization (DG) methods have not seen any images, cameras or motion from Human3.6M.

Method	MPJPE↓	PA-MPJPE(↓)	Task	Camera
Chen et al.[3]	136.1	–	DA	Implicit
Habekost et al. [6]	118.2	–	DA	Given
Chen et al. [4]	–	68.0	DA	Implicit
Kanazawa et al. [8] unpaired	106.8	66.5	DA	Implicit
Shimada et al. [25]	97.4	65.1	S	Given
Kanazawa et al. [8] paired	88.0	56.8	S	Implicit
Ours	87.9	66.9	**DG**	**Unseen**
Rhodin et al. [23]	66.8	51.6	S	Implicit
Kocabas et al. [10]	65.6	41.4	S	Implicit
Martinez et al. [15]	62.9	47.7	S	Implicit

there is still room for improving the proposed method's translation accuracy by generating an even larger dataset.

There are methods [25,27] that report the Human3.6m translation error we report in Table 2 and they are significantly better. This is simply due to the methods assuming known camera parameters. But when camera parameters are unknown, like for the CP dataset, these do not work. Hence it is impossible to infer the subject's translation in our CP dataset, which we also report in Table 2. We argue that implicit camera estimation is half of the work necessary for out model to infer the subject's translation and a comparison would be unfair.

Table 1 shows our camera estimation results compared to other deep learning methods on image data. We do not expect to outperform these models but merely show that the results are sensible and can be regressed from only 2D human motion. Also, only our method can infer the camera's height (inversely scaled to the human's size in the video). Note that our method can regress the camera parameters in one shot. We show this to convince our reader that our model can implicitly learn the camera estimation necessary for global pose estimation.

6   Conclusion

By using a large scale synthetic dataset coupled with DensePose [24] as a 2D human motion extractor and an one-shot regression network that encourages global information flow, we show that human performance capture is possible without externally calibrated cameras or visual understanding of the surroundings. We demonstrate that the camera's intrinsics and extrinsics can even be estimated explicitly. To our knowledge, by doing so we have created the first domain generalization approach for the popular Human3.6M [7] dataset. Our result is comparable with some supervised learning approaches and outperforms all domain adaptation based methods on Human3.6m's local pose performance.

References

1. Arora, S., Ge, R., Neyshabur, B., Zhang, Y.: Stronger generalization bounds for deep nets via a compression approach. In: ICML (2018)
2. Cao, Z., Simon, T., Wei, S.E., Sheikh, Y.: Realtime multi-person 2d pose estimation using part affinity fields. In: CVPR (2017)
3. Chen, C.H., Ramanan, D.: 3d human pose estimation = 2d pose estimation + matching. In: CVPR (2017)
4. Chen, C.H., et al.: Unsupervised 3d pose estimation with geometric self-supervision. In: CVPR (2019)
5. Fengxiang He, D.T.: Recent advances in deep learning theory. CoRR abs/2012.10931 (2020)
6. Habekost, J., Shiratori, T., Ye, Y., Komura, T.: Learning 3d global human motion estimation from unpaired, disjoint datasets. In: BMVC (2020)
7. Ionescu, C., Papava, D., Olaru, V., Sminchisescu, C.: Human3.6m: Large scale datasets and predictive methods for 3d human sensing in natural environments. IEEE Trans. Pattern Anal. Mach. Intell. **36**(7), 1325–1339 (2014)
8. Kanazawa, A., Black, M.J., Jacobs, D.W., Malik, J.: End-to-end recovery of human shape and pose. In: CVPR (2018)
9. Kanazawa, A., Zhang, J.Y., Felsen, P., Malik, J.: Learning 3d human dynamics from video. In: CVPR (2019)
10. Kocabas, M., Athanasiou, N., Black, M.J.: Vibe: video inference for human body pose and shape estimation (2019). arXiv:1912.05656
11. Kocabas, M., Huang, C.H.P., Tesch, J., Müller, L., Hilliges, O., Black, M.J.: SPEC: seeing people in the wild with an estimated camera. In: ICCV (2021)
12. Loper, M., Mahmood, N., Romero, J., Pons-Moll, G., Black, M.J.: SMPL: a skinned multi-person linear model. In: SIGGRAPH Asia (2015)
13. Loshchilov, I., Hutter, F.: Fixing weight decay regularization in adam. CoRR abs/1711.05101 (2017)
14. Mahmood, N., Ghorbani, N., Troje, N.F., Pons-Moll, G., Black, M.J.: Amass: archive of motion capture as surface shapes. In: ICCV (2019)
15. Martinez, J., Hossain, R., Romero, J., Little, J.J.: A simple yet effective baseline for 3d human pose estimation. In: ICCV (2017)
16. Mehta, D., et al.: Monocular 3d human pose estimation in the wild using improved CNN supervision. In: 3DV (2017)
17. Mehta, D., et al.: Vnect: real-time 3d human pose estimation with a single RGB camera. ACM Trans. Graphics (TOG) **36**(4), 1–14 (2017)

18. Newell, A., Yang, K., Deng, J.: Stacked hourglass networks for human pose estimation. In: Leibe, B., Matas, J., Sebe, N., Welling, M. (eds.) ECCV 2016. LNCS, vol. 9912, pp. 483–499. Springer, Cham (2016). https://doi.org/10.1007/978-3-319-46484-8_29

19. Pavlakos, G., Zhu, L., Zhou, X., Daniilidis, K.: Learning to estimate 3D human pose and shape from a single color image. In: CVPR (2018)

20. Pavllo, D., Feichtenhofer, C., Grangier, D., Auli, M.: 3d human pose estimation in video with temporal convolutions and semi-supervised training. arXiv abs/1811.11742 (2018)

21. Qi, C.R., Su, H., Mo, K., Guibas, L.J.: Pointnet: deep learning on point sets for 3d classification and segmentation. arXiv preprint arXiv:1612.00593 (2016)

22. Rempe, D., Birdal, T., Hertzmann, A., Yang, J., Sridhar, S., Guibas, L.J.: Humor: 3d human motion model for robust pose estimation. In: ICCV (2021)

23. Rhodin, H., et al.: Learning monocular 3d human pose estimation from multi-view images. In: CVPR (2020)

24. Guler, R.A., Natalia Neverova, I.K.: Densepose: dense human pose estimation in the wild. In: CVPR (2018)

25. Shimada, S., Golyanik, V., Xu, W., Theobalt, C.: Physcap: physically plausible monocular 3d motion capture in real time. ACM Trans. Graphics (TOG) **39**(6), 1–16 (2020)

26. Varol, G., et al.: Learning from synthetic humans. In: CVPR (2017)

27. Xie, K., Wang, T., Iqbal, U., Guo, Y., Fidler, S., Shkurti, F.: Physics-based human motion estimation and synthesis from videos. In: ICCV (2021)

28. Zhou, X., Huang, Q., Sun, X., Xue, X., Wei, Y.: Towards 3d human pose estimation in the wild: a weakly-supervised approach. In: ICCV (2017)

29. Zhu, R.: single view metrology in the wild. In: Vedaldi, A., Bischof, H., Brox, T., Frahm, J.-M. (eds.) ECCV 2020. LNCS, vol. 12356, pp. 316–333. Springer, Cham (2020). https://doi.org/10.1007/978-3-030-58621-8_19

Feature

Computation of 2D Discrete Geometric Moments Through Inclusion-Exclusion

Lidija Čomić[1] and Paola Magillo[2]([✉])

[1] Faculty of Technical Sciences, University of Novi Sad, Novi Sad, Serbia
comic@uns.ac.rs
[2] Department of Computer Science, Bioengineering, Robotics, and Systems Engineering, University of Genova, Genova, Italy
magillo@dibris.unige.it

Abstract. We propose a new formula for computing discrete geometric moments on 2D binary images. The new formula is based on the inclusion-exclusion principle, and is especially tailored for images coming from computer art, characterized by a prevalence of horizontal and vertical lines. On the target class of images, our formula reduces the number of pixels where calculations are to be performed.

1 Introduction

Geometric moments are a classic tool in image processing and pattern recognition. Based on geometric moments of order up to three, Hu [4] introduced a set of quantities, invariant to similarity transformations (translation, scaling and rotation), through which numerous shape descriptors have been defined. Many formulas for moments computation have been proposed (for a review, see [3]). We propose another one, based on inclusion-exclusion, i.e., on the sum of signed moments of overlapping axis-aligned rectangles. Our formula is especially suitable for images where the objects have a prevalence of vertical and horizontal lines in their contour. This is the case of most computer-produced art, including icons, signals, logos, etc.

2 Background Notions

We consider a bi-dimensional world having two colors, black and white, where the object of interest is black, and the background is white. This world can be continuous or digital. In the latter case, the world is an image, i.e., a raster of $N \times M$ pixels, each either black or white.

2.1 Geometric (Cartesian) Moments

For an object O in the continuous world, its geometric moment of order $p + q$ is defined as

$$m_{p,q}(O) = \int_O x^p y^q dx dy.$$

© Springer Nature Switzerland AG 2022
M. El Yacoubi et al. (Eds.): ICPRAI 2022, LNCS 13363, pp. 529–540, 2022.
https://doi.org/10.1007/978-3-031-09037-0_43

For a digital object O, the geometric moment is usually approximated by

$$m_{p,q}(O) = \sum_{(i,j)\in O} i^p j^q. \tag{1}$$

When the digital object is a rectangle R composed of pixels centered at points in $[I,J] \times [K,L] \cap \mathbb{N}^2$, with I, J, K, L integers,

$$m_{p,q}(R) = \sum_{i=I}^{J} i^p \sum_{j=K}^{L} j^q = (S_p(J) - S_p(I-1)) \cdot (S_q(L) - S_q(K-1)), \tag{2}$$

where S_p and S_q denote the sum of exponentials, defined as $S_k(n) = \sum_{h=1}^{n} h^k$.

In particular, if $I = K = 1$ then the rectangle $R(J,L)$ is determined by its upper right vertex with coordinates $(J + \frac{1}{2}, L + \frac{1}{2})$ and Formula (2) becomes

$$m_{p,q}(R(J,L)) = \sum_{i=1}^{J} i^p \sum_{j=1}^{L} j^q = S_p(J) \cdot S_q(L). \tag{3}$$

The sums S_k of exponentials, for $k \leq 3$ (which are the relevant values needed for moment invariants), are given by $S_0(n) = n$, $S_1(n) = n(n+1)/2$, $S_2(n) = n^3/3 + n^2/2 + n/6$, $S_3(n) = n^4/4 + n^3/2 + n^2/4$.

2.2   Green's Theorem

Green's theorem gives a connection between a double integral over a simply connected region and the line integral along the boundary of the region. We review briefly Green's theorem in the continuous case, and its discrete version.

If P and Q are continuous functions of two variables with continuous partial derivatives over a simply connected domain O with piece-wise smooth simple closed boundary ∂O, the continuous Green's theorem states that

$$\int_{\partial O} P dx + Q dy = \int_{O} \left(\frac{\partial Q}{\partial x} - \frac{\partial P}{\partial y} \right) dx dy,$$

with ∂O oriented counterclockwise. When applied to the computation of moments, Green's theorem is used to convert the double integral to a (non-unique) line integral. One (often used) solution of

$$x^p y^q = \frac{\partial Q}{\partial x} - \frac{\partial P}{\partial y},$$

is $P = \frac{1}{p+1} x^{p+1} y^q$ and $Q = 0$ [14].

The discrete version of Green's theorem, in the formulation proposed by Tang [13], states that

$$\sum_{(i,j)\in O} f(i,j) = \sum_{(i,j)\in \mathcal{C}(O)} \left(F_x(i,j) D_Y(i,j) + f(i,j) C_Y(i,j) \right), \tag{4}$$

where $\mathcal{C}(O)$ is the set of contour pixels of O (i.e., the pixels of O that are edge-adjacent to at least one white pixel), $F_x(i,j) = \sum_{n=0}^{i} f(n,j)$, $D_Y(i,j) = 1$ or -1 if (i,j) is the first or last pixel of a run (a maximal set of contiguous black pixels in one row) with length > 1, otherwise it is 0; $C_Y(i,j) = 1$ if (i,j) is the first pixel of a run, otherwise it is 0 (see Fig. 1).

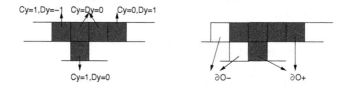

Fig. 1. Left: the values of C_Y and D_Y for a run consisting of more pixels (top) or of just one pixel (bottom); only pixels starting or ending a run give a non-zero contribution to the moments. Right: black pixels belonging to ∂O^+ and white pixels belonging to ∂O^- in the same configuration.

An equivalent formulation of the discrete version of the Green's theorem, proposed by Philips [6], states that

$$\sum_{(i,j)\in O} \nabla_x f(i,j) = \sum_{(i,j)\in\partial O^+} f(i,j) - \sum_{(i,j)\in\partial O^-} f(i,j), \tag{5}$$

where $\nabla_x f(i,j) = f(i,j) - f(i-1,j)$ and ∂O^+ is the set of black pixels with white right neighbor, while ∂O^- is the set of white pixels with black right neighbor (see Fig. 1).

3   Related Work

We are interested in the exact computation of discrete moments of digital objects. The relevant algorithms [3] either decompose the object into non-overlapping simple shapes, or they use some form of the discrete Green's theorem.

3.1   Decomposition-Based Algorithms

Algorithms in this class work on a decomposition of the object O, contained in the image, into non-overlapping rectangles. They are either designed for an image encoded in a specific data structure (quadtree [7] or run-length [10,11,16]) or they compute a decomposition in a pre-processing step [9,12].
    The δ-method proposed by Zakaria et al. [16] computes low-order moments of horizontally convex objects (i.e., with at most one run in each row). Li [5] generalized this algorithm to non-convex objects [2]. Spiliotis and Mertzios [10, 11] proposed another extension of [16], which first decomposes an object into

disjoint rectangular blocks by merging consecutive runs of equal spread and then computes the discrete moments of arbitrary order on the rectangles.

Sossa et al. [9] decompose the object into non-overlapping squares using morphological erosion. Their algorithm works also for objects with holes. Suk and Flusser [12] use distance transform to obtain the decomposition into squares.

The pre-processing stage, necessary to decompose the object, is expensive. Decomposition methods are convenient only if the object is compact (if it can be partitioned into a small number of squares) and a large number of moments is to be computed [12].

3.2   Boundary-Based Algorithms

Tang [13], Philips [6] and Yang and Albregtsen [15] proposed to use the discrete Green's theorem to compute low-order moments. In both formulas coming from the discrete Green's theorem (see Formulas (4) and (5) in Sect. 2.2), the only pixels giving a non-zero contribution to the sum are those lying on the contour of the object O, i.e, the pixels of O that are edge-adjacent to at least one white pixel.

The algorithm by Tang works on the cyclic sequence $(i_0, j_0), \ldots (i_l, j_l)$ of the contour pixels, which is given as a contour chain code. The used formula comes from (4) by taking $f(i, j) = i^p j^q$. This gives

$$F_x(i_n, j_n) = \sum_{h=0}^{i_n} f(h, j_n) = \sum_{h=0}^{i_n} h^p j_n^q = j_n^q S_p(i_n),$$

and

$$
\begin{aligned}
m_{p,q}(O) &= \sum_{(i,j) \in O} f(i,j) = \sum_{(i,j) \in O} i^p j^q \\
&= \sum_{n=0}^{l-1} \left(F_x(i_n, j_n) D_Y(i_n, j_n) + f(i_n, j_n) C_Y(i_n, j_n) \right) \\
&= \sum_{n=0}^{l-1} \left(F_x(i_n, j_n) D_Y(i_n, j_n) + i_n^p j_n^q C_Y(i_n, j_n) \right).
\end{aligned}
\tag{6}
$$

The algorithm by Philips [6] works on the runs, and applies the alternative formulation (5) of the discrete Green's theorem. The algorithm classifies the pixels during a raster scan. For the moment computation, Formula (5) is considered with $f(i, j) = g(i) j^q$, where $g(i)$ is such that $\nabla_x g(i) = i^p$. The moments are computed as

$$m_{p,q}(O) = \sum_{(i,j) \in \partial O^+} S_p(i) j^q - \sum_{(i,j) \in \partial O^-} S_p(i) j^q, \tag{7}$$

where ∂O^+ is the set of end pixels of the runs, and the immediate right neighbors of white pixels in ∂O^- are start pixels of the runs (see Fig. 1).

The obtained formula is the same as that of the δ-method of Zakaria et al. [16] (for horizontally convex objects), as formula (5) is equivalent to

$$\sum_{(i,j)\in O} f(i,j) = \sum_{(i,j)\in \partial O^+} \sum_{h=0}^{i} f(h,j) - \sum_{(i,j)\in \partial O^-} \sum_{h=0}^{i} f(h,j).$$

The algorithm by Yang and Albregtsen [15] considers the boundary of O (consisting of the edges between black and white pixels) instead of the contour of O (consisting of pixels). For horizontal edges, the term containing C_Y [13] vanishes. For vertical edges, $D_Y = \pm 1$ if the incident black pixel is the end pixel or the start pixel of a run, respectively. The final obtained formula is the same as that by Philips, but in [15] it is embedded within a contour following algorithm.

Flusser [1] and Flusser and Suk [2] improve on the algorithm by Philips by pre-calculating the sums $S_k(n)$, i.e., the integrals over the horizontal runs starting at the left image border. Sossa et al. [8] improved on the algorithm by Philips by computing some moments from runs in the x-direction (if $q > p$), and others from runs in the y-direction (if $q < p$) and simplifying the formulas by expressing them in terms of the pixels in O. Contour pixels are classified through the contour chain code. For objects with holes, the moment contributions of inner contours are subtracted from that of the outer contour.

4   Our Formula

We suppose that the object O is in the first quadrant, and contained in a rectangle of size $N \times M$. That is, O is a set of (black) pixels with integer coordinates (i,j) with $1 \le i \le N$ and $1 \le j \le M$. We pose no restrictions on the configuration of black pixels, so the object does not need to be (simply) connected, or convex.

The coordinates of the four vertices of the pixel (i,j) are $(i \pm \frac{1}{2}, j \pm \frac{1}{2})$. We consider the boundary ∂O as a set of line segments at inter-pixel level. We define the corner vertices of O as those vertices v such that the four incident pixels of v are not all white or all black, and are not two edge-adjacent white pixels and two edge-adjacent black pixels. The configurations of corner vertices are shown in Fig. 2.

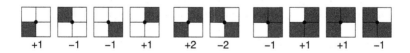

Fig. 2. Various configurations defining the corner vertices. The shown coefficient is associated with the lower left pixel of the configuration.

4.1   The Proposed Formula

We decompose the image into overlapping axis-aligned rectangles. Each rectangle is defined by the vertex $(\frac{1}{2}, \frac{1}{2})$ and by one corner vertex $(J + \frac{1}{2}, L + \frac{1}{2})$ of O. Figure 3 shows an object O and the considered rectangles. According to Formula (3), the moment of the rectangle associated with the corner vertex $(J + \frac{1}{2}, L + \frac{1}{2})$ is equal to $S_p(J) \cdot S_q(L)$.

The moments of O are then computed from rectangle moments through a simple inclusion-exclusion principle. We sum the moments of rectangles for each corner vertex in the boundary of O with the appropriate coefficient, shown in Fig. 2. Our formula for moment computation can be summarized as:

$$m_{p,q}(O) = \sum_{(x,y) \in \partial O} V(x,y) \cdot S_p(x - \frac{1}{2}) \cdot S_q(y - \frac{1}{2}) \tag{8}$$

where $V(x,y)$, called corner code, is non-zero for corners only, and its values are shown in Fig. 2. Note that $(x - \frac{1}{2}, y - \frac{1}{2})$ are the coordinates of the pixel having (x,y) as its upper right corner.

For the sample object O in the upper part of Fig. 3, $m_{0,0}(O) = 8$. We compute $m_{0,0}(O)$ as the sum over all the (non-degenerate) rectangles (see Fig. 3, bottom), and therefore we get $+12 - 6 + 4 - 1 + 2 - 8 + 5 = 8$.

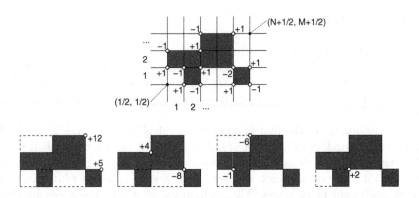

Fig. 3. Top: An object O consisting of 8 pixels, the limits N, M, its 13 corner pixels (marked with a white dot) with the coefficient of each. Bottom: the rectangles corresponding to each corner pixel (with the exception of those having $I = 0$ or $J = 0$, which are thus null rectangles), with the values of the associated summands in $m_{0,0}(O)$.

4.2   Proof of Correctness

Now, we prove that the value $m_{p,q}^R(O)$, computed by our Formula (8) is correct, i.e., equal to $m_{p,q}(O)$, for any object O. The proof is by induction on the number k of pixels in O. For the base case, $k = 0$, O is empty and trivially $m_{p,q}^R(O) = 0 = m_{p,q}(O)$.

We suppose that the formula is correct for objects with up to k pixels, $k \geq 0$, and let O be an object with $k + 1$ pixels. Let $P = (i, j)$ be the rightmost of the uppermost pixels in O. This means that the three vertex-adjacent pixels above P, and the one to the right of P are white (see Fig. 4).

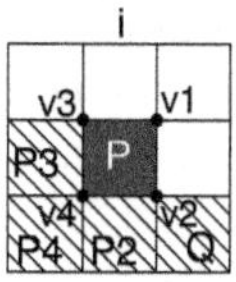

vert.	config.	contribution			vert.	config.	contribution		
		O	P	O'			O	P	O'
v_1		1	1	0	v_4		2	1	1
v_3		-1	-1	0	v_4		0	1	-1
v_3		0	-1	1	v_4		1	1	0
v_2		-2	-1	-1	v_4	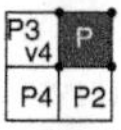	1	1	0
v_2		0	-1	1	v_4		1	1	0
v_2		-1	-1	0	v_4		-1	-2	1
v_2		-1	-1	0	v_4		0	1	-1
...	...	...			v_4	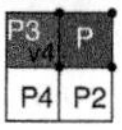	0	1	-1

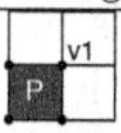

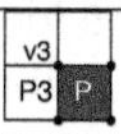

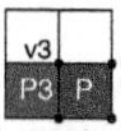

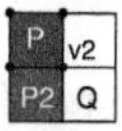

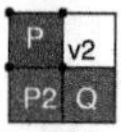

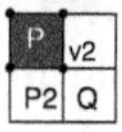

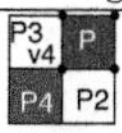

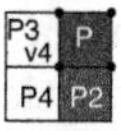

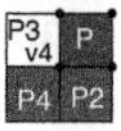

Fig. 4. Inductive step of the proof. Left: empty pixels are white, dashed pixels P_2, P_3, P_4 and Q can be black or white. Right: the contribution of each vertex v_1, v_2, v_3, v_4 to the moment of O, of P, and of $O' = O \setminus P$, in all possible configurations.

Let us remove P from O, obtaining O'. By inductive hypothesis, our formula computes correctly the moments of O' and of P. Since moments are additive, we can compute $m_{p,q}(O)$ as $m_{p,q}(O') + m_{p,q}(P)$, i.e., as $m_{p,q}^R(O') + m_{p,q}^R(P)$. We show that this is equal to $m_{p,q}^R(O)$.

Both $m_{p,q}^R(O') + m_{p,q}^R(P)$ and $m_{p,q}^R(O)$ are sums of corner contributions, with the coefficients shown in Fig. 2. Differences occur only at vertices v_1, v_2, v_3, v_4 (see Fig. 4). Each such vertex v_l is a corner in P, while it may or may not be a corner in O and O'. The table in Fig. 4 presents all possible cases, i.e., all possible configurations of pixels incident to v_l, for $l = 1 \ldots 4$, and shows the contribution of v_l to $m_{p,q}^R(O)$, $m_{p,q}^R(P)$, and $m_{p,q}^R(O')$.

As an example, let us consider the upper of the two rows concerning the contribution of the vertex v_3; in such case, v_3 is a corner in O and in P while it is not a corner in O'; its contribution has coefficient -1 in $m_{p,q}^R(O)$ and in $m_{p,q}^R(P)$, and 0 in $m_{p,q}^R(O')$. From the Table, we see that the contribution of the vertex v_l to $m_{p,q}^R(O)$ (first numeric column) is always equal to its contribution to $m_{p,q}^R(O') + m_{p,q}^R(P)$ (sum of the last two columns). Therefore $m_{p,q}^R(O') + m_{p,q}^R(P) = m_{p,q}^R(O)$ and thus $m_{p,q}^R(O) = m_{p,q}(O)$.

5   Experimental Validation

The contribution of this paper is in Formula (8). The used formula is just one component of a moment computation algorithm. Other components are the format of the input image and the procedure for pixel scanning. For example, an algorithm may scan a run-length encoded image, or it may follow a contour chain code, etc. Here, we consider those computational costs of an algorithm, which depend on the used formula: the number of pixels giving a non-zero contribution to the moment, and the number of arithmetic operations performed. For comparing our formula with others, we have embedded it into a simple raster scan. The implementation is in C language, using a library for big integers from https://github.com/dandclark/BigInt.

In Subsect. 5.1, we compare our formula with other representatives of the same class, i.e., boundary-based ones (see Sect. 3.2). In Subsect. 5.2, we compare it with a representative of the decomposition-based class (see Sect. 3.1).

5.1   Comparison with Other Boundary-Based Formulas

We compare our new Formula (8) with two classical formulas based on the discrete Green's theorem, namely Formula (6) used by Tang and Formula (7) used by Philips. We inserted the formulas into a simple image scanning algorithm. Being boundary-based, such formulas could be inserted into an algorithm operating on runs or contours. Our choice was guided by simplicity of implementation.

All the three considered formulas can be summarized as

$$m_{p,q} = \sum_{i,j} (\text{coefficient}(i,j) \cdot \text{ex}(i) \cdot \text{ey}(j))$$

or equivalently:

$$m_{p,q} = \sum_{j} \left(\text{ey}(j) \cdot \sum_{i} (\text{coefficient}(i,j) \cdot \text{ex}(i)) \right).$$

For our Formula (8), the coefficient is the corner code $V(i + \frac{1}{2}, j + \frac{1}{2})$ (see Sect. 4 and Fig. 2) and $\text{ex}(i) = S_p(i)$, $\text{ey}(j) = S_q(j)$. For Formula (6), the coefficients are actually two, D_y and C_y (see Sect. 2.2 and Fig. 1), $\text{ey}(j) = j^q$, while the inner contribution of the row, i.e., $\text{coefficient}(i,j) \cdot \text{ex}(i)$, consists of two terms $D_y \cdot S_p(i)$ and $C_y \cdot i^p$. For Formula (7), the coefficient is 1 or -1 if (i,j) belongs to ∂O^+ or ∂O^-, respectively (see Sect. 2.2 and Fig. 1), $\text{ex}(i) = S_p(i)$ and $\text{ey}(j) = j^q$.

The general pseudocode of the algorithm used for testing the formulas is shown in Fig. 5, where we assumed that the image containing the object has size $N \times M$, column coordinates are $i \in [1, N]$ and row coordinates are $j \in [1, M]$.

```
computeMoment(p, q)
1    m = 0 // the moment of order p+q
2    for j = 1 to M
3       a = 0 // the contribution of row j
4       for i = 1 to N
5          c = coefficient(i,j)
6          if (c not zero)
7             a = a + c * ex(i) // add the contribution of pixel (i,j)
8       m = m + a * ey(j) // add contrib. of row j
9    return m // the moment of order p+q
```

Fig. 5. General pseudocode of the algorithm used to test the formulas.

All three formulas need the values of $S_k(n)$. Similarly to [1] and [2], all such values are pre-computed and stored in a matrix.

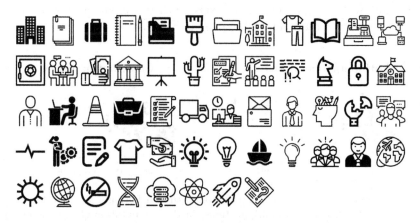

Fig. 6. Test inputs for the experiments. Each icon was used twice, the second time with a rotation of 90°. Icons are sorted from the best to the worst performance of our formula on them.

Our formula is especially suited for objects bounded mostly by axis-parallel lines, and therefore having few corners. Objects with such characteristics are common products of computer art, such as icons, signals, logos, etc. We considered a test set consisting of 56 icons from https://www.flaticon.com/free-icons/ (see Fig. 6), and their rotated versions, obtained by exchanging rows and columns. On such 112 test inputs, we computed moments $m_{p,q}$ with $p + q \leq 3$.

We compared the number of pixels contributing to the moment computation (i.e., those with a non-zero coefficient), and the number of performed multiplications and additions (not including the operations needed to compute the sums of exponentials, that are the same for the three formulas). Smaller numbers correspond to more efficient formulas. Formula (6) showed to be less efficient than Formula (7), therefore in the plots of Fig. 7 we compare our Formula (8) with (7) used by Philips. Most dots (precisely, 88 over 112) are above the bisecting line of the first quadrant, meaning that, on the corresponding test inputs, our formula performs better. The ratio of the number of contributing pixels with our formula over the one by Philips ranges from 0.05 to 1.85, with an average value around 0.67. The ratio of the number of operations ranges from 0.05 to 1.68, with an average value around 0.62.

The icons in Fig. 6 are sorted from the one giving the best performance (in the top-left corner, where all boundary lines are axis-parallel) to the one giving the worst performance (having no axis-parallel lines). In this last icon, as well as in its rotated version, almost each black pixel is incident to a corner, therefore our formula tests a large number of pixels. Such two input images are the two dots at the extreme right side of the plots in Fig. 7.

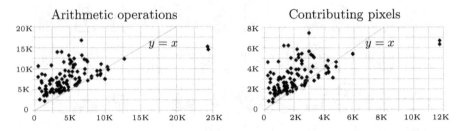

Fig. 7. Comparison of Formula (7) by Philips versus our Formula (8). Left: the number of operations (additions and multiplications) in the computation of a single moment. Right: the number of pixels contributing to the computation of moments (pixels with a non-zero coefficient). The horizontal axis is our formula, the vertical one is Formula (7). Each dot is a tested image.

5.2   Comparison with the Decomposition-Based Approach

We have chosen for the comparison the algorithm by Spiliotis and Mertzios [11], as it is the fastest in its class [3]. We applied the linear-time decomposition algorithm in [11], based on grouping runs having the same extension on consecutive rows. Then, we computed the moment of each block with Formula (2) for rectangles. This second stage is considered in the comparison.

The first plot in Fig. 8 compares the number of operations performed for moment computation by [11] and by our formula. As expected, [11] performs fewer operations than us, thanks to the block decomposition built in the preprocessing stage. Nevertheless, our number of operations is only between 1.5 and 2 times larger. The number of corners considered by our formula is about three times the number of blocks in [11], as shown in the second plot if Fig. 8, with the last image of Fig. 6 giving the exceptional ratio of 4.

If, on one hand, our formula doubles the number of necessary operations for moment computation, on the other hand it can directly accept the input image in many common encoding formats (raster, run-length, contour chain), while the one in [11], as well as all decomposition-based ones, needs to build and store the image block representation.

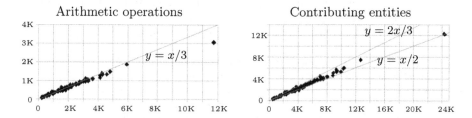

Fig. 8. Comparison of Formula (2) applied to the rectangles of the block decomposition by Spiliotis and Mertzios [11] versus our formula applied to the original image. Left: the number of operations. Right: the number of blocks in [11] versus our number of corners. The horizontal axis is our formula, the vertical one is [11]. Each dot is a tested image.

6   Summary and Future Work

We proposed a simple inclusion-exclusion based formula for the computation of discrete geometric moments of 2D binary images, and we showed that it is suitable for images with boundary composed mainly of horizontal and vertical lines. Experiments show that our formula performs fewer arithmetic operations than other boundary-based formulas. Compared with the decomposition-based approach, it performs a limited amount of extra operations, but methods in this class need to pre-process the given image, while our formula can compute the moments directly. We plan to extend this work to the computation of exact continuous geometric moments in 2D, as well as to images in arbitrary dimensions.

Acknowledgments. This research has been partially supported by the Ministry of Education, Science and Technological Development through project no. 451-03-68/2022-14/ 200156 "Innovative scientific and artistic research from the FTS (activity) domain".

References

1. Flusser, J.: Fast calculation of geometric moments of binary images. In: 22nd Workshop on Pattern Recognition and Medical Computer Vision, OAGM, pp. 265–274 (1998)

2. Flusser, J., Suk, T.: On the calculation of image moments. Technical Report 1946, Institute of Information Theory and Automation, Academy of Sciences of the Czech Republic (1999)
3. Flusser, J., Suk, T., Zitova, B.: 2D and 3D Image Analysis by Moments. John Wiley & Sons Ltd, 2016
4. Hu, M.-K.: Visual pattern recognition by moment invariants. IRE Trans. Inf. Theory **8**(2), 179–187 (1962)
5. Li, B.C.: A new computation of geometric moments. Pattern Recogn. **26**(1), 109–113 (1993)
6. Philips, W.: A new fast algorithm for moment computation. Pattern Recogn. **26**(11), 1619–1621 (1993)
7. Shneier, M.: Calculations of geometric properties using quadtrees. Comput. Graph. Image Proc. **16**, 296–302 (1981)
8. Sossa-Azuela, J.H., Mazaira-Morales, I., Ibarra-Zannatha, J.M.: An extension to Philips' algorithm for moment calculation. Computacion y Sistemas **3**(1), 5–16 (1999)
9. Sossa-Azuela, J.H., Yáñez-Márquez, C., Díaz-de-León S, J.L.: Computing geometric moments using morphological erosions. Pattern Recogn. **34**(2), 271–276 (2001)
10. Spiliotis, I.M., Mertzios, B.G.: Real-time computation of 2-d moments on block represented binary images on the scan line array processor. In: 8th European Signal Processing Conference, EUSIPCO, pp. 1–4 (1996)
11. Spiliotis, I.M., Mertzios, B.G.: Real-time computation of two-dimensional moments on binary images using image block representation. IEEE Trans. Image Process. **7**(11), 1609–1615 (1998)
12. Suk, T., Flusser, J.: Refined morphological methods of moment computation. In: 20th International Conference on Pattern Recognition, ICPR, pp. 966–970 (2010)
13. Tang, G.Y.: A discrete version of Green's theorem. IEEE Trans. Pattern Anal. Mach. Intell. **4**(3), 242–249 (1982)
14. Wilf, J.M., Cunningham, R.T.: Computing region moments from boundary representations. Technical Report NASA-CR-162685), N80–16767, National Aeronautics and Space Administration Jet Propulsion Laboratory California Institute of Technology Pasadena, California (1979)
15. Yang, L., Albregtsen, F.: Fast computation of invariant geometric moments: a new method giving correct results. In: 12th IAPR International Conference on Pattern Recognition, Conference A: Computer Vision & Image Processing, ICPR, vol. 1, pp. 201–204 (1994)
16. Zakaria, M.F., Vroomen, L.J., Zsombor-Murray, P.J., van Kessel, J.M.H.M.: Fast algorithm for the computation of moment invariants. Pattern Recogn. **20**(6), 639–643 (1987)

Feature Subset Selection for Detecting Fatigue in Runners Using Time Series Sensor Data

Bahavathy Kathirgamanathan[1(✉)], Cillian Buckley[2], Brian Caulfield[2,3], and Pádraig Cunningham[1]

[1] School of Computer Science, University College Dublin, Dublin, Ireland
bahavathy.kathirgamanathan@ucdconnect.ie
[2] School of Public Health, Physiotherapy and Sports Science, University College Dublin, Dublin, Ireland
[3] Insight Centre for Data Analytics, University College Dublin, Dublin, Ireland

Abstract. Time Series data collected from wearable sensors such as Inertial Measurement Units (IMU) are becoming popular for use in classification tasks in the exercise domain. The data from these IMU sensors tend to have multiple channels of data as well as the potential to augment new time series based features. However, this data also tends to have high correlations between the channels which means that often only a small subset of features are required for classification. A challenge in working with human movement data is that there tends to be inter-subject variabilities which makes it challenging to build a generalised model that works across subjects. In this work, the feasibility of generating generalisable feature subsets to predict fatigue in runners using a correlation based feature subset selection approach was investigated. It is shown that personalised classification systems where the feature selection is also tuned to the individual provides the best overall performance.

Keywords: Time-series analysis · Feature subset selection · Human movement data

1 Introduction

A particular characteristic of data coming from wearable sensors is that the data can be high dimension with sensors producing multiple quite correlated streams. For instance, 9 Degrees of Freedom (DoF) inertial measurement units, such as Shimmer sensors[1] produces accelerometer, gyroscope and magnetometer data, all in three dimensions. These time-series will typically be augmented with derived signals which further increases the dimension of the data. These time-series will be highly correlated and some may be uninformative so feature subset selection is a key concern. As each feature is a complete time-series, 'normal' feature selection methods may not be applicable.

---

[1] https://shimmersensing.com.

© Springer Nature Switzerland AG 2022
M. El Yacoubi et al. (Eds.): ICPRAI 2022, LNCS 13363, pp. 541–552, 2022.
https://doi.org/10.1007/978-3-031-09037-0_44

In this paper we assess the performance of a feature subset selection method for multi-dimension time-series data called Merit Score for Time-Series data (MSTS) [9] on Shimmer sensor data. The task is to distinguish between normal and fatigued running at a stride level. We are interested in the relative merits of global versus personalised classifiers and the performance of feature subset selection for both scenarios. The classifiers we consider are k-Nearest Neighbour (k-NN) using Dynamic Time Warping (DTW) and Rocket [5]. The specific research questions we consider are:

1. Is MSTS effective for this classification task?
2. Is it possible to develop a global classification system that will generalise across different runners?
3. If personalised classification systems are to be developed, does the feature selection process need to be specialised for each individual or can a generic feature subset be identified?

In the next section we provide an overview of the fatigue detection task and the data. An introduction to feature selection for time series and details of the MSTS method are then presented in Sect. 3. The evaluations are presented in Sect. 4 and the paper concludes with an outline of our plans for future work in Sect. 5.

2   Predicting Fatigue in Runners

Research shows that fatigue can increase the risk of injury for runners because higher impact accelerations can lead to overload injuries [12]. Furthermore, changes in running kinematics due to fatigue may be more pronounced in novice than in competitive runners [11]. These running injuries can occur due to a range of biomechanical factors [18]. Wearable Sensors such as the Shimmer sensors allow this biomechanical behaviour to be captured so that it can be objectively analysed.

Given that injury is a significant concern for runners it is important to be able to identify when fatigue is altering their running 'form'. In this paper we build on previous work on the identification of running fatigue using a single inertial measurement unit [4]. An effective feature selection methodology has been shown to be important in improving the efficacy of human movement data classification [13]. The previous study used aggregate statistics extracted from the signals such as mean, standard deviation, skewness, and kurtosis as the features for the model. This allowed classification in the standard feature vector framework. Our objective here is to work more directly with the time-series data using k-NN DTW and Rocket (see Sect. 2.2) and hence employ a feature subset selection rather than a feature extraction methodology. The two different approaches are discussed in more detail in Sect. 3.

2.1   Dataset

The dataset covers two 400 m runs by 18 recreational runners. The first run was at the participant's comfortable running pace and the second run was the

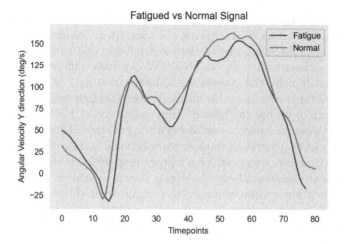

Fig. 1. A sample signal from the gyroscope in the y-direction for a fatigued stride vs a normal stride.

same following a fatigue intervention. More detail on the data collection protocol is presented in [4]. The runners wore lumbar mounted Shimmer sensors set to sample 256 Hz. Altogether, 18 time-series were considered:

- Acceleration (X,Y,Z)
- Gyroscope vectors (X,Y,Z)
- Magnetometer(X,Y,Z)
- Euler (Pitch, Roll, Yaw)
- Quaternion (W, X, Y, Z)
- Magnitude (Acceleration, Gyro) $M = \sqrt{X^2 + Y^2 + Z^2}$

The signals were filtered using a Butterworth filter of order $n = 5$. The Euler and Quaternion features were calculated on-board the sensor. The time-series were split into strides based on a characteristic foot-strike signal in the Y Acceleration time-series – two sample strides are shown in Fig. 1. The data was further divided into a training subject set (10/18 subjects) and a test subject set (8/18 subjects). Altogether there are 3417 normal and 3253 fatigued strides in the train set and 2366 normal and 2333 fatigued strides in the test set.

2.2 Personalised Vs Global Classification

Previous studies have shown that for some exercises the application of a personalised classifier can lead to substantial improvements in the performance [17]. To test this on our dataset, we compare the performance of a global and personalised classifier. There are a variety of time series classification techniques that are available and recent literature is available which evaluates these techniques [3,14]. In our evaluation, we use two classification techniques:

- **1-Nearest Neighbour (1-NN) with Dynamic Time Warping (DTW)** is commonly used as a benchmark classifier when working with time series as it is known for being one of the most reliable and simple approaches for time series classification [3]. k-NN-DTW can have different values of k set which may improve the classification, however as k=1 is a commonly used benchmark for time series, this has been used throughout our evaluations. In our evaluation, we use the tslearn[2] implementation of 1-NN-DTW [15].
- **Rocket** is a recent development and is a current state-of-the-art technique [5]. Rocket works by generating random convolutional kernels which are convolved along the time series to produce a feature map which is then used to train a simple linear classifier. Rocket has been shown to achieve good performance with a much lower computational load than other time-series classification techniques. In our evaluation, we use the sktime[3] implementation of Rocket [10] and we used the default 10,000 kernels and set a random_state of 42.

Global classification is done by training a model using the 10 subjects in the train set and testing on the 8 subjects in the test set. For the personalised models, each subject's data is split into a train (66%) and test (33%) sets and hold-out testing is conducted for each subject. The average of all the subjects is then calculated and reported as the personalised classifier score. The accuracy obtained from these classifications are presented in Table 1. These results show how for both classification techniques, the overall performance of the personalised classifier greatly outperforms that of the global classifier.

Table 1. Baseline accuracy for global vs personalised classification

Classifier	Global classifier	Personalised classifier
1-NN-DTW	0.55	0.97
Rocket	0.53	0.98

These baseline results clearly show the advantage personalised models have over global models. Next we assess the impact of feature subset selection on performance. We are particularly interested in whether each personalised model needs its own feature selection process or can a generic set of features be identified that is effective across all personalised models?

3   Feature Selection for Sensor Data

There are two common methods of feature selection that are used while working with multidimensional time series data, feature extraction and feature subset selection. In feature extraction, aggregate or summary statistics are extracted

---

[2] https://tslearn.readthedocs.io/en/stable/.
[3] https://www.sktime.org/en/stable/.

from the original data [13]. In feature subset selection, a subset of the original features themselves are selected by keeping the influential features and removing the redundant ones. Using feature subset selection and hence using the time series directly may provide some advantages over the feature extraction techniques that are generally used in the exercise classification domain. Feature subset selection provides scope for greater interpretability as well as less information loss as the features are from the original time series rather than abstract extracted features [20]. For example, with the running data, extracted features such as skewness and kurtosis may aid classification but don't provide much insight. Selecting the raw channels such as acceleration in a given direction can provide insights about when and where the deviation in running pattern is occurring.

The majority of studies that use Inertial Measurement Units (IMU's) for classification on human movement data use feature extraction techniques [13] as this allows traditional feature selection techniques such as Recursive Feature Elimination (RFE) to be used. However these techniques require each item in a column vector format which means any correlation between the features will be lost and hence these do not work well for multivariate time series [8]. There are few techniques that have been introduced for feature subset selection on time series. One such recent development assigns scores to feature subsets based on a k-NN strategy used to measure the shared information between time series [7]. Another popular technique is CLeVer which uses Principal Component Analysis (PCA) to give loadings to weight the contribution of each feature [19]. This however could be considered more for dimension reduction rather than feature subset selection. In this evaluation, we use a technique called MSTS which we previously introduced in [9]. This technique is described in more detail in Sect. 3.1 below.

3.1   Correlation Based Feature Subset Selection for Time Series

Correlation Based Feature Selection (CFS) is a technique that ranks feature subsets based on a merit score which is calculated from the correlations in the data [6]. CFS works on the principle that a 'good' feature subset should have features that are highly correlated to the class, yet uncorrelated with each other. MSTS is a technique which carries out CFS on time series data [9]. MSTS uses single feature predictions of the class labels to calculate a merit score which is based on feature-feature and feature-class correlations. Mutual Information (MI) is used to measure the correlations. The merit score for time series was measured using the following formula:

$$MSTS = \frac{k\overline{Y_{cf}}}{\sqrt{k + k(k-1)\overline{Y_{ff}}}} \tag{1}$$

where $\overline{Y_{cf}}$ and $\overline{Y_{ff}}$ are correlations calculated on the class labels predicted for the training data. $\overline{Y_{cf}}$ was calculated by averaging the feature-class correlations of all the features present in the subset. In this paper, the adjusted mutual information (AMI) score, which is a variation of MI to account for chance, is used to calculate the correlations [16]. k represents the number of features in the subset

The merit score is used as a means of ranking the suitability of each feature subset, however to select the 'best' feature subset for the given task, a Wrapper approach is used where the best 2-feature subset is found, then all 3-feature subsets that include this 2-feature subset is identified. From here the best feature subset is once again taken forward until there is no more improvement in the merit score. This technique was introduced and evaluated in [9] on datasets from the UEA multivariate time series archive [2]. In this work, we evaluate the technique on the real-life dataset obtained from runners before and after the fatiguing intervention.

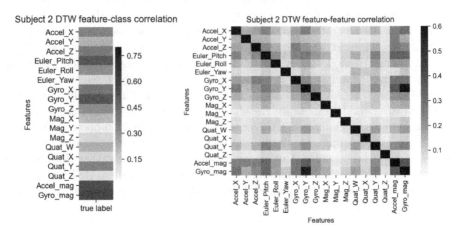

Fig. 2. Feature-Feature and Feature-Class correlations for Subject 2. Features Selected by MSTS (in order added): *Accel_mag, Gyro_mag, Euler_Pitch, Gyro_Y, Accel_Z, Gyro_X, Quat_Y, Gyro_Z, Euler_Roll, Accel_X*

Figures 2 and 3 help to illustrate how MSTS works. Figure 2, shows the feature-feature and feature-class correlations on one subjects data. In this example, CFS techniques should select feature combinations where the feature-class (Fig. 2a) is high and the feature-feature correlation (Fig. 2b) is low. In this example, Euler_pitch is selected as the third feature after Accel_mag and Gyro_mag despite having a slightly lower feature-class correlation than Gyro_Y. This is due to Gyro_Y being more correlated with the first two features selected than Euler_Pitch. Figure 3 shows how the feature subsets are selected and how as the merit score increases, the overall accuracy also increases. The plot illustrates the forward search strategy that is used to identify the best feature subset. Initially the blue dots represent the merit score vs accuracy for all two feature subsets, a third feature is then added to the subset with the highest merit score. This process is continued until there is no improvement in the merit score due to the addition of another feature.

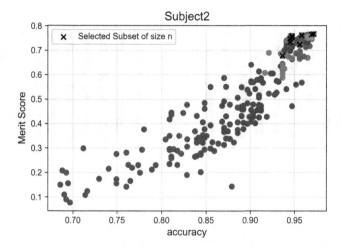

Fig. 3. Features selected at each iteration where the different colours indicate different subset sizes and the cross indicates the subset selected for each subset size

4   Evaluation

In this evaluation, we aim to investigate:

- The effectiveness of using MSTS to identify 'good' feature subsets to predict fatigue in running at an individual level.
- The feasibility of developing a global classification system to classify fatigue in running using a generic feature subset identified from the training subject set.

4.1   MSTS for Feature Subset Selection on Individuals

To evaluate the effectiveness of using MSTS to identify a personalised feature subset, the MSTS technique is evaluated on each of the ten subjects in the training set. This allowed for the identification of each subject's 'best' feature subset. Each subject in the training set had their data further split into a training and test set (33%) which was hold-out tested to check the performance of the personalised subsets at predicting fatigue in runners. The random seed for the train test split was maintained to ensure the same data was being used for each subject level evaluation. The MSTS technique can be used alongside any classifier of the users choice. In this evaluation, the two time series classification techniques of 1-NN-DTW and Rocket are used (see Sect. 2.2)

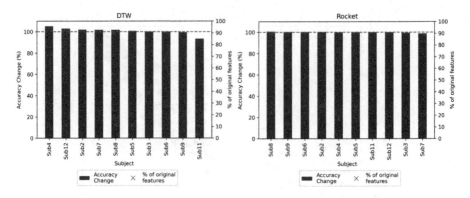

Fig. 4. Accuracy change (left axis) and % of original features used (right axis) of the personalised feature subset compared to the baseline which uses the full set of features using the classifiers DTW (Left) and Rocket (Right)

Performance of MSTS: Figure 4 shows the performance of the MSTS selected feature subset for each subject in the training set as well as the reduction in the number of features from the original feature set. These plots show that MSTS works well at classifying fatigue in runners and reduces the number of features required to obtain this good performance. In Fig. 4 it can be seen that for both DTW and Rocket the accuracy is maintained while the number of features required is hugely reduced across all the subjects. All the subjects in the training data set for both DTW and Rocket, required at most 60% of the total features and for many subjects, as little as 10% of the total features to maintain accuracy. This reduction in the features required will improve compute times and could simplify the data collection and processing. Although, a small difference, the MSTS selected subsets shows better improvement in the accuracy for DTW than Rocket, and this is likely because DTW had a lower accuracy overall to start with. This may also be due to the way Rocket works where there is a level of in-built feature selection which is based on the kernels that are selected. Although Rocket performs well without feature subset selection, the use of a feature subset selection technique such as MSTS will give more explainable output than what can be interpreted from the random kernels that are selected while using Rocket which is an important consideration while working in the sports domain.

Features Selected by MSTS: Figure 5 shows the features that were selected for each individual in the train set. There was some agreement between the features that were selected by each classifier. For example, features such as gyroscope and quaternion measures are selected more frequently by both classifiers. Similarly, features such as Euler_Yaw, Mag_Y, and Mag_Z were not selected by either classifier suggesting that they are features of less importance for this task. However, there are also some differences between the two classifiers, for example the acceleration measure is selected more often by Rocket than DTW. This could be in the nature of how both techniques work where DTW is mostly looking at the overall shape of the time series whereas Rocket may be good at learning using other attributes such as frequency or variance.

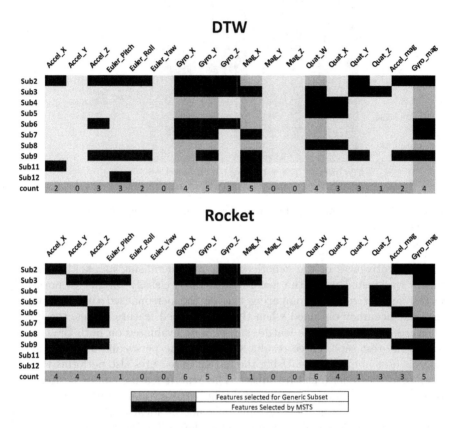

Fig. 5. Features selected by MSTS for each subject. Top: 1-NN-DTW classifier, Bottom: Rocket classifier

4.2   Generic Model Selection

Once the feature subsets for each individual was identified, the top five features that were selected most often by MSTS in the training subject set was selected as the 'generic subset'. Five was selected as the number of features to take as this was roughly the average number of features that was selected by MSTS across the individuals in the training set. The subsets were selected separately for 1-NN-DTW and Rocket. Figure 5 shows the features that were selected by each classifier. The two classifiers selected similar features with 4 of the 5 features the same.

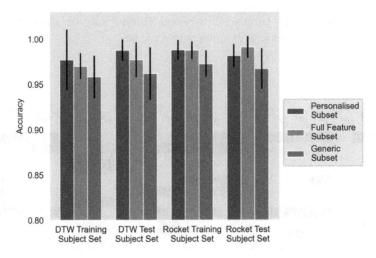

Fig. 6. Accuracy obtained for the three feature subsets using the rocket and 1-NN-DTW classifiers

The effectiveness of the generic subset at generalising across the different runners was tested using the generic subsets to classify fatigue vs normal in the test-subject set and comparing this to the personalised subsets. Figure 6 shows the accuracy obtained when the personalised feature subset, the full set of features, and the generic feature subset were evaluated on both the training set and the test sets. These results show that the personalised feature subset performs best in most cases. Using the full set of features also performs well and better than the generic feature subset. The generic feature subset performs the worst, however still manages to maintain the accuracy above 0.95. This suggests, that generalised classification systems may not be ideal in this domain as the inter-subject variation whilst running may be large. This evaluation supports the notion that running styles are heterogenous. An example of this is the known variation in foot-strike pattern with many runners hitting the ground with the rearfoot first while others hit with the midfoot or forefoot [1]. Thus, it may be required to group by running style prior to developing a global classifier.

Global classification systems would simplify the data collection process as the features that are not required need not be collected. Personalised feature subsets carry with them a downfall where most features would need to be collected even if they are to be discarded later on. However, the performance will be improved and compute times will be reduced compared to using the full set of features.

5   Conclusions and Future Work

The evaluations suggest that MSTS is effective as a means of identifying 'good' feature subsets for this fatigue prediction during running task. The evaluations also suggest that personalised classification systems perform well which supports previous studies [17] but also goes further to suggest that the feature selection process should also be customised to the individual for improved classification results.

MSTS was shown to be good for feature reduction while working with wearable sensor data. Reducing the features is valuable in this domain as it can aid in the explainability of the task. Additionally, knowing that some features are not required for the task means they could be excluded from data collection leading to cost savings as well as reduced compute times.

The generic feature subsets performed well across the individuals, however best performance was achieved with personalised feature subsets. Hence, ideally, the feature selection should also be personalised. Some patterns were able to be identified where some features were never selected by the algorithm. Hence even if an exact set of global features cannot be identified, some redundant features can be removed from the data collection process. Furthermore, this problem is specialised and hence this approach may suit other classification tasks where there is less inter-subject variability. Another area to investigate is in specialising the generic feature subset to different types of runners such as forefoot strikers, midfoot strikers or rearfoot strikers so instead of having a one-fit-all subset, there would be a few generic subsets to select from. This may improve the performance of global classifiers which would be an area to consider as future work.

Acknowledgements. This work has emanated from research conducted with the financial support of Science Foundation Ireland under the Grant number 18/CRT/6183. For the purpose of Open Access, the author has applied a CC BY public copyright license to any Author Accepted Manuscript version arising from this submission.

References

1. Asegawa, H.I.H., Amauchi, T.A.Y., Raemer, W.I.J.K.: Foot strike patterns of runners at the 15-Km. Strength Conditioning **21**(3), 888–893 (2007)
2. Bagnall, A., et al.: The UEA multivariate time series classification archive, pp. 1–36 (2018). http://arxiv.org/abs/1811.00075
3. Bagnall, A., Lines, J., Bostrom, A., Large, J., Keogh, E.: The great time series classification bake off: a review and experimental evaluation of recent algorithmic advances. Data Min. Knowl. Disc. **31**(3), 606–660 (2016). https://doi.org/10.1007/s10618-016-0483-9
4. Buckley, C., et al.: Binary classification of running fatigue using a single inertial measurement unit. In: 2017 IEEE 14th International Conference on Wearable and Implantable Body Sensor Networks, BSN, pp. 197–201. IEEE (2017)
5. Dempster, A., Petitjean, F., Webb, G.I.: ROCKET: exceptionally fast and accurate time series classification using random convolutional kernels. Data Min. Knowl. Disc. **34**(5), 1454–1495 (2020). https://doi.org/10.1007/s10618-020-00701-z
6. Hall, M.: Correlation-based feature selection for machine learning. Ph.D. thesis, Department of Computer Science, University of Waikato Hamilton (1999)
7. Ircio, J., Lojo, A., Mori, U., Lozano, J.A.: Mutual information based feature subset selection in multivariate time series classification. Pattern Recogn. **108**, 107525 (2020). https://doi.org/10.1016/j.patcog.2020.107525

8. Isabelle, G., Andre, E.: An introduction to variable and feature selection. J. Mach. Learn. Res. **3**, 1157–1182 (2003). https://doi.org/10.1016/j.aca.2011.07.027
9. Kathirgamanathan, B., Cunningham, P.: Correlation based feature subset selection for multivariate time-series data. arXiv preprint arXiv:2112.03705 (2021)
10. Löning, M., Kazakov, V., Bagnall, A., Lines, J., Ganesh, S., Király, F.J.: Sktime: a unified interface for machine learning with time series. arXiv (2019)
11. Maas, E., De Bie, J., Vanfleteren, R., Hoogkamer, W., Vanwanseele, B.: Novice runners show greater changes in kinematics with fatigue compared with competitive runners. Sports Biomech. **17**(3), 350–360 (2018)
12. Mizrahi, J., Verbitsky, O., Isakov, E., Daily, D.: Effect of fatigue on leg kinematics and impact acceleration in long distance running. Hum. Mov. Sci. **19**(2), 139–151 (2000)
13. O'Reilly, M.A., Johnston, W., Buckley, C., Whelan, D., Caulfield, B.: The influence of feature selection methods on exercise classification with inertial measurement units. In: 2017 IEEE 14th International Conference on Wearable and Implantable Body Sensor Networks, BSN 2017, pp. 193–196 (2017). https://doi.org/10.1109/BSN.2017.7936039
14. Pasos, A., Michael, R., James, F., Middlehurst, M., Bagnall, A.: The great multivariate time series classification bake off : a advances. Springer, US (2020).https://doi.org/10.1007/s10618-020-00727-3
15. Tavenard, R., et al.: Tslearn, a machine learning toolkit for time series data. J. Mach. Learn. Res. **21**(118), 1–6 (2020). http://jmlr.org/papers/v21/20-091.html
16. Vinh, N.X., Epps, J., Bailey, J.: Information theoretic measures for clusterings comparison: variants, properties, normalization and correction for chance. J. Mach. Learn. Res. **11**, 2837–2854 (2010)
17. Whelan, D.F., O'Reilly, M.A., Ward, T.E., Delahunt, E., Caulfield, B.: Technology in rehabilitation: comparing personalised and global classification methodologies in evaluating the squat exercise with wearable IMUs. Methods Inf. Med. **56**(5), 361–369 (2017). https://doi.org/10.3414/ME16-01-0141
18. Yamato, T.P., Saragiotto, B.T., Lopes, A.D.: A consensus definition of running-related injury in recreational runners: a modified Delphi approach. J. Orthop. Sports Phys. Ther. **45**(5), 375–380 (2015). https://doi.org/10.2519/jospt.2015.5741
19. Yang, K., Yoon, H., Shahabi, C.: CLeVer: a Feature Subset Selection Technique for Multivariate Time Series (Full Version). Tech. rep. (2005)
20. Yoon, H., Shahabi, C.: Feature subset selection on multivariate time series with extremely large spatial features. In: Proceedings - IEEE International Conference on Data Mining, ICDM 0238560, pp. 337–342 (2006). https://doi.org/10.1109/icdmw.2006.81

Compositing Foreground and Background Using Variational Autoencoders

Zezhen Zeng$^{(\boxtimes)}$, Jonathon Hare, and Adam Prügel-Bennett

University of Southampton, Southampton, UK
{zz8n17,jsh2,apb}@ecs.soton.ac.uk

Abstract. We consider the problem of composing images by combining an arbitrary foreground object to some background. To achieve this we use a factorized latent space. Thus we introduce a model called the "Background and Foreground VAE" (BFVAE) that can combine arbitrary foreground and background from an image dataset to generate unseen images. To enhance the quality of the generated images we also propose a VAE-GAN mixed model called "Latent Space Renderer-GAN" (LSR-GAN). This substantially reduces the blurriness of BFVAE images.

Keywords: Representation learning · VAE · Disentanglement

1 Introduction

Learning factorized representations of visual scenes is a challenging problem in computer vision. Human brains can process the realistic scene as a whole and decompose it into different parts using visual clues and prior knowledge. This cognitive ability also enables humans to imagine different scenes. Objects form the basis of humans' high-level cognition [36]. Thus, learning good object representations could be an important step towards making artificial intelligence closer to human intelligence. In visually inspecting a scene, one object is often attended to as the foreground and the rest of the scene is the background. There exists a considerable body of work learning representation for each object in a scene and achieve objects segmentation [3,14,28,32]. We argue that a good object representation should not only benefit the downstream tasks such as classification, or segmentation, but also enable generative models to create images conditioned on the object representations.

Our aim is to build a generative model for classes of images that allows us to alter the foreground objects independently of the background. This requires building a model that factorizes and composites these two part representations of the image. Existing works that can factorize the foreground and background of images are all based on hierarchical Generative Adversarial Networks [26,35,41]. Here we introduce a new VAE-based model that can be used to factorize the background and foreground objects in a continuous latent space and composite factors of those training images to generate new images in one shot. Compared to GAN-based models, our VAE-based models can infer the latent representation of existing images in addition to performing generation.

© Springer Nature Switzerland AG 2022
M. El Yacoubi et al. (Eds.): ICPRAI 2022, LNCS 13363, pp. 553–566, 2022.
https://doi.org/10.1007/978-3-031-09037-0_45

We consider the decomposition of an image x into a set of foreground pixels f and background pixels b such that

$$x = f \odot m + b \odot (1 - m), \qquad (1)$$

where m is the binary mask of the foreground and $\odot$ denotes elementwise multiplication. Thus we require a mask or bounding box to crop the foreground object f out, as shown in Fig. 1. Row C is the generated images of our model by combining different factors in row B. The background and foreground of images in row C are not totally the same as images in row A and row B, this is due to a trade-off between the similarity and reality in our model which will be addressed in the following section.

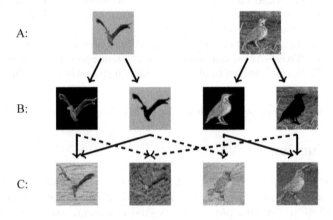

Fig. 1. Our model can disentangle the foreground and background of images and combine factors from different images to generate new images. Row A is the original images. Row B is the decomposition of Row A. Row C is the generations of combining different factors. Between row B and row C, the solid arrow means reconstruction and dashed arrow means generation.

We name this model the *Background and Foreground VAE* (BFVAE). BFVAE consists of two different VAEs: VAE-B and VAE-F. We train VAE-F on the foreground object, f, while the VAE-B encoder is given the full image, x, as input. We concatenate the latent representation for VAE-B with that of VAE-F before feeding it into the decoder of VAE-B. This operation encourages the encoder in VAE-B to ignore information about the foreground object as this is already encoded. It is crucial to use the full image, x, and not just the background image, b, as the input of VAE-B since the original information in x helps the model to generate pure background images without a hole when we use a pure black image as the input of VAE-F. It also helps to fix the hole when we exchange the foreground objects among images.

The drawback of VAE-based model is the generated images tend to be blurry, thus we propose another VAE-GAN mixed model which can generate high-quality images but also obtain an approximate latent space of a pre-trained

VAE model (BFVAE in this case). We name it Latent Space Renderer-GAN (or LSR-GAN). By feeding the output of the generator to the encoder of a pre-trained VAE, LSR-GAN is more stable and can avoid mode drops. In addition, we note that a different pre-processing operation of the images make a significant difference to the FID scores. Thus, we argue that it is necessary to clarify how the FID score is computed.

The main contributions of our work are fourfold:

- We propose a new VAE-based model called BFVAE that can composite the foreground and background of images and generate images by combining different factors.
- We introduce a VAE-GAN mixed model called LSR-GAN which enables us to generate high-quality images with the approximated disentangled latent space.
- We demonstrate that BFVAE can factorize the foreground and background representation and generate high-quality images when combined with LSR-GAN. Moreover, We show our model can obtain FID scores that are comparable to the state-of-the-art model.
- We demonstrate that BFVAE is able to factorize other factors when we have additional information available for training (like class labels).

2   Related Work

There are several papers on composition and decomposition of images [3,9,11,12, 14,27,28,34]. Genesis [12] tries to decompose image into object representations using a recurrent neural network which builds a strong relationship among each objects. All the models generate or reconstruct images part by part and stitch all the parts together.

Not many works focus on compositing images in a background-foreground manner. The existing models are all GAN-based model that generate foreground and background separately and recursively, the generated images are stitched at the final stages [26,35,41]. ReDO [5] can segment foreground objects from images by using a GAN but it can not change the shape of the original foreground. Only MixNMatch [26] can encode real data into discrete codes or feature maps (in the Feature-mode). Although MixNMatch and FineGAN [35] do not require masks of images nevertheless they both need bounding boxes and the number of categories for training. Our model generates the whole image in one shot while it can still learn a continuous factorized latent space. Moreover, the model can be trained either with or without supervision. And FBC-GAN [10] is another GAN-based model that generates the foreground and the background concurrently and independently.

There is a vast literature about learning disentangled representations based on deep generative models. Many unsupervised generative models have developed disentanglement in a latent space. GAN-type models are usually based on InfoGAN [7] while most VAE-type models are based on β-VAE [17]. There is a trade-off in β-VAE between disentanglement and reconstruction quality.

There are many attempts to solve this trade-off issue [6,21,42]. Both approaches modify the ELBO to avoid getting worse reconstructions while keeping the disentanglement. Kumar *et al.* [25] propose a VAE-based model that penalizing the covariance between latent dimensions without modifying the β value.

In contrast to unsupervised models, it is easier for supervised models to learn a factorized representation. VAEs have been used in a semi-supervised manner to factorize the class information and other information [8], or combinations of VAE and GAN aim to learn disentangled representations [29,30,38,40]. ML-VAE [1] is another VAE-based model that requires weak-supervision. In their work, they propose group supervision that uses a group of images with the same label instead of a single image to learn a separable latent space. Esser *et al.* [13] combine the U-Net [33] with a VAE and one extra encoder to learn a disentangled representation of human pose. Harsh *et al.* [15] is the closest work to our model, we both have two VAEs and a pair of inputs, while they use a different image with the same label and they also swap the factors during training (something we do not require in our model).

The VAE and GAN mixed models has been explored for a long time, and almost all the works train the VAE and GAN simultaneously [2,4,29,37], while our LSR-GAN requires a pre-trained VAE. Some methods feed the output of the decoder into the encoder [2,19,37] which is similar to our model. VEEGAN [37] introduces an encoder to the GAN and tries to train all the network simultaneously. However, only LSR-GAN tries to map the sample space into a latent space of a pre-trained VAE by maximum likelihood.

3   Model

In this section we describe the components of our model starting from the classic model of VAEs.

3.1   VAE

The Variational Autoencoder (VAE) [23] is a deep generative model that learns a distribution over observed data, $\boldsymbol{x}$, in terms of latent variables, $\boldsymbol{z}$. The original VAE approximates the intractable posterior by using a variational approximation to provide a tractable bound on the marginal log-likelihood called the evidence lower bound (ELBO)

$$\log p_\theta(\boldsymbol{x}) \geq \mathbb{E}_{\boldsymbol{z} \sim q_\phi(\boldsymbol{z}|\boldsymbol{x})}[\log p_\theta(\boldsymbol{x}|\boldsymbol{z})] - D_{KL}(q_\phi(\boldsymbol{z}|\boldsymbol{x})||p(\boldsymbol{z})). \tag{2}$$

Commonly, $q_\phi(\boldsymbol{z}|\boldsymbol{x})$ is the output of an inference network with parameters ϕ and $p_\theta(\boldsymbol{x}|\boldsymbol{z})$ is generated by a decoder network with parameters θ.

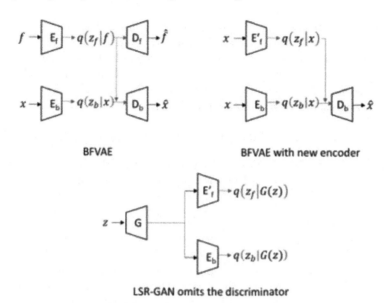

Fig. 2. The diagram of BFVAE, BFVAE with new encoder and the LSR-GAN which we omits the discriminator.

3.2 BFVAE

Starting from a mask m of the foreground object we can extract the foreground f from the image x using $f = x \odot m$. We use f and x as inputs to our two VAEs. The architecture of our model is shown in Fig. 2. For simplicity, we omit symbols of the parameters. The top network is VAE-F and it acts like a vanilla VAE. The encoder E_f generates a probability distribution, $q(z_f|f)$ that acts as a latent space representation of f. A sample from this distribution, z_f, is used by the decoder D_f to generate a reconstruction, $\hat{f}$, of the input f. The top VAE ensures the z_f contain representations of foreground objects. The bottom network is VAE-B. The original image, x, is given to the encoder, E_b that generates a probability distribution, $q(z_b|x)$. A latent variables z_b, is sampled from this distribution and concatenated with z_f. This concatenated vector is sent to decoder D_b that must reconstruct the original image. Thus, we modify the ELBO for VAE-B to be

$$\mathcal{L}_b = \mathbb{E}_{z \sim q(z|x)}\left[\log p(x|(z_b, z_f))\right] - D_{KL}(q(z_b|x)\|p(z_b)). \tag{3}$$

Since the input f does not contain any information about the background, it is assured that the latent variables z_f only contain information about the foreground. For VAE-B, the encoder can extract information about both foreground and background from x. When we train the decoder with both z_f and z_b, it can force z_b to discard the information about the foreground and only leave information about background. This also enable us to extract the pure background from images by using z_f obtained from a pure black image. In the initial stages of training, z_b contain all the information about the image. This makes the decoder of VAE-B prone to ignore z_f especially when the dataset is complicated. There are two methods to alleviate this issue. The first method is to set the size of z_b to be reasonably small, it forces the z_b to discard information, but this design makes it hard to find an accurate size for z_b. Thus, we recommend the second method which is turning the model into β-VAE,

$$\mathcal{L}_b = \mathbb{E}_{z \sim q(z|x)} \left[\log p(x|(z_b, z_f)) \right] - \beta D_{KL}(q(z_b|x)||p(z_b)) \tag{4}$$

It is well known (see, for example, Hoffman *et al.* [18] and Kim *et al.* [21]) that the expected KL term in Equation (4) can be rewritten as

$$\mathbb{E}_{p_{data(x)}}[D_{KL}(q(z_b|x)||p(z_b))] = D_{KL}(q(z_b)||p(z_b)) + I(x, z_b) \tag{5}$$

By setting $\beta > 1$, we penalize both terms on the right side of Eq. (5). Penalizing $D_{KL}(q(z_b)||p(z_b))$ encourages factorization of the latent space, while at the same time it pushes $q(z_b|x)$ towards a standard Gaussian distribution. But the most important part in BFVAE is that we penalize the mutual information term $I(x, z_b)$ which helps z_b to discard information about the foreground.

3.3   LSR-GAN

A prominent problem of vanilla VAEs is the blurriness of the output. Thus we introduce a VAE-GAN mixed model that can learn a latent space from BFVAE and generate high-quality images. The idea is that we pass the output $G(z)$ of the generator G into the two encoders of BFVAE, and ask the two encoders to map $G(z)$ to the latent vectors z that we used to generate $G(z)$. By doing this, the generator will generate an image with a latent space encoding, z, of the pre-trained BFVAE. It can be seen as a simple regularization term of the normal GAN loss function for the generator

$$\mathcal{L}_G = \mathbb{E}_{z \sim p_z(z)}[\log(D(G(z)))] + \lambda \log(q(z|(E_b(G(z)), E'_f(G(z)))) \tag{6}$$

where E_b means the encoder of VAE-B, and the $(E_b(G(z)), E'_f(G(z))$ in the second term represents the concatenation of $E_b(G(z))$ and $E'_f(G(z))$. We train a new encoder E'_f that can extract the z_f from $G(z)$, we freeze all the other parts of BFVAE and replace E_f with E'_f, then train the encoder with the original loss function. Note that when training the LSR-GAN we freeze the weights of the E_b and E'_f. The constant λ is an adjustable hyper-parameter providing a trade-off between how realistic the image looks and the similarity between reconstructions and real images. Although the idea is simple, it provides a powerful method to improve the image quality of BFVAE. The generator G can either be a new network or a pre-trained decoder of BFVAE. The pre-trained decoder can be a strong initialization for the generator when the generator meets with model collapse.

4   Experiments

In this section, we show that BFVAE can factorize the foreground and background efficiently and can composite factors from different images to generate high-quality images when we combine LSR-GAN with BFVAE. Our model achieves state-of-the-art FID scores on images of size 64×64 compared to baseline models. We show the results quantitatively and qualitatively on natural images (CUB [39], Stanforddogs [20] and Stanfordcars [24]). Moreover, we notice that our model can factorize other kinds of attributes in the image as long as we change the input of VAE-F (See details in the following context). We evaluate this on MNIST. We set $\beta = 8$ for Dogs dataset and $\beta = 5$ otherwise; λ is 1 for all datasets.

The architecture of the encoder is 4 layers CNN network with Batch Normalization and 2 layers fully connected network, and decoder consists of 5 layers CNN network. When we combine the BFVAE with LSR-GAN, we use 4 residual blocks in both encoder and decoder of BFVAE with downsampling and upsampling operation respectively. And we add one extra linear layer at the end of the encoder and the beginning of the decoder. The generator of LSR-GAN is similar to the decoder of BFVAE and the discriminator consists of 4 residual blocks with a spectral norm [31]. We apply orthogonal initialization to both LSR-GAN and the new Encoder E_f' and optimize the model using ADAM [22] optimizer with $\beta_1 = 0.5$ and $\beta_2 = 0.999$. We train the BFVAE and the new encoder E_f' for only 100 epochs and train the LSR-GAN for 600 epochs.

4.1   BFVAE with LSR-GAN

Due to the blurriness of images created by the VAE decoders, BFVAE cannot perform well on natural images. Thus, we use the LSR-GAN described above to generate high-quality images. We first train a new encoder E_f' before training the new generator. We find it is better to choose the same β value for VAE-B and VAE-F when we combine BFVAE with LSR-GAN. Our experiments use three datasets, the whole dataset of CUB, the training set of *Stanford cars* and 12000 images from *Stanford dogs* (120 classes ×100 images).

BFVAE+LSR-GAN obtains superior FID scores [16] compared to previous models for images of size 64×64. It is well-known that the number of images and the implementation (Pytorch or Tensorflow) we use to calculate FID can strongly affect the results. Moreover, we notice an additional pre-processing operation that can make differences to the results. Commonly, when we calculate the FID scores of the dataset we need to resize the original images to the same size of our generated images, whether we save the resized images and reload them or feed the resized images to the inception model directly makes a significant difference to the FID scores we obtain. Given the extreme sensitivity of FID scores to these details, it is necessary for the process of computing FID scores to be fully documented to make meaningful comparisons. Thus, we report two FID results of feeding resized images directly and saving resized images. The outputs of our model are saved as PNG image. (Given these changes are not noticeable to

Table 1. The FID scores (lower is better) of saving resized images (left part) and feeding resized images directly (right part) at 64 × 64 scale.

	FID (saved)			FID (directly)		
	CUB	Cars	Dogs	CUB	Cars	Dogs
SNGAN	41.63	42.67	54.85	53.45	43.83	69.54
LR-GAN	35.22	30.30	86.67	51.85	38.80	104.45
FineGAN	24.51	31.32	**33.66**	**16.79**	23.61	**39.43**
MixNMatch	28.25	37.42	36.62	20.63	25.53	44.42
LSR-GAN	**19.12**	**18.01**	44.22	28.15	**18.99**	61.54

humans it raises some concerns about how seriously we should take FID scores. However, given these are the standard metric in this field we present the results as honestly as we can.)

Quantitative Results. We evaluate FID on 10K randomly generated images of size 64×64 for three different datasets. For LR-GAN, FineGAN and MixNMatch, we use the authors' publicly-available code. For a fair comparison, we use the same architecture of our LSR-GAN to train a SNGAN. We also tried replacing the original discriminator of other models with the same discriminator we use in the LSR-GAN, but it does not improve the results for either FineGAN or MixNMatch. Thus, we present results with those models' original architectures. As shown in Table 1, the results in the two halves of the table are different even though the only difference is whether we saved the images or kept them in main memory (although saving images will introduce small errors due to truncation, these are not observable to a human viewer). This shows that the small difference in FID scores is not that meaningful. Comparing to previous models, our model is the best overall when we save the resized images while FineGAN is the best one otherwise. But our model has, by a considerable margin, the smallest number of parameters and training time. The size of LRGAN, FineGAN and MixNMatch's saved models are 65.6 MB, 158.7 MB and 336.7 MB respectively. The size of our BFVAE+LSR-GAN is only 22.1 MB.

Conditional Generation. In Fig. 3 we show images generated by our method on three datasets. The top row and the first column are both the input images of two encoders. The other images are generated by combining factors from the two different images. As mentioned before, there is a trade-off between the realism and the similarity of generated images when we train the LSR-GAN, so there is a slight difference between reconstructions and input images. In the last row, some images are not pure background images. Because the discriminator has never seen images without foreground and can easily classify a pure background image as fake, this prevents the generator from generating a pure background image for some backgrounds especially pure colour background (e.g. sky). For

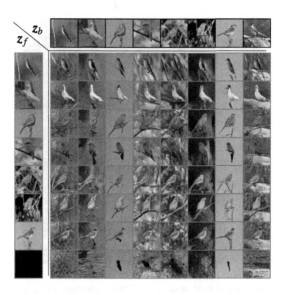

Fig. 3. Generation by swapping z_f and z_b. The top row and the first column are both the input images of two encoders.

the same reason, the background changes a little bit in the same column when the foreground is not harmonious with the background. This demonstrates how the LSR-GAN reduces its similarity when it tries to learn an approximate latent space of the pre-trained BFVAE. The nice part of this phenomena is the generator can adjust details in the background, such as the orientation of branches, to fit the foreground.

Continuous Latent Space. We demonstrate the continuity of the latent space learnt by BFVAE in Fig. 4 where we show the interpolation between two images. The top-left image and the bottom-right image are the original images. Other images are the interpolations between the two images. As we move along the axes, we change z_f or z_b. Both transitions between real images and fake images are smooth in the latent space, but it is obvious that even if we do not change z_b for each column, the birds (foreground) are slightly changing, this also happens for background in each row. The two reasons for this change are the same as above: firstly, the approximate latent space loses some similarity; and secondly, the discriminator can classify the unreal images like waterbirds on the branch or non-aquatic bird on the water as fake images, then the discriminator forces the generator to generate non-aquatic bird on a branch or waterbirds with water, which results in the slight change of both foregrounds and background even we do not change one of z_f and z_b. This change is also a trade-off between reality and similarity.

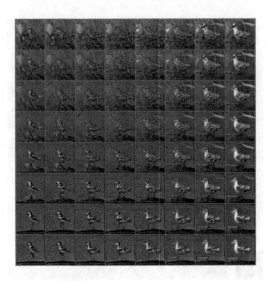

Fig. 4. Interpolation in the latent space, the left-top image and the right bottom image are the original images, others are the interpolations between the two images.

4.2 Substitute Attributes for Foreground

Apart from factorizing the background and foreground in the latent space, our model is also capable to factorize attributes such as style and content. The only thing we need to do is to substitute foreground images f with images that represent each different class, and x should be images from the same class as f. For example, if we want VAE-F to learn the information about digit label of MNIST, we choose 10 images from 10 classes randomly and use these 10 images as fixed input of VAE-F. This differs from previous work on conditional image generation as we use images instead of one-hot vectors as labels. Then the VAE-B will learn a latent space about the style of images. And Fig. 5 shows images generated using MNIST analogous to Fig. 4, where the top row is x and the first column is f. It can be observed that the generated images obtain class information from the first column and the style information from the top row.

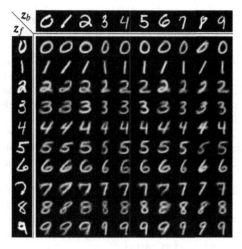

Fig. 5. Generation by swapping z_f and z_b on MNIST. The top row is x and the first column is f.

5 Discussion

Although several works have shown great success by representing scenes using their components [3,14,28], what defines a good object representation is still in discussion. We argue that a good object representation should also benefit the image generation task. We believe that enabling generative models to generate certain objects with random backgrounds should also be a property of good object representations.

Moreover, conditional image generation tasks such as the one discussed here are useful in clarifying what we require of a good image representation. After all the ability of dreaming and imagining scenes seem to be an intrinsic human ability. In the mammalian visual system there is plenty of evidence that scenes are disentangled in different areas of the visual cortex and later re-integrated to obtain a complete understanding of a scene. Although very much simplified the BFVAE makes a step towards learning such a disentangled representation of the foreground and background.

References

1. Bouchacourt, D., Tomioka, R., Nowozin, S.: Multi-level variational autoencoder: learning disentangled representations from grouped observations. In: Proceedings of the AAAI Conference on Artificial Intelligence (2018)
2. Brock, A., Lim, T., Ritchie, J.M., Weston, N.: Neural photo editing with introspective adversarial networks. In: Proceedings of International Conference on Learning Representations (2017)
3. Burgess, C.P., et al.: Monet: unsupervised scene decomposition and representation. arXiv preprint arXiv:1901.11390 (2019)

4. Che, T., Li, Y., Jacob, A.P., Bengio, Y., Li, W.: Mode regularized generative adversarial networks. In: Proceedings of International Conference on Learning Representations (2017)
5. Chen, M., Artières, T., Denoyer, L.: Unsupervised object segmentation by redrawing. In: Advances in Neural Information Processing Systems (2019)
6. Chen, T.Q., Li, X., Grosse, R.B., Duvenaud, D.K.: Isolating sources of disentanglement in variational autoencoders. In: Advances in Neural Information Processing Systems, pp. 2610–2620 (2018)
7. Chen, X., Duan, Y., Houthooft, R., Schulman, J., Sutskever, I., Abbeel, P.: InfoGAN: interpretable representation learning by information maximizing generative adversarial nets. In: Advances in Neural Information Processing Systems. pp. 2172–2180 (2016)
8. Cheung, B., Livezey, J.A., Bansal, A.K., Olshausen, B.A.: Discovering hidden factors of variation in deep networks. arXiv preprint arXiv:1412.6583 (2014)
9. Crawford, E., Pineau, J.: Spatially invariant unsupervised object detection with convolutional neural networks. In: Proceedings of the AAAI Conference on Artificial Intelligence. pp. 3412–3420 (2019)
10. Cui, K., Zhang, G., Zhan, F., Huang, J., Lu, S.: Fbc-gan: diverse and flexible image synthesis via foreground-background composition. arXiv preprint arXiv:2107.03166 (2021)
11. Dubrovina, A., Xia, F., Achlioptas, P., Shalah, M., Groscot, R., Guibas, L.J.: Composite shape modeling via latent space factorization. In: Proceedings of the IEEE International Conference on Computer Vision, pp. 8140–8149 (2019)
12. Engelcke, M., Kosiorek, A.R., Jones, O.P., Posner, I.: Genesis: generative scene inference and sampling with object-centric latent representations. In: International Conference on Learning Representations (2020)
13. Esser, P., Sutter, E., Ommer, B.: A variational u-net for conditional appearance and shape generation. In: Proceedings of the IEEE Conference on Computer Vision and Pattern Recognition. pp. 8857–8866 (2018)
14. Greff, K., et al.: Multi-object representation learning with iterative variational inference. In: International Conference on Machine Learning, pp. 2424–2433. PMLR (2019)
15. Harsh Jha, A., Anand, S., Singh, M., Veeravasarapu, V.: Disentangling factors of variation with cycle-consistent variational auto-encoders. In: Proceedings of the European Conference on Computer Vision (ECCV), pp. 805–820 (2018)
16. Heusel, M., Ramsauer, H., Unterthiner, T., Nessler, B., Hochreiter, S.: GANs trained by a two time-scale update rule converge to a local nash equilibrium. In: Advances in Neural Information Processing Systems, pp. 6626–6637 (2017)
17. Higgins, I., et al.: Beta-VAE: learning basic visual concepts with a constrained variational framework. In: Proceedings of International Conference on Learning Representations (2017)
18. Hoffman, M.D., Johnson, M.J.: Elbo surgery: yet another way to carve up the variational evidence lower bound. In: Workshop in Advances in Approximate Bayesian Inference (2016)
19. Huang, H., He, R., Sun, Z., Tan, T., et al.: IntroVAE: introspective variational autoencoders for photographic image synthesis. In: Advances in Neural Information Processing Systems, pp. 52–63 (2018)
20. Khosla, A., Jayadevaprakash, N., Yao, B., Fei-Fei, L.: Novel dataset for fine-grained image categorization. In: First Workshop on Fine-Grained Visual Categorization, IEEE Conference on Computer Vision and Pattern Recognition, Colorado Springs, CO (June 2011)

21. Kim, H., Mnih, A.: Disentangling by factorising. In: International Conference on Machine Learning, pp. 2649–2658. PMLR (2018)
22. Kingma, D.P., Ba, J.: Adam: a method for stochastic optimization. In: Proceedings of International Conference on Learning Representations (2015)
23. Kingma, D.P., Welling, M.: Auto-encoding variational bayes. In: Proceedings of International Conference on Learning Representations (2013)
24. Krause, J., Stark, M., Deng, J., Fei-Fei, L.: 3d object representations for fine-grained categorization. In: 4th International IEEE Workshop on 3D Representation and Recognition (3dRR-13), Sydney, Australia (2013)
25. Kumar, A., Sattigeri, P., Balakrishnan, A.: Variational inference of disentangled latent concepts from unlabeled observations. arXiv preprint arXiv:1711.00848 (2017)
26. Li, Y., Singh, K.K., Ojha, U., Lee, Y.J.: Mixnmatch: multifactor disentanglement and encoding for conditional image generation. In: Proceedings of the IEEE Conference on Computer Vision and Pattern Recognition (2020)
27. Lin, C.H., Yumer, E., Wang, O., Shechtman, E., Lucey, S.: ST-GAN: spatial transformer generative adversarial networks for image compositing. In: Proceedings of the IEEE Conference on Computer Vision and Pattern Recognition, pp. 9455–9464 (2018)
28. Lin, Z., et al.: Space: unsupervised object-oriented scene representation via spatial attention and decomposition. In: Proceedings of International Conference on Learning Representations (2020)
29. Makhzani, A., Shlens, J., Jaitly, N., Goodfellow, I., Frey, B.: Adversarial autoencoders. In: Proceedings of International Conference on Learning Representations (2016)
30. Mathieu, M.F., Zhao, J.J., Zhao, J., Ramesh, A., Sprechmann, P., LeCun, Y.: Disentangling factors of variation in deep representation using adversarial training. In: Advances in Neural Information Processing Systems, pp. 5040–5048 (2016)
31. Miyato, T., Kataoka, T., Koyama, M., Yoshida, Y.: Spectral normalization for generative adversarial networks. arXiv preprint arXiv:1802.05957 (2018)
32. Nash, C., et al.: The multi-entity variational autoencoder. In: NeurIPS Workshops (2017)
33. Ronneberger, O., Fischer, P., Brox, T.: U-Net: convolutional networks for biomedical image segmentation. In: Navab, N., Hornegger, J., Wells, W.M., Frangi, A.F. (eds.) MICCAI 2015. LNCS, vol. 9351, pp. 234–241. Springer, Cham (2015). https://doi.org/10.1007/978-3-319-24574-4_28
34. Schor, N., Katzir, O., Zhang, H., Cohen-Or, D.: Componet: learning to generate the unseen by part synthesis and composition. In: Proceedings of the IEEE International Conference on Computer Vision, pp. 8759–8768 (2019)
35. Singh, K.K., Ojha, U., Lee, Y.J.: Finegan: unsupervised hierarchical disentanglement for fine-grained object generation and discovery. In: Proceedings of the IEEE Conference on Computer Vision and Pattern Recognition (2019)
36. Spelke, E.S.: Principles of object perception. Cogn. Sci. 14(1), 29–56 (1990)
37. Srivastava, A., Valkov, L., Russell, C., Gutmann, M.U., Sutton, C.: VEEGAN: reducing mode collapse in GANs using implicit variational learning. In: Advances in Neural Information Processing Systems, pp. 3308–3318 (2017)
38. Szabó, A., Hu, Q., Portenier, T., Zwicker, M., Favaro, P.: Challenges in disentangling independent factors of variation. arXiv preprint arXiv:1711.02245 (2017)
39. Welinder, P., et al.: Caltech-ucsd birds 200 (2010)
40. Xiao, T., Hong, J., Ma, J.: DNA-GAN: learning disentangled representations from multi-attribute images. arXiv preprint arXiv:1711.05415 (2017)

41. Yang, J., Kannan, A., Batra, D., Parikh, D.: LR-GAN: layered recursive generative adversarial networks for image generation. arXiv preprint arXiv:1703.01560 (2017)
42. Zhao, S., Song, J., Ermon, S.: InfoVAE: information maximizing variational autoencoders. arXiv preprint arXiv:1706.02262 (2017)

Unsupervised Representation Learning via Information Compression

Zezhen Zeng$^{(\boxtimes)}$, Jonathon Hare, and Adam Prügel-Bennett

University of Southampton, Southampton, UK
{zz8n17,jsh2,apb}@ecs.soton.ac.uk

Abstract. This paper explores a new paradigm for decomposing an image by seeking a compressed representation of the image through an information bottleneck. The compression is achieved iteratively by refining the reconstruction by adding patches that reduce the residual error. This is achieved by a network that is given the current residual errors and proposes bounding boxes that are down-sampled and passed to a variational auto-encoder (VAE). This acts as the bottleneck. The latent code is decoded by the VAE decoder and up-sampled to correct the reconstruction within the bounding box. The objective is to minimise the size of the latent codes of the VAE and the length of code needed to transmit the residual error. The iterations end when the size of the latent code exceeds the reduction in transmitting the residual error. We show that a very simple implementation is capable of finding meaningful bounding boxes and using those bounding boxes for downstream applications. We compare our model with other unsupervised object discovery models.

Keywords: Unsupervised representation learning · VAE · Object discovery · Information bottleneck

1 Introduction

In the last few years there has been a significant research effort in developing unsupervised techniques in deep learning. A very prominent example of these methods is the variational auto-encoder (VAE) [12,16] that attempts to find latent representations to efficiently encode a dataset. A drawback of VAEs is that they represent the entire image. This is unlikely to lead to an efficient representation for many real-world images that depict multiple objects. Following the development of VAEs there have been a number of attempts to use unsupervised techniques for object location and segmentation within an image [1,3,4,9,13,14].

In this paper we will explore the use of a minimum description length cost function together with an information bottleneck to achieve unsupervised image understanding. The evidence lower bound (ELBO) of a VAE can be interpreted as a description length where the KL-divergence corresponds to a code length of the latent representation and the log-probability of the reconstruction error as the code length of the residual error (i.e. the error between the reconstruction and the original image). In our approach we will use multiple glimpses of an image

© Springer Nature Switzerland AG 2022
M. El Yacoubi et al. (Eds.): ICPRAI 2022, LNCS 13363, pp. 567–578, 2022.
https://doi.org/10.1007/978-3-031-09037-0_46

corresponding to a sequence of bounding boxes. These are resized to 8×8 patches and passed to a variational auto-encoder. The full reconstruction is built up from adding together the reconstructions from the VAE. This is done iteratively with each patch providing a correction between the current reconstruction and the true image. A spatial transformer is fed the current residual error and used to select the next bounding box. The overall cost function is the cost of the latent codes for all the bounding boxes together with the cost of the final residual error. We stop when the cost of transmitting the latent code is higher the reduction in the cost of transmitting the residual error. The spatial transformer and VAE is trained end-to-end by minimising the description cost of the images in a dataset.

Although we expect our approach to be very different to human eye movement nevertheless, there is a rough correspondence due to the restricted size of the fovea requiring multiple fixations of an image around areas of high interest and possible interpretational ambiguity [18]. We deliberately avoid building in any bias towards glimpsing complete objects, however, as we will see later, at least, in simple scenes this behaviour emerges. Our aim is not to build a state-of-the-art unsupervised object detector, but rather to investigate how a minimal implementation using minimum description length and an information bottle-neck will glimpse images. As we will demonstrate these glimpses can sometimes be used to solve downstream tasks that have competitive results with much more sophisticated approaches.

2   Related Work

There are several works on unsupervised object-centric representation learning and scene decomposition. MONet [1] applies a recurrent attention mechanism that produces deterministic soft masks for each component in the scene. They also use a VAE following their attention mechanism. Genesis [4] is similar to MONet and employs an RNN network after the encoder to infer the mask of objects and then uses another VAE to infer the object representations. Unlike MONet, all the modules in Genesis can be processed in parallel. IODINE [8] employs an amortized iterative refinement mechanism for the latent code, which is computationally expensive. Genesis-V2 [3] is the upgraded version of Genesis which replaces the RNN network with a semi-convolution embedding method. Other scene-mixture methods based on self-attention mechanism can also perform image decomposition and object representation learning [14,19].

The Attend-Infer-Repeat (AIR) [5] and the following work SPAIR[2] and SuPAIR [17] infer the object representation as "what", "where" and "pres" variables, where SPAIR infer an additional variable "depth". The "what" variable represents the shape and appearance of objects, the "where" contains the position and scale of objects and the "pres" variable is slightly different in the two models. In AIR, "pres" is a unary code which is formed of 1 and 0, where 0 means the termination of inference, while in SPAIR, "pres" is a binary variable that can be sampled from a Bernoulli distribution, where 0 represents no object in the corresponding cell. The image is encoded as a feature map which can be the same size as the original image or smaller size. Each cell in the feature map is processed with the nearby cells that have already been processed before. Thus, the whole process is sequential. However, such a sequential operation is time-consuming. The SPACE network [13] discards the nearby cells and processes all the cells fully parallel. The authors also add another network to infer the background components.

PermaKey [7] is a model that aims to extract object keypoints from images that take the error map between two feature maps as input. While our model takes the error map between two images as input directly to inference the position of objects.

3   Model

In this section we introduce our model in details.

3.1   Glimpsing Network

In our approach we iteratively build up a reconstruction. We use a glimpsing network that consists of a spatial transformer network that proposes the location of a bounding box and then resamples the image within that bounding box to create (in our case) a low-resolution patch of the original image. In our network at each iteration, the spatial transformer network is given the residual error between the current reconstruction and the input image. The glimpsing network selects a bounding box. Then the residual error, $\boldsymbol{\Delta}(t) = \boldsymbol{x} - \hat{\boldsymbol{x}}(t)$, within the bounding box is down-sampled to an 8×8 patch (with 3 colour channels) and fed to a VAE. The VAE produces a latent code $q(\boldsymbol{z}|\boldsymbol{\Delta}(t))$. This is used to create a reconstruction using the standard reparameterisation trick, which is then resized to the size of the original bounding box. This results in a reconstructed correction, $\hat{\boldsymbol{\Delta}}(t)$, which is then added to reconstruction to obtain an new reconstruction $\hat{\boldsymbol{x}}(t+1) =$

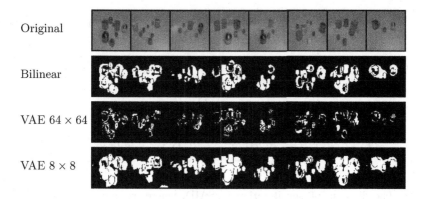

Fig. 1. The error maps of different compression methods. The first row is the original image, the next three rows are the error maps of bilinear interpolation, a VAE for 64×64 image and a VAE for 8×8 image which takes the downsampled version of the original images as input

$\hat{\boldsymbol{x}}(t) + \hat{\boldsymbol{\Delta}}(t)$ (note that $\hat{\boldsymbol{\Delta}}(t)$ only has non-zero values within the bounding box selected by the glimpsing network).

We use the standard information theoretic result that the cost of transmitting a random variable with a distribution $q(\boldsymbol{z}|\boldsymbol{\Delta}(t))$ relative to a distribution $p(\boldsymbol{z})$ is given by the KL-divergence (or relative entropy) $D_{KL}(q\|p)$. In our case we use the standard latent encoding $q(\boldsymbol{z}|\boldsymbol{\Delta}(t)) = \mathcal{N}\big(\boldsymbol{z}|\boldsymbol{\mu}, \mathrm{diag}(\boldsymbol{\sigma})\big)$ and standard prior $p(\boldsymbol{z}) = \mathcal{N}(\boldsymbol{z}|\boldsymbol{0}, \mathbf{I})$. The cost of communicating the residual error is given by $-\log\big(p(\boldsymbol{x} - \hat{\boldsymbol{x}})\big)$. We use the standard assumption that the residual errors are independent at each pixel and colour channel and normally distributed with mean 0 and standard deviation σ. To minimise the communication cost we choose σ^2 to be the empirical variance. In this case the cost of communicating the residual errors is, up to a constant, equal to $N \log(\sigma)$, where N is the number of pixels times the number of colour channels.

Note that provided both the sender and receiver have the same VAE decoder we can communicate an image by sending the set of latent codes (plus the position of the bounding box) and the residual error. (We assume that the dataset we are sending is so large that the cost of transmitting the VAE decoder is negligible). To train our spatial transformer and VAE we attempt to minimise this communication cost for a dataset of images.

A critical component of our approach is that we use an information bottleneck. That is, we down-sample our bounding box and feed this to a VAE. We illustrate the effect of this for images taken from the CLEVR [10] dataset in Fig. 1. In the first row we show the original images. In the second row we show the reconstruction error after down-sampling the whole image to an 8×8 image and then up-sampling using bilinear interpolation to the original size (64×64). In the third row we show the reconstruction loss if we use a vanilla VAE without down-sampling. Finally, we show the reconstruction loss when we down-sample to 8×8 encode that through a VAE and then up-sample the VAE reconstruction.

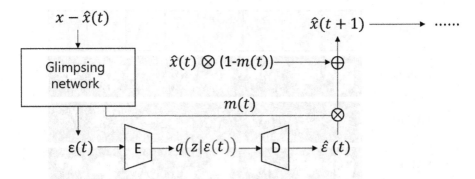

Fig. 2. The diagram of one iteration in SAID, where we omit the operation from position code $\boldsymbol{u}$ to $\boldsymbol{\epsilon}(t)$.

Figure 1 illustrates that due to the bottleneck we have high reconstruction error around the objects in the image. This error will drive the glimpse model towards parts of the scene of high complexity.

3.2   Model Architecture and Training

In keeping with our philosophy or keeping our model simple. Our glimpsing network consists of 2 layers of CNN and 2 layers of MLP. Each image is presented K times. At each presentation the input to the glimpsing network is the residual error, $\boldsymbol{\Delta}(t) = \boldsymbol{x} - \hat{\boldsymbol{x}}(t)$. The output of the glimpsing network provides the coordinates of the bounding box that is then resampled to create an 8×8 RGB image patch, $\boldsymbol{\epsilon}(t)$ that is used as the input to a standard VAE. In Fig. 2, we illustrate the structure of one iteration in our model. In the experiment, $\boldsymbol{\epsilon}(t)$ is the original image within the bounding box rather than the residual error (which is better for the downstream tasks). This also makes $\hat{\boldsymbol{x}}(t + 1) = (1 - \boldsymbol{m}(t)) \otimes \hat{\boldsymbol{x}}(t) + \boldsymbol{m}(t) \otimes \hat{\boldsymbol{\epsilon}}(t)$. where $\boldsymbol{m}(t)$ is a mask equal to 1 in the bounding box and 0 otherwise that obtained from the position code, and $\otimes$ denotes elementwise multiplication. Additionally, $\boldsymbol{m}(t)$ can be an alpha mask produced by the decoder of the VAE, the importance of the alpha mask will be investigated in the ablation study. The VAE reconstruction, $\hat{\boldsymbol{\epsilon}}(t)$, is reshaped to the original bounding box to create a correction to the reconstruction. Both encoder and decoder contain 4 layers of CNN with ReLU and 2 layers of MLP. We used a 10-dimensional latent representation. To train the VAE we minimise the standard ELBO loss function

$$\mathcal{L}_{vae} = - \log(p(\boldsymbol{\epsilon}(t)|\hat{\boldsymbol{\epsilon}}(t))) + D_{KL}\left(q(\boldsymbol{z}(t)|\boldsymbol{\epsilon}(t))\|\mathcal{N}(\boldsymbol{x}|\boldsymbol{0}, \mathbf{I})\right) \tag{1}$$

where $q(\boldsymbol{z}(t)|\boldsymbol{\epsilon}(t))$ is the distribution describing the latent. Note that the reconstruction $\hat{\boldsymbol{\epsilon}}$ is generated by sampling a latent vector from $q(\boldsymbol{z}(t)|\boldsymbol{\epsilon}(t))$ and feeding this to the decoder of the VAE.

Recall the glimpsing network predicts the position of the bounding box. We encode this through a position parameter $\boldsymbol{\mu} = (\mu_x, \mu_y)$ and width parameters $\boldsymbol{\sigma} = (\sigma_x, \sigma_y)$. Adding a bounding box at iteration t reduces the cost of communicating the residual error by

$$\mathcal{L}_{res} = - \log(p(\boldsymbol{\Delta}(t)) + \log(p(\boldsymbol{\Delta}(t - 1)) \tag{2}$$

but requires an additional cost

$$\mathcal{L}_{kl} = D_{KL}\left(q(\boldsymbol{z}(t)|\boldsymbol{\epsilon}(t))\|\mathcal{N}(\boldsymbol{x}|\boldsymbol{0}, \mathbf{I})\right). \tag{3}$$

Summing these two terms provide a loss function for the network that measures (up to an additive constant) the reduction in cost of communicating the image using the new latent code describing the correction to the residual error. Note that in using the trained network when this difference becomes positive then we stop glimpsing. In practice, training the glimpsing network with just these term leads to poor performance. To improve this we assume the parameters $\boldsymbol{\mu}$ and $\boldsymbol{\sigma}$

represent parameters of a normal distribution where we regularise them with an additional loss term

$$\mathcal{L}_{pos} = D_{KL}\left(\mathcal{N}(\boldsymbol{u}|\boldsymbol{\mu}, \boldsymbol{\sigma})\|p(\boldsymbol{u})\right). \tag{4}$$

This acts as a regularisation term for $\boldsymbol{\mu}$ and $\boldsymbol{\sigma}$. We call the whole network *Spatial Attention for Information Detection* (SAID).

We also considered two modified network architectures. In the first we learn an alpha channel so that the corrections are only applied to particular regions within the bounding box. In the second case we include an additional channel as the input, which we called *scope*. This is motivated by MONet [1] that uses the same idea. This scope channel can force the network to look at the area that has not been discovered even when there are areas that have been discovered before contain high error pixels. Initially we set $\boldsymbol{s}(0) = \boldsymbol{1}$. Recall that the mask, $\boldsymbol{m}(t)$, is defined to be 1 in the bounding box and 0 elsewhere. Then the scope is updated as

$$\boldsymbol{s}(t+1) = \boldsymbol{s}(t) \otimes (\boldsymbol{1} - \boldsymbol{m}(t)) \tag{5}$$

so the scope will be 0 where a bounding box has been proposed and 1 otherwise. Note that in our approach we learn after every iteration rather than build up a gradient over multiple iterations. This makes the learning problem for our system much simpler than methods such as MONet that applies the loss function only after making a series of bounding box proposals. We investigate the role of the alpha channel and scope in ablations studies described in Sect. 4.4.

4   Experiments

In this section we attempt to quantify the performance. Recall that the objective is to find glimpses that allows an image to be efficiently encoded through a bottleneck, so it will not necessarily find glimpses that correspond to objects. However, as we will show this is an emergent property of the network, at least for simple scenes. We therefore compare our model to two models, SPACE [13] and SPAIR [2] designed to find multiple objects in an image. To evaluate our model, we use three commonly used datasets in unsupervised object-centric representation learning models. The first dataset is Multi-dSprites, which is developed from dSprites [15] and each image consists of different shapes with different colour, the maximum number of objects in this dataset is 4. The second dataset is Multi-MNIST. For Multi-MNIST, we render MNIST digits of size 20×20 on a 84×84 canvas. The maximum number of objects in this dataset is 5. The last dataset is CLEVR [10]. For all the datasets we resize images into 64×64.

We trained our network, SAID, using the ADAM [11] optimizer with $\beta_1 = 0.5$ and $\beta_2 = 0.999$. We train our model for 200 epochs for all the datasets.

4.1   Quantitative Comparison

As a first test we consider object location on the Multi-MNIST dataset. Although object location is not an objective of our model, for the Multi-MNIST dataset the

Table 1. Comparison with respect to the quality of the bounding boxes in the Multi-MNIST. Results are averaged over 5 random seeds.

	AP	Object
	IoU Threshold $\in [0.1{:}0.1{:}0.9]$	Count error
SPAIR	0.501 ± 0.004	0.261 ± 0.032
SPACE	0.310 ± 0.041	0.031 ± 0.005
SAID	0.503 ± 0.005	0.810 ± 0.040

hand-written characters are well separated and so a natural choice of bounding box would be around each character. There are however situations where the bounding box only covers part of the objects or covers more than one object, as shown in Fig. 5. We perform a quantitative comparison of results on Multi-MNIST using two metrics with SPACE and SPAIR. The two metrics are the Average Precision (AP) and the Object Count Error. AP is a commonly used metric in object detection task [6] and the Object Count Error is the difference between the number of objects predicted by the models and the true number of digits [2]. For SPACE and SPAIR, we set the grid size as 3×3. For our model, we use the index of the iteration that the KL term of the VAE is smaller than improvements on the mean squared error as the number of objects, and we set $K = 5$ in training and $K = 9$ in AP measurement.

As shown in Table 1, our model achieves similar AP with SPAIR, SPACE has the worst AP. However, this result on Multi-MNIST does not reflect the ability of object detection. The reason is the ground truth bounding box we are using for MNIST in the AP calculation is larger than the digits, which degrades the AP result when the model returns a smaller bounding box while it still detects the objects well. In Fig. 3, the first row is the ground truth bounding box we can obtain in Multi-MNIST dataset, this brings disadvantages to the SPACE model in the AP calculation since the third row shows the bounding box of SPACE model is tighter than the ground truth and still maintain the accuracy. Our model does not perform well on the Object Count Error, since there is no z_{pres} in our model and the objective of our model is to find high error areas rather than find objects. Objects of high complexity are often selected more than once leading to a count error. We note that our stop criteria is applicable to any image and was not chosen to given an accurate object counts.

4.2 Downstream Task

Obviously a glimpsing model is only of value if the glimpses can be used in some downstream task. Here we consider the task of returning the sum of all the digits in a Multi-MNIST image. Each image contains 5 digits. This is a task that has previously been used to test unsupervised multi-object detection. We show the results on 80k training set and 20k test set. We compare our results to

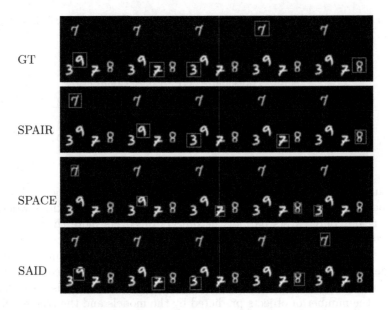

Fig. 3. Qualitative comparison between the bounding boxes found for different models. GT is the ground truth bounding boxes, SPAIR and SPACE are models developed by other authors while SAID is our model.

the SPACE and SPAIR models. We run implementation of all three models to ensure consistency.

For SPACE and our model, we use the same architecture of the encoder, and the channel of the latent space is 10. For SPAIR, we observered that the model tended to collapse at an early stage when we using these parameter setting. Thus, we maintain the original architecture of the encoder, but increase the channel of the latent space to 50 and the input size of the encoder is 15×15 rather than 8×8, which potentially brings benefits to the capacity of the encoder.

To compute the sum of the digits we construct a 3 layer MLP using the latent codes, $z(t)$, as inputs. The output of the MLP has a single output which we train to have the same numerical value as the digit (that is, the digit 3 should have an output of 3). When testing we add the outputs from each glimpse and then round that number to the nearest integer. We trained the MLP for 100 epochs. This is considerably simpler than the set up described in [2] who use an LSTM to perform the addition. We note that our method explicitly treats the glimpse for this problem as a set, where the result is invariant to the ordering of the glimpses. We also demonstrate the results by feeding the ground truth bounding box into the encoder rather than the predicted bounding box, which we note as GT. GT provides an estimated upper-bound on the performance we could achieve.

Table 2 shows the results of four models in 2 different conditions. Fixed represents a frozen encoder during the classifier training while Unfixed represents

Table 2. The performance on the downstream task of summing the digits in the images in Multi-MNIST is shown using the ground truth (GT) bounding boxes and bounding boxes found by SPAIR, SPACE and our network SAID. The results are computed by averaging over 5 runs with different random seeds.

	Fixed		Unfixed	
	Train	Test	Train	Test
GT	30.3% ± 1.2%	29.2% ± 1.1%	97.5% ± 0.9%	92.3% ± 1.1%
SPAIR	25.8% ± 2.2%	24.0% ± 2.1%	24.6% ± 1.5%	22.0% ± 1.1%
SPACE	15.1% ± 2.5%	14.4% ± 2.2%	42.3% ± 1.5%	30.1% ± 1.2%
SAID	22.3% ± 1.8%	21.3% ± 2.0%	57.8% ± 1.6%	31.9% ± 1.5%

an encoder tuning with the classifier. Due to the architecture issue, SPAIR performs best under Fixed but worst under Unfixed. Our model performs better than SPACE in both situations but there is still a huge gap between our model and the ground truth bounding box.

4.3 Generalization

Our model uses a very general principle that we believe can be widely used in different contexts. To explore this we look at out-of-distribution generalisation. That is, when we train on one dataset (here we use CLEVR) and use the model on a different dataset. We test the network on the Multi-dSprites and Multi-MNIST datasets. We set the maximum number of iteration $K = 10$ which the same as we used when training CLEVR, but we stop the iteration when the KL is larger than the reduction in code length of the reconstruction error. Results are shown in Fig. 4. The first row is the result for Multi-dSprites, the model trained on CLEVR can stop at reasonable iteration. But the model tends to infer more times on Multi-MNIST, we assume it is because the binary images are simpler to be transmitted than the RGB images, the VAE trained on CLEVR can transmit binary images efficiently no matter if the bounding box covers the digits correctly. The model can still locate the area of objects although some of the bounding boxes failed at covering one object.

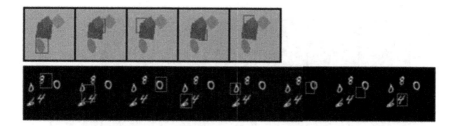

Fig. 4. Examples of bounding boxes found on the Multi-dSprites and Multi-MNIST dataset are shown for a network trained of the CLEVR dataset.

4.4   Ablation Study

The results we show in the previous section is trained with a scope channel and the input is the difference between the original image and a lossy image that has been downsampled to 8 × 8 and then upsampled to the original size through bilinear interpolation. Also, we have used an alpha mask instead of a binary mask when we blend the images. In this section, we show the importance of the scope channel and the alpha channel. We also show how the lossy image can affect the results when we use different methods to get the lossy version.

Table 3 shows the results on AP and Object Count Error, no alpha and no scope mean we remove the alpha channel and scope channel respectively. VAE8 means we use a 8 × 8 VAE to reconstruct the image after the downsample interpolation, as shown in Fig. 1. It can be observed that the alpha channel does not make a huge difference to the model while the model gets a degeneration performance when we remove the scope channel. Also, the model performs worse when we use a VAE to obtain the lossy version of images. This is because after using a 8 × 8 VAE, the error map tends to cover more background.

Table 3. The performance of ablation studies carried out on the Multi-MNIST dataset. The average precision in the detection of bounding boxes is presented together with the error in the count of the numberof objects. Different versions of SAID are compared.

	AP	Object
	IoU Threshold ∈ [0.1:0.1:0.9]	Count error
SAID (no alpha)	0.490 ± 0.008	0.731 ± 0.040
SAID (no scope)	0.341 ± 0.006	1.710 ± 0.110
SAID (VAE8)	0.452 ± 0.008	1.101 ± 0.031
SAID	0.503 ± 0.005	0.810 ± 0.040

4.5   CLEVR and Multi-dSprites

In the Multi-MNIST the objects are of approximately the same size and do not suffer from occlusion. Clearly, this is very different to real images. To explore these issues we tested our models on CLEVR and Multi-dSprites dataset.

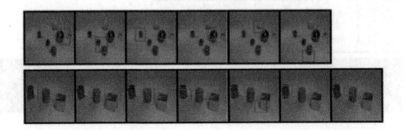

Fig. 5. Examples of bounding boxes found by SAID on the CLEVR dataset.

Figure 5 shows the results on CLEVR dataset and Fig. 6 shows the results on Multi-dSprites dataset, we set $K = 10$ for CLEVR and $K = 4$ for Multi-dSprites respectively. We stop the iteration when the KL divergences is greater than the reduction in transmitting the residual error. In Fig. 5, the first row, the size of objects is close to 8×8, the model can stop at the correct iteration and all the bounding boxes covers different objects, although the bounding boxes are less accurate. For the last row, the size of objects is much larger than 8×8. Our model tends to infer more than the number of objects, this is due to the limited bottleneck failing at transmitting the whole object at the first transmission. But for those big objects, the model returns more accurate bounding boxes compared to the first two rows. Since big objects tend to show a big error. In Fig. 6, our model does not stop after in a reasonable number of iterations. It has the same issue as CLEVR dataset that the bounding box tends to cover parts of shapes rather than the whole object. Also, our model cannot deal with overlap properly. In part we attribute this failure to the weakness of the attention network which struggles with finding bounding boxes of very different sizes.

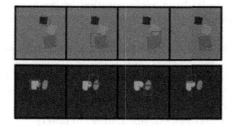

Fig. 6. Examples of bounding boxes found on the Multi-dSprites dataset.

5   Conclusion

Information compression provides a powerful tool for recognising structure in complex data sources. In this paper we have combined this with an information bottleneck to produce a glimpsing network that encodes images through a series of glimpses. By feeding the network the current residual error we can generate a series of bounding box proposals around parts of the image with high uncertainty in its reconstruction. We combine this with a VAE that can learn the common structures within an image (e.g. objects, or rather typical residual errors associated with objects). As the bounding boxes are rescaled, the structures being learned by the VAE are translation and scale invariant. We have shown that following these principles it is possible to train a very simple network that has comparable performance on object detection tasks to much more complex networks designed for multi-object detection. Our objective was to test as simple a network as possible to prove the power of this learning paradigm.

References

1. Burgess, C.P., et al.: MoNet: unsupervised scene decomposition and representation. arXiv preprint arXiv:1901.11390 (2019)
2. Crawford, E., Pineau, J.: Spatially invariant unsupervised object detection with convolutional neural networks. In: Proceedings of the AAAI Conference on Artificial Intelligence, pp. 3412–3420 (2019)
3. Engelcke, M., Jones, O.P., Posner, I.: Genesis-v2: inferring unordered object representations without iterative refinement. arXiv preprint arXiv:2104.09958 (2021)
4. Engelcke, M., Kosiorek, A.R., Jones, O.P., Posner, I.: Genesis: generative scene inference and sampling with object-centric latent representations. In: International Conference on Learning Representations (2020)
5. Eslami, S., et al.: Attend, infer, repeat: fast scene understanding with generative models. In: Advances in Neural Information Processing Systems (2016)
6. Everingham, M., Van Gool, L., Williams, C.K., Winn, J., Zisserman, A.: The pascal visual object classes (VOC) challenge. Int. J. Comput. Vis. **88**(2), 303–338 (2010)
7. Gopalakrishnan, A., van Steenkiste, S., Schmidhuber, J.: Unsupervised object keypoint learning using local spatial predictability. In: International Conference on Learning Representations (2021)
8. Greff, K., et al.: Multi-object representation learning with iterative variational inference. In: International Conference on Machine Learning, pp. 2424–2433. PMLR (2019)
9. Greff, K., Van Steenkiste, S., Schmidhuber, J.: Neural expectation maximization. In: Advances in Neural Information Processing Systems (2017)
10. Johnson, J., Hariharan, B., van der Maaten, L., Fei-Fei, L., Lawrence Zitnick, C., Girshick, R.: CLEVR: a diagnostic dataset for compositional language and elementary visual reasoning. In: Proceedings of the IEEE Conference on Computer Vision and Pattern Recognition, pp. 2901–2910 (2017)
11. Kingma, D.P., Ba, J.: Adam: a method for stochastic optimization. In: Proceedings of International Conference on Learning Representations (2015)
12. Kingma, D.P., Welling, M.: Auto-encoding variational bayes. In: Proceedings of International Conference on Learning Representations (2013)
13. Lin, Z., et al.: Space: Unsupervised object-oriented scene representation via spatial attention and decomposition. In: Proceedings of International Conference on Learning Representations (2020)
14. Locatello, F., et al.: Object-centric learning with slot attention. In: Advances in Neural Information Processing Systems (2020)
15. Matthey, L., Higgins, I., Hassabis, D., Lerchner, A.: dSprites: disentanglement testing sprites dataset (2017)
16. Rezende, D.J., Mohamed, S., Wierstra, D.: Stochastic backpropagation and approximate inference in deep generative models. In: Proceedings of the 31st International Conference on International Conference on Machine Learning (2014)
17. Stelzner, K., Peharz, R., Kersting, K.: Faster attend-infer-repeat with tractable probabilistic models. In: Chaudhuri, K., Salakhutdinov, R. (eds.) Proceedings of the 36th International Conference on Machine Learning. Proceedings of Machine Learning Research, vol. 97, pp. 5966–5975. PMLR, 09–15 June 2019
18. Stewart, E.E., Valsecchi, M., Schütz, A.C.: A review of interactions between peripheral and foveal vision. J. Vis. **20**(12), 2–2 (2020)
19. Van Steenkiste, S., Kurach, K., Schmidhuber, J., Gelly, S.: Investigating object compositionality in generative adversarial networks. Neural Netw. **130**, 309–325 (2020)

Remote Sensing Scene Classification Based on Covariance Pooling of Multi-layer CNN Features Guided by Saliency Maps

Sara Akodad[(⊠)] [iD], Lionel Bombrun[iD], Christian Germain[iD], and Yannick Berthoumieu[iD]

Université de Bordeaux, CNRS, IMS, UMR 5218, Groupe Signal et Image, 33405 Talence, France
{sara.akodad,lionel.bombrun,christian.germain, yannick.berthoumieu}@ims-bordeaux.fr

Abstract. The new generation of remote sensing imaging sensors enables high spatial, spectral and temporal resolution images with high revisit frequencies. These sensors allow the acquisition of multi-spectral and multi-temporal images. The availability of these data has raised the interest of the remote sensing community to develop novel machine learning strategies for supervised classification. This paper aims at introducing a novel supervised classification algorithm based on covariance pooling of multi-layer convolutional neural network (CNN) features. The basic idea consists in an ensemble learning approach based on covariance matrices estimation from CNN features. Then, after being projected on the log-Euclidean space, an SVM classifier is used to make a decision. In order to give more strength to relatively small objects of interest in the scene, we propose to incorporate the visual saliency map in the process. For that, inspired by the theory of robust statistics, a weighted covariance matrix estimator is considered. Larger weights are given to more salient regions. Finally, some experiments on remote sensing classification are conducted on the UC Merced land use dataset. The obtained results confirm the potential of the proposed approach in terms of classification scene accuracy. It demonstrates, besides the interest of exploiting second order statistics and adopting an ensemble learning approach, the benefit of incorporating visual saliency maps.

Keywords: Covariance pooling · Saliency map · Ensemble learning · Multi-layer CNN features

1 Introduction

The availability of multi-spectral and multi-temporal image datasets leads to the development of novel data processing techniques for many important and

Supported by CNES TEMPOSS project.

challenging applications, in particular, the classification task. A supervised classification algorithm aims at assigning a label to an image according to its content. To this end, the first methods which appeared were based on manually extracting and coding features from images with for instance the bag of words model (BoW) [1], the vector of locally aggregated descriptors (VLAD) [2] or the Fisher vectors (FV) [3]. Those latter methods have demonstrated interesting results in a wide range of applications such as image classification [3–5], text-retrieval, action and face recognition, etc. In the last decade, convolutional neural networks (CNN) [6] have achieved a great success in image recognition tasks by automatically extracting and learning a hierarchical feature representation from input images [6]. To take advantage of both coding strategies and deep learning methods, several authors have proposed hybrid architectures which permit the combination of CNN models with VLAD or FV vectors such as the Fisher network [7], the NetVLAD [8] and the Hybrid FV which consists in FV encoding of multi-layer CNN features [9].

On another side, several authors focus their researches on exploiting second order statistics in order to strengthen the feature representation. In particular, the use of covariance matrices has proven to be highly effective in various classification tasks including person re-identification, texture recognition, material categorization or EEG classification in brain-computer interfaces to cite a few of them [10–12]. However, Euclidean computational tools have to be adapted since symmetric positive definite (SPD) matrices do not lie on an Euclidean space but on a Riemannian manifold. Since then, coding methods were extended to covariance matrix descriptors which yields to the following strategies: the log-Euclidean bag of words (LE BoW), the bag of Riemannian words (BoRW) [13], the log-Euclidean vector of locally aggregated descriptors (LE VLAD) [10], the intrinsic Riemannian vector of locally aggregated descriptors (RVLAD), the Log-Euclidean Fisher vectors (LE FV) [14] and the Riemannian Fisher vectors (RFV) [15]. Meanwhile, in order to benefit of both second-order statistics and deep learning architectures, different second-order convolutional neural network architectures have recently been introduced [16–20]. The first try was the pooled covariance matrix from the outputs of a CNN model [16,17]. A different way to exploit second-order statistics in a deep neural network is the Riemannian SPD matrix network (SPDNet) [18]. Inspired by this work, Yu et al. have proposed in [19] an end-to-end training version of a second-order CNN (SO-CNN). Also, the Hybrid LE FV approach [14] encodes a set of covariance matrices coming from convolutional layer outputs of a pretrained CNN. Later, He et al. have proposed in [20] a multi-layer version: the multi-layer stacked covariance pooling (MSCP). Inspired by this work and the success of ensemble learning strategies, we have proposed in [21,22] an ensemble learning approach (ELCP) based on global covariance pooling of stacked convolutional features. Even if the ELCP approach has shown competitive results, it suffers from a main drawback: each pixel contributes equally during covariance pooling. Since the objective is to classify remote sensing images, this might be problematic. In fact, in a given scene, objects of interest of relatively small dimension could be assigned to the wrong class due to the predominant information of the environment. For example, in a scene of a golf course, or a storage tank, the surrounding environment of the object of interest (bunkers, tank) such as trees or urban areas can greatly affect the final decision. To solve this problem, we propose to exploit the visual saliency information [23]. The idea behind visual attention prediction is initially inspired by the behavior and the neural architecture of the human visual system. Its goal is to reduce the large amount of useless information carried by images and to focus on most relevant objects, also named *salient information*. It aims at simulating the human visual system by detecting pixels or regions that most attract human visual attention. Different types of saliency detection algorithms exist [24]. Especially, deep learning based methods have yielded a qualitative leap in performance such as superCNN [25] which is trained with sequences of color superpixels, and the DHSNet [26] which exploits the global context of the image before refining the details of the saliency map step by step. Recently, with the huge potential of generative adversarial networks (GANs), Pan *et al.* proposed the SalGan strategy in [27] to generate saliency maps by a combination of two CNN models.

The main contribution of this paper is to propose an ensemble learning approach which exploits saliency information during covariance pooling. It consists of computing a weighted covariance matrix which allows us to give more weight to small objects of interest. The paper is structured as follows, Sect. 2 presents and discusses the related works regarding the ensemble learning approach based on covariance pooling (ELCP). Then, Sect. 3 introduces the proposed approach. An application on remote sensing scene classification is next presented in Sect. 4. Finally, Sect. 5 concludes this paper and provides some perspectives for this work.

2   Related Works

Willing to exploit multi-layer CNN features richness and the multi-variate representations through second order statistics while involving an ensemble learning approach, we have introduced in [21] the ensemble learning covariance pooling (ELCP) architecture which consists in the extension of the multi-layer stacked covariance pooling (MSCP) approach [17]. The method aims at enhancing the classification performance by using different convolutional layer features of a CNN with various depth and combining different weak classifiers. This strategy ensures robustness of classification by fusing the decision obtained on different subsets. As described in Fig. 1, the principle of ELCP can be summarized as follows:

- First, multi-layer features are extracted where specific convolutional layers of a pretrained CNN model are considered. Each convolutional layer has its own spatial dimension. For example, in the case of the *VGG-16* model, the chosen layers are $conv_{3,3}$, $conv_{4,3}$ and $conv_{5,3}$. Their associated outputs are sized respectively $M_1 \in \mathbb{R}^{56 \times 56 \times 256}$, $M_2 \in \mathbb{R}^{28 \times 28 \times 512}$ and $M_3 \in \mathbb{R}^{14 \times 14 \times 512}$.
- These extracted feature maps M_1, M_2 and M_3 are stacked together to form a unique set of features. As the spatial dimension is not homogeneous, a

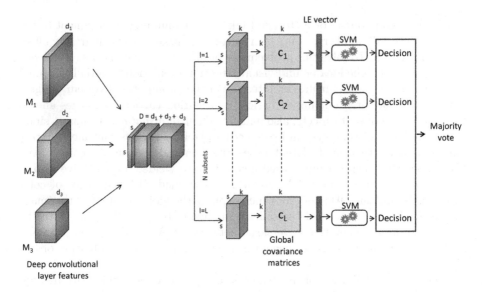

Fig. 1. Architecture of the ensemble learning approach for covariance pooling of multi-layer CNN features (ELCP) [21].

bilinear interpolation is applied allowing to downsample each feature map to the smallest size.

- Then, for each image, the produced stacked features are randomly partitioned into L subsets of k features. For each subset, the $k \times k$ sample covariance matrix is computed. Since covariance matrices are SPD matrices that lie on a Riemannian manifold, Euclidean tools are not adapted to compute distance between two matrices. The log-Euclidean metric is better suited. It consists in projecting the covariance matrices on a tangent space where Euclidean distance can be adopted. The mapping in the log-Euclidean space is performed with the log map operator [28] defined as:

$$\mathbf{C}^{LE} = \log \mathbf{C} = \mathbf{V} \, \mathrm{logm}(\mathbf{D}) \, \mathbf{V}^T, \tag{1}$$

where $\mathbf{C} = \mathbf{V}\mathbf{D}\mathbf{V}^T$ is the eigen decomposition of covariance matrix $\mathbf{C}$ and $\mathrm{logm}()$ is the matrix logarithm. Then, to obtain the log-Euclidean vector representation, a vectorization operation $\mathrm{Vec}()$ is performed such that:

$$\mathbf{x} = \mathrm{Vec}(\mathbf{X}) = \left[X_{11}, \sqrt{2}X_{12}, \ldots, \sqrt{2}X_{1k}, X_{22}, \sqrt{2}X_{23}, \ldots, X_{kk} \right]. \tag{2}$$

These operations lead to a transformation from a covariance matrix $\mathbf{C} \in \mathbb{R}^{k \times k}$ to a vector $\mathbf{c} \in \mathbb{R}^{\frac{k(k+1)}{2}}$ which corresponds to a multi-variate representation of each image.

- Finally, the log-Euclidean vectors computed for each subset are fed into an SVM classifier to obtain a decision. In the end, a majority vote is performed to elect the most represented decision among the L subsets.

3   Proposed Method: ELCP Guided by Saliency Maps (EL-SCP)

Visual saliency has been investigated in the computer vision literature in many different tasks, such as image classification and retrieval, semantic segmentation and object recognition [29,30]. It permits to identify parts of the input image which are the most important for classification.

In the ELCP approach, all the pixels of the image contribute equally during the estimation of the sample covariance matrix. This might be problematic when the objects of interest are of small dimension compared to the surrounding environment. In order to give more strength to those elements, several approaches can be considered to exploit saliency maps. The simplest one consists in using the ELCP approach where the input image is multiplied by the saliency map. But this approach loses the contextual information. To circumvent this drawback, we propose to exploit the saliency map on the CNN features. For that, we introduce a weighted covariance matrix estimator where the weights depend on the visual saliency. Larger weights will be given to more salient regions. In practice, each branch related to each subset in the ELCP approach shown in Fig. 1 is replaced by the one shown in Fig. 2 to form the proposed EL-SCP method.

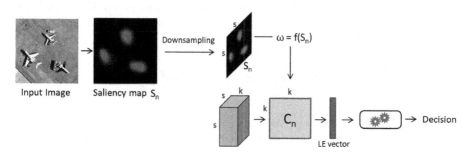

Fig. 2. Presentation of the proposed covariance pooling of CNN features guided by saliency maps.

3.1   Saliency Map Generation

Visual saliency describes the spatial locations in an image that attract the human attention. According to a bottom-up process, it consists in an exploration of the image by a human observer during a small duration and without any prior about its content. Inspired by generative adversarial networks (GANs), Pan *et al.* introduced in [27] the SalGAN architecture to estimate the saliency map of an input image. SalGAN, as illustrated in Fig. 3, is composed of two competing convolutional neural networks: a generator which allows the generation of saliency maps using a convolutional encoder-decoder architecture and a discriminator which tells whether the generated saliency map is real or fake.

The training of SalGAN is made through two competing convolutional neural networks:

- **Generator:**
  Permits the generation of saliency maps using a convolutional encoder-decoder architecture. The encoder part is similar to a pretrained VGG-16 network. Filter weights of the last layers are modified and trained for saliency prediction. The decoder is structured in a reversed order than the encoder. The final output of the generator is a saliency map having the same size as the input image. The values are normalized such that each pixel is in range $[0, 1]$.
- **Discriminator:**
  The convolutional network is constituted by kernel convolutions, pooling, fully connected layers and activation functions. It produces an output score which tells whether the input saliency map is real or fake. As shown in Fig. 3, this network is initially trained with a binary cross entropy (BCE) loss over the saliency maps.

3.2   Weighted Covariance Matrix Estimator

Inspired by the theory of robust statistics, we propose to consider a weighted covariance matrix estimator during the covariance pooling step. For a given set of k dimensional CNN features $\{\mathbf{x}_i\}_{i=1...N}$, the $k \times k$ weighted covariance matrix is:

$$\mathbf{C} = \sum_{i=1}^{N} \omega_i (\mathbf{x}_i - \mu)(\mathbf{x}_i - \mu)^T, \tag{3}$$

where μ is the weighted mean vector, *i.e.* $\mu = \sum_{i=1}^{N} \omega_i \mathbf{x}_i$, and ω_i is the weight assigned to pixel i and N the number of pixels. In order to give more strength to salient regions, weights are defined by:

$$\omega_i = \frac{\exp\left(\frac{s_i}{\sigma}\right)}{\sum_{j=1}^{N} \exp\left(\frac{s_j}{\sigma}\right)}, \tag{4}$$

where s_i is the saliency information obtained by SalGAN for pixel i and σ is a positive scalar parameter which controls the importance given to the saliency information. Note that when σ tends toward infinity, the weights ω_i are equal to $\frac{1}{N}$, the weighted covariance matrix vanishes to the sample covariance matrix and the proposed EL-SCP approach reduces to ELCP [21].

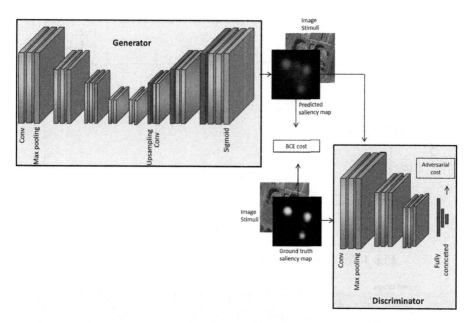

Fig. 3. Overall architecture of the SalGAN network involving a generator and a discriminator for producing a saliency map.

4 Experiments

This section summarizes some classification experiments on large scale scene remote sensing images on the UC Merced land use land cover dataset [31]. It is composed of 2 100 images partitioned into 21 classes. The size of each image is 256×256 pixels. In practice, for the ELCP architecture, parameters L and k are respectively set equal to 20 and 170 as recommended in [21]. The first experiment is a sensitivity analysis about the scalar parameter σ. For that 20% of images are used for training. Figure 4 draws the evolution of the overall accuracy as a function of σ in (4). As expected, when σ tends toward infinity, the proposed EL-SCP approach is equivalent to ELCP [21]. Note that the best results are obtained for $\sigma = 50$. This value will be retained in the following.

Actually, as illustrated in Fig. 5, for a low value of σ, little importance is given to the bottom bunker even though it is a major element to recognize the golf course. And on the other side, for a high value of σ, more importance is given to elements that are not much useful to predict the class, such as trees and grass that surround the bunkers. In practice, $\sigma = 50$ is a good trade-off and will be retained in the following.

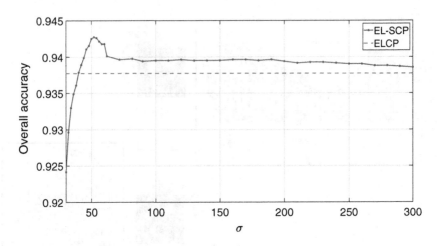

Fig. 4. Influence of σ parameter for 20% of training images.

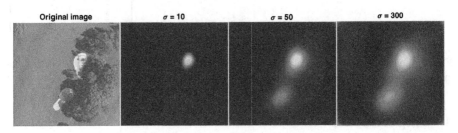

Fig. 5. Weight maps comparison for different parameter values σ.

Figure 6 shows the evolution of the classification performance with the percentage of training samples. Five benchmark approaches are considered. The first one, named VGG-16, consists of a simple transfer learning approach where features are extracted from VGG-16 model and classified with an SVM. The four other approaches are based on second-order features, namely MSCP [20], ELCP [21], Hybrid LE FV [14] and the proposed EL-SCP. As observed, EL-SCP allows to obtain competitive results compared to these state-of-the-art methods.

In order to analyze the pros and cons of the proposed EL-SCP approach over ELCP and MSCP, Table 1 shows the classification performance per class on the UC Merced dataset where only 10% of images are used for training. As it can be seen, EL-SCP performs better for most of the classes. Figure 7 shows some examples of images (with their corresponding saliency map). The three first images, belonging to (a) airplane, (b) tennis court and (c) storage tanks classes, are correctly classified only by EL-SCP, whereas the ELCP assigned them to runway, golf course and intersection classes, respectively. As observed, these images contain object of interest that are well captured by the saliency map. The proposed weighted covariance matrix estimator in EL-SCP allows hence to focus more on them, while for the ELCP, all pixels of the image contribute equally,

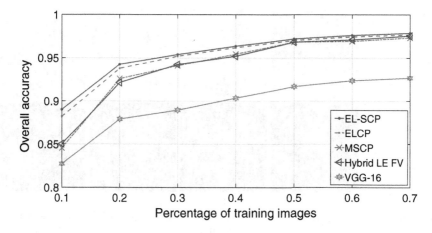

Fig. 6. Influence of the percentage of training sample on the classification accuracy.

the decision is therefore made on the basis of the whole image information and hence disregarding under-represented objects. In contrast, for very few images, there are some cases where the saliency map can be misguiding. This is the case of Fig. 7(d) which belongs to intersection class. Here, the saliency does not focus on the intersection but on the surrounding area. This image is hence assigned to the buildings class for EL-SCP whereas it is correctly classified by ELCP.

Table 1. Classification performance per class for 10% of training images: comparison between MSCP, ELCP and EL-SCP approaches.

Class	MSCP [20]	ELCP [21]	EL-SCP		Class	MSCP [20]	ELCP [21]	EL-SCP
1	80.8	**87.0**	86.8		12	66.8	**80.4**	78.8
2	85.4	88.2	**89.6**		13	66.4	**76.6**	74.0
3	66.2	75.4	**76.2**		14	66.6	**72.6**	72.4
4	81.2	**87.0**	86.0		15	66.6	80.4	**80.6**
5	66.2	71.6	**72.0**		16	88.8	**89.8**	89.6
6	85.4	**88.0**	**88.0**		17	69.8	**80.8**	79.8
7	57.6	60.4	**62.0**		18	78.0	81.6	**82.2**
8	88.4	86.2	**89.4**		19	66.0	79.8	**80.2**
9	66.0	83.4	**84.4**		20	58.2	67.6	**69.2**
10	79.4	80.0	**80.2**		21	59.8	67.8	**72.8**
11	84.4	88.2	**88.4**		**OA**	80.8	88.6	**89.0**

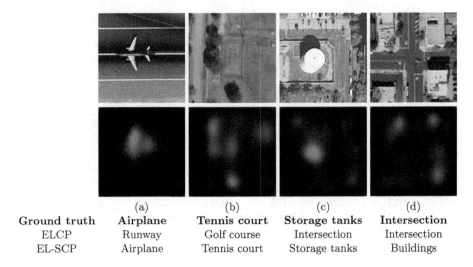

	(a) **Airplane**	(b) **Tennis court**	(c) **Storage tanks**	(d) **Intersection**
Ground truth	**Airplane**	**Tennis court**	**Storage tanks**	**Intersection**
ELCP	Runway	Golf course	Intersection	Intersection
EL-SCP	Airplane	Tennis court	Storage tanks	Buildings

Fig. 7. Examples of images on first row (and saliency maps on the second row) correctly classified only by EL-SCP: (a) airplane, (b) tennis court, (c) storage tanks; and only by ELCP: (d) intersection.

5   Conclusion

This paper has introduced a remote sensing scene classification algorithm based on a multi-variate representation of multi-layer convolutional neural network (CNN) features with the use of covariance pooling. Building on the success of deep neural networks, it consists of an ensemble learning approach where a weighted covariance matrix of multi-layer CNN features is computed for each subset. In order to give more importance to small objects of interest in the scene, the visual saliency map is computed with SalGAN and then used during covariance pooling. The largest weights are given to the most salient regions. Then, covariance matrices are projected in the log-Euclidean space and an SVM classifier is used to make a decision for each subset. In the end, a majority vote is performed to obtain the final decision. The experimental results on UC Merced dataset have illustrated the potential of the proposed approach compared to similar competitive state-of-the-art methods. Future works will include the proposition of a deep ensemble learning architecture that can be trained from end-to-end. In fact, the considered saliency maps are provided by a pre-trained model. The SalGAN model is not retrained on the dataset of interest but is only applied on a transfer learning procedure. To improve that, one can extend the proposed architecture to an end-to-end training process. In addition, the considered saliency map remains the same for each subset on the EL-SCP approach whatever the considered feature maps. This can be overcame by proposing a more adapted strategy where the saliency maps are estimated for each EL-SCP branch according to the considered subset features.

References

1. Sivic, J., Russell, B.C., Efros, A.A., Zisserman, A., Freeman, W.T.: Discovering objects and their location in images. In: Tenth IEEE International Conference on Computer Vision (ICCV 2005), October 2005, vol. 1, pp. 370–377 (2005)
2. Arandjelović, R., Zisserman, A.: All about VLAD. In: IEEE Conference on Computer Vision and Pattern Recognition, pp. 1578–1585 (2013)
3. Perronnin, F., Dance, C.: Fisher kernels on visual vocabularies for image categorization. In: IEEE Conference on Computer Vision and Pattern Recognition, pp. 1–8 (2007)
4. Douze, M., Ramisa, A., Schmid, C.: Combining attributes and Fisher vectors for efficient image retrieval. In: Proceedings of the IEEE Conference on Computer Vision and Pattern Recognition, pp. 745–752 (2011)
5. Sánchez, J., Perronnin, F., Mensink, T., Verbeek, J.: Image classification with the Fisher vector: theory and practice. Int. J. Comp. Vis. **105**(3), 222–245 (2013)
6. Krizhevsky, A., Sutskever, I., Hinton, G.E.: ImageNet classification with deep convolutional neural networks. In: Proceedings of the 25th International Conference on Neural Information Processing Systems, vol. 1, pp. 1097–1105, ser. NIPS 2012. Curran Associates Inc. (2012)
7. Simonyan, K., Vedaldi, A., Zisserman, A.: Deep Fisher networks for large-scale image classification. In: Proceedings of the 26th International Conference on Neural Information Processing Systems, vol. 1, pp. 163–171, ser. NIPS 2013. Curran Associates Inc. (2013)
8. Arandjelovic, R., Gronát, P., Torii, A., Pajdla, T., Sivic, J.: NetVLAD: CNN architecture for weakly supervised place recognition. CoRR, vol. abs/1511.07247 (2015)
9. Li, E., Xia, J., Du, P., Lin, C., Samat, A.: Integrating multilayer features of convolutional neural networks for remote sensing scene classification. IEEE Trans. Geosci. Remote Sens. **55**(10), 5653–5665 (2017)
10. Faraki, M., Harandi, M.T., Porikli, F.: More about VLAD: a leap from Euclidean to Riemannian manifolds. In: IEEE Conference on Computer Vision and Pattern Recognition, pp. 4951–4960 (2015)
11. Barachant, A., Bonnet, S., Congedo, M., Jutten, C.: Classification of covariance matrices using a Riemannian-based kernel for BCI applications. Neuro Comput. **112**, 172–178 (2013)
12. Said, S., Bombrun, L., Berthoumieu, Y.: Texture classification using Rao's distance on the space of covariance matrices. In: Nielsen, F., Barbaresco, F. (eds.) GSI 2015. LNCS, vol. 9389, pp. 371–378. Springer, Cham (2015). https://doi.org/10.1007/978-3-319-25040-3_40
13. Faraki, M., Harandi, M.T., Wiliem, A., Lovell, B.C.: Fisher tensors for classifying human epithelial cells. Pattern Recogn. **47**(7), 2348–2359 (2014)
14. Akodad, S., Bombrun, L., Yaacoub, C., Berthoumieu, Y., Germain, C.: Image classification based on log-Euclidean Fisher vectors for covariance matrix descriptors. In: International Conference on Image Processing Theory, Tools and Applications (IPTA), Xi-an, China, November 2018
15. Ilea, I., Bombrun, L., Said, S., Berthoumieu, Y.: Covariance matrices encoding based on the log-Euclidean and affine invariant Riemannian metrics. In: IEEE CVPRW, pp. 506–515, June 2018
16. Ionescu, C., Vantzos, O., Sminchisescu, C.: Matrix backpropagation for deep networks with structured layers. In: IEEE International Conference on Computer Vision (ICCV), pp. 2965–2973 (2015)

17. Acharya, D., Huang, Z., Paudel, D.P., Gool, L.V.: Covariance pooling for facial expression recognition. CoRR, vol. abs/1805.04855 (2018)
18. Huang, Z., Gool, L.V.: A Riemannian network for SPD matrix learning. In: AAAI Conference on Artificial Intelligence, pp. 2036–2042 (2017)
19. Yu, K., Salzmann, M.: Second-order convolutional neural networks. CoRR, vol. abs/1703.06817 (2017)
20. He, N., Fang, L., Li, S., Plaza, A., Plaza, J.: Remote sensing scene classification using multilayer stacked covariance pooling. IEEE Trans. Geosci. Remote Sens. **56**(12), 6899–6910 (2018)
21. Akodad, S., Vilfroy, S., Bombrun, L., Cavalcante, C.C., Germain, C., Berthoumieu, Y.: An ensemble learning approach for the classification of remote sensing scenes based on covariance pooling of CNN features. In: 2019 27th European Signal Processing Conference (EUSIPCO), September 2019, pp. 1–5 (2019)
22. Akodad, S., Bombrun, L., Xia, J., Berthoumieu, Y., Germain, C.: Ensemble learning approaches based on covariance pooling of CNN features for high resolution remote sensing scene classification. Remote Sens. **12**, 3292 (2020)
23. Itti, L., Koch, C., Niebur, E.: A model of saliency-based visual attention for rapid scene analysis. IEEE Trans. Pattern Anal. Mach. Intell. **20**, 1254–1259 (2009)
24. Cong, R., Lei, J., Fu, H., Cheng, M., Lin, W., Huang, Q.: Review of visual saliency detection with comprehensive information. CoRR, vol. abs/1803.03391 (2018)
25. He, S., Lau, R.W.H., Liu, W., Huang, Z., Yang, Q.: SuperCNN: a superpixelwise convolutional neural network for salient object detection. Int. J. Comp. Vis. **115**(3), 330–344 (2015)
26. Liu, N., Han, J.: DHSNet: deep hierarchical saliency network for salient object detection. In: 2016 IEEE CVPR, June 2016, pp. 678–686 (2016)
27. Pan, J., et al.: SalGAN: visual saliency prediction with generative adversarial networks. CoRR, vol. abs/1701.01081 (2017)
28. Arsigny, V., Fillard, P., Pennec, X., Ayache, N.: Log-Euclidean metrics for fast and simple calculus on diffusion tensors. Magn. Reson. Med. **56**(2), 411–421 (2006)
29. Moosmann, F., Larlus, D., Jurie, F.: Learning saliency maps for object categorization. In: International Workshop on The Representation and Use of Prior Knowledge in Vision (in ECCV 2006), Graz, Austria, May 2006
30. Gao, D., Vasconcelos, N.: Discriminant saliency for visual recognition from cluttered scenes. In: NIPS, vol. 17, January 2004
31. Yang, Y., Newsam, S.: Bag-of-visual-words and spatial extensions for land-use classification. In: Proceedings of the 18th SIGSPATIAL International Conference on Advances in Geographic Information Systems, ser. GIS 2010, pp. 270–279. ACM, New York (2010)

Attention Embedding ResNet for Pest Classification

Jinglin Wu[1] ⓘ, Shiqi Liang[1] ⓘ, Ning Bi[1,2] ⓘ, and Jun Tan[1,2(✉)] ⓘ

[1] School of Mathematics and Computational Science, Sun Yat-Sen University, Guangzhou 510275, People's Republic of China
{wujlin27,liangshq7}@mail2.sysu.edu.cn, {mcsbn, mcstj}@mail.sysu.edu.cn

[2] Guangdong Province Key Laboratory of Computational Science, Sun Yat-Sen University, Guangzhou 510275, People's Republic of China

Abstract. Agriculture drives the development of a country's economic system. Nowadays, due to population growth and continuous growth in demand for food, agriculture and food industry have become indispensable activities. However, pest has always been considered as a serious challenge affecting crop production. The main hazard of pest is the reduction of crop yields, which reduces food product and even causes famine in some areas. Therefore, the detection and classification of pest and their prevention play a vital role in agriculture. With the advancement of computer technology, accurate and rapid identification of pest can help avoid economic losses caused by pest. This article will carry out the task of pest classification based on the basic deep learning model. The main contributions are as follows: Based on the ResNet-50, different attention modules are introduced for different purposes designs, namely Efficient Channel Attention and Coordinate Attention. The former is an improved SE module, which can more effectively integrate the information between image channels and enhance the network's learning ability; the latter embeds location information into channel attention. It can obtain information in a larger area without introducing large overheads. Experimental results show that embedding the ECA attention module and CCO module improve network prediction accuracy by about 2%. And these two attention modules do not cause a substantial increase in the amount of calculation, so embedding the attention module is very useful for improving the network's learning ability.

Keywords: ResNet-50 · Efficient channel attention · Coordinate attention

1 Introduction

1.1 The Challenge of Pest Classification

Agriculture is one of the most important food sources in whole human history. Pest is one of the main factors affecting the yield of agricultural products. Accurate identification and classification of pest in time will help take preventive measures to ensure the yield of agricultural products and avoid economic losses. However, the existing neural networks

© Springer Nature Switzerland AG 2022
M. El Yacoubi et al. (Eds.): ICPRAI 2022, LNCS 13363, pp. 591–602, 2022.
https://doi.org/10.1007/978-3-031-09037-0_48

used for visual classification tasks mainly focus on common objects, such as strays and dogs. This limits the application of powerful deep learning techniques in specific fields (such as agriculture).

The key to carrying out targeted control work such as spraying pesticides for different types of pest, lies in automatically identification and classification of different pest. Therefore, the classification of pest plays a vital role in agricultural control, essential for food security and a stable agricultural economy. However, due to the wide variety of pest and the subtle differences between different types, identification and classification of pest relies heavily on the expertise of agricultural specialists. This process is not only time-consuming but also requires high labor costs. With the development of computer technology, automated pest identification technology has attracted more and more research attention.

However, the task of pest identification is largely different from existing work on object or animal classification because this task has some special characteristics. On the one hand, different pest species may have a high degree of similarity in appearance, which means that interspecific differences may be subtle. On the other hand, the scale of different pest varies greatly. For example, the same species may have different forms, including eggs, larvae, and adults. Another example is the smaller round ladybird, which varies greatly in scale compared with other larger and elongated pest.

1.2 Researches on Classification for Pest

As early as 2010, Bashish D A et al. [1] applied K-means clustering and neural network methods to identify and classify five kinds of diseases about leaf (early scorch, cotton-like mold, gray mold, late scorch, and white). It provided a fast, cheap, and accurate solution to detect plant leaf/stem diseases.

In 2014, Rothe P R et al. [2] proposed a method to automatically classify cotton leaf diseases by extracting features of leaf symptoms from digital images. They used the OTSU method to extract color and features about shape and a support vector machine (SVM) to classify the extracted features.

In 2016, Sladojevic S et al. [3] used CNN to build a new model for plants disease recognition. The model can not only accurately identify 13 different types of diseases from healthy plant leaves but also accurately distinguish plant leaves areas.

In 2017, Wang et al. [4] used apple black rot images to diagnose four different levels of plant diseases. They trained small convolutional neural networks of different depths and fine-tuned four latest deep model. The results show that fine-tuning the pre-trained depth model can significantly improve the performance of a small amount of data. The fine-tuned VGGNet-16 model has the best performance, with an accuracy of 90.4% on the test set. Ramcharan A et al. [5] used a dataset of cassava disease images. They applied transfer learning to identify three diseases and two types of pest damage. Their model, Inception-v3, was state of art at the time, and the classification accuracy of all types of pest was higher than 95%.

In 2018, Nanni L et al. [6] proposed an automatic classifier based on the saliency method and network fusion. They used three different saliency methods as image preprocessing and trained four different convolutional neural networks for each saliency method.

In 2018, Alfarisy A A et al. [7] constructed a network to detect rice diseases, and pest simultaneously. They used search engines to collect 4,511 images from four languages and applied deep learning to classify pest and diseases in rice fields. Their pre-trained CaffeNet model can achieve 87% accuracy.

In 2018, Wang D et al. [8] proposed a pest detection and identification system based on transfer learning to provide a basis for controlling pest and weeds and accurately spraying pesticides. This method can train and test ten kinds of tea pest with an accuracy rate of 93.84%, which is higher than most human experts and tradi-tional neural networks. Two kinds of weeds were used to verify the wide adaptability of the model, and the accuracy rate reached 98.92%.

In 2019, Mishra M et al. [9] believed that lighting, complex backgrounds, and partially visible or different pest in different directions would cause classification errors. They took the crop rice as an example and proposed a pest identification system to mitigate the above situations. They used morphology and skeletonization along with neural networks as classifiers and conducted experiments on datasets to compare their model with other popular classifiers.

In 2020, Bollis E [10] designed a weakly supervised learning process guided by saliency maps to automatically select regions of interest in the images, significantly reducing the annotation task. They conducted experiments on two large datasets to demonstrate models are very promising for pest and disease classification.

In 2021, Liu W [11] proposed a new residual block, DMF-ResNet, to learn multiscale representation. Three branches through each layer and an embedded module are designed to focus on feature fusion between channels. They conducted experiments on IP102 dataset and achieved 59.22% accuracy.

1.3 Pest Recognition Datasets

Several datasets for pest recognition have been set up in recent years as shown in Table 1. In 2019, Li et al. [13] collected 2200 aphids images to solve the problem of aphids causing a sharp decline in wheat, corn, and rapeseed output. Chen [14] et al. collected the Agricultural Diseases and Pest Research Library (IDADP), which includes 15 kinds of pest diseases, including three field crops of rice, wheat, and corn.

In 2019, Wu et al. published a large-scale dataset named IP102 for pest identification, including 102 species of pest and a total of 75,222 images. Examples of IP102 are shown in Fig. 1. Compared with the previous dataset, IP102 conforms to the diversity and category imbalance of pest distribution in the natural environment.

In 2020, Bollis [15] et al. collected 10816 images of 6 types of mites and named the database CPB.

Table 1. Pest and diseases datasets

Author	Name	Size	Year
Li et al.	Aphid	2200	2019
Chen et al.	IDADP	17624	2019
Wu et al.	IP102	75222	2019
Bollis et al.	CPB	10816	2020

Fig. 1. Pest images from IP102 Three examples from the IP102 data set. The first two images show large morphological differences between rice leaf rollers in different stages. The third one shows rice leaf cater-pillar, similar to rice leaf roller shown in the first image in appearance. Noisy backgrounds even make it harder to identify different pests.

1.4   Our Work

In order to advance the research on the identification and classification of pest through computer vision technology, this paper conducts experiments on the pest dataset, IP102 [12]. Firstly, the ResNet is built on the IP102 dataset. Furthermore, a more effective attention module is introduced, and the network's learning ability is enhanced by embedding different attention modules. For example, an improved SE module, ECA, is introduced to enhance the networks integration of information between channels and achieve the effect of improving network classification capabilities. Secondly, the CCO attention module with position-coding information is introduced to capture the direction and position-sensitive information of the images. We explain why embedding these two attention mechanisms is useful, driving the application and development of neural networks for pest identification and classification tasks.

2   Related Studies

2.1   ResNet

ResNet [16] was proposed by He K et al. Their research found that traditional convolutional neural networks are all obtained by stacking a series of convolutional layers. However, two problems will arise when stacking to a certain network depth. One is, the gradient disappears, or the gradient explodes. The other is, degradation problem. Therefore, they proposed two kinds of breakthrough designs enabling the network framework to have a deeper architecture and used Batch Normalization to accelerate training.

2.2 Attention Mechanism

Attention mechanism is a data processing method in machine learning, widely used in various machine learning tasks such as natural language processing, image recognition, and speech recognition.

In layman's terms, the attention mechanism hopes that the network can automatically learn the places that need attention in the picture or text sequence. For example, when looking at a picture, modules help models not distribute the attention equally to all pixels but distribute more attention to the place where people pay attention. From the perspective of realization, the attention mechanism generates a mask by adding a neural network operation, and the value on the mask is the score for evaluating the current point of interest.

The attention mechanism can be divided into:

1. Channel attention mechanism, generating a mask for the channel and scoring it, such as SE module.
2. Spatial attention mechanism, generating a mask and scoring the space, such as Spatial Attention Module.
3. Mixed domain attention mechanism: evaluating and scoring channel attention and spatial attention at the same time, such as BAM and CBAM.

3 Methodology

3.1 ECA: Efficient Channel Attention

We have already learned that by increasing the attention mechanism, the model can focus on some useful information, but how to design the network module so that the attention mechanism can pay more attention to the information that is useful to the result without increasing too much computation.

ECA [17] makes a trade-off between the performance and complexity, and the ECA module only brings a handful of parameters while significantly improving the model's performance. As shown in Fig. 2, by dissecting the channel attention module in SE [18] module, ECA takes appropriate cross-channel interaction can preserve performance while significantly decreasing model complexity.

The process of ECA-module is:

(1) Perform Global Average Pooling on the feature map to get a vector of 1*1*C;
(2) Complete the cross-channel information exchange through one-dimensional convolution.

The SE block used two FC layers to calculate the weights given the aggregation characteristics using GAP. While ECA generated channel weights by performing fast 1D-Conv of size k, so channel dimension C is determined to k.

The size of the convolution kernel of 1D-Conv is adaptive through a function, so that the layer with a larger number of channels can perform more cross channel interactions.

The calculation formula for the size of the adaptive convolution kernel is:

$$\psi(C) = \left| \frac{log_2 C}{\iota} + \frac{b}{\iota} \right|, \, and \, \iota = 2, b = 1 \tag{1}$$

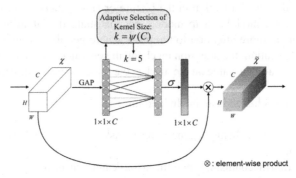

Fig. 2. Effective channel attention (ECA) module

ECA captures local cross-channel interactions by considering each channel and its k neighbors. Therefore, ECA can be effectively realized by fast one-dimensional convolution of size k, and the efficiency and effectiveness of ECA can be improved by adjusting k. Wang Q [17] proposes a function related to the channel dimension to determine k adaptively.

3.2 CCO: Coordinate Attention

Previous attention module largely paid more attention to the information fusion between channels, as shown in Fig. 3(a), but ignored the important information such as the position in the picture, the structure of the object, etc. Although some attention modules [19] try to use convolution to extracting local information as shown in Fig. 3(b). There is no progress in processing long-range dependencies information, which is very important for classification tasks.

CCO [20] captures long-range dependencies, along vertical and horizontal directions, and preserves precise positional information. In this way, CCO captures not only cross-channel but also direction-aware and position-sensitive information, which enables model to more accurately locate and capture the objects of interest.

Coordinate attention encodes both channel relationships and long-range dependencies with precise positional information in two steps: coordinate information embedding and coordinate attention generation, as shown in Fig. 3(c).

$$z_c^h(h) = \frac{1}{W} \sum_{0 \leq i < W} x_c(h, i) \tag{2}$$

$$z_c^w(w) = \frac{1}{H} \sum_{0 \leq j < H} x_c(j, w) \tag{3}$$

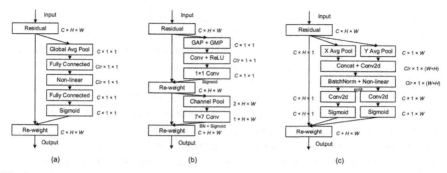

Fig. 3. Schematic comparison of the proposed coordinate attention block (c) to the classic SE channel attention block (a) and CBAM (b). Here, "GAP" and "GMP" refer to the global average pooling and global max pooling, respectively. "X Avg Pool" and "Y Avg Pool" refer to 1D horizontal global pooling and 1D vertical global pooling, respectively.

$$f = \delta\left(F_1\left(\left[z^h, z^w\right]\right)\right) \tag{4}$$

$$g^h = \sigma\left(F_h\left(f^h\right)\right) \quad and \quad g^w = \sigma\left(F_w\left(f^w\right)\right) \tag{5}$$

$$y_c(i,j) = x_c(i,j) \times g_c^h(i) \times g_c^w(j) \tag{6}$$

1. Factorize the global pooling as formulated into a pair of 1D feature encoding operations. The output of the c-th channel at height h can be written as (2), the output of the c-th channel at width w can be formulated as (3);
2. Concatenate the above results and then send them to a shared 1×1 convolutional transformation function F1, yielding f as (4);
3. Split f along the spatial dimension into two separate tensors, the outputs g^h and g^w are then expanded and used as attention weights, respectively, shown as (5), here $f^h \epsilon R^{C/r \times H}$ and $f^w \epsilon R^{C/r \times W}$;
4. The output of coordinate attention block Y can be written as (6).

By embeds location information into channel attention, CCO has the benefit of obtaining information in a larger area without introducing large overheads.

4 Experiment

4.1 Experimental Settings

We embed different attention modules into ResNet50 based on the IP102 dataset. The IP102 dataset contains 75,222 images for a total of 102 insect class, with an average of 737 samples per class. Following a roughly 6:1:3 division, IP102 is divided into 45095 training, 7508 validation, and 22619 test images for classification tasks.

The experimental environment in this article is running on Ubuntu server, the installed Pytorch version is 1.7.1, and the python version is 3.7.0. During the experiment, the loss function used by the model is cross-entropy, and the Adam optimizer is used during model training. The learning rate is 0.0001, batch size = 54, and epoch = 40.

We applied pre-processing steps on the input image of the size h × w, where h and w are its height and width, respectively. We resized the input image into h′ × w′, in which the original image's aspect ratio is kept.

Firstly, the smaller value between h and w is resized to 256. Then, the larger value is assigned by multiplying it with the ratio of the bigger value and the smaller value. Secondly, we applied the random crop data augmentation with the window size of 256 × 256 on the training phase to address the over-fitting problem. Finally, we applied the center crop method with the same window size as the training phase in the testing phase (Table 2).

Table 2. Architecture for ResNet-50 embedding attention module on IP102

Layers	Output size	50-layer
Convolutions	128 × 128	7 × 7 conv, stride 2
Pooling	64 × 64	3 × 3 Max pool, stride 2
Conv2_X	64 × 64	$\begin{bmatrix} 1 \times 1, 64 \\ 3 \times 3, 64 \\ 1 \times 1, 512 \end{bmatrix} \times 3$
Attention module	64 × 64	ECA/CCO
Conv3_X	64 × 64	$\begin{bmatrix} 1 \times 1, 128 \\ 3 \times 3, 128 \\ 1 \times 1, 512 \end{bmatrix} \times 4$
Attention module	32 × 32	ECA/CCO
Conv4_X	32 × 32	$\begin{bmatrix} 1 \times 1, 256 \\ 3 \times 3, 256 \\ 1 \times 1, 1024 \end{bmatrix} \times 6$
Attention module	16 × 16	ECA/CCO
Conv5_X	16 × 16	$\begin{bmatrix} 1 \times 1, 512 \\ 3 \times 3, 512 \\ 1 \times 1, 2048 \end{bmatrix} \times 3$
Convolutions	1 × 1	Average pool, 1000-d fc, softmax
Convolutions	1 × 1	Average pool, 102-d fc, softmax

4.2 Architecture

4.3 Comparison with Other Methods

Table 3. Accuracy (%) on the IP102 dataset by our models and other state of the art methods

Model	Depth	Acc(%)
AlexNet [22]	8	49.63
ResNet-50 [17]	50	57.39
ResNet-101 [17]	101	56.02
Pre-ResNet-50 [23]	50	55.86
VGG-16 [24]	16	54.43
Densenet-121 [25]	121	57.73
DMF-ResNet [11]	117	59.22
ResNet-50-ECA (ours)	**50**	**59.32**
ResNet-50-CCO (ours)	**50**	**59.29**

We embed ECA and CCO into the ResNet to compare with ResNet, PreResNet, and other state-of-the-art methods. The accuracy performance on the test set is reported in Table 3. As the results showed, ResNet-50-ECA achieved a 59.32% test accuracy on the test set, close to the DMF-ResNet while our model uses less backbone layer (ResNet50). We achieved the same accuracy as the model DMF using only a 50-layer ResNet. This means we get better results with fewer parameters, and we believe our model should perform better than other models at the same network depth. Based on these experiments, we empirically demonstrated the validness of our approach to IP102 dataset (Table 4).

4.4 Ablation Experiment

Building the basic ResNet on IP102, it can achieve a classification accuracy of 56.3%. If a simple SE module is embedded, the accuracy can be improved by about 2%. By adopting the improved SE module, ECA, the model is more accurate. The accuracy rises approximately 1%, indicating the effectiveness of the ECA module based on the SE module. The ECA module can effectively integrate the information between channels and improve the network's learning ability. The accuracy of ResNet-50-CCO reached 0.592, close to that of ResNet-50-ECA. However, the complexity of the CCO module is significantly increased compared with the ECA module, which can illustrate the effectiveness of the ECA module.

When the EPA module is embedded into the basic ResNet-50, there is almost no improvement in the accuracy of the network. When multiple attention modules are embedded into ResNet50, the accuracy does not increase significantly, indicating that information fusion is not a simple stacking Attention module. Designing information fusion is necessary to make the network have better learning ability.

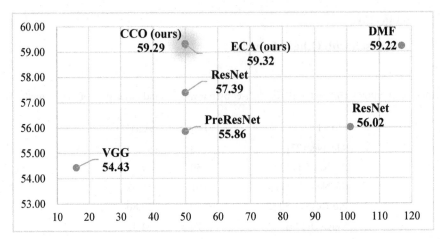

Fig. 4. Accuracy (%) on the IP102 dataset by our models and other state of the art methods. The Acc about our model, CCO and ECA is very close. And they achieve the highest Acc while using only 50 layers about the ResNet model.

Table 4. Experiment results

Model	Depth	Acc (%)
AlexNet [22]	8	49.63
ResNet-50 [17]	50	57.39
ResNet-101 [17]	101	56.02
Pre-ResNet-50 [23]	50	55.86
VGG-16 [24]	16	54.43
Densenet-121 [25]	121	57.73
DMF-ResNet [11]	117	59.22
ResNet-50-ECA (ours)	**50**	**59.32**
ResNet-50-CCO (ours)	**50**	**59.29**

4.5 Visualization of Experiment

From Fig. 4, we can recognize that the noise of the environment will greatly affect the accuracy of prediction; secondly, for small objects, it may be possible to design the network to focus on more global crop disease information to assist in identifying and classifying pest. At the same time, we found that due to the unbalanced distribution of samples, the recognition ability of some pest with a small number of training data was insufficient (Fig. 5).

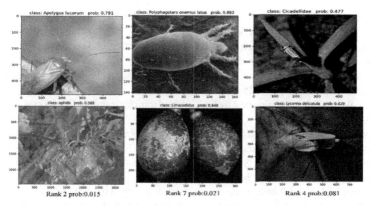

Fig. 5. The first column is Apolygus lucorum, the second column is Polyphagotars onemus latus, and the third column is Cicadellidae. The first row is the three examples the network classified correctly, the second column is the three examples the network misclassified, and prob gives the probability that the corresponding correct class.

5 Conclusion

To advance the research on the identification and classification of pest through neural network, this paper conducts experiments on the IP102 dataset. Firstly, the ResNet framework is built on the IP102 dataset. Furthermore, a more effective attention module is introduced, and the network's learning ability is enhanced by embedding attention modules. For example, an improved SE module, ECA, is introduced to enhance the network's integration of information between channels and achieve the effect of improving network classification capabilities. This module approximately increases 2% Acc of the model. Secondly, the CCO attention module with position-coding information is introduced to capture the direction and position-sensitive information of the picture. This module also improved 2% Acc about the model.

Acknowledgments. This work was supported by Guangdong Province Key Laboratory of Computational Science at the Sun Yat-sen University (2020B1212060032), the National Natural Science Foundation of China (Grant no. 11971491, 11471012).

References

1. Al Bashish, D., Braik, M., Bani-Ahmad, S.: A framework for detection and classification of plant leaf and stem diseases. In: 2010 international conference on signal and image processing IEEE, pp. 113–118 (2010)
2. Rothe, P., Kshirsagar, R.: Svm-based classifier system for recognition of cotton leaf diseases. Int. J. Emer. Technol. Comput. Appl. Sci. **7**(4), 427–432 (2014)
3. Sladojevic, S., Arsenovic, M., Anderla, A., et al.: Deep neural networks based recognition of plant diseases by leaf image classification. Comput. Intell. Neurosci. **2016**, 1–11 (2016)
4. Guan, W., Yu, S., Jianxin, W.: Automatic image-based plant disease severity estimation using deep learning. Comput. Intell. Neurosci. **2017**, 1–8 (2017)

5. Ramcharan, A., Baranowski, K., McCloskey, P., et al.: Deep learning for image-based cassava disease detection. Front. Plant Sci. **8**, 1–7 (2017)
6. Nanni, L., Maguolo, G., Pancino, F.: Pest image detection and recognition based on bio-inspired methods. Eco. Inform. **57**, 1–8 (2020)
7. Alfarisy, A.A., Chen, Q., Guo, M.: Deep learning based classification for paddy pest & diseases recognition. pp. 21–25 (2018)
8. Dawei, W., et al.: Recognition pest by image-based transfer learning. J. Sci. Food Agri. **99**(10), 4524–4531 (2019)
9. Mishra, M., Singh, P.K., Brahmachari, A., et al.: A robust pest identification system using morphological analysis in neural networks. Period. Eng. Nat. Sci. (PEN) **7**(1), 483–495 (2019)
10. Bollis, E., Pedrini, H., Avila, S.: Weakly supervised learning guided by activation mapping applied to a novel citrus pest benchmark. In: Proceedings of the IEEE/CVF Conference on Computer Vision and Pattern Recognition Workshops, pp. 310–319 (2020)
11. Liu, W., Wu, G., Ren, F.: Deep multi-branch fusion residual network for pest recognition. IEEE Trans. Cogn. Develop. Syst. **13**(3), 705–716 (2020)
12. Wu, X., Zhan, C., Lai, Y.K., et al.: Ip102: a large-scale benchmark dataset for insect pest recognition. In: Proceedings of the IEEE/CVF Conference on Computer Vision and Pattern Recognition, pp. 8787–8796 (2019)
13. Li, R., Wang, R., Xie, C., et al.: A coarse-to-fine network for aphid recognition and detection in the field. Biosys. Eng. **187**, 39–52 (2019)
14. Lei, C., Yuan, Y.: An image dataset for field crop disease identification. Chin. Sci. Citation Database **4**(4), 81–87 (2019)
15. Bollis, E., Pedrini, H., Avila, S.: Weakly supervised learning guided by activation mapping applied to a novel citrus pest benchmark. In: IEEE, pp. 1–10 (2020)
16. He, K., Zhang, X., Ren, S., et al.: Deep residual learning for image recognition. In: Proceedings of the IEEE Conference on Computer Vision and Pattern Recognition, pp. 770–778 (2016)
17. Wang, Q., Wu, B., Zhu, P., et al.: ECA-Net: efficient channel attention for deep convolutional neural networks. In: 2020 IEEE/CVF Conference on Computer Vision and Pattern Recognition (CVPR), pp. 11531–11539. IEEE (2020)
18. Jie, H., Li, S., Gang, S., et al.: Squeeze-and-excitation networks. IEEE Trans. Pattern Anal. Mach. Intell. **42**(8), 2011–2023 (2017)
19. Zhang, H., Zu, K., Lu, J., et al.: EPSANet: an efficient pyramid split attention block on convolutional neural network, pp. 1–12 (2021)
20. Hou, Q., Zhou, D., Feng J.: Coordinate Attention for Efficient Mobile Network Design, pp. 13708–13717 (2021)
21. Simonyan, K., Zisserman, A.: Very deep convolutional networks for large-scale image recognition. arXiv preprint arXiv:1409.1556 pp. 1–14 (2014)
22. Huang, G., Liu, Z., Laurens, V., et al.: Densely connected convolutional networks. In: IEEE Computer Society, pp. 2261–2269 (2016)

Multi Layered Feature Explanation Method for Convolutional Neural Networks

Luca Bourroux, Jenny Benois-Pineau$^{(\boxtimes)}$ ⓘ, Romain Bourqui ⓘ, and Romain Giot ⓘ

Univ. Bordeaux, CNRS, Bordeaux INP, LaBRI, UMR5800, 33400 Talence, France
`jenny.benois-pineau@u-bordeaux.fr`

Abstract. The most popular methods for Artificial Intelligence such as Deep Neural Networks are, for the vast majority, considered black boxes. It is necessary to explain their decisions to understand the input data which influence most the result.

Methods presented in this paper aim at an explanation in image classification tasks: which data in the input are the most important for the result. We further extend the Feature Explanation Method (FEM) from our previous work, transforming it into a multi-layered FEM (MLFEM). The evaluation of the method is designed by comparison of explanation maps with human Gaze Fixation Density maps (GFDM). We show that proposed MLFEM outperforms FEM and popular DNN explanation methods in terms of classical comparison metrics with GFDM.

Keywords: XAI · Features attribution · ResNet · Gaze fixation density maps

1 Introduction and Related Work

Deep learning (DL) approaches have become indispensable in data analysis and classification. Although the results of DL models have been exemplary, they lack transparency, which prevents a wide use of them in critical applications such as medical image analysis or security.

The need for explanations of Deep Neural Networks (DNN) decisions has led to an active research in eXplainable Artificial Intelligence (XAI). In the field of pattern recognition for images and videos, explanation of a DNN's decision consists in identifying the set of input pixels that have contributed the most into the decision [1]. A famous example of decisions on a wrong data is given by Ribeiro *et al.* [2]: here, a trained classifier wrongly used the presence of snow as the distinguishing feature between the *"Wolf"* and *"Husky"* classes. One of the ways to automatically verify if the DL classifier builds its decision on the

---

Supported by LaBRI.

M. El Yacoubi et al. (Eds.): ICPRAI 2022, LNCS 13363, pp. 603–614, 2022.
https://doi.org/10.1007/978-3-031-09037-0_49

adequate pattern in the input data is to compare the set of "important" pixels with human observations of visual content; we use this approach in this paper.

Ayyar *et al.* [1] analyzed the variety of explanations methods highlighting important patterns from the input image. Following their proposed taxonomy, we can identify "black-box" and "white-box" families of explanation methods. The "black-box" methods remain model agnostic and are applicable to any classifier, as they identify important pixels in images by masking different parts of the input and tracking induced decisions (*e.g.*, LIME [2] method). "White-box" methods, on the contrary, use the internal architecture of DNNs and can be subdivided into several groups. The first one concerns the methods based on linearization of the Deep-CNN. One of the first was the so-called Deconvolution Network (DeconvNet) proposed by Zeiler *et al.* [3]. The principle here was to build the mapping of the output score to the input space using reverse filters or "deconvolution" and thus identifying the important pixels. The methods based on gradient back-propagation such as a popular GradCam [4] or its further improved versions (*e.g.*, smoothgrad [5] or integrated gradients [6]) proceed by propagation of gradients from the last layers to the input with regard to the changed input. The important input information is located where the gradients are strong. The *Layered Relevance Propagation method* (LRP) [7] is also based on the same idea of back propagation, but without the need of gradient computations. Here, the relevance of neurons from the last decision layer through receptive fields in previous layers using the principle of conservation of the relevance at each layer allows identifying important input neurons-pixels. *Feature Explanation Method* (FEM) [8] (Sect. 2.1) is also based on backpropagation, but it is not linear in the sense that with the help of statistical filtering of the features of the last convolutional layer it identifies the most important ones. The various features maps are usually depicted using a heatmap overlaying the input image, explaining important regions in the input to the user.

Propagating information through subsequent layers, the Deep NNs loose high resolution information due to the cascaded convolutions and subsampling. Hence, it is logical to explore the DNN classifier a bit more, preserving important details in each conv layer which finally bring the classification decision. We assert that the fusion of explanations from several layers is a key to improve the final explanation. For this reason, we propose an extension of FEM, the Multi-Layered FEM (MLFEM), that relies on information fusion on feature importance from different layers. We study different strategies of fusion and benchmark them against Gaze Fixation Density Maps resulting from psycho-visual experiments on image databases.

The reminder of the paper is organized as follows. Section 2 presents our contribution - MLFEM, Sect. 3 gives the evaluation methodology, while results are reported in Sect. 4. Conclusion and perspectives are drown in Sect. 5.

2   Multi Layered Feature Explanation Method

Our method MLFEM is built upon FEM method [8]. The latter relies on the analysis of activations at the *last* conv layer of a CNN classifier. As each layer of a CNN embeds information at a different scale, we assume that computing FEM at several layers and fusing them would improve the quality of the feature attribution; this is the main idea of MLFEM. In the following, we briefly review FEM and describe the adaptations for MLFEM.

2.1 Reminder of Feature Explanation Method (FEM)

Feature Explanation Method (FEM) [8] is a recent algorithm used to produce an explanation map of the decision of a CNN. In opposite to other methods of the literature, it is class agnostic and does not need to provide a class of interest. FEM makes two hypotheses. The first is that strong features at the last convolutional layer will contribute the most in the final decision of the CNN in a classification task when pushed through fully connected layers. The second hypothesis will help us to select strong features. It assumes that the features in each feature map follow a Gaussian Distribution; this is a simplification hypothesis, but in case of large feature maps it could hold. At the last layer of convolution the strongest features are the representations of the most relevant regions in the input image. This comes from the interpretation of the "convolutional" part of a deep CNN as of a multiscaled pyramid with filtering, non-linear input signal transformations and subsampling [9].

By analyzing only the last layer of the CNN part of the model, one can get input pixels which contributed the most into the final decision. As FEM uses activations of the last layer of the CNN *after* the non-linearity (most likely ReLU) only *positive* features will be picked up. As FEM is class agnostic, it is not a problem if it emphasizes on some high activations that are negatively weighted in the next layer. Indeed the features remain important for the overall classification wether they vote for or against a specific class.

The last convolutional layer produces activations of size $(W \times H)$ for D feature maps f_i. D binary maps, $b_{i,i=1...D}$ corresponding to each of the D feature maps f_i are computed by selecting their strongest features: $f_i(x,y) \geq \mu_i + k\sigma_i$. Mean μ_i and standard deviation σ_i are individually estimated for each feature map f_i. In the same manner as the most important features are selected in each feature map f_i, the contribution of each map into decision is also weighted by a map-importance weight corresponding to μ_i. This will give us a saliency map $s = \sum b_i \mu_i$ of dimension $(W \times H)$ that is then upscaled to the resolution of the input image by linear interpolation. A min-max normalization is finally used to bring the domain from $\mathbb{R}^+$ to $[0,1]$ and obtain the final normalized map of feature importance S.

2.2 Principles of Multi Layered FEM (MLFEM)

In fact, FEM as presented previously can be applied on any layer of a CNN. We can merely pretend to truncate the model at a particular layer and see that FEM would work as is. The application of FEM on a CNN consisting of L convolutional layers will yield L different feature importance maps. As all importance maps are interpolated in FEM method we finally have L maps of

Block 1   Block 2   Block 3   Block 4   Block 5   Block 6   Block 7   Block 8

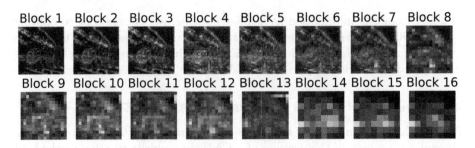

Block 9   Block 10   Block 11   Block 12   Block 13   Block 14   Block 15   Block 16

Fig. 1. FEM applied on every convolutional block of a typical ResNet50 architecture. Resolution is higher for the first layers.

the input resolution. The information provided by the maps is layer-dependent and it is interesting to fuse them. Now the question is how to obtain a single heat-map for the input highlighting the pixels which have contributed into the Netwok decision the most.

Let M be our convolutional neural network, with $l = 1, ..., L$ convolutional layers. Let us denote F_l a feature tensor obtained at each convolutional layer after the positive non-linearity (ReLU).

Let us denote by $H(F_l)$ the operator which implements FEM method yielding to a normalized importance map S_l of features F_l. The multi layered FEM pixel importance map is obtained by fusing all the importance maps S_l with a fusion operator $\bigoplus$: $S = \bigoplus_{l=1}^{L} S_l$.

The combination of L different maps can be done in a recursive manner. For each intermediary map S_l we will construct S as the combination of S and the current intermediary map S_l. We will then move along for each $l < L$. An alternative is to devise a fusion operator that takes a variable number of arguments to produce a single final feature importance map.

Intuition Behind Multi-layerd FEM. The reasoning for applying multiple times the same explanation method at different network's layers is the following. The network passes the input image through multiple layers of convolution. Convolution layers produce results that are position invariant. They are meant to pick up on spatially-local feature. With each step deeper in the network, the convolutional layer picks up on a more and more abstract concepts (see Fig. 1). The very first layers are generally performing edge detection while the later ones extract abstract concept like "face", "car" etc.

So different information is available at different points in the network. By combining the different activation maps at different points in the network, we can reconstruct a heatmap that takes advantage of all this scattered information.

2.3   Fusion Operators

We can apply quite a number of usual operators in data fusion. In our present work, we have appealed to the algebraic fusion operators, and to the fusion by a convolutional neural network trained with regard to the ground truth obtained from human observers of the content.

Algebraic Fusion Operators. applied in our work are presented below. They are applied individually to the element of the maps.

- The *max* operator $max(a, b)$ is the result of the *max* operation applied element wise to a and b. $max_{u,v}(a, b) = max(a_{u,v}, b_{u,v})$
- The weighted addition $add(a, b)$ is the result of the addition of a and b given a factor α. $add_{u,v}(a, b) = \alpha \cdot a_{u,v} + (1 - \alpha) \cdot b_{u,v}$
- The *top* operator. It is defined in relation to the *add* operator, taking only the top 50% features of b. $b'_i = b_i$ if $(b_i > \mu(b))$, 0 otherwise, top(a, b) = add(a, b')
- The *fem* operator. We can produce the same result as the FEM method would by using this fusion operator. $fem(a, b) = b$ it is also a special case of the *add* operator with $\alpha = 0$

The maximum is commutative: $max(a, b) = max(b, a)$, but the *add* and so the *top* operators are not: $add(a, b) \neq add(b, a)$, $top(a, b) \neq top(b, a)$. The *add* operation in fact constructs a geometric sequence. $\Sigma\alpha(1 - \alpha)^{l-1}S_l$. The normalization operator can also be applied, either at the end of the fusions or interleaved between each binary operator.

By the fact that *add* and *top* are not commutative they take advantage of the structure of data, namely, of the fact that the first operand of the operator is the cumulated map in the recursive fusion approach and can be more or less taken into account regulated by the parameter α.

Fusion by a Convolutional Neural Network. The idea here consists in training a light CNN m which input is the set of feature importance maps S_l from all layers of the CNN model M to be explained, interpolated to the resolution of input images of M. The training of m is fulfilled with regard to the ground truth expressing human perception of the visual content in the classification task. This perception is measured by Gaze Fixation Density Maps (GFDM) obtained in a psycho-visual experiment when human subjects observe images to classify them. We refer the reader to [10] for a detailed explanation of such an experiment. Human gaze fixations from a number of observers are recorded for each image by an eye-tracking device.

Then on each fixation (u, v) in the image plane, a 2D-Gaussian surface $N_{(u,v,\Sigma)}$ is centered with the mean vector $\mu = (u, v)^T$ and a diagonal covariance matrix Σ with equal σ^2 values on the principal diagonal. The scale parameter σ is defined from the geometry of the experiment to represent the projection of the fovea, into the image plane. Summing up and normalizing multi-Gaussian surface from different observers for the same image, its GFDM G is obtained. An example of such maps on the dataset from [10] is illustrated in Fig. 2.

We call this CNN-based fusion operator NET. As a light fusion CNN m we use a simple architecture. The input tensor consisting of intermediate importance

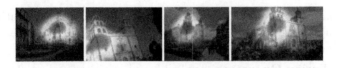

Fig. 2. Example of GFDMs on Mexculture database [10]

maps S_l is pushed through three successive convolution layers with pooling. They have the total effect of pooling the input tensor by a factor of 4 and multiplying the depth by a factor of 8. Lastly, a weighted sum is computed to output a final predicted 2D map. The loss function is the Euclidean loss, which is the mean square error between G and the application of NET operator to the input set of importance maps S_l. The fusion network m is trained on GFDMs of a training set of a given dataset. We present our datasets in Sect. 4.

2.4   Implementation of MLFEM on CNN Classifiers

The MLFEM is a white-box method and can be applied to any architecture of a CNN in visual classification tasks. Here we present the implementation of MLFEM for ResNet50 [11] architecture.

ResNet50. Contains 16 residual blocks; as a block is the natural unit of choice to apply FEM, we apply it to the output of each of them, after the activation function. This gives us 16 different applications of FEM to fuse. The goal is to maximize the different semantic meaning that one can extract: for ResNet50 we take advantage of the structure of the network.

ResNet50 used in our experiments is trained with the Adam optimizer [12], with a binary cross entropy for binary classification tasks and a categorical cross-entropy loss for multi-label classification tasks.

3   Evaluation of MLFEM Explanations

Methodology. In [1] and [13] the methodology of evaluation of explanation methods was proposed. It consists in the comparison of the pixel importance maps obtained by the network sensing with the maps expressing human perception of the same visual content. This perception is expressed by gaze fixation density maps we have presented in Sect. 2.3. Today, this methodology is possible thanks to public databases with the recorded gaze fixation of observers, like [10,14,15] and we will apply it to our MLFEM method with different fusion operators and compare with different explanation methods which generate pixel importance maps as MLFEM does.

Evaluation Metrics. Evaluating the relevance of pixel importance explanation maps is an open problem. There is no widely agreed upon metrics for assessing their quality. We propose to employ metrics widely used in psychovisual community for comparison of saliency maps[16]: the Pearson Correlation Coefficient and the Similarity metric. Pearson Correlation Coefficient(PCC) is defined as:

$$corr(x, y) = \frac{\sum_u^W \sum_v^H (x_{u,v} - \overline{x})(y_{u,v} - \overline{y})}{\sqrt{\sum_u^W \sum_v^H (x_{u,v} - \overline{x})^2}\sqrt{\sum_u^W \sum_v^H (y_{u,v} - \overline{y})^2}}$$

with $x_{u,v}$ being the value of the pixel at position (u, v) in one saliency map and $y_{u,v}$ in another.

The similarity metric is defined as such:

$$sim(x, y) = \sum min(x_{u,v}, y_{u,v})$$

Design of Experiments. To evaluate the proposed MLFEM method, we will perform three kinds of experiments: i) overall method comparison, ii) dependence on correct or wrong classification results, iii) sensitivity to clutter in the image.

Overall Method Comparison. We will compare pixel importance maps generated by MLFEM with different fusion methods and the reference methods such as FEM and GradCam [4] which remains the most popular in explanation methods generating pixel importance maps.

Dependence on Correct/Wrong Prediction. We divide the test dataset into images that were correctly categorized by the neural network M and those that were not. We will analyze if a drop in correlation with the ground trouth GFDMs is observed.

In the case of a drop, we can deduce that the convolutional part of the network did not pick up on the relevant features of the image. The fully connected part of the network will then not have the correct information in feature space to classify the image.

If the metrics do not change between correctly and wrongly classified images, we can presume that the fully connected part of M, given supposedly correct feature space information, was not able to classify the images. We can then add more fully connected layers to help the network categorize the inputs.

Sensitivity to Clutter. In case the image is cluttered, the GFDMs are dispersed as human attention is attracted by multiple singularities/objects in the image. It is reasonable to expect that the CNN allocates more importance to a strongest relevant region in the image. In this case, the similarity metrics between our explanation map and GFDMs will be lower than for images with low clutter effects.

4   Experiments and Results

4.1   Datasets

We have chosen three different datasets to work on. The first one is MexCulture [10]. It is composed of 284 images from four classes supplied with GFDMs.

Fig. 3. Sample of the data in Salicon database (with GFDM overlaid)

It is a subset of 12000 images of the Mexican architectural style: Modern, Pre-Hispanic and Colonial, there is also a rejection class. The dataset contains 2000 images for each category for training and 2000 other images for validation. The GFDM was constructed by instructing the subject to categorize the presented images. We have illustrated the GFDMs in Fig. 2.

The second one is Salicon [14]. It is composed of 15000 images of different (up to 80) categories, 10000 of them are supplied with GFDMs It is common to have multiple categories present for each image, hence these images are more cluttered than those from MexCulture dataset. To construct the GFDMs, the subjects were free to "look around" the image and expressed their attention by mouse pointing. We illustrate the GFMDs from this dataset in Fig. 3.

Finally, we use Cat2000 [15] as a third dataset. It is composed of 4000 images, 2000 with GFDM, each divided into 20 equally populated categories. The GFDMs were obtained from gaze fixations and the images are less cluttered.

4.2   Results

Overall Method Comparison. We compute two similarity metrics PCC and *sim* for each classified image of each dataset for every method (FEM, GradCam noted CAM and MLFEM with NET, ADD and TOP variantes) with regard to the GFDMs. To compare the methods between them, we compute a 2×2 matrix, comparing the number of times that a method m_a was better at explaining classification than a method m_b in terms of higher value of each metric. This will give us 6 matrices, 2 for each dataset, one for the comparison using PCC and another for the *sim* metric, see Fig. 4a, 4b, 4c.

In Figs. 5a, 5b distribution of the metrics in Salicon and Cat2000 datasets is plotted for every method compared to the GFDMs.

We can see here in Figs. 4a and 5a that the proposed MLFEM method is better suited for the explanation of ResNet 50 on the Salicon dataset. We achieve a mean correlation coefficient of, 0.70 whereas the GradCam method only achieves 0.37. We can also see that without resorting to learned fusion operator, FEM and ADD/TOP are better with, respectively, $0.38, 0.43, 0.41$ values of PCC. The *sim* metric behavior is the same. The trained NET fusion operator is the best in terms of both metrics. In Mexculture dataset, the NET operator is at least as good as other operators, see Fig. 4c. For Cat2000 dataset the conclusion is the same as for Salicon, as illustrated in 4b and 5b.

Dependence on Correct/Wrong Prediction. For Salicon, we are in a multi-label classification task with objects of several classes in the same image. We

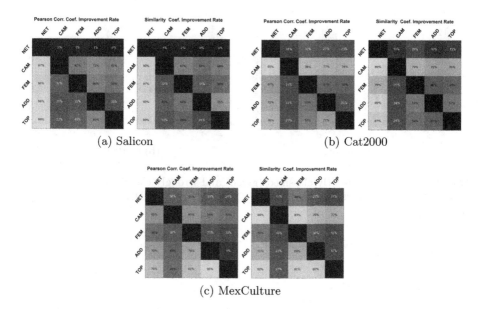

Fig. 4. Number of images with a better explanation by method m_a - column than with method m_b - line -on the Salicon, Cat2000 and MexCulture datasets.

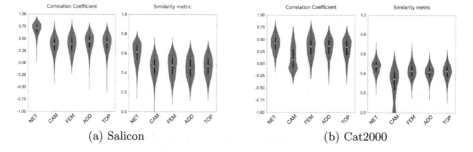

Fig. 5. Distribution of the different metrics for each explanation method for the Salicon and Cat2000 dataset.

count the number of times when every class present in an image is detected by the network: *i.e.*, the corresponding output neuron has an activation value larger than 0.5. as a correct prediction. When at least one class is not correctly predicted, this image is considered wrongly classified.

We do not see any significant effect of the correct/wrong categorization of the image on the quality of the explanation map (Figs. 6a and 6b diplay the average PCC and Similarity metrics for both correctly and wrongly classifed samples). For Salicon dataset (Fig. 6a), we have a small drop in the quality of explanation for miss-classified images (in red), a 3% drop in the PCC and no change in the *sim* metric. For Cat2000, Fig. 6b, a small increase of the quality

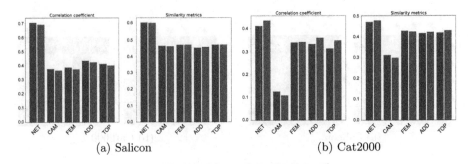

(a) Salicon   (b) Cat2000

Fig. 6. Metrics for correctly classified (green) and wrongly classified images (red) for the Salicon and Cat2000 dataset with NET, CAM, FEM, ADD, TOP. (Color figure online)

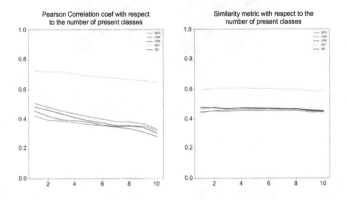

Fig. 7. The evolution of similarity metrics with regard to the number of classes present in the image to explain on the SALICON dataset.

of explanation for miss-classified images is observed. The PCC is 4% better, but there is practically no change for the similarity metric.

Sensitivity to Clutter. This experiment is conducted on Salicon dataset with different classes of objects present in the same image. We divide images into ten categories, with ith category containing images that have i different classes present in it. Then we can plot the mean of the different metrics as a function of the number of classes appearing in an image.

We can see in Fig. 7 that our hypothesis holds: the quality of our explanation drops when the number of classes present in an image increases. However, even in high clutter situation, our proposed method with NET fusion gives the best scores. The NET method only loses 11% of its performance measured by PCC, where the FEM method loses about 33%.

The similarity metric, however, shows a lower dependence in regard to the number of classes present in an input image. The implication of this merits further research in future works.

5   Conclusion

In this work, we have extended the method FEM for the explanation of decisions of CNN classifiers by introducing a Multi-Layered strategy: MLFEM. We showed its performance on the ResNet as the latter is nowadays the most efficient CNN classifier. Nevertheless, the method remains generic and applicable to any CNN whether it is residual or not.

We studied different fusion strategies of individual importance maps from each CNN layer. The evaluation has been performed accordingly to the evaluation method designed by us similarly with [13] which consists in the comparison of explanation maps with gaze fixation density maps (GFDM) of human observers. In terms of comparison metrics of explanation maps and GFDM, MLFEM achieves better performance than the similar state-of-the-art method GradCam and the original FEM. Over GradCam, we got an improvement of 89% for PCC on Salicon and 241% on Cat2000; the improvement of similarity metric is of 30% on Salicon and 51% on Cat2000. We got an improvement over FEM of 84% for PCC on Salicon and 20% on Cat2000; for similarity metric, the improvement is of 27% on Salicon and 9% on Cat2000.

We note that amongst the proposed fusion strategies, the "learnt" fusion operator achieves the best results according to the considered comparison metrics. Hence, the proposed MLFEM method better explains the decisions of the CNN classifier ResNet with regard to the human perception of the content in the classification tasks.

In the future works, it may be interesting to apply and adapt MLFEM to newly appeared transformer networks and to use it with another kind of data than images. In such a case, we will face the problem of definition of the ground truth for the evaluation methodology proposed. Hence, the proposed method opens multiple research questions which have to be addressed in the future.

References

1. Ayyar, M.P., Benois-Pineau, J., Zemmari, A.: White box methods for explanations of convolutional neural networks in image classification tasks (2021)
2. Ribeiro, M.T., Singh, S., Guestrin, C.: Why should i trust you? explaining the predictions of any classifier. In: Proceedings of the 22nd ACM SIGKDD International Conference on Knowledge Discovery and Data Mining, pp. 1135–1144 (2016)
3. Zeiler, M.D., Fergus, R.: Visualizing and understanding convolutional networks. In: Proceedings of European Conference on Computer Vision, pp. 818–833. Springer, Cham (2014). https://doi.org/10.48550/arXiv.1311.2901
4. Selvaraju, R.R., Cogswell, M., Das, A., Vedantam, R., Parikh, D., Batra, D.: Gradcam: visual explanations from deep networks via gradient-based localization. Int. J. Comput. Vis. **128**(2), 336–359 (2019)
5. Smilkov, D., Thorat, N., Kim, B., Viégas, F.B., Wattenberg, M.: Smoothgrad: removing noise by adding noise. CoRR, abs/1706.03825:1–10 (2017)
6. Sundararajan, M., Taly, A., Yan, Q.: Axiomatic attribution for deep networks. In: Proceedings of International Conference on Machine Learning, PMLR, pp. 3319–3328 (2017)

7. Bach, S., Binder, A., Montavon, G., Klauschen, F., Müller, K.R., Samek, W.: On pixel-wise explanations for non-linear classifier decisions by layer-wise relevance propagation. PLoS ONE **10**, e0130140 (2015)
8. Ahmed Asif Fuad, K., Martin, P.E., Giot, R., Bourqui, R., Benois-Pineau, J., Zemmari, A.: Features understanding in 3D CNNs for actions recognition in video. In: Tenth International Conference on Image Processing Theory, Tools and Applications, IPTA 2020, Paris, France, October 2020
9. Zemmari, A., Benois-Pineau, J.: Introducing Domain Knowledge. In: Deep Learning in Mining of Visual Content. SCS, pp. 87–97. Springer, Cham (2020). https://doi.org/10.1007/978-3-030-34376-7_9
10. Obeso, A.M., Benois-Pineau, J., García-Vázquez, M.S., Ramírez-Acosta, A.A.: Visual vs internal attention mechanisms in deep neural networks for image classification and object detection. Pattern Recognit. **123**, 108411 (2022)
11. Rousseau, F., Drumetz, L., Fablet, R.: Residual networks as flows of diffeomorphisms. J. Math. Imag. Vis. **62**, 04 (2020)
12. Kingma, D.P., Lei Ba, J.: A method for stochastic optimization, Adam (2017)
13. Jouis, G., Mouchère, H., Picarougne, F., Hardouin, A.: Anchors vs attention: Comparing XAI on a real-life use case. In: ICPR Workshops (3). LNCS, vol. 12663, pp. 219–227. Springer, Cham (2020). https://doi.org/10.1007/978-3-030-68796-0_16
14. Jiang, M., Huang, S., Duan, J., Zhao, Q.: Salicon: Saliency in context. In: The IEEE Conference on Computer Vision and Pattern Recognition, CVPR, vol. 6 (2015)
15. Borji, A., Itti, L.: CAT2000: a large scale fixation dataset for boosting saliency research. CoRR, abs/1505.03581 (2015)
16. Le Meur, O., Baccino, T.: Methods for comparing scanpaths and saliency maps: strengths and weaknesses. Behav. Res. Methods **45**(1), 251–266 (2012)

Bayesian Gate Mechanism for Multi-task Scale Learning

Shihao Wang and Hongwei Ge[✉]

Dalian University of Technology, Dalian, China
wang_sh@mail.dlut.edu.cn, gehw@dlut.edu.cn

Abstract. Multi-task learning demonstrates excellent performance in multiple domains of deep learning. Nevertheless, how to obtain knowledge beneficial to each task from the shared representation is a long-term challenge of multi-task deep learning. Simultaneously, insufficient information communication is a current issue in multi-task scale deep networks. In this paper, we propose a novel multi-task communication network on pixel-level prediction. Specifically, to realize the joint learning of high-scale and low-scale features in network decoding, we design a multi-scale multi-task knowledge communication module in the shared network decoder. A multi-task learning unit pool is utilized for communicating the constructed shared features among multiple tasks. Furthermore, we design the Bayesian knowledge gating mechanism to filter the information flow. By introducing the Bayesian deep learning method, uncertain shared features are gated in different communication stages of the shared network. Our experiments show that the proposed model can effectively improve the prediction performance in multiple vision tasks.

Keywords: Multi-task learning · Bayesian deep learning · Scene understanding

1 Introduction

In recent years, the performance of convolutional neural networks (CNN) has been significantly improved in many computer vision tasks, such as object detection [18], instance segmentation [10], and depth prediction [6]. Generally, a neural network only focuses on solving a single vision task. Yet, most problems in the real world are multimodal, so we must consider the consistency and complementarity between modalities. Utilizing deep learning approaches to solve multi-task problems is a promising research direction.

Compared with single task learning methods, multi-task learning has the advantages of less resource utilization and improved inference speed [23]. Multi-task approaches are used in various deep learning domains, such as natural language processing [7,20], image classification [17], and medical image processing [2].

© Springer Nature Switzerland AG 2022
M. El Yacoubi et al. (Eds.): ICPRAI 2022, LNCS 13363, pp. 615–626, 2022.
https://doi.org/10.1007/978-3-031-09037-0_50

Some recent work on multi-task learning attempts to introduce multi-scale concepts to enhance the scene understanding ability of models. Zhang et al. [26] execute task learning on coarse-to-fine scale sequences recursively to refine and facilitate semantic segmentation and depth prediction tasks. Simon et al. [22] perform multimodal distillation at multiple scales for information interaction.

Although existing work has demonstrated the effectiveness of multi-scale information interaction in visual multi-task learning, only limited scale information transfer exists in these methods. Simultaneously, multi-task deep learning still faces the following challenges. (1) The fused features constructed in some multi-task networks cannot contain enough shared information, further affecting the ability of each task to extract information. (2) How to develop an effective multi-tasking information transmission strategy. An exceptional communication mechanism handles the joint learning among multiple tasks, which drives each task to extract knowledge from the context and utilize signals from other members more effectively.

Based on the above, in this paper, we design a multi-task deep network with shared network structure improvements and the optimization strategy. We propose the Bayesian Multi-scale-task Network (BMSTN). The BMSTN consists of a bidirectional receptive field flow structure in the multi-task network encoding stage, which is designed to facilitate feature communication between scales and tasks. We also introduce a Bayesian deep learning method in the gate mechanism. Bayesian deep learning has been shown to improve the generalization ability of DNNs [25] and provide uncertainty representation. Specifically, in the early stage of information exchange, we use multiple sets of scale feature integration modules and task communication modules to learn and share knowledge alternately to realize the interaction between scale and task information. Higher-scale features learn subtle semantic information contained in local features of smaller receptive fields. Besides, in the MTL decoder backend, the features of the smaller receptive field comprehend the environmental relationship information contained in the higher-scale features. In the BMSTN, we also design a Bayesian gate mechanism. Through the Bayesian deep learning algorithm, this mechanism utilizes variational inference to fit the posterior distribution of gate parameters during network training. Bayesian principles balance the weights of task features and reduce the generation of negative transfer in multi-task networks. Furthermore, multi-task networks obtain practical knowledge of uncertain shared features through Bayesian inference.

The experimental results show that our method outperforms state-of-the-art approaches. In summary, this paper has the following contributions:

1. In this paper, we design a novel multi-scale multi-task network structure for computer vision tasks. It improves the prediction performance of each task by communicating information sufficiently between scales and tasks.
2. We introduce the concept of Bayesian deep learning and design the Bayesian knowledge gating unit. Each task extracts the required knowledge from shared features.

3. Experimental results show that our method has better performance than existing methods and demonstrates the method's effectiveness proposed in this paper.

2   Related Work

2.1   Multi-task Learning

Multi-task learning (MTL) captures domain-related information in the training process of related tasks, jointly optimizes multiple learning tasks, and uses shared knowledge to improve the generalization and prediction capabilities of the overall network. Multi-task methods in computer vision can be generally divided into task assignment and network structure design. Task assignment methods focus on formulating strategies and avoiding the problem of misleading task prediction caused by excessive preemption of shared learning resources by some subtasks. The current methods are mainly aimed at optimizing the MTL loss function. Some related works realize the optimal allocation of multiple tasks based on subtask loss variance [11], loss weight balance [4], dynamic task priority [8], inductive bias optimal solution [5], and so on.

Multi-task network structure methods can be further divided into encoder-focused methods and decoder-focused methods [23]. The encoder-focused network mainly focuses on multi-task feature learning communication in the head encoding stage of the network. This type of method mainly improves the performance of each task by learning the multilinear relationship between tasks [15], shared weight matrix [17,20], and attention module [14]. Decoder-focused networks focus on information communication and feature sharing between specific tasks during decoding. PAD-Net [24] use attention mechanism to extract multimodal information contained in shared spatial features.

2.2   Bayesian Deep Learning

Bayesian deep learning considers the aleatoric uncertainty and epistemic uncertainty that exists in traditional deep learning models. In the process of training the model, the weights and biases of the neural network are regarded as a series of distributions, forming an uncertainty estimation, so that Bayesian neural network has higher robustness and prediction performance than the traditional neural network.

The purpose of Bayesian inference algorithms is to fit or construct posterior distributions of parameters in deep neural networks. Calculating the complex posterior distribution of parameters is the current challenge for Bayesian deep learning. Modern Bayesian algorithms for deep neural networks are primarily based on Markov Chain Monte Carlo [3,25], Laplace [19], and variational inference methods [1,16]. Among them, SWAG [16] is a variational method that constructs a low-rank plus diagonal covariance matrix to fit the posterior distribution in the process of stochastic weight average.

Our proposed method introduces the SWAG algorithm and designs a Bayesian knowledge gating module in a multi-task network. This novel gating mechanism can reduce the computational complexity of Bayesian inference while making each specific task in the training process extract desired features from uncertain shared information.

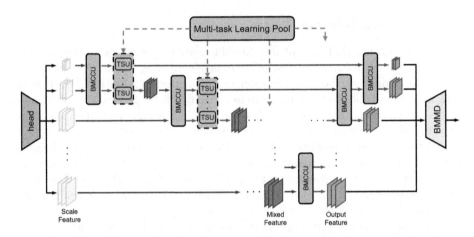

Fig. 1. An overview of Bayesian Multi-scale-task Network. BMSTN utilizes a single backbone as the encoder of the multi-task network to generate multi-scale shared features. Among them, MSTD is composed of several multi-scale communication modules (MSCM) and multi-task pools (MTLP). Among them, Bayesian Multi-Channel Communication Units (BMCCU) in MSCM communicates information among multiple input scale features. Task-sharing units in MTLP perform multi-task feature learning on scale-specific inputs and then output the features to the next BMCCU. Finally, Bayesian Multimodal Distillation (BMMD) processes the output features of the decoder and outputs the prediction results of multiple tasks.

3   Method

3.1   Overview

In this section, we describe Bayesian multi-scale-task deep learning networks designed for scene understanding and pixel-level task inference in dense prediction tasks for computer vision, such as semantic segmentation and depth prediction. Specifically, we propose the Multi-scale-task Decoder (MSTD) (Fig. 1), which enables scale information and task information to communicate effectively in the network coding stage. Bayesian deep learning strategies are used in the MTL decoder for task-specific and scale-specific features to learn beneficial representations from uncertain shared information. We describe the multi-task network structure and Bayesian optimization strategy, respectively.

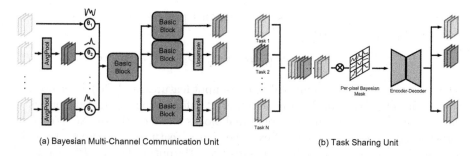

(a) Bayesian Multi-Channel Communication Unit   (b) Task Sharing Unit

Fig. 2. (a) The structure of the Bayesian Multi-Channel Communication Unit in the pre-order scale circulation process: larger-scale features are transformed into smaller-scale features through an average pooling layer. The Bayesian gating unit applies uncertainty weights to and gates the transformed shared representation. After the fusion operation, the shared scale features are refined in the information communication block and then upsampled to output different scale features. In the subsequent circulation process, the small-scale features are upsampled and fused with high-scale features. (b) In the task sharing unit, multiple task features at the same scale are filtered into different channel streams through pixel-wise Bayesian masks. After feature aggregation, the constructed global features output refined multi-task features through the autoencoder, which enables each task to learn an efficient representation of shared knowledge.

3.2   Multiple Scale-Task Decoder

A decoder-focused MTL network need consider designing a decoder that captures the commonalities and differences between tasks. The existing multi-scale and multi-task methods transmit feature information of different scales from low to high through the feature propagation module. However, this one-way propagation undoubtedly causes the limitation of information exchange and weakens the feature learning ability between scales and tasks. Therefore, we propose a decoder suitable for multi-task network, MSTD, which uses multi-scale communication modules and multi-task pool to realize bidirectional communication between different receptive field information and mutual learning between scale and task features.

Bayesian Multi-channel Communication Module. We design a novel structure for interactive learning of information from different receptive fields in the MTL encoder to communicate between multiple scales effectively. The structure consists of multiple BMCCUs. Each unit is responsible for processing the interaction of several adjacent scale information. Figure 2(a) shows that higher-scale features are pixel-aligned with the smallest-scale features through the average pooling layer during the pre-order scale circulation process. We then use the Bayesian gate θ to extract discriminative scale-specific features. The mechanism aims to adaptively gate features from multiple channels, deciding which features are needed and which ones need to be downweighted to avoid negative transfer between scales. Through this process, the multi-scale fusion feature M_{scale} is obtained:

$$M_{\text{scale}} = CONCAT\left(\theta_1 P_1^i, \theta_2 \mathcal{D}_2\left(P_2^i\right), \ldots, \theta_s \mathcal{D}_s\left(P_s^i\right)\right) \qquad (1)$$

where s is the number of input scales, P^i is input features, and $\mathcal{D}(\cdot)$ is the pooling operation. The rationale for the selection of information interaction blocks is flexible. In this work, we use convolutional blocks based on the ResNet structure for scale information exchange. Next, the shared features are restored to high-scale information by upsampling, so as to obtain the output feature P^o as follows:

$$P_j^o = \begin{cases} \mathcal{U}_j\left(\mathcal{F}_{scale}(M) \cdot f_j\right), j \neq 1 \cap j = 1, \ldots, s \\ \mathcal{F}_{scale}(M) \qquad\qquad\qquad , j = 1 \end{cases} \qquad (2)$$

where $\mathcal{F}(\cdot)$ is the convolution block function, and $\mathcal{U}(\cdot)$ is the upsampling operation. In this paper, we use the bilinear interpolation method.

From the global perspective of the decoder, the scale information in MSTD is designed to communicate bidirectionally: the larger-scale features first learn the refined local information from the smaller scale. In the latter stage of the decoder, the smaller-scale features then understand the scene information in the larger receptive field. This two-way communication mechanism can fully communicate the information of different receptive fields between scale information. In addition, the interaction between the Bayesian multi-channel communication module and the multi-task pool also improves the model's ability to understand multiscene semantics.

Multi-task Pool. This module aims to realize the information exchange between tasks and refine the multi-scale shared information. Figure 2(b) shows that the task-sharing unit first integrates the input N task features, then Bayesian masks apply pixel-level weights to the constructed features. The Bayesian structure can be viewed as an attention-like mechanism that filters the global task information flow to build a shared representation that contains less invalid information. The obtained shared task feature M_{task} is as follows:

$$M_{task} = CONCAT\left(\Theta_1 Q_1^i, \Theta_2 Q_2^i, \ldots, \Theta_N Q_N^i\right) \qquad (3)$$

where Θ is the mask matrix, and Q^i is the feature of each task. Next, M_{task} learns abstract shared representations through a set of auto-encoders, and finally outputs the features Q^o of different tasks as:

$$Q^o = \mathcal{F}_{task}\left(M_{task}\right) \qquad (4)$$

3.3   Bayesian Knowledge Gating Module

We design Bayesian gate structures for scale sharing, task sharing, and task distillation to improve the ability to extract abstract features at the cost of fewer network parameters. We consider that traditional deep learning models often misestimate noise and uncertainty factors. Moreover, there is uncertainty about the correspondence between semantic and geometric information in the MTL network. Therefore, we attempt to fit the uncertainty factors in the shared information by introducing Bayesian deep learning. The SWAG algorithm is a Bayesian method based on variational inference suitable for modern deep learning, which has shown its potential to improve performance in other vision tasks [13,16]. Our network uses this algorithm and is adaptively designed for the characteristics of the gated structure.

For dataset $\mathcal{D}$ and a deep network with parameter ω, according to Bayesian theorem, we can get the posterior $p(\omega \mid \mathcal{D})$ of the model:

$$p(\omega \mid \mathcal{D}) \propto p(\mathcal{D} \mid \omega)p(\omega) \tag{5}$$

where $p(\mathcal{D} \mid \omega)$ is the likelihood and $p(\omega)$ is the prior. In Bayesian deep learning, ω obeys a certain distribution, and the predicted distribution is:

$$p(y \mid \mathcal{D}, x) = \int p(y \mid \omega, x)p(\omega \mid \mathcal{D})d\omega \tag{6}$$

where x and y are the input and output of the test set, respectively. According to the SWAG algorithm, the representation of the multi-scale fusion feature M_{scale} and the shared task feature M_{task} in Sect. 2 is:

$$M_{scale} = CONCAT\left(\tilde{\theta}_1 P_1^i, \tilde{\theta}_2 \mathcal{D}_2\left(P_2^i\right), \ldots, \tilde{\theta}_s \mathcal{D}_s\left(P_s^i\right)\right), \tilde{\theta}_j \sim \mathcal{N}\left(\theta_j; \mu, \Sigma_j\right) \tag{7}$$

$$M_{task} = CONCAT\left(\widetilde{\Theta}_1 Q_1^i, \widetilde{\Theta}_2 Q_2^i, \ldots, \widetilde{\Theta}_N Q_N^i\right), \widetilde{\Theta}_k \sim \mathcal{N}\left(\Theta_k; \mu, \Sigma_k\right) \tag{8}$$

where Σ is the low-rank plus diagonal covariance matrix constructed during stochastic gradient descent. The gating parameters are obtained when the network predicts by sampling the posterior distribution using the Bayesian model averaging method.

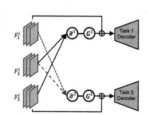

Fig. 3. Schematic diagram of Bayesian multimodal distillation. We obtain complementary information in other task features by adding a Bayesian gate mechanism.

Bayesian Multimodal Distillation. Multimodal distillation has been demonstrated to effectively acquire complementary information between tasks in various MTL networks [22,24]. In this paper, we propose a distillation scheme that applies a Bayesian gate mechanism. As shown in Fig. 3, the other feature maps

F related to the kth task are jointly refined by the Bayesian gate $\tilde{\sigma}$ and the attention map G after distillation. The multimodal information outputs the network prediction results through different task decoders. The whole distillation process can be expressed as:

$$F_k^o \leftarrow F_k^i + \sum_{l \neq k} \tilde{\sigma}_l^k G_l^k F_l^i, \tilde{\sigma}_l^k \sim \mathcal{N}\left(\sigma_l^k; \mu, \Sigma_l\right) \tag{9}$$

4   Experiment

To demonstrate the effectiveness of the proposed network, we conduct experiments on popular dense labeling benchmark datasets containing depth information, edge information, normal information, and semantic information. We detail our experimental evaluations below.

4.1   Experimental Setup

The Datasets. NYUD-v2 [9] dataset is an RGBD indoor dataset containing 1449 pairs of RGB and depth images with a resolution of 640×480, of which 795 are used for training and the remaining 654 pairs are used for testing. We obtain normal and semantic boundary information from other works [22,24]. Consistent with Work 2, during the training phase, we scale the input image randomly with a ratio of {1, 1.2, 1.5}, and we flip the data horizontally with a probability of 0.5.

Implementation Details. Unless otherwise specified, the head of all network structures uses the HRNet [21] architecture, and the parameters are pretrained by ImageNet [12]. The network is optimized using stochastic gradient descent with the weight decay and momentum set to 1×10^{-4} and 0.9, respectively. Total 200 epochs are used for NYUD-v2. The batch number is set to 4, and the learning rate parameter is 1×10^{-3}. MSTN starts building the covariance matrix at epoch 110. Our method is implemented based on the Pytorch library and runs on an Nvidia Tesla P40.

Loss Function. The linear weighted loss $L_{\text{total}} = \sum_i w_i L_i$ is used as the MTL loss in our experiments. We use cross-entropy loss with softmax classifier for the semantic segmentation task and L1 loss to measure the mean absolute error between output and label for depth estimation task. We use balanced cross-entropy loss and label-ignoring L1 loss for boundary detection and normal prediction. In the NYUD-v2 dataset, we set the weights for semantic segmentation and depth prediction tasks to 1.

Table 1. Comparison of our method with existing multi-task models on the NYUD-v2 dataset. Δ_{MTL} is the multi-task performance metric proposed in work [23]. (depth prediction and semantic segmentation as main tasks).

Method	Seg.	Depth						Δ_{MTL} ↑
	mIoU%↑	rmse↓	log rmse↓	δ_1 ↑	δ_2 ↑	δ_3 ↑	
Single task	29.98	–		–	–	–	–
	–	0.7294	0.2547	0.8230	0.9579	0.9901	–
MTL	30.87	0.7139	0.2557	0.8290	0.9582	0.9890	2.55
PadNet	32.39	0.6939	0.2412	0.8421	0.9647	0.9913	6.48
PadNet (E+N)	33.61	0.6816	0.2378	0.8482	0.9656	0.9919	9.33
MTINet	34.44	0.6343	0.2155	0.8828	0.9725	**0.9938**	13.95
MTI (E+N)	36.81	0.6166	**0.2095**	0.8830	**0.9737**	0.9933	19.12
MSTN	**38.44**	**0.6138**	0.2133	**0.8874**	0.9729	0.9924	**22.04**

Table 2. The IoU of some objects in the NYUDv2 dataset.

Method	IoU%								
	Dresser	Curtain	Floor	Door	Television	Toilet	Sink	Person	Books
PADNet	31.34	33.09	78.87	25.22	32.53	59.99	43.60	32.88	22.89
MTINet	33.84	33.59	80.60	**30.08**	34.30	59.90	48.05	40.03	20.31
Ours	**42.19**	**38.37**	**81.25**	29.58	**40.24**	**61.94**	**50.21**	**48.12**	**25.42**

4.2 Network Performance

We use mean Intersection over Union (mIoU) and root mean squared error(rmse) as metrics for evaluating semantic segmentation and depth prediction tasks, respectively. In the experiments, our main tasks focus on semantic segmentation (S) and depth prediction (D), with edge detection (E) and normal estimation (N) as auxiliary tasks. Table 1 shows the comparison of the accuracy of multiple models on the NYUD-v2 dataset. From the Table 1 and 2, we can see that the models employing multi-task learning improve the performance on most tasks beyond the single-task models, in which our model achieves the highest accuracy. Specifically, our model boosts the MTL performance over the single-task model, outstripping other encoder-focus multi-task models by at least 2.92%. Specifically, when the main tasks are semantic segmentation and depth prediction, our model improves the multi-task performance (+8.09%) compared with the state-of-art methods. After adding auxiliary tasks, the model learns the refined shared information, and the performance of the multi-task model is improved. In this case, the performance of MSTN also has certain advantages.

Visual Analysis. To account for the potential uncertainty between tasks, we propose introducing a Bayesian approach to the MTL network. Figure 4 shows the visualization results of NYUD-v2. We observe that in the living room scene (the first row in the figure), the package and paper on the table have depth

Table 3. Ablation study for the Bayesian gate mechanism on NYUD-v2. MG stands for Multimodal Distillation Gate. PG and BG represent the Gate structure of the BMCCU in the pre-order circulation and the post-order circulation, respectively. $b(\cdot)$ means to perform Bayesian inference processing.

Method	Seg.	Depth	Δ_{MTL} ↑
	mIoU↑	rmse↓	
MTS+MG	36.69	0.6334	+0.00
MTS+b (MG)	36.72	0.6270	+0.48
MTS+b (BG+MG)	37.61	0.6309	+1.71
MTS+b (PG+BG+MG)	38.44	0.6138	+4.27

information and no depth information, respectively. MSTN understands the implicit information to a certain extent and makes a comparatively correct classification of three objects in the semantic scene. The result shows that our proposed Bayesian multi-task network has a specific multimodal perception ability. And in most scenarios, the final predictions are further improved substantially.

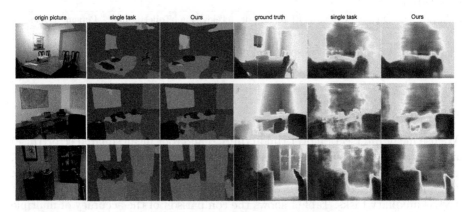

Fig. 4. Qualitative results on NYUD-v2. We compare the predictions made by a set of single-task models against the predictions made by our MSTN. Our method can perceive uncertainty across multiple modalities.

4.3   Ablation Study

An ablation experiment is developed to verify the effectiveness of the Bayesian gate mechanism. We take a multi-scale multi-task network containing 8 BMC-CUs as the baseline in the experiments. As shown in Table 3, compared with the original multi-task networks, the addition of Bayesian gate modules at different positions in the decoder will improve the multi-task performance. Specifically, we get the maximum promotion when all Bayesian gates are added to the module. After introducing the Bayesian deep learning algorithm, the gating performance is consistently better than that of the traditional gate structure (+0.48%, +1.71%, +4.27%). The experimental results show that adding

Bayesian gating to the pre-order scale circulation can significantly improve the performance of each task. We believe that the unknown information in the scale-sharing features generated by the head network provides insufficient prior knowledge. The Bayesian gate mechanism filters the feature stream, using uncertainty to capture the relative confidence between tasks, avoiding negatively impacting the overall performance of the predictions.

5   Conclusion

In this paper, in order to study the effective construction, extraction, and utilization of shared information in multi-task networks, we introduce the idea of Bayesian inference in multi-task learning and combine it with the gate mechanism. Moreover, a Multi-scale-task feature communication network is designed, which can enhance the comprehension ability of the model. We demonstrate the effectiveness of our method in experiments and show the potential of multi-task learning with visualization results. In the future, we will try to apply it to larger-scale deep networks and more computer vision tasks.

Acknowledgment. This work is supported by the National Natural Science Foundation of China (61976034), the Dalian Science and Technology Innovation Fund, China (2019J12GX035), and the Fundamental Research Funds for the Central Universities, China (DUT21YG106).

References

1. Blundell, C., Cornebise, J., Kavukcuoglu, K., Wierstra, D.: Weight uncertainty in neural network. In: International Conference on Machine Learning, PMLR, pp. 1613–1622 (2015)
2. Chen, S., Bortsova, G., García-Uceda Juárez, A., van Tulder, G., de Bruijne, M.: Multi-task attention-based semi-supervised learning for medical image segmentation. In: Shen, D., et al. (eds.) MICCAI 2019. LNCS, vol. 11766, pp. 457–465. Springer, Cham (2019). https://doi.org/10.1007/978-3-030-32248-9_51
3. Chen, T., Fox, E., Guestrin, C.: Stochastic gradient hamiltonian monte carlo. In: International conference on machine learning, PMLR, pp. 1683–1691 (2014)
4. Chen, Z., Badrinarayanan, V., Lee, C.Y., Rabinovich, A.: Gradnorm: gradient normalization for adaptive loss balancing in deep multitask networks. In: International Conference on Machine Learning, PMLR, pp. 794–803 (2018)
5. Désidéri, J.A.: Multiple-gradient descent algorithm (MGDA) for multiobjective optimization. C.R. Math. **350**(5–6), 313–318 (2012)
6. Eigen, D., Puhrsch, C., Fergus, R.: Depth map prediction from a single image using a multi-scale deep network. arXiv preprint arXiv:1406.2283 (2014)
7. Galassi, A., Lippi, M., Torroni, P.: Attention in natural language processing. IEEE Trans. Neural Netw. Learn. Syst. **32**(10), 4291–308 (2020)
8. Guo, M., Haque, A., Huang, D.-A., Yeung, S., Fei-Fei, L.: Dynamic task prioritization for multitask learning. In: Ferrari, V., Hebert, M., Sminchisescu, C., Weiss, Y. (eds.) ECCV 2018. LNCS, vol. 11220, pp. 282–299. Springer, Cham (2018). https://doi.org/10.1007/978-3-030-01270-0_17

9. Gupta, S., Arbelaez, P., Malik, J.: Perceptual organization and recognition of indoor scenes from RGB-D images. In: Proceedings of the IEEE Conference on Computer Vision and Pattern Recognition, CVPR, June 2013

10. He, K., Gkioxari, G., Dollár, P., Girshick, R.: Mask R-CNN. In: Proceedings of the IEEE International Conference on Computer Vision, pp. 2961–2969 (2017)

11. Kendall, A., Gal, Y., Cipolla, R.: Multi-task learning using uncertainty to weigh losses for scene geometry and semantics. In: Proceedings of the IEEE Conference On Computer Vision and Pattern Recognition, pp. 7482–7491 (2018)

12. Krizhevsky, A., Sutskever, I., Hinton, G.E.: Imagenet classification with deep convolutional neural networks. Adv. Neural. Inf. Process. Syst. **25**, 1097–1105 (2012)

13. Lawen, H., Ben-Cohen, A., Protter, M., Friedman, I., Zelnik-Manor, L.: Compact network training for person ReID. In: Proceedings of the 2020 International Conference on Multimedia Retrieval, pp. 164–171 (2020)

14. Liu, S., Johns, E., Davison, A.J.: End-to-end multi-task learning with attention. In: Proceedings of the IEEE/CVF Conference on Computer Vision and Pattern Recognition, pp. 1871–1880 (2019)

15. Long, M., Cao, Z., Wang, J., Yu, P.S.: Learning multiple tasks with multilinear relationship networks, pp. 1593–1602 (2017)

16. Maddox, W.J., Izmailov, P., Garipov, T., Vetrov, D.P., Wilson, A.G.: A simple baseline for bayesian uncertainty in deep learning. Adv. Neural. Inf. Process. Syst. **32**, 13153–13164 (2019)

17. Misra, I., Shrivastava, A., Gupta, A., Hebert, M.: Cross-stitch networks for multi-task learning. In: Proceedings of the IEEE conference on computer vision and pattern recognition, pp. 3994–4003 (2016)

18. Redmon, J., Divvala, S., Girshick, R., Farhadi, A.: You only look once: unified, real-time object detection. In: Proceedings of the IEEE Conference on Computer Vision and Pattern Recognition, pp. 779–788 (2016)

19. Ritter, H., Botev, A., Barber, D.: A scalable laplace approximation for neural networks. In: International Conference on Learning Representations (2018)

20. Ruder, S., Bingel, J., Augenstein, I., Søgaard, A.: Latent Multi-task Architecture Learning, vol. 33(01), pp. 4822–4829 (2019)

21. Sun, K., Xiao, B., Liu, D., Wang, J.: Deep high-resolution representation learning for human pose estimation. In: CVPR (2019)

22. Vandenhende, S., Georgoulis, S., Van Gool, L.: MTI-net: multi-scale task interaction networks for multi-task learning. In: Vedaldi, A., Bischof, H., Brox, T., Frahm, J.-M. (eds.) ECCV 2020. LNCS, vol. 12349, pp. 527–543. Springer, Cham (2020). https://doi.org/10.1007/978-3-030-58548-8_31

23. Vandenhende, S., Georgoulis, S., Van Gansbeke, W., Proesmans, M., Dai, D., Van Gool, L.: Multi-task learning for dense prediction tasks: a survey. IEEE Trans. Pattern Anal. Mach. Intell. (2021). https://doi.org/10.1109/TPAMI.2021.3054719

24. Xu, D., Ouyang, W., Wang, X., Sebe, N.: Pad-net: multi-tasks guided prediction-and-distillation network for simultaneous depth estimation and scene parsing, pp. 675–684 (2018)

25. Zhang, R., Li, C., Zhang, J., Chen, C., Wilson, A.G.: Cyclical stochastic gradient MCMC for bayesian deep learning. arXiv preprint arXiv:1902.03932 (2019)

26. Zhang, Z., Cui, Z., Xu, C., Jie, Z., Li, X., Yang, J.: Joint task-recursive learning for semantic segmentation and depth estimation. In: Ferrari, V., Hebert, M., Sminchisescu, C., Weiss, Y. (eds.) ECCV 2018. LNCS, vol. 11214, pp. 238–255. Springer, Cham (2018). https://doi.org/10.1007/978-3-030-01249-6_15

ASRSNet: Automatic Salient Region Selection Network for Few-Shot Fine-Grained Image Classification

Yi Liao[1], Weichuan Zhang[1], Yongsheng Gao[1(✉)], Changming Sun[2], and Xiaohan Yu[1]

[1] Griffith University, Brisbane, Australia
yi.liao2@griffithuni.edu.au, {yongsheng.gao,xiaohan.yu}@griffith.edu.au
[2] CSIRO, Data61, PO Box 76 ,Epping, NSW 1710, Australia
changming.sun@data61.csiro.au

Abstract. Few-shot learning for image classification aims at predicting unseen classes with only a few images. Recent works, especially the works on few-shot fine-grained image classification (FSFGIC), have achieved great progress. However, most of them neglected the spatial information and computed the distance between a query image and a support image directly, which may cause vagueness because the dominant objects can exist anywhere on images. A promising solution is to locate salient regions from images for discriminative feature representation learning. This paper develops an automatic salient region selection network without the use of a bounding box or part annotation mechanism for locating salient regions from images. Then a weighted average mechanism is introduced for facilitating a neural network to focus on those salient regions, optimizing the network, and performing the FSFGIC tasks. The experimental results on four benchmark datasets demonstrate the effectiveness of the proposed strategy.

Keywords: Few-shot fine-grained image classification · Discriminative feature representation learning · Automatic salient region selection network · Weighted average mechanism

1 Introduction

Few-shot fine-grained image classification (FSFGIC) methods refer to machine learning methods which aim to classify images belonging to subordinate object categories of the same entry-level category with only a few samples. In the last few years, FSFGIC has achieved stable progresses. The learning ability of deep neural networks [8, 26, 30] for recognizing the subtle differences between highly similar objects has been continuously improved. Meanwhile, a large number of fine-grained image datasets (e.g., CUB-200–2010 [4], Standard Cars [15], Aircraft [20], and Plant Disease [25]) have been collected by domain experts using complex rules to determine the accuracy of different types of object classification

© Springer Nature Switzerland AG 2022
M. El Yacoubi et al. (Eds.): ICPRAI 2022, LNCS 13363, pp. 627–638, 2022.
https://doi.org/10.1007/978-3-031-09037-0_51

methods and to assist researchers to improve the algorithms for achieving better performance on FSFGIC tasks.

Learning discriminative feature representation from images plays a key role on FSFGIC which is used not only to represent training samples but also to construct a classifier for performing FSFGIC tasks. The primal step of discriminative feature representation learning is to locate salient regions from images. Currently, a bounding box or part annotations mechanism [1,11,14,28] is widely applied for locating salient regions and performing object classification using the discriminative information from the selected regions. In this paper, an automatic salient region selection network without the use of a bounding box or part annotations mechanism is designed for learning discriminative feature representations and performing FSFGIC tasks. First, for each image, it is divided it into M parts equally. Then the image and its corresponding M sub-images are sent into a given neural network (e.g., Conv-64 F [30]) for training and obtaining feature descriptors. Second, the similarity between the query and support images is measured based on the obtained feature descriptors and they are named as basic similarity. Meanwhile, M similarities between M pairs of sub-images from query and support images are obtained based on their corresponding feature descriptors and named as sub-similarities. Third, if some sub-similarities are larger than the basic similarity, their corresponding sub-images are marked as salient regions and a weighted average mechanism is designed for a neural network to focus on these salient regions, optimizing the network, and performing the FSFGIC tasks. It is worth noting that if sub-similarities are less than the basic similarity in one episode, the designed neural network is optimized by using the basic similarity in this episode.

The main contributions in our proposed method comprise two aspects.

- An automatic salient region selection network is designed for discriminative feature representations learning and performing FSFGIC tasks. This designed network enables the salient regions on images to be detected automatically without the help of bounding box and annotation information.
- A weighed average mechanism is designed for enhancing the effect of discriminative features in the tasks of classifying fine-grained images.
- Experimental evaluation are performed on four public datasets, verifying the effectiveness of the proposed method in various FSFGIC tasks.

2   Related Work

In this section, we briefly introduce the existing FSFGIC related methods: fine-grained image classification methods, meta-learning based FSFGIC methods, and metric-learning based FSFGIC methods.

2.1   Fine-Grained Image Classification

Fine-grained image classification (FGIC) is an attractive topic in the computer vision research community. In FGIC, the training samples share the same class space with testing samples. Current regional feature based FGIC approaches try to discover salient regions from images without the help of bounding box and annotation information. Peng et al. [21] proposed an object-part attention model in which potential objects from images were detected and the most discriminative parts of the object were selected as feature representation. The classification accuracy is improved by 1.2% on dataset CUB-200–2010 [31]. Zhang et al. [32] proposed an approach by which all the potential object parts were generated by using selective search method [29] and the most discriminative object part was selected to form image representation according to its importance value computed with the help of Fisher Vector [23]. The approach improved classification accuracy by 3.5% on dataset CUB-200–2010 [31]. Therefore, locating the discriminative regions can boost classification performance in FGIC tasks.

2.2   Meta-learning Based FSFGIC Methods

Different from FGIC, The class space of training data and the class space of testing data are disjoint in FSFGIC. Meta-learning based FSFGIC is a branch of FSFGIC. Finn et al. [6] proposed a model-agnostic meta-learning (MAML) method by which any model is trained successively twice to obtain two groups of parameters. The new gradient for updating the model is computed using both groups of parameters. Cai et al. [3] proposed a memory matching network (MM-Net) where a contextual learner consisting of multiple bidirectional long-shot term memory (LSTM) [24] is devised to predict the parameters for the embedding network. Sachin et al. [22] proposed an LSTM-based optimizer by combining the standard gradient descent algorithm and the cell state of LSTM [9]. In this way, a novel gradient is obtained by training a LSTM network.

2.3   Metric-learning Based FSFGIC Methods

The existing metric-learning based FSFGIC methods usually consist of three steps. Firstly, the images including support images and query images are embedded into their image representations by embedding networks (e.g., Conv-64F [30]). Secondly, the distances between each query embeddings and all support embeddings are calculated by employing different distance metrics (e.g., cosine similarity [17], Euclidean distance [27], and Kullback-Leibler(KL) distance [16]). Thirdly, each query image is allocated to the support class according to the closest distance principle.

Snell et al. [27] proposed a prototypical network that employs the Euclidean distance for measuring the similarity between the support image representations and the query image representation. Li et al. [17] proposed a deep nearest neighbour neural network (DN4) using cosine similarity as the measurement.

In [16], an asymmetric Kullback-Leibler (KL) divergence was utilized to measure the relation of distribution between query image and support image. In [18], a covariance metric network is proposed to measure the relation between a query image and support categories. However, the aforementioned methods [16–18,27] did not deal with the spatial information discriminatively and calculated similarity distance between a query image and a support class directly without considering the effect of salient regions on images in FSFGIC.

Recently, many few-shot fine-grained learning research works focus on attention mechanisms. For example, Dong et al. [5] presented a novel ATL-Net in which a task adaptive attention module is designed to generate a relation matrix. The relation matrix consists of cosine similarity between each local representation of a query embedding and each local representation of one support class embeddings. All the local representations are processed by a convolution layer and filtered through a threshold. The weights of every image patch are decided by the threshold. However, the threshold is predicted by a multi-layer perceptron (MLP) trained on query embeddings. Therefore, the threshold will vary with various query images and the weights for semantic patches from query image are not stable enough. It should have negative influence on the final classification accuracy. Yan et al. [19] presented a novel method called dense classification in which the weights of each patch are learned through training on auxiliary data. The assumption is that the weights learned on auxiliary data are generic enough to be used for new classes.

Different from the methods above, our proposed method not only has an ability to automatically locate the semantic regions with aid of the comparison between image patch level similarity and image level similarity, but assigns a stable weight to most discriminative regions by using a weighted average mechanism.

3   Methodology

In this section, we first present a brief review of the problem definition of few-shot classification. Then we illustrate how to automatically select salient regions from images. Finally, a weighted average mechanism is designed for a neural network to focus on these salient regions, optimizing the network, and performing the FSFGIC tasks. The overview of the proposed framework for one-shot image classification is shown in Fig. 1.

3.1   Problem Definition

For an FSFGIC task, the target dataset $\mathcal{D}$ contains two parts: a support set $\mathcal{S}$ and a query set $\mathcal{Q}$. The small support set $\mathcal{S}$ includes C unseen classes, and each of which has K labeled samples. The query set $\mathcal{Q}$ contains J unlabeled samples. Displayed equations are centered and set on a separate line.

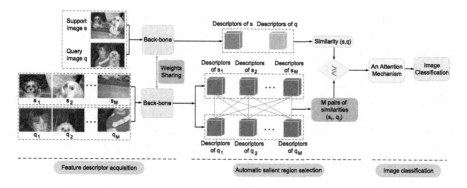

Fig. 1. The overall pipeline of our proposed automatic salient region selection framework. (1) Feature descriptor acquisition: support and query and their corresponding sub-images are sent into backbones for obtaining feature descriptors. (2) Automatic salient region selection: if some sub-similarities are larger than the basic similarity, their corresponding sub-images are marked as salient regions. (3) Image classification: a weighted average mechanism is designed for a neural network to focus on these salient regions and performing FSFGIC tasks.

$$\mathcal{D} = \left\{ \mathcal{S} = \left\{ (x_i, y_i)_{i=1}^{C \times K} \right\} \cup \mathcal{Q} = \left\{ (x_j)_{j=1}^{J} \right\} \right\}, \tag{1}$$

where $\mathcal{S} \cap \mathcal{Q} = \emptyset$, x_i and x_j denote fine-grained samples and $y_i \subset C$ represents the ground truth label of x_i. The goal of FSFGIC is to successfully classify x_j into its corresponding class in C in $\mathcal{S}$. Thus, the problem is denoted as a C-way K-shot task.

It is worth noting that the training samples of each class in FSFGIC are too limited to effectively learn transferable knowledge [33] for performing FSFGIC tasks. Then, an episodic training paradigm [30] with an auxiliary set $\mathcal{A}$, which has similar data distribution with $\mathcal{D}$, is applied to tackle the aforementioned problem as follows

$$\mathcal{A} = \left\{ \mathcal{E} = \left\{ (u_i, v_i)_{i=1}^{N} \right\} \cup \mathcal{F} = \left\{ (u_j, v_j)_{j=1}^{L} \right\} \right\}, \tag{2}$$

where u_i and u_j are fine-grained images, v_i and v_j are their corresponding labels; $\mathcal{E} \cup \mathcal{F} = \emptyset$, $\mathcal{D} \cup \mathcal{A} = \emptyset$. The auxiliary set A contains sufficient classes and labeled samples which are far larger than C and K respectively.

In each round of training, $\mathcal{A}$ is randomly separated into two parts: an auxiliary support set $\mathcal{G} = \left\{ (u_i, v_i)_{i=1}^{C \times K} \right\}$ and an auxiliary query set $\mathcal{H} = \left\{ (u_j, v_j)_{j=1}^{J} \right\}$. With $N >> C \times K$, $\mathcal{E}$ can mimic the composition of $\mathcal{S}$ in each iteration. Then $\mathcal{A}$ is employed to learn prior knowledge for training $\mathcal{S}$.

3.2 Automatic Salient Regions Selection for FSFGIC

Let s $(s \in \mathcal{S})$ and q $(q \in \mathcal{Q})$ denote a support image and a query image respectively. The support image s and query image q are divided into M (here $M = 36$) parts equally. Then sub-images (i.e., $s_1, s_2,..., s_M$) of support image s and sub-images (i.e., q_1, q_2,..., q_M) of query image q are obtained. Meanwhile, the sub-images and query and support images are resized into the same widths and they are sent into a given backbone (i.e., Conv-64F [30]) for training and obtaining their corresponding descriptors. Typically, after an input image x is sent into a backbone Θ, dhw-dimensional feature descriptors (i.e., $\Theta(x) \in R^{d \times (h \times w)}$) can be obtained where h and w denote the height and width of the feature tensor map respectively, d is the number of filters, and R represents real space. Therefore, the feature descriptors of the support image s, the query image q, the sub-images (i.e., s_1, s_2,...,s_M) of support image s, and the sub-images (i.e., q_1, q_2, ...,q_M) of query image q are obtained as

$$\begin{aligned}
\Psi^s &= [\Theta_1(s), \cdots, \Theta_\tau(s)], \\
\Psi^q &= [\Theta_1(q), \cdots, \Theta_\tau(q)], \\
\Psi^{s_l} &= [\Theta_1(s_l), \cdots, \Theta_\tau(s_l)], \\
\Psi^{q_l} &= [\Theta_1(q_l), \cdots, \Theta_\tau(q_l)], \ l = 1, \cdots, M,
\end{aligned} \tag{3}$$

where τ ($\tau = h \times w$) is the total number of descriptors for each image. In this work, a cosine measure is utilized for calculating the similarity between two different images based on the 1-nearest neighbor method [2]. Then the basic similarity between a query image and a support image is as follows,

$$\begin{aligned}
\Lambda(\Theta_t(s), \Theta_t(q)) &= \frac{\Theta_t(s)^T \Theta_t(q)}{\| \Theta_t(s_u) \| \cdot \| \Theta_t(q_v) \|}, \\
\Lambda(\Psi^s, \Psi^s) &= \max \{\Lambda(\Theta_1(s_u), \Theta_1(q_v)), \cdots, \Lambda(\Theta_\tau(s_u), \Theta_\tau(q_v))\}, \\
t &= 1, 2, \cdots, \tau.
\end{aligned} \tag{4}$$

The sub-similarities between the sub-images of a support image and the sub-images of a query image are as follows,

$$\begin{aligned}
\Lambda(\Theta_t(s_u), \Theta_t(q_v)) &= \frac{\Theta_t(s_u)^T \Theta_t(q_v)}{\| \Theta_t(s_u) \| \cdot \| \Theta_t(q_v) \|}, \\
\Lambda(\Psi^{s_u}, \Psi^{q_v}) &= \max \{\Lambda(\Theta_1(s_u), \Theta_1(q_v)), \cdots, \Lambda(\Theta_\tau(s_u), \Theta_\tau(q_v))\}, \\
t &= 1, 2, \cdots, \tau, \ u = 1, 2, \cdots, M, \ v = 1, 2, \cdots, M.
\end{aligned} \tag{5}$$

From Eq. (5), an $M \times M$ sub-similarity matrix ζ_1 can be obtained. Then we first find the maximum value in the subsimilarity matrix ζ_1 and its corresponding row i and column j which is denoted as $\eta_1 = \zeta_1(i, j)$. If η_1 is larger than its corresponding basic similarity, the sub-image pair between the i-th sub-image of the support image and the j-th subimage of the query image are marked as a pair of salient regions. Second, we delete the i-th row and j-th column of the matrix ζ_1 and construct a new $(M - 1) \times (M - 1)$ matrix ζ_2. Then we find the maximum value in matrix ζ_2 and its corresponding row u and column v which is denoted as $\eta_2 = \zeta_2(u, v)$. If η_2 is also larger than its corresponding basic similarity, we will continue to perform this operation until the maximum value η_{k+1} of the $(k + 1)$-th sub-similarity matrix is less than the basic similarity. Finally, k pairs of sub-images corresponding to the k sub-similarities are marked as salient regions, and a weighted average β is presented on the k subsimilarities (i.e., η_1, η_2, ..., η_k) for representing the similarity between the support image and the query image as follows

$$\beta(s,q) = \frac{1}{\sum_{i=1}^{k} \eta_i}(\eta_1^2 + \eta_2^2 + \cdots + \eta_k^2). \tag{6}$$

It is worth noting that if η_1 is less than the basic similarity, the similarity between the support and query images is represented by

$$\beta(s,q) = \Lambda(\Psi^s, \Psi^q). \tag{7}$$

Furthermore, the similarity between query image q and class C is calculated which is named as image-to-class similarity measure [16] as follows,

$$\xi(q,C) = \sum_{j=1}^{\tau} \beta(s^j, q), \tag{8}$$

where s^j represents the j-th support image in class C. Then the Adam optimization method [13] with a cross-entropy loss is used to train the whole network for learning the parameters and performing FSFGIC tasks. The detailed process is listed as Algorithm 1.

Algorithm 1: Salient regions selection mechanism

    Input: sub-similarity matrix ζ_1, M
    Output: $\beta(s,q)$
1 $k = 0, t = 0, s = 0$;
2 **while** $k \leq M$ **do**
3     $k = k + 1$;
4     $\eta_k = \max(\zeta_k)$;
5   **if** $\eta_k \geq \Lambda(\Psi^s, \Psi^s)$ **then**
6        $(i,j) = \operatorname{argmax}(\zeta_k)$;
7   η_{k+1} is contructed by i-th row and j-th column are deleted from η_k;
8        $t = t + \eta_k$;
9        $s = s + \eta_k^2$;
10   **else**
11   break;
12   **end**
13 **end**
14 $\beta(s,q) = \frac{t}{s}$;
15 **return** $\beta(s,q)$

---

4 Experiment

4.1 Datasets

Our proposed network is evaluated on four fine-grained datasets, i.e., the Stanford Dogs [12], Stanford Cars [15], CUB-200–2010 [31], and Plant Disease [25] datasets. The Stanford Dogs dataset consists of 120 dog classes with 20,580 samples. The Stanford Cars dataset consists of 196 car classes with 16,185 samples. The CUB-200–2010 dataset consists of 200 bird classes with 6,033 samples. The Plant Disease dataset consists of 38 plant disease classes with 54,306 samples. For fair performance comparisons, we follow the same data split as used in [17] that are illustrated in Table 1.

Table 1. The class split of four fine-grained datasets. N_{train}, N_{val}, and N_{test} are the numbers of classes in the auxiliary set, validation set, and test set respectively.

Dataset	N_{train}	N_{val}	N_{test}
Stanford Dogs	70	20	30
Stanford Cars	130	17	49
CUB-200–2010	130	20	50
Plant Disease	20	10	8

4.2 Experimental Setup

In this work, both the 5-way 1-shot and 5-way 5-shot FSFGIC tasks are performed on the four datasets. We follow the basic feature extraction network (i.e., Conv-64F [30]). Each input image is resized to 84×84. Then we have $h = w = 21$, $d = 64$, and $\tau = 441$. Random crop, random color transformations, random horizontal flips, and random rotations are utilized for data augmentation. There are 300,000 episodes which are randomly sampled and constructed for training the proposed models by utilizing the episodic training paradigm [30]. For each episode, 15 query samples per class are randomly selected for the four datasets. The Adam optimization method [13] is utilized for training the models using 30 epochs. The learning rate is initially set as 0.001 and multiplied by 0.5 for every 100,000 episodes. In the testing stage, 600 episodes are randomly constructed from the testing set for obtaining the classification results. The top-1 mean accuracy is employed as the evaluation criteria. The above process is repeated five times and the final mean results are obtained as the classification accuracy for FSFGIC. Meanwhile, the 95% confidence intervals are obtained and reported.

4.3 Performance Comparison

The experimental results of eight state-of-the-art metric learning methods (i.e., Matching Net (M-Net) [30], Prototypical Net (P-Net) [27], GNN [7], CovaMNet

Table 2. Comparison results on Stanford Dogs and Stanford Cars datasets

Model	5-way Accuracy (%)			
	Stanford Dogs		Stanford Cars	
	1-shot	5-shot	1-shot	5-shot
M-Net [30]	35.80 ± 0.99	47.50 ± 1.03	34.80 ± 0.98	44.70 ± 1.03
P-Net [27]	37.59 ± 1.00	48.19 ± 1.03	40.90 ± 1.01	52.93 ± 1.03
GNN [7]	46.98 ± 0.98	62.27 ± 0.95	55.85 ± 0.97	71.25 ± 0.89
CovaMNet [18]	49.10 ± 0.76	63.04 ± 0.65	56.65 ± 0.86	71.33 ± 0.62
DN4 [17]	45.73 ± 0.76	66.33 ± 0.66	61.51 ± 0.85	89.60 ± 0.44
PABN+$_{cpt}$ [10]	45.65 ± 0.71	61.24 ± 0.62	54.44 ± 0.71	67.36 ± 0.61
LRPABN$_{cpt}$ [10]	45.72 ± 0.75	60.94 ± 0.66	60.28 ± 0.76	73.29 ± 0.58
ATL-Net [5]	54.49 ± 0.92	73.20 ± 0.69	$\mathbf{67.95 \pm 0.84}$	89.16 ± 0.48
Proposed ASRSNET	$\mathbf{54.97 \pm 0.88}$	$\mathbf{73.21 \pm 0.57}$	64.33 ± 0.75	$\mathbf{91.15 \pm 0.78}$

[18], DN4 [17], PABN+$_{cpt}$ [10], LRPABN$_{cpt}$ [10], and ATL-Net [5]) and the proposed method on the four datasets are summarized in Table 2 and Table 3. It is worth noting that the accuracies of the seven other methods are also tested on the same feature extraction network (i.e., Conv-64F [30]). For three fine-grained datasets, i.e., the Stanford Dogs [12], Stanford Cars [15], CUB-200–2010 [31], we use the officially provided results for all the other methods. For the Plant Disease [25] dataset, we utilize the codes provided to test their corresponding results. Because the codes for PABN+$_{cpt}$ [10] and LRPABN$_{cpt}$ [10] are not provided, we leave them blank on the Plant Disease dataset.

It can be found from Table 2 and Table 3 that the proposed method gets steady and notable improvements on almost all FSFGIC tasks. For the 5-way 5-shot task, the proposed method achieves the best performance on four fine-grained datasets. For the 5-way 1-shot task, the proposed method also achieves the best performance on Standford Dogs, CUB-200–2010, and Plant Disease and achieves the second best performance on Standford Cars. For the 5-way 1-shot and 5-way 5-shot FSFGIC tasks on the CUB-200–2010 dataset, our proposed method achieves 41.56%, 71.65%, 23.73%, 22.33%, 20.65%, 1.22%, 0.78%, and 5.28% improvements and 38%, 81.34%, 28.92%, 28.78%,0.25%, 9.90%, 0.95%, and 6.56% improvements over M-Net, P-Net, GNN, CovaMNet, DN4, PABN+$_{cpt}$, LRPABN$_{cpt}$, and ATL-Net respectively. Such improvements demonstrate the ability of ASRSNET for effectively highlighting the feature representation in salient regions in images and making the similarity measure between the samples within the same class larger and the similarity measure between samples from different classes smaller with limited training samples.

Table 3. Comparison results on Plant Disease and CUB-200–2010 datasets.

Model	5-way Accuracy (%)			
	Plant Disease		CUB-200–2010	
	1-shot	5-shot	1-shot	5-shot
M-Net [30]	62.93 ± 0.94	80.55 ± 0.93	45.30 ± 1.03	59.50 ± 1.01
P-Net [27]	64.97 ± 0.85	82.73 ± 0.91	37.36 ± 1.00	45.28 ± 1.03
GNN [7]	69.85 ± 0.91	88.69 ± 0.79	51.83 ± 0.98	63.69 ± 0.64
CovaMNet [18]	70.72 ± 0.89	88.92 ± 0.81	52.42 ± 0.76	63.76 ± 0.64
DN4 [17]	72.47 ± 0.76	90.68 ± 0.44	53.15 ± 0.84	81.90 ± 0.60
PABN+$_{cpt}$ [10]	–	–	63.36 ± 0.80	74.71 ± 0.60
LRPABN$_{cpt}$ [10]	–	–	63.23 ± 0.77	76.06 ± 0.58
ATL-Net [5]	72.18 ± 0.92	90.11 ± 0.65	60.91 ± 0.91	77.05 ± 0.67
Proposed ASRSNET	**73.58±0.87**	**91.76±0.79**	**64.13±0.85**	**82.11±0.72**

5   Conclusion

Current few-shot metric-based learning methods have improved classification accuracy greatly in FSFGIC tasks. However, they computed similarity distance between a query image and a support class directly without considering the effect of salient regions on images. Such image-level based similarity resulted in a vagueness problem because the dominant objects can exist anywhere on images. In this paper, a novel automatic salient region selection network without the use of a bounding box or part annotation mechanism is proposed for obtaining salient region pairs from query and support images, aiming to locate the more discriminative regions for improving the representation ability of neural networks trained by few samples. Meanwhile, it donates an advanced approach to alleviating vagueness problem for the FSFGIC research community. Furthermore, a weighted average mechanism is designed for facilitating a neural network to focus on those salient regions, optimizing the network, and enhance the classification accuracy for FSFGIC tasks. The effectiveness of our proposed method has been demonstrated through experiments on four benchmark fine-grained datasets.

References

1. Berg, T., Liu, J., Woo Lee, S., Alexander, M.L., Jacobs, D.W., Belhumeur, P.N.: Birdsnap: Large-scale fine-grained visual categorization of birds. In: Proceedings of the IEEE Conference on Computer Vision and Pattern Recognition, pp. 2011–2018 (2014)
2. Boiman, O., Shechtman, E., Irani, M.: In defense of nearest-neighbor based image classification. In: Proceedings of the IEEE Conference on Computer Vision and Pattern Recognition, pp. 1–8 (2008)

3. Cai, Q., Pan, Y., Yao, T., Yan, C., Mei, T.: Memory Matching Networks for One-Shot Image Recognition. In: Proceedings of the IEEE Conference on Computer Vision and Pattern Recognition, pp. 4080–4088 (2018)

4. Cathrine Wah, S.B., Peter Welinder, P.P., Belongie, S.: The caltech-ucsd birds-200-2011 dataset. California Institute of Technology (2011)

5. Dong, C., Li, W., Huo, J., Gu, Z., Gao, Y.: Learning task-aware local representations for few-shot learning. In: Proceedings of the Twenty-Ninth International Conference on International Joint Conferences on Artificial Intelligence, pp. 716–722 (2021)

6. Finn, C., Abbeel, P., Levine, S.: Model-agnostic meta-learning for fast adaptation of deep networks. In: Proceedings of International Conference on Machine Learning, pp. 1126–1135 (2017)

7. Garcia, V., Bruna, J.: Few-shot learning with graph neural networks. In: Proceedings of the International Conference on Learning Representations (2018)

8. He, K., Zhang, X., Ren, S., Sun, J.: Deep residual learning for image recognition. In: Proceedings of the IEEE Conference on Computer Vision and Pattern Recognition, vol. 2016, pp. 770–778 (2016)

9. Hochreiter, S., Schmidhuber, J.: Long short-term memory. Neural Comput. **9**(8), 1735–1780 (1997). https://doi.org/10.1162/neco.1997.9.8.1735

10. Huang, H., Zhang, J., Zhang, J., Xu, J., Wu, Q.: Low-rank pairwise alignment bilinear network for few-shot fine-grained image classification. IEEE Trans. Multimedia **23**, 1666–1680 (2021). https://doi.org/10.1109/TMM.2020.3001510

11. Huang, S., Xu, Z., Tao, D., Zhang, Y.: Part-stacked cnn for fine-grained visual categorization. In: Proceedings of the IEEE Conference on Computer Vision and Pattern Recognition, pp. 1173–1182 (2016)

12. Khosla, A., Jayadevaprakash, N., Yao, B., Li, F.F.: Novel dataset for fine-grained image categorization: stanford dogs. In: Proceedings of the IEEE Conference on Computer Vision and Pattern Recognition Workshop on Fine-Grained Visual Categorization (2011)

13. Kingma, D.P., Ba, J.: Adam: a method for stochastic optimization. In: Proceedings of the International Conference on Learning Representations (2015)

14. Krause, J., Jin, H., Yang, J., Fei-Fei, L.: Fine-grained recognition without part annotations. In: Proceedings of the IEEE Conference on Computer Vision and Pattern Recognition, pp. 5546–5555 (2015)

15. Krause, J., Stark, M., Deng, J., Fei-Fei, L.: 3D object representations for fine-grained categorization. In: Proceedings of the IEEE International Conference on Computer Vision Workshops, pp. 554–561 (2013)

16. Li, W., Wang, L., Huo, J., Shi, Y., Gao, Y., Luo, J.: Asymmetric distribution measure for few-shot learning. arXiv preprint arXiv:2002.00153 (2020)

17. Li, W., Wang, L., Xu, J., Huo, J., Gao, Y., Luo, J.: Revisiting local descriptor based image-to-class measure for few-shot learning. In: Proceedings of the IEEE Conference on Computer Vision and Pattern Recognition, pp. 7260–7268 (2019)

18. Li, W., Xu, J., Huo, J., Wang, L., Gao, Y., Luo, J.: Distribution consistency based covariance metric networks for few-shot learning. In: Proceedings of the Association for the Advancement of Artificial Intelligence, pp. 8642–8649 (2019)

19. Lifchitz, Y., Avrithis, Y., Picard, S., Bursuc, A.: Dense classification and implanting for few-shot learning. In: Proceedings of the IEEE Conference on Computer Vision and Pattern Recognition, pp. 9258–9267 (2019)

20. Maji, S., Rahtu, E., Kannala, J., Blaschko, M., Vedaldi, A.: Fine-grained visual classification of aircraft. arXiv Preprint arXiv:1306.5151 (2013)

21. Peng, Y., He, X., Zhao, J.: Object-part attention model for fine-grained image classification. IEEE Trans. Image Process. **27**(3), 1487–1500 (2017)
22. Ravi, S., Larochelle, H.: Optimization as a model for few-shot learning. In: Proceedings of International Conference on Learning Representations (2017)
23. Sánchez, J., Perronnin, F., Mensink, T., Verbeek, J.: Image classification with the fisher vector: theory and practice. Int. J. Comput. Vision **105**(3), 222–245 (2013)
24. Schuster, M., Paliwal, K.K.: Bidirectional recurrent neural networks. IEEE Trans. Signal Process. **45**(11), 2673–2681 (1997). https://doi.org/10.1109/78.650093
25. Sharma, S.R.: Plant disease (2018). https://www.kaggle.com/saroz014/plant-disease
26. Simonyan, K., Zisserman, A.: Very deep convolutional networks for large-scale image recognition. In: Proceedings of the International Conference on Learning Representations, pp. 770–784 (2015)
27. Snell, J., Swersky, K., Zemel, R.S.: Prototypical networks for few-shot learning. In: Conference on Neural Information Processing Systems, pp. 4077–4087 (2017)
28. Sun, X., Xv, H., Dong, J., Zhou, H., Chen, C., Li, Q.: Few-shot learning for domain-specific fine-grained image classification. IEEE Trans. Industr. Electron. **68**(4), 3588–3598 (2020)
29. Uijlings, J.R., Van De Sande, K.E., Gevers, T., Smeulders, A.W.: Selective search for object recognition. Int. J. Comput. Vision **104**(2), 154–171 (2013)
30. Vinyals, O., Blundell, C., Lillicrap, T., Wierstra, D., et al.: Matching networks for one shot learning. In: Conference on Neural Information Processing Systems, vol. 29, pp. 3630–3638 (2016)
31. Welinder, P., et al.: Caltech-UCSD birds 200. California Institute of Technology (2010)
32. Zhang, Y., et al.: Weakly supervised fine-grained categorization with part-based image representation. IEEE Trans. Image Process. **25**(4), 1713–1725 (2016)
33. Zhangy, W., Liuy, X., Xue, Z., Gao, Y., Sun, C.: Ndpnet: A novel non-linear data projection network for few-shot fine-grained image classification. arXiv preprint arXiv:2106.06988 (2021)

Face Age Progression with Attribute Manipulation

Sinzith Tatikonda[1]([✉]), Athira Nambiar[2]([✉]), and Anurag Mittal[1]

[1] Department of Computer Science and Engineering,
Indian Institute of Technology Madras, Chennai, India
`sinzithtatikonda@gmail.com, amittal@cse.iitm.ac.in`
[2] Department of Computational Intelligence,
SRM Institute of Science and Technology, Chennai, India
`athiram@srmist.edu.in`

Abstract. The human face is one of the predominant means of person recognition. Human faces are affected by many factors *i.e.* time, attributes, weather, and other subject-specific variations. Although face aging has been studied in the past, the impact of the aforesaid factors, especially, the effect of attributes on the aging process were unexplored. In this paper, we propose a novel holistic "Face Age progression With Attribute Manipulation" (FAWAM) model that generates face images at different ages while simultaneously varying attributes and other subject specific characteristics. We address the task in a bottom-up manner, considering both age and attributes submodules. For face aging, we use an attribute-conscious face aging model with a pyramidal generative adversarial network that can model age-specific facial changes while maintaining intrinsic subject specific characteristics. For facial attribute manipulation, the age processed facial image is manipulated with desired attributes while preserving other details unchanged, leveraging an attribute generative adversarial network architecture. Our proposed model achieves significant qualitative as well as quantitative performance results.

1 Introduction

In this paper, we address a novel *"Face Age Progression With Attribute Manipulation"* task *i.e.* upon a given young face input image, aesthetically render the effects of facial aging along with simultaneously manipulating facial attributes. This has great practical application in forensics, entertainment, investigation etc. With the development of deep convolutional neural network (CNNs) and large scale labeled datasets, significant advances have been made recently in Computer Vision. Although facial aging and attribute manipulation has been addressed independently as two active research areas, their mutual impact hasn't studied much. This work investigates some initial comprehensive study in this direction. The motivation of this work is from basic human recognition ability, as humans can recognize their peers even after a long time and with attribute variations. To understand how does the machine recognize this, it is required to understand the process of aging and facial attribute analysis.

© Springer Nature Switzerland AG 2022
M. El Yacoubi et al. (Eds.): ICPRAI 2022, LNCS 13363, pp. 639–652, 2022.
https://doi.org/10.1007/978-3-031-09037-0_52

The intrinsic complexity of physical aging, the influences from other external factors such as pose, illumination, and expression (PIE) variations and the shortage of labeled aging data collectively make face age progression a difficult problem. Two important key targets of face aging are to achieve aging accuracy and identity permanence [22]. After the early attempts based on skin's anatomical structure and mechanical simulations, data-driven approaches gained more popularity either by applying the prototype of aging details to test faces [8] or by modeling the relationship between facial changes and corresponding ages [18,21]. Further, significant improvement on the aging results were reported while using deep generative networks towards image generation [4,7] with more appealing aging effects and less ghosting artifacts (Fig. 1).

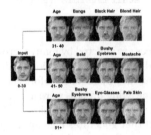

Fig. 1. Demonstration of our "Face aging with attribute manipulation" (FAWAM) results. Images in each row are the attribute manipulated output images corresponding to different age clusters.

The facial attribute manipulation problem addresses face editing via manipulating single/multiple attributes *i.e.* haircolor, glasses, expression etc. One major challenge associated with this is the difficulty in collecting annotated images of a particular person with varying attributes. However, with the arrival of deep neural network techniques and large scale datasets [14], considerable advancements in the field has been witnessed. In particular, generative models such as variational auto-encoder (VAE) and generative adversarial network (GAN) are employed to bring out significant facial attribute editing. The encoder-decoder architecture is one of the most effective solutions for using a single model for multiple attribute manipulation. To this end, many key works such as VAE/GAN [10], IcGAN [15], Fader networks [9], AttGAN [6] etc. were reported in the past. Nonetheless, such works considered age only as an attribute element and consequently, age gains only very little importance compared to the attribute factor.

In this work, we address a high-level and generic framework named "Face age progression with attribute manipulation (FAWAM)" wherein both the aging and attribute manipulation counterparts get equal roles to play, with which the model can exclusively render a particular attribute for a specific age group. In other words, our model makes it possible to visualize the aged image (in different ranges 30+, 40+, 50+) alongwith a variety of choices of attributes *i.e.* how a person will look like in future with beard/bald head/grey hair etc. The aging submodule of FAWAM leverages pyramidal GAN architecture [22] whereas the attribute manipulation submodule uses AttGAN [6]. Since there was no common large-scale dataset available towards both face aging and attribute manipulation tasks simultaneously, each module is trained independently on its respective dataset; whereas the testing is carried out in an end-to-end manner. Extensive baseline studies, performance analysis and ablation studies are carried out on CelebA, CACD, FGNET and UTK-face datasets.

The major contributions of this study are: (1) Proposal of a novel FAWAM model that bestows equal significant roles for age and attribute components during image synthesis; a task not well explored in the past. (2) Extensive experiments on multiple datasets that verify the effectiveness and robustness of our FAWAM model i.e. the influence of age on attribute and vice versa, clearly enhances the synthesised image quality.

2   Related Works

2.1   Face Aging

The early works on aging exploited physical models and skin anatomy, to simulate the aging progression of facial muscles. Later, many data-driven approaches came to prominence where they leveraged training faces to learn aging pattern. In this regard, many recent works exploited GANs to improve the results by synthesising faces with corresponding aging factors. Wang et al. [21] proposed a model by mapping the faces in a tensor space and the age-related details were added on top of that. Similarly, Yang et al. [23] tackled it as a multi-attribute decomposition problem, and the age progression was incorporated by manipulating the age component to the target age group. Further, deep generative networks were used for generating smooth versions of real-looking faces across different ages, for e.g. [20] and S2GAN [5]. One of the most popular recent work leveraged pyramidal architecture of GANs [22] towards age transformation, also by taking the advantage from individual-dependent critic to keep the identity cue stable, as well as multi-pathway discriminator to refine aging details. We build our FAWAM model upon Pyramidal GAN architecture.

2.2   Facial Attribute Manipulation

Facial attribute manipulation can be achieved via: (a) Optimization based methods [11,19] or (b) Learning based methods [9,12]. The former uses CNN based architectures and try to minimize the attribute loss of given face and set of different attribute faces as in CNAI [11]. However, the training of such optimization-based methods is laborious and time consuming. The latter one employ residual learning strategy that minimizes the objective loss function. Li et al. [12] proposed a model to edit attribute in a face image using an adversarial attribute loss and a deep identity feature loss. Another work [16] leverages dual residual learning strategy to train two networks, simultaneously to add/remove a specific attribute. Its downside is the necessity of different models for different attributes. To overcome this practical constraint, single model for multiple facial attribute editing was proposed e.g., attribute manipulation is achieved in VAE/GAN [10] by modifying the latent representation. In Fader Networks [9], an adversarial process upon the latent representation of an autoencoder is carried out to learn the attribute-invariant representation. The decoder generates the edited result based on the arbitrary attribute vector. Another work AttGAN [6] uses an encoder-decoder architecture that is inspired by the VAE/GAN [10] and Fader Networks [9]. It models the relation between the latent representation and the attributes.

Although many aging and attribute manipulation tasks were reported in the literature, their mutual influence is not well addressed. The key novelty of this work is the proposal of an ensemble model *i.e.* FAWAM, that can simultaneously incorporate both age and attribute components with equal importance, while synthesising the image.

3   Proposed Architecture for Face Age Progression with Attribute Manipulation

In this section, we describe our novel architecture designed towards the task of *Face age progression with attribute manipulation*(FAWAM). The holistic architecture of our proposed FAWAM model is explained in Sect. 3.1. The internal architecture of Face Aging (FA) and Attribute Manipulation (AM) submodules are described in detail in Sect. 3.2 and 3.3 respectively.

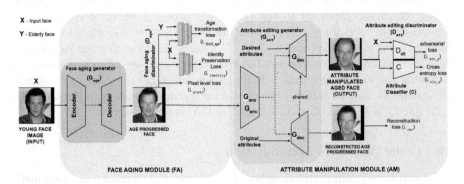

Fig. 2. Framework of the proposed Face Age Progression With Attribute Manipulation (FAWAM) model. For a young input face image, the architecture provides attribute manipulated aged face image output. (Example shows "51+" aged face, with "bald" attribute.)

3.1 Overview of Our Proposed FAWAM Model

The key objective of our model is to generate the aged attribute manipulated face image as the output, while providing a young face and the desired attributes as the input. To achieve this goal, we address this complex task in a bottom-up fashion, by addressing it as two separate modules *i.e.* Face Aging (FA) and Attribute Manipulation (AM). Although we can treat *age* as an attribute (like, gender, glasses etc.), in this study we wish to provide equal importance (probability) to both the *aging* as well as *attribute* factors. Hence, we treat them as separate modules and combine them in a comprehensive manner.

The overall architecture is shown in Fig. 2. The base network for both FA and AM modules is GAN architecture. Initially, the model is fed with the young facial input image. It is given to the face aging module, which is internally comprised of face aging generator and a face aging discriminator. Using three key loss functions *i.e.*, Identity preservation loss for maintaining the identity, GAN loss for aging and pixel level loss in image space, the network is trained to produce the age progressed face as the output of FA module. Further, this aged image is given as the input to the attribute manipulation module. Here, in addition to the image, we also provide the attribute as the second input. Using both of these inputs, AM module, that internally consists of an attribute editing generator and attribute editing discriminator, produces the attribute manipulated aged face as the final output. To obtain these manipulations we employ adversarial loss, cross entropy loss and reconstruction loss. More details on the internal architecture of each sub-module and the methodology adopted are described in detail in the Sects. 3.2, 3.3.

3.2 Face Aging Module

We have implemented the Face Aging (FA) module by using pyramidal GAN architecture proposed by Yang et al. [22]. This model has CNN based architecture for generator (G_{age}) to learn the age transformation effects of face image, and the training critic has squared euclidean loss, GAN loss and identity loss. In discriminator, we have VGG-16 [17] structure which captures the properties from exact pixel values to high-level age-specific information, this module leverages intrinsic pyramid hierarchy. The pyramid discriminator at multiple levels tries to advance and simulate the face aging effects. This method works on different face samples having different variations in posture, expression, etc.

Generator (G_{age}). As shown in Fig. 2, the Generator takes young face images as input, and generates age-progressed face images as output. The input image is passed through three convolutional layers for encoding it into latent space. This would capture the facial properties that tends to be constant with time. Then we have four residual blocks for capturing similar features shared by input and output faces. Then a decoder with three deconvolutional layers for the age progression to the target image space. We have got 3×3 convolutional kernels with a stride of two Paddings are added to make sure that input and output have equivalent size. Every convolutional layers is followed by Instance Normalization and ReLU non-linearity activation.

Discriminator (D_{age}). The input to discriminator (D_{age}) would be young faces, elderly faces and output of Generator(generated images). The discriminator is termed as system critic because it has previous knowledge of the data density. The Discriminator network D_{age} is so introduced, such that it outputs a scalar quantity $D_{age}(x)$ representing with what probability x comes from the data. The distribution of the generated faces P_g (we denote the distribution of young face images as $x \sim P_{young}$, then generated ones as $G_{age}(x) \sim P_g$) is meant to be equivalent to the distribution P_{old} once optimality is reached. To attain more satisfying and realistic age specific facial details, the true young face images and the generated age transformed face images are passed to D_{age} as negative samples and the real elderly face images as positive samples. ϕ_{age} is pre-trained for multi label classification task of age estimation for the VGG-16 structure [17] and after convergence, we remove the fully connected layers and integrate it into the framework.

Objective Function: The objective function of face aging module is combination of pixel level loss ($\mathcal{L}_{pixel}$), identity preservation loss ($\mathcal{L}_{identity}$), and Age transformation loss ($\mathcal{L}_{GAN_{Gage}}$) i.e. discriminator loss.

$$\mathcal{L}_{G_{age}} = \lambda_a \mathcal{L}_{GAN_{Gage}} + \lambda_p \mathcal{L}_{pixel} + \lambda_i \mathcal{L}_{identity} \tag{1}$$

$$\mathcal{L}_{D_{age}} = \mathcal{L}_{GAN_{Dage}} \tag{2}$$

We train G_{age} and D_{age} iteratively till they will learn age transformation effects and then finally G_{age} would learn the transformation and D_{age} would become a reliable reckoner.

3.3 Attribute Manipulation Module

We use GAN and encoder-decoder architecture for attribute-manipulation task. By using the encoder-decoder architecture, face attribute editing is achieved by decoding the latent representation of the given face conditioned on the desired attributes. In this work, we apply attribute classification constraint to the generated image to verify the desired change of attributes. Then reconstruction learning is used to preserve attribute-excluding details. Besides, the adversarial learning is used for realistic changes. These three components cooperate with each other for facial attribute editing.

Framework: The framework of face attribute editing module is shown in Fig. 2. It has GAN architecture. The generator comprises of two basic sub-networks, i.e. an encoder $G_{att-enc}$ and a decoder $G_{att-dec}$. The discriminator(D_{att}) consists a stack of convolutional layers followed by fully connected layers, and the classifier(C) has a similar architecture and shares all convolutional layers with D_{att}. The encoder($G_{att-enc}$) is a stack of convolutional layers and the decoder($G_{att-dec}$) is a stack of de-convolutional layers.

Objective Function: The objective function of face attribute editing module is combination of attribute classification constraint($\mathcal{L}_{cls_g}$), the reconstruction loss($\mathcal{L}_{rec}$) and the adversarial loss($\mathcal{L}_{adv_g}$). The objective for the encoder and decoder is formulated in Eq. (3) and for the discriminator and the attribute classifier is formulated in Eq. (4)

$$\min_{G_{att-enc},G_{att-dec}} \mathcal{L}_{enc,dec} = \lambda_1 \mathcal{L}_{rec} + \lambda_2 \mathcal{L}_{cls_g} + \mathcal{L}_{adv_g} \tag{3}$$

$$\min_{D_{att},C} \mathcal{L}_{dis,cls} = \lambda_3 \mathcal{L}_{cls_c} + \mathcal{L}_{adv_d} \tag{4}$$

4 Experimental Results

4.1 Datasets

CACD: This dataset is proposed by [3]. It contains 163,446 face images of 2,000 celebrities captured in less controlled conditions. Besides large variations in PIE, images in CACD are accumulated through Google Image Search, making it a difficult and challenging dataset.

FGNET: This dataset is proposed by [2]. It contains 1,002 images from 82 individuals. The age span is 0–69 years, there are 6–18 images per subject and average age is 15.54 years. It is used for testing.

UTK-Face: This dataset is proposed by [24], it has 20,000 images of age ranging from 0 to 116 years. These images are collected from Google and Bing search engines. 68 landmarks are defined with cropped and aligned faces.

CelebA: CelebFaces Attributes Dataset (CelebA) is a large-scale face attributes dataset, proposed by [14], contains 202,599 number of face images of various celebrities, 10,177 unique identities, 40 binary attribute annotations per image and 5 landmark locations. Thirteen attributes with strong visual impact are chosen in all our experiments, including *Bald, Bangs, Black Hair, Blond Hair, Brown Hair, Bushy Eyebrows, Eye-glasses, Gender, Mouth Open, Mustache, No Beard, Pale Skin.*

4.2 Implementation Details

Regarding the FA module, We follow age span of 10 years [23] for every aging cluster; we train separately for different age clusters. We use Adam optimizer for both generator and discriminator, with the learning rate of 1×10^{-4}, batch size of 8 and weight decay of 0.5 for $50,000$ iterations. The trade-off parameters are set to $\lambda_p = 0.20, \lambda_a = 750.00$ and $\lambda_i = 0.005$, for CACD. We update discriminator for each iteration, use the aging and identity critics for every generator iteration, and use the pixel level critic for each 5 generator iterations. For the AM module, the model is trained by Adam optimizer ($\beta_1 = 0.5, \beta_2 = 0.999$) with the batch size of 32 and the learning rate of 0.0002. The coefficients for the losses are set as: $\lambda_1 = 100, \lambda_2 = 10$, and $\lambda_3 = 1$, which aims to make the loss values be in the same order of magnitude.

4.3   Face Aging Module Results

In this section, we discuss the experimental analysis and aging performance evaluation of the FA module, both qualitatively and quantitatively.

Qualitative Results: The visualizations of age progressed results on CACD are shown in Fig. 3. We depict the result of face aging in different age clusters *i.e.* [31–40], [41–50], [51+], following most of the prior face aging analysis criteria in the field as in [13,22]. Results show that even with different facial attributes the model tries to give visually realistic and smooth aging effects.

Quantitative Results: We carry out two kinds of quantitative analysis for verification; *i.e.* the aging accuracy and the identity permanence. The former deals with vivid aging effects and their span, whereas the latter measures identity/familiarity between two face images. In order to measure these results, we use online face analysis tool FACE++ api [1].

Identity preservation can be verified by using a pair of image that is input image and generated image, The result is verification confidence (probability value) between two images, *i.e.* how close the images are, higher the confidence higher the closeness to image. The verification results are given in the Table 1 on CACD, FGNET and UTK face datasets. As can be seen in Table 1, as age increases, the confidence decreases due to physical constraints occurred as part of aging.

The change in facial age should be in correspondence with real aging and the predicted result should be satisfying with the age cluster of it. We use face analysis tool Face++ [1] to verify aging accuracy. Age is calculated on each generated image from the respective age cluster and average is presented as

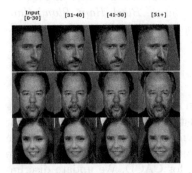

Fig. 3. Aging effects on CACD Dataset for the baseline FA module. The first image in each row is the original face image and the next 3 images are in [31–40], [41–50] and [51+] age clusters.

Table 1. Face verification results for facial aging module (values are in %)

Dataset	Test	Verification confidence		
		Age [31–40]	Age [41–50]	Age [51+]
CACD	Age [0–30]	92.1	89.32	84.8
	Age [31–40]	–	92.4	91.13
	Age [41–50]	–	–	93.5
FGNET	Age [0–30]	93.2	89.8	85.4
	Age [31–40]	–	91.3	89.2
	Age [41–50]	–	–	92.7
UTK	Age [0–30]	91.2	89.8	85.4

accuracy. The results of aging accuracy are given in Table 2 for CACD, FGNET datasets on the age clusters [31–40], [41–50], [51+]. We can observe that the predicted age clusters belong to the intended category. However, in the 31+ category, the average age is slightly greater than the cluster's age, this is due to the data density of faces in their ages. The standard deviation is also calculated on all the synthesized faces.

Table 2. Age estimation results for facial aging module (values are mean of predicted age).

Dataset	Age-clusters		
	[31–40]	[41–50]	[51+]
CACD	44.8± 6.2	49.2± 7.05	53.42± 7.42
FGNET	43.2± 5.4	51.4± 8.41	58.1± 7.25

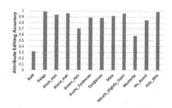

Fig. 4. Attribute editing accuracy of Attribute Manipulation module (Higher the Better).

4.4 Attribute Manipulation Module Results

In this section, we describe the experimental analysis and evaluation of the AM module in detail.

Qualitative Results: Figure 5 shows the result of facial attribute editing. These are for single attribute editing for each image. This model preserves all attribute excluding details like face identity, background and illumination. Our model accurately edits local and global attributes as can be seen in Fig. 5. We have used 12 attributes for training on CelebA dataset. The attributes like eyeglasses, black hair, bangs, blond hair are edited more realistically.

Quantitative Results: For evaluating the facial attribute editing accuracy, we use facial attribute classifier trained on CelebA dataset. If the generated image attribute is same as the desired one by the classifier then it is a valid generation. Figure 4 shows the attribute accuracy, as can be seen the model achieves good results for bangs, gender, pale skin, eyeglasses with 99.01%, 91.6%, 99.1% and 88.3% accuracy, respectively. We can observe that bald, mustache, are less accurate due to the difficulty in modelling and less samples in dataset.

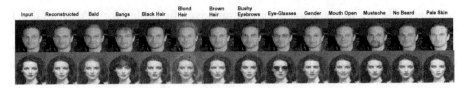

Fig. 5. Results of facial attribute editing on CelebA dataset for the baseline AM module. For each attribute, editing is to invert the attribute, e.g., edit No-Beard to Beard etc.

4.5   FAWAM Results

Here we explain the results of our proposed FAWAM model. For our problem at hand, we have two inputs *i.e.* young image as well as the attribute. From the proposed model we first obtain the aged face from FA module and then apply attribute editing using AM module.

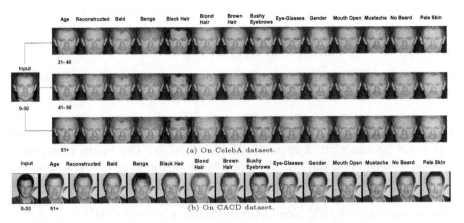

Fig. 6. Results of our proposed FAWAM model. (a) On CelebA dataset: For a given input, the first image in each output row shows the aged face and the remaining images are attribute manipulated for respective age. (b) On CACD dataset: Attribute manipulated images corresponding to the [51+] age cluster.

Visualization Results for our FAWAM Model: FAWAM results for a single input image that produce multi-aged and single-attribute images as outputs are shown in Fig. 6. From the results, we can see that for different aging clusters, there is a subtle difference in their attributes produced owing to the aging factor, which is a significant realistic advantage of our proposed model.

Visual Fidelity: Figure 7a displays face images showing cheeks region. We can observe that the synthesised images are photo-realistic that clearly depict the age-related features such as wrinkles, thin lips etc. Figure 7b and Fig. 7c show the attributes incorporated along with aging for beard, mustache and bushy eyebrows respectively.

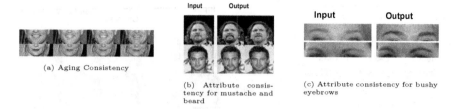

(a) Aging Consistency

(b) Attribute consistency for mustache and beard

(c) Attribute consistency for bushy eyebrows

Fig. 7. Illustration of visual fidelity

Quantitative Results: Figure 8 shows the attribute accuracy of our FAWAM model. The model achieves good results for bangs, gender, pale skin, eyeglasses with 98.07%, 90.4%, 97.6% and 85.0% of accuracies, respectively. We also perform the facial verification as shown in Table 3 on CelebA dataset for the test images. We perform verification only on CelebA dataset due the availability of attributes. Since this study marks one of the first works on *face aging along with attribute manipulation*, the results in this paper bestow the **state-of-the-art** for the problem. Nevertheless, we provide SOTA comparison of the earlier works in respective subtasks *i.e.* Face Aging and Attribute Manipulation to our FAWAM results in Fig. 9 and 10. It is observed that our model outperforms in terms of aging quality, visual fidelity and aesthetics rendering.

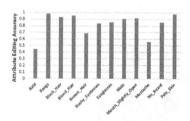

Fig. 8. Attribute editing accuracy of proposed FAWAM model (Higher the Better).

Table 3. Face verification results for our proposed FAWAM model on **CelebA** Dataset (values are in %)

Test	Verification confidence		
	Age [31–40]	Age [41–50]	Age [51+]
Young	92.5	88.6	84.02
Old	–	91.2	89.4

Ablation Studies: Here we demonstrate various ablation studies carried out on our model. We show the possibility of **multi-attribute editing,***i.e.* to concurrently manipulate multiple facial attributes. The resulting images are shown in Fig. 11. Another study is conducted to study the **impact of attribute intensity**. We applied probabilistic attribute tuning, which showed the degree of the impact of a particular attribute on the image. The results for the same are shown in Fig. 12, for an attribute intensity control of 20% per image across the row. We can see that the simulated output results are smooth and continuous, highlighting the effectiveness of our model.

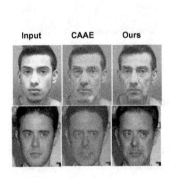

Input   CAAE   Ours

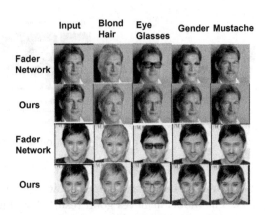

Input   Blond Hair   Eye Glasses   Gender Mustache

Fader Network

Ours

Fader Network

Ours

Fig. 9. State-of-the-art comparison on Face aging: of FAWAM model vs CAAE [24]

Fig. 10. State-of-the-art comparison on Attribute Manipulation: FAWAM vs Fader Networks [9]

Input   Bangs Eye-Glasses   Input   Bangs Blond Hair   Input   Gender Black Hair

Fig. 11. Multi facial attribute editing on CelebA dataset.

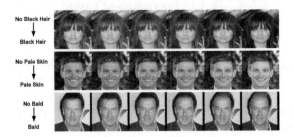

No Black Hair → Black Hair

No Pale Skin → Pale Skin

No Bald → Bald

Fig. 12. Illustration of attribute intensity control.

5   Conclusions

We proposed a novel holistic model towards Face age progression with attribute manipulation (FAWAM). We addressed the task by leveraging face aging (FA) module and attribute manipulation (AM) module, which are independent of each other and provide equal importance while image rendering. For the FA module, leveraging pyramidal GAN model is able to come up with age-specific changes along with identity preservation. Regarding the AM module, the synthesised aged face undergoes attribute manipulation for desired change of attributes, visually realistic editing and to preserve attribute-excluding details. Extensive analysis of our FAWAM model is carried out in a bottom up manner, the achieved attribute-manipulated aged imageries and the quantitative evaluations clearly confirm the effectiveness and robustness of the proposed method. Our future works include dual-discriminator based GAN for further improvements.

References

1. Face++, May 2020. https://www.faceplusplus.com/
2. The FG-net aging database, May 2020. http://www-prima.inrialpes.fr/FGnet/
3. Chen, B.C., Chen, C.S., Hsu, W.H.: Face recognition and retrieval using cross-age reference coding with cross-age celebrity dataset. IEEE Trans. Multimedia 17(6), 804–815 (2015)
4. Goodfellow, I., et al.: Generative adversarial nets. In: NIPS, pp. 2672–2680 (2014)
5. He, Z., Kan, M., Shan, S., Chen, X.: S2gan: share aging factors across ages and share aging trends among individuals. In: ICCV, pp. 9440–9449 (2019)
6. He, Z., Zuo, W., Kan, M., Shan, S., Chen, X.: Attgan: facial attribute editing by only changing what you want. IEEE Trans. Image Process. 28(11), 5464–5478 (2019)
7. Isola, P., Zhu, J.Y., Zhou, T., Efros, A.A.: Image-to-image translation with conditional adversarial networks. In: CVPR, pp. 1125–1134 (2017)
8. Kemelmacher-Shlizerman, I., Suwajanakorn, S., Seitz, S.M.: Illumination-aware age progression. In: CVPR, pp. 3334–3341 (2014)
9. Lample, G., Zeghidour, N., Usunier, N., Bordes, A., Denoyer, L., Ranzato, M.: Fader networks: manipulating images by sliding attributes. In: NIPS
10. Larsen, A.B.L., Sønderby, S.K., Larochelle, H., Winther, O.: Autoencoding beyond pixels using a learned similarity metric. In: ICML, pp. 1558–1566 (2016)
11. Li, M., Zuo, W., Zhang, D.: Convolutional network for attribute-driven and identity-preserving human face generation. arXiv:1608.06434 (2016)
12. Li, M., Zuo, W., Zhang, D.: Deep identity-aware transfer of facial attributes. arXiv preprint arXiv:1610.05586 (2016)
13. Liu, Y., Li, Q., Sun, Z.: Attribute-aware face aging with wavelet-based generative adversarial networks. In: CVPR, pp. 11877–11886 (2019)
14. Liu, Z., Luo, P., Wang, X., Tang, X.: Deep learning face attributes in the wild. In: Proceedings of ICCV, December 2015
15. Perarnau, G., Van De Weijer, J., Raducanu, B., Álvarez, J.M.: Invertible conditional GANs for image editing. arXiv preprint arXiv:1611.06355 (2016)
16. Shen, W., Liu, R.: Learning residual images for face attribute manipulation. In: CVPR, pp. 4030–4038 (2017)
17. Simonyan, K., Zisserman, A.: Very deep convolutional networks for large-scale image recognition. arXiv preprint arXiv:1409.1556 (2014)
18. Suo, J., Chen, X., Shan, S., Gao, W., Dai, Q.: A concatenational graph evolution aging model. TPAMI 34(11), 2083–2096 (2012)
19. Upchurch, P., et al.: Deep feature interpolation for image content changes. In: CVPR (2017)
20. Wang, W., et al.: Recurrent face aging. In: CVPR, pp. 2378–2386 (2016)
21. Wang, Y., Zhang, Z., Li, W., Jiang, F.: Combining tensor space analysis and active appearance models for aging effect simulation on face images. IEEE Trans. Syst. Man Cybern. Part B 42(4), 1107–1118 (2012)

22. Yang, H., Huang, D., Wang, Y., Jain, A.K.: Learning face age progression: a pyramid architecture of GANs. In: CVPR, pp. 31–39 (2018)
23. Yang, H., Huang, D., Wang, Y., Wang, H., Tang, Y.: Face aging effect simulation using hidden factor analysis joint sparse representation. IEEE Trans. Image Process. **25**(6), 2493–2507 (2016)
24. Zhang, Z., Song, Y., Qi, H.: Age progression/regression by conditional adversarial autoencoder. In: CVPR (2017)

Random Dilated Shapelet Transform: A New Approach for Time Series Shapelets

Antoine Guillaume[1,2(✉)] [ID], Christel Vrain[1] [ID], and Wael Elloumi[2] [ID]

[1] Univ. Orléans, INSA Centre Val de Loire, LIFO EA 4022, 45067 Orléans, France
`christel.vrain@univ-orleans.fr`
[2] Worldline, Blois, France
{`antoine.guillaume,wael.elloumi`}`@worldline.com`

Abstract. Shapelet-based algorithms are widely used for time series classification because of their ease of interpretation, but they are currently outperformed by recent state-of-the-art approaches. We present a new formulation of time series shapelets including the notion of dilation, and we introduce a new shapelet feature to enhance their discriminative power for classification. Experiments performed on 112 datasets show that our method improves on the state-of-the-art shapelet algorithm, and achieves comparable accuracy to recent state-of-the-art approaches, without sacrificing neither scalability, nor interpretability.

Keywords: Time series · Shapelets · Classification

1 Introduction

Time series occur in a multitude of domains, covering a wide range of applications, which have impacts in many parts of society. The ever-increasing quantity of data and the publications of laws regarding models interpretability are setting new constraints for applications across industries.

Recent research in time series classification produced highly accurate classifiers, using either deep learning approaches [10], or meta-ensemble methods [13,18]. Despite being the most accurate approaches, they are among the slowest, which make them hard to apply on use-cases with huge amount of data. Other methods, based on random approaches, notably the RandOm Convolutional KErnel Transform (ROCKET) [4], achieve comparable accuracy with extreme scalability. Even though recent works on post-hoc methods and specific frameworks [5] improved the interpretability of those approaches, they lack a "by design" interpretability.

On the other hand, time series shapelets [25] have been widely used in time series classification for their ease of interpretation, which is a critical aspect to some application domains such as health and security. The downside is that shapelet algorithms are often outperformed by recent approaches, both in terms of accuracy and scalability. Most Shapelet approaches tried to solve the scalability issues

© Springer Nature Switzerland AG 2022
M. El Yacoubi et al. (Eds.): ICPRAI 2022, LNCS 13363, pp. 653–664, 2022.
https://doi.org/10.1007/978-3-031-09037-0_53

at the expense of some classification accuracy, notably through the use of symbolic approximation techniques [11], while others used random shapelets [24]. Recently, a symbolic sequence ensemble learning [19] method was proposed, which improved the predictive power of approximation-based methods, while other work focused on finding a new discriminative feature [7] to consider during the extraction process.

In this work, we present the Random Dilated Shapelet Transform, an adaptation of time series shapelets that includes the notion of dilation, one of the core mechanism of the success of convolutional kernel approaches. We also extend on the work of [7] and introduce a new feature to enhance the discriminative power of shapelets. Our contributions can be summarized as follows:

- an adaptation of time series shapelets allowing the use of dilation, and a feature to capture a new discriminative property of shapelets,
- an interpretable, scalable and accurate shapelet algorithm, which allows shapelet based algorithm to catch-up with the state-of-the-art,
- an experimental study about the sensitivity of our method parameters and a comparative study against the state-of-the-art algorithms for time series classification.

2   Background

In this section, we present a brief review of time series classification, and make a focus on shapelet methods. From now on, we use calligraphic font $(\mathcal{X})$ to denote a collection of elements (e.g. a set of time series), capital (X) for one element (e.g. a time series), and lowercase (x) for a value of this element. In this work we consider supervised classification: the ensemble of input time series will be denoted by $\mathcal{X} = \{X_1, ..., X_n\}$ with $X_i = \{x_1, ..., x_m\}$ a time series and $Y = \{y_1, ..., y_n\}$ their respective classes.

2.1   Time Series Classification

We present a brief overview of the algorithms identified as state-of-the-art and used in our experimental section, and we report the reader to a recent review [1] for a more detailed view of the field.

- **Shapelet Transform Classifier (STC)** [2], is regarded as a state of the art for shapelet algorithms in terms of accuracy. This algorithm iteratively initializes new shapelets, assesses their discriminative power, and removes those that are too similar. The goal being to maximize the discriminative power of an ensemble of shapelets. A Rotation Forest is then applied as a classifier.
- **Temporal Dictionary Ensemble (TDE)** [17] is an ensemble of dictionary-based classifiers. It uses some variants of the BOSS classifier [20] and WEASEL [21], as base estimators and optimizes their parameters through a Gaussian process.

- **Diverse Representation Canonical Interval Forest Classifier (DrCIF)** [18], is an extension of the CIF algorithm [16]. After selecting random intervals from different representations of the time series, it uses the Catch22 [14] method to extract a feature matrix.
- **RandOm Convolutional KErnel Transform (ROCKET)** [4], randomly generates a huge set of convolutional kernels, and extracts as features the maximum and the proportion of positive values of the convolution for each time series and each kernel. It is followed by a Ridge classifier. An ensemble version of this method, called ARSENAL, was introduced by [18].
- **Inception-Time** [10] is an ensemble of Inception networks, which introduce Inception modules as replacement for traditional fully convolutional layers, notably to mitigate the vanishing gradient problem.
- **Hierarchical Vote Collective of Transformation-based Ensembles (HC1)** [13]is a meta-ensemble classifier using a variety of time series classifiers, such as STC, with a novel ensemble learning scheme which estimate the weight of each base classifier in the final decision. This estimation is based on performance in a 10-fold validation scheme.

  Variants of this method were developed, such as TS-CHIEF [22] and HC2 [18], that both modify the set of base classifiers to improve accuracy. HC2 also modified the meta-ensemble procedure, using a Out-Of-Bag estimate instead of a 10-fold validation to estimate the performance of each base classifier, which improved scalability compared to HC1.

2.2 Shapelets

Shapelets [25] were originally defined as time series subsequences representative of class membership. In the following, we define a shapelet S as a vector $S = \{s_1, ..., s_l\}$ with l its length. All shapelet-based algorithms have the same protocol to extract features from a shapelet S and a time series $X = \{x_1, ..., x_m\}$, by using a distance vector $f(S, X) = \{f_1, ..., f_{m-(l-1)}\}$ defined as :

$$f_i = \sqrt{\sum_{j=1}^{l} (X_{i+(j-1)} - s_j)^2} \tag{1}$$

In this definition, a point f_i is simply the Euclidean distance between S and the subsequence of length l starting at index i in X. The minimum value of $f(S, X)$ is then extracted as a feature, which can be interpreted as an indicator of the presence of the pattern represented by S in X. A popular variant of this distance function consists in using a z-normalized Euclidean distance, where S and all subsequences of X are z-normalized independently, allowing to add scale invariance to the translation invariance of the initial formulation. Then, as presented in the Shapelet Transform [12], by using a set of shapelets $\mathcal{S}$, one can then transform an ensemble of time series $\mathcal{X}$ into a feature matrix of shape $(|\mathcal{X}|, |\mathcal{S}|)$, and use it as input in a non-temporal classifier such as a decision tree.

The step of generating and selecting shapelet candidates is the main difference between most approaches. In order to speed up the exhaustive search, Fast Shapelet [11] use input discretization, while Ultra Fast Shapelet [24] use random sampling. FLAG [8] build shapelets location indicators from the data to reduce the set of admissible candidates, and GENDIS [23] use an evolutionary algorithm initialized by a clustering on the set of possible candidates. Learning Time Series Shapelet [6] use a gradient-descent optimization that iteratively change the values of a set of shapelets. MrSEQL [19], while not strictly speaking a shapelet algorithm, searches for discriminative symbolic sequences in a variety of symbolic representations of the inputs.

Since the publication of Localized Random Shapelet (LRS) [7], which showed the benefit of extracting $argmin\ d(S, X)$ to discriminate time series based on the location of the minimum between S and X, it has been included in most recent approaches. Based on their results, we will also use this feature in our method.

3   Proposed Method

In this section, we introduce the main components of our method: the use of dilation in the shapelet formulation and the features extracted from the distance vector between a shapelet and a time series. We put emphasis on the dilation and on the Shapelet Occurrence feature that are new contributions to shapelet algorithms. We give some simple visual examples to illustrate these notions, and report the visualization on real data to the experimental section.

3.1   Dilated Shapelets

To introduce the notion of dilation in shapelets, we define now a shapelet S as $S = \{\{v_1, ..., v_l\}, d\}$ with l the length parameter and d the dilation parameter. In practice, the dilation is used in the distance function f, where each value of the shapelet will be compared to a dilated subsequence of the input time series. More formally, consider a time series $X = \{x_1, ..., x_m\}$ and a dilated shapelet S, we now define $f(S, X) = \{f_1, ..., f_{m-(l-1) \times d}\}$ as :

$$f_i = \sqrt{\sum_{j=1}^{l}(X_{i+(j-1) \times d} - s_j)^2} \tag{2}$$

The interest of using dilation in shapelets is to make them non-contiguous subsequences. It allows a shapelet to either match a non-contiguous pattern, or a contiguous one, by focusing on key points of the pattern without covering it entirely, as illustrated in Fig. 1. Note that this formulation is equivalent to the original shapelet formulation when $d = 1$.

3.2   Shapelet Occurrence Feature

If we consider a shapelet S and two time series X_1 and X_2, we can imagine multiple ways of discriminating X_1 and X_2 using S.

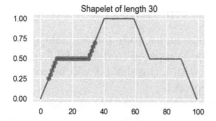
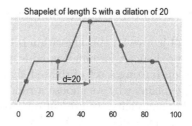

Fig. 1. An example of two possible shapelets (in orange), positioned on a synthetic pattern (in blue): (a) one without dilation, and (b) a much smaller one but with dilation (Color figure online)

- S can be present in X_1 but not in X_2. This is captured by $min\ f(S, X_i)$, with smaller distances indicating better matches between the shapelet and the series.
- S can be present in both series, but not at the same place. This is captured by the $argmin$ feature introduced by LRS [7].
- S can be present in both series, but not at the same scale. In this case, a normalized distance would not be able to discriminate the series.
- S can be present in both series, but occurs a different number of times in X_1 compared to X_2. This is captured by a new feature, called Shapelet Occurrence (SO).

Those points are illustrated in Fig. 2. Deciding whether scaling is important or not is highly dependent on the application, but without prior knowledge, one cannot know which to choose. For this reason, we introduce a parameter in Sect. 3.3 allowing to tune the amount of normalized shapelets.

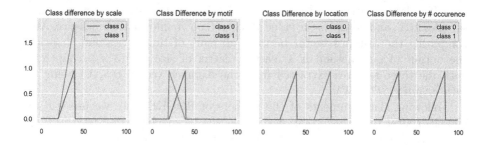

Fig. 2. Synthetic examples of possible discriminative properties between two classes

To the best of our knowledge, the number of occurrences of a shapelet has never been considered as a feature. This requires another modification to the definition of S as $S = \{\{v_1, ..., v_l\}, d, \lambda\}$, with λ a threshold allowing us to compute the Shapelet Occurrence (SO) feature as $SO = |\{i|f(S, X)_i < \lambda\}|$. Although the parameter λ could be set randomly, we discuss in Sect. 3.3 a method to set the value of this threshold.

3.3 Random Dilated Shapelet Transform (RDST)

Our objective for this algorithm is to produce an accurate but scalable approach. As our shapelet formulation adds attributes compared to the initial formulation [25], optimizing a set of dilated shapelets with a threshold λ will be costly, and this explains why we choose a random approach.

For simplicity, we present our approach in the context of univariate and even length time series, with $\mathcal{X} = \{X_1, ..., X_n\}$ a set of time series ($X_i = \{x_1, ..., x_m\}$) and $Y = \{y_1, ..., y_n\}$ their respective classes. Our method takes as input four parameters that are: $n\_shapelets$ the number of shapelets to generate, L a set of possible lengths for the shapelets, p_norm the proportion of shapelets that will use z-normalization, and $(P_1, P_2) \in [0, 100]$ a pair used as percentile bounds for the sampling of the threshold λ.

Given the definition of a shapelet $S = \{\{v_1, ..., v_l\}, d, \lambda\}$, we initialize each parameter as follows:

- the length l is uniformly drawn from L,
- the dilation d, in the same way as ROCKET [4], is set to $d = \lfloor 2^x \rfloor$ with x uniformly drawn in $[0, log_2 \frac{m}{l}]$,
- we randomly choose whether the shapelet will use a z-normalized distance with probability p_norm,
- for setting the values, a sample X is uniformly drawn from $\mathcal{X}$, and an admissible start point i (given l, d) is randomly selected. Then, values are set to $[X_i, ..., X_{i+(l-1)\times d}]$.
- finally, given a shapelet S, to fix the value of λ, we take a sample X from the same class as the one used for extracting the shapelet value, and uniformly draw a value between the two percentiles (P_1, P_2) of $f(S, X)$.

The strategy employed to find λ is a classic trade-off between time and accuracy. If scalability was not a focus, we could compute the distance vector for more samples in $\mathcal{X}$, and optimize the value of λ based on an information measure. After computing the distance vector between all pairs of time series and shapelets, the output of our method is a feature matrix of size $(|\mathcal{X}|, 3 \times n\_shapelets)$, with the three features extracted from the distance vector $f(S, X)$ being the $min, argmin, SO(S, X)$.

Following the arguments of the authors of ROCKET [4], we use a Ridge Classifier after the transformation of $\mathcal{X}$, as the L2 regularization used in Ridge is of critical importance due to the high number of features that are generated, while being scalable and interpretable.

4 Experiments

Our focus in this section is to study the influence of the four parameters of our method on classification accuracy, as well as comparing its performance to recent state-of-the-art approaches. All the experiments were run on a DELL PowerEdge R730 on Debian 9 with 2 XEON E5-2630 Corei7 (92 cores) and 64GB of RAM.

We provide a python package[1] using community standards to run the method and the interpretability tool on any dataset, along with all result tables, and reproducibility instructions for our experiments.

In the following, we use the 112 univariate datasets from the UCR archive [3] and when comparing to state-of-the-art results, we use the same resamples scheme as the one used in their experiments. We use critical difference diagrams to display the mean ranks of objects, with cliques (formed by horizontal bars) computed using the Wilcoxon-Holm post-hoc analysis [9], with a p-value of 0.05. A clique indicates that the accuracy difference between objects is not statistically significant.

4.1   Sensitivity Analysis

We conduct a sensitivity analysis on the four input parameters of our algorithm and their effect on classification accuracy on 40 datasets selected randomly, with raw results and selected datasets in a specific file in the online repository. For each parameter analysis, all other parameters remain fixed at the following default values : $n\_shapelets = 10000$, $p\_norm = 0.9$, $L = [7, 9, 11]$, $P1 = 5$ and $P2 = 15$. Figure 3 and Fig. 4 give the mean accuracy ranks of each method over the 40 datasets, with the accuracy of each method and each dataset computed as the mean of the same 10 resamples. Given the tested set of values, the most impactful parameter is the number of shapelets, with a noticeable increase in performance above 10000 shapelets. All other parameters only display minor gains and thus seem to be stable. Based on those results, for all further experiments we set as default parameters $n\_shapelets = 10000$, $p\_norm = 0.8$, $L = [11]$ and $P1 = 5$, $P2 = 10$, and report results for datasets used in sensitivity analysis and the others.

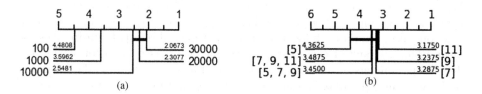

Fig. 3. Accuracy ranks for (a) different number of shapelets, and (b) different shapelet lengths

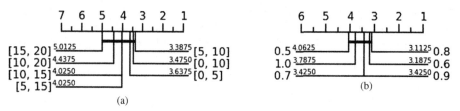

Fig. 4. Accuracy ranks for (a) different percentiles bounds, and (b) proportion of z-normalized shapelets

---

[1] https://github.com/baraline/convst.

4.2 Scalability

We perform a comparison of the scalability of our approach against Hive-Cote 1.0 (HC1), Hive-Cote 2.0 (HC2), DrCIF, ROCKET, and the Shapelet Transform Classifier (STC). Note that when used as a component in HC1 and HC2, STC is by default subject to a time contract of two hours. Except from this default configuration in HC1 and HC2, we are not setting any time contract in other algorithms. Both STC and RDST are by default sampling 10000 shapelets, and ROCKET use 10000 kernels.

We are aware that the runtime of HC1, HC2 and STC could be reduced with time contracts. But, as our goal in this section is to contextualize the gain in classification accuracy against the time complexity of each method, we present the results with the time contracts used to generate the accuracy results of the next section.

We use the Crop Dataset and the Rock Dataset of the UCR archive for evaluating the scalability respectively on the number of time series and their length. As all competing algorithms implemented in the sktime package of [15] can use parallel processing, we set each algorithm to use 90 cores. Figure 5 reports the mean training time over 10 resamples, showing the very competitive scalability of RDST. Note that due to job time limitation on our machine and the computational cost of HC2, we could not consider all samples for the Crop dataset. We report the reader interested in the implementation details of our algorithm to the web page of the project.

4.3 Comparative Study

We present the results of our comparative study using the mean accuracy over the same 30 resamples for each of the 112 datasets as HC2 [18] used in their study, and compare our approach against their experimental result. Figure 6 gives the mean accuracy rank of each method over the 40 datasets used for setting the defaults parameters in sensitivity analysis, and for the 72 others. The full result tables including standard deviation per dataset and more visualizations of the results are available online as supplementary materials.

Given the scalability and simplicity of our method, having an accuracy comparable to the prior developments of HC2 and to deep learning approaches is a very promising result. Notably for future developments where focus would shift to accuracy rather than scalability. For reference, using RDST without any distance normalization is equivalent to STC in terms of mean accuracy rank, with the same protocol as above.

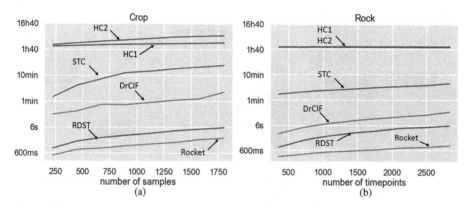

Fig. 5. Result of the scalability study of the competing algorithms for current state-of-the-art, for (a) number of time series and (b) time series length. Y-axis use log-scale.

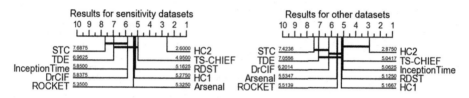

Fig. 6. Mean accuracy ranks of each method for the 40 dataset used in sensitivity analysis and the 72 others.

4.4 Interpretability

Given a set of M shapelets, RDST generates $3M$ features. Each feature is linked to a weight for each class in the Ridge classifier, as it is trained in a one-vs-all fashion. Given a class, we can then visualize either global or local information. Locally, we can inspect a shapelet to show how it discriminates the current class, and where the shapelet is positioned with either training or testing data, as shown in Fig. 7. Globally, we can display the distribution of weights for each feature type (min, arg min and SO) or by shapelet characteristics such as length, dilation, or use of normalization as shown in Fig. 8. While this only provides a basic interpretation of the results, we believe a more formal framework could be developed to extract explanations from this data.

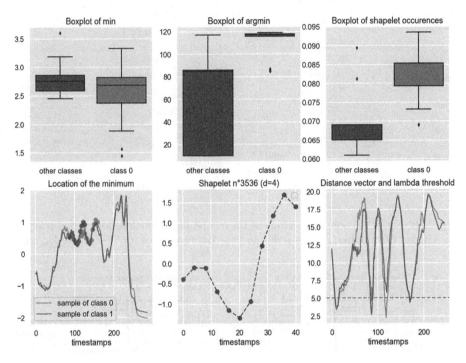

Fig. 7. The most important shapelet for class 0 of the Coffee dataset, according to weights of the Ridge classifier, with distribution displayed on the testing data, and two testing samples for visualization.

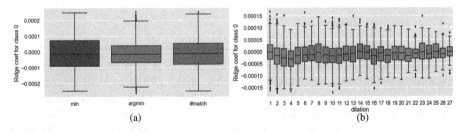

Fig. 8. A global interpretation of RDST, with (a) distribution of weights for each type of feature, and (b) distribution of weights per dilation.

5   Conclusions and Future Work

The Random Dilated Shapelet Transform introduces new ways of increasing the global performance of shapelet algorithms, notably through the use of dilation, allowing the use of small non-contiguous subsequences as shapelets, efficiently covering areas of interest in the data. We have shown in our experiments that this new method improves on the state-of-the-art for shapelet algorithms with a good scalability compared to most of the approaches. This work offers many perspectives for future work, notably a generalized version to process uneven length or multivariate time series, as well as modifications of the shapelet generation process to better leverage class information. A more formal explainability framework is also one of our main priorities with this work, since being able to extract clear and visual explanations for domain experts is an extremely desirable property.

Acknowledgements. This work is supported by the ANRT CIFRE grant n°2019/0281 in partnership with Worldline and the University of Orléans.

References

1. Bagnall, A., Lines, J., Bostrom, A., Large, J., Keogh, E.: The great multivariate time series classification bake off: a review and experimental evaluation of recent algorithmic advances. Data Mining Knowl. Discov. **35**, 401–449 (2020)
2. Bostrom, A., Bagnall, A.: Binary Shapelet transform for multiclass time series classification. In: Madria, S., Hara, T. (eds.) DaWaK 2015. LNCS, vol. 9263, pp. 257–269. Springer, Cham (2015). https://doi.org/10.1007/978-3-319-22729-0_20
3. Dau, H.A., et al.: The UCR time series archive (2019)
4. Dempster, A., Petitjean, F., Webb, G.: Rocket: exceptionally fast and accurate time series classification using random convolutional kernels. Data Mining Knowl. Discov. **34** (2020)
5. Fauvel, K., Masson, V., Fromont, E.: A performance-explainability framework to benchmark machine learning methods: application to multivariate time series classifiers. In: IJCAI-PRICAI 2020 - Workshop on Explainable Artificial Intelligence (XAI), pp. 1–8. Yokohama, Japan, January 2021
6. Grabocka, J., Schilling, N., Wistuba, M., Schmidt-Thieme, L.: Learning time-series shapelets. In: Proceedings of the 20th ACM SIGKDD International Conference on Knowledge Discovery and Data Mining, pp. 392–401. KDD 2014, Association for Computing Machinery, New York, NY, USA (2014)
7. Guilleme, M., Malinowski, S., Tavenard, R., Renard, X.: Localized random Shapelets. In: International Workshop on Advanced Analysis and Learning on Temporal Data, pp. 85–97. Wurzburg, Germany (2019)
8. Hou, L., Kwok, J.T., Zurada, J.M.: Efficient learning of timeseries Shapelets. In: Proceedings of the Thirtieth AAAI Conference on Artificial Intelligence, pp. 1209–1215. AAAI 2016, AAAI Press (2016)
9. Ismail Fawaz, H., Forestier, G., Weber, J., Idoumghar, L., Muller, P.-A.: Deep learning for time series classification: a review. Data Min. Knowl. Discov. **33**(4), 917–963 (2019). https://doi.org/10.1007/s10618-019-00619-1
10. Ismail Fawaz, H., et al.: Inceptiontime: finding Alexnet for time series classification. Data Min. Knowl. Discov. **34**, 1–27 (2020)
11. Keogh, E.J., Rakthanmanon, T.: Fast Shapelets: a scalable algorithm for discovering time series Shapelets. In: SDM (2013)
12. Lines, J., Davis, L.M., Hills, J., Bagnall, A.: A Shapelet transform for time series classification. In: Proceedings of the 18th ACM SIGKDD International Conference on Knowledge Discovery and Data Mining, pp. 289–297. KDD 2012, Association for Computing Machinery, New York, NY, USA (2012)

13. Lines, J., Taylor, S., Bagnall, A.: Hive-cote: the hierarchical vote collective of transformation-based ensembles for time series classification. In: 2016 IEEE 16th International Conference on Data Mining (ICDM), pp. 1041–1046 (2016)
14. Lubba, C.H., Sethi, S., Knaute, P., Schultz, S., Fulcher, B., Jones, N.: catch22: canonical time-series characteristics: selected through highly comparative time-series analysis. Data Min. Knowl. Discov. **33** (2019)
15. Löning, M., et al.: alan-turing-institute/sktime: v0.8.2, October 2021
16. Middlehurst, M., Large, J., Bagnall, A.: The canonical interval forest (CIF) classifier for time series classification. In: 2020 IEEE International Conference on Big Data (Big Data), pp. 188–195 (2020)
17. Middlehurst, M., Large, J., Cawley, G., Bagnall, A.: The temporal dictionary ensemble (TDE) classifier for time series classification. In: Hutter, F., Kersting, K., Lijffijt, J., Valera, I. (eds.) Machine Learning and Knowledge Discovery in Databases, pp. 660–676. Springer International Publishing, Cham (2021)
18. Middlehurst, M., Large, J., Flynn, M., Lines, J., Bostrom, A., Bagnall, A.: Hive-cote 2.0: a new meta ensemble for time series classification. Mach. Learn. **110** (2021)
19. Nguyen, T., Gsponer, S., Ilie, I., O'reilly, M., Ifrim, G.: Interpretable time series classification using linear models and multi-resolution multi-domain symbolic representations. Data Min. Knowl. Discov. **33**(4), 1183–1222 (2019)
20. Schäfer, P.: The boss is concerned with time series classification in the presence of noise. Data Min. Knowl. Discov. **29**, 1505–1530 (2014)
21. Schäfer, P., Leser, U.: Fast and accurate time series classification with weasel. In: Proceedings of the 2017 ACM on Conference on Information and Knowledge Management, pp. 637–646. CIKM 2017, Association for Computing Machinery, New York, NY, USA (2017)
22. Shifaz, A., Pelletier, C., Petitjean, F., Webb, G.: TS-chief: a scalable and accurate forest algorithm for time series classification. Data Min. Knowl. Discov. **34** (2020)
23. Vandewiele, G., Ongenae, F., De Turck, F.: Gendis: genetic discovery of shapelets. Sensors **21**(4) (2021)
24. Wistuba, M., Grabocka, J., Schmidt-Thieme, L.: Ultra-fast shapelets for time series classification. ArXiv abs/1503.05018 (2015)
25. Ye, L., Keogh, E.: Time series shapelets: A new primitive for data mining. In: Proceedings of the 15th ACM SIGKDD International Conference on Knowledge Discovery and Data Mining, pp. 947–956. KDD 2009, Association for Computing Machinery, New York, NY, USA (2009)

Guiding Random Walks by Effective Resistance for Effective Node Embedding

Abderaouf Gacem[1], Mohammed Haddad[1], Hamida Seba[1(⊠)], Gaetan Berthe[1], and Michel Habib[2]

[1] Univ Lyon, UCBL, CNRS, INSA Lyon, LIRIS, UMR5205, Villeurbanne, France
{abderaouf.gacem,mohammed.haddad,hamida.seba}@univ-lyon1.fr,
gaetan.berthe@ens-lyon.fr
[2] IRIF, CNRS & Paris City University, Paris, France
habib@irif.fr

Abstract. One of the most effective and successful approaches to construct effective Euclidean representation of graphs, *i.e.*, embedding, are based on random walks. This solution allows to learn a latent representation by capturing nodes similarities from a series of walk contexts while optimizing the likelihood of preserving their neighborhood in the Euclidean space. In this paper, we address the question of enhancing the existing random walks based methods by making the walk generation process aware of the global graph structure. To this end, we propose a node embedding method based on random walks guided by weights calculated considering a macro observation of the graph structure rather than a micro one. Experimental results on both synthetic and real-world networks show that our computed embedding allows to reach better accuracy rates on two tasks: node classification and link prediction.

Keywords: Node embedding · Representation learning · Random walks · Effective resistance

1 Introduction

Graph data structures are of interest due to the diversity of their use cases (communication, road traffic, biology, e-commerce, ...) on which many tasks can be formulated as node, edge, or graph prediction and regression problems. In order for these tasks to be solved by the undeniably successful machine learning vector-based or matrix-based algorithms, graphs structural data has to be embedded, i.e., mapped to a low-dimension vectorial representation. Seduced by the success achieved by automating representation learning in language modeling and computer vision, several graph representation learning solutions have been proposed [2]. Among them are random walks based methods which have been proved to be successful and have thus been subject to a series of improvements along the past years [1,5,12]. These methods use node contexts generated by random walks on

Supported by Agence National de Recherche under Grant No ANR-20-CE23-0002.

the graph structure the same way sentences are used as a context for words in a bulk of text. The representation learning is done while maximizing the closeness in the continuous space of the nodes appearing frequently in the same context on the graph. These methods output embeddings which are task agnostic [7] which means that they can be used on any designed downstream task afterwards. Deepwalk [12] initiated the concept of using the Skipgram model used for text embedding with a series of node sequences. Node2vec [5] introduced an improvement which consists on guiding the random walks taking in consideration the current node and the last visited one. Node2vec guides the walks based on a local consideration of neighborhoods of nodes and is incapable of perceiving the communities boundaries that most real graphs are consisted of. To deal with this issue, several methods, generally referred to by role-based, consider motifs and connected components while learning the embedding [7]. However, they introduce an extra computation effort because they need to detect these motifs beforehand.

In this work, we study the possibility of designing guided random walks generated with an awareness of the graph connected components. To this end, we propose a graph embedding method based on random walks guided by weights calculated considering a global observation of the graph structure rather than a local one. This macro view is assured by treating the graph as an electrical network where we use the effective resistance as the core of the proposed guided walks. The obtained walks carry more meaning than the ones generated on a local neighborhood basis because the effective resistance reflects the communities distribution of the nodes. Furthermore, we show that our method can be put in cooperation with existing ones to achieve better results. To evaluate our approach, we undertake several experiments and compare with strong baselines on standard graphs downstream tasks, namely (1) node classification: where a model predicts a class of a node given its embedding, and (2) edge classification: where given an embedding of a pair of nodes, a model predicts whether a connection between the pair should exist on the graph or not. Our results show that our embedding allows to reach a better accuracy rate on a variety of graph configurations.

The remainder of the paper is organized as follows: Sect. 2 reviews existing approaches to graph embedding. Section 3 presents our approach and defines effective resistance. Section 4 gives our experimental settings and results. Section 5 concludes the paper by outlining the research perspectives opened by this work.

2   Related Work

There is a wide range of techniques to embed graphs, from handcraft feature engineering, graph kernels, spectral analogy on graphs, to deep learning. The latter was largely exploited with a variety of models [2]. Deep learning for graph embedding started with a pioneer node embedding technique named DeepWalk [12] that was inspired by Word2Vec [11] which uses Skipgram to embed text. Deepwalk treats a graph of nodes as corpus of words. It generates sentences or a series of ordered sequences generated through random walks over the connections. The sequence construction starts by selecting a starting node v, then a new node u is repeatedly selected from the set of the last node neighbor N_v in the sequence, the transition probability to u is

$$P(v_i = u | v_{i-1} = v) = \frac{w_{vu}}{\sum_{o \in N_v} w_{vo}} \tag{1}$$

where w_{uv} is the weight associated to the edge (u, v). Once the set of sequences is ready, we can invoke Skipgram for it is unaware of the established analogy, as long as the input format matches its requirement. Node2Vec [5] extends Deep-Walk by a flexible framework that guides the random walk either in depth or in breadth. For this end, the transition probability in Eq. 1 is modified to $P(v_i = u | v_{i-1} = v, v_{i-2} = t) = \frac{\alpha(u,t)w_{vu}}{Z}$ where Z is the normalization factor and the walk guide $\alpha(u, t)$ is determined according to the distance d_{ut} between nodes u and t. As depicted in Fig. 1 (b), the walk guide is either $\frac{1}{p}$ if $d_{ut} = 0$, 1 if $d_{ut} = 1$, or $\frac{1}{q}$ if $d_{ut} = 2$. p and q are the parameter factors to control the random walks and give them more sense than the uniform ones. Despite the showed improvement of the embedding quality, the guidance Node2Vec provides is based on a very local awareness of the graph structure. On the other hand, "Don't_walk, Skip" [13] is based on giving the walks a larger sight over the neighborhood of nodes, allowing immediate connection and co-appearing context between distant nodes via skipping intermediate ones during the walk. Other approaches, not based on random walks, also addressed this problem. We can cite role-based embedding technique [7] which captures higher level features such as motifs in their representation learning. However these methods are time consuming. Another branch of graph representation techniques are Graph Neural Network (GNN) that use convolution like operations on graphs to build a single pipeline designed for a particular task. GNNs strength relies on exploiting node/edges attributes to discover affinities while conditioning the model on graph structure (via the adjacency matrix for example) [8].

Our approach takes advantages of the simplicity of random walks while introducing a global knowledge about the graph. This is possible by guiding the walks by computed weights that have been proved to measure how strongly nodes are connected.

3   Guiding Random Walks with Effective Resistance

3.1   Preliminaries

An undirected graph $G = (V, E)$ is 2-sets structure: a set V of n nodes ($n = |V|$), and a set E of m edges ($m = |E|$) each linking a pair of nodes. A graph can be described by an adjacency matrix A of size n^2. If G is unweighted, then an entry a_{ij} is equal to 1 if nodes v_i and v_j are connected, i.e., $(v_i, v_j) \in E$, and equal to 0 otherwise. For weighted graphs, a_{ij} is equal to w_{ij}, a value that scores the edge (v_i, v_j) over the other ones. The diagonal matrix D stores the node degrees

$(d_{ii} = degree(v_i))$. The Laplacian matrix of G is noted L, where $L = D - A$. For an undirected graph, L is a real symmetric matrix, all its eigenvalues are real. It is also possible to verify that $\lambda_0 = 0$ is an eigenvalue of L [3]. Therefore, L^{-1} does not exist.

Effective Resistance: To consider the graph as an electrical network, each edge is seen as a resistor whose resistance is equal to $R_{ij} = 1/w_{ij}$. Then, the absence of a connection corresponds to having a resistor of infinite resistance. In such a network, *Ohm* law states that $V = RI$, i.e., the potential that drops across a resistor is equal to the current flowing over it times its resistance. Moreover, if we define a current flowing over an edge (u_1, u_2) as $i(u_1, u_2) = -i(u_2, u_1)$, then according to Kirchhoff law, all the current entering the edges of node u in the graph must exit u to an external source. Thus:

$$i_{ext}(u_1) = \sum_{(u_1,u_2)\in E} i(u_1, u_2) = \sum_{(u_1,u_2)\in E} \frac{v(u_2) - v(u_1)}{R_{u_1 u_2}} \tag{2}$$

With v being a vector of potential voltages at the graph nodes. [14] shows that Eq. 2 is equivalent in matrix format to $i_{ext} = Lv$

The effective resistance between two nodes u_i and u_j in an electrical network is the resistance of the entire network when we treat it as one complex resistor. Let's consider nodes u_i and u_j as entering and exiting points respectively in an electrical network. We reduce the rest of the network to a single edge (u_i, u_j). Then, for a flow of one unit of current from u_i to u_j, the voltages induced at the internal nodes is given by resolving Eq. 2. Let L^+ be the pseudo-inverse matrix of L [14]. The solution is then $v = L^+ i_{ext} = L^+(e_i - e_j)$ where e_i is a one dimension vector of size n with the $i - th$ entry set to 1 while all the other ones are set to 0. Spielman and Srivastava [14] show that the measure of the needed potential difference between u_i and u_j to realize this current flow, gives us the effective resistance between u_i and u_j defined by $R_{eff}(i,j) = (e_i - e_j)^T L^+(e_i - e_j)$. We note that computing L^+ is expensive. This motivated several attempts on approximating the effective resistance. We refer the reader to the work of Spielman et al. [14,15] for further details.

Representation Learning: The ultimate goal is to generate a set of generated meaningful sequences from the graph and leverage them to learn a continuous vector representation of the graph using the Skipgram model, i.e., learning a mapping function $\Phi : V \longmapsto \mathbb{R}^d$, d being the embedding dimension. The learning process is done while predicting the context of a node v_i given a sequence in the set $P(v_{i+1}, \dots, v_{i+t} | \Phi(v_i))$. In order for the model to maximize this probability, it works on minimizing $[-\log P(v_{i+1}, \dots, v_{i+t} | \Phi(v_i))]$. Since it is challenging to compute this quantity, we follow Node2Vec procedure which benefits from negative sampling in order to optimize the Softmax probability [5].

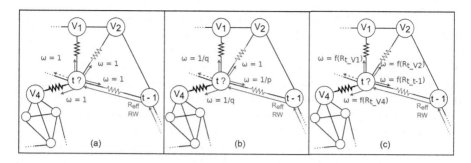

Fig. 1. Visualization of random walk running strategies

3.2 Effective Resistance as a Walk Guide

There is an established connection between random walks and electrical networks. In fact, the probability of a random walk starting at v_i to hit v_j before
returning to v_i is given by [4]:

$$P = \frac{1}{degree(v_i)R_{eff}(i,j)} \tag{3}$$

Moreover, it is proved that edges connecting nodes from the same community
have smaller effective resistance. Which means that gates between communities
are the ones with higher effective resistance [4].

We propose to use the effective resistance measure to induce a weight on the
edges. Therefore, running random walks will result on having guided sequences
based on a macro view of the graph, allowing us to surf in and out of communities,
explore unprivileged paths, and thus capture structural and role similarities, even
those of distant nodes. The weights in Eq. 1 are then redefined as follows:

$$w_{vu} = f(R_{eff}(u,v)) \tag{4}$$

Given this transition probability, we can see that the guided random walks
are still a Markovian process, which means that the sampling efficiency can be
improved by selecting a window of k nodes out of a reused walk of length $l > k$
per starting node. The effective resistance as a walk guide (f being the identity
function) would then encourage the random walk to remain within a connected
component of the graph and prevent it from degenerating after few steps as in
an expander graph. R_{eff} inverse as a walk guide would encourage the walks
to extract distant nodes' similarities and prevent them from being trapped and
generating walks with redundant nodes that cause an unbalanced appearances
on the sequences fed to the Skipgram.

In Fig. 1, we take an example of a walk that went, through edge $(t - 1, t)$,
from node $t - 1$ to node t which is located at the frontier between two connected
components in the graph. To determine the next step, which could be a node
from the set $\{v_1, v_2, v_3, v_4\}$, we consider three scenarios of the exploration guide

ω: In Fig. 1 (a), no walk guide is used, the transition probability is left unchanged, which gives the four nodes the same chance to be selected. We can clearly see that the fact of t being a frontier node is ignored. This is the behaviour of random walks as generated by DeepWalk. Figure 1 (b) illustrates how Node2Vec walks proceed. We can see that nodes $\{v_2, v_3, v_4\}$ have the same chance to be selected despite the fact that the future steps of the walks would generate a completely different neighbourhood if v_4 is chosen over the rest of the nodes. That is due to the process of calculating the walk guide. In fact, a neighbour from a different connected component is treated in a same way as long as it is located within two hops from the node visited at $t-1$. While in Fig. 1 (c), we can tell by the weight on the edges that choosing v_4 will lead to a whole new neighbourhood. So, we can act accordingly to guide the random walk by picking an appropriate function f that turns the effective Resistance measure into a walk guide the gives the walks more sense regarding the coherence of the selected context.

3.3 Combining Guided and Regular Random Walks

There are many possible running strategies for random walks, resulting in different learned feature representations, and there is no universal one suitable for all kind of datasets. We show then, that combining sequences uniformly generated with guided ones based on effective resistance improves the accuracy of the downstream tasks. Which proves that the guided walks allow to have a more informative sequences and thus extract more relevant and non-obvious similarities.

We proceed in two different ways as shown in Fig. 2: 1) we can either enrich the dataset of sequences fed to Skipgram as in Fig. 2 (b) and let it learn the structural features gathered by the random walks, or 2) perform two learning phases, collect the two sets of embeddings and concatenate them to form the final embeddings. Figure 2 (a) does not necessarily mean that the two Skipgram models are distinct, the first one might be used as a pre-trained model for the second phase, which helps with the convergence speed.

4 Experimentation

In this comparative study, we evaluate how the learned embedding from the resistance guided walks performs compared to two state-of-the-art embedding models *DeepWalk* [12] and *Node2vec* [5] on *Node Classification task* and *Link Prediction*. We first consider pure Resistance guided walks, then 1) we combine uniform and resistance guided walks, and then 2) we combine the two independently learned embeddings (see Fig. 2). Specifically, we focus on answering the following research question: To what extent does introducing the effective resistance as a walk guide impact the overall performance of node classification and link prediction tasks?

4.1 Datasets

For our experiments, we used a synthetic benchmark and three real-world networks:

- **LFR benchmark**[1] (Lancichinetti-Fortunato-Radicchi) which emulates real social networks characteristics. The generated graphs have n nodes with k average degree. The degrees are sampled from a power law distribution. Each node shares a fraction $1 - \mu$ of its links with nodes of its community (μ is called the mixing parameter). The sizes of the communities are also sampled from a power law distribution but the exponent is different. The benchmark is composed of two groups of datasets: *LFR-A* and *LFR-B*; For each graph of n nodes in *LFR-A* (resp. *LFR-B*), the class size goes from $0.05n$ to $0.2n$ nodes (resp. 10 to $0.1n$ nodes) and the average node degree is 25 (resp. 20).
- **email-Eu-core network** [9]: This network was generated using email data from a large European research institution. A connection (u, v) means that a person u sent person v at least one email. The dataset is formed of 1005 nodes and 25571 edges. Each individual belongs to exactly one of 42 departments at the research institute. The challenge compared to LFR instances is that the number of classes is larger and the density is smaller which makes it harder to correctly predict links.
- **Flickr & BlogCatalog** [10]: Flickr is build upon users interaction via photo sharing on an image and video hosting website. It is formed of 7575 nodes and 239738 edges. The users are distributed among 9 groups which are used as labels. BlogCatalog is build upon users following each others on a blog posting platform. The network has 5196 node and 171743 connections. The users are labeled by one of the 6 predefined domain interests

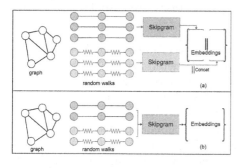

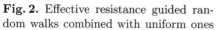

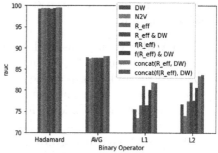

Fig. 2. Effective resistance guided random walks combined with uniform ones

Fig. 3. AUC results for link prediction on email-EU-Core dataset

---

[1] link to LFR benchmark: https://doi.org/10.5281/zenodo.4450167.

Table 1. Accuracy score for node classification on LFR benchmark dataset (acc ± std). The reported results are the average of 10 runs over 5 instances of each dataset configuration.

Dataset	n	μ	DW	N2V	R_eff	DW + R_eff	$f(R\_eff)$	DW +$f(R\_eff)$
LFR-A	300	20	96,69% ± 0,90	**97,03% ± 1,03**	94,46% ± 2,06	96,63% ± 1,41	94,94% ± 2,08	96,86% ± 1,20
	300	41	73,21% ± 2,75	73,28% ± 1,20	72,53% ± 1,30	73,69% ± 2,83	70,24% ± 4,65	**76,49% ± 3,17**
	300	51	57,99% ± 5,07	58,18% ± 2,78	59,52% ± 2,95	57,98% ± 4,35	57,02% ± 1,01	**60,21% ± 1,20**
	300	61	40,47% ± 5,18	43,36% ± 3,68	41,51% ± 3,05	**45,16% ± 3,34**	44,26% ± 5,97	43,40% ± 5,30
	300	80	23,17% ± 1,62	27,49% ± 1,65	23,81% ± 2,08	26,13% ± 1,74	26,59% ± 5,71	**27,55% ± 4,66**
	600	41	94,18% ± 0,84	**95,07% ± 0,70**	93,87% ± 1,24	94,65% ± 1,31	93,81% ± 0,35	94,52% ± 1,29
	600	51	77,65% ± 2,96	**81,59% ± 0,99**	77,95% ± 1,26	79,25% ± 0,61	79,06% ± 1,46	79,65% ± 1,88
	600	61	51,74% ± 1,77	50,16% ± 0,64	48,55% ± 3,84	**51,78% ± 1,95**	47,01% ± 5,61	51,49% ± 2,60
	600	80	23,26% ± 2,89	21,10% ± 2,85	22,36% ± 2,00	**25,45% ± 1,24**	20,97% ± 3,60	23,16% ± 6,04
	1200	51	90,24% ± 2,45	90,90% ± 1,21	90,63% ± 1,49	**90,91% ± 1,74**	90,05% ± 0,94	90,40% ± 0,89
	1200	61	**62,16% ± 3,79**	60,05% ± 5,53	60,06% ± 5,22	61,30% ± 4,35	60,63% ± 4,90	61,61% ± 5,25
	1200	80	20,50% ± 1,17	19,60% ± 3,01	20,48% ± 1,06	**20,95% ± 0,33**	19,88% ± 1,00	19,84% ± 0,88
LFR-B	300	20	89,35% ± 2,55	88,67% ± 1,79	88,81% ± 1,47	88,66% ± 4,29	**91,04% ± 2,58**	90,35% ± 2,54
	300	41	68,83% ± 7,52	68,68% ± 4,12	70,40% ± 3,08	71,43% ± 6,73	**71,45% ± 6,73**	68,67% ± 6,82
	300	51	49,06% ± 6,54	50,93% ± 5,95	49,86% ± 5,65	49,86% ± 5,76	52,14% ± 7,15	**52,70% ± 6,91**
	300	61	34,61% ± 3,57	36,13% ± 1,37	**38,26% ± 3,88**	35,72% ± 2,16	35,13% ± 4,05	35,39% ± 3,37
	300	80	15,69% ± 2,37	12,65% ± 1,62	**16,44% ± 3,63**	15,41% ± 0,63	13,95% ± 0,63	14,62% ± 0,61
	600	41	95,25% ± 1,62	95,26% ± 0,78	95,26% ± 1,42	95,31% ± 1,32	95,50% ± 1,32	**95,90% ± 1,38**
	600	51	82,84% ± 1,30	85,36% ± 1,10	83,49% ± 2,97	86,13% ± 3,37	83,58% ± 3,37	**86,83% ± 1,10**
	600	61	61,38% ± 6,75	63,06% ± 1,37	60,09% ± 2,51	61,50% ± 4,51	61,27% ± 1,05	**63,48% ± 5,52**
	600	80	13,87% ± 1,90	15,53% ± 0,79	15,59% ± 2,25	16,44% ± 1,34	15,60% ± 1,86	**16,72% ± 2,37**
	1200	51	**95,16% ± 0,61**	94,92% ± 1,01	94,08% ± 0,65	94,20% ± 0,52	94,46% ± 0,52	94,65% ± 0,83
	1200	61	73,10% ± 2,11	71,98% ± 2,41	72,45% ± 1,56	72,85% ± 2,33	72,90% ± 2,35	**73,21% ± 2,13**
	1200	80	18,74% ± 0,96	19,05% ± 0,95	18,42% ± 2,14	**19,74% ± 1,08**	17,83% ± 1,21	18,53% ± 1,74
	2400	51	95,86% ± 1,19	96,38% ± 1,15	95,82% ± 1,30	**96,39% ± 1,54**	95,61% ± 1,54	95,87% ± 1,09
	2400	61	81,26% ± 2,70	82,11% ± 2,43	81,70% ± 2,98	81,90% ± 2,58	82,19% ± 2,58	**82,44% ± 2,98**
	2400	80	17,29% ± 1,33	18,61% ± 1,59	18,35% ± 1,59	19,13% ± 1,53	18,24% ± 2,06	**19,41% ± 1,14**

(n, μ) are the LFR datasets' generation parameters.

4.2   Evaluation Tasks

In order to perform the downstream evaluation tasks, we start by getting the embeddings using:

– **DeepWalk:** We use this method for it is a pioneer work on graph embedding based on random walks. As for the hyper-parameters, we explore the domain $5, 10, 20$ for walk length crossed with $5, 10, 20$ domain for walks per node.

– **Node2Vec:** It is an improvement of Deepwalk based on a guided random walk generation. We adopt the values $p = 0.5$, $q = 2$ as hyper-parameters since they gave the best performance on the original reported results.

– **Effective Resistance guided walks:** Our first variant, we use the effective resistance as weight on the graph edges. The generated walks are then guided accordingly. We explore the same domains of walk length and walks per node as the previous methods.

– f(**Effective Resistance) guided walks:** We also use the effective resistance to induce edge weights. We chose function $f : x \rightarrow e^{-x}$ for its smoothness. We expect, by doing so, to prevent the walks from being trapped and encourage inter components paths.

Table 2. Accuracy score for node classification on real-world datasets (acc ± std)

Dataset	DW	N2V	R_eff	$f(R\_eff)$
email-Eu-Core	69.66% ± 1.22	69.76% ± 1.15	70.33% ± 1.58	70.56% ± 1.67
flickr	48.93% ± 0.99	49.67% ± 0.57	50.37% ± 1.12	49.12% ± 0.41
blogcatalog	74,67% ± 0,87	73,93% ± 0,44	75,41% ± 0,94	74,18% ± 0,75
	DW + R_eff	DW $\oplus R\_eff$	DW + $f(R\_eff)$	DW $\oplus f(R\_eff)$
email-Eu-Core	70.11% ± 1.56	69.89% ± 1.05	70.33% ± 1.94	**71.23% ± 1.23**
flickr	48.74% ± 0.51	46.88% ± 0.60	47.72% ± 0.80	**51.27% ± 0.78**
blogcatalog	74,51% ± 0,38	75,00% ± 0,85	74,92% ± 1,13	**75,49% ± 1,34**

$\oplus$ is a concatenation operator.

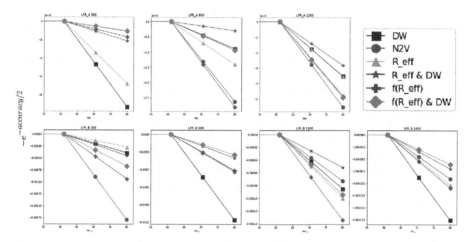

Fig. 4. Accuracy dropping speed on LFR node classification

- **Deepwalk combined with Effective Resistance:** In order to enrich the
  sequences set normally fed to the Skipgram in Deepwalk, we inject incremental
  amounts of effective resistance guided walks into the set before the start of
  the learning procedure. We also run tests by combining effective resistance
  guided learned embedding with the regular one by concatenating the two of
  them as explained in Sect. 3.

The same Skipgram architecture is used for all the methods using negative sampling rather than Softmax for evaluation fairness, and it is trained for 100 epochs,
with a learning rate of 0.01. We use Adam optimizer, and the resulting embedding dimension for all the methods is of 128. We pick random instances from a
number of *LFR* configurations, preprocess the graph when necessary, and report
the average accuracy as well as the standard deviation over the executions.
We evaluate the learned latent node representation on two tasks:

– A standard supervised classification for nodes: Given a vector representation of the nodes, we train a model on predicting its class. This downstream task reflects the quality of the embeddings and servers to show whether effective resistance guided walks help to gather additional relevant information over the existing strategies. We used a multi-class logistic regression from scikit-learn python library where accuracy is the score function. And we set the size of the training set (proportion of labeled nodes) to 30% for all the instances that the model is trained on.

– Link prediction: which is a task where a model is expected to detect missing connections. In order to evaluate the learned embeddings on this task, a preprocessing on the graph dataset as well as on node embeddings is needed. For the graph dataset, we begin by removing a proportion of the existing edges (20% for our tests) to be our test set, we give the edges on the test and training the label '1', we generate as many false edges as the original ones and we give them the label '0', we take 20% of the false edges and assign them to the test set, the rest goes to the training set. Then, we can train a logistic regression model on classifying test set edges into 'true' or 'false' categories, therefore it will be able predict whether a new edge is eligible or not. The training being done on edges, edge embeddings must be inferred from the learned node embeddings. For this preprocessing, we adopt Node2Vec methodology for efficiency and test fairness. We calculate (u, v) embedding by aggregating the node embeddings of u and v with a binary operation. We use the same binary operators as Node2Vec which are: Average; Hadamard product; L1 and L2 distances [5]. Area under the receiver operating characteristic curve (AUC) [6] is the criteria used to measure the quality of link prediction. AUC is the probability that a model ranks a true edge higher than a false one.

For each dataset, multiple sets of embeddings are learned since we explore multiple combinations of hyper-parameters for generating random walks. We report the average of the results achieved by the best hyper-parameters for all the methods. While we split the dataset randomly, we use the same splits to evaluate the embeddings learned by all the methods. All data and source code are available through https://gitlab.liris.cnrs.fr/agacem/rw_effective_resistance.

4.3   Results and Discussion

Table 1 shows the accuracy of the classification score on both LFR datasets. It is the average accuracy scored over five random instances picked for each (n, μ) configuration. After ensuring a fair trial for all the methods in the table, we can see that the latent representation learned by our method outscores or closely tails both Deepwalk and Node2Vec nearly 90% of the time. For the $DW + R_{eff}$ column, we additionally explore a domain of 25%, 50% and 75% percentage amount of Resistance guided walks injected to enrich the conventional set of sequences leveraged by the Skipgram of DeepWalk. Table 2 reports the accuracy score of node classification for the real word datasets, we can see that $DW \oplus f(R_{eff}$ gets the best score which proves the usefulness of combining two sets of learned embeddings and also shows that the new embeddings contains insightful characteristic graph traits lacked in the original ones. As a matter of fact, combining uniform and effective resistance based guided walks is quite distinctively the best performance over all. This supports the claim that using the effective resistance as a walk guide enables generating paths with more relevant information to encode similarities. It is also worth pointing out that when the class sizes are relatively large (LFR-A use case), having more than 50% of shared connections with non-related nodes, would cause the walk to degenerate after few steps. This is prevented by guiding the walk by the actual effective distance on the edges, meaning that the walks are encouraged to stay in local neighborhood which generates walks with meaningful contexts of coappearing nodes. On the other hand, one it comes to smaller groups of similar nodes (LFR-B), enriching the sequences by walks guided by the inverse of effective resistance contributes to escape traps and redundant neighborhood. This means that the set of sequences used to learn the embeddings is not unbalanced, and thus allows them to be more generative and accurate. This shows the potential of guiding the walks through the network when the weights inducing function is well selected. This actually opens a large research question on what other type of similarities can be captured using other functions to guide walks. This leads us to another interesting opening, namely replacing the induction function by a neural network to be trained along the embedding. Thus, extending the unsupervised Skipgram method to a semi supervised one, with a generalized walk guide to be learned. It's quite predictable that all the methods perform poorly on use cases where 80% of nodes connections are with unrelated neighbours. In fact, it is an extreme scenario rather rare to occur in real situations. Figure 4 shows the dropping of accuracy as the mixing parameter grows. We applied $x \longmapsto -\exp(-x/2)$ function to the accuracy in order to change the scale and thus clearly see the difference between the methods as it is difficult to distinguish it otherwise. We can see that introducing the effective resistance helps to decrease the accuracy dropping speed. This is explained by the fact that when the connections start to make no sense as the mixing parameter grows, the walk guide helps to make sense of the random walks by selecting the meaningful paths. For link prediction, Fig. 3 shows AUC results for all the methods using the four binary operators. We can see that the score using Hadamard product reaches 99% for all the methods with a slight advantage for effective resistance based methods. What is worth mentioning is the enhancement of edge embeddings using the other operators while using effective resistance based methods especially when they are combined with the regular ones. The fact that the walk guide is computed over edges properties makes the embeddings more suitable for edge-based tasks. We report only Email-Eu-Core results since we got very similar ones for the other datasets.

5   Conclusion and Future Work

In this paper, we used effective resistance to propose a random walk based method for robust node embeddings. For this end, we treated the graph structure as an electrical network, and leveraged the resistance distance to guide the random walks towards paths that showed, through the experiments, to be more representative and helpful in capturing more relevant similarities for the downstream tasks. We also presented a general framework for guiding random walks by using a non linear transformation of the effective resistance. This framework is extensible by learning a more sophisticated function using a neural network and embed the nodes in a semi-supervised fashion. We have shown that our proposed strategy can be integrated in a collaboration fashion to enrich the sequences fed to Skipgram. It would be interesting for future work to explore this walk guiding strategy for graph and edge embedding on an even more challenging network setting, to explore its results on more datasets and other applications.

References

1. Ahmed, N., et al.: Role-based graph embeddings. IEEE Trans. Knowl. Data Eng. (2020)
2. Cai, H., Zheng, V., Chang, K.C.C.: A comprehensive survey of graph embedding: problems, techniques, and applications. IEEE Trans. Knowl. Data Eng. **30**(9), 1616–1637 (2018)
3. Chandra, A.K., Raghavan, P., Ruzzo, W.L., Smolensky, R., Tiwari, P.: The electrical resistance of a graph captures its commute and cover times. Comput. Complex. **6**(4), 312–340 (1997)
4. Doyle, P.G., Snell, J.L.: Random Walks and Electric Networks, vol. 22. American Mathematical Soc. (1984)
5. Grover, A., Leskovec, J.: node2vec: scalable feature learning for networks. In: Proceedings of the 22nd ACM SIGKDD, pp. 855–864. ACM (2016)
6. Hanley, J.A., McNeil, B.J.: The meaning and use of the area under a receiver operating characteristic (ROC) curve. Radiology **143**(1), 29–36 (1982)
7. Jiao, P., et al.: A survey on role-oriented network embedding. IEEE Trans. Big Data (2021)
8. Kipf, T.N., Welling, M.: Semi-supervised classification with graph convolutional networks. In: 5th International Conference on Learning Representations (2017)
9. Leskovec, J., Sosič, R.: SNAP: a general-purpose network analysis and graph-mining library. ACM Trans. Intell. Syst. Technol. (TIST) **8**(1), 1 (2016)
10. Meng, Z., Liang, S., Fang, J., Xiao, T.: Semi-supervisedly co-embedding attributed networks. In: Advances in Neural Information Processing Systems, vol. 32 (2019)
11. Mikolov, T., Chen, K., Corrado, G., Dean, J.: Efficient estimation of word representations in vector space. In: 1st International Conference on Learning Representations (2013)
12. Perozzi, B., Al-Rfou, R., Skiena, S.: DeepWalk: online learning of social representations. In: The 20th ACM SIGKDD, pp. 701–710 (2014)
13. Perozzi, B., Kulkarni, V., Chen, H., Skiena, S.: Don't walk, skip!: Online learning of multi-scale network embeddings. In: Proceedings of the 2017 IEEE/ACM International Conference on Advances in Social Networks Analysis and Mining, pp. 258–265 (2017)
14. Spielman, D.A., Srivastava, N.: Graph sparsification by effective resistances. SIAM J. Comput. **40**(6), 1913–1926 (2011)
15. Spielman, D.A., Teng, S.: A local clustering algorithm for massive graphs and its application to nearly linear time graph partitioning. SIAM J. Comput. **42**(1), 1–26 (2013)

An Oculomotor Digital Parkinson Biomarker from a Deep Riemannian Representation

Juan Olmos[1] , Antoine Manzanera[2] , and Fabio Martínez[1](✉)

[1] Biomedical Imaging, Vision and Learning Laboratory (BIVL2ab),
Universidad Industrial de Santander (UIS), Cra 27 Calle 9 Ciudad Universitaria,
Bucaramanga, Colombia
`jaolmosr@correo.uis.edu.co`, `famarcar@saber.uis.edu.co`
[2] U2IS, ENSTA Paris, Institut Polytechnique de Paris, 828 Boulevard des
Maréchaux, 91762 Palaiseau, CEDEX, France
`antoine.manzanera@ensta-paris.fr`

Abstract. Parkinson's disease (PD) is characterized by motor alterations and associated with dopamine neurotransmitters degeneration, affecting 3% of the population over 65 years of age. Today, there is no definitive biomarker for an early diagnosis and progression characterization. Recently, oculomotor alterations have shown promising evidence to quantify PD patterns. Current capture and oculomotor setups however require sophisticated protocols, limiting the analysis to coarse measures that poorly exploit alterations and restrict their standard use in clinical environments. Computational based deep learning strategies today bring a robust alternative by discovering in video sequences hidden patterns associated to the disease. However, these approaches are dependent on large training data volumes to cover the variability of patterns of interest. This work introduces a novel strategy that exploits data geometry within a deep Riemannian manifold, withstanding data scarcity and discovering oculomotor PD hidden patterns. First, oculomotor information is encoded as symmetric matrices that capture second order statistics of deep features computed by a convolutional scheme. These symmetric matrices then form an embedded representation, which is decoded by a Riemannian network to discriminate Parkinsonian patients w.r.t a control population. The proposed strategy, evaluated on a fixational eye experiment, proves to be a promising approach to represent PD patterns.

Keywords: Oculomotor patterns · Parkinson's disease classification · SPD pooling · Deep non-linear learning · Riemannian manifold

1 Introduction

Neurological diseases are currently the major cause of disability across the world [5]. Parkinson's disease (PD) is the second most common neurodegenerative disorder, affecting around 2–3% of the global population over the age of 65. Actually,

ⓒ Springer Nature Switzerland AG 2022
M. El Yacoubi et al. (Eds.): ICPRAI 2022, LNCS 13363, pp. 677–687, 2022.
https://doi.org/10.1007/978-3-031-09037-0_55

this disease reports a prevalence around 22%, being the neurological disorder of fastest growth world-around [5,16]. The PD is related to the disruption of the dopamine neurotransmitters that control voluntary movement, producing in consequence alterations in the patient's movement. Currently, this disease has no cure, but the early and personalized treatment planning is fundamental to slow down motor symptoms and disabilities. Nonetheless, today there is no definitive disease biomarker and the diagnosis is commonly subject to observational analysis, reporting errors up to 24% [16,19]. In the literature have been done multiple efforts to characterize and measure motor disabilities correlated with PD. However, the motion patterns related to tremor in hands, disabilities during gait and trunk rigidity [22], are mostly captured at an advanced stage of the disease. More recently, different studies have experimentally supported the hypothesis of a strong correlation of oculomotor patterns with PD, even at early stages [4,8,22]. These patterns, however, are collected from sophisticated capture devices that simplify eye dynamic to global displacement trajectories, making difficult to address the wide range of disease evolution.

Computational approaches have emerged as an alternative to support the quantification of motor patterns directly from video analysis. More recently, deep learning approaches have revealed determining advantages to discover hidden patterns and to characterize kinematic descriptors in the modelling of gait videos, eye movement disorders, cerebrospinal data and tracking eye movement, among many others [9,21]. These deep strategies however require a huge amount of training information to deal with observation variability and the quantification of proper hidden variables demand deeper architectures to discriminate the data [13,21]. These requirements are rarely realistic in clinical scenarios with large pattern variability, and where annotated examples are difficult to get, above all in the task of discovering motor anomalies associated with PD. To avoid such challenging training scheme, some works have used a collection of convolutional responses extracted from the first layers of a Convolutional Neural Network (CNN) architecture previously trained on a general natural image classification problem [17]. Subsequently, different works propose pooling methods to compact these representations in low dimension descriptors using Symmetric Positive Definite (SPD) matrices that summarize feature statistics [2,17]. However, these matrices belong to a Riemannian manifold, making it necessary to design proper methods regarding the geometric structure [3,11]. Despite current efforts, manifold learning methods still use shallow learning and machine learning algorithms need been redesigned to take into account data geometry [11].

This work introduces a novel digital biomarker that captures discriminatory PD fixational eye patterns, following a Riemannian deep representation, that compactly codes in symmetric matrices second order statistics of deep convolutional features. For this purpose, each video sequence is transformed in spatiotemporal slices that recover tiny tremor patterns, during ocular fixation experiment. From this input, an end-to-end learning process is herein proposed through a hybrid deep network, whose first layers are convolutional (CNN) and last layers are Riemannian (SPDNet). The CNN module projects the input slices to deep features, which are then summarized in symmetric positive embedding matrices, allowing to exploit feature correlations that are related to visual observations. Hence, these embedding matrices feed the Riemannian module, that focus on non-linear learning, while preserving geometry of input SPD data, achieving a discrimination between Parkinsonian and control classes. The result is a method able to discriminate between oculomotor patterns of patients diagnosed with the disease and a control population.

2   Proposed Method

We hypothesize that symmetric positive embedding vectors are key to discover new PD biomarkers from deep oculomotor patterns. In this work, we designed an end-to-end Riemannian deep strategy (ConvSPD network) that uses spatio-temporal slice observations of a fixational experiment. Each slice is overcompletely represented by convolutional deep features, which in turn are summarized in symmetric embedding vectors and finally exploited by a Riemannian module to carry out the classification task. The proposed representation preserves the Riemannian geometry of data and robustly discriminates Parkinson patients from a control population. Figure 1 summarizes the proposed pipeline.

2.1   Convolutional Module and Symmetric Pooling Representation

A convolutional scheme is here introduced as the first part of the proposed approach to represent slices of oculomotor sequences. More precisely, this CNN module learns to extract early to mid-level (textural) features, to capture relevant patterns in eye micro-movements during fixational experiment. The convolutional representation is structured in several layers, hierarchically organized to progressively increase the time × space receptive field, as well as the semantic level w.r.t. Parkinsonian classification.

In the deepest layer, the corresponding D feature maps form a tensor $X \in \mathbb{R}^{D \times W \times H}$, where (W, H) are the dimensions of the feature maps, resulting from the successive convolutional and pooling processes along the representation. This embedding tensor X, is then summarized in a special symmetric positive embedding matrix by computing second-order statistics from such description [2,20]. To this end, we implement a special pooling layer (*SPDpool*) that summarizes the information from the last layer into a symmetric positive embedding matrix (SPD matrix).

In general SPD matrices aim to compute second order statistics to recover similarities among features. For instance, by taking the inner product of all pairs of feature vectors, some works propose correlation volumes to compute visual similarities between pixels [18]. In this work, if we suppose that $(k - 1)$ is the index of the last convolutional layer, we re-organize the embedding tensor X in a matrix named X_{k-1} with D rows and $W \times H$ columns. Then we compute the outer product of X_{k-1} with itself. Then, the proposed SPDpool layer calculates: $X_k = f_{SPDpool}(X_{k-1}) = \frac{1}{W \times H} X_{k-1} X_{k-1}^T$. This way, the (i, j) element of X_k is the inner product (correlation) between the i-th feature map and the j-th

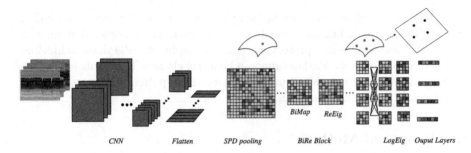

Fig. 1. Architecture of the proposed ConvSPD network. Starting from a collection of space × time slice images summarizing the oculomotor video sequence, a CNN module first projects them to an overcomplete embedding of deep features. These features are then flattened and compacted using a SPD pooling layer. The classification is finally performed by a Riemannian non-linear SPDNet module.

feature map. This provides second order statistics, and has been used to measure statistical discrepancy [14]. Here, the resultant symmetric positive embedding $D \times D$ matrix allows to capture the most statistically relevant relationships in the previous CNN module, with respect to the Parkinson classification task.

2.2   Riemmanian Module Structure

In the same way as the SPD Gram matrix was used in [6] and [7] to model texture and pictorial style respectively, we may consider the Parkinsonian stage of the patient as a stationary parameter, in the sense that it will affect the ocumolotor action independently on the temporal position (phase) of the movement. In short, the oculomotor task (fixation or tracking) represents the "content" (layout) of the input slices, whereas the stage of the disease represents their "style". However, unlike [7], who use Gram matrices in their loss function, we choose to go on working with stationary features that may be interpreted in terms of distributions, by completing the CNN module by a Riemannian SPD network.

Then, once obtained the SPD embedding, we maintain the deep representation while taking into account the Riemmanian geometry of SPD matrices. We then base the next processing layers on the SPDNet framework, that carries out a deep non-linear representation [11]. This requires the codification of special layers, such as: *BiMap*, *ReEig*, and *LogEig*. We now describe the respective Riemmanian layers and their particular learning procedure.

The BiMap layer is a fully connected layer designed to generate a new bank of more compact and discriminative SPD matrices by a bilinear mapping

$$X_k = W_k X_{k-1} W_k^T. \tag{1}$$

Here, $X_{k-1} \in S_{++}^{d_{k-1}}$ is the input $d_{k-1} \times d_{k-1}$ SPD matrix of the layer $(k-1)$, and $W_k \in \mathbb{R}_*^{d_k \times d_{k-1}}$ is the transformation matrix (connection weight). Similarly to the CNN, the sizes of the SPD matrices decrease from layer to layer, i.e.

$d_k < d_{k-1}$, and the *BiMap* layer actually uses m different weight matrices $\{W_k^{(i)}\}_{i=1}^m$ in order to generate m SPD matrices $\{X_k^{(i)}\}_{i=1}^m$ in the k-th layer.

The *ReEig layer* was inspired by rectified linear units (ReLU) of CNNs. It is composed of a non-linear function to improve the training process by rectifying the SPD matrices:

$$X_k = U_{k-1} \max(\varepsilon I, \Sigma_{k-1}) U_{k-1}^T,$$

where U_{k-1} and Σ_{k-1} come from the eigen decomposition $X_{k-1} = U_{k-1} \Sigma_{k-1} U_{k-1}^T$. Here, $\varepsilon \in \mathbb{R}_+^*$ is a rectification threshold, I is the identity matrix and Σ_{k-1} the diagonal matrix of the eigenvalues of X_{k-1}. This operation tunes up the eigenvalues avoiding non-positiveness and improving the discriminative performance.

The *LogEig layer* results from the necessity to project SPD matrices back to Euclidean space where the classifiers are designed. In Riemannian manifolds we can attach each point to a flat tangent space with a vector space structure. This structure ease classic Euclidean computations. To map elements here is used the Riemannian logarithm map. To facilitate the computing and work on the same tangent space, we map the SPD matrix X_{k-1} onto the tangent space at the identity by

$$X_k = \log(X_{k-1}) = U_{k-1} \log(\Sigma_{k-1}) U_{k-1}^T.$$

Thereafter, the output layers correspond to the classic final layers of neural networks, e.g. a flatten layer or a fully connected layer, and the final output layer should be a softmax operation.

Learning Scheme. The proposed ConvSPD was trained following a classic back-propagation in convolutional module, but for LogEig and ReEig Riemmanian layers was taken into account structured derivatives in propagation [12]. Besides, to learn weights of the *BiMap* layers (Eq. 1) it is necessary to consider special optimization constraints. To generate consistent SPD matrices and achieve a feasible optimization, connection weights are non squared, orthogonal, and row full-rank matrices. That implies these weights matrices lie in a compact *Stiefel manifold* $St(d_k, d_{k-1})$ [11]. To calculate the gradient, in the equation (1) the steepest descent direction with respect to W_k on the Stiefel manifold is given by

$$\widetilde{\nabla} L_{W_k^t}^{(k)} = \nabla L_{W_k^t}^{(k)} - \nabla L_{W_k^t}^{(k)} \left(W_k^t\right)^T W_k^t \tag{2}$$

which is the tangent component obtained by subtracting the normal component to the Euclidean gradient $\nabla L_{W_k^t}^{(k)}$. Finally, the step of gradient descent for the connection weights is

$$W_k^{t+1} = \Gamma \left(W_k^t - \alpha \widetilde{\nabla} L_{W_k^t}^{(k)}\right) \tag{3}$$

where Γ is a retraction operation to get back to the Stiefel manifold, and α is the learning rate [11]. Given some ξ in the tangent component, by the orthogonal constrain, the retraction map is reduced to the calculus of the Q factor of the polar decomposition of $W_k^t + \xi$ [1].

3　Experimental Setup

3.1　Dataset Description

A total of 13 PD patients (average age of 72.3 ± 7.4) and 13 control subjects (average age of 72.2 ± 6.1) were captured and analyzed for evaluating the proposed approach. A camera with a temporal resolution of 60 fps was fixed in front of the subjects to capture their upper face region. Participants were invited to sit and observe a simple stimulus as illustrated in Fig. 2(a). A single fixation period of 5 s was set and individual eyes were manually cropped to 210×140 pixels by centering the first frame to the center of the pupil, to obtain the sequences of interest. In total, 5 video sequences were obtained for each participant. Subjects with different disease degree progression were selected to include inter-subject variability. With the help of a physical therapist, PD patients were categorized into the Hoehn-Yahr rating scale. A total of five patients were categorized in stage two, six patients in stage three, and two patients in stage four. The dataset was approved by an Ethic Committee. Written informed consent was obtained for every participant. To our knowledge, there is no public dataset containing more eye movement videos for Parkinson stage prediction.

For spatio-temporal slice computation, each video being considered as a volume $\{I(x, y, t)\}_{x=1, y=1, t=1}^{W, H, N}$, with spatial dimension $W \times H$ and N frames, we choose 4 radial directions $\theta_i \in \{0°, 45°, 90°, 135°\}$ around the center, and cut the video volume along each direction as illustrated in Fig. 2(a). The output is then four 2d slice images $S_\theta(x, t)$, each one recording subtle eye displacements, capturing potential oculomotor alterations related with PD.

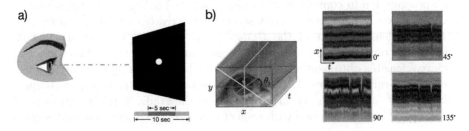

Fig. 2. Dataset: (a) Ocular fixation task. (b) 2D Video slices representation of eye movements.

3.2　Network Configuration

For the convolutional module, the weights were initialized from a pre-trained ResNet-18 architecture [10], which has a total of 8 convolutional blocks. Regarding the Riemannian module, we implement BiRe blocks (a BiMap layer, followed by a ReEig layer), which reduce the input dimension by half. A total of four models were herein evaluated using the following architecture:

- A convolutional module using only the first $N = \{2, 4, 6, 8\}$ convolutional blocks, which outputs 64, 128, 256 and 512 feature maps of size 53×75, 27×38, 14×19 and 7×10 respectively.
- A pooling layer using $f_{SPDpool}$.
- A Riemannian module with 3 BiRe blocks and a LogEig layer.
- Output layers: a flatten layer, a fully connected layer, and a softmax dedicated to classification output.

We call this hybrid model a ConvSPD N-th block model, which is trainable end-to-end starting from video slices while learning convolutional and Riemannian structures.

A Leave one out cross validation scheme was carried out to evaluate the performance of the proposed models. In such sense, each fold leaves one patient for testing while the remaining are used for training, for a total of 26 experiments.

During training and validation, we also recover the resultant Riemmanian representation, encoded in SPD embedding matrices. We compute distances among these matrices, that represent points in the learned Riemmanian manifold, to measure the discriminatory capability of such representation. We use the Riemannian distance $d_R(x, y) = \| \log_x(y) \|_x$, where x, y are embedding points, $\log(\cdot)$ is the Riemannian logarithm map and $\| \cdot \|_x$ an *affine-invariant* norm [15]. With the class-labeled data, we consider two disjoint sets P (Parkinsonian) and C (control) in the manifold, respectively. Therefore we define the separation metric as the Riemannian distance between P and C, as

$$d_R(P, C) = \frac{1}{|P||C|} \sum_{x \in P} \sum_{y \in C} d_R(x, y).$$

4 Evaluation and Results

In the proposed architecture, a deeper convolutional module produces more feature maps but with a smaller size. Therefore, a first validation of the proposed approach was carried out varying the number of convolutional blocks previous to the SPD pooling layer. Such validation was carried out according to the classification task, measuring the sensitivity, specificity, precision, accuracy, and F1-Score of each model respectively. Table 1 summarizes performance achieved from the different configurations, achieving outstanding accuracy scores, above 90% for all validations. In all metrics it is visible that intermediate and deep blocks aid the network to achieve better results. This way, mid-level feature maps support the ConvSPD 4th-Block model to accurately predict PD patients with an accuracy of 97.7%. Moreover, the results of ConvSPD 4th-Block and 6th-Block enhance the trade-off between the size and the number of features, where small features (ConvSPD 8th-Block) turn out to be statistically insufficient and few features (ConvSPD 2nd-Block) limit the measurement of similarities. As comparison with standard convolutional nets, we implement the complete ResNet-18 CNN, achieving only an accuracy of 94.26%, with a relative more complex architecture and a total of 11.7M parameters. As baseline comparison, we compared with a machine learning approach that classifies SPD matrices constructed from convolutional responses [17]. Under the same data validation conditions, this approach reports an accuracy of 87.7%, 10% less than the proposed end-to-end ConvSPD 4th-Block model.

Table 1. Classification results of the proposed ConvSPD N-th block models for $N = 2, 4, 6, 8$.

Model	Sen(%)	Spe(%)	Pr(%)	Acc(%)	F1(%)	Parameters	Time
ConvSPD 8th-Block	94.4	94.4	94.4	94.4	94.4	11.6M	1.63 s
ConvSPD 6th-Block	95.4	94.4	94.4	94.9	94.9	2.83M	0.88 s
ConvSPD 4th-Block	97.2	98.5	98.4	**97.8**	97.8	0.70M	0.54 s
ConvSPD 2nd-Block	94.9	93.1	93.2	94.0	94.0	0.16M	0.27 s

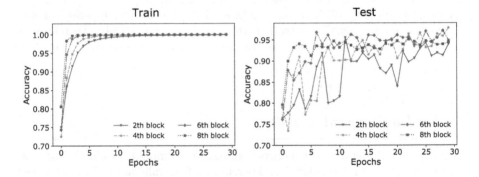

Fig. 3. Convergence of the models

The convergence of the proposed approach was also analyzed to measure the stability of the SPD component together with convolutional representation. Figure 3 shows the effective convergence performance for all models. Besides, deeper models present a rapid and stable convergence as expected, thanks to the wide receptive field. On the other hand, since shallow models have feature maps with less semantics, these results show the ability of the Riemannian module to improve the networks generalization.

The inference time of the proposed descriptor is determinant to be implemented in clinical scenarios, and routine validation of PD patients. For this reason, the Table 1also reports the inference time and the total number of parameters, that requires each of the validated configurations. Inference time refers to the time that takes the model to forward the video slices data and produce a prediction. We can observe that the increasing between models is exponential, the inference time almost doubles, and the number of parameters is quadrupled. However, the ConvSPD 2nd-Block and ConvSPD 4th-Block are significantly light models, and all models except ConvSPD 8th-Block compute the inference in acceptable time (< 1 s). From this, we can see how the ConvSPD 4th-Block model with almost 20 times fewer parameters outperforms the complete Convolutional model. The implementation of clinical routine requires a trade-off between computational inference time, parameters of the representation to define computational architecture, but also sufficient precision to support diagnosis and following.

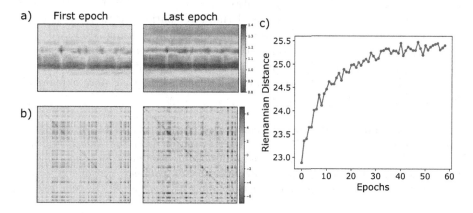

Fig. 4. Analysis of ConvSPD structures. We take sample activations extracted from the ConvSPD 4th-Block model. **a)** Average activations from the second block of the convolutional module on the first (left panel) and last (right panel) epoch. **b)** SPD matrices from the third BiRe block of the Riemannian module on the first (left panel) and last (right panel) epoch. **c)** Evolution of the average Riemannian distance between Parkinson and Control subjects on the test sets.

As visual analysis, we recover the feature maps from PD patients of the 2nd-Block at first and last epochs. For this last experiment, instead of carrying out a cross validation, two random subjects were chosen for each class, and the rest was used for training a ConvSPD *4th-Block* model one time. In Fig. 4a) is illustrated an average of these maps, observing the evolution of the model to detect areas of interest in the slice. Specifically, the model focus on the center of slices, indicating that the ConvSPD use eye movement information for the quantification. Similarly, in Fig. 4b) we illustrate the average of the SPD matrices extracted from the third BiRe block. It is observed that the Riemannian module effectively enriches the relationship between different features, while reducing the importance of others. Finally, we measure the average Riemannian distance between the two classes in the test set during training, see Fig. 4c). Here can be seen a growing trend of the distance, showing the ability of the network to learn Riemannian mappings that separate the SPD matrices, which traduces in a discriminative method. This result evidences the contribution of the Riemannian structures to the discrimination between control and PD patients.

5   Conclusions and Future Work

This paper introduced a Riemannian deep model with the capability to recover Parkinsonian oculomotor patterns under a classification task scheme. For this purpose, video sliced data was provided to represent ocular fixation abnormalities. The whole deep representation integrates convolutional and Riemannian modules to effectively discriminate between Parkinson and Control population. In a clinical scenario with few observations, the use of intermediate SPD representations produce stable results considering inter-patients variability. Furthermore, the ConvSPD improves classification performance using SPD structures and results in a lightweight model able to accurately predict in a reasonable inference time. Future works include new experiments with larger datasets and a backward analysis to discover potential relationships that may explain the disease.

Acknowledgments. The recorded dataset was possible thanks to the support of the Parkinson foundation FAMPAS and the institution *Asilo San Rafael*. Additionally, acknowledgments to the Universidad Industrial de Santander for supporting this research registered by the project: *Cuantificación de patrones locomotores para el diagnóstico y seguimiento remoto en zonas de difícil acceso*, with SIVIE code 2697.

References

1. Absil, P.A., Mahony, R., Sepulchre, R.: Optimization Algorithms on Matrix Manifolds. Princeton University Press, Princeton (2009)
2. Acharya, D., Huang, Z., Pani Paudel, D., Van Gool, L.: Covariance pooling for facial expression recognition. In: Proceedings of the IEEE Conference on Computer Vision and Pattern Recognition Workshops, pp. 367–374 (2018)
3. Bronstein, M.M., Bruna, J., LeCun, Y., Szlam, A., Vandergheynst, P.: Geometric deep learning: going beyond Euclidean data. IEEE Signal Process. Mag. **34**(4), 18–42 (2017). https://doi.org/10.1109/MSP.2017.2693418
4. Chan, F., Armstrong, I.T., Pari, G., Riopelle, R.J., Munoz, D.P.: Deficits in saccadic eye-movement control in Parkinson's disease. Neuropsychologia **43**, 784–796 (2005)
5. Dorsey, E.R., Elbaz, A., Nichols, E., Abd-Allah, F., Abdelalim, A., Adsuar, J.C., et al.: Global, regional, and national burden of Parkinson's disease, 1990–2016: a systematic analysis for the global burden of disease study 2016. Lancet Neurol. **17**(11), 939–953 (2018)
6. Gatys, L., Ecker, A.S., Bethge, M.: Texture synthesis using convolutional neural networks. In: Advances in Neural Information Processing Systems, vol. 28 (2015)
7. Gatys, L.A., Ecker, A.S., Bethge, M.: Image style transfer using convolutional neural networks. In: IEEE Conference on Computer Vision and Pattern Recognition (CVPR), pp. 2414–2423 (2016)

8. Gitchel, G.T., Wetzel, P.A., Baron, M.S.: Pervasive ocular tremor in patients with Parkinson disease. Arch. Neurol. **69**, 1011–1017 (2012)

9. Guayacán, L.C., Rangel, E., Martínez, F.: Towards understanding spatio-temporal parkinsonian patterns from salient regions of a 3D convolutional network. In: 2020 42nd Annual International Conference of the IEEE Engineering in Medicine & Biology Society (EMBC), pp. 3688–3691. IEEE (2020)

10. He, K., Zhang, X., Ren, S., Sun, J.: Deep residual learning for image recognition. In: Proceedings of the IEEE Conference on Computer Vision and Pattern Recognition, pp. 770–778 (2016)

11. Huang, Z., Van Gool, L.: A Riemannian network for SPD matrix learning. In: Thirty-First AAAI Conference on Artificial Intelligence, vol. 31, no. 1 (2017)

12. Ionescu, C., Vantzos, O., Sminchisescu, C.: Matrix backpropagation for deep networks with structured layers. In: Proceedings of the IEEE International Conference on Computer Vision, pp. 2965–2973 (2015)

13. Li, P., Xie, J., Wang, Q., Zuo, W.: Is second-order information helpful for large-scale visual recognition? In: Proceedings of the IEEE International Conference on Computer Vision, pp. 2070–2078 (2017)

14. Li, Y., Wang, N., Liu, J., Hou, X.: Demystifying neural style transfer. arXiv preprint arXiv:1701.01036 (2017)

15. Pennec, X., Fillard, P., Ayache, N.: A Riemannian framework for tensor computing. Int. J. Comput. Vis. **66**(1), 41–66 (2006)

16. Poewe, W., Seppi, K., Tanner, C.M., Halliday, G.M., Brundin, P., Volkmann, J., et al.: Parkinson disease. Nat. Rev. Disease Primers **3**(1), 1–21 (2017)

17. Salazar, I., Pertuz, S., Contreras, W., Martínez, F.: A convolutional oculomotor representation to model Parkinsonian fixational patterns from magnified videos. Pattern Anal. Appl. **24**(2), 445–457 (2021)

18. Teed, Z., Deng, J.: RAFT: recurrent all-pairs field transforms for optical flow. In: Vedaldi, A., Bischof, H., Brox, T., Frahm, J.-M. (eds.) ECCV 2020. LNCS, vol. 12347, pp. 402–419. Springer, Cham (2020). https://doi.org/10.1007/978-3-030-58536-5_24

19. Tolosa, E., Garrido, A., Scholz, S.W., Poewe, W.: Challenges in the diagnosis of Parkinson's disease. Lancet Neurol. **20**(5), 385–397 (2021)

20. Wang, Q., Xie, J., Zuo, W., Zhang, L., Li, P.: Deep CNNs meet global covariance pooling: better representation and generalization. IEEE Trans. Pattern Anal. Mach. Intell. **43**, 2582–2597 (2020)

21. Wang, W., Lee, J., Harrou, F., Sun, Y.: Early detection of Parkinson's disease using deep learning and machine learning. IEEE Access **8**, 147635–147646 (2020)

22. Weil, R.S., Schrag, A.E., Warren, J.D., Crutch, S.J., Lees, A.J., Morris, H.R.: Visual dysfunction in Parkinson's disease. Brain J. Neurol. **139**(11), 2827–2843 (2016)

Pruning Neural Nets by Optimal Neuron Merging

Felix Goldberg$^{(\boxtimes)}$ ⓘ, Yackov Lubarsky, Alexei Gaissinski, Dan Botchan, and Pavel Kisilev

Toga Networks Ltd., HaHarash Street 4, Hod Hasharon, Israel
{felix.goldberg,yackov.lubarsky,alexei.gaissinski,dan.botchan, pavel.kisilev}@toganetworks.com

Abstract. We present a new method for structured pruning of neural networks, based on the recently proposed neuron merging trick in which following a pruning operation, the weights of the *next* layer are suitably modified. By a rigorous mathematical analysis of the neuron merging technique we prove an upper bound on the reconstruction error. This bound defines a new objective function for pruning-and-merging. Our new optimal algorithm provably achieves the lowest objective cost among all possible prune-and-merge strategies. We also show empirically that nuclear norm regularization can be used to obtain even better pruning-and-merging accuracy; this finding is supported by our theoretical analysis.

Keywords: Network pruning · Neuron merging · Facility location

1 Introduction

Modern Deep Neural Network (DNN) architectures are constantly growing at a frenetic rate, in order to be able to learn models that accommodate ever larger and more complex data. Developing methodologies to create compact DNNs that perform efficiently during run-time by pruning away large portions of the original networks while retaining the accuracy thus becomes imperative.

Our goal in this paper is to present a new pruning method, Optimal Neuron Merging based Pruning (ONMP, for short), that has the following attractive properties: (i) Data-free pruning criterion (ii) No dependence on the training protocol (iii) Solid theoretical foundation (iv) Strong empirical results.

Pruning usually incurs a significant accuracy loss. To mitigate this, a rather complex and resource-hungry re-training procedures must be applied to attain/recover good results [11,19]. For instance, the highly-regarded Network Slimming method [13] requires 160 epochs of non-standard training before pruning and the same number for re-training.

Our inspiration and point of departure is the paper [9] which introduced the neuron merging technique. After briefly surveying relevant literature in Sect. 1.1 we give in Sect. 2 a brief account of neuron merging. Our exposition is based on

© Springer Nature Switzerland AG 2022
M. El Yacoubi et al. (Eds.): ICPRAI 2022, LNCS 13363, pp. 688–699, 2022.
https://doi.org/10.1007/978-3-031-09037-0_56

[9] with the addition of the so-called "selection matrix" which helps to clarify and formalize the method. For a very effective visual presentation we strongly urge the reader to refer to Fig. 2 of [9] which we could not reproduce here for reasons of space.

Then in Sect. 3 we introduce our own novel analysis and the new optimal prune-and-merge algorithm derived from it. Section 4 discusses a further development whereas by a minor modification of the training regime the results can be further improved. Experiments, conclusions, and references follow in due course.

1.1   Related Work

Our work falls within the class of *filter pruning* methods [5,6,14] that remove whole filters or neurons from the network. This is currently the most common approach to *structured* pruning because it can be easily leveraged by existing hardware. For a discussion of the relative merits of pruning techniques at various granularity levels see [15]. For more general excellent recent surveys see [8,21].

Our focus will be on the activations of each layer and we shall obtain a bound on the maximum possible discrepancy between the pre-pruning and post-pruning activations. Earlier works (e.g. [7,12,14,24]) have also taken preserving the activations as their guiding principle but they pursued it in a data-driven way. Data-driven methods are often considered more accurate than current data-free methods but they are also more cumbersome and susceptible to domain drift.

Another popular approach is to adjust the training loss in a way that should reduce the accuracy hit incurred when the model is pruned. [2,13,22] are examples of such algorithms. This requires either re-training or fine-tuning of the model before pruning can be done. In contrast, our method can be applied directly to a pre-trained network.

Since our new method is based on a universal bound for activation discrepancy that holds over *all possible* data points, it allows us to bridge the chasm between data-driven and data-free methods. It does not require access to training data, operating instead on the similarities between filters.

The idea of basing the pruning criterion on the similarities between the filters has already appeared a number of times in the literature; the recent FPGM method [6] is one of the most successful examples. However, FPGM and the other methods driven by the similarities between the filters are based on a heuristic analysis.

2   Background: Pruning and Merging

Denote by W_i the weight matrix of layer i of the network. For a fully-connected layer, the layer itself is essentially the weight matrix[1]. For a convolutional layer, each filter of the layer i is rastered into a column of W_i. The dimensions of W_i

---

[1] The bias also needs to be taken into account - see [9, Section 6.1] for details how to do that.

are $N_i \times N_{i+1}$. Suppose that we wish to retain only $P_{i+1} = p$ of the N_{i+1} output neurons of layer i, where $0 < P_{i+1} < N_{i+1}$.

Definition 1. *Let $C^p(W_i)$ be the set of all submatrices formed by choosing p columns from W_i.*

Definition 2. *Let $\mathbf{P_1}$ be the set of those nonnegative matrices that have at most one nonzero entry in each column.*

Define the $N_{i+1} \times P_{i+1}$ selection matrix J be the unique $\{0,1\}$ matrix satisfying $W_i J = Y_i$, where Y_i is a column submatrix of W_i.

Consider now the effect of pruning on the next layer $i + 1$. Since the output neurons of layer i are actually the input neurons of layer $i + 1$, the weight matrix W_{i+1} after pruning becomes a smaller matrix $\hat{W}_{i+1} \in \mathbb{R}^{P_{i+1} \times N_{i+2}}$. The expression for $\hat{W}_{i+1}$ can be conveniently written down using the selection matrix:

$$\hat{W}_{i+1} = J^T W_{i+1}.$$

The standard pruning scheme can be written down as Algorithm 1.

Algorithm 1. Naive Layerwise Prune

Input: weight matrices W_i, W_{i+1}
Parameter: p, pruning method $\mathcal{A}$
1: $Y_i = \mathcal{A}(W_i) \in C^p(W_i)$
2: $W_i \mapsto Y_i$
3: $W_{i+1} \mapsto J^T W_{i+1}$

Let us now see what happens to the activation of layer $i + 1$ as a result of pruning. For an input vector $x \in \mathbb{R}^{N_i}$ it is given by:

$$\mathbf{a}_{i+1}(x) = W_{i+1}^T f(W_i^T x), \tag{1}$$

where f is the non-linear activation function used in the network.

After pruning with Algorithm 1 the activation becomes:

$$\mathbf{a}_{i+1}^{\text{pruned}}(x) = \hat{W}_{i+1}^T f(Y_i^T x) = W_{i+1}^T J f(Y_i^T x). \tag{2}$$

So the activation error incurred as a result of pruning is:

$$\mathbf{a}_{i+1}(x) - \mathbf{a}_{i+1}^{\text{pruned}}(x) = W_{i+1}^T \Big(f(W_i^T x) - J f(Y_i^T x) \Big). \tag{3}$$

2.1   Error Propagation in Pruning

Consider again Equation (3) which measures the post-pruning reconstruction error of the activation. If we could find a way to minimize its right-hand side, we would be in possession of a better pruning scheme.

Theorem 1. *[9] Let f be the ReLU function and let $Z \in \mathbb{R}^{p \times n}$. Then*

$$f(Z^T v) = Z^T f(v) \text{ for every } v \in \mathbb{R}^p \tag{4}$$

if and only if $Z \in \mathbf{P_1}$.

Since the selection matrix J defined earlier clearly satisfies $J^T \in \mathbf{P_1}$, we can use Theorem 1 to slightly modify (3):

$$\mathbf{a}_{i+1}(x) - \mathbf{a}_{i+1}^{\text{pruned}}(x) = W_{i+1}^T \Big(f(W_i^T x) - f(J Y_i^T x) \Big). \tag{5}$$

We are now ready to interpret Eq. (5) in a new way: the matrix W_i is *approximated* by $Y_i J^T$ and the equation describes the *propagation of error* from this approximation to the layer $i + 1$ activation.

2.2   Pruning-and-Merging

The neuron merging scheme of [9] calls for replacing the approximation $W_i \approx Y_i J^T$ with one with a smaller error so that the error propagation equation (5) ensures a smaller activation reconstruction error. To be able to use Theorem 1 (which powers the whole scheme) this approximation must be of the form

$$W_i \approx Y_i Z_i, \ Z_i \in \mathbf{P_1}. \tag{6}$$

In [9] a heuristic method called MostSim was proposed to find for a given column submatrix Y_i of W_i a matrix $Z_i \in \mathbf{P_1}$ that minimizes the approximation error. We will show in Sect. 3.1 that this method indeed recovers the optimal Z_i for a *fixed* Y_i.

Our new contribution will go one step further: we will show that *both* Y_i and Z_i can be chosen in a joint way that obtains the smallest possible approximation error, instead of using an external sub-algorithm to first choose Y_i.

Let us write down as Algorithm 2 the prune-and-merge method of [9].

Algorithm 2. Agnostic Layerwise Prune-and-Merge

Input: weight matrices W_i, W_{i+1}
Parameter: p, $\mathcal{A}$, parameter t for MostSim
1: $Y_i = \mathcal{A}(W_i) \in C^p(W_i)$
2: MostSim$(W_i, Y_i, t) \mapsto Z_i$
3: $W_i \mapsto Y_i$
4: $W_{i+1} \mapsto Z_i W_{i+1}$

---

3   New Method: Optimal Pruning-and-merging

Let us first give a rigorous formulation of the relative error bound for merging:

Theorem 2. *Let* W_i, W_{i+1} *be the weight matrices for layers* $i, i+1$, *let* Y_i *be a column submatrix of* W_i, *and let* $Z_i \in \mathbf{P_1}$. *Then:*

$$\max_{x \neq 0} \frac{||\mathbf{a}_{i+1}(x) - \mathbf{a}_{i+1}^{merged}(x)||}{||x||} \leq ||W_{i+1}||_2 \cdot ||W_i - Y_i Z_i||_2.$$

The proof of the theorem is omitted for reasons of space. Now, Theorem 2 suggests a way to define an optimality notion for pruning-and-merging algorithms. Note that we are using the slightly larger Frobenius norm instead of the (spectral) 2-norm in the theorem. This relaxation is crucial to the solution.

Problem 1. *Find an optimal pruning algorithm that will take as input the weight matrix* W_i *and a fixed number* p *and return a column submatrix* Y_i^* *of* W_i *and a* $Z_i^* \in \mathbf{P_1}$ *that satisfy*

$$Y_i^*, Z_i^* = \underset{\substack{Y_i \in C^p(W_i) \\ Z_i \in \mathbf{P_1}}}{arg\ min}\ ||W_i - Y_i Z_i||_F.$$

3.1   Solution of Problem 1, Step I

Because we are dealing with the Frobenius norm, the approximation error $||W_i - Y_i Z_i||_F$ can be decomposed into a sum of N_i columnwise errors that can be dealt with separately. Formally, if we let $\sigma(j)$ be the row index of the single non-zero entry in the jth column of Z_i, then:

$$||W_i - Y_i Z_i||_F^2 = \sum_{j=1}^{N_j} ||\mathbf{w}_j - (Z_i)_{\sigma(j),j} \mathbf{y}_{\sigma(j)}||^2. \tag{7}$$

So Problem 1 becomes equivalent to minimizing the right-hand side of (7). As the summands are independent of each other, the optimal matrix Z_i for a fixed Y_i can be computed by choosing for each j the row index $\sigma(j)$ and the scalar value $(Z_i)_{\sigma(j),j}$ so that $||\mathbf{w}_j - (Z_i)_{\sigma(j),j} \mathbf{y}_{\sigma(j)}||$ is minimized.

The choice of $\sigma(j)$ can be easily accomplished with the help of the following

Lemma 1. *Let* $\mathbf{w}$ *and* $\mathbf{y}$ *be real-valued vectors. Then the minimum of* $||\mathbf{w} - \lambda \mathbf{y}||$ *over* $\lambda \in \mathbb{R}$ *is obtained at*

$$\lambda = \frac{\mathbf{w}^T \mathbf{y}}{||\mathbf{y}||^2}.$$

Proof. The vector projection of $\mathbf{w}$ on $\mathbf{y}$ is given by $\frac{\mathbf{w}^T \mathbf{y}}{||\mathbf{y}||^2}\mathbf{y}$. Since this is the multiple of $\mathbf{y}$ closest to $\mathbf{w}$, the claim follows immediately.

We then choose $\sigma(j)$ to yield the smallest norm for the residual.

Algorithm 3. Layerwise Optimal Prune-and-Merge

Input: weight matrices W_i, W_{i+1}
Parameter: p

1: Calculate the approximation costs $c(\mathbf{w_1}, \mathbf{w_2})$ for every two distinct columns $\mathbf{w_1}, \mathbf{w_2} \in W_i$ using (8)
2: Solve the p-median problem for W_i and $c(\cdot, \cdot) \mapsto Y_i$
3: MostSim$(W_i, Y_i, 0) \mapsto Z_i$
4: $W_i \mapsto Y_i$
5: $W_{i+1} \mapsto Z_i W_{i+1}$

Remark. *If the angle between the vectors* $\mathbf{w}$ *and* $\mathbf{y}$ *is more than* $\frac{\pi}{2}$, *then the optimal* λ *computed in Lemma 1 will be negative and we will have to re-set it to zero, because* Z_i *must stay in* $\mathbf{P^1}$.

The preceding argument formalizes and validates the optimality of the Most-Sim heuristic suggested in [9] to compute Z_i for an Y_i obtained by an arbitrary $\mathcal{A}$. Their proviso regarding non-acute angles is equivalent to setting $t = 0$ in MostSim.

3.2   Solution of Problem 1, Step II

Observe that after the first step we have arrived at a formulation of the optimality criterion that actually no longer depends on the unknown Y_i and Z_i. Instead we can express the criterion entirely in terms of the mutual relations between the columns of W_i.

Essentially we have here a weighted graph G_{W_i} whose vertices are the columns of W_i and there is a cost associated with approximating vertex $\mathbf{w}$ by vertex $\mathbf{v}$, given by the formula:

$$c(\mathbf{w}, \mathbf{v}) = \begin{cases} ||\mathbf{w} - \frac{\mathbf{w}^T \mathbf{v}}{||\mathbf{v}||^2} \cdot \mathbf{w}||, & \text{if } \angle(\mathbf{w}, \mathbf{v}) \leq \frac{\pi}{2} \\ \infty, & \text{otherwise} \end{cases} \tag{8}$$

So we can now re-state Problem 1 in an equivalent formulation:

Problem 1' *Find an algorithm that will take as input the graph* G_{W_i} *and a fixed number* p *and return a subset of vertices* $S \subseteq V(G_{W_i})$ *so that the following is satisfied:*

$$S = \underset{\substack{S \subseteq V(G_{W_i}) \\ |S|=p}}{\arg\min} \sum_{\mathbf{w} \in V(G_{W_i})} \min_{\mathbf{y} \in S} c(\mathbf{w}, \mathbf{y}).$$

Fortunately, Problem 1' is precisely an instance of the well-known p-**median problem** [1,3,18]. Although it is NP-Hard, instances of moderate size can be solved quite efficiently using the standard mixed integer linear programming formulation. Our new method is formally stated as Algorithm 3.

4   Nuclear Norm Regularization for Better Pruning

We have formulated optimal pruning-and-merging as essentially a combinatorial problem. The precise nature of the problem in each instance depends, however, on the geometric configuration presented by the columns of the weight matrix W_i. The question now arises whether we can "encourage" the training process to produce weight matrices more amenable to our type of approximation.

More rigorously speaking, recall that the Theorem 2 contained the term $||W_{i+1}||_2$ which we earlier took as fixed. But what if it could be also minimized?

To this end, let us consider a W_i with zero approximation error. Clearly, such a W_i must have p columns such that all other columns are positive multiples of them. This implies that $\text{rank} W_i = p$. This is the property we will seek to encourage during training.

However, we cannot directly regularize over $\text{rank} W_i$ itself, since its derivative is zero almost everywhere. Therefore we resort to the standard method of regularizing over the so-called nuclear norm $||W_i||_*$ (a.k.a. the trace norm or the Schatten 1-norm), which is defined as the sum of all singular values of W_i. It is well-known that the nuclear norm is the convex envelope of the matrix rank and it is often used as a proxy for matrix rank [16, 17].

5   Experiments

We evaluate our method on two standard image classification benchmarks: CIFAR [10] and ILSVRC-2012 [20]. We use mainly ResNet [4] and WideResNet [23] architectures, which allow us to cover different network sizes and pruning rates.

To conduct the experiments we use the PyTorch framework. We use pre-trained weights that are available as part of the framework for ResNet on CIFAR-10 and ILSVRC-2012 datasets where possible.

Our filter pruning scheme is similar to that of [9] - we prune only the internal layers inside the residual blocks to avoid misalignment in the shortcut connections. Similarly to [6] all layers are pruned with the same prune/keep ratio. To solve the p-median problem we use the PyScipOpt package.

All experiments are conducted on a server machine with 8 GTX 2080 TI GPUs. The bulk of our training experiments are the fine-tuning of the ILSVRC-2012 [20] models. The p-median algorithm typically runs at negligible cost.

5.1   Prune and Merge Evaluation

In this set of experiments we test the validation error immediately after pruning a pre-trained network, and then after applying the merging algorithm.

We compare our method (ONMP) to three baseline pruning criteria followed by the weight merging step. Namely, the pruning methods are 'L1-norm', 'L2-norm' and single-shot FPGM [6].

Table 1. Prune and Merge results on ILSVRC-2012. P and M refer to validation error after pruning and merging respectively, and (M-B) presents the error difference between the merged network and the (unpruned) baseline. FLOPs represent the percentage of pruned FLOPs and Params the number of parameters in the pruned network. We mark in bold the best result in each column.

Method	Top-1 Error(%)			Top-5 Error(%)			FLOPs	Params
	P	M	M-B	P	M	M-B	(%)	
ResNet-18	30.36			11.02				
L1	74.41	59.09	28.74	50.80	33.32	22.31	20%	9.464M
L2	64.65	55.61	25.25	40.00	30.22	19.20		
FPGM	61.61	54.64	24.29	37.45	29.42	18.40		
ONMP	**61.50**	**54.57**	**24.21**	**36.20**	**29.20**	**18.18**		
L1	93.30	79.60	49.24	83.32	58.11	47.09	30%	8.371M
L2	86.11	77.59	47.24	69.78	55.81	44.79		
FPGM	86.57	74.95	44.59	71.03	52.40	41.38		
ONMP	**85.84**	**72.88**	**42.52**	**68.83**	**49.62**	**38.60**		
ResNet-34	26.73			8.57				
L1	59.39	46.62	19.89	32.66	21.69	13.12	20%	17.522M
L2	57.19	44.30	17.57	31.32	20.32	11.75		
FPGM	56.55	44.61	17.88	30.97	20.49	11.92		
ONMP	**56.05**	**43.91**	**17.18**	**30.03**	**19.95**	**11.38**		
L1	87.42	64.67	37.93	70.61	39.13	30.56	30%	15.430M
L2	**82.98**	**60.78**	**34.04**	**64.09**	**35.44**	**26.87**		
FPGM	84.26	62.03	35.30	66.56	36.97	28.40		
ONMP	84.18	61.50	34.77	65.53	36.20	27.63		
WRN-50-2	21.53			5.93				
L1	59.64	33.88	12.35	35.47	13.13	7.19	30%	52.170M
L2	61.15	32.42	10.88	37.66	12.01	6.08		
FPGM	63.70	32.71	11.18	40.51	12.31	6.37		
ONMP	**55.91**	**31.87**	**10.33**	**31.77**	**11.53**	**5.60**		

Remark. *It is important to stress that in the experiments in this section we are comparing against the original prune-and-merge method of [9] for three different options of the choice of $\mathcal{A} \in \{$ L1, L2, FPGM $\}$.*

CIFAR-10. We test our method on ResNet-56 and various Wide-ResNet architectures with a 50% pruning ratio. Table 2 confirms that our optimal prune-and-merge algorithm achieves best results for this dataset over all the tested architectures.

We tested our algorithm on WRN 16–4, 28–4 and 40–4 architectures.

ILSVRC-2012. We tested our method on ResNet-18 and ResNet-34 networks with three pruning rates: 10%, 20% and 30%. As shown in Table 1 our method has the best performance over the ResNet-18 architecure.

Table 2. Prune and Merge results on CIFAR-10. The column notations are same as in Table 1.

Method	Top-1 Error(%)			FLOPs	Params
	P	M	M-B	(%)	
ResNet-56	6.61				
L1	60.65	38.47	31.86	50%	0.425M
L2	**57.84**	38.32	31.71		
FPGM	62.45	41.21	34.6		
ONMP	68.75	**37.54**	**30.93**		
WRN-16-4	4.8				
L1	51.82	25.4	20.6	50%	1.395M
L2	51.59	27.48	22.68		
FPGM	**51.15**	24.78	19.98		
ONMP	58.22	**20.99**	**16.19**		
WRN-40-4	4.07				
L1	30.51	13.77	9.7	50%	4.491M
L2	30.62	12.7	8.63		
FPGM	30.21	12.91	8.84		
ONMP	**27.77**	**11.17**	**7.1**		

Table 3. ResNet results on CIFAR-10 with Fine-tune.

Depth	Method	Baseline Err. (%)	Accelerated Err. (%)	Err. Inc. (%)	FLOPs (%)
20	FPGM	7.80	9.38	1.58	54
	ONMP	8.25	9.46	**1.21**	56
32	FPGM	7.37	8.07	0.70	54
	ONMP	7.37	7.94	**0.57**	56
56	FPGM	6.41	6.51	**0.10**	53
	ONMP	6.61	6.99	0.38	57
110	FPGM	6.32	6.26	−0.06	53
	ONMP	6.32	6.13	**−0.19**	57

Table 4. Results on ILSVRC-2012 with Fine-tune.

Depth	Method	Baseline Top-1 Err. (%)	Accelerated Top-1 Err. (%)	Err. Inc. (%)	Baseline Top-5 Err. (%)	Accelerated Top-5 Err. (%)	Err. Inc. (%)	FLOPs (%)
18	FPGM	29.72	31.59	1.87	10.37	11.52	1.15	41.8%
	ONMP	30.24	31.72	**1.48**	10.92	11.59	**0.67**	41.9%
34	FPGM	26.08	27.37	1.29	8.38	8.92	0.54	41.1 %
	ONMP	26.69	27.47	**0.78**	8.57	9.04	**0.47**	43.6 %
50	FPGM	23.85	24.41	0.56	7.13	7.37	0.24	42.2%
	ONMP	23.87	24.27	**0.4**	7.13	7.23	**0.10**	39.5 %
101	FPGM	22.63	22.68	**0.05**	6.44	6.44	0	42.2%
	ONMP	22.62	22.77	0.15	6.46	6.44	**−0.02**	42.6%

5.2   Prune, Merge and Fine-tune

Here we test our pruning algorithm using the prune then fine-tune paradigm. In this setting the pretrained network is pruned and then retrained using the standard SGD training. We use 160 epochs for CIFAR-10 and 100 epochs for ILSVRC-2012 [20]. In the case of CIFAR-10, we repeat each experiment 3 times and report the mean value. We compare our method to the iterative version of FPGM [6] which to the best of our knowledge is the current SOTA for data-free algorithms.

It should be noted that our pruning algorithm is applied in a single-shot manner while FPGM is iteratively applied at each epoch, which we believe gives a slight initial advantage to FPGM in terms of being able to recover from pruning errors in subsequent training steps.

CIFAR-10. For CIFAR-10 with fine-tuning, we test our ONMP method on ResNet-20, 32, 56 and 110.

ILSVRC-2012. For ILSVRC-2012, we test our ONMP method on ResNet-18, 34, 50 and 101. Table 4 summarizes the results.

Table 5. Nuclear norm regularization. Prune+merge error at 50% FLOPs after training from scratch ResNet-56 on CIFAR-10. The first row is the model error without pruning.

Method	No reg.	Nuc. norm reg.
–	6.61	9.45
L1	38.47	41.60
L2	38.32	48.90
FPGM	41.21	53.22
ONMP	37.54	**28.26**

5.3   Nuclear Norm Regularization

To evaluate the effect of nuclear norm regularization we define a regularization loss term $L_{nuc} = \sum_{i=1}^{L} ||W_i||_* / N_{i+1}$ where W_i and N_{i+1} are as described before, and L is the number of layers. The overall training loss is a linear combination of standard classification cross-entropy loss L_{cls} and the regularizer: $L = L_{cls} + \lambda L_{nuc}$. We train ResNet-56 from scratch on the CIFAR-10 dataset with and without our regularization, and compare the error after pruning and merging. The value of λ is set to 1.0.

Table 5 summarizes the results. Figure 1 shows the ranks and nuclear norms of ResNet-56 layers at different training epochs. As expected, in the regularized model the weight ranks go down as the training progresses. In contrast, the weight matrices of the non-regularized model remain full-rank.

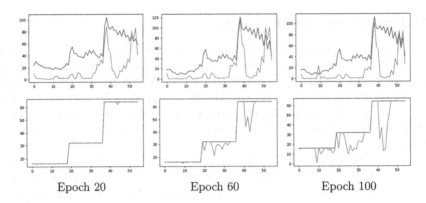

Epoch 20   Epoch 60   Epoch 100

Fig. 1. The effect of nuclear norm regularization when training ResNet-56 from scratch on CIFAR-10. From left to right, the nuclear norm (top) and rank (bottom) of the convolutional layer weights at epochs 20, 60 and 100. Orange lines indicate a model trained with nuclear norm regularization, blue shows normal training. The x-axis represents the layer index. (Color figure online)

6   Conclusions

We have presented a mathematical analysis of the neuron merging technique and used it to derive a new optimal prune-and-merge method based on a criterion that minimizes a strong upper bound on the activation reconstruction error.

Our experimental results prove that the proposed method outperforms the competing filter pruning methods in the prune-merge setting, including the SOTA FPGM method, in almost all experiments.

References

1. Church, R.L.: Beamr: an exact and approximate model for the p-median problem. Comput. Operat. Res. **35**(2), 417–426 (2008)
2. Enderich, L., Timm, F., Burgard, W.: Holistic filter pruning for efficient deep neural networks. In: Proceedings of the IEEE/CVF Winter Conference on Applications of Computer Vision, pp. 2596–2605 (2021)
3. Hakimi, S.L.: Optimum distribution of switching centers in a communication network and some related graph theoretic problems. Oper. Res. **13**(3), 462–475 (1965)
4. He, K., Zhang, X., Ren, S., Sun, J.: Deep residual learning for image recognition. In: Proceedings of the IEEE Conference on Computer Vision and Pattern Recognition, pp. 770–778 (2016)
5. He, Y., Kang, G., Dong, X., Fu, Y., Yang, Y.: Soft filter pruning for accelerating deep convolutional neural networks. arXiv preprint arXiv:1808.06866 (2018)
6. He, Y., Liu, P., Wang, Z., Hu, Z., Yang, Y.: Filter pruning via geometric median for deep convolutional neural networks acceleration. In: Proceedings of the IEEE Conference on Computer Vision and Pattern Recognition, pp. 4340–4349 (2019)
7. He, Y., Zhang, X., Sun, J.: Channel pruning for accelerating very deep neural networks. In: Proceedings of the IEEE Conference on Computer Vision and Pattern Recognition, pp. 1389–1397 (2017)

8. Hoefler, T., Alistarh, D., Ben-Nun, T., Dryden, N., Peste, A.: Sparsity in deep learning: pruning and growth for efficient inference and training in neural networks. arXiv preprint arXiv:2102.00554 (2021)
9. Kim, W., Kim, S., Park, M., Jeon, G.: Neuron merging: compensating for pruned neurons. In: Advances in Neural Information Processing Systems, vol. 33 (2020)
10. Krizhevsky, A., Hinton, G., et al.: Learning multiple layers of features from tiny images (2009)
11. Le, D.H., Hua, B.S.: Network pruning that matters: a case study on retraining variants. In: International Conference on Learning Representations (2021). https://openreview.net/forum?id=Cb54AMqHQFP
12. Li, T., Li, J., Liu, Z., Zhang, C.: Few sample knowledge distillation for efficient network compression. In: Proceedings of the IEEE/CVF Conference on Computer Vision and Pattern Recognition, pp. 14639–14647 (2020)
13. Liu, Z., Li, J., Shen, Z., Huang, G., Yan, S., Zhang, C.: Learning efficient convolutional networks through network slimming. In: Proceedings of the IEEE International Conference on Computer Vision, pp. 2736–2744 (2017)
14. Luo, J.H., Wu, J., Lin, W.: Thinet: a filter level pruning method for deep neural network compression. In: Proceedings of the IEEE International Conference on Computer Vision, pp. 5058–5066 (2017)
15. Mao, H., et al.: Exploring the granularity of sparsity in convolutional neural networks. In: Proceedings of the IEEE Conference on Computer Vision and Pattern Recognition Workshops, pp. 13–20 (2017)
16. Nie, F., Huang, H., Ding, C.: Low-rank matrix recovery via efficient Schatten p-norm minimization. In: Twenty-sixth AAAI Conference on Artificial Intelligence (2012)
17. Recht, B., Xu, W., Hassibi, B.: Necessary and sufficient conditions for success of the nuclear norm heuristic for rank minimization. In: 2008 47th IEEE Conference on Decision and Control, pp. 3065–3070. IEEE (2008)
18. Reese, J.: Solution methods for the p-median problem: an annotated bibliography. Netw. Int. J. **48**(3), 125–142 (2006)
19. Renda, A., Frankle, J., Carbin, M.: Comparing rewinding and fine-tuning in neural network pruning. In: International Conference on Learning Representations (2020). https://openreview.net/forum?id=S1gSj0NKvB
20. Russakovsky, O., et al.: Imagenet large scale visual recognition challenge. Int. J. Comput. Vis. **115**(3), 211–252 (2015)
21. Vadera, S., Ameen, S.: Methods for pruning deep neural networks. arXiv preprint arXiv:2011.00241 (2020)
22. You, Z., Yan, K., Ye, J., Ma, M., Wang, P.: Gate decorator: Global filter pruning method for accelerating deep convolutional neural networks. arXiv preprint arXiv:1909.08174 (2019)
23. Zagoruyko, S., Komodakis, N.: Wide residual networks. arXiv preprint arXiv:1605.07146 (2016)
24. Zhou, D., et al.: Go wide, then narrow: efficient training of deep thin networks. In: International Conference on Machine Learning, pp. 11546–11555. PMLR (2020)

Correction to: Learning Document Graphs with Attention for Image Manipulation Detection

Hailey Joren, Otkrist Gupta, and Dan Raviv

Correction to:
Chapter "Learning Document Graphs with Attention
for Image Manipulation Detection" in: M. El Yacoubi et al.
(Eds.): *Pattern Recognition and Artificial Intelligence,*
LNCS 13363, https://doi.org/10.1007/978-3-031-09037-0_22

In an older version of this paper, there was error in the author name, "Hailey James" and email-ID were incorrect. This has been corrected to "Hailey Joren" with email-ID.

The updated original version of this chapter can be found at
https://doi.org/10.1007/978-3-031-09037-0_22

© Springer Nature Switzerland AG 2023
M. El Yacoubi et al. (Eds.): ICPRAI 2022, LNCS 13363, p. C1, 2023.
https://doi.org/10.1007/978-3-031-09037-0_57

Author Index

Printed in the United States
by Baker & Taylor Publisher Services